UNITED STATES GOVERNMENT AND POLITICS

Preparing for the Advanced Placement® Examination

D0064465

David Wolfford teaches Advanced Placement® U.S. Government and Politics at Mariemont High School in Cincinnati, Ohio, and has served as an AP® Reader. He has a B.A. in Secondary Education and an M.A. in Constitutional and Legal History, both from the University of Kentucky. He has conducted historical research projects on school desegregation and American political history. David has published in historical journals, such as *Ohio Valley History* and *Kentucky Humanities*. He has written on government, politics, and campaigns for national magazines and Cincinnati newspapers. He is a James Madison Fellow, a National Board certified teacher, and a regular contributor to *Social Education*.

Reviewers

David LaShomb
Consultant, College Board
Advanced Technologies Academy
AP® U.S. Government and Politics
Las Vegas, Nevada

Louis Magnon
Department of History and Political Science
San Antonio College
San Antonio, Texas

Eileen Sheehy
Billings West High School
AP® U.S. Government and Politics
Billings, Montana

David M. Seiter
Northridge High School
AP® U.S. Government and Politics
Layton, Utah

Brian Stevens
Consultant, College Board
Coldwater High School
AP® U.S. Government and Politics
Coldwater, Michigan

UNITED STATES GOVERNMENT AND POLITICS

Preparing for the Advanced Placement® Examination

David Wolfford

AMSCO SCHOOL PUBLICATIONS, INC. ,
a division of Perfection Learning®

AMSCO

*This book is dedicated to Mika, Maya, and Miki,
whose sacrifices made it possible. It is also dedicated
to my students, the "Warriors," who have made teaching
government and politics fun.*

United States Government and Politics: Preparing for the Advanced Placement® Examination
is one of a series of AP® social studies texts first launched with *United States History: Preparing for the
Advanced Placement® Examination.*

6 7 8 9 EBM 22 21 20 19 18 17

When ordering this book, please specify:

Softcover: ISBN 978-1-62974-855-9 or 1488201
Ebook edition: ISBN 978-1-62974-945-7 or 14882D

Printed in the United States of America

Contents

Preface   xi

Introduction   xii

Unit 1: Constitutional Underpinnings   1

Chapter 1 The Constitution   2

American Independence and Early
  National Government   2

An Ineffective Confederation and a Call for
  New Government   8

The Constitution in Practice   18

  Is That Constitutional? *Texas v. Johnson*   21

  Think as a Political Scientist: Analyze, Interpret,
    and Synthesize *Federalist #10* and *Federalist #51*   23

Multiple-Choice Questions   24

Free-Response Questions   27

  Writing: Understand the Task   27

Chapter 2 Federalism   28

Federalism Defined   28

The New Republic to the New Deal   31

Contemporary Federalism   38

  Think as a Political Scientist: Determine
    Relationships, Patterns, or Trends in
    Federal Grants   40

Returning Authority to the States   41

  Is That Constitutional? *United States v. Lopez*   43

Multiple-Choice Questions   47

Free-Response Questions   50

  Writing: Use Active Voice   50

Unit Review   51

  Think as a Political Scientist: Construct a Visual
    and Formulate an Argument About Federalism   51

Unit 2: Political Beliefs and Behaviors   52

Chapter 3 Public Opinion   53

    The Roots of Public Opinion   53

    Political Socialization   57

    Measuring Public Opinion   61

        Think as a Political Scientist: Assess the Credibility
of a Public Opinion Poll   66

    Multiple-Choice Questions   70

    Free-Response Questions   73

        Writing: Use Transitions   74

Chapter 4 Political Participation   75

    Participation and Voting   75

        Is That Constitutional? *Minor v. Happerset*   81

    Voting and Nonvoting   83

    Voting Blocs and Behaviors   86

    Voting Reform and Current Trends   91

        Think as a Political Scientist: Formulate and
Support an Argument to a Public Official   97

    Multiple-Choice Questions   98

    Free-Response Questions   101

        Writing: Be Objective   102

Unit Review   103

        Think as a Political Scientist: Construct a Graph
of a President's Approval Rating   103

Unit 3: Political Parties, Interest Groups, and Mass Media   104

Chapter 5 Political Parties   105

    History of the Two-Party System   105

    Is That Constitutional? *Smith v. Allwright*   111

    Contemporary Parties   116

    Minor Parties   122

    Parties and Patterns   126

    Multiple-Choice Questions   128

    Free-Response Questions   130

        Writing: Be Specific   131

Chapter 6 Campaigns and Elections   132

History of Campaigns and Elections   132

Congressional Campaigns   136

Road to the White House   140

Campaign Finance   145

Is That Constitutional? *Buckley v. Valeo*   148

Think as a Political Scientist: Present Accurate
Information on Your Representative's War Chest   151

Multiple-Choice Questions   152

Free-Response Questions   155

Writing: Notice and Use Dates   156

Chapter 7 Interest Groups   157

Early Interest Groups   157

Proliferation   160

Groups and Members   164

Influencing Policy   167

Is That Constitutional? *Citizens United v. FEC*   173

Ethics and Reform   175

Think as a Political Scientist: Determine
Relationships, Patterns, or Trends   178

Multiple-Choice Questions   179

Free-Response Questions   182

Writing: Answer Completely   182

Chapter 8 Media   183

History of Government and the Press   183

The Roles of Media   189

Government's Relationship with the Media   190

Think as a Political Scientist: Formulate and Refine
Inquiries on the Role of the Press   193

Freedom of the Press   194

Is That Constitutional? *New York Times v. Sullivan*   196

Contemporary Reporting and New Media   201

Ethical Lapses in Journalism   204

Multiple-Choice Questions   208

Free-Response Questions   210

Writing: Use Proper Names   210

Unit Review   211

Think as a Political Scientist: Analyze, Interpret,
and Synthesize Each Party's Platform   211

Unit 4: The Institutions of National Government   212

Chapter 9 Congress   213
    History of Congress   213
    Powers of Congress   219
    The Legislative Institution   221
        Is That Constitutional? *Shaw v. Reno*   225
    Organization of the Legislative Process   228
        Think as a Political Scientist: Present Accurate
          Visual Information About Congressional
          Committee Leadership, Members, and Activities   234
    Contemporary Congress   237
    Multiple-Choice Questions   241
    Free-Response Questions   243
        Writing: Plan   243

Chapter 10 The Presidency   244
    Creating and Developing the Presidency   244
    Presidential Elections   250
    Presidential Roles   254
    The Vice President   262
    Administering the Executive Branch   263
        Is That Constitutional? *Humphrey's Executor v.
          United States*   269
        Think as a Political Scientist: Evaluate the
          President's Cabinet   271
    Multiple-Choice Questions   273
    Free-Response Questions   276
        Writing: Consider Your Options   276

Chapter 11 The Bureaucracy   277
    History, Growth, and Reform   277
    The Bureaucracy Today   281
        Is That Constitutional? *INS v. Chadha*   289
    Bureaucratic Culture and Contemporary Issues   290
    Multiple-Choice Questions   294
    Free-Response Questions   297
        Writing: Make Clear Divisions   297

Chapter 12 The Judiciary   298
    Article III and the Federal Courts   298
    History of the Supreme Court   304

The Modern Supreme Court 310

The Courts and Other Branches of Government 315

Multiple-Choice Questions 322

Free-Response Questions 325

Writing: Use Concise Language 325

Unit Review 326

Think as a Political Scientist: Analyze and Interpret
a President's Inaugural Address 326

Unit 5: Civil Rights and Civil Liberties 327

Chapter 13 Civil Rights 328

Civil Rights for African Americans 328

The NAACP Seeks Justice and Equality 331

Civil Rights in Congress 334

Is That Constitutional? *Heart of
Atlanta v. United States* 339

Fulfilling the Spirit of *Brown* 342

Women's Rights 344

Gay Rights and Equality 348

Affirmative Action 352

Think as a Political Scientist: Analyze, Interpret,
and Synthesize Information on African-American
Suffrage 355

Multiple-Choice Questions 356

Free-Response Questions 359

Writing: Avoid First Person 359

Chapter 14 Civil Liberties 360

A Culture of Civil Liberties 360

Free Speech and Free Press 364

Church and State 370

Due Process 374

Civil Liberties and National Security 379

Think as a Political Scientist: Interpret
Snyder v. Phelps 383

Multiple-Choice Questions 384

Free-Response Questions 387

Writing: Use Disciplinary Conventions 387

Unit Review   388

    Think as a Political Scientist: Apply Disciplinary
      Theories and Concepts in Researching a Civil
      Rights Organization   388

Unit 6: Public Policy   389

Chapter 15 Domestic Policy   390

    Policymaking   390

    Social Welfare Policy   392

    Environmental Policy   394

    Labor Policy   395

      Think as a Political Scientist: Analyze and Interpret
       a Political Cartoon on Environmental Policy   396

    Economic Policy   397

    Monetary Policy   400

    Fiscal Policy   402

      Is That Constitutional? *Pollack v. Farmers'*
       Loan and Trust Co.   403

      Multiple-Choice Questions   413

      Free-Response Questions   416

      Writing: Use Strong and Varied Examples   417

Chapter 16 Foreign and Military Policy   418

    Creating Foreign and Military Policy   418

    A Brief History of War and Diplomacy   427

      Is That Constitutional? *Youngstown Sheet*
       & Tube v. Sawyer   433

    Human Rights and Strategic Interest   437

      Think as a Political Scientist: Analyze and
       Interpret World Maps of U.S. Foreign Policy   441

      Multiple-Choice Questions   443

      Free-Response Questions   446

      Writing: Use Style Conventions   446

Unit Review   447

    Think as a Political Scientist: Formulate and
      Refine Relevant Inquiries on Presidential Budgets   447

Practice Exam   448

United States Constitution   466

Bibliography   484

Index   489

Preface

United States Government and Politics: Preparing for the Advanced Placement® Examination explains the American political system and is designed to enhance student performance on the Advanced Placement® U.S. Government and Politics exam. The text includes a good mix of colorful history, modern political examples, and relevant statistics. Accounts of political personalities and historic events aid understanding and provide examples for students to use when answering the exam's free-response questions. The practice questions in this book—both the free-response and multiple-choice questions—parallel the questions asked on the national exam.

This up-to-date book reflects contemporary trends in Congress, the presidency, and the courts, and it includes data from the 2014 midterm elections. The essentials of government and politics in this book are drawn from the author's research projects, political reporting, and years of classroom teaching. Sources are cited and a bibliography provided in part to recommend these sources—organizational Web sites, government reports, relevant articles, classic political works, and cutting-edge books—for those who want more information and insights.

This book fills the gap between a test prep handbook and a college-level political science textbook. It is thorough enough to be a student's go-to book, especially if used in conjunction with college-level resources and online sources. It can be read gradually over an entire school year or in just a few weeks for a year-end review.

I would like to thank for their inspiration and counsel my dad, George Wolfford; history professor David Hamilton; and friends and colleagues Luke Wiseman, Dan Ruff, and Matt Litton. Special thanks go to Brian Stevens, a mentor and a reviewer of this volume. Also thanks to David LaShomb, Tony Magnon, David Seiter, and Eileen Sheehy for improving the book. Thanks to editor Carol Francis for her ideas and for her care of the project and to Perfection Learning for publishing my work. More than any, thanks to Mika, Maya, and Miki.

David Wolfford, January 2015

INTRODUCTION

Congratulations on accepting the challenge to learn and master United States government at an accelerated level. *United States Government and Politics: Preparing for the Advanced Placement® Examination* will enhance your knowledge of the United States government and improve your performance on the national AP® exam. This introduction explains the test and the overall content of the course. Sixteen chapters follow with extensive coverage of political history, contemporary events, relevant terms, and practice questions.

The College Board's Advanced Placement® program started in 1955. The U.S. Government and Politics section began in 1987. In 2014, more than 8,500 high schools offered the AP® government and politics course, and nearly 270,000 students took the national exam. The vast majority took the class in their senior year. Nearly 3,000 colleges accepted these scores and awarded credit in place of course work.

Taking an Advanced Placement® course and exam has many benefits. The depth and rigor will give you extensive information on this relevant subject. Some high schools award a weighted grade for AP® courses. The course will also help prepare you for college, sharpening your skills in analyzing and interpreting data. Taking AP® courses may allow you to save time and money by bypassing college courses later, depending on how your prospective college regards these exams. Additionally, prospective colleges consider your enrollment and performance in these courses as they determine admissions and award scholarships. One College Board study found that 85 percent of colleges view students' AP® experience favorably as they consider admissions decisions, and 31 percent report considering it when determining scholarship awards.

The exam is given in early May, but you must register earlier in the year. Check your school's guidance department or the College Board's Web site for details, fees, and deadlines.

Please note: This book prepares you for the U.S. Government and Politics exam, not the separate Comparative Government and Politics course, which compares various national governments.

Course Content

The topics of the course and exam include the creation and development of the United States government and the functions and processes of government today. Overarching questions include: How do elections work and how are they won? How do the three branches interact to create law and policy? How are people in this democracy linked to government institutions? Following political news on a regular basis, whether in a newspaper, on the evening news, or via the Internet, will enhance your understanding of government and politics.

The chart below summarizes what you should be able to do in order to succeed on the exam.

How to Succeed on the Exam
• Know important terms, names, and events relevant to U.S. government and politics
• Understand patterns of political behavior and their consequences
• Examine and analyze data and ideas conveyed in illustrations
• Critically analyze institutions and political concepts

American Political History

Knowing American history and recognizing names, dates, and events will provide a useful context for this course, though this is not a history course or exam. Perhaps you've already had a high school U.S. history course. Recall the important eras and their relevance to politics. For example, the American founding included an intense dispute between the American colonists and Great Britain about a lack of democratic representation and liberty. You will be expected to know the American Revolution's legal and political (not military) history, the ideas in the Declaration of Independence, and the creation and ratification of the Constitution.

You need not know every president, but knowing something about a few leading presidents—their terms in office, impact, and accomplishments—will help you cement your understanding of key political events and forces. For example, the first presidents—Washington, Adams, Jefferson, Madison, and Monroe—shaped the office. When the nation elected Andrew Jackson, political participation expanded and public campaigns formed. Abraham Lincoln served as chief executive during the Civil War, 1861–1865. Theodore Roosevelt took office in 1901, and his cousin Franklin Roosevelt in 1933. For more recent presidents and their legacies, consult the table in Chapter 10 on page 261.

Other key historical personalities are relevant to shaping the American government as well. Leading Federalists James Madison and Alexander Hamilton promoted a strong national government. Chief Justice John Marshall became the father of the Supreme Court, serving during its formative era, 1801–1837. Alexis de Tocqueville, an upper-class Frenchman, toured the United States about 50 years after its founding and recorded his observations of early American politics in his classic work, *Democracy in America*. In the early 1900s, Speaker of the House Joe Cannon ruled Congress with an iron fist. During the Civil Rights Movement of the 1950s and 1960s, Thurgood Marshall, a civil rights attorney and later Supreme Court justice, led in desegregating America. Though individuals' names generally do not appear on the exam, knowing historical figures will provide you with strong examples to use as you answer the free-response questions.

Understanding Modern Politics

The exam covers the federal government, but you will also need to know something about state and local governments and their authority. For example, state legislators redraw Congressional districts every ten years and fund schools, prisons, and highways. A city's mayor heads the local government's executive branch, with police and parks departments under his or her administration. A county judge holds criminal and civil court to determine if and how the law should be applied. The main focus of the course, however, is on the three branches of government outlined in the Constitution and how people and groups interact with these institutions to create public policy. The relationship between the federal and state governments is a recurring theme in understanding the challenges of federalism.

Most government action takes place "inside the beltway"—the Washington, D.C., area encircled by Interstate 495. Congress convenes on Capitol Hill, the president lives and works in the White House, and the Supreme Court justices hear cases in their building nearby. These institutions are the policymaking bodies that create the law and define how it is carried out. The press, or media, report to citizens on the work of these branches. Interest groups and political parties try to influence all three branches in different ways. These different entities work together and at odds with one another to accomplish their separate goals.

In addition to the federal government, which includes hundreds of agencies and more than two million employees, each state has a legislature, a governor, and a court system. Countless municipal or city governments and school boards create a web of policies. Our complex system is designed to address a variety of viewpoints while ultimately adopting only those few ideas the masses can largely agree on. This is the basis of **pluralism**, a system through which public policies result from compromise among competing groups. With pluralism, we create a **consensus government** to satisfy most participants most of the time.

Where Does the Power Lie?

Officially, national political power and authority rests with "We the people" as introduced in the Preamble of the Constitution. To ensure the ideals of a government by the people, the Constitution defines the structure of Congress, the qualifications for president, and the jurisdiction of the courts. Actual government policies, however, depend on who holds these offices and how they approach their duties. In many instances, public policy is created after a competition between the political elites (upper-level politicians) and the rank and file (voters).

Those who subscribe to the elite theory of government claim that big businesses, political elites, and those with money and resources may dominate the policymaking process. But pluralists counter that because such political resources and access to the media are so widely scattered, no single elite has a monopoly on power. Pluralists also argue that the many levels of government and the officials within each branch bring a variety of views and divide the power to prevent one sector of society or one view from dominating.

Exam Content

The exam, course, and this book cover six large areas described below. The rough percentages represent their value on the exam.

Topics
I. Constitutional Underpinnings (5–15%)
II. Political Beliefs and Behaviors (10–20%)
III. Political Parties, Interest Groups, and Mass Media (10–20%)
IV. Institutions of National Government (35–45%)
V. Civil Rights and Civil Liberties (5–15%)
VI. Public Policy (5–15%)

Constitutional Underpinnings The first topic focuses on the historical creation of the United States federal government. It includes the struggle between the American colonists and the British government, the Revolutionary War, the infant U.S. government under the failed Articles of Confederation, and the creation of the Constitution and the Bill of Rights. Knowing the Constitution in detail is very beneficial for your success in the course and on the exam. A copy of it is provided in the back of this book beginning on page 462. The "Underpinnings" section also considers the arguments offered for and against the Bill of Rights and how American federalism developed, largely after Supreme Court rulings.

Political Beliefs and Behaviors This broad topic covers such questions as why American citizens fall into different political categories and what forces or experiences cause a person to develop political beliefs. Parents and family are the major influences in how a child thinks, and they shape a new voter's behavior. Demographics, religion, school, geographic location, race, and countless other factors contribute to this political socialization process. People who have any degree of opinion on politics possess an **ideology**. A wide range of ideologies exist, but Americans often divide these into two simple camps, conservative and liberal.

Beliefs and behaviors also influence the degree to which people participate in politics and public life. Different demographic groups—men, African Americans, women, and young adults—began to participate in politics (usually by voting) at different points in history. Some groups participate more than others and hold well-defined beliefs. Citizens participate in different forms beyond voting, such as contacting lawmakers, joining an interest group, writing a letter to the editor, or contributing to a political campaign.

Political Parties, Interest Groups, and Mass Media This topic focuses on the ways in which political parties, interest groups, and mass media impact the political process. These organizations are sometimes referred to as **linkage institutions** because they link people to the government. Political parties—Democrats, Republicans, and others—represent a certain broad ideology and try to impact the creation of law that reflects that ideology. Parties recruit and nominate candidates for public office who are favorable to their viewpoints. They also finance campaigns, meet with lawmakers, and try to further their platform goals.

Interest groups are smaller organizations with more specific concerns and goals. These groups engage in politics in a variety of ways. Interest groups take part in political campaigns, testify before Congress, and place persuasive ads in newspapers and on television. They also form political action committees (PACs) to donate money to candidates. The mass media include nationally influential newspapers such as the *Washington Post* and *New York Times*, network and cable television news shows, Internet sources, and the local press. Public opinion polling, too, is a form of mass media. Polling measures political beliefs and behaviors and informs the government about citizens' views and desires.

Institutions of National Government This topic covers the four governing institutions—Congress, the Presidency, the Bureaucracy, and the Judiciary—that are found within the three branches of government (legislative, executive, and judicial) defined in Articles I, II, and III of the Constitution. The Bureaucracy is the president's administration, from Cabinet-level advisors down to national park rangers. Government sub-units include the House and Senate, committees within Congress, federal departments and agencies, and the lower U.S. courts.

In the unit on institutions, you will learn about the legislative process, presidential decision making, and how the Supreme Court accepts and decides cases. These institutions have unique relationships with one another, some defined in the Constitution and some developed over history.

Civil Rights and Civil Liberties Civil rights generally refer to citizens' basic rights to freedom and to humane, equal treatment. Civil rights quests usually involve the struggle for certain groups—African Americans, other ethnic minorities, women, or gays and lesbians—seeking equality under the law. The AP® Government and Politics Examination emphasizes women's suffrage and the historic rise of women in political participation as well as African Americans in the post-Civil War era and during the Civil Rights Movement from the 1950s through the 1970s.

Civil liberties refer to a citizen's political freedoms, such as the right to free speech, freedom of religion, a fair criminal justice process, and basic privacy. After reading Chapter 14, you will understand the division of church and state, the limits of free speech in the public square, and the line between an individual's right and society's responsibilities. Understanding civil rights and liberties requires solid knowledge of the Supreme Court's role and its many landmark decisions.

Public Policy The term "policy" simply refers to the way government does business. Each branch of government plays a role in shaping public policy. Congressional acts that define crimes or guide citizen behavior are generally clear-cut statements of policy. The manner in which the executive branch enforces the law also defines policy. How a court interprets a law can further shape its application. The way the president or State Department interacts with other nations determines foreign policy. In fact, policy is formed by thousands of governmental participants. Democrats and Republicans differ on policies regarding social issues (abortion and gay marriage, for example) and economic issues (such as taxation). Chapters 15 and 16 discuss the particulars of social welfare, environmental, economic, labor, foreign, and military policies.

The Exam

You will be allotted two hours and 25 minutes to take the exam. First is a 45-minute session to answer all 60 multiple-choice questions; next is a 100-minute session to answer four free-response questions (FRQs). The exams are written by a team of college faculty and experienced AP® teachers. A full practice exam is included at the end of this book.

Timing of the Exam
• Two hours and 25 minutes
• Multiple-Choice: 60 questions in 45 minutes
• Essay: Four FRQ prompts in 100 minutes

Multiple-Choice

The 60 multiple-choice questions take a variety of forms and go through a rigorous revision process. Some exam questions are reused over the years to ensure a consistency from year to year. You must always choose from five options, A through E, and there is never more than one correct answer. Some questions simply test your knowledge of course terms from a particular chapter, while many others measure your full understanding, application, and analysis of government and politics across the chapters.

Within the next few pages are some sample questions. These examples are similar to questions from past released AP® exams, designed to challenge you at the end of your preparation. At the end of each chapter in this book you will find ten similar questions based on the chapter's specific subject.

Standard Advice As with most multiple-choice tests, determine what exactly the question is asking and then select the best answer. If an early answer option in (A) or (B) looks extremely obvious, still read and consider the remaining options to confirm or reconsider your first impressions. For questions that you do not immediately know, use the process of elimination. Rule out, and actually mark through, the impossible options to narrow your choice. Since there is no added penalty for guessing, if you do not know the answer, make your best guess.

When you see a challenging or time-consuming question, remember time is limited. You are allotted an average of 45 seconds per question. You should pass the midpoint of the exam, question #30, at about 20 to 22 minutes into the first portion of the test. At times it will be better to skip a tough question (be sure to leave that spot blank on the answer form) and continue on through the test. Return and answer those questions if you have time after you have gone through all 60. The example questions that follow are challenging. If you're just beginning your preparation, you could elect to read and attempt these later.

Question Styles

The multiple-choice questions fall into a handful of categories, from simple definitions to text-based analysis. The following are common question styles on the AP® exam.

Simple Definitions Of the 60 questions, about 12 to 15 will require you to know a simple definition.

1. Which of the following early American documents signaled the colonies' political break from Great Britain?

    (A) Articles of Confederation

    (B) Declaration of Independence

    (C) Constitution

    (D) Bill of Rights

    (E) The opinion in *Marbury v. Madison*

These definition-style questions present a question or the first part of a sentence, and then you select the correct answer or the ending that completes the statement correctly. The answer to this question is (B). The Declaration of Independence did as its name suggests: it declared American independence from Great Britain. The other documents were equally important in the founding, and you will learn more about them in Chapter 1. Here's another simple definition question:

2. What type of bill covers a number of diverse topics?

    (A) Private bill

    (B) Pork barrel bill

    (C) Continuing resolution

    (D) Omnibus bill

    (E) Supplemental

The correct answer is (D). The term *omnibus bill* simply means an all-encompassing bill that has come about after much political trading on the floor of Congress. If you didn't know that at this point, don't worry. Once you read Chapter 9 you'll better understand the legislative process and such terms. Each chapter in the book ends with a chart showing key terms, names, and events covered in the chapter. You can use these charts as a study guide to review definitions of terms as you prepare for the exam.

Conceptual Questions Several questions will call on you to compare or contrast two elements of U.S. government. Others will require a deep understanding of the inner workings of federal institutions. And still others will touch on multiple parts of the AP® Government and Politics curriculum, perhaps requiring knowledge from multiple topics across chapters. Following are two examples:

3. A key difference between the Secretary of Defense and the Chairman of the Joint Chiefs of Staff is that
    (A) one is appointed by the president and the other is appointed by the Secretary of State
    (B) one is a civilian, and one is uniformed military personnel
    (C) the Secretary of Defense is more attuned to ground maneuvers and combat readiness, while the Chairman of the Joint Chiefs oversees the budget process
    (D) the Secretary of Defense must be approved by the Senate, while the Chairman of the Joint Chiefs does not need that approval
    (E) one serves at the pleasure of the president; one has a lifetime term

To answer this challenging and specific question, you would have to know the concepts underlying these two executive branch positions, their roles, and how they get their jobs. The answer is (B).

4. Which of the following regarding the Supreme Court's interpretation of free speech is true?
    (A) Students have no rights to free speech in schools.
    (B) Profanity and obscenity are among the most protected forms of speech.
    (C) The Court has usually upheld free speech, as long as no one is offended.
    (D) The Supreme Court has never ruled on free speech.
    (E) When petitioned, the Supreme Court has tended to restrain speech.

To correctly answer this question you must know quite a bit about the Supreme Court's record with free speech cases. The Court has ruled on speech many times; thus (D) is wrong. You must also know and understand the concept of "protected speech" and the essential legal definition of profanity and obscenity, as well as how the court views each. The correct answer is (E).

Reverse Multiple-Choice You will see some questions where you must find an untrue statement or an exception to a trend. The College Board capitalizes the key word in these questions, such as NOT, EXCEPT, or LEAST. About 10 percent of the multiple-choice questions will take this form. But even with the all-caps serving as a flag, you should actually circle the capitalized word on the test copy to remind you to look for the "incorrect answer" or the exception as you read down the list of options. Too often, students know the concept or idea in the question but forget the question's orientation under pressure during the exam, even after reading it seconds before. Here are some examples.

5. Low voter turnout can be attributed to all of the following EXCEPT
   (A) an aging America
   (B) weakened political parties
   (C) registration requirements
   (D) disillusionment with politics and government
   (E) frequency of elections

As you read down the list, did you keep in mind which of these would NOT cause low voter turnout? It is (A). Older citizens actually vote more reliably than younger ones. According to the U.S. Census, the two oldest age-brackets measured turned out to vote in higher numbers than any other. The 18- to 24-year-old bloc consistently has turned out at the lowest rates. All the other points do cause people to participate less in voting.

6. Which of the following groups would be LEAST likely to have organized a national interest group or PAC?
   (A) Environmentalists
   (B) Temporary workers
   (C) Teachers
   (D) Gun manufacturers
   (E) Home builders

The answer is (B). Interest groups rely on resources, such as money and members, to operate. All the other groups, professionals and profit makers, are more likely than temporary workers—who lack money, resources, and political experience—to have the resources to develop an organized presence in politics.

If it helps you to do so, you can reword these questions for another way to understand them. For example, you might reword #6 to "All of these groups have the resources to create a national interest groups or PACs EXCEPT…"

Roman Numerals List You will see two or three questions that offer a Roman numeral list and ask you to choose one or more from the list to answer the question. Take this example.

7. Which of the following are linkage institutions?

   I. House of Representatives
   II. Presidency
   III. Interest Groups
   IV. Democratic Party

   (A) I only
   (B) I and II
   (C) I, II, and III
   (D) II and III
   (E) III and IV

The answer is (E) because linkage institutions are those that are not actually part of the government but that link the citizenry to official government institutions. Interest groups and parties satisfy that definition, as would the media if listed.

Questions with Illustrations A few questions will be accompanied by illustrations. These illustrations are usually tables or graphs that present statistical data displaying some type of political trend. You might also see a map. Examine this graphic that explains primary voting in the Democratic Party 1968–1984.

8. Which of the following can be determined from the table on the next page?
   (A) The number of state primaries remained the same for the presidential elections from 1968 to 1984.
   (B) The percentage of delegates awarded to Democratic candidates via primary elections continually rose over the period listed.
   (C) As primary elections became more frequent, so did media attention dedicated to those primaries.
   (D) When more states held primaries, more citizens voted.
   (E) Voter participation for the period shown peaked in 1976 presidential primaries.

Primary Votes and Delegate Selection 1968–1984 Democratic Party			
Year	State Primaries	Total Votes Cast	Delegates via Primary (percent)
1968	15	7,535,069	40.2
1972	21	15,993,965	65.3
1976	27	16,052,652	76.0
1980	34	18,747,825	71.8
1984	29	18,009,217	52.4

This question requires you to examine a simple table that shows the number of states holding primaries, the total number of citizens who voted in each of the presidential primary elections, and the percentage of Democratic delegates that were earned by the primary vote. This course will help you fully understand the nomination process. But for the purposes of answering this question, you need not fully understand it. You can tell that the number of states holding presidential primaries gradually increased until 1980, as did the number of voters. Option (C) is likely true, but it is not depicted in the table. The answer is (D).

Historic Work or Passage Sometimes a question will refer to a passage from the Constitution, the *Federalist Papers*, a Supreme Court opinion, or some other notable text. Even if you are not familiar with the historic quote, read the passage closely and consider the question that follows. (Sometimes you don't even need to recognize the quote or the authority or even relate your answer to either). For the question that follows, consider this quote:

> "It sometimes happens in a people divided in opinions that when the equilibrium between the parties comes to be upset, one of them acquires an irresistible preponderance. It crushes all obstacle, overwhelms its adversary, and exploits the entire society to its profit."
> —Alexis de Tocqueville, *Democracy in America*

9. The statement above is a commentary on which of the following?
   (A) Line-item veto
   (B) The rule of law
   (C) Partisanship and majority rule
   (D) The filibuster
   (E) Impeachment

De Tocqueville said this in observance of how the majority party can run roughshod over the minority party; thus the correct answer is (C).

Watch Out for "Always" and "Never" Government and politics are far from exact sciences. There are exceptions to every rule. Therefore, when you see multiple-choice questions followed by options that include such absolute words as "never," "always," or "none," be wary. Take this question:

10. Which of the following statements about the Electoral College is accurate?
    (A) The winner of the Electoral College never actually wins the popular vote.
    (B) To win the Electoral College, the candidate must win a majority of electoral votes.
    (C) All of the states use the winner-take-all system.
    (D) Historically, presidential electors have always voted the same as the people.
    (E) If there is no winner in the Electoral College, the sitting president decides the winner.

You've probably heard that (A) is possible, but this result has happened only four times in history. Many particulars of the Electoral College system can be determined by states. Most states use the "winner-take-all system, but some do not. (D) is typical and some states have created laws requiring this policy, but in the past, electors did not have to consider the people's vote as strongly as they do now. For (E), the system dictates that if there is no winner, the election goes into the House of Representatives to be decided. The House provides a large, people's body to determine the candidate. The president is but one official who may even be a contender for re-election. The system calls for a separation of powers. This process of elimination leaves (B) as the correct answer.

Released Exams: Multiple-Choice Overview

The College Board has released previous exams for your review. An analysis of these exams provides insight into what topics, terms, and structures tend to be covered. Some topics invariably repeat. Some show up on the exam only occasionally. A topic's appearance on a released exam, though, is no guarantee it will be on the exam you will take, which could be substantially different in topics covered from the released exams.

Free-Response Questions (FRQs)

The free-response section of the exam consists of four questions you must answer in 100 minutes. These questions draw from multiple topics within the course and are of equal weight, each worth one-eighth of the test. You should spend roughly 25 minutes on each.

These FRQs usually begin with an introductory sentence or two that reveal the thrust of the question and provide focus. Subprompts or questions labeled (a), (b), and so on, follow. Sometimes you have choices; other times you do not. Consider this example that deals with African-American suffrage:

1. The Fifteenth Amendment to the Constitution prohibits the U.S. government and the states from denying or abridging citizens' right to vote "on account of race, color, or previous condition of servitude." After ratification of the Fifteenth Amendment, some states circumvented the amendment to prevent African Americans from voting.

    (a) Identify and describe one past policy or custom states used to evade the Fifteenth Amendment.

    (b) Identify and describe a second past policy or custom states used to evade the Fifteenth Amendment.

    (c) Select one example you provided in (a) or (b) and explain why the policy or custom was effective in evading the Constitution to suppress African-American voting.

    (d) Select one policy you provided in (a) or (b) and explain how it came to an end.

This question presents a short passage from the Fifteenth Amendment to the Constitution and calls on the students' knowledge of how states continued to deny suffrage to African Americans. Acceptable answers for (a) and (b) include the literacy tests, grandfather clause, poll tax, white primary, gerrymandering, and others, all of which are covered in Chapter 13. In answering this question, carefully note the wording, which asks you to identify "past" customs or policies, Voter ID laws and disproportionate handling of black and white voter precincts, while relevant issues today, would not fit the time frame required in the answer.

Parts (c) and (d) call for a higher level of thinking and explanation. Part (c) calls on you to explain how these policies worked and what impact they had. Section (d) asks you to explain how these came to an end. The grandfather clause was struck down with a Supreme Court decision in 1915 in *Guinn v. United States*; the poll tax stopped with the Twenty-fourth Amendment; the literacy test ceased after the Voting Rights Act and a subsequent court ruling. There are more possibilities.

A survey of the past twelve AP® exams reveals some frequency of free-response topics. Recurring themes include presidential elections and the road to the White House; the division of powers and interaction among the branches of government, especially between Congress and the president; the inner workings of Congress—the legislative process, committee system, and leadership roles; interest groups and their activities; and economic policies such as the federal budget, Social Security, or federal grants programs. One cannot, however, predict the questions. It is entirely possible to see four questions that have nothing to do with the above topics.

Illustrations

You may see one FRQ (and also a multiple-choice question) with an accompanying illustration. Some are tables or graphs with such information as election data, public opinion polling, or budgeted public monies. You may also see a map, and each exam will likely include one political cartoon.

Political cartoons, whether historic or recent, reveal the opinions of the cartoonists at the time. Following is a 2004 depiction of the two presidential candidates, incumbent George Bush and then-Senator John Kerry. As you examine the cartoon, look for symbols and words that help you understand it, and then try to answer the questions below. Most questions accompanying political cartoons ask for the cartoonist's viewpoint.

Source: Graeme MacKay

2. Public opinion and formal debates play unique roles in political campaigns and elections.

   (a) Explain two effects of public opinion on political campaigns.

   (b) Identify one challenge for candidates regarding formal debates.

   (c) Identify one impact/effect of formal debates.

   (d) Explain the cartoonist's viewpoint of televised presidential debates.

This question discusses political debates in campaign season. Notice the cartoon is from the 2004 election, but for choices (a)–(c), you did not need the cartoon, nor were correct answers limited to examples from presidential candidates. For (d), you do not need to recall or know much about this 2004 election debate, but you can likely tell that the cartoonist thought that one candidate, John Kerry on the left, needed to project a "less academic" persona, and President George W. Bush needed to appear "less cowboy." Both candidates were trying for the middle, undecided voters. You would not have to know these candidates or mention the year to earn the points for this type of question.

Instructions

Free-response prompts use a variety of terms that direct you to answer in a certain way. Depending on the level of difficulty, the different terms carry different point values. Prompts that ask you to "identify" are typically worth fewer points because these call on you to merely write a sentence or so without explanation. Sometimes the prompts will call on you to "describe" or "explain," which requires more knowledge, higher thinking, and more writing. Therefore these verbs should signal you to provide more information and elaboration. The most common FRQ pattern is to identify and then explain.

Rubrics and Reading

A mix of AP® high school government teachers and political science college professors convene at the AP® Reading to grade the entire national batch of responses. The readers follow a rubric or scoring guide, a prescribed checklist of possible answers. The test-taker either earns points or does not based on how well the answers match the rubric. When taking the exam, try to anticipate the rubric and try to cover all points.

Different prompts have different points possible. For example, Question 2 above would likely be scored on a six-point rubric—that is, two points for the explanation in (a), one point for each correct identification in (b) and (c), and then two points for (d), which once again calls on the test-taker to explain more details. Readers might be given a scoring guide like the one on the following page to evaluate answers to this free-response question.

Question 2 Scoring Guide *5 points*

Part (a): 2 points
One point is earned for each of two correct explanations of the impact of public opinion on political campaigns, including:

- will determine the winner
- could provide a mandate for governing
- shapes a campaign strategy
- reveals the interest or intensity of the electorate

Part (b): 1 point
One point is earned for the correct identification of a challenge regarding formal debates, including:

- preparing
- whether to accept/attend the debate
- the rules/terms of the debate
- potential gaffes
- concern for appealing to the undecided
- spinning the debate to media

Part (c): 1 point
One point is earned for the correct identification of the impact of formal debates, including:

- can alter public opinion
- can cause one candidate to win or lose
- allows candidates to project image
- allows candidates to convey policy messages
- allows voters to compare candidates

Part (d): 2 points
Two points are earned for a possible explanation of the cartoonist's viewpoint, including:

- there is too much emphasis on image/appearance and not enough on substance
- candidates may not really be examples of the images they project
- the public may be too easily swayed by oversimplified images
- the public is not easily fooled by candidates' debate performances
- debate prep is too influenced by consultants/focus groups
- candidates overprepare/try too hard

Though each FRQ may be worth a different number of points, each question is weighted the same. As you read questions, underline the key verbs and the number of examples you must give and anticipate how many total topic points you are expected to make.

Political Science Thinking Skills

In addition to in-depth content, practice questions at the end of each chapter, and a final full Practice Exam, this book provides support for developing and practicing thinking skills essential to effective understanding of government and politics. At least three times in each unit you will see "Think as a Political Scientist" in a gray tinted box. This instruction and the practice activities accompanying it will help you develop critical thinking skills in three key areas: exploring processes for **inquiring** into political science topics, **analyzing evidence** discovered in a political science inquiry, and **communicating** your political science findings to others.

Inquiring No research effort will be worth the trouble without a clearly formulated and refined focus for inquiry. Developing a highly targeted objective for research is a skill with multiple steps. You may start with nothing more than a hunch, but delving into research on only a hunch will yield little more than scattered information. With some preliminary research, however, you can begin to see the possible definitions of your research focus and develop a refined inquiry. With this focus to guide you, you can systematically begin identifying and evaluating the most appropriate methods, techniques, and evidence for your research.

Analyzing Evidence To sort through the evidence you accumulate, you use additional critical thinking skills. You **apply the theories and concepts of political science**—economic theories, political theories, concepts of democratic fairness and equality, for a few examples—as you evaluate the information and evidence in your sources. You also use both **qualitative information** expressed in narrative, open-ended form such as you might find in a biography or news report, and you use **quantitative information** expressed in numbers, statistics, and polls to **determine relationships, patterns, and trends** in different places at different times. You also carefully evaluate the credibility of your sources, questioning possible biases or outdated information. You analyze, interpret, and synthesize into a coherent understanding both the textual and visual information you have gathered to fill out your inquiry.

Communicating You use another set of critical thinking skills as you prepare to present your findings to others. You develop a claim and **formulate an argument** that you can back up with the appropriate evidence. You **present the evidence** in your argument clearly and coherently, making sure it is accurate. When necessary, you **construct and use visuals**, such as maps, graphs, and diagrams, to communicate information best expressed in that way.

Mastering these skills will help you succeed on the exam and throughout your college years.

Exam Day

Wake up in time to relax and eat a normal breakfast. Bring two #2 pencils for the multiple-choice section, two black or blue ink pens for the free-response section, and a watch. Wear comfortable clothing suitable for a cold or hot testing room. Do not bring any government books, laptops, or cellphones. Follow the general advice below to make the most of your testing experience.

General Advice and Tips

- Read the question fully to determine what the question is ultimately asking.
- Use scratch paper to brainstorm, prewrite, and outline your response.
- When possible, use real names, dates, events, or court cases as examples. Though not required, these will help you convey your points with strength. Once you've completed this book, you'll have many examples to offer.
- If the prompt calls on you to take a position, be sure to do so.
- Do not open with an overly general introduction. Get to your point.
- Try to be accurate and use correct spelling, dates, and names, but don't sweat particulars.
- If you are not familiar with a free-response topic, still attempt it. Answer fully any part you can, and try the other parts. One of the four questions will seem more difficult, or at least less familiar, than the others.
- Practice the standard rules of writing. Evaluate and proofread your essay. Read over and correct any mistakes.

Overall Scoring and Credit

The exams are graded in early June and reported back to you and your high school in mid-summer. You can earn between zero and five points.

Scoring on the Exam

5	Extremely well qualified
4	Well qualified
3	Qualified
2	Possibly qualified
1	No recommendation

Many colleges award credit for a score of three or better; some require a five; and occasionally prestigious universities do not recognize the AP® Government and Politics exam at all. The College Board equates a score of five to an A in a college-level class, a four to an A-, B+, or B, and a three to roughly a B-, C+, or C.

In 2014, nearly 12 percent of those taking the exam earned a score of five. More than 12 percent received a four and 26 percent earned a three. About 25 percent earned a two, and roughly another 25 percent earned a one. So considering a score of three as passing, just over half of students passed the exam. Many colleges allow students with a passing grade on the AP exam to bypass a class titled *American Politics* or *Political Science 101*. To help you plan for the exam, the College Board provides a site to connect with universities across the nation. Use it to find how your college regards the exam and what score they require. www.collegeboard.com/ap/creditpolicy

A Final Note

Large numbers of Americans, especially independents and young adults, mistrust politicians and the partisan talking heads on cable TV and are turned off by the political process. If you feel this way, you are very normal. However, don't let an understandable irritation with polarizing partisans hamper your chances for success as a student or diminish your performance on the exam. You are primarily a student observer. As you begin in-depth preparation for the exam, though, you may find that as you learn more about the United States government, you can move from observer to participant.

UNIT 1: Constitutional Underpinnings

Chapter 1 *The Constitution*

Chapter 2 *Federalism*

After suffering a decade of imposed tax laws and rights violations, the American colonists presented the Declaration of Independence to the British Crown to break away from British control. The U.S. government at first operated under the Articles of Confederation, a weak form of government, until delegates convened in Philadelphia in 1787 to draft the Constitution. After a public debate between Federalists, who endorsed the plan, and Anti-Federalists, who opposed the plan, the states ultimately ratified the Constitution.

The Constitution defined the three branches of government, relations among the states, national and state powers, and the process to alter, or amend, the document itself. Chief among its provisions are the checks and balances which keep any one branch from becoming too powerful. Also, the amendment process allowed for a swift addition of the Bill of Rights and a total of 27 amendments.

The Constitution established federalism, a system of government that divides the power between the national and state governments. As new national concerns have surfaced, Congress has used its power to set policies to address these issues consistently throughout the states. The federal government has awarded large financial grants to encourage state action and has simply mandated others. Yet, states use their power to maintain jurisdiction over schools, marriages and divorces, criminal law enforcement, wills, deeds, motor-vehicle law, and several other aspects of life. Through state referenda, citizens have recently made unique and variant changes on gambling, gay marriage, and the legalization of marijuana.

Key Concepts

Constitutional Underpinnings of United States Government

- Considerations that influenced the formulation and adoption of the Constitution
- Separation of powers
- Checks and balances
- Federalism
- Theories of democratic government

Source: *AP® United States Government and Politics Course and Exam Description*

The Constitution

"I doubt whether any other Convention we can obtain, may be able to make a better Constitution. From such an assembly can a perfect production be expected? It therefore astonishes me, Sir, to find this system approaching so near perfection as it does."

—Ben Franklin on the Proposed Constitution, 1787

Essential Question: What historical and philosophical influences shaped the United States system of government?

The United States Constitution is the document that provides the guidelines for the national government. Drafted in Philadelphia in 1787 and officially ratified in 1788, the Constitution defines governing principles, national offices, functions, and limitations. It created the legislative, executive, and judicial branches; defined federalism and the relationship among the states; and provided for a method to alter, or amend, the document. In 1789, Congress passed and the states ratified the first ten amendments to the Constitution, known as the Bill of Rights. Seventeen amendments have been added since.

Because the Constitution is the blueprint for government, knowing and understanding this document is essential to this course and to understanding American government. The full text of the Constitution is printed in the back of this book. When reading about particular provisions or clauses, turn to it for reference. Keep good notes on key passages and their importance. These practices will help you master the content and overall structure of the document.

American Independence and Early National Government

The Constitution and the new government it defines did not come into being easily. It took a war with Great Britain, a governing experiment, and a three-year struggle to create a more perfect union.

In the 1770s, after a century of British rule in the American colonies, the colonists and England's King George III came to an impasse after Parliament passed a series of tax laws. Leaders from the 13 colonies challenged British authority. They were inspired by philosophers from the Enlightenment who had argued for natural, God-given rights and for a **social contract** between a democratic government and the people. If a government violated the understood compact between the state and the governed, they argued, then the people could take that power back. After a successful military campaign, the leading American revolutionaries became the Founding

TIMELINE

1764	Parliament passes Sugar Act
1765	Parliament passes Stamp Act
1770	Boston Massacre
1773	Boston Tea Party
1774	First Continental Congress
1775	Battles of Lexington and Concord
1776	Declaration of Independence
1781	Articles of Confederation ratified
1783	Treaty of Paris
1786	Shays Rebellion
1787	Constitutional Convention
1789	President Washington, Congress elected
1789	Congress Proposes Bill of Rights
1790	Rhode Island, the 13th State, ratifies Constitution
1791	Bill of Rights ratified

Source: Allyn Cox, Architect of the Capitol
The First Continental Congress

Source: archive.org
Shays Rebellion

Source: Library of Congress
Constitution

Fathers of the new nation. After a failed attempt to govern themselves during the 1780s under the Articles of Confederation, a stronger framework—the Constitution—became necessary for the United States to transition from a loose collection of sovereign states into a united republic.

The Road to Revolution

England's King George III and Parliament passed laws that restricted the colonists' freedoms and taxed them to help finance the Crown's empire. With plentiful land and resources, the North American colonies were among Britain's most financially successful properties in an otherwise financially challenging time. Decades of wars and imperial endeavors had ravaged the British treasury. The popular saying at the time, "The sun never sets on the British Empire," literally defined the expansive nature of the realm because the sun shone on British land somewhere on the globe 24 hours a day, seven days a week. Maintaining such a far-flung empire required revenue. The Sugar Act was Britain's first attempt at increasing revenue. Soon the Stamp Act, which taxed colonists who transacted legal documents, the Tea Act, and other acts followed.

The colonists organized to oppose the acts. Some colonists opposed the taxes on a practical, economic basis, but most outspoken American leaders took a principled position against the laws because Parliament created these without any colonial representation. No colonist expected the democratic representation Americans value today. At the time only men with property could cast votes in England and in American elections, but colonists felt the Crown's complete disregard for any representation at all violated the Enlightenment philosophies they so revered.

"No taxation without representation!" demanded the colonists. The British government responded unapologetically and declared the colonists were "virtually represented." They reminded colonists that most citizens residing throughout the British Isles, about 90 percent, could not vote. Members of Parliament insisted they still considered the colonists' best interests.

Tensions increased as protesters refused to abide by the new laws and the British government doubled-down to enforce them. Royal courts tried and convicted protesters unfairly. The British government violated the ideas of free speech, free assembly, and free press by exacting punishments when colonists spoke, gathered, or published in opposition. Colonial leaders attempted at first to negotiate a peaceful relationship through the Olive Branch Petition to King George, a symbolic act of peace in which they pledged loyalty but also made clear their grievances. The King rejected that petition, and the colonies mobilized for revolt.

In Boston, the Sons of Liberty created an organized force that expanded to cities throughout the colonies. Among the leading advocates for freedom in the Sons of Liberty were John and Samuel Adams. Others, such as Benjamin Franklin, Patrick Henry, and Thomas Jefferson, also vocally criticized British lawmakers. Pamphleteers such as Thomas Paine and David Ramsey published treatises that argued for a break from Britain.

Influence of Enlightenment Thought

The Sons of Liberty and other advocates for freedom drew on Enlightenment political theory. It had been developed when the principles of rationalism that had unlocked doors to the natural world during the Scientific Revolution were applied to the social world as well. Especially influential were the writings of English philosopher **John Locke** (1632–1704) and Swiss-born philosopher Jean-Jacques Rousseau (1712–1778).

John Locke and Natural Law Locke argued that **natural law** is the law of God, and that this law is acknowledged through human sense and reason. He proposed that under natural law—in a state of nature—people were born free and equal. According to this law, Locke reasoned,

> . . . no one can be . . . subjected to the political power of another, without his own consent. The only way whereby any one divests himself of his natural liberty, and puts on the bonds of civil society, is by agreeing with other men to join and unite into a community, for their comfortable, safe, and peaceable living one amongst another, in a secure enjoyment of their properties. . . . When any number of men have so consented to make one community or government, they are thereby presently incorporated, and make one body politic, wherein the majority have a right to act and conclude the rest. (*Second Treatise of Government, Ch. 8, Sec. 95*)

Locke argued further that natural law not only entitled but obligated people to rebel when the rule of kings did not respect the consent of the governed.

Jean-Jacques Rousseau and the Social Contract Rousseau was much influenced by Locke. He spoke for those "intending their minds" away from an irrational and oppressive political order, away from a governmental theory that rested in divine right of kings and clergy to rule and misrule. The opening sentence of his influential treatise, *The Social Contract*, dramatically lays out a key human problem: "Man was born free, and he is everywhere in chains." The social contract he describes is the agreement of free and equal people to abandon certain natural rights in order to find freedom in a single body politic committed to the general good. He envisioned a sovereignty—the will of the people—as the authority for making laws, and a government of officials to carry out the laws.

French philosopher Montesquieu (1689–1755), like Rousseau, recognized both the sovereign and administrative aspects of governmental power. He argued for the separation of powers in the administrative government, comprised of the executive, legislative, and judicial branches.

Enlightenment thought was well known among English colonists in North America. According to historian Carl Becker, "Most Americans had absorbed Locke's works as a kind of political gospel." The American revolutionaries believed that men were entitled to "life, liberty, and property," and that these cannot be taken away except under laws created through the consent of the governed. The lack of colonial representation in Parliament, taxation without consent, and subsequent violations of liberty violated those fundamental rights.

Declaring Independence

American-British tensions rose to new heights during 1774 and 1775, beginning with the battles at Lexington and Concord in Massachusetts. By the summer of 1776, the Continental Congress commissioned a committee of five men—Thomas Jefferson, John Adams, Benjamin Franklin, Roger Sherman, and Robert Livingston—to draft an official statement to summarize the colonists' views. In that document, which became the **Declaration of Independence,** these men justified the break from Britain and proclaimed to the world the reasons for independence. The Declaration created a moral and legal justification for the rebellion.

Thomas Jefferson was the primary author and drew from Locke and other Enlightenment philosophers. The opening paragraph, for example, asserts that the colonists are acting to protect "the separate and equal station to which the Laws of Nature and of Nature's God entitle them." The document goes on to declare that men "are endowed by their creator with certain unalienable rights...[and] to secure these rights, governments are instituted among men, deriving their powers from the consent of the governed." It asserts that "all

THE 13 ORIGINAL COLONIES

men are created equal" and that people are entitled to "life, liberty, and the pursuit of happiness." After laying the philosophical foundation, the Declaration goes on to list "a long train of abuses and usurpations" the English Crown had committed, including dissolving the colonial legislatures, keeping standing armies in peacetime and depriving accused Americans of jury trials. Congress approved the final draft of the Declaration on July 4, 1776, marking the official birth of the United States.

The Declaration was just that—a declaration to the King, Parliament, and the world to justify the new, independent United States. It expresses the philosophical underpinnings of the new nation—Enlightenment ideals applied to a very specific situation—and when it was distributed and read publicly it helped to rally colonists to the cause. It was not intended as a plan for governing the new nation. It does not create any governmental bodies, offices, or policy-making procedures that could actually guarantee all the human entitlements Enlightenment philosophers upheld. On *equality*, for example, until Congress and the states added the Fourteenth Amendment's equal protection clause to the Constitution, governments did not have to treat citizens equally. And, unfortunately, we don't have a full legal right to "happiness" even today—how could such a personal matter be guaranteed?

During the war, Americans instituted the Continental Congress to govern the American states collectively, and they began to formalize their ideas for a permanent government. The war raged on until General George Washington's army defeated the British at Yorktown, Virginia, in 1781. An official peace was negotiated in 1783 with the Treaty of Paris.

The Articles of Confederation

As soon as the states declared independence, they realized a more formal relationship among them could only assist their cause. The Continental Congress created a committee of 13 men to draft the **Articles of Confederation,** a series of statements that defined the initial national government and redefined the former colonies as states. Though the Articles of Confederation were not officially ratified by the states until 1781, the Continental Congress legislated during wartime with a wide array of powers to adopt commercial codes, establish and maintain an army, define crimes against the United States, and negotiate foreign affairs abroad. This document defined "the firm league of friendship" that existed among the states, which had delegated a few powers to the national government. The Articles provide that "each state retains its sovereignty, freedom and independence."

How to apportion states' representation in the newly designed Confederation Congress beset the nation with controversy from the very beginning. Some leaders recognized the merits of giving greater representation to the more populated states, something the Virginia delegation pushed for early on. Leaders from smaller states opposed representation based on population. After a furious debate, the authors of the Articles created an equal representation system—each state received one vote in the Congress.

The Confederation Congress continued to meet in New York. States appointed delegations of up to seven men that voted as a unit. National legislation required the votes of at least nine states to pass. A unanimous vote of all 13 was required to alter or amend the existing Articles of Confederation. The Articles entitled the Congress to engage in international diplomacy, to declare war, and to acquire territory. They provided protection of religion and speech. They provided for **extradition**—that is, states were expected to extradite, or return, fugitives to states where they had committed crimes and runaway slaves to states they had fled. The document encouraged a free flow of commerce among the states. It required that states provide a public, fair government and that Congress could sit as a court in disputes between states.

Following are some of the key provisions of the Articles of Confederation.

Articles of Confederation

- "Each state retains its sovereignty, freedom, and independence, and every Power, [not]...expressly delegated to the United States, in Congress assembled."

- "In determining questions in the United States, in Congress assembled, each State shall have one vote."

- "The United States in Congress assembled, shall have the sole and exclusive right and power of determining on peace and war."

- "Full faith and credit shall be given in each of these States to the records, acts, and judicial proceedings of the courts and magistrates of every other State."

- "Congress assembled shall also be the last resort on appeal in all disputes and differences now subsisting or that hereafter may arise between two or more States."

An Ineffective Confederation and a Call for New Government

The Articles of Confederation provided a weak system for the new United States and prevented leaders from making much domestic progress. The requirements that nine states must agree in order to enact federal law and that all states must agree in order to amend the system of government proved daunting. The Congress could not tax the people directly. The national government could not raise or maintain an army. There was no national court system or national currency. The Congress encouraged but could not regulate commerce among the states. The system had rendered the Confederation Congress ineffective. In fact, the stagnation and a degree of anarchy threatened the health of the nation. The country faced a high war debt, and foreign creditors lost faith in this new nation. States quarreled over boundary disputes. Interstate trade was chaotic.

Shays Rebellion and Response

A regional rebellion signaled the height of disruption. In western Massachusetts in 1786, a large group of impoverished farmers, many Revolutionary War veterans, lost their farms to mortgage foreclosures and failure to pay taxes. Daniel Shays, a former captain in the Continental army, led the group who demanded that the government ease financial pressures by printing more money, lightening taxes, and suspending mortgages. They grabbed their muskets and challenged the Massachusetts government. The state raised a small army with donations from the wealthy citizenry in an attempt to put down the uprising. Several skirmishes occurred, and three of Shays's men were killed. The movement soon collapsed, but Shays rebellion, along with irregularities in commerce, made leaders realize the need to revise government. A small group convened in Annapolis, Maryland, to discuss the concerns. This convention addressed trade and the untapped economic potential of the new United States. Little was accomplished, however, except to secure a recommendation for Congress to call a more comprehensive convention.

Congress scheduled the much larger convention for May of 1787 in Philadelphia. By then few Americans viewed the Articles of Confederation as sufficient. John Adams, who was serving in Congress, argued that a man's "country" was still his state, and for his Massachusetts delegation, the Congress was "our embassy." There was little sense of national unity.

The Constitutional Convention in Philadelphia

The Confederation Congress called the convention "for the sole and express purpose of revising the Articles of Confederation." By the time the process was over, critics pointed to the extralegal manner in which the Articles were replaced by a new system of government. In May 1787, delegates from neighboring states began to arrive to Independence Hall (the Pennsylvania State House) to get an early start on improving national governance. Among the first to arrive was 36-year-old Virginia lawyer **James Madison,** and he was well prepared for the deliberations. His friend and fellow planter Thomas Jefferson was serving in Paris as the U.S. ambassador to France, and he sent Madison books from Europe on ancient governments, both successful and failed examples. Though Madison was not the most vocal at the convention, his influence in creating the plan for the new government has earned him the nickname "Father of the Constitution."

Other noteworthy delegates came from 12 states (Rhode Island chose to not participate). These included George Washington, who served as a cooling force during heated debate. In fact, Washington's participation alone elevated the validity of the meeting and the endeavor to enhance government. Another influential founder, Alexander Hamilton, Washington's aide-de-camp during the war, proved annoying at the meetings for his long-winded speeches and his reverence for monarchy. Benjamin Franklin, the elder statesman at age 81, offered his experience as one who had participated in the drafting of the Declaration, the Articles themselves, and the Treaty of Paris with Britain. He also held distinction in discovery, invention, and civic endeavors.

James Madison, the "Father of the Constitution"

In addition to these leading statesmen, others in attendance included future Supreme Court justices, cabinet members, and notable congressmen. Nearly three-fourths of the delegates had served in the Continental Congress. Several had helped draft their state constitutions. Eight had also signed the Declaration of Independence. Twenty-one had fought in the Revolutionary War.

Once a quorum (enough present to conduct business) of states arrived, the convention established some basic ground rules. The delegates unanimously elected General Washington, the most revered man in the room, as president of the convention. All delegates had an opportunity to speak uninterrupted but then had to wait for any other delegates responding before speaking again. States would vote as units, and a simple majority would carry the state's vote. Perhaps the most controversial rule was that those attending the convention had to keep everything secret during the proceedings until the entire plan was ready to present to the public. The controversy and intense viewpoints from across the land had the potential to incite exaggerated rumors. Opponents of the convention would feed on any information, or misinformation, to dismantle this plan. So the delegates kept the windows closed and the proceedings quiet for the duration of the convention.

The Virginia Plan Numerous plans were presented to the convention to improve the workings of the national government. Virginia's governor Edmund Randolph introduced what was later dubbed the **Virginia Plan**. Written largely by Madison, the plan created a three-branch system of government defined by 15 resolves. It called for a national executive to administer the business of state, a judiciary, and a **bicameral**, or two-house, legislature. The people would elect a lower house that would then elect members of an upper house. This plan became the blueprint for the Constitution. The Virginia Plan also made the national government supreme over the states and offered the ideas for a multi-tiered court system and the **separation of powers**, defining the distinct responsibilities and limits of each branch to keep any one branch from becoming too powerful. Delegates discussed and intensely debated the plan, as the smaller states began to fear the overwhelming representation larger states would have.

The New Jersey Plan William Paterson of New Jersey introduced a counter-proposal for government. **The New Jersey Plan**, as it came to be known, differed from Randolph's proposal in important ways. It assured that states would retain sovereignty; it proposed that the national legislature would have only limited and defined powers; and it included no provision for national courts. Two other distinct differences between Paterson's plan and the Virginia Plan lay in how representation would be apportioned and whether or not the new government would be "federal," a collection of sovereign states gathered to govern, or "national," a unified authority with absolute sovereignty over the entire nation as well as the individual states.

The Great Compromise Representation had been the frustration of the Americans since they began seeking independence. The more populated states felt they deserved a stronger voice in making national policy decisions. The smaller states sought to retain an equal footing. Finally, Roger Sherman of Connecticut offered the **Great Compromise** (the Connecticut Compromise). Sherman's proposal created a two-house Congress composed of a **House of Representatives** and a **Senate**. His plan satisfied both those wanting population as the criteria for awarding seats in a legislature, because House seats would be awarded based on population, and those wanting equal representation, because the Senate would receive two senators from each state, regardless of the state's size.

Slavery and the Three-Fifths Compromise Another compromise would be necessary before the question of representation was settled, however. Delegates from nonslave states questioned how slaves would be counted in determining representation. Since slaves did not have the right to vote, those who were able to vote in slave states would have more sway than voters in nonslave states if slaves were counted in the population. Roger Sherman once more put forward a compromise, this time with Pennsylvania delegate James Wilson. They introduced and Congress accepted the **Three-Fifths Compromise**. The northern and southern delegates agreed to count only three of every five slaves to determine representation in the House after the three-fifths compromise.

Two other issues regarding slavery were also debated and addressed in the Constitution, although the words "slave" and "slavery" do not appear in the document. Delegates questioned whether the states or the federal government should have the power to control or regulate slavery. They also debated how to handle slave insurrection, or runaways. Delegates resolved the first matter by prohibiting Congress from stopping the international slave trade for 20 years after ratification of the Constitution. And they resolved the second with an extradition clause that addressed how states should handle runaway slaves.

Other compromises would be necessary during the summer-long convention in Philadelphia. Delegates debated whether or not the United States needed a president or chief executive, how such an officer should be elected, what powers the federal government would have, and what powers the states would retain. The delegates who desired stronger states' rights and feared a national centralization of power wanted a limited list of powers granted to the federal government. The term "federal" at the time meant a loose collection of states gathered for a common purpose, with the states ultimately retaining sovereignty, which was the very relationship defined under the Articles of Confederation. A national government, however, would make the national lawmaking body supreme and create a stronger union instead of a loose collection of states. Delegates also considered what types of laws the Congress could make and what citizen rights to protect. What resulted from "a bundle of compromises" was the U.S. Constitution.

The Proposed Constitutional Structure

On September 17, 1787, thirty-nine delegates put their signatures to the Constitution. Once the plan for national government was complete, the proposed Constitution contained seven articles with a host of provisions. The document opens with the **Preamble,** a sort of mission statement, that begins "We the people" and outlines the purposes of the new government, such as "establishing justice" and providing for a "common defense."

The plan for government included three separate branches—legislative, executive, and judicial—each having unique powers and each able to block the other with the designed **checks and balances.** It included an executive president to serve as commander in chief and a Congress that could tax, borrow, and regulate commerce. It also called for a Supreme Court and a plan for lower courts and the **Electoral College System** to elect the president. The Committee of Style composed the final wording of the Constitution (the original final draft is in the hand of Pennsylvania's Gouverneur Morris) and the standard for ratification was defined. Once nine state conventions ratified this Constitution, it would go into effect.

The resulting document created the legislative, executive, and judicial branches defined in the first three articles, a separation of powers among the branches, and the qualifications and terms for offices. It also included sections regarding the relations among the states, the amendment process, and national supremacy.

Article I The House and Senate differ in ways beyond their allotment of seats. House members are elected by the people every two years. In contrast, state legislatures would elect senators, who were then beholden to state governments (this provision was later changed by the Seventeenth Amendment). The House became the more representative, or more democratic, institution. The differing age requirements, 25 for House members and 30 for Senators, and the fact that senators represent the state at large while House members represent localities create a different dynamic in each body.

Article I has 10 sections and is the longest article, revealing the Framers' concern for representative lawmaking and their reverence for the legislative branch. Sections 8, 9, and 10 detail the powers and limitations of Congress and the powers of the states. The Framers identified a limited list of **enumerated powers** included in Section 8, which include the powers to tax, borrow money, raise an army, create a postal system, address piracy on the seas, define the immigration and naturalization process, and a few others. The **commerce clause** empowers the Congress to "regulate commerce with other nations, and among the several states."

The final clause in Section 8 is the **necessary and proper clause**, or **elastic clause**. This provision states, "The Congress shall have the power…to make all laws which shall be necessary and proper for carrying into execution the foregoing powers." Since this power goes beyond the explicitly enumerated powers, the elastic clause is said to grant *implicit* powers. After a fierce debate, the Framers included this to assure the Congress some flexibility in legislating.

Section 9 lists what Congress *cannot* do. For example, the federal legislature cannot tax exported goods. Congress cannot take away the right of *habeas corpus* (the right to be formally charged after an arrest), cannot pass bills of attainder (legislative acts declaring one guilty of a crime) or *ex post facto* laws (making an act illegal after one has committed it). Nor can Congress grant any title of nobility. Section 10 lists powers the states are denied. States cannot, for example, enter into treaties with other countries, coin money, or tax exports.

Article II How to create and define the office of president in Article II stirred one of the more heated discussions in Philadelphia. The rebellion against a monarch made the populace concerned about one-person rule. However, the lack of leadership under the Articles of Confederation and the need for an executive to take care of the nation's business made the creation of the presidency inevitable. Article II lays out the requirements to assume this office and the executive's role. The president must be 35 years old, a natural born citizen, and a resident of the United States for at least 14 years. As commander in chief, the president oversees and manages the U.S. military. As head of state, the president receives foreign ambassadors and sends U.S. ambassadors abroad.

Article III The need for national courts led to Article III, which defines the judiciary. The Framers only mentioned one actual court, the Supreme Court, but they empowered Congress to create inferior courts. The federal courts have jurisdiction over cases involving federal law, disputes between states, and concerns that involve government officials. The president appoints Supreme Court justices and other federal judges, with approval of the Senate. These judges serve "during good behavior," which in practice often means life terms.

Article IV Article IV defines relations among the states. It includes the **"full faith and credit"** clause that requires states to be open about their laws and encourages states to respect one another's laws. It also requires that "the citizens of each state shall be entitled to all privileges and immunities of citizens in the several states." In other words, on most issues states cannot play favorites with their own citizens or exclude outsiders from basic privileges and immunities. For example, if a Nebraska police officer pulls over an Oklahoma driver, the officer of one state will honor the driver's license from another. If a California man is accused of a crime in Alabama, he'll get the same protections and immunities as an accused Alabama defendant. Article IV also addresses the extradition process for fugitives who have committed state crimes.

Article V Delegates in Philadelphia realized the Constitution would prove imperfect and that it would occasionally require some changes. That is why Article V defines the amendment process. There are two different ways to propose an amendment and two different ways to ratify amendments. The Congress can propose an amendment with a two-thirds vote in each house. Two-thirds of state legislatures can also propose by calling a convention to propose an amendment. To ratify the proposal, three-fourths of the state legislatures must agree to it, or three-fourths of state conventions. All successful amendments have been passed by Congress and all but one, the Twenty-First Amendment to repeal prohibition of alcohol, were ratified by state legislatures. The Framers included the alternative method to propose or ratify in case sitting governments refused the people's wishes.

Article VI To avoid the lack of unification experienced under the Articles of Confederation and to unite the nation under stronger national policy, Article VI was included to establish **national supremacy**. "This Constitution, and the Laws of the United States," the **supremacy clause** declares, "shall be the supreme Law of the Land."

Article VII In this article, the Framers outlined the process by which this new plan would be put into place. Rather than relying on existing state legislatures that might refrain from giving up power or delay the ratification process, Article VII declares the Constitution would go into effect when the ninth state convention approved it. This design for ratification, opponents and later historians would argue, was yet another extralegal method in the process.

The Original U.S. Constitution	
Article I	The Legislative Branch
Article II	The Executive Branch
Article III	The Judiciary
Article IV	Relations among States
Article V	Amendment Process
Article VI	National Supremacy
Article VII	Ratification Process

When the Framers finished the final draft of the Constitution, not all were present in Independence Hall. As most remaining men attached their names to the document, three stood by and refused to sign it. Edmund Randolph was one. He had watched as the convention altered the Virginia Plan he introduced in May. George Mason, the chief author of Virginia's Declaration of Rights, was another. He refused to sign because the Constitution had no federal bill of rights. The Constitution's lack of a detailed list of rights became the national debate over the following year. Finally, Massachusetts delegate Elbridge Gerry did not agree to the new plan. The delegates departed Philadelphia wondering what the future held and if their months of work, debate, and detailed plans were for naught. Leaders and citizens fell into two camps: those for and those against the new plan.

Ratification

James Madison returned to New York to serve in the Confederation Congress and immediately began working toward ratification, which looked promising early on. During December 1787, three states quickly voted to ratify. Two more states joined in January 1788. Of the first five state ratifying conventions, three approved the Constitution unanimously. The other two did so with strong majorities. Nonetheless, the future of the Republic was uncertain. Massachusetts proved reluctant, and leading opponents of the Constitution criticized the plan in newspapers and in circulating pamphlets.

Support for the Constitution With the insistence of fellow pro-Constitution Virginians, Madison named himself a candidate for his state's ratifying convention to be held in Richmond. From New York, he began writing a series of essays for publication to argue in favor of this new plan. He soon joined fellow delegate Alexander Hamilton and New York Governor John Jay in writing a series of essays that explained the Framers' intentions. These authors adopted the name *The Federalist* to assure citizens that they had created a federal system and that states, in the main, had not lost their importance (today these essays are commonly called **The Federalist Papers**). The so-called Federalists also wanted to allay fears that their plan would subject people in the states to abuses by this new national government.

Of the 85 essays that Madison, Hamilton, and Jay penned, numbers 10 and 51 are often cited because these address the concern for special interests and the system of checks and balances. *Federalist #10* speaks of factions, or interested groups in government, whether a majority or a minority, "united and actuated by some common passion or interest adverse to the rights of other citizens." Publius, a Federalist pen name, stated that men of like mind might begin to dominate government for their own ends rather than for the public good. He explained how no plan for government can eliminate factions entirely, but noted that the Framers had created a system to stall and frustrate factions and thus limit their effects. They created not a pure democracy at the national level, but rather a representative republic that had to consider the interests of varied people from across many miles of land. America even at its birth was one of the most expansive countries in the world, and varied factions arriving from New England and from Georgia would neutralize one another. The advantage, Madison said, "is enjoyed by a large over a small republic, and enjoyed by the union over the State composing it."

Federalist #51 points to the separation of powers as a guard against tyranny. "If men were angels, no government would be necessary," Publius stated, admitting that devious men were inevitably going to make their way into government at some future point. "You must first enable the government to control the governed," the essay explained, "and in the next place, force it to control itself." Madison also stated how each branch had devices to prevent any one branch from becoming too powerful, how bicameralism would serve as a check within the legislature. He also elaborated that a president, armed with the power of **veto**, could stop a runaway legislature that threatened the people's freedoms. The fact that state and federal governments would be distinct, separate, and sovereign in their own spheres would also prevent an accumulation of power in one spot. The Framers wanted a democracy in which the people ruled, but Madison pointed out a concern for the "tyranny of the majority," the possibility that the majority could run roughshod over minorities who should be afforded liberties. The Framers' governmental design with checks and balances, judges' life terms, and other devices would limit this tyranny.

BY THE NUMBERS Ratifying the Constitution			
State	**Date**	**For**	**Against**
Delaware	December 1787	30	0
Pennsylvania	December 1787	46	23
New Jersey	December 1787	38	0
Georgia	January 1788	26	0
Connecticut	January 1788	128	40
Massachusetts	February 1788	187	168
Maryland	April 1788	63	11
South Carolina	May 1788	149	73
New Hampshire	June 1788	57	47
Virginia	June 1788	89	79
New York	July 1788	30	27
North Carolina	November 1789	194	77
Rhode Island	May 1790	34	32

What do the numbers show? Which states ratified early, and which states took longer? What states ratified the Constitution by slim margins? Which were unanimous? Which state's ratification put the Constitution into effect?

Opposition to the Constitution Opponents of the Constitution, including Virginia's Patrick Henry and George Mason, desired a federal government more like the one under the Articles. Madison and his colleagues' attaching the "Federalist" name to their cause preempted opponents from claiming the label. Opponents then became known as **Anti-Federalists** for lack of a better term. The irony was that the Anti-Federalists argued for a truly federal government as defined, while the Federalists advocated a national system with some loss of state sovereignty. The Anti-Federalist concerns came from the recent experience with an autocratic ruling country. Some feared a single executive might replicate a monarchical king, potentially limiting state and individual rights. Congress's power to tax, to control a standing army, and to do anything else it felt "necessary and proper" made the Anti-Federalists wary. The thick veil of secrecy in which designing men had conspired to draft the document made Anti-Federalists and much of the general public suspicious.

Newspapers published the text of the Constitution and essays for and against it. Some state conventions had remarkably close votes, but the Federalists won the day, with New Hampshire becoming the ninth state to ratify. Yet most agreed without New York and Virginia, the new Republic might stumble. Both of these states did ratify, but only after contentious debate and close votes. The government was underway by 1789. Congress began meeting and President Washington took office. North Carolina and then Rhode Island ratified, resulting in ratification by all 13 states.

A Bill of Rights

George Mason's concern that the original Constitution had no bill of rights disturbed many others as well. Those who fought for independence argued that a bill of rights was necessary to secure the liberties earned through the revolution. The document framed in Philadelphia lacked a guarantee of free speech in Congress. There were no protections against aggressive prosecution, and no promise against cruel and unusual punishments. The Constitution did, however, include a few basic rights.

Rights in the Original Constitution
No religious tests to hold federal office
Right to jury trials in criminal cases
Neither Congress nor the states can pass a bill of attainder
Neither Congress nor the states can pass *ex post facto* laws
Congress cannot suspend *habeas corpus* rights except in wartime

The Anti-Federalists and some pro-Constitution leaders felt a list of rights was needed to complete the Philadelphia mission. There was opposition, however. One leading opponent was James Madison. He called bills of rights "parchment barriers," mere paper blocks to injustices and tyranny that could prevail if the government itself did not have provisions, such as checks and balances, to prevent such tyranny. He offered as examples minorities who had suffered at the will of majorities in states that did in fact have bills of rights. He also felt that by listing all the rights the federal government could not take away, a right could be inadvertently overlooked and the new federal government *could* later take it away. He felt the constitution never entitled the new federal government to take away any rights in the first place, so why was it necessary to list those that could not be taken away in the future?

The debate for or against adding a bill of rights overlapped the series of ratifying conventions that occurred throughout 1787–1790. With the efforts of the Federalists, as well as assurances that amendments protecting personal rights would be added, the large, later states ratified and joined the Union. Additionally, as the new Congress began meeting in 1789, delegates petitioned for these rights. Madison and the Congress compiled the many concerns into the amendments that became the **Bill of Rights**. The Bill of Rights was fully ratified by 1791.

The Bill of Rights includes many essential rights, most of which were violated under the oppressive British regime. The First Amendment declares freedoms of religion, speech, press, assembly, and protest. Dissent was the engine for revolution and was guaranteed permissible under the new American system of government. Therefore, Congress and the people put a high priority on the right to express political ideas, even if unpopular. Other amendments protect private property, due process, and fair trials and prevent cruel and unusual punishments. The Tenth Amendment prevents the federal government from taking any powers that are reserved to the states. The text of the Bill of Rights begins on page 476.

Selected Rights in the Bill of Rights	
Amendment I	Freedoms of religion, speech, press, assembly, and protest
Amendment II	Right to bear arms
Amendment III	No quartering of troops
Amendment IV	No unreasonable searches or seizures
Amendment V	Indictment, double jeopardy, protection against self incrimination, due process
Amendment VI	Speedy, public trial by jury of peers, cross examination, right to defense counsel
Amendment VII	Lawsuits and juries
Amendment VIII	No cruel or unusual punishments, no excessive fines
Amendment IX	Listing rights here doesn't deny others
Amendment X	Delegated and reserved powers

The Constitution in Practice

The Framers included several governing themes. They ensured a level of democracy by mandating elections for members of Congress and the president. **Popular sovereignty**—the people as the ultimate ruling authority—is evident in the Preamble, in the ratification process, and in the amendment process. Yet instead of creating a democracy, the Constitution creates a representative republic that limits government and tempers hasty, even if popular, ideas. The three branches share powers at the national level, and the national and state governments divide and share power as well under federalism. The Bill of Rights guarantees citizens a series of civil liberties. The Constitution's flexibility has empowered the government to face unforeseen circumstances and has allowed the people to add 27 total amendments.

A Democratic Republic

The Framers wanted the citizen representation of a democracy, but on the national level, they created a **representative republic**, a collection of sovereign states to gather for the national interest, national needs, and national defense. To promote popular sovereignty, the Framers required popular elections every two years for House members, but those were the only popular elections they put in the original Constitution. State legislatures elected their senators until 1913. The states name their electors to the Electoral College, and then the Electoral College elects the president.

Separation of Powers

The Framers made the legislative, executive, and judicial branches distinct in their own powers and responsibilities to dilute power among the three branches. Earlier in school you might have learned that "the legislature makes the law, the executive branch enforces the law, and the judicial branch interprets the law." This simplification overlooks the fact that all three branches can establish law and policy, but it does highlight the basic function of each branch. The legislature is the most numerous and representative branch, and it brings the people's ideas and opinions into the government. The president is ultimately the authority to enforce the law and to carry out Congress's policies, so the president and his administration shape the law in carrying it out through policy. The judiciary, appointed by the president and approved by the Senate, hears disputes and interprets laws and their application.

Checks and Balances

The limiting powers each branch has on the others are especially clear in the lawmaking process. A bill (a proposed law) can originate in either the House or Senate and must pass both bodies with a simple majority (50 percent plus one). Then the bill is presented to the president, who may sign it into law if in agreement with the proposal. Or, exercising executive checks and balances, the president may reject it with a **veto.** If after 10 days the president has done neither, the bill becomes law. If the president receives the bill at the end of a legislative session, his refusal to sign is known as a **pocket veto** and has the effect of killing the bill.

After the president consents to a law, it is entered into the United States Code, our body of federal laws and statutes. If the president vetoes a popular bill, the Congress, each house acting separately, can reverse the veto with a **two-thirds override,** which requires the support of a super majority. Congress overrode President George W. Bush's veto of the bill funding stem cell research in 2007, for example. Presidents must present their objections and reasons for vetoing to the house in which the bill originated. Congress can consider the president's explanation and reintroduce legislation with changes, or it can try to bypass the veto. Overriding a veto is extremely challenging because it means two-thirds or more of legislators (and supposedly two-thirds of the country) must agree on something, a tough standard to meet.

The Framers placed additional checks on power, such as the **impeachment** process and the Senate's right to provide **advice and consent** on presidential appointments. An impeachment is an accusation, an indictment of wrongdoing. Article I, Section II claims the House "shall have the sole power of impeachment." If a simple majority of the House wants to accuse the president, a federal judge, or other official of wrongdoing, members draft and vote on a bill of impeachment. If passed, the accused official can respond and defend himself or herself in front of the Senate in a trial. The Chief Justice presides as the judge. The Senate acts as a jury and casts a vote to keep or remove the president. A guilty verdict, or removal, requires a two-thirds vote. Two presidents have been impeached, Andrew Johnson, Lincoln's successor, and Bill Clinton for abuse of office and accusations of lying under oath. After their trials, the Senate did not remove either because the charges did not reach the standard of "treason, bribery, or other high crimes or misdemeanors." President Richard Nixon, the only president to resign, did so because he feared an impeachment from the House. The House has impeached several federal judges and the Senate has removed some of them.

The Framers gave the president the right to appoint "by and with the advice and consent of the Senate...ambassadors, other public ministers and consuls, judges of the Supreme Court." The president appoints the cabinet (secretaries of state and defense, for example), judges, and heads of agencies, but only if the Senate approves.

Article III doesn't say much about the proposed court system. Nor does Article III mention the concept of **judicial review**. This judicial check on power became a national reality a few years after the drafting of the Constitution. Chief Justice John Marshall initiated the custom in a complicated dispute between William Marbury and then-Secretary of State James Madison in 1803. Marshall interpreted part of the relevant law as a violation of the Constitution and simply declared it null and void.

In his *Marbury v. Madison* (1803) opinion, Marshall stated unequivocally that "a law repugnant to the Constitution is void; and that courts, as well as other departments, are bound by that instrument." Since this landmark decision, judicial review has often become a major step in finalizing law. In modern times, the Supreme Court and lower courts have exercised review to protect liberties and to properly initiate policy. Courts can use this power to check the legislature, the executive, or state actions.

Federalism

Federalism is the balance of power among a central, national authority and state or regional authorities. Assigning different powers to the federal and state governments had been a vital issue at the Constitutional Convention. Congress and the president have unique powers defining their responsibilities and limits. The states are denied certain powers. And the Tenth Amendment ensures that the states have delegated to the federal government only those powers enumerated in the document and that all other powers are reserved to the states.

Is That Constitutional? *Texas v. Johnson* (1989)

Can state or federal governments make burning the U.S. flag in protest a criminal act? No. Such a law is a violation of the First Amendment's free speech clause.

In 1984 at the Republican National Convention in Dallas, Gregory Lee Johnson burned a U.S. flag outside the convention hall to protest President Reagan's policies. Authorities arrested Johnson and charged him with a crime under a Texas law that prevented flag desecration. He was convicted, sentenced to a year in prison, and charged a $2,000 fine.

Johnson claimed the law violated his First Amendment right to free speech. The Supreme Court had ruled much earlier that speech inciting others to imminent lawlessness or violent conduct may be abridged. But this protest was an expression that transmitted a message. "If there is a bedrock principle underlying the First Amendment," Justice William Brennan wrote, "it is that government may not prohibit the expression of an idea simply because society finds the idea itself offensive or disagreeable." The Court's decision struck down the Texas state law in order to protect free speech.

Countless Americans disagreed. With popular backing, Congress passed the Flag Protection Act the same year, making flag desecration criminal at the federal level. As soon as Congress acted, protesters tested the law on the steps of the U.S. Capitol. The Court voided the federal law in *United States v. Eichman* in 1990. Since then a movement to add a flag desecration amendment to the Constitution has surfaced. In fact, the House has passed an amendment proposal with the necessary two-thirds, but the Senate has not. So for now, neither states nor Congress can prevent burning a flag in protest.

National Supremacy

Article VI to the Constitution stipulates supremacy of national laws and government. The Anti-Federalists heavily questioned this provision. Included to assure compliance of the acts of Congress and treaties with other nations, the supremacy clause has placed the national government in some respects above the states in the areas of law delegated to the federal government. For example, in coining or printing money, international diplomacy, or national defense, the federal government is the exclusive authority. Yet, as we will see in the following chapter, Congress cannot claim national supremacy on distinctly **reserved powers**.

Limited Government

The Constitution reveals the Framers' commitment to limited government. The lawmaking process is slow and designed for gridlock among the branches to discuss, debate, and rewrite legislation before it is fully passed. Bicameralism ensures an extra step within the chief lawmaking branch. A president can veto popular ideas that may pass both houses too quickly without full consideration of the proposed law. The Bill of Rights serves as a broad limitation over an array of issues. Congress cannot establish a religion, abridge free speech, or arrest suspects without following a particular due process procedure. And the Tenth Amendment ultimately prevents Congress from actions beyond those limited in Article I, Section 8.

Flexibility

Limited government was important, but the Framers had the foresight to ensure flexibility. These men had seen much change in their generation and suspected that unforeseen events and changes in society might require revolutionary changes in national policy and in the Constitution. That's why they included the "necessary and proper clause" and the amendment process. The first allows Congress to legislate on matters closely related to the expressed powers. The amendment process has allowed for the Bill of Rights, women's suffrage, a redefined presidency, and national income taxes, among other changes.

REFLECT ON THE ESSENTIAL QUESTION

Essential Question: *What historical and philosophical influences shaped the United States system of government?* On separate paper, complete a chart like the one below to gather details to answer that question.

Political Philosophy of the Time	Historical Events and Forces

---

THINK AS A POLITICAL SCIENTIST: ANALYZE, INTERPRET, AND SYNTHESIZE *FEDERALIST #10* AND *FEDERALIST #51*

When you **analyze** a source, you take it apart and identify the elements that make it up. For example, if you analyzed the Constitution on the most obvious level, you would note there were three main parts: the Preamble, the Articles, and the Amendments. Each of these parts could be analyzed further. For example, within the Articles section, there are seven separate Articles.

When you **interpret** a source, you use critical thinking skills to understand what it means. You consider the time, place, and circumstance in which it was created and how that context might affect the meaning. You consider the author and apply what you may already know about the author to your understanding of the text. You ask how this source fits into (or stands apart from) the author's other ideas.

When you **synthesize** information, you pull together the information into a unified and coherent understanding. You identify different perspectives, and you draw in what you already may have known about the subject and fit all the pieces together in a new whole.

Practice: Read the *Federalist Papers #10* and *#51* on the Library of Congress Web site. Analyze and interpret them to determine how they fit into and/or stand apart from prevailing ideas of the times and to understand the implications they have for a future government and society. Then write a synthesis of what you learned through your analysis and interpretation. Pay special attention to these passages:

Federalist #10 "The very ambitions of leaders, human passions, and diversity of interests have, at various times, divided mankind into parties, and inflamed animosity, making them more apt to oppress each other than cooperate for their common good."

"The obvious inference is that the causes of faction cannot be removed and relief can only be sought in the means of controlling its effects."

"Hence, it clearly appears that the same advantage a Republic has over a democracy, controlling the effects of faction, is enjoyed by a larger over a small republic, and enjoyed by the Union over the States composing it."

Federalist #51 "You must first enable the government to control the governed, and in the next place, force it to control itself."

"The remedy for this is to divide the legislature into different houses and make them . . . as little connected with each other as the nature of their common functions and their common dependence on the society will allow."

KEY TERMS, NAMES, AND EVENTS

advice and consent

Anti-Federalists

Articles of Confederation

bicameral

Bill of Rights

checks and balances

commerce clause

Declaration of Independence

Electoral College System

enumerated powers

extradition

Federalist Papers

federalism

Federalists

Great Compromise

House of Representatives

impeachment

James Madison

John Locke

judicial review

Marbury v. Madison (1803)

national supremacy

natural law

necessary and proper (elastic) clause

New Jersey Plan

pocket veto

popular sovereignty

Preamble

representative republic

reserved powers

Senate

separation of powers

social contract

supremacy clause

Texas v. Johnson (1989)

two-thirds override

United States v. Eichman (1990)

veto

Virginia Plan

MULTIPLE-CHOICE QUESTIONS

1. The American colonists revolted against the British government
   (A) in the 1750s
   (B) in search of social equality
   (C) motivated by a lack of representation and ideas of Enlightened thinkers
   (D) by creating a two-house legislature
   (E) to end slavery

2. The ratification of the U.S. Constitution
   (A) followed the amendment process outlined in the Articles of Confederation
   (B) was done by the legislatures of the several states
   (C) required the consent of nine state-ratifying conventions
   (D) did not occur until the Bill of Rights was fully ratified
   (E) is defined in Article II

3. Which amendment in the Bill of Rights guarantees the right of free speech?

(A) First Amendment

(B) Second Amendment

(C) Fourth Amendment

(D) Eighth Amendment

(E) Tenth Amendment

4. The Framers had a commitment to a limited, representative republic. Which is the most democratic institution that represents that commitment?

(A) U.S. Senate

(B) Supreme Court

(C) House of Representatives

(D) Electoral College

(E) Cabinet

5. A chief argument in James Madison's *Federalist #10* is

(A) a Bill of Rights is necessary to secure liberty

(B) free speech should be added to the Constitution

(C) judicial review will prevent harsh laws against the citizenry

(D) a large, diverse republic and checks and balances will tame factions

(E) that New York should oppose ratification of the Constitution

6. All of the following are examples of checks and balances EXCEPT

(A) a president vetoes a bill passed by Congress

(B) the Senate majority leader reorganizes the Senate calendar for bringing a floor vote

(C) the Supreme Court declares a law unconstitutional

(D) the House impeaches a president

(E) two-thirds of the House and Senate override a president's veto

7. Which statement about the Constitution and slavery is true?
   (A) The original Constitution freed the slaves because it proclaimed "all men are created equal."
   (B) The Constitution required counting slaves the same as counting whites to determine representation.
   (C) The Constitution expressly denied slaves and African Americans the right to vote.
   (D) The original Constitution limited Congress's regulation of the slave trade and called on northern states to extradite fugitive slaves.
   (E) The Framers nearly abolished slavery at the Constitutional Convention.

8. Which statement regarding the American founding is true?
   (A) The Constitution was drafted at the First Continental Congress.
   (B) The Declaration of Independence was drafted after the states ratified the Constitution.
   (C) The Framers in Philadelphia included the Bill of Rights in the Constitution.
   (D) The new Congress met before the final state joined the Union.
   (E) George Washington was elected president of the United States, and then the Articles of Confederation were put into effect.

9. One benefit of the Articles of Confederation was they allowed the Congress to
   (A) declare peace and war
   (B) tax the people directly
   (C) keep a standing army
   (D) regulate interstate commerce
   (E) easily amend them

10. Which statement about impeachment under the Constitution is true?
    (A) An impeachment is the removal of a president.
    (B) No president has ever been impeached.
    (C) The House can impeach presidents, not other federal officials.
    (D) The House can impeach officials for "treason, bribery, or other high crimes or misdemeanors."
    (E) The Constitution declares the Senate can impeach, but only for felonies.

Question

1. Leading American statesmen drew from varied experiences to create the U.S. Constitution and the Bill of Rights in a unique, representative manner, though historians argue about whether the founders created the new government in an extralegal manner.

   (a) Identify and describe two critical political events in the founding of the United States.
   (b) Identify and explain one reason why the manner in which the Constitution was created can be viewed as acceptable and necessary.
   (c) Identify and explain one reason why the manner in which the Constitution was created can be viewed as improper or extralegal.

Question

2. The Framers of the Constitution and the Bill of Rights created a plan for a national government that had limitations but was also very flexible.

   (a) Identify and explain two constitutional principles that show the Framers' commitment to limiting the federal government.

   (b) Identify and explain two constitutional principles that allow government to be flexible.

WRITING: UNDERSTAND THE TASK

When answering a free-response question, focus on the exact task that section of the prompt calls for. For example, both questions above ask you to **identify** and either **describe** or **explain**. The verbs *identify* and *describe* call for recalling straightforward information or processes. The verb *explain*, however, calls for showing how the specific recalled information demonstrates a general concept or how events or concepts are related. Also, for each lettered item, notice how many examples you must provide. The total across these will be the number of points that question is worth.

2

Federalism

"The government of the Union, though limited in its powers, is supreme within its sphere of action."

— Chief Justice John Marshall in *McCulloch v. Maryland,* 1819

Essential Question: How has federalism shaped the administration of public policy, and how do state, local, and national governments work within the federal framework today?

The Framers of the U.S. Constitution had to balance the powers of Congress and the federal government at the national level with the other powers held by the states. Where the power ultimately lies, however, has been a source of controversy since 1787. The national legislature has stretched its powers in trying to address national needs, while states have tried to maintain their sovereignty. In this chapter you will gain a better understanding of the evolution of federalism, how Congress's authority and modern function have blurred the line between state and national jurisdictions, and how modern leaders have tried to return much authority to the states.

Federalism Defined

In creating and empowering the new federal government, the Constitution's Framers debated where power should lie. The experience of having just defeated a tyrannical central government in London to secure liberty locally did not make the idea of centralizing power in the new United States very attractive. **Federalism**, the sharing of power between a central government and equally sovereign regional governments, became a key part of the framework to secure liberty while also dividing respective powers among multiple authorities.

Today, Canada, Australia, Germany, and other nations have a federal system. Some others have **unitary governments**, those with a single governing authority in a central capital with uniform law throughout the land. These include the United Kingdom, France, Italy, and Japan.

Under the original American federal system, the states had more authority than the nation. Recall that the Articles of Confederation (pages 7–8) merely created a firm league of friendship among the states. The revolutionaries created the Confederation government of the 1780s mainly for national defense and to engage in diplomatic relations with other countries. The Articles held that the national government derived all of its powers from the states.

By that time, every state had its own constitution, several with an attached bill of rights. All states had a legislature, defined crimes (such as murder and theft), and courts for criminal trials. The Framers focused on new national concerns, such as regulating commerce, building roads, coining money, defending the country, and defining immigration.

Provisions Defining Federalism

The foundation for federalism can be found in various parts of the original Constitution and the Bill of Rights. National needs require consistency across state lines, such as having uniform weights and measures and a national currency. To establish this consistency, Article I enables Congress to legislate on military and diplomatic affairs and international and interstate commerce. It also allows Congress to define such crimes as counterfeiting, mail fraud, immigration violations, and piracy. The Framers also put limits on Congress with Article I, Section 9.

Constitutional Provisions That Guide Federalism	
Article I, Section 8	Enumerated powers of Congress, including the "necessary and proper"clause
Article I, Section 9	Powers denied Congress, no regulating slave trade before 1808; states to be treated uniformly
Article I, Section 10	Powers denied to the states, such as treaties; impairing contracts
Article IV	Full faith and credit; privileges and immunities; extradition
Article VI	Supremacy of the national government
Ninth Amendment	Rights not listed reserved by the people
Tenth Amendment	Powers not delegated to the federal government reserved by the states

Later provisions define the relations among the states and national supremacy. Article IV explains full faith and credit, protections of privileges and immunities, and extradition. The article requires each state to give **full faith and credit** "to the public acts, records, and judicial proceedings of every other state." In other words, states must regard and honor one another's governments and laws. The **privileges and immunities clause** declares "citizens of each state shall be entitled to all privileges and immunities of citizens in the several states." States have created laws to protect their own residents or to give them priority over nonresidents, but the Supreme Court has struck down most of them based on this clause. States can, however, charge different college tuition prices for in-state and out-of-state students, largely because in-state students and their families have long paid into the state's tax system that supports state colleges. The **extradition** clause obligates states to deliver captured fugitive criminals back to the state where they committed the original crime.

Article VI, commonly called the *supremacy clause*, places national law above state authority. National law, however, is limited by the enumerated list of Congress's powers in Article I, Section 8. (See page 12.) But when a congressional act is enacted and constitutional, states cannot disregard it.

The States States already had prisons, state militias, and other services when the federal system was created. The Framers left these concerns up to the states, along with the management of elections, marriage laws, and maintaining deeds and records. Skeptics and Anti-Federalists desired an expressed guarantee in the Constitution to assure the preservation of states' rights. It came in the form of Amendment X. "The powers not delegated to the United States," the amendment declares, "are reserved to the states."

States have **police powers**, or powers to create and enforce laws on health, safety, and morals. These concerns encompass much of state budgets today. States fund and operate hospitals and clinics. Law enforcement is predominantly composed of state personnel. States can set their own laws on speed limits, seat belts, and smoking in public places.

The terms of the **Tenth Amendment** distinguish the two governing spheres. The **delegated powers** are those the states have delegated to the federal government, listed in Article I, Section 8, and in the job descriptions for the president and the courts in Articles II and III, respectively. The **reserved powers** are not specifically listed, and thus any powers not mentioned remain with the states. Some powers are held by authorities at both levels, state and federal. These are called **concurrent powers**. The states and the nation can both lay and collect taxes, define crimes, run court systems, and improve lands.

Federalism: A Sharing of Powers

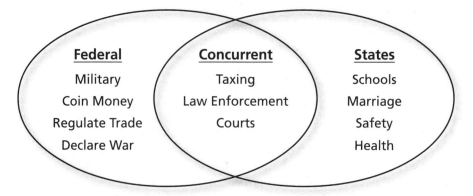

Federal	Concurrent	States
Military	Taxing	Schools
Coin Money	Law Enforcement	Marriage
Regulate Trade	Courts	Safety
Declare War		Health

Overlap and Uncertainty

States generally honored marriage licenses from other states, but the legalization of same-sex marriages in some states caused other states to expressly refuse recognition of these marriages. Opposing states rewrote their marriage laws and added amendments to their state constitutions to define marriage as between a man and a woman only. This controversy put Article IV in direct conflict with Amendment X. The full faith and credit clause suggests that if Vermont sanctioned the marriage of two gay men, Missouri would have to honor it. Yet the reserved powers clause in the Tenth Amendment grants Missouri's right to define marriage within its borders. The Supreme Court settled this dispute in 2015 in *Obergefell v. Hodges*, ruling 5-4 that the right to same-sex marriage was guaranteed by the due process clause and the equal protection clause in the Fourteenth Amendment.

Federalism leaves schools, elections, and most law enforcement up to the states. Why, then, do we have a national Department of Education, the Federal Elections Commission, and a Federal Bureau of Investigation? These questions will be answered in the next section as you learn how the new nation began to walk a delicate line that divided state and federal power, how the Supreme Court has defined federalism, and how Congress became keenly interested in issues of education, political campaigns, and crime.

Powers Delegated to the Federal Government	Powers Reserved by the States
Declaring war	Regulating health and morals
Coining money	Safety regulations
Taxing	Incorporating cities and companies
Regulating interstate commerce	Defining legal relationships: marriage, divorce, wills
Defining immigration and naturalization	Operating schools

The New Republic to the New Deal

In 1788, in one of its final acts, the outgoing Confederation Congress directed states to choose presidential electors to vote for the nation's first president. With Virginia now in the Union, few doubted that George Washington was the best man for the job. He would oversee the birth of a federal system that would look drastically different after Franklin Roosevelt's New Deal went into effect.

Washington's Golden Age

On February 4, 1789, electors unanimously elected Washington with their first ballot. His leadership at the Constitutional Convention, his endorsement of the new plan for government, and his alliance with Madison, Hamilton, and others made him a Federalist of the first order (though Washington would criticize the developing political parties). The same group that advocated ratification also pioneered establishing a strong national government. As historians Stanley Elkins and Eric McKitrick recap, the initial congressional elections sent mostly Federalist-minded men to the national legislature. Only 11 Anti-Federalists filled the 59 elected seats in the first House of Representatives, and only two Anti-Federalists served in the 20-member Senate. This dynamic in Congress and the leadership of Washington resulted in a mainly unified federal government that accomplished much during its first term. Congress designed the courts, declared the District of Columbia the new capital city, and created national financial institutions.

Beginning Divisions As Washington and his Federalist colleagues steered the new ship of state, national politics divided Americans into two camps. The familiar debate over national strength versus states' rights and individual liberties continued to shape the United States into a two-party nation. Though political parties as we know them did not yet exist, the Federalists faced off against the Democrat-Republicans led by Thomas Jefferson and later James Madison. Several showdowns between state and national authorities and between these two groups defined the era and shaped the interpretation of the Constitution.

One of the first pressing issues arose around Congress's creation of a national bank. Washington requested opinions on the bank idea from his secretaries, Jefferson and Hamilton, who clashed mightily on the bank question and on how to interpret the Constitution. Jefferson expressed that the bank was improper and that Congress had no power to create it. He was a **strict constructionist**, one who believes the Constitution should be interpreted literally, or strictly construed. Hamilton generally believed that if the Constitution did not forbid something, then it permitted it. Jefferson, on the other hand, believed that what the Constitution did not expressly permit, it forbade. Washington and the Federalist Congress went with Hamilton and established the first Bank of the United States in 1791.

Whiskey Rebellion Another controversy brewed after a federal tax burdened whiskey distillers of the backcountry. Opponents sharply challenged the new national government and refused to pay federal tax collectors. President Washington summoned the militia of several states. About 13,000 soldiers rallied to Washington's call and easily put down the rebellion. But the incident strengthened the developing Jeffersonian faction. It also called the growing federal power into question. Numerous Federalist foes condemned the administration for its brutal display of force.

John Adams and the Jeffersonians

As Washington headed into retirement, Vice President John Adams barely defeated Jefferson in an electoral vote of 71 to 68, which, at the time, gave Jefferson the vice presidency. Adams continued to establish policies to strengthen the nation that also widened the gap between his followers and Jefferson's. In a time of nearly full-scale war against the French, Adams and the Federalist Congress passed the Alien and Sedition Acts. These laws empowered the federal government to jail any dissenters against the government's cause or deport foreigners who posed any threat to the United States. Many outspoken newspaper editors criticized Adams for this policy and were indicted under the law. The Sedition Act, in the minds of many, violated the First Amendment and sent many political converts over to Jefferson's camp.

As Adams's administration jailed its detractors, Jefferson responded to the new laws while also developing a larger philosophy of the **compact theory**, which held that the 13 sovereign states, in creating the federal government, had entered into a compact or contract regarding its jurisdiction. The states created the national government and thus could judge whether federal authorities had broken the compact by overstepping the limited authority they granted in the first place. Jefferson felt if the Federalists could stamp out free speech and free press with these harsh measures, they could soon violate other liberties in the compact. So, in secret to avoid prosecution, he penned a series of resolutions to address this violation. The Kentucky legislature passed these in 1798. Jefferson's friend and developing ally on the states' rights front, James Madison, penned a similar set of sentiments for the Virginia legislature to pass. The Kentucky and Virginia Resolutions became the bedrock ideas for the Jeffersonian movement and the Anti-Federalists' resurgence.

Ultimately the resolutions declared the states' right to **nullification**, the right to declare null and void any federal law if a state thought the law violated the Constitution. The Alien and Sedition laws expired and Adams left office before opponents could challenge these in the courts, but the South's reserved right to nullification continued over the ensuing decades, leading to the Civil War. South Carolina Senator John Calhoun, an outspoken defender of slavery, revived the idea in the years leading up to the Civil War. Calhoun argued that if the national government attempted to ban slavery, the states had the right to void such acts. Calhoun did not live to see the Civil War, but his ideas led to the South's secession. Ever since the Union's victory in the conflict, the doctrine of nullification has disappeared and the federal Union has proven indissoluble.

The Supreme Court Shapes Federalism

"Has the government of the United States power to make law on every subject?" delegate John Marshall asked at the Virginia ratifying convention in Richmond in 1788. Then he quickly asserted that the new federal judiciary "would declare void" any law going against the Constitution. In 1801, outgoing president John Adams appointed Marshall as Chief Justice of the Supreme Court. Taking the seat as Jefferson became president, the two men served as leading rivals in the Federalist-states' rights debate as the nation entered the nineteenth century.

McCulloch v. Maryland The U.S. bank controversy arose again. The state of Maryland, among others, questioned the legality of a congressionally created bank in Baltimore where James McCulloch was the chief cashier. The Constitution does not explicitly mention that Congress has the power "to create a bank." So Maryland passed a law requiring all banks within its borders not incorporated by the state to pay a $15,000 tax to force the U.S. bank out of state and to overcome the federal government's power. When McCulloch refused to pay the tax, the state brought the case to court. On appeal, the case of *McCulloch v. Maryland* (1819) landed in John Marshall's Supreme Court.

The dispute centered on two central questions. One, can Congress create a bank? And two, can a state tax federal institutions? The Court's opinion was a resounding victory for the national government. Marshall sided with McCulloch and both strengthened the power of Congress and made the states more subservient to the federal government.

Article I, Section 8, contains no expressed power for Congress to create a bank, strict constructionists had argued, but it did contain the phrases "coin money," "borrow money," "collect taxes," determine "laws on bankruptcies," and "punish counterfeiting." Banking was therefore very much the federal government's business, and supporters argued that a bank was "necessary and proper." John Marshall's Court agreed. He also strongly denounced the state's attempt to tax the national government, saying, "The power to tax involves the power to destroy." Invoking both the elastic and the supremacy clauses for the first time with this landmark case, the Court doubly strengthened the federal government. It broadened what Congress could do, denoting its **implied powers** in the Constitution (those not specifically listed in the Constitution but deriving from the elastic clause), and it declared that constitutional federal law will override state law. National leaders have since become involved with many more national issues that the federal government handles under the necessary and proper clause. Examples include education, health, welfare, disaster relief, and economic planning.

Gibbons v. Ogden Five years after *McCulloch*, the issue of regulating commerce came to a head in Marshall's Court. Article I's commerce clause states that Congress can regulate commerce "with foreign nations, and among the states, and with the Indian tribes." Its phrasing that Congress will assume regulation of commerce is clear enough, but *where* and *when* Congress could do so created problems for competing steamboat operators.

In the case of *Gibbons v. Ogden* (1824), a dispute arose around the monopoly granted to steamboat inventor Robert Fulton. New York's legislature granted Fulton the exclusive rights to operate his steamboat on the Hudson River, a chief thoroughfare in the northeast at the time. At the same time, Congress had authorized and licensed a Coast Guard ship to sail on the same waterway, claiming the right of the federal government to oversee the coastal and inland waterways. Fulton and the government of New York wanted to sustain the monopoly and argued that the commerce clause empowered Congress to regulate only actual goods. Marshall and the Supreme Court decided in favor of the federal government, declaring that the federal government is in charge of commerce and certifying Congress's authority over most commercial activity.

The *Gibbons* decision cleared the air temporarily. Since the national government did not engage in too much legislation regarding commerce at the time, the decision eventually led to a system of **dual federalism** in which the national government is supreme in its sphere—having the authority given it in Article I—and the states are equally supreme in their own sphere. Article I entitled Congress to legislate on commerce "among the states," while it did not forbid the states from regulating commerce within their borders. Chief Justice Marshall did qualify that states still had some rights to commerce, rejecting an exclusive national authority over internal commercial activity. This became known as **selective exclusiveness**—a doctrine asserting that when the commodity requires a national uniform rule, only Congress may regulate.

For years, this system worked because commerce and trade were mainly local, with fewer goods crossing state lines than they do today. Congress's relative inaction in regulating commerce until the Industrial Revolution allowed dual federalism to prevail. As the nation's business, manufacturing, transportation, and communication advanced, Congress became more and more interested in legislating business matters. Organized labor, reformers, and progressive leaders focused the national agenda on regulating the railroads, the factories, and the banks and on breaking up monopolies. On some occasions, the federal government crossed into the states' domain on the strength of the commerce clause—the most frequently contested congressional power—and on some occasions lost.

National Concerns, State Obligations

State and federal governments generally followed dual federalism into the early twentieth century. However, this practice gave way as Congress's increased use of the commerce clause empowered it to legislate on a variety of state concerns.

The Progressive Movement brought much federal legislation that created a power play over commerce authority. In the early 1900s, democracy became stronger through a variety of government reforms. The Sixteenth Amendment, for example, created the federal income tax and expanded Congress's reach of regulation. The Seventeenth Amendment made senators accountable to the people instead of to the state governments. Voters then put reformers in office who wanted to clean up the railroads, factories, and corrupt government.

As the nation grew and citizens became more mobile, the nation's problems, much like its goods, began to travel across state borders. The police powers originally left up to the states now became national in scope, and Congress created the Federal Bureau of Investigation (FBI). Reformers pressured Congress to act on issues when states refused or could not act. Since the Constitution nowhere gave Congress the direct power to legislate to improve safety, health, and morals, it began to rely on its regulatory power on commerce to reach national goals of decreasing crime, making the workplace safer, and ensuring equality among citizens. The commerce clause served as the primary vehicle for such legislation. For example, the Mann Act of 1910 forbade the transportation of women across state lines for immoral purposes to crack down on prostitution. The Automobile Theft Act of 1915 made it a federal offense to knowingly drive a stolen car across state lines. Since then, Congress has made racketeering, drug dealing, and bank robbery federal crimes (though they remain illegal at the state level as well). The federal executive can enforce these laws even if the criminal activity is entirely contained in one state.

The Supreme Court Stretches the Commerce Clause

The Supreme Court, however, disappointed reformers and issued a few setbacks. The conservative Court declared that corporations as well as individuals were protected by the Constitution, and it questioned many health and safety regulations through the era. For example, when Congress passed a law prohibiting a company from hiring and forcing children to work in factories, the Supreme Court blocked it. In *Hammer v. Daggenhart* (1918), the Court ruled that the evils of child labor were entirely in manufacturing, not commerce, and child labor was thus outside congressional authority. The Court ruled it was constitutional for Congress to prohibit spoiled food and drugs but not to violate the liberty of contract, drawing a line between manufacturing as creating goods and commerce as an exchange of goods. By the 1920s, however, the Court relied on Justice Oliver Wendell Holmes's words, which said the shipment of cattle from one state to another for slaughter and sale constituted "a typical, constantly recurring course" and thus made such commerce subject to national authority.

After President Franklin Roosevelt initiated his New Deal programs during the Great Depression, a power play began between Congress and the Court that ultimately allowed the national legislature to assume broad powers under the interstate commerce authority. Specifically, the Court upheld Congress's right to create a national minimum wage law with the Fair Labor Standards Act of 1938. The act barred the shipment and transaction of commerce across state lines for firms failing to pay employees at least $0.25 per hour. The Court upheld the act and overturned the *Hammer* decision.

Two centuries of Court interpretations, a drastic turn by the Court to broaden the scope of the interstate commerce clause, and prevailing attitudes of the last two generations have shaped American federalism into its current form. Congress has won more battles than the states in claiming authority on commerce-related legislation. But as you will see with the *Lopez* case later in this chapter (page 43), the Court does not always entitle Congress to legislate under the guise of regulating commerce.

Federal Grant Program

The overlap of federal and state authority is probably nowhere more obvious than in the federal grant program. In advancing the constitutional definition of federalism, Congress has dedicated itself to addressing national issues with federal dollars. Congress collects federal tax revenues and distributes these funds to the states to take care of particular national concerns. This process has different names, such as **revenue sharing, cooperative federalism,** or **fiscal federalism**. For decades, the federal government has encouraged, and at times required, states and localities to address safety, crime, education, and civil rights. Congress has largely done this by directing federal funds to states that qualify for aid. These **grants-in-aid** programs have developed over a 200-year history and picked up steadily during the Progressive Era, with FDR's New Deal, and then under President Lyndon Johnson's Great Society program of the 1960s. This financial aid helps states take care of basic state needs. Grants come in different forms with different requirements, and they sometimes stretch the limits of constitutionality. Political realities in Washington and at the local level explain why these grants have gone through so many variations.

Grants Through the Mid-1900s Grants are as old as the Republic. After the Americans earned independence and attained the vast lands west of the Appalachian Mountains, high-ranking soldiers received land grants for their service in the Revolution. The federal government later granted large sums of money to states so they could maintain militias. In 1862, Congress passed the Morrill Land Grant Act. It allowed Congress to parcel out large tracts of land to encourage states to build colleges. Soon, colleges and universities grew in the Midwest and beyond. In more modern times, Congress has provided money to states to take care of improvements in the environment, education, unemployment, interstate highways, welfare, and health care.

In the early 1900s, most grants were grants-in-aid with conditions attached. These conditions suited the federal government because they made administration convenient. Congress used them to prod state governments to modernize. States had to match federal grants with state funds, secure statewide uniformity, and create agencies to report to the federal government. Congress started using grants heavily in 1916 to fund road construction as the automobile became central to American society and as roads became central to economic improvement.

Source: Lewis Wickes Hine, Library of Congress

The Court's decision in *Hammer v. Daggenhart* (1918) put children who worked in manufacturing, sometimes against their will, beyond the jurisdiction of the federal government. That decision was later overturned.

The federal income tax caused the national treasury to grow exponentially. With these extra financial resources, Congress addressed concerns that were traditionally out of its jurisdiction. Additionally, larger numbers of people who had gained the right to vote pressed for more government reform and action. Women and other groups began voting and engaging in civic endeavors that resulted in the national government addressing more of society's concerns.

The economic crisis that followed, the Great Depression, caused the federal government to grow more, largely by implementing more grants. Traditionally, states, localities, and private charitable organizations provided relief for the poor. By 1935, most states had enacted laws to aid impoverished mothers and the aged. State funds did not always cover this effort, so President Franklin D. Roosevelt and Congress were required to address the issue.

Contemporary Federalism

Though state officials are well-schooled in the reserved powers clause of the Tenth Amendment and can see the conflict of interest by accepting federal funds, they also find it challenging to turn away federal money to handle state concerns. States do not necessarily want to cede their authority, but at the same time they want the funds to carry out state needs. The federal government has decided many times to pay the bill, as long as the states follow federal guidelines while taking care of the issue. Grants with particular congressional guidelines or requirements are known as **categorical grants**.

National Concerns of the 1960s and 1970s During the 1960s and 1970s several movements brought new federal initiatives. The fight for civil rights and school desegregation, the desire for clean air and clean water, and the concern for crime gained the interest of Washington. Once again, federal dollars spoke loudly to local officials. The 1964 Civil Rights Act, for example, withheld federal dollars from schools that did not fully desegregate its students. Under President Johnson, the federal government increased the number of grants to address poverty and health care.

Congress also began to redefine the grants process to give more decision-making power to local authorities. Some states felt grants had too many **strings**, or specific requirements, attached. In 1966, Congress introduced **block grants**. Block grants differ from categorical grants in that they offer larger sums of money to the states to take care of some large, overarching purpose, without the strings of the categorical grants. Democrats led the efforts for the early block grants, such as the Partnership for Health program approved in 1966 and the Safe Streets program created in 1968.

When Republican Richard Nixon became president in 1969, he wanted to return greater authority to local governments. A believer in clear boundaries between state and federal jurisdictions, Nixon desired a mix of block grants, revenue sharing, and welfare reform. Additionally, mayors and urban leaders saw a politicization of the grants process and the way the government awarded monies. They wanted the system revamped. Many other individuals in the field wanted to consolidate and decentralize the grant process and favored block grants over categorical grants. They believed federal agencies had little understanding of how local offices implemented particular programs.

In 1971, Nixon proposed to meld one-third of all federal programs into six loosely defined mega-grants, an initiative called "special revenue sharing." He wanted to consolidate 129 different programs into six block grants in the fields of transportation, education, rural development, law enforcement, community development, and employment training. He didn't achieve this goal for reasons we will discuss, but in 1972, general revenue sharing provided more than $6.1 billion annually in "no strings" grants to virtually all general-purpose governments. Congress passed two major block grants: the Comprehensive Employment and Training Act of 1973 (CETA) and the Community Development Block Grant program (CDBG) in 1974. By 1976, Congress had created three more large block grants.

Fiscal conservatives, who also favored local control, liked Nixon's plan. The result of his changes contributed to a phenomenon of mixing state and federal authority that had already begun. The classic explanation of our federal, state, and local governments often comes with a diagram of a layer cake with the federal government on top, the states in the middle, and the local government on the bottom. Everything is orderly and stacked. The flow of federal money to the various state and local governments, and even private charitable groups, however, has more recently created what is termed **marble cake federalism** because the lines are not straight and even. Federalism has become a hodgepodge of government authorities and has even mixed with the private sector. Federal grants are awarded to local nonprofits that help develop and clean up communities.

As soon as Nixon tried to steer federal money to states in larger, less restrictive ways, members of Congress realized the authority and benefits they would lose. Block grants, being larger, fewer, and with fewer strings than categorical grants, took away Congress's role of oversight. Congress was losing control and individual members felt some responsibility to provide federal dollars to their districts in a more specific way. From a political standpoint, block grants denied individual representatives and senators the ability to claim credit. Chairmen of relevant congressional committees, too, had suddenly lost control over the process.

What was the result? The number of categorical grants increased dramatically, while block grants subsided. Congress passed only five block grants during the period from 1966 to 1980. Categorical grants with strings or conditions of aid became the norm again. In addition to the political benefits congressional members experienced, grant recipients at the state and local levels enjoyed categorical grants. Special interest groups could lobby Congress for funding their causes. State agencies, such as those that support state health care or road construction, depend on federal aid and appreciate these grants. Community groups and nonprofit agencies thrive on these as well.

THINK AS A POLITICAL SCIENTIST: DETERMINE RELATIONSHIPS, PATTERNS, AND TRENDS IN FEDERAL GRANTS

Often you will be interpreting and applying information presented in the form of charts, graphs, and tables. For an accurate understanding of that information, begin by reading the title, labels, and contents of the chart, graph, or table. Be sure you understand the exact purpose of the information and exactly what the numbers represent. For example, are they percentages or amounts? If they refer to money, are the amounts expressed in constant dollars (adjusted for inflation) or real (nominal) dollars? Are the numbers expressed in thousands, millions, or billions?

Once you are sure you understand the purpose, labels, and contents of the informational illustration, look for patterns and relationships. For example, do the numbers go up or down in a predictable pattern? If there is a sudden change in a pattern, how can you explain it? Is there a clear trend visible in the information? Apply the information you gain from your interpretation of a visual source to your understanding of the subject at hand.

Practice: Carefully study the table below. Explain the table's information, trends, patterns, and variations. Answer these questions:

- How many overall federal dollars did state and local governments rely on during the years shown?

- What percent of the federal budget went to state and local projects?

- When do you see increases or decreases? What events or priorities might explain these?

Total Federal Outlays for State and Local Grants, 1955–1985		
Year	**(in billions of constant dollars)**	**Percentage of Total Federal Outlays**
1955	24.4	4.7
1960	45.3	7.6
1965	65.9	9.2
1970	123.7	12.3
1975	186.8	15.0
1980	227.0	15.5
1985	189.6	11.2

Source: *OMB Historical Tables, FY 2014*

Returning Authority to the States

The post-New Deal trend of fiscal federalism has experienced a mixed appreciation from state and local administrators. And Conservatives have pushed to reduce federal taxes and return to state and local control over the reserved powers. "It is my intention to curb the size and influence of the Federal establishment," President Ronald Reagan declared as he took his oath in 1981, "and to demand recognition of the distinction between the powers granted to the Federal Government and those reserved to the states or the people." Reagan followed with initiatives meant to define a **New Federalism** that he had promised.

Grants in the 1980s and Beyond

"In Two Words, Yes And No"

Source: Herblock

Political cartoonists use both words and images to convey their viewpoints. What point about federalism is the cartoonist making with the words and images above? (For more on interpreting political cartoons, see page 396.)

The federal government has created a dilemma for the states because states have come to depend on these grants. The strings can also be costly. Building projects, which make up a large share of these programs, require the local government to pay prevailing wages to its construction workers. Recipients must be careful of their project's impact on the region, and they must follow federally imposed hiring guidelines. State officials all too often see the otherwise enticing funds as not so attractive.

The federal government offered states one notable categorical grant in the early 1980s as a way to both satisfy the upkeep of highways and to ease the national drunk driving problem. Congress offered large sums of money to states on the condition that states increase their drinking age to 21. Studies showed that making 21 the legal drinking age would likely decrease the number of fatalities on the highways. Most states complied with the National Minimum Drinking Age Act of 1984 to secure these precious dollars. South Dakota, however, challenged these strings.

In *South Dakota v. Dole,* the Supreme Court ruled that Congress did have the power to set conditions of the drinking age for states to receive federal dollars for highway repair and construction. Congressional restrictions on grants to the states are constitutional if they meet certain requirements. They must be for the general welfare of the public and cannot be ambiguous. Conditions must be related to the federal interest in particular national projects or programs, and they must not run afoul of other constitutional provisions. That is, Congress cannot use a conditional grant to induce states to engage in unconstitutional activities. South Dakota lost and Congress continued creating and controlling strings.

Mandates With strings, states receive federal monies in exchange for following guidelines. Federal mandates, on the other hand, require states to comply with a federal directive sometimes with and sometimes without the allure and reward of funds. The legislative, executive, or judicial branches can issue mandates in various forms. Mandates often address civil rights and environmental concerns. Federal statutes require state environmental agencies to meet national clean air and water requirements. Significant intergovernmental regulations in the late '80s and early '90s include the Clean Air Act Amendments, the Americans with Disabilities Act (ADA), Civil Rights Restoration Act, Family and Medical Leave Act, and the National Voter Registration Act (also known as the Motor Voter law).

The **Clean Air Act,** originally passed in 1970, set requirements and timetables for dealing with urban smog, acid rain, and toxic pollutants. The **Americans with Disabilities Act** made public sector buildings and transportation systems accessible for disabled individuals. Cities and states had to make their buildings wheelchair accessible and install wheelchair lifts. The mandate imposed, according to the Congressional Budget Office's best estimates, as much as $1 billion in additional costs on states and localities. The Clean Air Act Amendments imposed $250 to $300 million annually, and the cost of the Motor Voter Law would reach $100 million over five years.

The federal courts have also issued mandates to ensure state or local governing bodies act in certain ways. Judges have decreed that cities redefine their hiring practices to prevent discrimination. They have placed firm restrictions on federal housing projects. In the early 1970s, federal judges mandated that public schools arrange appropriate black-to-white enrollment ratios, essentially mandating busing for racial balance.

Devolution Americans generally agree that issues such as education and health care have become national in scope. In 1990, 75 percent of Americans believed the nation was spending too little on education and environmental protection; 72 percent said the same about health care. But people questioned whether the federal government in Washington could take care of these issues. They wanted Washington to pay, but they also wanted local control.

By 1994, the Republican Party, especially those in the House of Representatives, began a call for **devolution**—devolving some of the responsibilities assumed by the federal government over the years back onto the states. Prior to the 1994 elections, House Majority Leader Newt Gingrich led the House Republicans and congressional candidates in front of the Capitol building to push for a Contract with America, calling for "the end of government that is too big, too intrusive, and too easy with the people's money." An overwhelming Republican victory followed with a plan to return this power and those dollars to the states. With bipartisan support and President Bill Clinton's signature, they managed to pass the Unfunded Mandates Reform Act and the Personal Responsibility and Work Opportunity Reconciliation Act. The first denied Congress the ability to issue unfunded mandates, laws that were taking up some 30 percent of state budgets. The second restructured the welfare system to return much authority and distribution of welfare dollars—Medicaid, for example—to the states. As Clinton declared in a 1996 address, "The era of big government is over."

 Is That Constitutional? *United States v. Lopez* (1995)

Does Congress have the authority to outlaw guns near schools under the commerce clause?

No. Congress passed the Gun-Free School Zones Act in 1990 in hopes of preventing gun violence at or near schools. In 1992, senior Alfonzo Lopez carried a .38 caliber handgun and bullets into a San Antonio high school. On an anonymous tip, school authorities confronted him, obtained the gun, and reported the infraction to the federal police. Lopez was indicted, tried, and sentenced in federal court for violating the statute. He challenged the ruling in the Supreme Court on the grounds that the federal government has no right to regulate specific behavior at a state-run school. The United States argued that the connections of guns and drug dealing made this an area under the federal legislative jurisdiction and Congress's commerce power.

The Court sided with Lopez, refusing to let Congress invoke the commerce clause. "It is difficult to perceive any limitation on federal power," Justice William Rehnquist wrote. ". . . [I]f we were to accept the government's arguments, we are hard pressed to posit any activity by an individual that Congress is without power to regulate." Congress had stretched its commerce power too far. Most states have regulations on guns and where one can legally carry a firearm. That is where the Supreme Court said this authority should stay.

Education: National Goals, State Management

The Constitution and the federal government left the creation and management of schools largely to the states until the 1960s. There has always been a national concern for an educated citizenry, but the racial desegregation of public schools and the Cold War competition with the Soviet Union in the 1950s caused education to move up the national agenda. President Johnson, a former teacher himself, and Congress passed the Elementary and Secondary Education Act in 1965. The law was as much an assault on poverty as it was reform of education, ensuring that lesser-funded schools received adequate resources. State officials generally welcomed the law because of the federal government's hands-off approach to school management and the broad discretion it gave local authorities on how to spend federal monies.

By the end of Johnson's term, federal aid to education totaled $4 billion. By the late 1970s, Congress created a new seat for the Secretary of Education in the president's cabinet and an entire Department of Education. In the 1980s and 1990s, presidents and members of Congress found education a topic that almost all voters cared about and wanted to improve.

The most sweeping changes in federal education law that caused consternation between the states and the national government came in the form of the **No Child Left Behind Act (NCLB)**. After campaigning to end an "education recession," George W. Bush gained bipartisan support for NCLB and signed the bill in early 2002. The new law brought Republicans and Democrats together to improve the nation's education system. The law declares that every child can learn and that schools and states should be held accountable. The act calls for "highly qualified" teachers in the core subjects in every classroom, the use of proven teaching methods, and the threat of sanctions on underperforming schools. No Child Left Behind pushes for classroom lessons and methods that research has proven effective and it gives parents information and choices about their child's education.

With these requirements and rewards also came greater emphasis on testing and the cloud of federal intervention. NCLB requires that students show annual yearly progress (AYP) through federally required and regulated tests. Underperforming schools can be reconstituted, replacing the administration and teaching staff.

Public support for the law was strong and widespread at its passage, but many teachers, administrators, and state governments have come to criticize NCLB. Part of the frustration is that Congress provides only 8 percent of the total funding for education nationwide, while it has increased the Department of Education's powers over the nation's schools. Some of its goals are just not realistic. Nearly 80 percent of U.S. schools will be labeled failures as they cannot reach the idealistic goals and deadlines. One education professor at Harvard University called the bill the "single largest expansion of federal power over the nation's education system in history." Several states agree. State and local officials complain of the law's restrictions and added management tasks.

President Obama's **Race to the Top** initiative offered incentives for states to adopt new national standards or develop their own that require students to be college- or career-ready at graduation. As the federal government tries to revamp the law, coming to a consensus on educational changes will be difficult. Traditionalists and those adhering to the Tenth Amendment argue that most of NCLB should disappear. Others, especially civil rights groups and advocates for the poor, see a need to keep the federal government involved as a watchdog on the states.

State and federal governments continue to push and pull to determine who will ultimately govern and fund education and an array of other services. The Federalism design intentionally dilutes governmental power and assures much local control over police powers, the management of state prisons, and internal roads. Yet Congress, taking care of citizens' concerns, will continue to act on national matters to improve the United States.

Federalism Terms	
Dual Federalism	National and state governments remain supreme in their own spheres, a Supreme Court doctrine common from the Civil War until the New Deal
Cooperative Federalism	The intermingled relationships among the national, state, and local governments to deliver services to citizens
Fiscal Federalism	The pattern of taxing, spending, and providing federal grants to state and local governments
New Federalism	A return to more distinct lines of responsibility for federal and state governments, begun by President Ronald Reagan
Revenue Sharing	A policy under fiscal federalism that requires both national and local funds for programs
Devolution	The continued effort to return original reserved powers to the states

Source: Florida Stop Common Core Coalition

In response to the Race to the Top initiative, many states adopted the Common Core State Standards. Members of the Florida Stop Common Core Coalition and Florida Parents R.I.S.E., like citizens in many other states, have protested these standards, believing their adoption has weakened local control of education and allowed the federal government to overreach.

REFLECT ON THE ESSENTIAL QUESTION

Essential Question: *How has federalism shaped the administration of public policy, and how do state, local, and national governments work within the federal framework today?* On separate paper, complete a chart like the one below to gather details to answer that question.

Federalism in History	Federalism Today

KEY TERMS, NAMES, AND EVENTS

Americans with Disabilities Act	fiscal federalism	police powers
block grants	full faith and credit clause	privileges and immunities clause
categorical grants	*Gibbons v. Ogden (1824)*	reserved powers
Clean Air Act (1970)	grants-in-aid	revenue sharing
compact theory	implied powers	selective exclusiveness
concurrent powers	mandates	*South Dakota v. Dole (1987)*
conditions of aid/strings	marble cake federalism	strict constructionist
cooperative federalism	*McCulloch v. Maryland (1819)*	strings
delegated powers	New Federalism	Tenth Amendment
devolution	No Child Left Behind Act (2002)	unitary government
dual federalism	nullification	*United States v. Lopez (1995)*
extradition		Whiskey Rebellion
federalism		

1. The states' reserved powers doctrine can be found in
    (A) Article I
    (B) Article II
    (C) Article III
    (D) the First Amendment
    (E) the Tenth Amendment

2. Which statement accurately describes federalism?
    (A) Federalism is a governing system that places a national authority above regional authority.
    (B) Federalism is exclusive to the United States.
    (C) Federalism did not exist in the United States until after the Civil War.
    (D) Federalism is a sharing of powers between national and regional governments.
    (E) Federalism is only possible because of the supremacy clause.

3. Which of the following showed support for the compact theory of the Constitution?
    (A) The framing of the necessary and proper clause in Philadelphia
    (B) The ratification of the Constitution
    (C) The Union's victory in the Civil War
    (D) The passage of the Virginia and Kentucky Resolutions
    (E) The Supreme Court's decision in *McCulloch v. Maryland*

4. Alexander Hamilton and Thomas Jefferson differed most greatly in their views of
    (A) declaring independence
    (B) writing the Constitution
    (C) ratifying the Constitution
    (D) Congress creating a bank
    (E) keeping the Articles of Confederation

5. All of the following nations have federal governments EXCEPT
   (A) the United States
   (B) the United Kingdom
   (C) Canada
   (D) Australia
   (E) Germany

6. The chief difference between block grants and categorical grants is
   (A) categorical grants are for particular, well-defined purposes and projects with strings attached, while block grants address some larger purpose
   (B) block grants are more popular today than categorical grants
   (C) categorical grants are given to states, while block grants are given to the federal government at large
   (D) members of Congress prefer giving federal dollars broadly rather than to local governments within their districts
   (E) block grants are for education and health; categorical grants help pay for crime prevention and protecting the environment

7. All of the following contributed to the widening of federal authority over interstate commerce EXCEPT
   (A) *Gibbons v. Ogden*
   (B) progressive reforms
   (C) presidential initiatives
   (D) pressing needs in times of crisis
   (E) *United States v. Lopez*

8. Which of the following regarding grants-in-aid is true?
   (A) Mayors and governors have never liked federal grants.
   (B) The first federal grants occurred in the 1960s.
   (C) State leaders have willingly ceded authority in exchange for federal funds to carry out state needs.
   (D) Grants rarely have restrictions or guidelines.
   (E) Such grants cannot address health, safety, or morals.

9. How have movements led by President Reagan in the 1980s and President Clinton and the congressional Republicans in the 1990s addressed the flow of federal money?

(A) They created the line-item veto, which still stands today.

(B) They reformed the federal welfare system to devolve responsibility on the states.

(C) They discouraged the private sector from engaging in public services.

(D) They increased taxes and asserted greater federal authority in the distribution of monies.

(E) They together nominated liberal judges to uphold their policies.

Federal Grants from the Top Five Departments FY 2011	
Department of Health and Human Services	$332 B
Department of Transportation	$25.7 B
Department of Agriculture	$23.3 B
Department of Education	$17.3 B
Department of Housing and Urban Development	$6.7 B

Source: www.usaspending.gov

10. Based on the chapter reading and the above table, which statement is true?

(A) More federal dollars go toward states' education and farming than any other concern.

(B) The constitutional lines on federalism prevent the national government from assisting with state responsibilities.

(C) Grants appear to assist the inner-city interests, not rural interests.

(D) The top grantor of federal dollars is the Department of Health and Human Services because it handles Medicare and Social Security.

(E) The federal government no longer awards grants.

Question

1. The United States has a unique system of federal government.

   (a) Define federalism.

   (b) Identify and explain one constitutional provision that strengthens the federal government's powers in relation to the states.

   (c) Identify and explain one constitutional provision that maintains states' sovereignty.

   (d) Select one of the following Supreme Court rulings and explain how the ruling shaped the U.S. federal system.
   - *McCulloch v. Maryland* (1819)
   - *Gibbons v. Ogden* (1924)
   - *United States v. Lopez* (1995)

Question

2. The federal government has developed a complex system of attaining national goals by awarding federal grants.

   (a) Identify and explain two reasons why this system was developed.

   (b) Identify and explain two restraints or guidelines Congress uses in this system.

WRITING: USE ACTIVE VOICE

Free-response questions usually ask you to explain how some facet of government works. You'll find that government institutions, noted politicians, historic figures, and actual laws become the subjects of your answers. Make them the subjects of your sentences as well by using the active voice. When explaining some government action, such as the *McCulloch* case in Question 1, write "Congress created a bank," rather than "A bank was created." The second sentence, which hides the subject in the passive voice, leaves the reader wondering who created the bank. Or, write, "The Supreme Court declared the Gun-Free School Zones Act unconstitutional," rather than "The law was declared unconstitutional." This approach allows you to add one more bit of information, to show your expertise, and to present a clear response.

UNIT 1: Review

Revolutionaries and American leaders established the United States government, which culminated in the creation of the Constitution. The same concerns that brought independence—a lack of representation, an autocratic centralized government, and violations of liberties—coupled with powerful political theory from Enlightenment philosophers shaped the design of the U.S. government. After a failed experiment under the Articles of Confederation, leaders created a new federal government that was national in character.

The union of states assumed unique and limited powers, the states assumed others, and some powers were concurrent. The "necessary and proper" clause, Congress's right to regulate interstate commerce, the full faith and credit clause, and the Tenth Amendment guide federalism. Starting with *McCulloch v. Maryland,* the Supreme Court has more often emboldened Congress's commerce power and authority; and the federal government, through grants and mandates, has created and funded national initiatives in spite of some overlap with states' reserved powers. In more recent years, however, Congress has slowed this trend and devolved some powers back on the states.

Since 1789, the Constitution, its alterations, and its government have endured. The written, transparent guidelines for government have allowed the United States to operate largely uninterrupted on the same basic plan. Never has the country missed an election. Leaders have been democratically pushed out of office without bloodshed. And our courts have settled intense, divisive matters of law to solve national crises.

THINK AS A POLITICAL SCIENTIST: CONSTRUCT A VISUAL AND FORMULATE AN ARGUMENT ABOUT FEDERALISM

Construct a timeline that orders and explains key events that have defined American federalism. Be sure to include events before and after the drafting of the Constitution. Also include acts of Congress, the president, and the Supreme Court that have shaped the Constitution and the practice of federalism. For each event, include the accurate year and add a brief note explaining the event's relevance.

When you have completed your timeline, use it to draft an argument that characterizes James Madison's vision for the new nation and that asserts and supports a claim on how closely contemporary federalism aligns with Madison's vision.

UNIT 2: Political Beliefs and Behaviors

Chapter 3 *Public Opinion*

Chapter 4 *Political Participation*

What the public thinks and how that thinking is conveyed to government officials are factors in shaping public policies. Professionals try to measure public opinion for a variety of reasons, using a method that makes the results as accurate as possible. Analysts and citizens alike should consider the legitimacy of a poll as much as its general finding, since if its method is faulty, its findings will be as well.

Public opinion changes, but the factors that help determine public opinion remain fairly constant. Voters' backgrounds, professions, and a range of demographic traits all have an impact on their political opinions. The family has the largest impact, since it is an early source of political information and understanding.

At the time of the American founding, only the elite classes could vote. Since then, however, state laws, constitutional amendments, and subsequent congressional statutes have expanded voting rights to nearly all men and women over the age of 18. Voting participation, however, has fluctuated over the last 20 years.

Key Concepts

Political Beliefs and Behaviors

- Beliefs that citizens hold about their government and its leaders
- Processes by which citizens learn about politics
- The nature, sources, and consequences of public opinion
- The ways in which citizens vote and otherwise participate in political life
- Factors that influence citizens to differ from one another in terms of political beliefs and behaviors

Source: *AP® United States Government and Politics Course and Exam Description*

3

Public Opinion

"Polls can help make government more efficient and responsive; they can improve the quality of candidates for public office; they can make this a truer democracy."

—George Gallup, 1965

Essential Question: How do Americans form opinions, and how do these opinions influence government?

Public opinion is the grand, collective set of beliefs the public holds. Sometimes public opinion forms a clear consensus. For example, nearly everyone agrees children should attend school and that the government should punish violent criminals. However, Americans also disagree on many issues. For example, exactly what topics should schools teach? What is the appropriate punishment for premeditated murder? Policymakers try to answer these questions in a society of diverse, constantly shifting views. The Framers built processes into the Constitution to temper rash governmental action influenced by public opinion. Federal judges, for example, are given life terms so they can make fair, even if unpopular, decisions. The Electoral College system tempered public passions in electing the president.

The Roots of Public Opinion

How is public opinion formed? Why do certain members of society have dramatically different opinions from others? What forces cause different people to think in different ways? What groups tend to cluster around certain beliefs, and why? Those who study public opinion and its role in governance have developed some answers to these questions.

Ideology

People take positions on public issues and develop a political philosophy on how government should act in line with their ideology. An ideology is a comprehensive and mutually consistent set of ideas. When there are two or more sides to an issue, voters tend to fall into different camps, either a conservative or a liberal ideology or philosophy. However, this diverse nation has a variety of ideologies that overlap one another.

Regardless of ideology, for example, most Americans agree that the government should regulate dangerous industries, educate children at public expense, and protect free speech, at least to a degree. Everyone wants a strong economy and national security. These are **valence issues**—concerns or policies that are viewed in the same way by people with a variety of ideologies. When political candidates debate valence issues, "the dialogue can be like a debate between the nearly identical Tweedledee and Tweedledum," says congressional elections expert Paul Herrnson.

Wedge issues, in contrast, sharply divide the public. These include the issues of abortion and the 2003 invasion and later occupation of Iraq. The more divisive issues tend to hold a high **saliency**, or importance, to an individual or a group. For senior citizens, for example, questions about reform of the Social Security system hold high saliency. For people 18 to 20 years old, the legal drinking age may have high saliency.

The Liberal-Conservative Spectrum For lack of a better system, political scientists use the terms **liberal** and **conservative**, as well as "left" and "right," to label each end of an ideological continuum. Most Americans are **moderate** and never fall fully into one camp or the other. Many others may fall into a conservative way of thinking on some issues while holding liberal beliefs on others.

The two leading political parties—Democrats and Republicans—tend to embody the liberal and the conservative ideology, respectively. Yet labeling the two parties as liberal or conservative is an oversimplification. Some self-described conservatives want nothing to do with the Republican Party, and many Democrats dislike the "liberal" label.

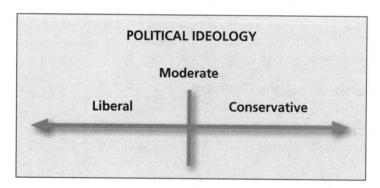

The meaning of the terms *liberal* and *conservative* has changed over history. In early America, a "liberal" government was one that did little. Thomas Jefferson believed in a high degree of liberty, declaring that a government that governs best is one that governs least. With this statement, Jefferson described the government's liberal approach toward the people, allowing citizen freedom, a free flow of ideas, free markets, fewer laws, and fewer restrictions. This construct on the word continued into the late nineteenth century.

In the Progressive Era, the federal government expanded its activity, going outside the confines of traditional government. In the 1930s, Democratic

President Franklin Roosevelt proposed a "liberal" plan for emergency legislation. His New Deal agenda was new and revolutionary. The government took on new responsibilities in ways it never had. The government acted in a liberal way, less constrained by tradition or limitations that guided earlier governments. Since the 1930s, the term *liberal* has usually meant open to allowing the government to flexibly expand beyond established constraints.

The term *conservative* describes those who believe in following tradition and having reverence for authority. Modern-day conservatives often invoke Jefferson and argue that government should do less and thus allow its people more freedom. Arizona Senator Barry Goldwater, the 1964 Republican presidential nominee, embraced the conservative label and published his book, *The Conscience of a Conservative*, en route to his nomination. He and much of his party felt Roosevelt's party had unwisely altered the role of government. Goldwater and his party wanted less economic regulation and more responsibility on the citizenry. Many conservatives call themselves "fiscal conservatives" because they want to see less taxation and less government spending overall.

Since FDR's presidency and Goldwater's nomination, these political terms have further evolved, and now it is difficult to know exactly what they mean. Roosevelt would likely not support some of the more liberal goals of the Democratic Party today, and Goldwater, in retirement, supported Democratic President Bill Clinton's initiatives to open the door for gays in the military. Additionally, an array of cultural and social issues that came to the forefront in the 1960s and 1970s changed the dynamic between those who consider themselves conservative and those who consider themselves liberal, and thus also changed the terms' meanings.

Traditional Christian voters, family values groups, and others who oppose abortion and gay marriage and support prayer in school have adopted the conservative label and have aligned themselves with the Republican Party. However, policies that restrict abortion, censor controversial material in books or magazines, or seek to more tightly define marriage actually require more, not less, law and regulation. For supporters of these policies, then, the label conservative is not necessarily accurate. People who believe in more regulation on industry, stronger gun control, and the value of diversity are generally seen as liberal. But when government acts to establish these goals, Jefferson might say, it is not necessarily acting liberally in relation to the rights of the people.

Off the Line If you have trouble finding the precise line between liberal and conservative, you are not alone. Cleavages, or gaps, in public opinion make understanding where the public stands on issues even more difficult. Few people, even regular party members, agree with every conservative or every liberal idea. Many people simply do not fall on the linear continuum diagrammed on page 54 but rather align themselves with one of several other notable political philosophies: **libertarian, populist**, or **progressive**.

Libertarian voters generally oppose government intervention or regulation. As their name suggests, they have a high regard for civil liberties, those rights outlined in the Bill of Rights. They oppose censorship, want lower taxes, and dislike government-imposed morality. Though a small Libertarian Party exists, more citizens claim the libertarian (small "l") label than formally belong to the Libertarian Party. In 2008, Libertarian Party candidate Bob Barr received less than one percent of the national vote. Libertarian-minded citizens can be found in both the Republican and Democratic Parties. In short, they are conservative on fiscal or economic issues, such as government spending or raising the minimum wage, while they are liberal on moral or social issues. Most are pro-choice on abortion and believe in equal treatment of gays. As Nick Gillespie and Matt Welch write of libertarians in their book *Declaration of Independents*, "We believe that you should be able to think what you want, live where you want, trade for what you want, eat what you want, smoke what you want, and wed whom you want."

Populists have a very different profile. They generally attend a Protestant church and follow fundamental Christian ideas: love thy neighbor, contribute to charity, and follow a strict moral code. More populists can be found in the South and Midwest than along each American coast. They tend to come from working-class families. In many ways, they think like the Democrat and Populist Party candidate a century ago, William Jennings Bryan. Bryan was an influential Nebraska congressman in the late 1800s who fought for farmers and factory workers, for more regulation on corporations to protect the working class. He was also a deeply religious man who invoked Christian principles. He is remembered especially for an impassioned 1896 "Cross of Gold" speech that criticized the gold standard for U.S. currency and his public support for Tennessee's anti-evolution law during the Scopes Trial of 1925. A modern-day populist would largely agree with Bryan, favoring the freedom to pray in public schools while also supporting a higher minimum wage and a solid welfare system.

The Progressive Movement grew in cities from roots in the Republican Party. It peaked in the United States in the early 1900s when reformers challenged government corruption that ran counter to the values of equality, individualism, democracy, and advancement. At that time, the Republican Party split into its two wings: conservative and progressive. Progressives criticized traditional political establishments that concentrated too much power in one place, such as government and business. To be sure, progressives were capitalists, but they also looked out for workers. Modern progressives are aligned with labor unions. They believe in workers' rights over corporate rights, and they believe the wealthier classes should pay a much larger percentage of taxes than they currently do.

With some variation, about 40 to 50 percent of America is moderate, nearly 30 percent consider themselves conservative, and about 20 percent consider themselves liberal. Bear in mind, when asked this question, every respondent holds a slightly different definition of these terms. Also, notice how self-described liberals come in third, yet the Democratic Party (with which most liberals align) has been strong and popular in its current form for two generations. A poll that asks voters if they are "moderate," "conservative," or "liberal" is starkly different from one that asks if respondents are "Democrat," "Republican," or "independent."

The American National Election Study found in 2008 that 51 percent claimed to be Democrats or leaning Democrat, 37 percent called themselves Republicans, and only 11 percent claimed to be independent. In answering a parallel question, only 32 percent considered themselves "strongly partisan." The Democratic Party won more elections in 2008, supporting the study's findings. Two years later, however, Republicans won more House and Senate seats. A large swath of the populace finds itself between these ideologies and between the two-party organizations, going back and forth from election to election. Many voters feel no need to be consistent when consistency is defined by party platforms, political scientists, and pollsters.

Political Socialization

If you try to pinpoint yourself with an X on the ideological spectrum shown on page 54, where would you fall? Would you be on the continuum at all, or would you fall into one of the other ideologies you read about? If you are not sure, think of someone you know, maybe a parent or good friend, and decide where that person might fall. Just how did you or the person you chose arrive at that point on the continuum? What influences or factors caused you, or anyone, to think about politics and policy in particular ways?

Political socialization is the process by which one develops political opinions. The process begins as soon as one is old enough to start forming opinions on public matters, and it never really ends. Attending college, getting married, purchasing a home, and having children can have an enormous impact on one's thinking. Even career politicians whose positions are well known modify or switch somewhat due to an evolving world with countless circumstances. Every political constituent and political participant is affected by a variety of influences that assist in political development.

Source: Thinkstock
Family is the most important influence in shaping political development.

Family

The single biggest influence on one's political socialization is family. As children begin to inquire about world events or local issues, parents begin to explain these. Most moms or dads have some degree of opinion that will likely influence their children. At the dinner table, families discuss "kitchen table politics," considering events currently happening and what impact they might have on the family.

Children can differ from their parents in political opinions. Teenagers who strongly differ from their parents in nonpolitical ways may find themselves adopting far different political views as well. Moms and dads often differ from each other anyway. Younger voters vote less frequently than older ones and, not surprisingly, have less consistent views. Citizens aged 18–24 are not solidly aligned with their parents in great numbers, yet those who hold strong opinions do not veer far from their parents. Studies show that among high school seniors, only about 10 percent identified with the party opposite their parents.

The children's magazine *Weekly Reader* has conducted a poll, unscientific though it may be, on presidential elections since 1956. Responding children generally answer as their parents would, and thus the massive sample becomes reflective of the parent population at large. The *Weekly Reader* presidential poll has been wrong only one time in its entire history.

How do these children differ from their elders once they reach adulthood or after they have voted in a few elections? About 60 percent of adults carry the same **party identification** as their parents, including independents. Most who differ from their parents proclaim political independence instead of aligning with the opposite party.

School and College

Both teachers and peer groups can have a large impact on students' beliefs. In school, topics come up in classes that may allow a teacher to influence students politically, intentionally or not. There is no solid evidence that the K–12 experience makes one more conservative or liberal.

College campuses are places where professional scholars and students can discuss new ideas and explore revolutionary theories. Colleges have more flexible rules than the average high school. College deans and professors encourage a free flow of ideas in classroom discussion. Such openness and a more diverse student body today than a generation ago have caused colleges to forge a certain open-mindedness that lends itself to liberalism.

From the 1950s to the early 1980s, fewer high school graduates attended college than do so today. In fact, in 1968 only about 13 percent of Americans had a four-year college degree. In 2012, more than 33 percent of Americans aged 24–29 had attended college and earned a degree. Because such large numbers of people attend college and because so many post-college forces impact one's beliefs, it is not possible to say that people with an undergraduate degree tend to adhere to one particular ideology.

Graduate school, however, is a different story. When researchers examine voters with advanced degrees—people with master's and doctoral degrees—they find they more frequently vote Democratic and hold more liberal attitudes. This could be due in part to the fact that more college professors are liberal than conservative. A study by Daniel Klein found that across all disciplines, Democrats get 15 votes from college professors for every one vote going to a Republican. Another study showed that nearly 48 percent of college faculty consider themselves liberal, while just about 14 percent call themselves conservative.

Religion

Churches and other places of worship also influence individuals' political thought. The National Election Study estimates that 33 percent of Americans attend church on a weekly or near-weekly basis. Churches are more ideological and convey a more coherent philosophy than does a typical school. There are so many different churches, religions, and sects in this nation that there is no way to say how religion in general influences where the average voter lies on the political spectrum. However, people who attend church are more likely than those who don't to vote or participate in politics in other ways.

Specific religious affiliations, though, can be directly tied to a political stance. Fundamentalists and Evangelical Christians have a strong political presence in the South and somewhat in the Midwest. Fundamentalists believe in a literal interpretation of the Holy Bible. Evangelicals promote the Christian faith. Both tend to take conservative positions and vote Republican. Catholics have traditionally voted with the Democratic Party, though their vote is not as attached to Democratic candidates today. Jews make up a small part of the national electorate and tend to vote for Democrats.

Race and Ethnicity

Race and ethnic heritage are other factors that play a major role in determining one's outlook on the world and how one votes. African Americans have closely allied with the Democratic Party since 1932 and even more strongly since the Civil Rights Movement of the 1960s. Hispanics, in recent years, have cast more Democratic than Republican votes, usually by 55 to 65 percent. Asian Americans vote more often with the conservative Republican Party, though exit polls in 2012 showed Asian American support for President Obama. New American citizens or voters with strong ties to a foreign country will consider their votes in the context of their culture or how an issue might affect the relationship between the United States and their country of origin.

Location

Geographic location plays a key role in the way people think or approach certain issues. For example, for a century after the Civil War, the most identifiable Democratic region was the South. The party went through a long-term metamorphosis that shifted that affiliation (Chapter 5). A close look at

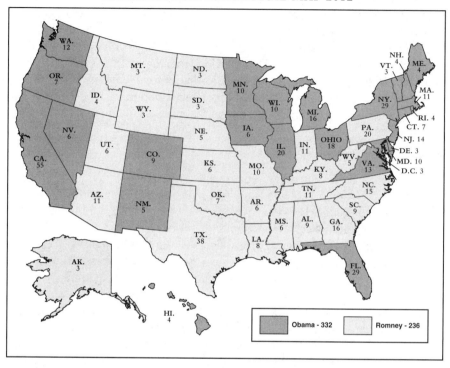

Electoral College results from a recent election will give you some indication where the two parties, and thus the two ideologies, are strong or weak. The candidate with the most votes in each state received the electoral votes for that state.

In the Northeast, Democrats dominate and more liberal policies prevail: higher tax rates, for example, fund more services, such as public transportation. Vermont and Massachusetts were among the first states to legalize civil unions and gay marriage. New York has followed. Democrats dominate the congressional delegations from New England, New York, and New Jersey. California and other western states also lean Democratic with liberal philosophies, having a strong concern for the environment and a tolerance for diverse lifestyles.

The South is more influenced by conservative Christian values than are the Northeast and West. Southern states contain higher percentages of gun ownership than in other regions and are less friendly to organized labor. The South is more religious than other parts of the country. Church attendance is higher, and voters are decidedly more Protestant. Roughly 76 percent of the South is Protestant versus about 49 percent for the remainder of the nation. There is also a high concern for issues related to farming and agriculture.

Republicans have enjoyed southern majorities in the last several national elections, but there are still many southern voters that remain Democrat, reflecting generations of party loyalty and the growth of southern cities. The working-class southerner may side with the Democratic Party on economic issues such as worker pay and employee benefits, but these same working-class voters want tighter immigration enforcement, and they tend to vote with traditional values in mind.

Measuring Public Opinion

Who cares about public opinion? Professionals in several different fields want to know what others think. In a capitalist society, manufacturers of products and providers of services want to know their customers' desires in order to better serve them and to increase sales. Marketing firms hold taste tests or include product surveys with packaged goods. Before fully launching a new product, companies allow small groups to test new prototypes and take their feedback into account.

Candidates running for office need to know their chances of winning, which groups support them, and which ones do not. Once elected, members of Congress want to know how their constituents regard proposed bills and how they view different types of government spending. These elected officials can determine public opinion by reading letters or emails, holding a town hall meeting, or conducting a survey in their districts. News services rely on public opinion polls in order to report to readers and viewers. Academics and political scientists also have an interest in the public's viewpoints. And average Americans want to know what others think to put their own opinions into context.

Polling is the most reliable way to assess public opinion. It entails posing well-developed, objective questions to a small group of people to find out what a much larger group thinks. Public opinion polling developed in the early to mid-twentieth century and now follows a sophisticated methodology.

Polling History

Polling has evolved from making ballpark estimates to an accurate, reliable science. In the 1860s, newspapers conducted **straw polls**—simple, non-scientific tallies of 50 or 60 selected voters to make rough predictions on upcoming elections. Formal polling and scientific surveys began to surface around 1900 and gained legitimacy in the 1920s and 1930s.

One notable poll, *Literary Digest's* **1936 poll** of presidential candidates, offers an insight into methodology. The popular magazine began conducting this survey through mailed questionnaires in 1916. It successfully predicted the victorious candidate in every contest from 1920 through 1932, proving to be an authority on the process. The magazine's luck ran out in 1936 when it incorrectly predicted that Kansas Republican Alfred Landon would defeat incumbent president Franklin D. Roosevelt.

Literary Digest obtained a large sampling of American adults from state auto registration lists and phone books. Then it mailed out 10 million letters with a questionnaire and a sample ballot for would-be voters to mark whom they would choose on election day, Landon or Roosevelt. Two million people responded. Once the magazine tallied the vote, it projected Landon would win with 57 percent of the vote, while FDR would receive only 43 percent.

In reality, Roosevelt won his second presidential election in a complete landslide over Landon and went on to win two more elections. The drastic miscalculation by *Literary Digest* caused people to question polling. The misread is understandable, however, if you consider the magazine's procedure. Only people who owned a car or a telephone received the questionnaire. In the middle of the Great Depression, this sample did not mirror average America, but rather the upper-middle class. A higher percentage of this sample favored Landon and the Republican Party. We'll discuss this notoriously problematic survey more, but we should first look at who got it right in 1936: George Gallup.

George Gallup is the father of modern public opinion polling. In college, Gallup researched newspaper readership and the effects of advertising. He became vastly interested in what he termed *The Pulse of America*, a title for one of his books. Working at a New York marketing firm, he began looking into elections and forecasting their results.

Elmo Roper and Lou Harris also established themselves as polling leaders. Roper began as a jewelry salesman, where he learned the value of trying to determine customers' opinions. Lou Harris, one of Roper's protégés, created Harris and Associates in 1956 and became one of the first professional pollsters to work for a presidential candidate, John F. Kennedy, in 1960. He became a leader in polling for the next generation.

Since the groundbreaking efforts of Gallup, Roper, and Harris, the field of measuring Americans' views has become its own industry. Many universities have established polling centers, and major television networks and large newspapers have created their own polling departments.

POLLING ORGANIZATIONS
Gallup
Harris Interactive
Zogby International
Rasmussen Reports
Quinnipiac University

Methodology

Pollsters take great pains to ensure their measurements are legitimate and reflective of the public. With modern technology, they have honed methods Gallup, Roper, and Harris pioneered. Today, researchers must construct a questionnaire with properly worded and properly ordered questions, select a representative sample, correctly interview the respondents, analyze the data appropriately, and draw the correct conclusions.

Pollsters must carefully phrase survey questions to not skew the results. The wording should be objective, not emotionally charged. Poll results on highly emotional issues such as abortion, gay marriage, and affirmative action can be totally distorted depending on the wording. On foreign aid, imagine how the following two questions would bring noticeably different results: "Should the U.S. provide foreign aid to other nations while American children suffer from hunger?" and "Should the U.S. give foreign aid to other nations to help them resist terrorism?"

Despite the complexity of issues explored, good polls avoid open-ended questions that allow for lengthy and uncontrolled responses and instead ask closed-ended questions that require a "yes" or "no," "agree" or "disagree," or multiple-choice answer. These allow for more conclusive results and for a quantifiable presentation, often with a chart or graph.

Question order can greatly impact the results. According to polling expert Herbert Asher, in a 2002 poll on President George W. Bush's performance, researchers tried the same basic questions but in a different sequence. When people were asked first about the performance of the president and then the direction of the country, the president fared better. If they were asked about the state of the country first, which many said was bad, then the president's approval dropped by 6 percent.

Most political questions are complicated and require more than a simple for-or-against orientation. In considering how the public views the legality of abortion, for example, researchers found that only 28 percent of Americans believe abortion should be legal under all circumstances, while many more say it should be legal only under certain circumstances, as the chart below shows.

BY THE NUMBERS When Should Abortion Be Legal?	
When a woman's life is endangered	84%
When a woman's physical health is endangered	81%
When the pregnancy was caused by rape or incest	78%
When the woman's mental health is endangered	64%
When there is evidence the baby may be physically or mentally impaired	53%
When the woman or family cannot afford to raise the child	34%

Source: R. Michael Alvarez and John Brehm, Hard Choices, Easy Answers, 2002. © Princeton University Press

What do the numbers show? How does wording the question differently affect opinions? How do people differ on the legality of abortion? What factors in the question make the policy more or less favorable?

Who is polled is just as important as the question's nature and wording. The pollster takes a **sample**, a group of people meant to represent the large group in question, known as the **universe**. Let's say you are trying to figure out students' pizza preference. If the school has 750 students, you need not ask everyone to determine what the majority wants. How many should you ask?

Surely you should ask more than two or three friends. After asking 30 students, you find that 25 preferred pepperoni pizza and only five preferred anchovy pizza. Should you keep asking, or do you have a pretty good idea? Probably the latter, but that would depend on who you asked and how you found them.

Pollsters work hard to find the right sample of the right size. Today a national poll with a proper sample needs to have about 1,500 respondents. A properly collected sample of citizens is reliably reflective of the universe. The larger the sample, the more reflective it is, so asking 1,600 respondents is better than 1,500. Yet the size of a sample is not as nearly as important as its representativeness.

Pollsters must obtain a **random sample**. That is, every single member of the universe must have an equal chance of selection. A reporter or marketer standing on a street corner asking questions to passersby may determine some indication of public opinion, but this system is not random, and not every person in that universe has an equal chance at being interviewed. Those who do not walk in that area have no chance of selection. Surveys that require respondents to go to the survey, whether approaching the researcher on the street or logging onto an Internet poll, are self-selected and thus not a cross section of the overall population.

The pollster must find a way to potentially reach everyone in the universe. Though *Literary Digest* erred with phone books in 1936, telephone ownership has dramatically increased. Since the 1980s, pollsters have used telephones as the primary contact for surveys, though concerns still exist. For example, roughly 30 percent of the populace has an unlisted number either by choice or because of mobility. To make polling more reliable and efficient, pollsters use **random-digit dialing**. A computer randomly calls possible numbers in a given area until enough people respond to establish a sample.

Once the pollster has enough respondents, he or she checks to see if the demographics in the sample are reflective of those of the universe. If disproportionately more women than men answer the phone and take the poll, the pollster will remove some female respondents from the sample in order to balance it. If a congressional district contains roughly 25 percent African Americans in the population, the sample needs to mirror that. Assuring this balance is known as **stratification**.

Even the most cautious survey with appropriate sampling techniques cannot guarantee absolute precision. The only way to know what everyone thinks is to ask everyone and hope they are entirely honest, both of which are impossible. Every poll has a **margin of error**. The sample size and the margin of error have an inverse relationship. That is, as the sample gets larger, the margin of error decreases. The way to determine this **sampling error**, the difference between poll outcomes, is to measure the outcomes in two or more polls. For example, the same basic poll with two similar samples revealed that 55 percent of the first sample opposed a particular congressional bill, while 58 percent of the second sample favored the law. This poll has a sampling error of 3 percent. A margin of error of plus-or-minus 4 percent or less is usually considered satisfactory.

The simplest yet most perplexing problem in public opinion polling is the presence of nonattitudes. Many people do not have strong opinions on the issues of the day, or they are uninformed or simply concerned about their privacy. Just over half of eligible voters actually cast votes in presidential elections. Matters of extreme importance to journalists and policymakers may not matter at all to average citizens. Pollsters now offer an "I don't know" option. When offering a middle or noncommittal option in a given poll, pollsters find that, on average, 25 percent more people choose it.

Another phenomenon affecting polls is the high frequency of uninformed citizens responding. Political scientist Herb Asher explains a poll asking about the repeal of the Public Affairs Act. In reality, no such act or repeal effort existed, but fully 43 percent of those questioned had an opinion of the non-existent law. Pollsters often ask screening questions to establish a respondent's knowledge or to ensure they are registered voters, such as "Do you plan to vote in the November election?" Such a question, however, does not eliminate the problem entirely. In fact, more than 90 percent of people answering phone surveys claim they will vote, but far fewer do so. Discerning polls may even ask, "Where do you vote?" or "On what day is the election?" to increase the chances that the respondent is a bona fide voter.

How the interviewer contacts and interacts with the respondent and how the respondent views the interviewer can also impact a poll. The difference between mailed questionnaires and telephone interviews are stark. People are more honest or frank with the anonymity of a paper questionnaire than a live telephone call. Some studies show women and men answering differently to male or female callers. Eighty-four percent of females agreed to a woman's right to choose an abortion when interviewed by females, while only 64 percent gave a pro-choice response to a male caller. Race, or perceived race, can matter as well. Asher claims African Americans are more critical of the political and criminal justice system to black interviewers while more supportive or positive to white interviewers. White respondents are less likely to reveal attitudes of racial hostility when interviewed by blacks than by whites.

Still other problems exist because not everyone conducting a poll is an objective journalist or an academic. Fund-raising under the guise of polling has cheapened polling's reputation. Political parties and candidates use phone and mail surveys to assess where their followers stand and then ask for a donation. Also, **push polling** via telephone has become a common practice. This is basically a telephone poll with an ulterior motive. Rather than a series of neutral questions meant to determine public opinion on a candidate, the caller, or more commonly a tape-recorded voice, offers positive points about the candidate or negative points about the opponent. Sometimes the voice takes an almost sinister tone. The call may end with a request for a vote on election day or to not vote for the other candidate.

Internet polling can be problematic due to self-selection, administration, and the nature of people who go online. When directed toward an Internet poll, only those strongly motivated will participate. With some online polls, there's no limit to how many times one can take it. Internet users also tend to be younger, better educated, more affluent, white, and suburban and do not represent a genuine cross section of society.

THINK AS A POLITICAL SCIENTIST: ASSESS THE CREDIBILITY OF A PUBLIC OPINION POLL

Your research and any conclusions you draw from it are no better than the credibility and reliability of your sources. To assess the credibility of most informational sources, ask yourself these questions.

Is the source current? Be sure to avoid out-of-date information.

Is the author an established authority in the field?

Is the source free from obvious bias?

Can you verify the information in other sources?

When assessing poll results and other collected data, you also need to evaluate the methodology of the study. Review pages 62–65 to identify possible problems in polling methodology.

Practice: Examine the parts of the fictional poll below to assess its credibility. In what ways did this poll follow appropriate methodology? In what ways did it not? What might be some concerns of validity?

REAL CURRENT POLITICS: "GOV. SAMUELS PREDICTED TO WIN ELECTORAL COLLEGE"

Question: "If the presidential election were today, would you vote for Bill Samuels, John Knox (order alternated), or another candidate?"

Results:

Samuels	37
Knox	33
Other	21
No choice	9

Sample: 233 likely voters answering prerecorded landline survey in NY, TX, CA   Sept. 17–19

Media and Polling

Reporters refer to polls to convey the views of the citizenry. One examination of three leading news magazines showed that roughly 30 percent of their cover stories cited public opinion polls. Nightly television news broadcasts provide polling results to accompany their reports. Journalists' quest to explain public opinion is a good thing; however, the modern media's use and misuse of polling is not.

In reporting on political campaigns, reporters can begin to sound like an announcer at a horse race, concentrating on which candidate is ahead and which candidate is behind, instead of focusing on the issues, candidates' views, or qualifications. A conflict of interest exists when polling departments are located down the hall from newsrooms. When CBS, the *Washington Post,* or local news stations conduct their own polls, they become not just the reporters of news but creators of the same with no critique of their own methods and a less than objective analysis.

The difference in how an academic analyst and a journalist approach polls can sometimes distort the big picture. One Gallup poll about attitudes on race relations caused differing headlines in national newspapers. *USA Today* printed atop its front page, "Poll: Whites Increasingly Accept Blacks," while the *New York Times* chose as its title, "New Survey Shows Americans Pessimistic on Race Relations." How could the same poll results bring such differing headlines?

As Frank Newport, editor of the Gallup Poll, tells us, the nature of modern journalism is in direct conflict with the proper approach to measuring citizens' views. Good reporting is sharply focused with relatively unambiguous conclusions. Good survey research, however, often reveals uncertainty, ambiguity, and low levels of public interest on matters of public policy. Reporters with tight deadlines don't have the time to study, reflect on, or contemplate poll results, particularly at election time. News reporting needs to be dramatic enough to raise interest yet simple enough to be digested quickly. Poll findings are often complex, equivocal, and not necessarily easy to explain. When placed against the mandates of journalism, scientific measures of public opinion on complicated issues do not always translate well into sound bites and brief headlines.

Source: iStockphoto

Exit polls are a staple of election days but can yield misleading results, as in 2004 when they suggested John Kerry would win the presidency.

Polls that examine complex issues give inconclusive results. Uncertain answers irritate average viewers who do not delve into the intricacies of public opinion. An astute pollster could convey ambiguous poll findings, but television news is dependent on good, interesting, and simple video. A talking head who can convey a full understanding will simply bore most viewers. Newport offers this list of how news reporters handle poll findings:

Reporting Poll Results
Clearly positive or clearly negative findings are more likely reported than mixed findings.
A single conclusion makes a better story than a complex or uncertain explanation.
A poll finding that contradicts conventional wisdom is cited more than one that confirms it.
A finding that can be boldly stated at the beginning of a news story will be used sooner than one that must follow with an explanation.

Common Measurements

Pollsters use different kinds of polls to gather information at different times. **Tracking polls** ask people the same or similar questions over time to "track" the path of public opinion. These are used heavily during election season to show how public opinion changes or to assess a candidate's strength. Candidates also use these to shape their campaigns. **Exit polls** are conducted outside a polling place on election day to predict the outcome of the election, to gain insight into the thoughts and behaviors of voters, or to analyze demographic voting trends.

Focus groups are small groups of citizens—10 to 40 people—gathered to hold conversations about issues or candidates. These are obviously much smaller samples, but they allow for elaboration of views. In 1988, when Vice President George H. W. Bush's team heard a focus group reveal a strong disdain for his opponent's anti-death penalty position, Bush's team created commercials to emphasize Massachusetts Governor Michael Dukakis's unpopular positions. As political analysts Mark Halperin and John Heilemann report, Republican presidential candidate Mitt Romney began wearing jeans more often when campaigning in the 2012 election after focus groups responded more positively to him in jeans than in formal clothes.

Researchers have measured presidential approval regularly since the 1930s. Pollsters simply ask whether or not the respondent approves, yes or no, of the president's job performance, usually over a three-day period. Presidential approval on average tends to hover above 50 percent. Some of the highest presidential **approval ratings** have come when the nation prospers, especially economically, or when the country finds itself in a crisis and rallies around its elected chief. Two of the highest presidential approval ratings were recorded on the days immediately following Harry Truman's decision to drop the atomic bombs on Japan to end World War II and following the terrorist attacks of September 11, 2001, in support for George W. Bush. Approval ratings, however, can change drastically. Truman found himself in a tight election three years later and at a low rating of 22 percent approval when he fired World War II hero General Douglas MacArthur during the Korean conflict. President Bush left office in 2009 with one of the lower approval ratings on record, 29 percent.

The "right-track-wrong-track" question is commonly asked to determine Americans' satisfaction with government leaders. A positive right-track response usually means incumbents will fare well in their re-election campaigns, while a high wrong-track response will make incumbents uncomfortable. The generic party ballot simply asks respondents if they will be voting for "Republicans" or "Democrats" during an upcoming election without mentioning candidates' names to determine the parties' relative strength.

REFLECT ON THE ESSENTIAL QUESTION

Essential Question: *How do Americans form opinions, and how do these opinions influence government?* On separate paper, complete a chart like the one below to gather details to answer that question.

How Public Opinion Forms	How Public Opinion Influences Government

1936 *Literary Digest* poll	party identification	sampling error
approval ratings	political socialization	stratification
conservative	populist	straw poll
exit polls	progressive	tracking poll
focus group	push polling	universe
liberal	random-digit dialing	valence issues
libertarian	random sample	wedge issues
margin of error	saliency	
moderate	sample	

MULTIPLE-CHOICE QUESTIONS

1. Which of the following statements regarding the Founding Fathers and public opinion is true?

   (A) There was no concern for public opinion at the American founding.

   (B) The Framers of the Constitution knew public opinion would not matter in American governance.

   (C) The Framers included in the Constitution devices to temper the forces of public opinion.

   (D) The American public generally opposed the Revolutionary War and the break from Britain.

   (E) Of the institutions the Framers created, the Electoral College is the most responsive to public opinion.

2. The single largest influence on a person's political socialization is

   (A) where the person attended school

   (B) the influence of his or her parents and family

   (C) what sources of media the person uses

   (D) the person's religion

   (E) what party was in power when the person was born

3. A self-described fiscal conservative would have the highest concern for which of the following?

   (A) A bill to make flag burning illegal

   (B) A bill to increase taxes on incomes

   (C) A Supreme Court decision that legalizes gay marriage

   (D) A proposal to lengthen the waiting period to purchase a gun

   (E) A student giving a prayer at a home football game

4. What is the adequate sample size for a national public opinion poll?

   (A) 100

   (B) 150

   (C) 1,500

   (D) 10,000

   (E) 150,000

5. Which of the following about public opinion polling is true?

   (A) Measuring public opinion is unnecessary because government officials don't have to consider public opinion.

   (B) If conducted properly, public opinion polls are reliable indicators of actual public opinion.

   (C) The demographic makeup of a sample makes no difference in the poll.

   (D) The news media give full discussions to ambiguous poll results.

   (E) Sample size matters more than sample representativeness.

6. The *Literary Digest* survey that incorrectly predicted the 1936 presidential election was incorrect because

   (A) it was the first national poll ever conducted

   (B) the sample was too small

   (C) the questions were loaded

   (D) the sample was not reflective of the population at large

   (E) it relied too heavily on the Internet

7. A libertarian would most likely

   (A) favor a tax increase for more government services

   (B) vote to legalize gambling

   (C) favor prayer in public schools

   (D) seek to increase the minimum wage

   (E) favor a ban on smoking in public

8. Which of the following about polling and measuring nonattitudes is true?

   (A) Pollsters never offer an "I don't know" option as a poll response.

   (B) Respondents are highly honest about their voting habits.

   (C) Respondents never answer a question on an unfamiliar issue.

   (D) More legitimate polls ask screening questions to verify the respondent's firmness of opinion or their likelihood as a voter.

   (E) Offering a middle choice usually generates only about 5 percent noncommittal answers.

Presidential Job Approval Over Term (Leaving Office)		
President	Percent Approving	Terms
George W. Bush (R)	38%	2
Bill Clinton (D)	68%	2
George H.W. Bush (R)	56%	1
Ronald Reagan (R)	63%	2
Jimmy Carter (D)	34%	1

Source: Surveys by American Research Group, PSRA/Newsweek, and Gallup Organization. Data provided by the Roper Center Archives.

9. Which statement below is backed by the data in the table above?

   (A) Presidents usually enjoy higher ratings when they enter office than when they leave.

   (B) During this period, the Democratic presidents left office with higher approval ratings than all the Republican presidents.

   (C) All two-term presidents had noticeably higher approval ratings upon leaving office than did one-term presidents.

   (D) Of those presidents shown in the table, Bill Clinton had the highest end-of-term approval rating.

   (E) Congressional approval is usually higher than the president's approval.

10. All of the following are legitimate criticisms of the media's use of polls EXCEPT

(A) media outlets tend to promote rather than critique their own measures and findings

(B) polling in campaign season encourages horse race journalism

(C) today's journalism requires simple reporting and conclusive answers, and many poll results do not offer that

(D) different newspapers can report the same poll in entirely different ways

(E) newspapers and TV reports do not emphasize polling enough

FREE-RESPONSE QUESTIONS

Question

1. Understanding public opinion is essential in a democracy, and accurately measuring public opinion can be challenging.

(a) Explain why each person listed below would benefit from knowing and understanding public opinion on an issue.

- A member of Congress
- A member of the media

(b) Identify and describe two methods necessary to ensure a public opinion poll is valid.

(c) Identify and describe one additional way to measure public opinion other than scientific polling or surveys.

GALLUP TRACKING POLL

"If the election were today, who would you vote for,
Barack Obama or John McCain?"

(The order of names was alternated for each respondent.)

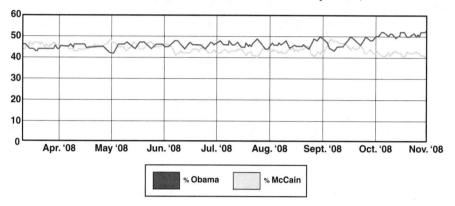

Question

2. Pollsters use surveys to predict elections. Look at the graph above, which shows how voters responded to the Gallup poll question.

   (a) Identify one trend in the 2008 presidential campaign poll depicted in the graph.

   (b) Identify and explain two polling methods that can influence a voter's response to poll questions.

   (c) Identify and explain two influences that shape a citizen's political opinions.

WRITING: USE TRANSITIONS

Seeing relationships is a key skill in interpreting data and transforming information into insight. Use transitions in your writing to highlight the relationships you find. *In contrast, on the other hand, in a similar way,* and *yet another* are just a few examples of words that show how ideas are related.

4

Political Participation

"It [universal suffrage] is found among populations placed on different rungs of the social ladder. I have had occasion to see its effects in diverse places and among races of men whom language, religion, or mores render almost strangers to one another."

—Alexis de Tocqueville, *Democracy in America, 1835*

Essential Question: How do Americans participate in the political world?

In November 2012, some 132 million people, nearly 62 percent of America's **voting-age population**, cast a vote in the presidential election, according to the U.S. Census Bureau. It was the highest **voter turnout** since 1960. Citizen participation in public affairs, whether more active or by voting alone, gives policymakers an insight into the public's views. Until the 1820s through the 1840s, only property-owning men could vote. Today, three constitutional amendments expanding the right to vote make the United States one of the world's most open democracies. Who is participating today, and at what levels? This chapter examines the history of voting, government's management of the voting process, and election trends.

Participation and Voting

Americans can get involved in public life in many ways. At a fundamental level, anytime people gather into community groups—through little league teams or library book clubs or neighborhood associations—they are participating in civil society and contributing to the spirit of public life. They might also participate in citizens' organizations with a political emphasis, such as special interest groups related to immigration reform, civil rights for people with disabilities, or environmental protection. These groups use the power of their membership to exert pressure on policymakers and sometimes on corporations.

Some organizations, such as the NAACP and the National Organization for Women, help to plan demonstrations and protests to express their views on matters of concern to them and to call attention to those concerns in the media. Individuals not affiliated with organized groups can also take part in these protests, as many have done in the mass movements that rallied citizens to protest racial discrimination and the war in Vietnam in the 1960s. The sheer number of people voicing protest to government policies alerts lawmakers to the power voters could wield to remove unresponsive politicians when the next election rolls around.

With guarantees of free speech, citizens can also write letters to the editor to express their feelings on a local or national issue. They can donate to a political cause, to a political party, or to a candidate. (See Chapters 6 and 7.) Public officials are often accessible via telephone and email. People can ask questions or express concerns at a town hall meeting. Citizens can run for office themselves. These are all forms of political participation.

The most common form of political participation, however, is voting. Every four years a large percentage of Americans, known as the **electorate**, "go to the polls" to cast a vote for the American president and lower offices. Elections of all kinds occur in other years at the local, state, and federal levels, giving political scientists and government students much data to tabulate and analyze.

The Framers decided states were the best judges for determining **suffrage**, or which citizens are qualified to vote, and the management of elections. There is little mention of voting or elections in the Constitution. Article I includes that "The Times, Places and Manner of holding Elections for Senators and Representatives, shall be prescribed in each State by the Legislature thereof," but Congress may "make or alter such Regulations." It also states "Each House shall be the Judge of the Elections, Returns and Qualifications of its own Members." With constitutional amendments and subsequent federal law, Congress has some oversight on elections, but administering elections is a state responsibility.

Congress has set federal elections to occur every two years, in even years, on the Tuesday after the first Monday in November. The congressional and presidential terms begin the next January. States also hold elections for offices from governor to school board member. In several states citizens can also change the law with elections. Through ballot **initiatives**, citizens gather the necessary number of signatures of registered voters to place a proposal on the ballot. This initiative could be to create a law, such as a statewide smoking ban or legalization of marijuana. A similar procedure known as a **referendum** can repeal an unpopular law. Some states allow citizens to **recall** elected officials in the middle of their elected term. The people can also decide tax rates in a formal election with levies. None of these measures exists at the national level.

Most states require a voter to register in advance of an election and to be 18 years old, a citizen of the United States, a resident of the state where voting will take place, and a nonfelon. States can constitutionally require **voter registration** 30 days in advance of the election so county boards of elections can create and maintain the voter rolls, or poll books.

For purposes of voting, counties and cities are subdivided into **wards**, which are broken into **precincts**. A precinct is a small geographic area of about 500–1,000 voters, all who vote at an assigned **polling place**, often a school or community center. States can allow 17-year-olds to vote, and many do so in the primary elections if the voter will be 18 by the date of the general election in November. A state elections official oversees the process statewide, while the county-level boards of elections tabulate and report the election returns. Typically, winning candidates are known late on election night or by the following day, but election authorities do not certify the election for days or weeks while they verify the count.

An Expanding Electorate

The **franchise**, or right to vote, was extended to white working-class men in the United States much earlier than in other countries. Even before the American Revolution, historians estimate, as many as half of white men had suffrage of some level in the colonies.

Madison biographer Richard Labunski recounts voter participation in one of the first congressional elections, in which future presidents James Madison and James Monroe competed for the U.S. House seat representing eight Virginia counties. The 1790 census shows about 50,000 total nonslaves lived in the congressional district, an average of 6,357 per county. Virginia required its voters to be male, twenty-one or older, and to own fifty acres of property or twenty-five acres and a house. There were 5,189 men eligible to vote. The unusually cold election day ended with 2,280 votes, 44 percent of the total eligible. Madison won and served in the first House of Representatives. Today, Virginia's seventh congressional district overlaps much of the same area as it did in 1789. In the 2010 midterm election, more than 233,000 citizens voted, about 40 percent of the voting-age population.

The first presidential election (1789) was decided on the basis of a different kind of participation—that of the political elites. The Constitution calls for state legislatures to appoint electors who then later elect the president. On a designated day, every state's electors meet in their capitals to cast votes for the president. There was no popular vote for George Washington, but every one of the 69 electors cast their first ballots for Washington. By the 1800 presidential election, five of 16 states used popular elections to name the electors.

State governments typically did not grant suffrage equally. The Constitution forbade religious tests for federal office but did not prevent such tests in determining who could vote. In addition to religious tests, states imposed property requirements and poll taxes. They also barred women, African Americans, and immigrants from the political process. Courageous activists worked for more than 100 years to persuade states to alter voting practices and state laws and to ratify amendments to extend suffrage. Until they were enfranchised, citizens participated in politics in the only channels available to them—through protest and expression of opinion in other ways.

Jacksonian Era Voter participation continued to grow in the 1830s. President **Andrew Jackson**, a popular leader and advocate for expanding suffrage to all white men, was influential in increasing citizen participation. Jackson embodied the common man, the non-son-of-privilege who bravely rose through military ranks and through Congress to become the seventh president of the United States. He called for the end of the property requirement to vote. It was during and around his time in office that universal male suffrage became a reality, greatly increasing voter turnout. In 1824, four candidates tallied a collective 350,671 votes. Four years later the popular vote total reached 1,155,350. By 1830, almost all states had removed the property requirement.

The citizenry, too, played a role in pushing to expand the right to vote to those beyond property owners. In 1829 a Rhode Island gathering of some 300 demonstrators petitioned the state's general assembly for the extension of suffrage. It was finally granted in 1840. North Carolina was the last state to abandon the property requirement in 1856.

This expansion of the electorate brought about the need for organized political parties to connect leaders to increased numbers of citizen-voters. Parties began to hold conventions at all levels. These became the barometer for public opinion. By the end of the 1830s, parties used national conventions to nominate presidential candidates. The political scene in the post-Jackson era included a greater number of gatherings than before the extension of suffrage. Rallies, banners, and songs became permanent fixtures on political campaigns.

Suffrage by Constitutional Amendment

America had yet to give the franchise to blacks, women, and other minorities. This situation changed with the passage of three constitutional amendments: the Fifteenth, Nineteenth, and Twenty-sixth. Two other amendments, the Twenty-third and Twenty-fourth, extended suffrage further. These allowed residents of the nation's capital to vote for the president and outlawed poll taxes.

Suffrage Amendments

- **Fifteenth Amendment**: Citizens shall not be denied the right to vote by the states or the United States "on account of race, color, or previous condition of servitude."

- **Nineteenth Amendment**: Citizens shall not be denied the right to vote by the states or the United States "on account of sex."

- **Twenty-third Amendment**: For presidential and vice presidential elections, "the District constituting the seat of government" shall appoint a number of electors "in no event more than the least populous State."

- **Twenty-fourth Amendment**: Citizens shall not be denied the right to vote by states or the United States "by reason of failure to pay any poll tax or other tax."

- **Twenty-sixth Amendment**: Citizens "eighteen years of age or older" shall not be denied the right to vote by the states or the United States "on account of age."

African-American Suffrage As suffrage expanded in its first phase, legislatures and groups of people discussed the potential for free blacks to vote. In the 1830s, six northern states permitted blacks to vote. After the North defeated the South in the Civil War, Congress passed the Reconstruction Amendments that freed the slaves, made them citizens, and gave them a vote. The **Fifteenth Amendment**, ratified in 1870, gave former slaves and free blacks the right to vote and was the first federal mandate affecting state voting requirements.

The Fifteenth Amendment, like the other amendments, passed through a northern-dominated Congress without southern support. The federal government enforced the amendment during Reconstruction when African Americans voted in large numbers. The Union Army's continued presence in the former Confederacy ensured that blacks could vote, and several were elected to public office. In 1876, Rutherford B. Hayes won a disputed presidential election and soon after withdrew Union troops from the South. A decade later, as the era of Jim Crow began, southern legislatures segregated their citizens and established loopholes to circumvent the Fifteenth Amendment. White citizens, including members of the Ku Klux Klan, intimidated and abused blacks to turn them away from the polls.

Several southern states denied suffrage to African Americans as they began requiring property or literacy qualifications to vote. Several states elevated the **literacy test** into their state constitutions. The **poll tax**—a simple fee required to vote—became one of the most effective ways to discourage the potential black voter. And the **grandfather clause**, which allowed states to recognize a registering voter as it would have recognized his grandfather, prevented scores of blacks from voting, while it allowed illiterate and poor whites to circumvent the literacy test and poll tax requirements.

These state-level loopholes suppressed the black vote but never explicitly violated the letter of the Constitution because they never prevented blacks from voting, "on account of race, color, or previous condition of servitude." The impact on black voting was demonstrated by the number of registered black voters in Louisiana as the state sought to alter the law. Historian C. Vann Woodward reveals that in 1896, the state had 130,334 registered black voters, and African Americans outnumbered registered white voters in 26 parishes (counties). By 1900, white voters dominated every parish, and by 1904, only 1,342 blacks were on the poll books and registered to vote.

The **white primary**, too, became a popular method for southern states to keep African Americans from voting. State Democratic Party organizations set rules for their primaries, defining their membership as white men's clubs. By 1915, thirteen southern states had established the white primary. A generation of intimidation, lynching, and a host of public policies to prevent blacks from voting resulted in a steady decline in turnout that began as soon as the Union pulled out of the South. Black voting reached an all-time low in the 1920s.

The growing quest for equality and the post-World War II Civil Rights Movement brought the greatest increases in African American turnout in a century. Some inroads to making the Fifteenth Amendment a reality had been made. In 1915, in *Guinn v. United States*, the Supreme Court ruled the grandfather clause unconstitutional. In 1944, the Court declared the white primary a violation of the Constitution's equal protection clause in *Smith v. Allwright*. One estimate of southern black registration before and after the white primary shows a statewide increase from 151,000 to 595,000 registered voters. Southern black voter turnout increased from 4.5 percent in 1940 to 12.5 in 1947. The Democratic Party included a pro-civil rights plank in its 1948 platform that called for equal treatment and fairness. The Civil Rights Movement of the 1950s and 1960s caused greater increases in voter participation following key congressional acts, additional Supreme Court rulings, and one more constitutional amendment.

The 1957 **Civil Rights Act**, the first such bill since Reconstruction, addressed discrimination in voter registration and established the U.S. Office of Civil Rights, an enforcement agency in the Justice Department. Before World War II, about 3 percent of the South's black voting-age populace was registered. In 1964, that percentage varied from 6 to 66 percent, averaging 36 percent.

The expansive 1964 Civil Rights Act also addressed voting. That same year Congress passed and the states ratified the **Twenty-fourth Amendment**, which outlawed poll taxes in any federal elections. By the time the amendment was introduced in Congress in 1962, only four states still charged such a tax. The Supreme Court later ruled taxes on any elections unconstitutional.

The 1965 **Voting Rights Act** was the most effective bill to bring the black populace into the political process. This law outlawed literacy tests and put states with low voter turnout on the watch of the Justice Department. The law gave the department jurisdiction over states that had any type of voting test and less than 50 percent turnout in the 1964 election. These states became subject to federal election examiners and the **preclearance** provision of the act's Section Five. If these states attempted to invent new, creative loopholes to diminish black suffrage, the federal government could stop them. By 1967, black voter registration in six southern states increased from about 30 to more than 50 percent. African Americans soon held office in greater numbers. The original law expired in 1971, but Congress has renewed the Voting Rights Act several times since.

Recently, the preclearance provision landed in the Supreme Court. Shelby County, Alabama, challenged the 1965 point of law, and the Court declared in a 5-to-4 decision that this section of the law imposes burdens that are no longer responsive to current conditions.

Women's Suffrage The push for women's suffrage began in the mid-1800s. Wyoming, Idaho, and Utah were among the first states to admit women to the polls. In the late 1800s, women entered the workplace and, later, in World War I served the nation on the home front. Women's suffrage became a national reality with passage of the **Nineteenth Amendment** in 1920.

Activists had worked hard and courageously to secure the amendment's passage. Susan B. Anthony became a leading suffragist. She spoke at political conventions and helped organize different associations. In 1872, in direct violation of New York law, she walked into a polling place and cast a vote. She was tried and convicted by an all-male jury.

Is That Constitutional? *Minor v. Happerset* (1875)

If a state denies a woman the right to vote, is that a violation of the Constitution? According to the Supreme Court in ***Minor v. Happerset*** (1875), no.

The National Women's Suffrage Association brought suit. Several constitutional provisions were addressed, such as the Fourteenth Amendment's citizenship clause and other parts. The group failed to show that the authors of the amendment intended for the federal government to take away from states the right to define voting qualifications. The Court ruled that citizenship conferred "membership of a nation and nothing more." States would still define suffrage. That would change with further amendment to the Constitution.

Suffragists continued the fight. By 1914, eleven states allowed women to vote. In the 1916 election, both major political parties endorsed the concept of women's suffrage in their platforms, and Montana elected the first woman to Congress, Jeanette Rankin. More western states granted suffrage to women, while eastern and southern states did so later. Women's groups picketed the White House to persuade President Woodrow Wilson to get behind the cause. He finally supported the amendment, and it was ratified in 1920.

What impact did the amendment have on voter turnout for women, and how did it impact elections after 1920? One University of Chicago study found that in Chicago, turnout for women was at 46 percent in the 1920 general election (Chicago had had women's suffrage since 1913). The university also did a survey of the April 1923 city mayoral race. Only 35 percent of women showed up, several responding that it wasn't a woman's place to engage in politics or that the act would offend their husbands. In the same city, men turned out in much higher numbers. In 1920, men outvoted women 75 to 46 percent, and in 1923, 63 to 35 percent. Some men expected their wives to avoid the election process, but other men embraced their wives' participation. Men's view of election day changed because the social activity in the presence of women put a respectability to the process that hadn't existed when it was an entirely men's affair. Drunken behavior and bold temperament might have ruled the day before, but some observers recounted post-Nineteenth Amendment elections as "more like Sunday" where manners were improved. Females became more and more accustomed to voting and became active participants in politics.

The District of Columbia The Electoral College system awards each state the same number of electors that it has senators and representatives. Washington, D.C., is not a state and had no electors until passage of the **Twenty-third Amendment**. The Founding Fathers were skeptical and concerned about the potential political influence of those living in and near the nation's capital. When they created the federal government, a debate ensued about the location of the national seat of government. Delegates at the constitutional convention feared the advantages a state might gain if it also housed the capital city. The Constitution therefore empowers Congress to "exercise exclusive Legislation in all Cases whatsoever, over such District…[to] become the Seat of the Government of the United States." After short terms of government in New York City and Philadelphia, the national capital moved to Washington, D.C., on a parcel of land ceded by Virginia and Maryland. The town's population remained small for decades, but as the role of government and the size of the town grew, the permanent population of citizens desired representation.

The Constitution, however, does not give this district "state" status, and therefore it has no voting representatives in the House or the Senate and no presidential electors. The nation's least populous state, Wyoming, has 544,270 residents represented by three total members to Congress and three electoral votes. The District of Columbia has 599,657 residents with no voting representation in Congress. The **Twenty-third Amendment** provides that the District shall appoint electors, but never more than those of the smallest state so that the District never has stronger influence than the smallest state. In 1964, the District voted for Democrat Lyndon Johnson and has voted for the Democratic candidate every year since.

Young Adults States used to generally require voters to be 21 years old. In the post-World War II years, however, a move to enfranchise 18-year-olds

WOMEN'S SUFFRAGE BEFORE THE NINETEENTH AMENDMENT

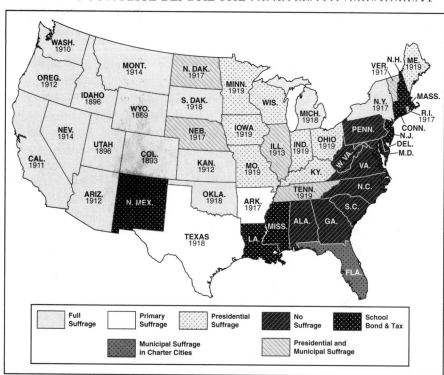

gained momentum. The president and Congress had sent scores of 18-, 19-, and 20-year-old draftees to Vietnam, most of whom had no right to vote for president or Congress. Some states, however allowed residents under 21 to vote, and four states allowed 18-year-olds to vote. In 1970, Congress passed amendments to the 1965 Voting Rights Act that lowered the national voting age to 18 for presidential and congressional elections. States challenged the new law in the Supreme Court based on reserved powers. The Court narrowly ruled that Congress did have the authority to set a voting age on *federal* elections but not for state and local offices. This ruling prompted Congress to pass the **Twenty-sixth Amendment** on June 30, 1971, which prevents states from denying citizens 18 and over the right to vote.

The rapid ratification of the measure with strong majorities in each state put younger citizens on the road to voting. President Nixon proclaimed that some 11 million young men and women who "have participated in the life of our nation through their work, their studies, and their sacrifices for its defense now are to be fully included in the electoral process of our country." Some 25 million new potential voters would participate in the 1972 election.

As the election neared, most political commentators predicted this new voting bloc would help Democrat George McGovern, an avid anti-war candidate, defeat incumbent Richard Nixon. McGovern was counting on this newly enfranchised group to elect him. The turnout among young voters, however, was roughly 42 percent, much lower than the population at large. President Nixon won re-election with the largest landslide in history.

Voting and Nonvoting

During the late nineteenth century, voter turnout rose to the highest levels in American history. Some estimates show that up to 90 percent of the legal electorate voted. As more and more people went to the polls, and as politicians had to court the masses, election corruption increased. Manipulation of the ballot box and other fraudulent practices became common. Some voters were bribed, some denied. Candidates sometimes had to pay large sums to get on the ballot. In urban settings, local ward bosses directed their thugs to intimidate voters, including many new Americans. Free alcohol, payments, and threats of getting fired from a job persuaded voters to vote a certain way. Large groups of voters moved from poll to poll, casting multiple ballots on election day. These "repeaters" were urged to "vote early and vote often." A generation of machine politics and patronage dominated from the precinct up to the national level. Powerful personalities with an ethnic or other unique following ruled bodies of government from state to state and became the faces of politics.

Election schemes brought the need for voter registration. Registration enables the government to prepare for an election, verify a voter's qualifications, and assign a voter to one particular polling place to prevent repeating. Registration systems and requirements vary state to state. The Supreme Court ruled in *Dunn v. Blumstein* that a one-year requirement was unconstitutional and wasn't necessary to prevent fraud or to manage elections. Today, no state can require registration beyond 30 days before an election. Voters can also vote by **absentee ballot**. If a voter cannot make it to the polls on election day, he or she can mail a completed ballot instead. Some states enable voters to vote by mail without a reason, and some allow early voting in person.

The machine's corrupt brand of democracy also caused Progressive Era reformers to adopt the **Australian ballot** in order to make elections fair. First used in Australia in 1872, by 1892, 33 U.S. states had adopted it. Before this change, parties had printed and controlled their own ballots, arranging them to benefit the party. To prevent this problem, the Australian ballot 1) is printed and distributed at public expense, 2) must show all candidates' names, 3) is available only at the polling places, and 4) is completed in private.

How Much Participation?

The United States is a leader in democracy, a nation that preserves the right to expression, dissent, representation, and participation, although it wasn't until the mid-1900s that all adult citizens had realistic ballot access. Ironically, during the same era from the Depression into the 1970s, voter turnout took a noticeable drop. From 1928 to 1968, the November turnout in presidential election years hovered generally just over 60 percent. In 1972, an election year that embraced a new voting bloc of young voters, turnout dipped down to 57 percent. The anti-government feelings about the unpopular Vietnam War and later Nixon's Watergate scandal resulted in a number of people disengaging from politics. Party loyalty in elections became weaker and weaker. The connection between money and elections further disturbed Americans and required Congress to regulate the flow of dollars through campaigns. From 1972 to 2000, presidential election turnout hovered above 50 percent. Into the twenty-first century, presidential election turnout has risen.

Measuring Turnout

Voter turnout is simply the number of voters who actually cast votes as a percentage of the voting-age population. Different organizations measure voter turnout in different ways. As a percentage of *registered* voters, voter turnout is high. Of those citizens registered to vote, 89.6 percent voted in 2008. More commonly, political scientists measure turnout as the percentage of those who voted out of the potential *voting-age* population. But that method includes some who cannot vote. Advocates of measuring turnout based on the total *voting-eligible* population argue this measure is a better indicator of citizen participation than turnout based on voting-age population because it discounts ineligible felons and undocumented immigrants who are old enough to vote but cannot legally.

Turnout varies based on the type of election. More voters show up for the presidential contest than any other. In no presidential election from 1972 until 2000 did turnout rise higher than 60 percent, with its lowest, 51.4 percent, in 1996. What would cause nearly half of the nation to not participate in the election? This **voter apathy**, a simple lack of concern for the election, has different causes. Some citizens feel no **political efficacy**, or sense of effectiveness with their vote. Voters who vote for losing candidates, or voters who did not experience a desired change with their vote (maybe hoping for a better economy) lack efficacy and may steer away from participation and voting. Some nonvoters are simply satisfied with the way things are.

In the last three presidential elections, voter turnout has crossed and remained above the 60 percent mark. The U.S. Census reported that 63.8 percent voted in 2004, 63.6 voted in 2008, and 61.8 percent voted in 2012. The graph below, using data from the Center for Democracy and Election Management at American University, shows the trend in voter turnout from 1960 to 2008. Each method of gathering election data is somewhat different. For this reason, voting percentages may vary from source to source.

VOTER TURNOUT IN PRESIDENTIAL ELECTIONS, 1960-2008

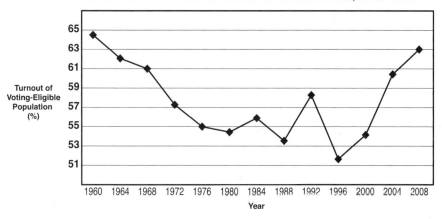

Congressional midterm elections, those federal elections that occur mid-way through a president's term, have lower turnouts. From 1974 through the late 1990s, the turnout hovered above 33 percent. It has grown to 40 percent in more recent years.

Voter turnout in the United States is lower than that of other advanced democracies. One reason for this difference is that states make voting a two-step process—registering and then voting. In many developed nations, the government registers the populace on a national level, removing one institutional block to voting. Additionally, voter turnout in Western European nations is high because elections occur less frequently than in the United States and for fewer offices. In America, citizens may vote several times per year in elections for various offices and issues. Every two years a federal election typically requires a two-stage campaign, one for the primary, and a second for the general election. Some states' elections for governor and state legislative offices occur in odd years. These many voting opportunities in the United States diminish the individual value of each election, bringing down the average voter turnout.

BY THE NUMBERS Voter Turnout in Selected Democracies	
Country	**Turnout**
Denmark	83.2
Australia	82.7
Italy	79.1
Netherlands	77.5
Spain	77.2
France	76.8
Germany	71.9
Israel	71.2
Portugal	69.2
Japan	66.6
United Kingdom	58.3
United States	**58.2**
Switzerland	39.8

Source: The International Institute for Democracy and Electoral Assistance (http://www.idea.int/vt/)

What do the numbers show? What countries lead in voter turnout? Which countries have the lowest turnout? What are the different reasons why turnout would be high or low?

Several factors determine levels of participation. There is a strong correlation between age, education, personal income, and voter turnout. The older, better-educated, wealthier voters show up to vote in higher numbers. Activists, people who attend church, military veterans, and members of civic organizations also turn out to vote in higher numbers.

Voting Blocs and Behaviors

Certain demographic groups will think alike on certain issues and tend to favor one ideology, or often one political party, over another. Anyone who identifies with a party, whether actively or casually, will likely vote for candidates from that party. This **party identification** is the easiest way to predict a voter's habits. For example, people who contribute to the party or just refer to themselves as "a Democrat" will vote for fellow Democrats.

Political scientists analyze voter turnout and reveal noticeable trends about how people of various demographics, or **voting blocs**, participate in politics.

Men and Women One of the easiest ways to divide and analyze voters is along gender lines. Men and women act differently with their votes based on their respective worldviews. The **gender gap** is the difference in their views and how these are expressed at the voting booth. Women tend to oppose harsh punishments and the death penalty more than men; they favor government spending on welfare; and they are less war-prone. These leanings have resulted in more women voting with the Democratic than the Republican Party. Men tend to believe in a harder line against accused criminals and are more fiscally conservative; they have a tendency to vote Republican.

Since the 1980 election, women turn out to vote in slightly higher numbers than men. Although women as a whole favor Democrats, there is a division among females who are married and unmarried. In 2000, the unmarried female population strongly voted with Democrats. Single women care about health care, employment, education, job security, and retirement benefits. On the other hand, in the 2002 midterms, 56 percent of married women voted for Republican candidates compared to 39 percent of unmarried women. Married women tend to be "moral traditionalists," having concerns for the institutions of marriage and traditional family. Both married and unmarried women contribute to their lead in turnout: in 2008, 65.7 percent of women voted, while 61.5 percent of men did so. According to a 2012 *Washington Post* exit poll, 55 percent of women voters sided with Democratic President Barack Obama. Roughly 52 percent of men voted for Republican candidate Mitt Romney.

Young Voters After receiving the vote in 1972 and turning out in surprisingly low numbers in that election, the nation's youngest voters developed a reputation as the voting bloc with the lowest turnout. Reasons include their undeveloped views of candidates, lack of strong views on issues, lack of full understanding of politics, and mobility. Working a full-time career job, owning a home, heading a family, and running a business are all things that make people notice the details of public policy, and for most people 18 to 24 years old, these activities are still in the future. Yet young voter turnout and interest in politics have risen. Eighteen- to 24-year-olds turned out at 30 percent in 1996, 38 percent in 2000, and nearly 47 percent in 2004. A census report on the 2012 election shows the 18- to 24-year-old bloc fell to 41.2 percent.

Authors Dan Balz and Haynes Johnson report that younger voters are becoming much more involved at the polls and more politically and socially active beyond election day. After a steady turning away from public life, public service, and political and social activism, student interest is on the rise as young people move from the center of the ideological spectrum. The 2008 election was the largest turnout in twenty years for voters under 30. Self-described liberals were among the highest since 1975—38 percent—while only 23 percent considered themselves conservative. Nearly three-fourths believed the government should do more to control the sale of handguns and should give greater support for gay rights. More than 60 percent favored offering legal same-sex marital status. More than two-to-one favored abolishing the death penalty and legalizing marijuana. Eighty-eight percent thought the government should do more for the environment.

Seniors At the other end of the age spectrum, senior citizens vote in reliably high numbers. In 2012, voter turnout among those 65 and over was nearly 72 percent. Older citizens have much experience and understanding of the political process, they've developed regular voting habits, and they likely have more at stake—the government handles Social Security, Medicare, tax and inheritance law, veterans benefits, and a host of other issues that are important to seniors.

African Americans The disenfranchising and intimidation of would-be black voters in the South for generations created a consistently low voter turnout among African Americans, making the South a region with a historically low voter turnout overall. The 1965 **Voting Rights Act** gave birth to a new generation of black voters. Turnout among African Americans in presidential elections has risen gradually from 53 percent in 1996 to more than 66 percent in 2012.

Because the Republican Party of the Civil War and Reconstruction eras freed the slaves and enfranchised African Americans, first-generation black voters largely sided with the Republican Party. By 1932, however, these voters began a relationship with Franklin Roosevelt and the Democratic Party on a national level, which only became stronger under Democratic presidents Truman, Kennedy, and Johnson, all of whom supported civil rights.

Blacks tend to have a less favorable view of the criminal justice system than whites. A recent University of Cincinnati poll shows that African Americans favor abolishing the death penalty by 51 percent, compared with 23 percent of white respondents. They also want less attention and money focused on international affairs and foreign policy and more on Americans in need. Black voters generally support welfare programs, and in a 2004 study, blacks were roughly twice as likely to favor increased federal aid to the poor. These views have aligned African American voters with the Democratic Party, and Democrats have supported causes for urban populations, the working class, and civil rights.

According to Gallup, black voters supported 1988 Democratic presidential candidate Michael Dukakis with 88 percent and 2004 Democrat John Kerry with 93 percent. The PEW Research Center estimated that 95 percent of the black populace voted for Democrat Barack Obama, and some exit polls suggest 99 percent. When the 113th Congress opened in 2013, there were 44 African American members, all but one a Democrat. An additional 1.7 million black voters voted in 2012. African Americans turned out in greater number than whites; 66.2 percent of blacks voted, while 64.1 percent of whites did so.

Hispanics Hispanics are the fastest growing minority in the United States, now well over 43 million. Hispanics live in large numbers in the southwestern and western states, the Sunbelt states, New York, and Florida. Hispanic turnout rose from 2.5 million nationally in 1980 to more than 11 million in 2012. Hispanics turn out in lower percentages than whites and blacks. Hispanic participation was 44 percent in 1996 and peaked at 50 percent in 2008. About

1.4 million more Hispanics voted in 2012 than had in 2008, but the turnout rate dropped to 48 percent. Nine Latinos served in Congress in 1980; 37 did so as the 113th Congress opened in 2013. Twenty-seven of those are Democrats; 10 are Republicans.

The Latino voting population contributed to Democratic successes of 2006 and 2008 when fully 67 percent voted for Obama. They have sided with Democrats on urban, minority, and labor issues. Also, conflict over immigration laws has created a wedge between Hispanic voters and conservative lawmakers. Heightened rhetoric and a Republican desire for strict requirements for citizenship have driven Hispanics closer to Democrats.

Asian Americans Asian Americans come mostly from Japan, China, Korea, and Vietnam. They make up only about 3 percent of the U.S. voting population, though that figure is higher in the West Coast states. They have concerns like other minorities for civil liberties and equal protection, but for years Asian Americans have voted conservatively. This pattern may be because the Republican Party has pushed for fewer regulations on business, and because conservative values often align with ethical beliefs in Asian cultures. Yet in 2012, exit polls reveal that roughly 73 percent of Asians voted for Obama.

Voter Turnout Among Blocs	
Voting Bloc	**Turnout**
Males	61.5
Females	65.7
Whites	66.1
Black	64.7
Hispanic	49.9
Asian	47.6
18 to 24	48.5
65 to 74	72.4
No High School Diploma	39.4

Source: U.S. Census, 2010

Evangelicals Fundamentalist and Evangelical Christians tend to hold conservative beliefs. They have become ardent supporters of the Republican Party and have joined Republicans to create the "religious right." Televangelists and leaders of conservative family-oriented groups have large followings and thus some political influence. Fundamentalists, who take the Holy Bible literally, generally do not believe in human evolution and would rather their sons or daughters not be taught this science in public schools. They are a strong political force in the South and Midwest.

Catholics The Catholic faith is defined largely by papal decrees (the Pope's orders) from Rome, which have established some strict rules and beliefs. Anti-immigrant and anti-Catholic sentiment in the Antebellum period gave birth to secret societies, such as the "Know Nothing" or American Party, focused on alienating Catholics and the foreign born. By 1856, Democrats began a strong relationship with Catholics when they criticized Know Nothings' call for religious tests and instead called for a "spirit of tolerance" in their platform.

The relationship with the Democrats continued into the twentieth century, as Catholics played a large role in the machine politics of the urban North. Democrats have nominated Catholics for president three times: Al Smith in 1928, John Kennedy in 1960, and John Kerry in 2004. Only Kennedy won.

Today, the Catholic vote is no longer a monolith; it straddles the ideological spectrum. Catholics, roughly 25 percent of the country, overlap so many other demographics—rich and poor, young and old, white and Latino—that they defy categorization. Catholic doctrine from the Vatican doesn't fall on just one side of the American ideological spectrum. The Papacy generally denounces birth control and abortion, for example, thereby aligning with Republican ideals; yet the church opposes the death penalty, a position taken by more Democrats than Republicans.

Many Catholics no longer practice or strictly follow the moral teachings of the Church. "Cafeteria Catholics," those who pick and choose elements of the religion, reject the church's teaching on abortion, promiscuity, birth control, homosexuality, euthanasia, or cloning. As Catholic voting expert George Marlin explains, by 2004, approximately 70 percent of the congressional Catholic membership had cast pro-choice votes. A recent finding of the National Election Study shows that 36 percent of Catholics identify themselves as conservative, while 35 percent say they are moderate, and 29 percent claim to be liberal. In 2004, Republican incumbent George W. Bush defeated Democratic challenger John Kerry 51 to 48 percent among all voters, yet Kerry won 52 percent of the Catholic vote, while Bush received about 47 percent of Catholics. In 2008, Democrat Barack Obama beat Republican John McCain 54 to 45 among Catholics, but 53 to 46 overall.

Jews Jews vote in large numbers and vote mainly with the Democrats. Jewish voters comprise a small fraction of the electorate, about 2 percent, but their participation in elections averages about 10 percent higher than the general population. Some estimates show that roughly 90 percent of Jews vote.

Jewish-American political history parallels American Catholic history—with ethnic, often immigrant, minorities occupying larger, northern urban centers. Subject to discrimination, Jews have developed strong concerns about the power of the state and infringements on civil liberties. Jewish voters place a high priority on privacy, on ensuring basic rights for the accused, and supporting charities. These factors have caused the Jewish vote to swing in a liberal direction.

The first measurable Jewish vote went to Woodrow Wilson with 55 percent in 1916. The 1920s Red Scare sent many Socialist Jews, fearing the "Communist" label, toward the Democratic Party. When the United States entered World War II and later defeated the Jews' worst enemy—Adolf Hitler and Nazi Germany—FDR gained full backing from American Jewish voters. When his successor Harry Truman embraced the idea of creating a Jewish state in the Middle East in what became Israel, it sealed a generation of Jewish support for Democrats. From 1952 to 1968, Jewish support for Democratic presidential candidates ran 20 to 30 percent higher than that of the general population. According to exit polls, nearly 70 percent of Jews voted for Obama over Republican challenger Mitt Romney in 2012.

Business Community Entrepreneurs, leaders in the business community, CEOs of companies, shareholders, and much of the upper class tend to embrace a conservative political philosophy. These voters are driven by economic concerns. They are not all wealthy. The small business owner is also in this bloc. These people believe in capitalist principles. They want less, not more, interference by the state in the business world. They want less regulation that is pushed for by environmentalists and consumer rights groups. They want lower taxes and an ability to make more profits. This voting profile usually results in their voting Republican.

Labor and Unions The wage earner, the craftsman, and the factory line worker tend to view politics through the lens of the workplace and often in line with their labor union. Since their rise in the late 1800s and early 1900s, labor unions such as the American Federation of Labor have supported government-mandated fair wage laws, child labor laws, safety regulations in the workplace, and fairness on the job. Aligned with Socialists in their earlier years, the labor unions struck a tight relationship with FDR's party during the implementation of New Deal policies. Unions have lost much of their influence today, and membership is down from the prior generation. About 7 percent of Americans belong to a labor union. Laborers and most unions are loyal to the Democratic Party.

Voting Reform and Current Trends

The federal government generally stayed out of the administration of elections until constitutional amendments and congressional acts changed its role. In the early 1970s, the creation of the Federal Elections Commission to regulate campaign funding brought the federal government further into the business of regulating elections. More recently, the **motor-voter law** of the late 1990s and the **Help America Vote Act** passed in 2002 both involve the federal government in elections.

Congress and National Voting Regulations

Congress passed the **National Voter Registration Act** (**NVRA**) of 1993 to increase citizen participation and to alleviate the burden of registration. The NVRA resulted from efforts that began in the early 1980s when voter mobilization groups and activists came up with four goals: national standards and enforcement of voter registration, election-day registration, mail registration, and government agency-based registration. The final goal allows citizens to register at state-run agencies, such as the bureaus of motor vehicles (hence the "motor-voter law" nickname). After much modification from the original plan—the final law did not require states to allow election-day registration—supporters secured passage with President Clinton's signature in 1993.

The bill met strong Republican opposition. President George H.W. Bush had vetoed it in 1992. When it passed in 1993, it did so with an obvious partisan vote. Fully 90 percent of congressional Republicans opposed the law, while 95 percent of Democrats supported it. Only 11 House Republicans voted for its passage, and only after adding a provision that required states to periodically purge their voter rolls. The conservative *Washington Times* called it the "date that shattered the nation's civic sense."

The partisan divide on this law exists for different reasons. The two major parties have clear differences on who should bear the burden of voter registration. Republicans tend to deny that registration is a challenge, while Democrats want the government to make voting more accessible. The cost to oversee the effects of motor-voter brought more opposition from Republicans, as did their view of the law's infringement on states' reserved powers. The parties' chief source of disagreement on this issue, however, may relate to perceptions about practical political consequences. Many believe that a higher turnout inevitably helps the Democratic Party. The reality is that, over time, increasing turnout shows no significant long-term effect to either party.

The NVRA increases the number of eligible citizens who register to vote in elections for federal office, expands the number of locations one can register, and protects the integrity of elections by ensuring accurate voter rolls are maintained. It requires states to make available a voter registration application at driver's license bureaus, public libraries, city and county clerk's offices, public schools, and fishing and hunting bureaus. It also requires states to accept registration by mail. States can remove voters for reasons of mental incapacity, criminal conviction, death, and relocation. Ultimately, the NVRA ensured that one's right to vote trumps bureaucratic or legal technicalities in becoming an eligible voter.

Election-day registration causes an increase in voter turnout, though the increase varies and at times is negligible. In 1996, using same-day registration for the first time, New Hampshire experienced a nearly 10 percent increase in turnout. But when Idaho offered it, turnout went up only 0.2 percent. The NVRA resulted in nationwide registration climbing to 76 percent in 1996,

5.65 points over 1992 and 8.61 over 1994. In reality, the law has not increased registration of either party, but it has increased the number of independent registrants. It has not increased voter turnout substantially.

A 2010 U.S. census report shows that 21 percent of voters registered at a county registration office; another 21 percent did so at a motor vehicle agency. More than 13 percent mailed in their registration, and 6 percent reported registering at the polls on election day (a few states do that), at a school, hospital, campus, or registration booth.

2000 Election and the Help America Vote Act

Activists, election officials, and voting watchdogs monitor registration policies, voter turnout, and election-day irregularities to enhance participation. The 2000 presidential election, one of the closest and most controversial elections ever, brought great attention to voting processes and heightened concern for election reform. Texas Governor George W. Bush and Vice President Al Gore had campaigned in a tight race, and the results were tied up with a series of events in Florida's election that greatly impacted states' voting procedures.

Florida's vote was extremely close. A confusing punch-card ballot, which allowed for fragments of paper called *chads* to remain attached to the ballot even after a hole was punched, made vote counting complicated. That problem as well as an unlikely turnout in four Democratic counties encouraged Al Gore to call for a recount. This request for a recount brought 36 days of suspense and a total of 47 lawsuits or hearings. The U.S. Supreme Court ultimately ruled that no recount should take place. Bush received 537 more popular votes than Gore in Florida, and therefore won 271 electoral votes to win the presidency (270 is the smallest majority), though Gore won about a half-million more popular votes nationwide.

Similar problems had occurred in previous elections, but never with this attention. States and Congress responded by trying to prevent another Florida 2000. More and more states have quit using the type of ballot used in Florida. Since the "hanging chad" debacle, 75 percent of the nation has changed the way it votes. Elections are more accurate. There is less chance that voters will make mistakes, and more safeguards are in place if they do. Access has been expanded, and millions now vote by mail.

Many changes came as a result of the **Help America Vote Act (HAVA)**, which Congress passed in 2002 in response to the Bush-Gore election. The law imposes a number of requirements on states, mostly to create national standards for voting and election management. All states had to upgrade their voting systems to an electronic format. The law requires states to replace punch card and lever systems, and Congress set aside federal money for that purpose.

HAVA also addresses voting for the disabled. States and counties must make the polling places accessible for blind and the physically handicapped voters to "ensure full participation in the electoral process." Largely due to the confusion among Florida's voters in 2000, the law requires states to use a system that allows the voter to glance at his or her choices before confirming the vote, whether in bubbling in a ballot to be scanned or looking at a screen after making choices, to give voters an opportunity to change their vote if they made a mistake. To prevent voter fraud, registering voters must provide a driver's license or the last four digits of a Social Security number that must be verified at the polling place on election day. The law also makes sure that military personnel serving overseas are provided with absentee ballots, registration forms, and election information.

With the Internet so essential in daily lives, many believe it is only a matter of time until voting can be done remotely online. There are some good arguments both for and against the Internet as an avenue for voting. Using the Internet would make it much easier for voters to cast their ballots. It could lower the cost of holding elections. No longer would bad weather, long lines, or confusion over the assigned polling place be valid excuses for nonvoting. Younger generations are more computer savvy, and thus implementing Internet voting might cause an increased participation among a low-turnout bloc. College students could bypass requests for an absentee ballot and just vote from their dorm rooms.

Opponents have equally compelling arguments why Internet voting should be avoided. The first concern among opponents is security. A second is that Internet voting would favor certain socioeconomic classes of people. Researchers R. Michael Alvarez and Thad Hall report that individuals who connect to the Internet tend to be white, wealthy, well-educated, and male. Such a "digital divide" could pit those voters with excellent ballot access against those without it. There is also a developing divide in quality of Internet access. The urban, wealthy, and typically white areas of the United States have higher-speed Internet access. The final criticism of Internet voting is that voting from a distance may further alienate Americans from public participation, from that annual ritual of going to the polls in the name of civic duty.

Some states have experimented with Internet voting. Arizona pioneered it in the 2000 Democratic presidential primary. With only three months of preparation, the state sent out an assigned PIN to all registered Democrats for voter identification. E-voting was set for a four-day period. Voters used their PIN and clicked boxes for presidential and congressional candidates. The PIN was then "punched" so it couldn't be used again. The process took the voter about two minutes. Turnout was spectacular. Nearly twice as many voters used the Internet as those who traveled to the polling places or who mailed in ballots. Overall turnout was double of any Democratic primary since 1984.

More states are experimenting with Internet voting after Congress passed the Military and Overseas Voter Empowerment Act. This law mandates that states send out absentee ballots to members of the military and those living abroad at least 45 days before the election. It also requires states to make electronic delivery of these ballots an option. These recent experiments forecast Internet voting as a reality, yet several of these jurisdictions experienced problems. Independent groups with an eye on elections feel the threats to election security outweigh the convenience of the process.

Convenience Voting

Beyond the Internet, states have implemented a variety of measures to make voting more convenient. These include voting by mail, early voting, election-day registration, and no-excuse absentee voting.

Today, a handful of states offer election-day registration at the same polling places where voting takes place. A greater number of states, 31, are offering early voting. Citizens can report to their county boards of elections early and fill out a ballot. This option allows voters to avoid long lines, and it can ensure they won't miss the election. Twenty-nine states have begun no-excuse absentee voting. For years, states have allowed residents to vote early via absentee ballot if the voter was out of town on business, vacation, or residing in another state. College students are able to vote by absentee while away at school. States have found that allowing voters to vote via absentee alleviates long lines, cuts costs, and allows for a quicker count.

Has all the convenience increased turnout? According to voting expert Curtis Gans, mail voting, no-excuse absentee voting, early voting, and even election-day registration does not help turnout. Half of the states that offered election-day registration experienced a decrease in turnout. Maine was down 3.5 percent. The overall lowest turnout states in 2008 had variations of convenience voting. Oregon, with entirely mail-in voting, had lost 2.8 percent in its turnout.

Voter Apathy

Compared to the turnout in other nations and in the United States in past years, politically active people might be ashamed of America's level of participation. The sacrifices of women a century ago and of civil rights leaders in the last generation may seem in vain when we consider the low voter turnout during the 1970s, 1980s, and 1990s. Nonvoting, however, can also be the result of satisfaction with government. Many people

Source: Thinkstock

Many young people became active in public life through the Occupy Movement, which protests income inequality and the influence of corporations on government. Its slogan, "We are the 99%," refers to the concentration of wealth in the top-earning 1% of the population. This picture shows an Occupy Los Angeles march in September, 2011, the year the movement was launched.

are generally satisfied and don't feel the need to participate. Others do so only on select occasions because the United States has so many opportunities to express political opinion. The high number of elections leads to a lower turnout because not all citizens vote in every election. Some of the nonvoters get involved in other ways, by volunteering in their communities, for example.

If we had an election and everyone showed up, would it change the outcome of elections? Probably not. The result would likely parallel the results already seen. Many believe that Democrats suffer from the underrepresented vote (blacks, poor, and uneducated, for example) and would thus benefit from a sudden increase in voting. However, studies show that those who don't vote differ in ideology just like those who do vote. The pendulum between Democratic and Republican victories over the years has swung left and right as independents have changed their minds. Three high turnouts in presidential elections in the last 75 years occurred in 1952, 1968, and 2004, when the GOP won. Two of the lowest turnouts were in 1948 and 1996, yet the Democratic candidate won.

REFLECT ON THE ESSENTIAL QUESTION

Essential Question: *How do Americans participate in the political world?* On separate paper, complete a chart like the one below to gather details to answer that question.

Ways People Participate in Politics	Examples

When you **formulate an argument**, you go through several processes of refinement. For example, you might have a general feeling that your city council should not vote to close the local branch of your library, as it is considering. From that general feeling, the first step in formulating an argument is to develop a **claim,** a statement you assert to be true: The library is too important a public facility to be closed. Then you look for **appropriate evidence** to support your claim, to prove that it is true. You might begin researching the benefits of libraries on the performance of children in school or the relationship between branch libraries and the level of teenage crime. You may also find that the city council is experiencing a budget shortfall and cannot both keep the local branch of the library open and support the public health clinic. Your research leads you to examine your original claim and refine it based on your new information. Maybe your refined claim is "City council should actively seek alternate funding for the clinic and continue to keep the branch library open." Now the evidence you provide to support your claim can be very focused and should show that other funding is available for the health clinic and that the benefits of the branch library are worth city funding.

Practice: Write a public official expressing your reasoned position on an issue of concern. Formulate and refine an argument for or against a law or policy or governmental action or inaction and support it with appropriate evidence. Follow the process below.

- Find a public issue that concerns you. It could be the nation's most recent involvement in the Middle East or the potholes in your local streets.

- Become well acquainted with the issue through research in a variety of print and online sources. If appropriate, talk to local experts or perhaps contact local offices.

- Find a poll or some measure of public opinion on the issue. What do other citizens, constituents, and your neighbors think? How are they affected? How do their views and the impact of the issue on your neighbors affect your argument?

- What specific position do you take? Develop a well-reasoned claim, refined through research, and support it with relevant and sufficient evidence appropriate to the topic.

- Select the appropriate public official and present your argument in a formal letter.

absentee ballot

Andrew Jackson

Australian ballot

Civil Rights Act (1957, 1964)

electorate

Fifteenth Amendment

franchise

gender gap

grandfather clause

Help America Vote Act (2002)

initiative

literacy test

Minor v. Happerset (1875)

National Voter Registration Act (motor-voter law) (1993)

Nineteenth Amendment

party identification

political efficacy

poll tax

polling place

precinct

preclearance

recall

referendum

suffrage

Twenty-fourth Amendment

Twenty-sixth Amendment

Twenty-third Amendment

voter apathy

voter registration

voter turnout

voting-age population

voting blocs

Voting Rights Act (1965)

ward

white primary

MULTIPLE-CHOICE QUESTIONS

1. Which of the following statements about voter registration is true?
    (A) Most states require voters to register 60 days in advance of the election.
    (B) Voter registration comes with fees and thus prevents eager voters from the process.
    (C) The number of American registered voters nearly doubled after implementation of the motor-voter law.
    (D) Voter registration began as a system a century ago to prevent voter fraud.
    (E) Most states allow voters to vote without being registered.

2. In the District of Columbia, people voted in the presidential election for the first time in which year?
    (A) 1800
    (B) 1860
    (C) 1960
    (D) 1964
    (E) 1972

3. When people under 21 were granted the constitutional right to vote in 1972, they
   (A) turned out to vote in higher numbers than the rest of the electorate
   (B) turned out to vote in similar numbers as other age groups
   (C) turned out to vote in lower numbers than the rest of the electorate
   (D) voted overwhelmingly for challenger George McGovern, enabling him to defeat President Nixon
   (E) boycotted the election entirely

4. The National Voter Registration Act, commonly called the "motor-voter" law,
   (A) was passed by Congress in 1980
   (B) was generally supported by Republicans
   (C) increased voter registration considerably but increased actual turnout only slightly
   (D) was signed into law by Republican President George H.W. Bush
   (E) requires states to offer Internet voting

5. Which of the following statements about Catholic voters is true?
   (A) Catholic voters today vote overwhelmingly for the Democratic Party.
   (B) Catholic voters have voted with the Democratic Party over much of their history.
   (C) The Catholic vote is stronger in the rural and southern parts of America.
   (D) Several Catholics have served as president.
   (E) Catholic members of Congress always vote in a pro-life manner on abortion issues.

6. Which of the following statements accurately reflects the 2000 presidential election?
   (A) The same candidate who won the national popular vote also won the overall electoral vote.
   (B) The election was close and prolonged in California.
   (C) Al Gore won the presidency after a hand recount.
   (D) The 2000 presidential election was followed by further disregard to election management and ballot accuracy.
   (E) The 2000 election was an error-prone election that brought national election reform.

7. African American voters have voted with the Democratic Party in the modern era for all of the following reasons EXCEPT

(A) Democratic leaders and Democratic presidents have supported civil rights legislation

(B) Democratic officials have acted to assist urban population

(C) the 1948 Democratic platform included a call for equal treatment

(D) a greater number of African-American officials are members of the Democratic Party

(E) southern states' use of the white primary

Top Reasons for Not Voting	
Too Busy	17.5%
Illness/Disability	14.9%
Not Interested	13.4%
Didn't Like Candidates/Issues	12.9%
Out of Town	8.8%
Registration Problems	6.0%

Source: U.S. Census, 2010

8. Which statement below is supported by data in the table above?

(A) Voter registration problems are the most common reason for nonvoting.

(B) More citizens are engaging with the media instead of voting.

(C) If more states offered absentee balloting, voter apathy would decrease.

(D) More than one-fourth of nonvoters either lacked interest or didn't like the candidates.

(E) Voter mobility is the number one cause for low turnout.

9. Which statement about voter turnout is accurate?

(A) Voter turnout in presidential elections has generally hovered over 50 percent from the 1970s through the 1990s.

(B) Voter turnout has never crossed 60 percent.

(C) Voter turnout was higher before 2000 than after 2000.

(D) Men turn out to vote in higher numbers than women.

(E) Turnout in the United States exceeds that of all European countries.

10. A small geographic area from which voters are assigned a voting location is a

(A) precinct

(B) polling place

(C) ballot access

(D) gerrymander

(E) district

FREE-RESPONSE QUESTIONS

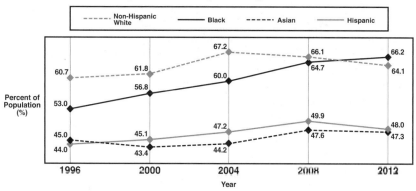

VOTING RATES IN PRESIDENTIAL ELECTIONS
by Race and Hispanic Origin: 1996–2012

Source: U.S. Census Bureau

Question

1. Political scientists study voter turnout and the voting patterns of different ethnic and minority groups.

   (a) Identify two trends in the graph.

   (b) For each trend you identified in (a), identify and explain two factors that may cause this trend.

   (c) Identify and describe two reasons eligible voters do not vote.

Question

2. The American electorate has greatly expanded since the founding of the United States.

Select two categories below. For each category, describe two changes that increased the size of the electorate and explain how those changes impacted the American electoral process.

- Constitutional amendments
- Congressional acts
- Supreme Court decisions

WRITING: BE OBJECTIVE

When answering your free-response questions, remember to establish and maintain a formal style. Also avoid stating your opinions or revealing your ideology as a liberal or conservative. Instead, provide ample and relevant facts, examples, and reasons to support your statements.

UNIT 2: Review

Those in government need to understand public opinion to create democratic laws. Opinion polls are useful to the news media, politicians, and academics. Polling has its limits as well as its benefits. A poll is only valid if it has properly worded questions and a representative sample (recall the 1936 *Literary Digest* debacle). In measuring public opinion, pollsters find that Americans fall into many political categories. People following liberal or conservative ideology tend to align with the Democrats or Republicans, respectively. The largest segment of the United States, however, is moderate and made up of independent voters and nonvoters. Countless other ideologies also exist. These are formed by many factors in the political socialization process, such as the influence of family, schooling, religion, and geographic region.

Political participation reached new heights during the Jacksonian era, when most men became eligible to vote and scores of citizens began to take part in campaigns and elections. The large remainder of the populace was added to the electorate over the following century. African Americans, women, and then 18-year-olds were granted full suffrage via constitutional amendments. Voting blocs or identified groups tend to vote in certain patterns or favor one party. Is America's participation at its full potential? Democracy advocates continue to work to increase ballot access and to make every citizen's vote count.

THINK AS A POLITICAL SCIENTIST: CONSTRUCT A GRAPH OF A PRESIDENT'S APPROVAL RATING

Using one of the Web sources below, select a recent president and examine that president's approval rating while in office. What major shifts in public opinion occurred? What were the highs and lows? When did these occur? Plot three distinct approval ratings on your own line chart, with dates on the *x-axis* and approval percentages on the *y-axis*. You can create your graph either on paper with a ruler or on a computer using a graphing program.

Then, using online newspapers, databases, timelines, or other sources, determine what brought the high or low approval ratings. Explain your findings in a brief paper or place quotes from reliable sources next to the high or low points on your chart. Or you could arrange the chart, with minimal text, atop an accompanying paragraph that explains the shifts of opinion in context.

The Roper Center: http://www.ropercenter.uconn.edu/. Go to "Presidential Approval."

The American Presidency Project: http://www.presidency.ucsb.edu/. Under "Data" you will find "Presidential Job Approval."

UNIT 3: Political Parties, Interest Groups, and Mass Media

Chapter 5 Political Parties

Chapter 6 Campaigns and Elections

Chapter 7 Interest Groups

Chapter 8 The Media

On the edge of U.S. government, organized groups interact with government to shape policy. These so-called linkage institutions—political parties, interest groups, and the media—link the people with the government. Many favor particular candidates and push members of government to take certain actions. They tell the citizenry what the government is doing or not doing. Two political parties, Democrats and Republicans, have dominated politics, though minor parties come and go. They battle back and forth for control of the government. On a national, state, and local level, parties recruit candidates, campaign, and play watchdog when the other party is in power.

Elections are held for offices from president to sheriff. Presidential candidates spend massive amounts of money as they travel a hard road to the White House through a series of primary elections, a national convention, and televised debates. Congressional and state candidates also compete in distinct yet smaller campaigns en route to office.

Interest groups adopt formal goals and raise money for their causes. Some are larger and more powerful than others and thus have more influence. They engage in several activities in Washington, D.C., and throughout America in the hopes of influencing the law.

The media are also a major force in U.S. politics. The press shapes public opinion, voter perceptions, campaign strategies, and the agenda. For this reason, candidates and members of government have a symbiotic and conflict-prone relationship with the media.

Key Concepts

Political Parties, Interest Groups, and Mass Media

- Political parties and elections
- Interest groups, including political action committees (PACs)
- The mass media

Source: *AP® United States Government and Politics Course and Exam Description*

Political Parties

"The common and continual mischiefs of the spirit of party are sufficient to make it the interest and duty of a wise people to discourage and restrain it."
—George Washington in his farewell address, 1797

Essential Question: How have individuals coalesced into organized political groups, and how do these groups influence policy?

Political parties are organized groups of people who have similar political ideologies and goals and who work to have candidates elected to public office to represent those ideologies and goals. Political parties nominate candidates for office, create platforms that define their ideas and goals, register like-minded people to vote, and govern in hopes of implementing their desired public policy. The parties make up one of the institutions that link the citizenry to the government. Two major parties, Democrats and Republicans, have dominated U.S. politics for more than 150 years. Both of these coalitions operate in every state.

Political parties began to develop in the aftermath of American independence. Like George Washington in his farewell address, most people agreed that parties were mischievous. The founders viewed political parties as factions driven by self-interest instead of by the desire to enhance the well-being of the nation. Yet it seems that when like-minded people desire certain policy changes in a democratic society, organized parties are the inevitable result. In this chapter, you will read about the history and development of the **two-party system**, how Republicans and Democrats operate today, and the role of **minor parties** in American politics.

History of the Two-Party System

A national two-party political system began with the creation of the nation during the Constitutional Convention. Leading Americans fell into two camps regarding the proposed Constitution: those who favored ratification and those who opposed it. Those supporting the Constitution and backing a stronger national government took the name Federalists, while those opposed became Anti-Federalists. After the states ratified the document, these factions remained.

Federalists kept their name, while those favoring less government and stronger states' rights took the name Republicans, or **Democrat-Republicans**.

Since the beginning of the party system, two parties have dominated. At certain points, new parties have emerged and old ones have faded into the background. Additionally, large groups of voters have switched allegiance from one party to another over divisive issues or in times of crisis. These political **realignments** are changes "in underlying electoral forces due to changes in party identification," according to the *Oxford Concise Dictionary of Politics*. They are marked by **critical elections**, those that reveal sharp, lasting changes in loyalties to political parties. A political realignment has occurred five times in U.S. history, each realignment marking the emergence of a different party system. There are at least two types of realignments: (1) a party is so badly defeated it fades into obscurity as a new party emerges, or (2) large blocs of voters shift allegiance from one party to another.

Politics and Party in Early America

Parties began as loose **caucuses** of notable politicians connected by region. Federalist presidents George Washington and later John Adams became standard bearers of this national party. Secretary of the Treasury Alexander Hamilton also contributed to the party's growth and philosophy. These Federalists generally believed in a loose interpretation of the Constitution, and they encouraged the federal government to act strongly in the national interest. They favored investing in roads, canals, and a national bank.

By 1800, growing numbers of people opposed the Federalists. In Washington's cabinet, Thomas Jefferson stood philosophically against some of the administration's decisions. He began to rival Hamilton and later John Adams. Jefferson believed in limited government, protection of civil liberties, and an emphasis on states' rights. Though he is now regarded as the Father of the Constitution, James Madison joined Jefferson in the fight to maintain states' rights. These Jeffersonians called themselves **Republicans** because they believed they had to defend the republic created under the Constitution. They also stood for democratic principles and eventually became known as Democrat-Republicans.

In a close contest that marked the nation's first realignment, the presidential election of 1800 placed Jefferson into the presidency. The Federalists never again elected another president. Instead, Jefferson, Madison, and then James Monroe governed with Jeffersonian principles over the course of six presidential terms, firmly planting the Jeffersonian philosophy into the national mindset. The Federalist presence in Congress disappeared.

Jacksonian Democracy

After 24 years of Virginians dominating the presidency, the 1824 election served as another landmark. Many voters in the West (Kentucky, Tennessee, and Indiana at the time) and South wanted war hero and former congressman

Andrew Jackson to become president. Multiple candidates entered this race, including John Quincy Adams and Henry Clay. With few defining issues, the campaign soon became a battle of personalities. Jackson was the most popular candidate with the common voter but did not earn the required number of electoral votes, an outcome that forced the House of Representatives to elect the president. After a political deal that became known as the corrupt bargain, the House elected Adams. The halls of government in Washington had just handed the presidency to a candidate who came in second place in the popular vote. The "corrupt bargain" served as a rallying point for Jackson's supporters to develop the Democratic Party.

Jackson's Coalition Jackson's Democratic Party was built from the bottom up rather than the top down. The party believed in limited government, opposed the national bank, and generally accepted states' rule on many issues, including slavery. The Democratic Party also wanted fewer government-mandated laws and restrictions and greater freedom for the people. A strong **coalition**—a group united for a greater cause—united squarely behind Jackson and opposed Adams.

By 1828, suffrage had expanded to give non-landowning males the right to vote. Only two states that year, Delaware and South Carolina, chose electors via their legislatures. All others had allowed a popular vote. Jackson ran again and won. The turnout was very high. Three times as many voters cast ballots in 1828 as had in 1824. A realignment had taken place, and Jackson's Democratic Party began to dominate. He advocated expanded suffrage and economic equality, and he opposed government intervention in state affairs. The party won the White House in most elections until 1860.

Whigs As the Jacksonian Democracy came to represent smaller western farmers and common voters, a loose collection of malcontents and fierce Jackson opponents denounced his arrogance in office. Jackson thwarted many of Congress's initiatives and refused to enforce decisions made by the Supreme Court. Routinely vetoing Congress, he was dubbed King Andrew I.

The Adams-Clay faction created a more formal party called the **Whigs**. They chose this name to show that their beliefs matched those of the English Whigs of the mother country. In the United States as in England, the Whigs opposed autocratic rule. Alleging that Jackson had overstepped presidential boundaries, the Whigs tried to elect a presidential candidate on a platform of national improvement.

American Whigs favored expansion, investment, and aggressive federal involvement in internal improvements. Led by Daniel Webster and Henry Clay, the Whigs rose to prominence only to be outdone by the stronger Democratic Party. The Whigs did send two candidates to the White House—William Henry Harrison and Zachary Taylor, both war heroes who likely carried the election more on personal following than on adherence to party ideology. From 1832, when the Democrats held their first national **party convention**, until 1860, the Democratic Party won the presidency in every election except two.

Republican Ascendancy

The 1850s marked a controversial time of intense division on the issue of slavery. Some northern Democrats felt the southern-western coalition did not represent them. These disgruntled Democrats became part of an alliance formed of abolitionists and old Whigs. This group came together at a gathering in Ripon, Wisconsin, in 1854 and at a later convention in Michigan. They gathered in part to oppose the Kansas-Nebraska Act, which overrode the Missouri Compromise law that prevented slavery in northern states and territories. The Kansas-Nebraska Act allowed new states to choose slave or free status by exercising **popular sovereignty**—leaving the ultimate authority with the people—through a popular vote. This alliance held its first national convention in Philadelphia in 1856, nominating John C. Fremont, who ran under the Free Soil banner—a political initiative focused on the single issue of opposition to slavery. Fremont lost to Democrat James Buchanan. At its next convention in Chicago in 1860, the party assumed the "Republican" label and nominated Abraham Lincoln. Also in 1860, the Democratic Party split into north-south factions and hosted two different conventions, nominating a candidate from each region. This split diluted the Democratic vote and allowed Lincoln to win the presidency with nearly every northern state.

The 1860 election marked the third national realignment. Though the Republican Party was technically a third party at the time—the last third party to win the White House—it quickly began to dominate national politics. Today the Republicans are often referred to as the **Grand Old Party**, or **GOP**.

Southern states feared northern sanctions on slavery and rejected Lincoln's victory—which came without one southern vote. Southern representatives and senators withdrew from Congress and their states seceded to form the Confederacy, leaving their seats empty during the ensuing Civil War. President Lincoln became a strong commander-in-chief, and the Republicans also held the majority in Congress.

Republicans managed the war and the Reconstruction period that followed. The so-called Radical Republicans were harsh on the South and thus cemented the North–South political division, pitting northern Republicans against southern Democrats for a century. The "Solid South" became the stronghold for Democratic politics for the next century.

From postwar Reconstruction until the 1920s, the Republicans largely controlled national politics while Democrats dominated the South. From Lincoln's 1860 victory until Democrat Woodrow Wilson's victory in 1912, the only Democrat to hold the presidency was Grover Cleveland. Republicans also held most seats in Congress during these years. Republicans joined with big business while the Democrats courted the working class and labor. Democrats still wanted less governmental control in the economic sector and felt government should play as small a role as possible. Republicans were a party of economic nationalism, guiding the economy, expanding railroads, and advocating custom duties to protect the American workforce.

1896 Realignment

America witnessed another realignment period during the era of big business and expansion. The critical 1896 election realigned voters along economic lines. The economic depressions of the 1880s and 1890s (or *panics*, as they were often called in those years) hit the South and the Midwest hard. Third parties such as the Greenbacks and Populists sought a fair deal for the working class. Voters in the South and West tended to be Christian fundamentalists, while the growing urban political base was Catholic. Disagreement over issues of immigration, prohibition of alcohol, and the public approach to parochial schools divided the two sides.

For the 1896 presidential election, congressman and orator William Jennings Bryan captured the Democratic nomination. The Populist Party also endorsed him. Anti-Bryan Democrats realigned themselves with the Republican Party, which nominated William McKinley. The Republicans were aligned with big business, industry, capitalists, and urban interests. Republicans also took in some Catholics, Lutherans, and immigrant groups who feared the anti-liquor stance of so many in the evolving Democratic Party. As Democratic legislatures began to regulate industry to protect laborers, conservative Republican judges declared such regulations unconstitutional. These differences began the division that continues today between Republican free-market capitalists and Democrats who favor regulation. Republicans continued to align themselves with Wall Street and favored a hands-off approach to business.

Source: Clifford Berryman, Library of Congress

The 1928 presidential election pitted Democrat Al Smith against Republican Herbert Hoover. When interpreting a political cartoon, first notice the symbols and read the labels. What symbols does the cartoonist provide to indicate the party that nominated each candidate? What are the tools of persuasion in campaigning?

The Depression and the Democrats

During the Great Depression, the Democrats rebuilt a strong national party and caught the attention of voters in need of a strong government in tough economic times. In 1932, the party's presidential candidate and new standard bearer, Franklin D. Roosevelt, offered the New Deal programs to assist the needy and to restore the nation economically. The party also began rebranding itself in an attempt to revive the economy, invest in people, preserve civil rights and civil liberties, and include greater numbers of participants in democracy. FDR's more liberal approach during the crisis—managing the economy, increased regulations, and an elevated welfare state—differed greatly from that of the party's father, Jackson.

New Deal Coalition Roosevelt's followers and rank-and-file party members included the working class, southerners, Catholics, urban dwellers, and others affected by the Depression. The Democrats joined with labor unions and sought their financial support during elections. African Americans had been loyal Republicans from emancipation to the Depression, but they left the party of Lincoln for the party of Roosevelt. The **New Deal coalition** elected FDR four times. His leadership during the economic crisis and through most of World War II allowed the Democrats to dominate Congress for another generation.

Source: Franklin D. Roosevelt Presidential Library and Museum

Franklin Roosevelt's public works programs employed the unemployed and boosted the nation's infrastructure. It's no wonder such a large coalition of voters supported FDR and his Democratic Party well after the New Deal. Roosevelt is pictured in the center of the photo with his wife Eleanor beside him.

Partial Realignment Along Issues and Region

The 1932 election is the most recent critical election in which a full national realignment took place. Since then, particular groups have shifted party loyalties and others have deserted the parties altogether. For example, southern whites departed the New Deal coalition as the Democrats elevated concerns for civil rights.

 Is That Constitutional? *Smith v. Allwright* (1944)

When the Texas Democratic Party prevented African Americans from participating in the party's primary election, did it violate the Fifteenth Amendment?

After 1890, in the state of Texas and elsewhere in the South, the Democratic Party denied African Americans participation in the primary elections. The resulting election was called the **white primary**. During the Democrats' hold on the Solid South at that time, most officeholders were determined in the primary election rather than in the general election in November. This loophole essentially removed blacks from participating in the part of the electoral process that invariably picked the candidate.

Political parties are private institutions that are not funded by the government and are not subject to the Constitution in defining their members. Proponents of the white primary argued that general voters were free to vote in November. Lonnie Smith, a black Texan, tried to vote in the 1940 primary and was denied the right by S. S. Allwright, a county elections official. With the assistance of the National Association for the Advancement of Colored People (NAACP), Smith's case went before the Supreme Court in 1944. Attorney Thurgood Marshall argued that the party was so intertwined with elections and government in this process that the Constitution did, in fact, apply.

Did the action violate the Constitution? Yes. The Court admitted the party was a voluntary association but argued that state statutes governed the selection of party leaders and that the party operated primary elections under state authority. A state cannot permit a private organization to practice racial discrimination in elections. In *Smith v. Allwright*, the Court outlawed the white primary and strengthened black suffrage.

Civil Rights A mix of Republicans and Democrats favored legal equality among the races. The northern liberal wing of the Democratic Party was the more aggressive in pushing for civil rights policy. President Harry Truman integrated the armed services in 1948, placing blacks and whites together in the military. At the Democratic convention that year, delegates from Mississippi and Alabama walked out in protest after northern Democrats spoke in favor of civil rights from the convention stage. These southern conservatives joined the States' Rights Party (the "Dixiecrats") and nominated segregationist South Carolina Governor Strom Thurmond for president. Thurmond carried five states in the Deep South.

In the 1960s, the liberal wing of the Democratic Party led in passing landmark civil rights legislation, which Democratic President Lyndon Johnson wholeheartedly supported. Southern conservatives, who had been Democrats for more than a century, began to oppose their leadership and flock toward the more conservative Republican Party.

This shift became apparent in the 1964 presidential election between President Johnson and Arizona Republican Barry Goldwater. Johnson quietly predicted the Democratic Party would lose the South for a generation when he signed the Civil Rights Act that summer. LBJ handily won the election, but he lost the heart of the South to Goldwater. Since then, the Democratic Party's affection for affirmative action, strong protection of civil liberties, and inclusion of diverse party membership have led to a great number of liberal members.

Conservatism Meanwhile, the Republicans' conservatives, led by senators Robert Taft, Richard Nixon, Barry Goldwater, and eventually President Ronald Reagan, believed in an agenda of less taxation, less federal power, and greater states' rights.

The Republican Party has come to embrace capitalism and free markets. Conservatives argued against minimum wage and some labor laws during the Depression. Republicans won support of small business owners and those who oppose government growth and encourage a mainly hands-off approach to governing.

The Republican Party has also come to stand for a tough stance on law and order. During the late 1960s and early 1970s, Supreme Court decisions extended some rights of accused criminals, upsetting law enforcement and many conservatives. The Republicans promised to get tough on law and order. Additionally, decisions involving such issues as racial integration of public schools and legalized abortion convinced many conservative voters to join the Republican Party.

Religious factions such as the Christian Coalition, made up of evangelical voters and dominant in the South, have further strengthened the GOP in that region. Social and moral concerns have also divided the U.S. electorate and affected party loyalties. After America had gone through the turbulence of antiwar protests, free love, and general experimentation in the 1960s and 1970s, public policy changed to address new, reactionary attitudes.

Values Voters Traditionalists generally opposed radical changes and have relied on influences from the church. A conservative–liberal gap widened during and after the 1960s. By 1973, the *Roe v. Wade* decision, which prevented states from outlawing abortion, divided the nation and added women voters to the Democratic Party. The "religious right" also came together over the issue. As President Reagan came to power, a conservative coalition of family-values voters came with him. Televangelists such as Jerry Falwell, Pat Robertson, and scores of their followers entered the political realm. The culture wars—conflicts between liberal and conservative ideologies—of the recent decades have widened the gap between the parties on the social issues.

Party Systems and Realignment Periods		
1789–1800	**Federalists** won ratification of the Constitution and the presidency for the first three terms.	**Anti-Federalists** opposed strong national government and favored states' rights and civil liberties.
1800–1824	**Federalists** maintained beliefs in a loose interpretation of the Constitution to strengthen the nation.	**Republicans** (Jeffersonians) put less emphasis on a strong Union and more on states' rights.
1824–1860	**Democrats** (Jacksonians) encouraged greater participation in politics and gained a Southern and Western following.	**Whigs** were a loose band of eastern capitalists, bankers, and merchants who wanted internal improvements and stronger national government.
1860–1896	**Democrats** became the second-place party, aligned with the South and the wage earner and sent only Grover Cleveland to the White House.	**Republicans** freed the slaves, reconstructed the Union, and aligned with industrial interests.
1896–1932	**Democrats** join with Populists to represent the Southern and Midwestern farmers, workers, and Protestant reformers.	**Republicans** continue to dominate after a realignment based on economic factors.
1932–Present	The Great Depression created the **New Deal coalition** around FDR's programs. **Democrats** have dominated politics.	**Republicans** have taken on a *laissez-faire* approach to economic regulation and a brand of conservatism that reflects limited government.

Divided Government and a Disillusioned Electorate

In the period following 1968, a party **dealignment** occurred. The unpopular Vietnam War and Nixon's Watergate scandal brought mistrust of the government and the parties that controlled it. Voter turnout dropped over the next three decades. Party loyalty decreased, apparently from an increased number of independent voters and **ticket splitting**, which is voting for candidates on both sides of the ballot.

Divided government, when one party controls Congress and the other occupies the White House, has been common at the federal level. One party has generally dominated the legislative branch, while the other has more frequently held the presidency. Democrats won a majority of House seats in every Congress from 1954 until 1994 and a majority in the Senate during most of those same years. Yet Republicans Dwight Eisenhower, Richard Nixon, Ronald Reagan, and George H. W. Bush held the presidency during many of those years. In Congress, Republicans experienced a resurgence of power with their 1994 landslide success, but Bill Clinton won the presidency in 1996. George W. Bush enjoyed six of his eight years with a Republican Congress. He then faced Democratic majorities in the House and Senate during his final two years.

Historian James McGregor Burns once explained how four groups actually make up the two parties. First, there's the "Democratic presidential party" still deeply rooted in FDR's New Deal and Johnson's Great Society. Second, the Democrats had maintained a Dixiecrat-influenced southern wing of the party in Congress that has largely disappeared. Republicans have divided into the eastern establishment of northern internationalists who question the New Deal but don't wholly oppose it, and what Burns terms "the suburban station-wagon set," dominated by working middle-class whites that were staunchly anticommunist a generation ago.

Some in the Republican Party have taken on a more isolationist, parochial, small-business-oriented, conservative tone than others. In many ways, Republicans are divided between the Wall Street Republicans who associate with corporate values and the Main Street Republicans who focus on small-town virtues. At the party's national conventions, northeastern candidates have faced off against other Republican leaders from the Midwest or South. In more recent years, the GOP has supported conservative issues such as agricultural subsidies, moral values, and the right to own firearms. Many congressional Republican leaders in the 1990s came from the South. The Solid South that Democrats relied on from Reconstruction through the New Deal no longer exists.

A realignment cannot be determined the day after an election. Nor does a switch in party power in and of itself signal a realignment. For example, when the Republican Party enjoyed two presidential victories and six years of party dominance in both the Congress and the presidency, the parties had not experienced realignment. The same basic voting blocs supported each party. As Democrats returned to power in 2008, winning both the Congress and the presidency, their victories came not because of a lasting shift of support by certain groups but rather because reliably Democratic voters turned out in higher numbers, and independents gravitated toward them.

BY THE NUMBERS President, Runner-up, and Majority Party in Congress				
Year	President	Runner-up	House	Senate
1968	Nixon (R)	Humphrey (D)	DEM	DEM
1970			DEM	DEM
1972	Nixon (R)	McGovern (D)	DEM	DEM
1974			DEM	DEM
1976	Carter (D)	Ford (R)	DEM	DEM
1978			DEM	DEM
1980	Reagan (R)	Carter (D)	DEM	REP
1982			DEM	REP
1984	Reagan (R)	Mondale (D)	DEM	REP
1986			DEM	DEM
1988	Bush, G. H. W. (R)	Dukakis (D)	DEM	DEM
1990			DEM	DEM
1992	Clinton (D)	Bush (R)	DEM	DEM
1994			REP	REP
1996	Clinton (D)	Dole (R)	REP	REP
1998			REP	REP
2000	Bush, G. W. (R)	Gore (D)	REP	REP
2002			REP	REP
2004	Bush, G. W. (R)	Kerry (D)	REP	REP
2006			DEM	DEM
2008	Obama (D)	McCain (R)	DEM	DEM
2010			REP	DEM
2012	Obama (D)	Romney (R)	REP	DEM
2014			REP	REP

What do the numbers show? Since 1968, in how many Congresses did Democrats hold the majority? How many did Republicans dominate? In what years do you see a president governing with a Congress dominated by the opposing party? In which years was the Congress split? In what elections do you see a change in party power? What caused these changes?

Contemporary Parties

Today's two major parties operate like large companies with national headquarters in Washington. Both the Republican and Democratic Parties have a strong organization made up of several organizational elements—the chair, other leaders, the national convention, party committees, and the platform.

National Party Structure

Both the **Democratic National Committee (DNC)** and the **Republican National Committee (RNC)** comprise a hierarchy of hundreds of employees and a complex network dedicated to furthering party goals. Each committee includes public leaders and other elite activists. The RNC and DNC meet formally every four years at their national conventions and on occasion between presidential elections to sharpen policy initiatives and to increase their influence.

National Chairs The **party chairperson** is the chief strategist and spokesperson. Though a leading official such as the president or an outspoken congressional leader tends to be the public face of the party, the chairperson runs the party machinery. He or she appears on political television shows and at major party events. The chair guides the party's daily operations, such as building up the membership, seeking funding, recruiting quality candidates for office, and conveying to voters the party philosophy. Both parties elect their chairs by a vote of the committee. Leading Republicans and Democrats campaign for the chair's spot. At a designated gathering in a large city, each party's committee hears speeches and then votes for the new chair. The position is nongovernmental, though some chairs have simultaneously served in the Senate or as state governors. Some famous party chairpersons include Republicans Bob Dole and George H. W. Bush and Democrats Ed Rendell and Howard Dean. Republicans recently chose Reince Priebus and the Democrats Debbie Wasserman Schultz as their respective chairs.

Both the RNC and the DNC have subcommittees that take care of recruitment, maintain communications and get-out-the-vote operations, and draft the party platform. Employees conduct surveys to ensure the party's philosophy aligns with that of its members and vice versa. Staffers meet with interest groups that have similar goals. They also regularly meet with their congressional leaders to further their policy agenda.

The Hill Committees Both parties have non-lawmaking committees in each house of Congress, which are organized to win seats in the House and Senate. These are sometimes referred to as the Hill Committees. Members are actual members of Congress as well. The chair of each committee holds a leadership position in his or her respective house. All four of these Hill committees have permanent offices and support staff. They recruit candidates and try to re-elect incumbents. They conduct polls, help candidates with fund-raising activities, contribute to campaigns, create political ads, and purchase television time. Candidates seeking election spend great amounts of time and energy seeking the endorsements and resources of the Hill Committees.

Party Committees in Congress
National Republican Senatorial Committee (NRSC)
National Republican Congressional Committee (NRCC)
Democratic Senatorial Campaign Committee (DSCC)
Democratic Congressional Campaign Committee (DCCC)

State and Local Parties Every state has a statewide party organization. Usually headquartered in the state's capital city, this organization carries out many of the same activities as the national party. The state party chairperson makes public appearances on local television and works to recruit new members and register voters. Within states, many counties have a party chair as well. At the state and county levels, population size and the history of the local party determine the strength of the party organization. Some chairs are full-time employees that collect a salary. Some parties have permanent office space or their own building. County-level chairpersons from less populated counties operate effectively out of their homes with nothing more than a basic Web page and a box of voter registration cards.

All these organizational elements at various levels create a mammoth party operation that is loosely structured across state lines. The national party chairperson and the national committees are at the top of this operation, but no official hierarchy really exists. There is no firm top-down flow of money, ideas, or directives. State and local organizations can operate independently of the national party committee. Popular, self-funded candidates often have more influence on campaigns than the local party. At times, state or local parties will differ from the national party on a policy stance or on candidate endorsements.

National Conventions

The parties' most momentous occasion is the national convention, which takes place every four years. Since the 1830s, Democrats and some short-lived parties have held conventions in major cities across the United States. Republicans have held national conventions since 1856. Today, delegates from all 50 states and U.S. territories convene in a single arena to create their platform and to nominate candidates for president and vice president. These patriotic galas are covered on primetime television and in other major media. The nominee's acceptance speech is the culminating event.

History The convention system to nominate the party's candidate replaced the unpopular caucus system common in the early 1800s. With caucuses, groups of like-minded congressional members had generally nominated presidential candidates from among themselves. Small gatherings of interested men struck political deals in Washington boardinghouses and meeting rooms. The corrupt bargain and unpopular "King Caucus" gave way to the convention system in Jackson's era. Increased voter eligibility and participation in elections (with the notable exception of women) caused more Americans to gain interest in politics. Local and state conventions included greater numbers of participants from a broader swath of the citizenry. National conventions began to parallel these smaller gatherings.

The first national party convention took place in Baltimore in 1831. The short-lived Anti-Masonic Party convened to nominate a presidential candidate. This party wanted to end the secret Masonic order's influence on the presidency.

The Democrats held their first national convention the next year in the same city. The party endorsed incumbent Andrew Jackson. The Whigs also met there in 1832 to nominate Henry Clay. Over the next decades, conventions served as events to draw up platforms and nominate the party's presidential candidate. Baltimore, a midpoint along the East Coast, became the host city for national political conventions for a generation.

These conventions took place in large churches or in music halls. Attendance hovered between 150 and 500 people. Delegates came from most states. By the 1850s, the parties began to choose other cities for these events. The Whigs held conventions in several cities in Pennsylvania. The Democrats departed Baltimore for Cincinnati in 1856. The new Republican Party held its first conventions in Philadelphia and then in Chicago. Minor parties, such as the **Know-Nothings**, Liberal Republicans, Prohibitionists, and Greenbacks, all organized and nominated presidential candidates at conventions.

For nearly 200 years, conventions have been grand spectacles. Contentious balloting has at times gone on for days. States' delegates arrive to nominate their favorite sons. Some delegations have marched out in protest. During the mid-1800s, there were rowdy encounters between delegates brandishing weapons. The longest convention battle for a nominee occurred in 1924 when it took 103 votes before the Democratic Party nominated John W. Davis. Such intense competitions have led to floor fights where intense wheeling and dealing finally vaulted candidates over the top. Promises of appointments to high-level positions sometimes served as political capital to persuade delegates or to convince potential rivals to step out of the contest. The last brokered convention—where results were determined by bargaining and multiple ballots—occurred in 1952, which was also the last time that multiple ballots were required.

The 1968 Democratic Convention and After

The 1968 Democratic Convention in Chicago revealed deep divisions within the party. Old-line conservative party regulars who favored Vice President Hubert Humphrey faced off with the anti-Vietnam War wing, who favored Senator Eugene McCarthy. Dominated by party **elites** and older members, the convention nominated Humphrey while antiwar protesters battled in the streets with the Chicago police. Only 16 states had used a primary election in the nominating process, none of which Humphrey won. To many, this outcome did not reflect the will of the **rank and file** or perhaps even the majority of the party. It brought great attention to the party's imperfect and undemocratic nominating procedure. Few women, African Americans, or young party members served as delegates. The Democrats lost the election to Richard Nixon and saw a need to bring peace within their ranks and to shape the nominating system to fairly reflect the makeup of party membership.

McGovern-Fraser Commission The Democratic Party created the **McGovern-Fraser Commission** to examine, consider, and ultimately rewrite convention rules. Headed by Senator George McGovern, the commission brought significant changes that ensured minorities, women, and younger voters representation at future conventions. A decade later, after having won only one presidential contest, largely as a reaction to Nixon's Watergate scandal, the Democrats radically modified the system's emphasis on the party's rank-and-file voting to give more independence to the party's elites. The party created **superdelegates**, high-ranking delegates not beholden to any state primary vote. Superdelegates include members of Congress, governors, mayors of large cities, and other party regulars that comprise roughly 20 percent of the Democratic delegates.

Source: Stan Honda / Getty Images

U.S. Senator Marco Rubio of Florida introduced presidential nominee Mitt Romney on the final day of the 2012 Republican National Convention in Tampa, Florida. The venue seated about 20,000 people and featured giant video display screens. More than 30 million viewers watched the convention at home.

Party Ideology and Platforms

The modern Republican Party holds a conservative party doctrine. Republicans for decades have preached against wasteful spending and for a strong national defense, limited regulation of businesses, and maintaining traditions. Democrats, on the other hand, with a strong following in cities and among academics on college campuses, believe strongly in civil rights, women's rights, and civil liberties. Democrats also desire more government services to solve public problems and greater regulations to protect the environment.

Platforms Divisions certainly exist within both major parties. At no time do all party members agree on all the issues. The best way to determine a party's primary ideology is to read its **platform**, or list of principles and plans it hopes to enact. Yet another organizational element, the platform is somewhat of a contract between the members and its elected officials. Party members argue over the wording of this document during drafting. The arguments have even caused some parties to split up.

In addition to basic principles, the party platforms drafted in 2012 include the legacies of the party's noted historical heroes, some specific proposals, and accusations against the opposite party. Below and on the next page are some selected quotes from both the Democratic and Republican platforms on a wide range of issues.

Democratic Party Platform 2012

- **On health care for the poor:** "We will strengthen Medicaid and oppose efforts to block grant the program, slash its funding, and leave millions more without health insurance."

- **On equal rights for women:** "We are committed to ensuring full equality for women: we reaffirm our support for the Equal Rights Amendment."

- **On equality and sexual orientation:** "…all Americans deserve the same chance to pursue happiness, earn a living, be safe in their communities, serve their country, and take care of the ones they love…[regardless of sexual orientation]."

- **On immigration:** "Democrats are strongly committed to enacting comprehensive immigration reform that supports our economic goals and reflects our values as both a nation of laws and a nation of immigrants."

- **On climate change:** "We affirm the science of climate change, commit to significantly reducing the pollution that causes climate change, and know we have to meet this challenge by driving smart policies that lead to greater growth in clean energy generation and result in a range of economic and social benefits."

- **On abortion:** "The Democratic Party strongly and unequivocally supports *Roe v. Wade* and a woman's right to make decisions regarding her pregnancy, including a safe and legal abortion, regardless of ability to pay."

These statements reveal why each party has a unique following of voters. The Democrats have proven they are an inclusive party that works for minority rights. Republicans, on the other hand, rely on conservative voters who support a limit on gun regulation, anti-abortion legislation, and fundamentalist Christian values. The electoral map of recent years shows these same trends geographically. The Democratic Party generally carries the more liberal northeastern states, while Republicans carry most of the South and rural West. Democrats increased their votes among women, African Americans, and the fastest-growing minority in the United States, Hispanics. These voters helped Barack Obama win in 2008 and 2012.

Republican Party Platform 2012

- **On government-funded support:** "Our vision of an opportunity society stands in stark contrast to the current Administration's policies that expand entitlements and guarantees, create new public programs, and provide expensive government bailouts."
- **On the death penalty:** "Courts should have the option of imposing the death penalty in capital murder cases."
- **On marriage:** "…we believe that marriage, the union of one man and one woman, must be upheld as the national standard, a goal to stand for, encourage, and promote through laws governing marriage."
- **On immigration:** "…we oppose any form of amnesty of those who, by intentionally violating the law, disadvantage those who have obeyed it."
- **On gun control:** "…we call on the governing authority to pass laws consistent with the Supreme Court's decisions in the *District of Columbia v. Heller* and *McDonald v. Chicago* cases, which upheld the fundamental right to keep and bear arms for self-defense."
- **On abortion:** "We oppose using public revenues to promote or perform abortion or fund organizations which perform or advocate it and will not fund or subsidize health care which includes abortion coverage."

Democrats and Republicans also tend to disagree on economic matters and issues related to law and order. Democrats, for example, tend to support increasing government services for the poor, including health care, and they tend to support regulations on business to promote environmental quality and equal rights. Republicans tend to strongly oppose wasteful government spending and the expansion of entitlements while strongly supporting a strong national defense. They also tend to support only limited government regulation of business. On law and order, Democrats tend to prefer rehabilitation for prisoners over punishment and often oppose the death penalty. Republicans tend to favor full prison sentences with few opportunities for parole and, as their platform states, they support the right of courts to impose the death penalty in certain cases.

Minor Parties

Though a two-party system has generally dominated the American political scene, competitive **minor parties**, often called *third parties*, have surfaced and played a distinct role. Technically, the Jacksonian Democrats and Lincoln's Republicans began as minor parties. Since President Lincoln's victory in 1860, however, no minor party has won the White House, but several third-party movements have met with different levels of success. These lesser-known groups have sent members to Congress, added amendments to the Constitution, and forced the larger parties to take note of them and their ideas.

Minor Party Types and Historic Examples

As parties were coming into their own during the antebellum period, several national groups sought to place their candidates into office. Some were **single-issue parties** created to advance a particular policy or to solve one particular political concern. These included the Anti-Masonic Party, the **Free Soil Party**, and the American Party, commonly known as the "Know-Nothings." These parties wanted, respectively, to wrest presidential control from Masons, free the slaves, and put tighter restrictions on immigration and citizenship.

In the later nineteenth century, America experienced growth in minor party activity. As the Republican Party struggled to define its ideology, some of its own members left to create new parties. These **splinter parties**, also called factional or **bolter parties**, often broke off from a larger existing party due to an ideology differing from that of party leaders. The Liberal Republicans, for example, met in 1872 to oppose incumbent Republican Ulysses S. Grant. This group, led by intellectuals, senators, and newspaper editors, felt the Grant administration and the Radical Republicans in Congress were too harsh on the South during Reconstruction. They thought the party should be more liberal in reconstructing the nation and in allowing the South to return to normalcy. Splinter parties often form around a strong political personality.

Several economic crises occurred in the late 1800s that sparked the creation of **economic protest parties**, those with strong concerns about economic conditions. The Populist and Greenback parties grew out of movements that sought to restructure America's economic situation and to ease the plight of workers. In 1892, the Populists, whose support was strongest in the agricultural South and West, gathered in Omaha to nominate James Weaver for president. Weaver won 22 electoral votes in a few western states but finished a distant third behind the Democratic and Republican nominees. The Populist Party merged into the Democratic Party, but it had proven its place in American politics.

The Socialist Party grew out of a concern for equality, especially economic equality. This party could be classified as an economic protest, or as an **ideological party**, one that follows a prescribed ideology. Also called *doctrinal* parties, these have a comprehensive view of government and policy that differs greatly from that of the two major parties. The Socialist Party took on such causes as child labor and the minimum wage. It also addressed foreign policy positions and other domestic concerns.

The Libertarian Party today espouses the general libertarian philosophy discussed in Chapter three. (See pages 55–56.)

Although there is some overlap, minor parties fall into four general categories, as shown in the chart below.

Minor Party Types and Examples
Ideological parties: Socialist, Libertarian
Splinter parties: Bull Moose, American Independent
Economic protest parties: Greenback, Populist
Single-issue parties: Free Soil, American (Know-Nothings), Prohibition, Green

Parties in the 1900s

In the twentieth century, emerging third parties generally resulted from party splintering. Popular figures in both major parties have periodically differed with their colleagues. When principles or goals drastically differed, these protest leaders left their parties and took large factions with them. Some examples include leaders of progressive ideals in the early 1900s and outraged southern spokesmen seeking states' rights over civil rights at midcentury.

Progressives After **Theodore Roosevelt** served as president (1901–1909), he felt that Republican leadership, including his successor William Howard Taft, had forsaken such progressive issues as trust busting—government efforts to break up corporate trusts and monopolies—and environmental conservation. The party divided along its conservative and progressive wings. The conservative Taft favored limited government and minimal interference in business, while Roosevelt, a proponent of enhanced workers' rights, challenged big business. Toward the end of Taft's term, Roosevelt sought his party's nomination to replace him. As usual, the party nominated the incumbent. A strong personality with a loyal following, Roosevelt refused to accept defeat; he ran for office as the Progressive Party nominee. In the general election, he outdid his Republican rival, earning 88 electoral votes to Taft's eight. But the Republican-conservative vote was diluted and split, allowing Democratic nominee Woodrow Wilson to win the presidency.

The Progressive Party continued to be a player in national politics. Progressives held governorships and seats in Congress. Popular Wisconsin Governor Robert La Follette ran for president as the Progressive nominee in 1924. This former Republican wanted to aggressively initiate progressive ideals that conservative President Calvin Coolidge did not support. La Follette had a following in some locales, but in the end he won only Wisconsin.

Dixiecrats After World War II, the debate over civil rights for African Americans became a central issue. The Democratic Party had for a century been the party of the white South, which cared little about black voters. But nationwide a great division in the party developed along this issue. Democratic President Harry Truman had integrated the military. Minnesota Democratic Senate candidate and later presidential nominee Hubert Humphrey gave a powerful pro-civil rights speech at the 1948 Democratic convention that favored integration and fair treatment of black Americans. In response, much of the southern delegation joined the States' Rights Party to nominate J. Strom Thurmond to run as the Dixiecrat candidate. Thurmond carried four states in the Deep South and forced Truman into a close election with New York Republican Thomas Dewey.

Twenty years later, in 1968, civil rights had come a long way. Yet many white southerners still felt that Congress, presidents, and the Supreme Court had gone too far in dictating new rules of racial equality to the states. Segregationist Alabama Governor George Wallace was unable to secure the Democratic nomination and instead created the American Independent Party. Wallace's party had many of the same goals and the same following as Thurmond's 1948 faction. Wallace earned the electoral votes from five states in Dixie and certainly contributed to Republican Richard Nixon's victory.

Modern Third Parties

Since 1968, there have been additional national candidates seeking office under a different banner from the two major parties. But since Wallace's 1968 attempt, no presidential candidate has won a plurality in any one state, and therefore none has ever earned one electoral vote. In 1980, Illinois Congressman John Anderson ran as an independent with little success. Texas oil tycoon **H. Ross Perot** burst onto the political scene in 1992 to run for president as an independent. Funded largely from his own wealth, Perot created **United We Stand America** and campaigned in every state. He won nearly 20 percent of the national popular vote. But with no strong following in any one state, he failed to earn any electoral votes.

Representatives, senators, and governors have also campaigned as independents or with lesser-known parties in recent years. Former pro wrestler Jesse "The Body" Ventura won the Minnesota governor's seat as the **Reform Party** candidate (Perot's party became the Reform Party). A handful of national politicians have either won as independents or proclaimed their independence after winning office. Vermont's Senator Jim Jeffords, Connecticut's Joe Lieberman, and former New York Mayor Michael Bloomberg have all shaken their party labels in recent years.

Minor Party Candidates and Independent Political Leaders	
Recent Minor Party Presidential Candidates	Becoming Independent
• **H. Ross Perot**—Texas millionaire ran with United We Stand America, 1992 and 1996	• **Jim Jeffords**—Vermont Republican Senator, 2001
• **Ralph Nader**—Consumer advocate ran with the Green Party, 1996 and 2000	• **Joe Lieberman**—Connecticut Democratic Senator, 2006
• **Pat Buchanan**—Conservative aide to Nixon and Reagan ran with Reform Party, 2000	• **Michael Bloomberg**—New York Republican Mayor, 2007

Limited Success

No minor party has won the presidency since 1860, and no third party has risen to second place in the meantime. This begs the question: What is the role of minor parties, and why would anyone even pay attention to these temporary organizations? Minor parties often play the role of **spoiler**, not winning the election but causing another candidate to lose. Minor parties were spoilers when Teddy Roosevelt ran in 1912 and when George Wallace ran in 1968.

Many minor party candidates have gained sizable followings that got the attention of the major parties. After election results come in, major parties must reconsider minor parties' political power and policy positions. In some cases, one or the other major party has adopted the minor party's platform or modified its own in hopes of attracting the minor party's followers.

Competing with Republicans and Democrats Minor parties have a difficult time competing with the Republicans and Democrats. Unlike European nations or other industrialized democracies, the United States is unique in its two-party system. The minor parties that come and go cannot effectively participate in the political process in America for a variety of reasons. Two major reasons are the division of public opinion and the institutional features of our elections.

Public issues, especially those that are controversial, are often divided into simple dichotomies. People are *for* or *against* higher taxes, abortion, gun control, or a minimum wage increase. This viewpoint encourages parties to take a pro or con position that simplifies, often unfairly, the public debate regarding these concerns. This simplification and dichotomization forces the electorate into two camps.

Institutional Blocks The institutional reasons for the dominance of the two major parties are many and complex. First, the United States generally has what are called **single-member districts** for elective office. In single-member districts, the candidate who wins the most votes, or a plurality in a field of candidates, wins that office. In other nations, proportional representation exists. Multiple parties compete for office, and voters cast ballots for the party they favor. After the election those offices are filled proportionally. For example, a party that wins 30 percent of the votes cast in the election is then awarded 30 percent of the seats in that parliament or governing body. This method encourages and rewards third parties, even if minimally. In most elections in the United States, however, if three or more candidates seek an office, the candidate winning the most votes—even if it is with a minority of the total—wins the office outright. There is no rewarding second, much less third, place.

Money and Resources Minor party candidates also have a steeper hill to climb in terms of financing, ballot access, and exposure. Both the Republican and Democratic Parties have organized operations to raise money to convince donors of their candidates' ability to win—and by so doing attract more donors. Full-time employees at the DNC and RNC constantly seek funding between elections. Political candidates in minor parties cannot compete financially.

Independents also have a difficult time with ballot access. Every state has a prescribed method for candidates to place their names on the ballot. It usually involves a modest fee and many signatures. Favored candidates in the Republican and Democratic Parties can simply dispatch party regulars and volunteers throughout a state's counties to collect signatures for the ballot petition. Green Party, Libertarian, or independent candidates must first secure assistance or collect those signatures themselves. Since the ballot petition requires thousands of registered voters, this task alone is daunting and discouraging to would-be third-party candidates.

The major parties try to keep minor parties off ballots, especially if the potential minor party candidate poses competition. For example, Democrats felt that Ralph Nader's presence in the 2000 election cut away at Al Gore's chances to win. Had Nader not been on the ballot in several states, Democrats predicted, Gore likely would have won. Instead he lost by a close margin to George W. Bush. In 2004, the Democratic Party fought legal battles in several crucial states to keep Nader off the ballot.

The media tend not to cover minor party candidates. Reporters are less likely to show up at an event held for a minor candidate. Independents are often not invited to public debates or televised forums at the local and national levels.

Parties and Patterns

Political parties are a unique part of American history. They are responsible for creating many national customs, involving greater numbers of people in the electoral process, and elevating political leaders into national office. Since the first political contests before the Republic was created, most citizens have fallen into two camps, or coalitions, of national government. This two-party system has seen five political realignments. The last one occurred in 1932. Since then, the Democrats have espoused an ideology that supports workers, provides more services to the populace, and in recent years, revolves on an attitude of inclusion and diversity. Republicans have generally aligned with big and small businesses, the religious right, and gun owners. Political parties serve as a check on one another, one that ideally moderates government decisions but can at times bring about the party bickering seen in the debt crisis in the 2010s. Parties provide an identity that simplifies the task of parsing major issues for members. Since the

1960s, voter disillusionment and changing times have made voters less loyal to the parties. There has been a rise in independents and an increase in ticket splitting. Minor parties have risen and fallen and have at times deeply affected elections as spoilers or as contributing blocs to coalitions.

REFLECT ON THE ESSENTIAL QUESTION

Essential Question: *How have individuals coalesced into organized political groups, and how do these groups influence policy?* On separate paper, complete a chart like the one below to gather details to answer that question.

Organized Political Groups	How They Influence Policy

KEY TERMS, NAMES, AND EVENTS

caucus
coalition
critical election
dealignment
Democratic Congressional Campaign Committee (DCCC)
Democratic National Committee (DNC)
Democratic Senatorial Campaign Committee (DSCC)
Democrat-Republicans
divided government
economic protest parties
elites
Free Soil Party
Grand Old Party (GOP)

H. Ross Perot
ideological party
Know-Nothings
McGovern-Fraser Commission
minor parties
National Republican Congressional Committee (NRCC)
National Republican Senatorial Committee (NRSC)
New Deal coalition
party chairperson
party convention
platform
popular sovereignty
rank and file
realignments

Reform Party
Republican National Committee (RNC)
Republicans
single-issue parties
single-member district
splinter/bolter parties
spoiler
superdelegates
Theodore Roosevelt
ticket splitting
two-party system
United We Stand America
Whigs
white primary

1. All of the following contributed to the realignment of the two major parties EXCEPT
   (A) the Democratic Party's presence in the South
   (B) New Deal legislation
   (C) partisan differences about entering World War II
   (D) civil rights legislation of the 1950s and 1960s
   (E) concern for social and moral values

2. African American voters generally supported the Republican Party until 1932 most likely due to
   (A) the early Republican Party's commitment to emancipation and civil rights
   (B) views of early Republican presidents like Thomas Jefferson and Andrew Jackson
   (C) FDR's affirmative action goals
   (D) increased employment for African Americans during the Great Depression
   (E) the Republican party's relationship to big business

3. The modern Democratic and Republican national conventions differ in that
   (A) one occurs biannually, and one occurs every four years
   (B) one has shown a stronger commitment to naming minorities, young voters, and women as delegates to its convention
   (C) one nominates a presidential candidate, and one nominates the vice presidential candidate
   (D) the Republican convention always occurs before the Democratic convention
   (E) Democratic conventions have always been smooth, and consensus has always been strong

4. A liberal candidate running for the U.S. House of Representatives would seek the assistance and resources of
   (A) the Republican National Committee
   (B) the Republican chairperson
   (C) the Progressive Party
   (D) the National Republican Senatorial Committee
   (E) the Democratic Congressional Campaign Committee

5. The Bull Moose and Dixiecrat Parties are examples of which type of minor party?

(A) Economic protest

(B) Ideological

(C) Splinter

(D) Single-issue

(E) Victorious

6. Which of the following points would most likely be part of the Democratic Party's national platform?

(A) Protecting gun owners' rights

(B) Dismantling welfare

(C) Outlawing labor unions

(D) Contributing more military troops abroad

(E) Expanding voting and increasing participation in politics

7. Which of the following statements most accurately reflects modern political parties?

(A) State and local party organizations must follow all ideas and directives of the national party.

(B) The press is rarely critical of party activity.

(C) Democrats and Republicans engage each other only in the public eye.

(D) Local party organizations support candidates and coordinate events.

(E) Political parties campaign for candidates but don't enter the public policymaking arena.

8. All of the following are impediments to minor parties gaining strength in the United States EXCEPT

(A) a lack of resources

(B) ballot access

(C) laws that bar minor parties

(D) single-member districts

(E) the Electoral College system

9. After altering its convention-delegate system in the early 1970s, the Democratic Party created which of these to give more voice to party elites?

(A) Doubled voting strength of office holders

(B) Superdelegates

(C) Iowa Caucus

(D) Blanket primary

(E) McGovern-Fraser Commission

10. Which statement about American political parties is true?

(A) The Republican Party has dominated the South since the party's inception.

(B) African Americans consistently have voted with the Republican Party since the 1950s.

(C) The Solid South refers to the Democrats' following in the region for roughly a century.

(D) The sitting president usually serves as national party chairperson.

(E) Teddy Roosevelt was able to win the presidency as a minor party candidate.

FREE-RESPONSE QUESTIONS

Question

1. Two major ideological parties have dominated U.S. politics and have organizational elements to further their policy goals.

(a) Describe the ideologies or views of the two major U.S. political parties with regard to two of the following:

- economic concerns
- social issues
- law and order

(b) Identify two of the following party organizational elements and explain how each serves to advance the party's goals.

- national chairperson
- national convention
- national committee
- congressional campaign committees

Question

2. Two parties have dominated American politics and elections over most of United States history. However, minor parties have surfaced and competed with the major parties.

(a) Identify and describe one minor party that has competed in a presidential election since 1900.

(b) Identify and describe one type of minor party and provide an example.

(c) Explain how a minor party can succeed on a national level besides winning the presidency.

WRITING: BE SPECIFIC

Both of these free-response questions require the introduction or discussion of actual formal groups or individuals. Be sure to name specific parties and their types. Using examples of specific individuals to articulate your answer will also strengthen your writing. For example, in Question 1, naming a current or recent national chairperson, such as Democrat Debbie Wasserman Schultz or Republican Reince Priebus, would enhance your answer, even though knowing them isn't required. Any other historic chairperson would also be effective. Also be specific about the year or location of a noted convention you discuss. In answering Question 2, naming actual candidates in addition to parties or states that voted for them will give your answer the specificity it needs to be clear and strong.

Source: Dreamstime

Democratic Congresswomen Nita Lowey (NY) and Debbie Wasserman Schultz (FL), who became the 52nd Chair of the Democratic Party National Committee in 2011, share the podium at the American Israel Public Affairs Committee Policy Conference in 2012.

6

Campaigns and Elections

"I am not the candidate of black America … I am not the candidate of the women's movement … I am the candidate of the people of America."
—Shirley Chisholm, announcement at press conference, 1972

Essential Question: How do U.S. citizens choose their elected officials in a free and fair society?

Federal elections are held on the first Tuesday after the first Monday in November in even years. States administer additional elections, though some federal law applies. Many candidates work long hours and withstand heavy scrutiny as they attempt to win office. Each must create a campaign organization, raise large sums of money, and effectively communicate a strong message. For partisan races (mayor, city council, and board of education elections are typically nonpartisan races), candidates must first win a primary election and then compete in the November general election. Though she did not win her quest for the Democratic nomination in 1972, African-American Congresswoman Shirley Chisholm later reflected, "The next time a woman runs, or a black, a Jew or anyone from a group that the country is 'not ready' to elect to its highest office . . . he or she will be taken seriously from the start."

History of Campaigns and Elections

Campaign events have evolved over time from quiet, humble contests among financially established statesmen to television and ad wars that rely too often on **sound bites**—short, simple phrases sometimes used to oversimplify a politician's position and cast a positive or negative light. As voting audiences grew, politicians used new techniques to reach them. As participation grew, the presidential nominating method developed to include more voters. Different methods have been developed over the years to nominate presidential candidates.

Early Campaigns

In 1789, during America's first presidential election, each state's legislators named their electors. The electors then met in their respective state capitals and cast their first votes for George Washington. Though popular-vote elections were held for state and local elections in those days, most states required voters to be landowners. A decade later, as political parties began to develop, more voters took part in presidential elections as the contests became much more competitive.

The 1800 presidential contest produced one of the closest elections in history. Incumbent President John Adams faced Thomas Jefferson, Aaron Burr, and others. Jefferson and Burr tied in the electoral vote, and no candidate secured the required majority. After the House of Representatives balloted for weeks, Jefferson prevailed.

Rise of the Caucus After Washington, D. C., became the seat of national government, **congressional caucuses**, private gatherings of like-minded congressional members, took on the task of nominating presidential candidates. But as suffrage expanded, voters became wary and suspicious of the caucus system. Rank-and-file members of the party felt their leaders sometimes disregarded their favored candidates. Party members across the country disliked what they dubbed "backroom deals" in Washington, where politicians exchanged political favors while disregarding the voice of the people. In the 1830s, national conventions replaced the caucus system of nomination.

Rise of the Political Campaign During Andrew Jackson's presidency (1829–1837), most states removed the property requirement in order to allow almost all white men to vote. States also conducted popular elections to name presidential electors instead of having their state legislatures select them. As the common citizen's opinion began to matter more, each party developed strategies to craft and communicate its message.

Political campaigning soon rose to an art form characterized by festivities, barbecues, and picnics. Campaigners made up slogans, popularized political songs, and held dinners and street rallies, all focused on one candidate presented as embodying the party's ideals and goals. French political thinker and historian Alexis de Tocqueville, touring the United States at the time, observed, "Parties in the United States as elsewhere feel the need to group themselves around one man in order more easily to reach the intelligence of the crowd . . . [and] make use of the name of the presidential candidate as a symbol."

The presidential campaign of 1840 was the first in which candidates appealed directly to large crowds. Pro-candidate banners, buttons, pamphlets, merchandise, and theme songs became campaign mainstays. The contest pitted Whig party nominee William Henry Harrison against incumbent Democrat Martin Van Buren. Harrison, the hero of the Battle of Tippecanoe, a pivotal 1811 clash between the U.S. Army and a confederation of Native American tribes, chose John Tyler as his running mate. Their effective and memorable slogan was "Tippecanoe and Tyler too."

One Democratic newspaper criticized Harrison by suggesting that he drank too much. It claimed that Harrison would do just as much good for the country if he spent his years in a log cabin with a jug of whiskey as he would taking up the office of president. Harrison and his followers capitalized on the remark in what became known as the Log Cabin Campaign. So-called Log Cabin newspapers promoted Harrison's events as he traveled the Midwest. On election day, some 80 percent of eligible voters came out to cast their ballots.

Harrison won his bid for the presidency, and the nation realized the importance of paying attention to national campaigns.

Machine Politics and Reform

After the Civil War, parties organized around a **political machine**, the party organization that rewarded jobs and services for votes and support and that punished the disloyal, especially in the urban North where well-connected party bosses controlled public decisions, public money, and many jobs.

Large numbers of immigrants were entering the United States primarily in search of jobs and the right to vote. The local political boss could provide both. In return, the newcomer owed the boss patronage, loyalty, and kickbacks. American-born citizens also filled up the cities and became dependent on party bosses. Bosses operated from the precinct level up to the national level. These were men with strong personalities who could command a large following; they ruled bodies of government and became some of the most familiar faces in politics. Nationally known bosses included New York City's corrupt William Marcy Tweed and Cleveland's Mark Hanna, senator, Republican chairman, and presidential kingmaker.

In this era of machine politics, bosses placed pawns in important positions and engaged in bogus elections. According to author Kate Kelly, in one New Jersey case, authorities discovered more than a thousand illegal voters within a single county. Campaigners brought gangs in from Philadelphia and paid one or two dollars to each for a vote. Campaigning became a rough business. Machine thugs often beat voters who did not follow orders, and sometimes law enforcement, at the mercy of the local boss, arrested noncompliant voters.

Primary Elections

The notorious era of boss-driven nominations led to the development of the **primary election**. This is an intraparty system by which declared party members (voters who identify with a particular party) nominate candidates in advance of the November **general election**, the election that determines the winner of the office. Primaries moved the party's nomination from the hands of a few party leaders to the rank-and-file membership. Originally called the "direct primary" because voters could choose candidates directly, the primary has become essential to winning public office in nearly every state.

The First Primaries Primary elections first appeared in northern cities, and by 1900 several city and state governments had initiated some type of primary election. Wisconsin first mandated the statewide primary in 1903 largely due to the efforts of Governor Robert La Follette. "Put aside the caucus and convention," said La Follette. "They answer no purpose further than to give respectable form to political robbery." Other states followed. By 1916, 20 states held presidential primaries. The next year, 32 states required primary nominations for statewide offices. Yet the average number of state primaries shrunk to about 15 over the following decades. State party committees or caucuses continued to endorse presidential candidates, and where states held primaries, convention delegates did not have to follow the statewide presidential primary party vote.

Primaries in the 1960s For the 1960 Democratic presidential contest, Senator Lyndon Johnson opted out of all primaries and announced his candidacy just prior to the convention. John F. Kennedy chose to compete in only seven of the 16 primary elections held that year, and he won nomination on the convention's first ballot. Eight years later Vice President Hubert Humphrey won the party's nomination in Chicago without winning a single state primary. This outcome led to more states implementing binding primaries—those that require state delegates to vote at the convention to reflect the citizens' choice.

Contemporary Primaries Today, most states hold a primary election. For years, the **closed primary** was standard. In a closed primary, voters must declare their party affiliation in advance of the election, typically when they register to vote. The **open primary**, used by about half of the states today, allows voters to declare party affiliation on election day. Poll workers hand these voters one party's ballot from which they select candidates.

The rarest primary is the **blanket primary.** California and other western states pioneered the blanket primary, which allows voters to cast votes for candidates in multiple parties. In other words, voters can cast a **split ticket**, picking Republicans in some races and Democrats in others. Independent and moderate voters like the freedom and flexibility of the blanket primary, but the parties and state lawmakers do not. Blanket primaries require no party commitment on the part of the voter. Partisan voters can attempt to sabotage the opposing party's front-runner by voting for the less qualified candidate. Only Alaska and Washington use the blanket primary. It is rare because partisans usually decide the state's primary election procedures.

California voters, however, instituted a nonpartisan primary in 2010. This new runoff system includes all candidates—both party members and independents. The top two vote-getters, regardless of party affiliation, compete for office in the general election. The quest for inclusiveness created a unique dynamic that caused the press to dub it the "jungle primary" because the winners emerge through the law of the jungle—survival of the fittest without regard to party. But as *Los Angeles Times* columnist Harold Meyerson points out, this system is not without problems. The party that runs fewer candidates tends to win office. Because California is a heavily Democratic state, the party tends to run more Democratic candidates in the primary, diluting the vote and often assuring two Republicans advancing to the general election. As far as turning out more voters, the most recent California primary had one of the lowest turnouts ever.

Contemporary Elections

Elections have become more frequent and more regulated. For decades, states administered elections exclusively under their reserved powers without any federal interference, and for the most part they still do. They determine how voter registration will work, which type of ballot voters will use, and what time polling places will open and close. At the federal level, Congress has addressed voting with constitutional amendments and civil rights laws. It places limits on campaign donations, and it created the **Federal Elections Commission**, an agency charged with enforcing campaign finance law. Additionally, federal courts have ruled on the constitutionality of state election procedures.

Who Governs Elections?	
State	**Federal**
Sets times and locations for elections, most dates	Sets date for federal, general elections
Chooses format of ballot and how to file for candidacy	Has judicial jurisdiction on election policy
Creates rules and procedures for voter registration	Addresses suffrage in constitutional amendments
Draws congressional district lines	Enforces relevant civil rights legislation
Certifies election results days after election day	Administers and enforces campaign finance rules

Counties and cities are divided into voting jurisdictions, which are typically broken down into precincts. After the election, poll workers send the completed ballots to a central location—the Board of Elections in most states—to be counted and reported to the public and the press.

Congressional Campaigns

All House candidates and one-third of Senate candidates run for election every two years. Federal elections that take place halfway through a president's term are called **midterm elections**. To compete in a modern campaign for the U.S. House or Senate, a candidate must create a networked organization that resembles a small corporation, spend much of his or her own money, solicit hundreds of donors for contributions, and sacrifice many hours and days to the process. Senator Sherrod Brown of Ohio explains how a candidate "must hire a staff and make wise use of volunteers . . . craft a cogent, clear message . . . budget carefully in spending money on mail, radio, television and printed material . . . and be able to successfully sell the product—himself—to the public and to the media." Large campaigns divide these tasks into several categories, such as management, public relations, research, fund-raising, advertising, and voter mobilization.

Fund-raising

Since running a campaign is expensive, raising money is a high priority. Some candidates finance their own campaigns, but most rely on the party organization and thousands of individual donors for contributions. The size of a candidate's **war chest**, or bank account for campaigning, can play a role in determining victory or loss. The campaign for financial resources begins long before the campaign for votes. Fund-raising allows candidates to test their chances. Those who can gather funds begin to prove a level of support that makes them viable.

About half of all House candidates raise more than $1 million for their campaigns, and some have even crossed the $8 million mark. Overall in 2012, House incumbents spent on average $1,664,902. To raise that over a two-year period, each incumbent had to raise nearly $16,000 per week. Senate candidates begin raising money much earlier than House candidates and devote more time to soliciting cash. Their quest for dollars is also more national in scope. Senate candidates spend an average of $12 million. For her first re-election campaign, then-Senator Hillary Clinton led the pack in 2006 with $39.8 million raised.

To collect these donations, candidates spend about one-fourth of their campaign schedule making personal phone calls and holding formal fund-raisers. The Internet came into use as a campaign and fund-raising tool in 1998. By 2002, 57 percent of all House candidates and virtually every Senate candidate used the Web or email to gather funds. This type of solicitation is free, compared with the average of $3 to $4 spent on every direct mail request. Candidates also hold cocktail parties, picnics, and formal dinners with higher-level officials or celebrities as guest speakers. The sitting president or other party leaders can yield a big take. During the 2006 midterm campaigns, 23 Republican incumbents who hosted a visit by President Bush raised 159 percent more money than GOP incumbents who had not hosted such a visit.

Connecting with the Public

To win an election, candidates must understand what voters think. A typical campaign spends about 3 percent of its resources on polling and surveys to gather this information. Candidates also want to build a base of support and mobilize members of their coalition to the voting booths. Polling can help candidates frame their message. It helps determine which words or phrases to use in speeches and advertising. Campaigns occasionally use tracking polls to gain feedback after changing campaign strategy. They may also hold focus groups, and incumbents rely on constituent communication over their term. Candidates also keep an eye on Internet blogs, listen to radio call-in shows, and talk with party leaders and political activists to find out what the public wants.

Campaigns also set up registration tables at county fairs and on college campuses. They gather addresses from voter registration lists and mail out promotional pieces that highlight the candidate's accomplishments and often include photos of him or her alongside spouse and family. Campaigns also conduct robocalls, automated mass phone calls that promote or denounce a candidate.

Showcasing the Candidate Most voters, like most shoppers, make their decision based on limited information with only a small amount of consideration. For this reason, electronic and social media, television, and focus groups are essential to winning an election. A candidate's message is often centered on common themes of decency, loyalty, and hard work.

A typical campaign is divided into three phases: the biography, the issues, and the attack. Successful candidates have a unique story to tell. Campaign literature and television ads show candidates in previous public service, on playgrounds with children, on a front porch with family, or in church. These images attract a wide variety of voters. After the biography is told, a debate over the issues begins as voters shop for their candidate. Consultants and professionals believe issues-oriented campaigns motivate large numbers of people to come out and vote. In 2004, for example, conservative groups placed anti-gay marriage amendments on several state ballots to bring traditional-values voters to the polls to vote for Republican candidates.

Defining the Opponent Candidates competing for the independent voter find it necessary to draw sharp contrasts between themselves and their opponents. An attack phase begins later in the race, often motivated by desperation. Underdogs sometimes resort to cheap shots and work hard to expose inconsistencies in their opponent's voting records. Campaigns do opposition research to reveal their opponent's missteps or any unpopular positions he or she has taken in the past. Aides and staffers comb over the *Congressional Record*, old interview transcripts, and newspaper articles to search for damaging quotes. They also analyze an opponent's donor list in order to spotlight special-interest donations or out-of-state money.

Debates As the election nears, candidates participate in formal public debates, highly structured events with strict rules governing response time and conduct. These events are risky because candidates can suffer from gaffes (verbal slips) or from rough appearances. Incumbents and front-runners typically avoid debates because they have everything to lose and little to gain. Appearing on a stage with a lesser-known competitor usually helps the underdog. For races with large fields, those organizations sponsoring the debates typically determine which candidates get to participate.

Television Appearances The average adult watches about three and a half hours of TV per day. About three-quarters of all voters say television is where they obtain most of their information about elections. Candidates rely on two forms of TV: the visual and the spot. A **visual** is a short news segment showing the candidate in action—touring a factory, speaking to a civic club, visiting a classroom, or appearing at a political rally. Candidates send out press releases announcing their events, usually scheduled early enough in the day to make the evening news. This is free media coverage because, unlike expensive television commercials, the campaign does not have to pay for it. A campaign **spot**, on the other hand, is a short, expensive commercial. In fact, the most costly part of nearly any campaign is television advertising. Veteran Democratic speechwriter and campaign consultant Bob Shrum laments, "Things are measured by when a campaign will go on television, or if they can and to what degree they can saturate the air waves." The typical modern spot includes great emphasis on imagery, action-oriented themes, emotional messages, negative characterizations of the opponent, and quick production turnaround.

Incumbents vs. Challengers

With so many officials seeking re-election, many races have an incumbent vs. challenger dynamic. The **incumbent** is the officeholder seeking re-election. With rare exception, the incumbent has a stronger chance of winning than the challenger.

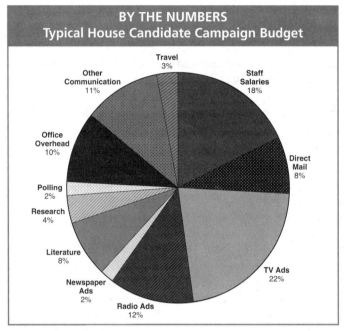

BY THE NUMBERS
Typical House Candidate Campaign Budget

Travel 3%
Other Communication 11%
Staff Salaries 18%
Office Overhead 10%
Direct Mail 8%
Polling 2%
Research 4%
Literature 8%
TV Ads 22%
Newspaper Ads 2%
Radio Ads 12%

Source: Paul S. Herrnson, *Congressional Elections*, 2008

What do the numbers show? What are the chief expenses in a House campaign? What portion of a candidate's expenditures are for marketing/showcasing the candidate? What percent goes to support staff or some type of research?

The incumbent's financial and electoral advantage is so daunting to challengers that it often dissuades them from ever entering the race. House incumbents tend to win re-election more than 90 percent of the time. Senators have an incumbency advantage too, but theirs is not quite as strong. Incumbents capitalize on their popularity and war chest, showering their districts with mail and email throughout the congressional term. During campaign season, they purchase commercials and load up the district with yard signs while ignoring their opponent and sometimes refusing to take part in public debates.

Name Recognition Incumbents have several built-in advantages. Name recognition is a powerful factor. For two or more years, all federal incumbents have appeared in the news, advocated legislation, and sent newsletters back to constituent voters. Nine out of ten voters recognize their House member's name, while fewer than six out of ten recognize that of the challenger.

Money Incumbents nearly always have more money than challengers because they are highly visible and often popular, and they can exploit the advantages of the office. **Political action committees (PACs)**, formal groups formed from interest groups, donate heavily to incumbents. Party leaders and the Hill Committees (page 116) realize the advantage incumbents have and invariably support the incumbent when he or she is challenged in a primary. In the general elections, House representatives receive roughly three times as much money as their challengers. Challengers receive a mere 9 percent of their donations from PACs, while House incumbents collect about 39 percent of their war chests from these groups. PACs give $12 to an incumbent for every $1 they donate to a challenger.

Presence A substantial number of incumbents keep a small campaign staff or maintain a campaign office between elections. Officeholders can provide services to constituents, including answering questions about issues of concern to voters, such as Medicare and bringing more federal dollars back home.

The Role of the Economy Certainly not all incumbents win. The single greatest predictor of an incumbent's loss is a poor economy. In hard economic times, the voting public holds incumbents and their party responsible. In midterm elections, regardless of the condition of the economy, the president's party usually loses some seats in Congress. Based on results from five recent midterm elections, the president's party lost an average of 26.4 House seats and 3.6 Senate seats.

Congressional candidates can often ride the popularity of their party's presidential candidate. When presidents win by wide margins, congressional candidates down the ballot typically do well also. This is called the **coattail effect**.

Some states require an election by a majority of voters. If no candidate receives a majority of votes, the top two vote-getters compete in a **runoff election**, basically guaranteeing a majority vote for one or the other.

Road to the White House

The U.S. presidential race is more complex, more expensive, and more involved than any other election. The road to the White House is long and arduous. Layers of rules, differing party structures, and varying state election laws complicate the process, making the quest for the presidency a state-by-state contest. A presidential campaign requires two or more years of advance work, tenacity, and a loyal and committed support system to make it through two fierce competitions—securing the party's nomination and winning a majority of electoral votes.

Running for President

Before presidential hopefuls formally announce their candidacy, they test the waters. Realizing the rigorous campaign and high price tag involved, most start early, touring the country and making television appearances. Some presidential candidates author a book, typically a memoir that relies heavily on their political philosophy.

The race essentially begins during a phase called the **invisible primary**, sometimes called the money primary, as candidates compete in polls and appear with political commentators. Long before any actual campaign, media personalities begin to declare who is fit to run. As commentators mention political notables, a potential field develops. Candidates include governors, senators, congressional members, and occasional leaders from the business world. They must appear "presidential," with a stately aura and a very clean public and private record, to encourage donations and political endorsements. Cable networks and political organizations eventually hold debates among primary contenders leading up to the election year and into the primary season.

Primaries and Caucuses

To win the presidential nomination, candidates must first win state primary elections or caucuses. Technically, primary voters cast votes for candidates to attend the convention and, with their vote, advise those delegates whom to nominate at the national convention. The Republican and Democratic rules for nomination differ, but both require a majority of votes by the appointed delegates at the convention. To win the nomination, candidates must win the requisite number of these state contests from January into the summer.

Iowa Caucuses Since 1976, the Iowa caucuses have taken place first. **Caucuses** differ from primary elections. These gatherings of like-minded party members parallel the idea of the congressional caucuses discussed earlier (page 133). Across Iowa, rank-and-file party members meet at community centers, schools, and private homes to discuss candidates and then take a vote. In comparison to elections, caucuses are inconvenient. Their two-hour commitment makes attendance hard for some voters, especially those who might have to skip work. Others are intimidated by the public discussion and the pressures at the gathering. Iowa caucus-goers essentially stand before friends, neighbors, and strangers and declare their support for a candidate. These dedicated voters hold strong opinions and often fall on the far left or far right of the ideological spectrum, thus causing more liberal or conservative figures to win nominations.

New Hampshire Primary New Hampshire follows Iowa. Candidates travel the state and hold town hall forums. Candidates spend time and money to seek the endorsement of the *Manchester Union-Journal*. They campaign in grocery stores and on the streets of relatively small New Hampshire towns. During this time, the voters heavily engage these presidential candidates. When asked their opinion on particular candidates, a typical New Hampshire voter might respond, "I don't know if I'm comfortable with him; I've only met him twice."

Pivotal events play out in New Hampshire, and many candidates' hopes of nomination end there. In 1980, Ronald Reagan defeated George H.W. Bush and began his climb to the nomination, leaving Bush behind.

Candidates cautiously frame their primary election night speeches to paint themselves as front-runners. In 1992, the news came to light that Bill Clinton had been part of a sex scandal, but he survived his diminished poll numbers to earn a second-place spot in New Hampshire. During his speech late that night, Clinton confidently referred to himself as "The Comeback Kid." This sound bite made its way into headlines that gave the impression Clinton had actually won the New Hampshire primary.

Front-loading Iowa and New Hampshire receive immense national attention during these events. Campaign teams and the national media converge on these states well in advance of election day. Hotels and restaurants fill with out-of-state customers bringing massive revenues. Politically, these states hold more influence than those that conduct their elections much later. This reality has brought on **front-loading**—states scheduling their primaries and caucuses earlier and earlier to boost their political clout and to enhance their tourism. As some states have scheduled earlier, Iowa and New Hampshire, not to be outdone, have moved their events even earlier. Front-loading has moved the initial contests to early January of the election year.

Following Iowa and New Hampshire, candidates then travel an uncertain path through several more states, hoping to secure enough delegates to win the nomination. In recent years, South Carolina has followed New Hampshire. The South Carolina primary has served as a barometer for the southern voting bloc. In the spring—these days as early as February—several states hold primaries on the same Tuesday. **Super Tuesday** began as a coordinated regional primary. It was initially dubbed "the tarmac primary" because candidates had only enough time to land on an airport's tarmac for a speech before flying off to the next state.

State Delegates States determine their convention delegates in different ways and hold them to differing rules. Some states give their delegates complete independence at the convention. Some presidential primaries are binding on "pledged delegates." But even in those cases, states differ on how these delegates are awarded. Some operate by congressional district. Some use a statewide winner-take-all system, and some use a proportional distribution for assigning delegates. For instance, if Candidate A receives 60 percent and Candidate B receives 40 percent of the popular primary vote, the state sends the corresponding percentage of delegates to the national gathering. In 2012, both parties used a proportional system of awarding delegates. The Democrats' superdelegates discussed in Chapter 5 also leave room for uncertainty in the process.

The complicated path to the convention is far from perfect. Because front-loading has pushed this contest to the opening of the calendar year, some have suggested holding a nationwide primary on a designated day to simplify the process and to curb the disproportional influence of the front-loaded states. Others have proposed rotating the dates of primaries on a regional basis. Compressing the primary schedule would perhaps make for a more efficient, less expensive contest.

Contemporary Conventions

The party conventions have become less suspenseful in modern times because the nominees are determined long before the convention date. Both parties have altered rules and formulas for state delegation strength. In the Democratic convention, strength has shifted away from the South and toward the North and West, while Republican voting strength is in the southern and western states. Democrats take into account the strength of each state's electoral vote and compare it to the record of how the state has cast votes for Democratic candidates in past general elections. Republicans place more value on the number of GOP representatives in Congress from those states and whether states have cast their electoral votes for Republican presidential candidates. In other words, Democrats give more delegates to large states, while Republicans give extra delegates to loyal ones. Democrats have also instituted the idea of "fair reflection" to balance delegates by age, gender, and race in relation to the superdelegates or party elders. Republicans do not bind their delegates, so GOP delegates can vote against the state's primary results. The Republican Party has a reputation for less inclusion of minority delegates, and this shows at the convention. In 2004, only 17 percent of GOP delegates were minorities.

BY THE NUMBERS Presidential Nominations (Selected Conventions)			
Year & Convention	Candidates on First Ballot (in order of votes received)	Eventual Nominee	Required Ballots
1924 Dem	William Gibbs McAdoo, Al Smith, James Cox, John W. Davis	Davis	103
1932 Dem	Franklin Roosevelt, Al Smith, John Nance Garner	Roosevelt	4
1952 GOP	Dwight Eisenhower, Robert Taft, Earl Warren	Eisenhower	1
1960 Dem	John Kennedy, Lyndon Johnson	Kennedy	1
1968 Dem	Hubert Humphrey, Eugene McCarthy, George McGovern	Humphrey	1
1976 GOP	Gerald Ford, Ronald Reagan	Ford	1
1980 GOP	Ronald Reagan, John Anderson	Reagan	1
1992 Dem	Bill Clinton, Jerry Brown	Clinton	1

What do the numbers show? Who were the party nominees in selected years? How frequently is the leader on the first ballot the final nominee? How many ballots are usually required to choose the party's candidate? How frequently did a losing candidate receive the party's nomination in a later convention?

The General Election

The general election season starts after party nominations and kicks into high gear after Labor Day weekend. Candidates fly around the country, stopping at key locations to deliver speeches. As the public and press begin to compare the two major party candidates, the issues become more sharply defined. Different groups and surrogates (spokespersons) support each candidate and appear on cable shows. The major party candidates debate, usually in three televised events over the course of several weeks. The vice presidential candidates usually debate once. Major newspapers endorse one candidate in their editorial pages. The media's daily coverage provides constant updates about which candidate is ahead and behind as measured by public opinion polls and campaign funding. By November, candidates have traveled to most states and have spent millions of dollars.

Electoral College The **Electoral College** system is both a revered and a frustrating part of the presidential election—one that shapes a presidential candidate's strategy. The system to elect the president has several features. The "college" is actually a simultaneous gathering of **electors** in their respective capital cities to vote on the same day. The Framers included this system in Article II of the Constitution to temper public opinion and to allow the more informed statesmen to select a consensus president. State and federal law and party custom also affect the process. Each state has the same number of electors as it has members of Congress; however, these electors cannot also be senators or representatives.

Alterations to the Electoral System Originally, the Constitution provided that each elector cast one vote for each of his top two choices for president. The winner became president and the runner-up became vice president. The Twelfth Amendment altered the system so that electors cast one vote for president and another for vice president. To win, candidates must earn a majority of the electoral votes. The **Twenty-third Amendment**, ratified in 1961, gave Washington, D. C., the number of electors no larger than that of the smallest state, three. This brings the electoral vote total to 538—435 for the House Representatives total, plus 100 for the Senate seats, plus the three votes for the District of Columbia. The candidate who earns 270 electoral votes, a simple majority, will become president. If no presidential candidate receives a majority, then the U.S. House of Representatives votes, by delegations, choosing from among the top three candidates. Each state casts one vote for president, and whichever candidate receives 26 states or more wins. The Senate would then determine the vice president in the same manner.

Winner-Take-All Today, most states require their pledged electors (people already committed to a party's ticket) to follow the election day popular vote. Besides, electors are typically long-time partisans or career politicians who are ultimately appointed by the state party. The candidate who wins the **plurality** of the popular vote (the most, even if not the majority) in a given state will ultimately receive all that state's electoral votes. This is known as the **winner-take-all** system. Only Nebraska and Maine allow for a split in their electoral votes and award electors by congressional district rather than on a statewide basis.

In early December, electors meet in state capitals and cast their votes. The ballots are transported to Washington in locked boxes. When Congress opens in January, the sitting vice president counts these votes before a joint session of Congress. Since most states now require their electors to follow the popular vote, the electoral vote total essentially becomes known on election night in November. Television newscasters typically show a U.S. map with Republican victories depicted in red and Democratic victories in blue. Soon after popular votes are tabulated, losing candidates publicly concede and the winner gives a victory speech. The constitutionally required procedures that follow—states' electors voting in December and the Congress counting those votes in January—thus become more formal ceremony than suspenseful events.

Four times in American history the winner of the popular vote did not win the electoral vote. Al Gore's loss to George W. Bush in 2000 is the most recent example. This possibility has led some to criticize the electoral college system. Others see the process as a way to ensure balance and to guarantee that a consensus candidate becomes president. Gallup has found that more than 60 percent of those polled want a constitutional amendment to change the electoral system, while only about 33 percent want to keep it in its current form. A proposed constitutional amendment to scrap the system and replace it with a popular vote has been offered repeatedly in Congress for years.

Benefits of the Electoral College	Drawbacks of the Electoral College
• States retain their importance in electing the president.	• One candidate can win the popular vote and not win the electoral vote.
• Candidates must campaign and seek votes in most states rather than only heavily populated states.	• Electoral vote strength is higher, per capita, in smaller states.
• The practice guarantees a consensus president with broad support.	• The winner-take-all system discourages those who voted for the runner-up.
• States retain primacy if the election goes into the House and Senate.	• If the election goes to the House and Senate, these delegations can vote independently of their states.

Though the election is not fully determined until Congress counts the electoral votes, the American public usually knows the winner by the day following the election. If the officeholder wins by a strong margin, he or she might view it as a **mandate**, an electoral victory resulting from campaign promises, for the policies and programs articulated during the campaign.

Campaign Finance

"There are two things that are important in politics," asserted political boss Mark Hanna more than 100 years ago. "The first is money, and I can't remember what the second is." Hanna was not the first, nor the last, politician to realize that money is at the heart of politics. James Madison, for instance, lost his 1777 bid for re-election to the Virginia legislature because he did not spend the money to provide liquor at his rallies. The entanglement of money and politics reached new levels during the Industrial Revolution. Robber barons and captains of industry became fixtures in the political process largely due to their concern over the federal government's regulation of commerce. In the 1960s, television became the primary vehicle to communicate a candidate's message. The high cost of airtime made money even more essential, and thus campaigns became more susceptible to corruption. Congress has addressed campaign finance through a handful of laws during the twentieth century, especially in the 1970s. Since then, campaign finance law has taken some twists and turns with subsequent acts and Supreme Court decisions.

Early Regulation

As industry grew, corporations competed for government contracts and supported officeholders with campaign donations to gain access and influence. This situation escalated, and, after a 1905 scandal involving New York insurance companies, the federal government began to address it. "All contributions by corporations to any political committee or for any political purpose should be forbidden by law," Teddy Roosevelt stated in his 1905 message to Congress. "Directors should not be permitted to use stockholders' money for such purposes." This brought about the first federal ban on donations from federally incorporated businesses. The law applied to only a few companies, and it was hardly enforced. Over the next 60 years, Congress passed similar measures that required disclosure of all donations and a cap on candidates' total spending. These laws did not stop wealthy donors from gaining influence. In the 1928 election, 1 percent of donors to both political parties contributed more than half the money spent by the parties.

By the end of the Great Depression, the Democratic Party had made a firm alliance with labor unions and began to rely on them for income. Republican legislators responded by limiting labor's influence. The Taft-Hartley Act, among other measures, banned unions from making direct contributions to political candidates. Yet these regulations did little to curtail money's influence. Unions, corporations, and their leaders ignored the federal laws or found loopholes that allowed them to contribute indirectly.

The 1960 presidential election between John F. Kennedy and Richard Nixon proved a turning point in campaign spending. Television played a major role with the famous debates and with expensive campaign commercials. Kennedy's successor, Lyndon Johnson, expressed his concern about money and elections in his 1966 State of the Union address. Over the 1960s, the costs of national campaigns brought even greater attention to the issue.

Source: Granger, NYC

Television raised the financial stakes in campaigns, and it also shone a spotlight on image and appearance. In 1960, John Kennedy and Richard Nixon participated in the first nationally televised debate.

What do the numbers show? What happened to the cost of presidential campaigns in the post-World War II era? Which party spent more during each cycle? How often did the higher-spending party win the election? What factors may have caused the trend(s) in this table?

The Federal Elections Commission

In 1971, Congress passed the **Federal Elections Campaign Act (FECA)**, which tightened reporting requirements and limited candidates' expenditures. Americans became further concerned as the known total spent in the 1972 presidential race between Richard Nixon and George McGovern reached $91 million. As the Watergate scandal unfolded, Americans became disenchanted with their president and with the flow of money in national politics. The White House-sponsored Watergate break-in was not initially about money, but investigators and reporters soon realized how donors had subverted the groundbreaking yet incomplete 1971 act. Congress followed up with the 1974 amendment to the FECA.

The 1974 law prevented donors from giving more than $1,000 to any federal candidate and more than $5,000 to a political committee. It capped the total a candidate could donate to his or her campaign and set a maximum on how much the campaign could spend. The law created the **Federal Elections Commission (FEC)** to monitor and enforce the regulations. It also defined **political action committees**, declaring that they must have at least 50 members, must donate to at least five candidates, and must register with the FEC at least six months in advance of the election. The points below summarize the key provisions of the Federal Elections Campaign Act.

Key Provisions of the Federal Elections Campaign Act
• Limited an individual's contributions to $1,000
• Limited a candidate's own contribution to $50,000
• Defined and regulated donations of political action committees (PACs)
• Created a voluntary public fund to assist viable presidential candidates

Is That Constitutional? *Buckley vs. Valeo* (1976)

Does limiting overall expenditures and campaign donations violate the First Amendment's free speech clause? Yes and no. In January 1975, a large group of conservatives and liberals joined to overturn the FECA in the courts. Conservative New York Senator James Buckley teamed up with Democratic senator and past presidential candidate Eugene McCarthy, the American Civil Liberties Union, and the American Conservative Union to file suit against Secretary of the U.S. Senate Francis Valeo. They argued that the law unconstitutionally limited free speech. The lower courts upheld the law, but Buckley and the others appealed to the Supreme Court. In 1976 the Court upheld the $1,000 limit on individual donations and the $5,000 limit on PAC donations, claiming these were not violations of free speech. However, the Court also ruled that Congress cannot limit a candidate's spending of his or her own money, nor can it place a maximum on the overall receipts or expenditures for a campaign.

The FEC has unique structural traits so it can carry out several responsibilities. The FEC's board of commissioners is appointed by the president and approved by the Senate to oversee election law. This commission always has an equal number of Democrats and Republicans. The FEC requires candidates to register, or file for candidacy, and to report campaign donations and expenses quarterly. A candidate's entire balance sheet is available to the government and the public. The FEC has a staff of professionals that maintains these records and places the information online. At the site www.fec.gov, you can see which individuals or PACs contributed to the candidates and in what amounts. The FEC also has a legal department that prosecutes candidates who do not follow the prescribed laws. From 1980 to 2005, the FEC was involved in more than 530 court cases and prevailed in 90 percent of the cases that went to court. From 2000 to 2013, the commission closed 2,623 cases and issued fines to candidates for late filing and non-filing that amounted to nearly $5 million.

After *Buckley,* Congress and the Court ultimately reached consensus that unlimited donations make for unfair elections. Money continued to play an all-important role while FEC officials and politicians began a game of cat and mouse during subsequent election seasons. Regardless of how the Court ruled in *Buckley*, television advertising and money gained increased importance in campaigns while interest groups, politicians, and lawyers found loopholes in the law.

Matching Money The Federal Elections Commission continued to enforce the donor limits. Candidates, however, could once again dig deeply into their own pockets. Also in 1976, the national government established a system to offer some public financial support for presidential candidates who met the qualifications. In this system today, everyone who files a tax return is asked if they want to contribute $3. The federal government then uses that voluntarily donated money to match specified donations given to candidates in both the primary and general elections. In short, the federal government will match, dollar for dollar, all individual donations of $250 or less. To qualify, candidates must contribute no more than $50,000 of their own money. They must also raise at least $5,000 in each of 20 states in increments of $250 or less. The guidelines for the federal matching money ensure that candidates have a broad base of support from smaller donors. Minor party candidates can qualify for matching money too, but only if the party's candidate won more than 5 percent of the vote in the prior election. This is the only public finance system for candidates across the United States.

The FECA only addressed money going directly to and from a candidate's treasury. If a non-candidate wanted to spend money to impact an election— say, to buy a radio ad for or against a candidate—there were no limits. **Hard money**, donations given directly to a candidate, could be traced and regulated. But **soft money**, cash donations to a party or interest group, was not tracked. So the party could flood a congressional district with television ads that paint the opponent in a bad light, causing large, ultimately untraceable spending on electioneering at the end of a campaign. Unsurprisingly, soft money spending escalated.

In 1980, presidential candidate John Connally of Texas opted not to accept the matching money. For Connally and many financially well-off presidential candidates, it is more practical to pad the war chest with their own dollars than to seek matches to small donations. In 2000, George W. Bush also declined partial federal matching money. That year, total candidate spending reached a new high, $607 million (both primary and general elections).

This situation brought greater attention to soft money's influence on elections and highlighted how much that influence was able to subvert the spirit of the 1970s reforms. Senators John McCain and Russ Feingold had pushed for greater campaign finance regulations since the mid-1990s. After some modification, the **Bipartisan Campaign Reform Act (BCRA)** of 2002 finally passed the House with a 240–189 vote and the Senate with 60–40 vote. President Bush reluctantly signed the bill. The act banned soft money contributions to the national parties, increased the limits on hard money donations to $2,000 from individuals with an adjustment for inflation, $5,000 from PACs, and $25,000 from the national parties per election cycle. The law also placed an aggregate limit on how much an individual could donate to multiple candidates in a two-year cycle.

The BCRA prohibited corporations, trade associations, and labor organizations from paying for electioneering communications using campaign treasury money within 60 days of the general election and 30 days of a primary. The McCain-Feingold law also requires candidates to explicitly acknowledge approval of all TV ads. Television spots for federal candidates now must state, "I'm [candidate's name] and I approve this message."

Though the law was dubbed bipartisan, the vote in Congress and the reaction to the law has been somewhat partisan. Again an odd grouping of opponents joined to oppose the bill. McCain's Senate colleague Mitch McConnell of Kentucky, the ACLU, the AFL-CIO, and free speech advocates fought the law. In *McConnell v. FEC* (2003), the law was largely upheld. In the 2010 case of *Citizens United v. FEC*, which will be discussed in Chapter 7, the Supreme Court ruled that corporations have a right to free speech and cannot be denied that right in the final days before an election. The Court ruled in *McCutcheon v. FEC* (2013) that the free speech clause prevents Congress from limiting the aggregate total an individual may donate to various candidates.

REFLECT ON THE ESSENTIAL QUESTION

Essential Question: *How do U.S. citizens choose their elected officials in a free and fair society?* On a separate paper, complete a chart like the one below to gather details to answer that question.

Key Terms, Names, and Events (page 152)	The Significance of Each Term in Fair and Free Elections

Source: Steve Sisney / AP Images

On January 21, 2012, the second anniversary of the *Citizens United* decision, citizens in Oklahoma City gathered to protest the ruling.

To communicate information in the most effective and efficient way possible, researchers need to use a variety of tools, including both text and visuals such as graphs, diagrams, maps, photos, and artwork.

When you construct a visual, you synthesize text information by putting it into a new format. This process can help you emphasize important text information. Using visuals can also help you condense complex information and put it into a form that will be easily understood.

A visual should be as simple as possible while including all the graphic and textual information necessary to communicate its message. For example, if you were going to use a visual to show the evolution of U.S. campaign finance reform, you might create a timeline that tracks the dates of major changes to campaign finance policies over time. Or you might create a table or graph to compare campaign expenditures and distributions during several different election campaigns over a particular period of time.

You will need to be aware of formatting elements such as titles, headings, captions, and keys. These will help you to organize your information in the most effective way possible.

Practice: Present the war chest of your congressional representative or candidate. First, research your representative, congressional candidate, or other federal donations and expenditures at the FEC website (www.fec.gov). Then construct a chart, table, or other visual to communicate a trend you find there. For example, your visual might explain the chronology of donations and expenses, compare revenues from large and small donors or from individual vs. PACs, or outline donor demographics.

MULTIPLE-CHOICE QUESTIONS

1. Which type of primary election allows voters to declare their party affiliation on election day?

   (A) Blanket

   (B) Open

   (C) Closed

   (D) Runoff

   (E) Invisible

2. Which is the first official contest for presidential candidates seeking their party's nomination?

   (A) New Hampshire primary

   (B) Iowa caucuses

   (C) National convention

   (D) Televised debates between Republican and Democratic nominees

   (E) The vote in the Electoral College

3. The 2002 Bipartisan Campaign Reform Act

   (A) bans advertising for or against candidates

   (B) has decreased the amount spent in national elections

   (C) assures that citizens can donate whatever amount they want

   (D) was struck down in *Buckley v. Valeo*

   (E) limits soft money donations and requires candidates' explicit approval of all TV ads

4. Which of the following statements regarding public or televised debates in a campaign is true?

(A) Incumbents and front-runners desire more public debates.

(B) For televised debates, all candidates are entitled to participate.

(C) Candidates can be damaged by verbal slips and missteps.

(D) Election law states candidates must debate publicly.

(E) Debates are typically advantageous to the Democratic candidate.

5. What is the most expensive element of a political campaign?

(A) Television advertising

(B) Consultants and pollsters

(C) Journalists' interviews

(D) Yard signs and flyers

(E) Appearances on television news broadcasts

6. Which statement is accurate concerning incumbent candidates?

(A) The major parties rarely nominate incumbents as presidential candidates.

(B) Political action committees prefer to donate to challengers over incumbents.

(C) House incumbents tend to win re-election at higher rates than Senate incumbents.

(D) Incumbent candidates only succeed during hard economic times.

(E) Voters will not recognize an incumbent's name as quickly as a challenger's name.

7. Which statement regarding the Electoral College is true?

(A) The United States no longer uses the Electoral College system to elect the president.

(B) In order to win the presidency, a candidate must win a majority of electoral votes.

(C) No president has ever won the popular vote and not the electoral vote.

(D) Every state uses the winner-take-all system.

(E) If no candidate receives a majority, the U.S. Senate decides the presidential election.

President and Congress, Party in Power After General Elections, 1988–2002				
Year	President (party, % popular vote, electoral votes)	Runner-up (party, % popular vote, electoral votes)	House (seats by party)	Senate (seats by party)
1988	Bush (R) 53.4%; 426	Dukakis (D) 45.6%; 111	DEM 262; REP 173	DEM 55; REP 45
1990			DEM 267; REP 167	DEM 56; REP 44
1992	Clinton (D) 43.0%; 370	Bush (R) 37.4%; 168 Perot 18.9%; 0	DEM 258; REP 176	DEM 57; REP 43
1994			REP 230; DEM 204	REP 53; DEM 47
1996	Clinton (D) 49.2%; 379	Dole (R) 40.7%; 159 Perot 8.4%; 0	REP 228; DEM 206	REP 55; DEM 45
1998			REP 223; DEM 211	REP 54; DEM 46
2000	Bush (R) 47.9%; 271	Gore (D) 48.4%; 266	REP 220; DEM 215	REP 50; DEM 50
2002			REP 229; DEM 204	REP 51; DEM 48

8. Which of the following is true based on the information provided in the table?

    (A) Presidents rarely win the Electoral College vote.

    (B) The same party held the presidency from 1988 to 2002.

    (C) American elections can result in divided government.

    (D) Bob Dole won the presidency in 1996.

    (E) Democrats held the majority of seats in the House for most of the above period.

9. Which statement regarding front-loading is true?

    (A) States like Nebraska and Maine have scheduled their elections earlier than others.

    (B) Front-loading allows some states to cast electoral votes before others.

    (C) House elections are held earlier than Senate elections.

    (D) Some states schedule presidential primaries early to gain influence and revenues.

    (E) Front-loading occurs when election officials place a candidate at the top of the ballot.

10. Which statement about money and elections is true?

(A) The U.S. election system matches all dollars raised by presidential candidates.

(B) Corporations and labor unions can donate directly to federal campaigns as long as those donations are recorded and made public.

(C) There is no correlation between the money a candidate spends and electoral success.

(D) If willing to waive potential matching money, a candidate can donate unlimited amounts to his or her own campaign.

(E) The Federal Elections Commission was declared an unconstitutional body in *Buckley v. Valeo*.

FREE-RESPONSE QUESTIONS

Question

1. The Electoral College system was designed to award the office of president to a consensus candidate, yet some argue the system has prevented representative democracy.

(a) Identify and explain one feature of the Electoral College system that is intended to elect a consensus candidate for president.

(b) Identify and explain one feature of the Electoral College that prevents representative democracy.

(c) Identify one potential change to the Electoral College system and explain how this change could improve the presidential election process.

Question

2. Since the 1970s, competing views and governing institutions have established campaign finance regulation for federal elections.

(a) Identify and explain one responsibility of the Federal Elections Commission.

(b) Identify and explain one structural trait that allows the FEC to enforce campaign finance law.

(c) Select two elements of campaign finance below and explain how these elements impact campaign finance policy or enforcement.
- First Amendment
- Soft money
- *Buckley v. Valeo*
- Political action committees

WRITING: NOTICE AND USE DATES

In studying U.S. government and politics, you must also have some understanding of American history, dates, and sequences. This course is not a history course, nor will you be taking a history exam, but dates and sequences can be relevant to your answers.

Dates have been used as limiters in past FRQs. That is, they have set the timeframe your answer must address. In #2 on page 155, for example, the FRQ calls for post-1970 activity, so you know you should limit your discussion to relevant events or facts after 1970.

Correct dates can also help you strengthen your explanations. If you choose *Buckley v. Valeo* in question 2, including the date would only improve your response even though you are not required to know it.

7

Interest Groups

"By a faction, I mean a group of citizens ... united and actuated by some common passion or interest, adverse to the rights of other citizens, or to the aggregate interests of the community."

—James Madison, *Federalist #10, 1787*

Essential Question: How do citizens, businesses, and other interests influence lawmaking and policy in this country, and how has government regulated their actions?

At any level of government, people differ on the question of how to shape the law. Some citizens naturally become part of formal groups based on their common beliefs. James Madison and other founders expressed concern about factions, groups of "interested" men motivated by the pursuit of wealth, religious beliefs, or alliances with other countries. Today, these special interests, sometimes referred to as pressure groups or lobbies, are concerned with corporate profits, workers' rights, the environment, product safety, or other issues. Historic and recent accounts of bribery, scandal, and other unethical tactics have shaped the public's impression of these groups. Yet, the First Amendment guarantees the right of special interests to operate and express opinions.

Early Interest Groups

The first major growth of organized interests occurred in the late 1800s and continued throughout the Progressive Era. America rapidly went from being an agrarian economy to being a manufacturing nation. Immigrants arrived on both coasts, bringing a wide variety of viewpoints into the country. Factory workers banded together for protection against their bosses. War veterans returning from armed conflicts looked to the government for benefits. Women and minorities sought equality, justice, and the right to vote. Congress began taking on new issues, such as regulating railroads, addressing child labor, supporting farmers, and generally passing legislation that would advance the nation. As democracy increased, the masses pushed to have their voices heard.

Industrial Revolution

America's Industrial Revolution pitted corporate interests against the laboring class when manufacturing and railroad firms sent men to influence decisions in Washington. As more and more influential "lobby men" roamed the Capitol, these interests became known as the "third house of Congress."

Labor Organizes The American Federation of Labor (AFL) organized in 1886 under the leadership of Samuel Gompers. Initially the organization had about 140,000 members. The AFL's most useful tool was the labor strike—skilled workers simply banding together and refusing to work until the company met their demands. In 1892, the federation went on strike at Homestead near Pittsburg against Carnegie Steel. In 1893, Socialist Eugene Debs organized the American Railway Union. Within one year it had 150,000 members. In 1894 alone, about 750,000 total workers were on strike throughout the United States.

Labor unions also entered the political arena and pushed for legislation that protected workers against unhealthy and hazardous conditions. New state (and sometimes national) laws addressed child labor, maximum workday hours, and eventually minimum wage. Gompers met with lawmakers in New York and Washington. Debs became a working-class hero and ran five times for president as the Socialist Party candidate.

Corporations Respond Businesses soon organized in response to the growing labor movement. The National Association of Manufacturers (NAM) was founded in 1895. The U.S. Chamber of Commerce formed in 1912 from the many local chambers of commerce in cities across the country. Heavily financed, the NAM and the Chamber became deeply involved in politics. They both backed conservative presidential candidate William Howard Taft. The number of **trade associations** grew from about 800 in 1914 to 1,500 in 1923.

Organizing Progressives

The Progressive Era was a fertile period of American reform beyond labor issues. The growing country and the rise in immigration resulted in a push for greater levels of democracy and policies to assist the average American. The push for a women's suffrage amendment had been growing. African-American leaders and compassionate northern intellectuals sought to ease racial strife in both the South and the North. The Women's Christian Temperance Union wanted to eliminate consumption of alcohol. Many believed that the nation's cities had become overcrowded, filthy denizens of vice, and various groups formed to clean them up.

Constitutional Amendments The passage of three amendments—the Sixteenth, Seventeenth, and Nineteenth—contributed to interest group growth and activity. First, the **Sixteenth Amendment** empowered Congress to tax individual incomes, which enhanced the national treasury and encouraged groups to push for more services. The **Seventeenth Amendment** empowered citizens to elect their U.S. senators directly, replacing the old system in which state legislators and party caucuses picked the senators. Senators now had to consider the views of all voters, not just the elites. When the **Nineteenth**

Amendment guaranteed women the right to vote, it doubled the potential voting population. Caring and civic-minded women drew attention to urban decay, child labor, alcoholism, and other humanitarian concerns.

Progressive Era Interest Groups		
Group	Purpose	Founded
Veterans of Foreign Wars	To secure rights for military veterans	1899
National Association for the Advancement of Colored People	To advocate for racial justice and civil rights	1909
Urban League (originally called Committee on Urban Conditions Among Negroes)	To prevent discrimination, especially in northern cities	1910
U.S. Chamber of Commerce	To unify businesses and protect commercial affairs	1912
Anti-Defamation League	To stop bigotry and defamation of Jewish people	1913
American Farm Bureau	To make farming more profitable; to secure farmers' benefits	1919
American Legion	To assist war veterans, service members, and communities	1919
League of Women Voters	To assure good government	1920
American Civil Liberties Union	To guarantee free speech, separation of church and state, and fair trials	1920

Strong Interests and Government Concern

As the above table shows, national groups represented a variety of interests, and all wanted some influence on governmental decisions. President Woodrow Wilson often expressed his frustration over the tactics lobbyists employed. "Washington has seldom seen so numerous, so industrious, or so insidious a lobby," he once lamented when corporations opposed his tariff bill. "The newspapers are being filled with paid advertisements calculated to mislead the judgments of public men ... [and] the public opinion of the country itself."

The Roaring Twenties were boom times for several industries, including radio, automobiles, and utilities. After the 1929 stock market crash, the Great Depression leveled the United States economically, which led many to believe that business elites held too much power over workers. President Franklin Roosevelt's New Deal assisted unions and created a better balance of power between corporate interests and workers' rights. The **Wagner Act** guaranteed the right to strike and allowed unions to bargain collectively.

Exposing Lobbying Alabama Senator Hugo Black investigated one utility company's 1930s lobbying effort, as recounted by Kenneth Crawford in *The Pressure Boys*. Black became suspicious when very similarly worded letters opposing a bill to regulate electric utilities began to flood Capitol Hill. Black exposed the scheme when a 19-year-old Western Union messenger testified before the investigating Senate committee. A gas and electric company had paid a group of telegraph messenger boys to persuade Pennsylvania citizens to send telegrams opposing the bill to their congressmen. The company provided the talking points for the messages. One congressman received 816 of these telegrams in two days, mostly from citizens with last names that began with A, B, or C. As it turned out, the young messenger had pulled the names from a phone book starting from the beginning.

"The lobby has reached such a position of power that it threatens government itself," an outraged Senator Black said in a radio address. He went on to condemn the lobby's "capacity for evil, its greed, trickery, deception, and fraud." To Black's dismay, it turned out that the utility company had done nothing illegal, and this tactic continues today with email.

Proliferation

Since Madison wrote *Federalist #10*, the United States has developed into a complex web of viewpoints, each seeking to influence government at the national, state, and local levels. The nation's constitutional arrangement of government encourages voices in all three branches of government and at all three levels. This **pluralism**, a multitude of views that ultimately results in a consensus government, has intensified the ongoing competition among interests. Most of today's interest groups were created after World War II. The most rapid acceleration of organized interests resulted from events that took place during the 1960s. This increase in lobbying the government came about for many reasons. Postwar social movements created new organizations and strengthened old ones. The economic prosperity of the 1950s and 1960s brought middle-class affluence and shifted priorities for average citizens. As government grew and assumed new responsibilities, citizens came to expect more, and they organized to petition the government for assistance.

Social Movements, 1955–75

After World War II, workers' concerns, civil rights and women's equality, environmental pollution, and a rising consumer consciousness were the focus of leading social movements. Backing for these causes expanded during the turbulent 1960s as citizens began to rely less on political parties with general platforms and more on interest groups with very specific goals.

Labor The power of labor organizations reached new levels in the 1950s. In 1955 the American Federation of Labor merged with the Congress of Industrial Organizations (CIO), a large union composed of steelworkers, miners, and unskilled workers. The AFL-CIO became the leading voice for the working class. American union membership peaked in 1954 with roughly 28 percent of all households belonging to unions. In 1964, the nation's largest truckers' union, the Teamsters, signed a freight agreement that protected truckers across the country and increased the union's power. Union membership hovered near 1950s' levels until the early 1980s. Today, about 13 percent of households, or about 7 percent of American workers, belong to organized labor. The AFL-CIO includes 57 smaller unions, including the United Mine Workers and United Automobile, Aerospace and Agricultural Implement Workers of America, with about 12 million total members.

Civil Rights The National Association for the Advancement of Colored People (NAACP) and the Urban League were founded in 1909 and 1910, respectively, to seek racial equality and social fairness for African Americans. In the 1950s and 1960s, these groups experienced a dramatic rise in membership, which increased their influence in Washington. NAACP attorneys worked tirelessly to organize black communities to seek legal redress in the courts. The Urban League worked to increase membership to enhance its influence. Additional civil rights groups surfaced and grew. The Congress on Racial Equality (CORE) was founded at the University of Chicago and became instrumental in the nonviolent civil disobedience effort to desegregate lunch counters. Reverend Martin Luther King's Southern Christian Leadership Conference (SCLC), an organization of leading black southern clergymen, began a national publishing effort to create public awareness of racist conditions in the South. And the Student Non-Violent Coordinating Committee (SNCC) was a leading force in the dangerous Freedom Rides to integrate interstate bus lines and terminals. Whether in the courts, in the streets, or on Capitol Hill, most changes to civil rights policy and legislation resulted from these organizations' efforts.

Women's Movement A growing number of women entered public office. Federal laws began to address fair hiring, equal pay, and workplace discrimination. Both the 1963 Equal Pay Act and the 1964 Civil Rights Act addressed occupational equality.

Leading feminist Betty Friedan wrote *The Feminine Mystique* in 1963 and formed the National Organization for Women (NOW) in 1966. NOW had 200 chapters by the early 1970s and was joined by the National Women's Political Caucus and the National Association for the Repeal of Abortion Laws (NARAL) to create a coalition for feminist causes. These groups brought congressional passage of the Equal Rights Amendment (which failed in the state ratification battle) and Title IX, which brought more focus and funding equality to men's and women's school athletics. They also fought for the *Roe v. Wade* Supreme Court decision that prevented states from outlawing abortion.

Environmental Movement As activists drew attention to mistreatment of blacks and women, they also generated a consciousness about the misuse of our environment. Marine biologist Rachel Carson's best-selling book *Silent Spring* (1962) made a dramatic impact. Carson criticized the use of insecticides and other pesticides that harmed birds and other wildlife. Her chosen title referenced the decreased bird population that silenced an otherwise cheerful springtime. Organizations such as the Sierra Club, the Wilderness Society, and the Audubon Society expanded their goals and quadrupled their membership.

In 1963 and 1964, Congress passed the first Clean Water Act and Clean Air Act, respectively. The years of disregard of pollution and chemical dumping into the nation's waterways reached a crisis point in 1969 when Cleveland's

Cuyahoga River was so inundated with chemicals that it actually caught on fire. This crisis led to even stronger legislation and the creation of the Environmental Protection Agency in 1970. Earth Day became an annual event to focus on how Americans could help to preserve the environment.

Consumer Movement Consumers and their advocates began to demand that manufacturers take responsibility for making products safe. No longer was *caveat emptor* ("let the buyer beware") the guiding principle in the exchange of goods and services. In 1962 President Kennedy put forth a Consumers' Bill of Rights meant to challenge manufacturers and guarantee citizens' rights to product safety, information, and selection. By the end of the decade, the Consumer's Union established a Washington office, and activists formed the Consumer Federation of America. With new access to sometimes troubling consumer information, the nation's confidence in major companies dropped from 55 percent in 1966 to 27 percent in 1971.

Ralph Nader emerged as America's chief consumer advocate. As early as 1959 he published articles in *The Nation* condemning the auto industry. "It is clear Detroit is designing automobiles for style, cost, performance, and calculated obsolescence," Nader wrote, "but not for safety." In 1965 he published *Unsafe at Any Speed*, an exposé of the industry, especially General Motors' sporty Corvair. To counter Nader's accusations, GM hired private detectives to tail and discredit, and even blackmail him. When this effort came to light, a congressional committee summoned GM's president to testify and to apologize to Nader. That publicity that helped catapult Nader's book sales and his career. In 1966, Congress also passed the National Traffic and Motor Vehicle Safety Act, which, among other things, required seat belts in all new cars.

Constitutional Principles That Generate Groups

The American system of government, with policymaking bodies in multiple branches at multiple levels, is one factor in the the rise of interest groups.

Three Branches The three separate and equal branches of government, Madison argued in *The Federalist*, would prevent the domination and influence of factions or interests. However, modern interest groups have become adept at influencing policies in all three branches. Within each branch there are people and entities—individual members of Congress, a president's appointed staff, agency directors, and scores of federal courts—that have helped to increase special interest groups' efforts.

Federalism The division of powers among national and state governments has encouraged lobbying not only in Washington but also in every state capital across the land. State governments are based on the federal model: within each state branch is a multi-member legislature, state agencies, and various courts, all of which provide targets for interest groups. County and city governments also make major decisions on school funding, road construction, fire departments, water works, and garbage collection. Many of the national interest groups, such as the Fraternal Order of Police (FOP) or national teachers' unions, have local chapters to influence local decisions. Thus interests have an incentive to meet not only with national and state legislators but also with mayors, county administrators, and city council members.

First Amendment Those who wish to silence the voices of powerful interests need look no further than the First Amendment to understand why they can't. Interest groups are legal and constitutional because the amendment protects free speech, free association, and the right to petition the government. In response to escalating lobbying efforts over the years, however, Congress began in 1946 to require lobbyists to register with the House or Senate. The Supreme Court upheld lobbyists' registration requirements but also declared in *United States v. Harriss* (1954) that the First Amendment ensures anyone or any group the right to lobby.

Citizen Expectation and Involvement

The people's rising expectations of their government has also contributed to the proliferation of interest groups. The more government offers to the public, the more the populace will continue to expect of the government. Through such programs as FDR's New Deal and the Great Society programs of the 1960s, the federal government increased programs and services. In 1945, Congress had 135 committees and subcommittees. By 1975 there were 313. Interest groups could no longer rely on connections with congressional leaders alone. They needed connections with committee chairpersons, key members, and staffers.

In recent times, new media forms and changing government customs have allowed people outside of Washington to keep abreast of the events and actions within the capital. Congress opened its committee hearings decades ago, and today these are televised. Roll call votes are more accessible as well. This visibility enables groups and their members to monitor and understand government, which in turn allows them to find effective ways to influence it.

Mobilization and Counter-Mobilization

In some ways, as author Robert Kaiser reports, Washington politics parallels Isaac Newton's third law of motion: every action seems to produce an equal and opposite reaction. Group growth results from successive waves of mobilization and counter-mobilization. The late 1800s labor movement brought manufacturing and trade associations. The rise of consumers' rights and environmental organizations in the 1960s caused pro-business groups to react in the 1970s.

The 1980s animal rights movement and the reaction that followed provide an interesting example. The People for the Ethical Treatment of Animals (PETA) and other groups against animal cruelty campaign for vegetarianism and against the use of animal products such as wool, milk, meat, and eggs. PETA grew from about 20,000 members in 1984 to more than half a million in 2001. A recent estimate tabulated the total membership of animal rights groups at 10 million.

PETA's protests and expectations—it recommended Ben and Jerry's use human breast milk instead of cows' milk for its ice cream—have encouraged an anti-animal rights movement. Farm and medical groups have joined the countercause. Examples include the Incurably Ill For Animal Research, the Foundation for Animal Health (an offshoot of the American Medical Association), and Putting People First. These groups complain that animal rights organizations "insist every form of life is equal: humans and dogs and slugs and cockroaches," and claim to speak for the average American who "eats meat, drinks milk, benefits from medical research, wears leather, wool, and fur, hunts, and fishes, and owns a pet and goes to the zoo."

Groups and Members

Interest groups fall into a handful of categories. These consist of institutional (corporate and intergovernmental groups), professional, ideological, member-based, and public interest groups. There is some overlap among these. For example, business groups want to make profits, but they also have a distinct ideology when it comes to taxation and business regulation. Likewise, citizens groups have members who may pay modest dues, but these groups mostly push for laws that benefit society at large. Nonprofit interest organizations fall into two categories based on their tax classification. The **501(c)(3)** organizations, such as churches and certain hospitals, receive tax deductions for charitable donations and can influence government, but they cannot lobby government officials or donate to campaigns. By comparison, **501(c)(4)** groups, such as certain social welfare organizations, can lobby and campaign.

Institutional Groups

Institutional groups break down into several different categories, including intergovernmental groups, professional associations, and corporations.

Intergovernmental Groups The U.S. system of redistributing federal revenues through the state governments encourages government-associated interest groups. Governors, mayors, and members of state legislatures are all interested in receiving funding from Washington. The federal grants system and marble cake federalism discussed in Chapter 2 increase state, county, and city interest in national policy. Governments and their employees—police, firefighters, EMTs, and sanitation workers—have a keen interest in government rules that affect their jobs and funding that impacts their salaries. This interest has created the **intergovernmental lobby**, which includes the National Governors Association, the National League of Cities, and the U.S. Conference of Mayors, all of which have offices in the nation's capital.

Professional Associations Unlike labor unions that might represent pipefitters or carpenters, **professional associations** typically represent particular white-collar professions. Examples include the American Medical Association (AMA) and the American Bar Association (ABA). They are concerned with business success and the laws that guide their trade. Police and teachers unions, such as the Fraternal Order of Police or the National Education Association, are often associated with the labor force, but in many ways they fall into this category. The AMA endorsed the 2010 Affordable Care Act. The ABA rates judicial nominees and testifies before Congress about proposed crime bills.

Corporations In the 1970s, the consumer and environmental movements brought an increase in business and free enterprise lobbyists. The National Association of Manufacturers and the U.S. Chamber of Commerce merged resources to form a joint political action committee. By the late 1970s, both groups had convinced Congress to deregulate. The Chamber's membership grew at a rate of 30 percent per year, expanding its $20 million budget and 50,000 members to $65 million and 215,000 members by 1983.

The Business Roundtable, formed in 1973, represents firms that account for nearly half of the nation's gross domestic product. New conservative **think tanks**—research institutions, often with specific ideological goals— emerged and old ones revived, such as the American Enterprise Institute and the Heritage Foundation, largely to counter the more liberal ideas coming from philanthropic foundations.

As writer John Judis explains, in 1971, only 175 businesses registered lobbyists in Washington. By 1982, there were 2,445 companies that had paid lobbyists. The number of corporate offices in the capital jumped from 50 in 1961 to 500 in 1978 and to 1,300 by 1986. By 1978, 1,800 trade associations were headquartered in the nation's capital. Today, Washington has an army of lawyers and public relations experts whose job it is to represent corporate interests and lobby the government for their corporate clients.

Member Groups

Most groups have a defined membership and member fees, typically ranging from $15 to $40 annually. (Corporate and professional associations typically charge much higher fees.) When groups seek to change or protect a law, they represent their members and even nonmembers who have not joined. For example, there are many more African Americans that approve of the NAACP's goals and support their actions than there are actual NAACP members. There are more gun advocates than members of the National Rifle Association (NRA). These nonmembers choose not to bear the participation costs of time and fees but do benefit from the associated group's efforts. This results in what is known as the **free rider** problem. Groups that push for a collective benefit for a large group inevitably have free riders.

To encourage membership, interest groups offer incentives. **Purposive incentives** are those that give the joiner some philosophical satisfaction. They realize their money will contribute to some worthy cause. **Solidary incentives** are those that allow people of like mind to gather on occasion. Many groups offer **material incentives**, such as travel discounts, subscriptions to magazines or newsletters, or complimentary items such as bags or jackets.

One study found that the average interest group member's annual income is $17,000 higher than the national average, and that 43 percent of interest group members have advanced degrees, suggesting that interest group membership has an **upper-class bias**. Though annual membership fees in most interest groups are modest, critics argue that the trend results in policies that favor the higher socioeconomic classes.

Public Interest Groups

As opposed to special interest groups, **public interest groups** are geared to improve life or government for the masses. Fully 30 percent of such groups have formed since 1975, and they constitute about one-fifth of all groups represented in Washington.

Common Cause In 1970, Republican John Gardner, Lyndon Johnson's Secretary of Health, Education, and Welfare, took what he called the biggest gamble of his career to create Common Cause. "Everybody's organized but the people," Garner declared when he put out the call to recruit members to build "a true citizens' lobby." Within six months Common Cause had more than 100,000 members. The antiwar movement and the post-Watergate reform mindset contributed to the group's early popularity. Common Cause's accomplishments include the **Twenty-sixth Amendment** to grant voting rights to those 18 and over, campaign finance laws, transparent government, and other voting reforms. More recently, the group pushed for the Bipartisan Campaign Reform (McCain-Feingold) Act and the 2007 lobbying regulations. Today Common Cause has nearly 400,000 members and 38 state offices.

Public Citizen With money from a legal settlement with General Motors, Ralph Nader joined with other consumer advocates to create Public Citizen in 1971. He hired bright, aggressive lawyers who came to be known as Nader's Raiders. In 1974, *U.S. News and World Report* ranked Nader as the fourth most influential man in America. Carrying out ideals similar to those that Nader had emphasized in the 1960s—consumers' rights and open government—Public Citizen tries to ensure that all citizens are represented in the halls of power. It fights against undemocratic trade agreements and provides a "countervailing force to corporate power." Nader went on to create other watchdog organizations, such as the Center for Responsive Law and Congress Watch, to address the concerns of ordinary citizens who don't have the resources to organize and lobby government.

Ideological and Single-Issue Groups

Some groups have very specific goals or are concerned about one particular area of the law. Three powerful and effective groups are the National Rifle Association, the American Civil Liberties Union, and the American Association of Retired Persons.

National Rifle Association The National Rifle Association has gone from post–Civil War marksmen's club to pro-gun beltway powerhouse. Its original charter was to improve the marksmanship of military soldiers. After a 1968 gun control and crime law, this **single-issue group** appealed to sportsmen and Second Amendment advocates. Its revised 1977 charter states the NRA is "generally to encourage the lawful ownership and use of small arms by citizens of good repute."

In 2001 *Fortune* magazine named the NRA the most powerful lobby in America. Hundreds of employees work at its Fairfax, Virginia, headquarters. The NRA appeals to law enforcement officers and outdoorsmen with insurance policies, discounts, and its magazine *American Rifleman*. The group holds periodic local dinners for "Friends of the NRA" to raise money. The annual convention provides a chance for gun enthusiasts to mingle and view the newest firearms, and attendance reaches beyond 50,000.

The Brady Bill, which mandates automatic waiting periods and background checks for handgun purchasers, along with the 1992 election of President Bill Clinton, caused NRA membership to soar from 2.5 million to 3.4 million, with many free riders deciding to join. The NRA endorses candidates from both major political parties but heavily favors Republicans. From 1978 to 2000 the organization spent more than $26 million in elections; $22.5 million went to GOP candidates and $4.3 went to Democrats.

American Civil Liberties Union Activists created the American Civil Liberties Union after World War I to counteract government's authoritarian interpretation of the First Amendment. At that time, the federal government deported radicals and threw dissenters of the war and the military draft in jail. Guaranteeing free expression became the ACLU's central mission. In 1925, the organization went up against Tennessee state law to defend John Scopes's right to teach evolution in a public school.

Over the following decades, the ACLU opened state affiliates and took on other civil liberties violations. It remains very active, serving as a watchdog for free speech, fair trials, and racial justice and against overly aggressive law enforcement. In 2010, its executive director predicted in its ninetieth anniversary newsletter, "Same sex marriage will spread ... to achieve national legitimacy ... marijuana will continue to gain acceptance as a medical treatment ... and the United States will finally abolish the death penalty." The ACLU has about half a million members, about 200 attorneys, a presence on Capitol Hill, and chapters in all 50 states.

American Association of Retired Persons The American Association of Retired Persons (AARP) has the largest membership of any interest group in the nation. AARP has twice the membership of the AFL-CIO, its own zip code in Washington, and its own registered in-house lobbyists. Its magazine has the largest circulation of any monthly publication in the country. People age 50 and over can join by paying $16 per year. The organization's main concerns are members' health, financial stability and livelihood, and the Social Security system. "AARP seeks to attract a membership as diverse as America itself," its Web site claims. With such a large, high voter-turnout membership, elected officials tend to pay very close attention to AARP.

Influencing Policy

Interest groups take on a variety of activities using a variety of techniques. **Insider strategies** quietly persuade government decision makers through exclusive access. The most common form of insider activity is **direct lobbying** of legislators. **Outsider strategies** involve lawsuits or get-out-the vote drives. Groups also try to sway public opinion by issuing press releases, writing op-ed articles for newspapers, appearing as experts on television, and purchasing print and TV advertising. They also mobilize their membership to call or write legislators on pending laws or to swing an election.

Lobbying Legislators

The term **lobbying** came into vogue in the mid-1600s when the anteroom of the British House of Commons became known as "the lobby." **Lobbyists** were present at the first session of the U.S. Congress in 1789. As Kaiser reports, wealthy New York merchants engaged House and Senate members to delay action on a tariff bill they thought would hurt their profits. They soon employed what would become a classic tactic—a good dinner with plenty of alcohol to help create the type of warm, friendly atmosphere the favor seeker needed to make his case.

Lobbyists attend Washington social gatherings to develop relationships through their contacts who have **access** to government officials. They monitor legislators' proposed bills and votes. They assess which lawmakers support their cause and which do not. They also help draft bills that their congressional allies introduce. They find which lawmakers are undecided and try to bring them over to their side. "Influence peddler" is a derogatory term for a lobbyist, but influencing lawmakers is exactly what lobbyists try to do.

Give and Take Lobbyists want access to legislators, and Congress members appreciate the information lobbyists can provide. Senators and house members represent the individual constituents living in their districts. Sometimes so-called special interests actually represent large swaths of a given constituency. A lobbyist for a defense contractor that sells fighter jets to the Pentagon represents his company but might also speak for hundreds of plant workers. Democracy purists argue that a lawmaker should disregard a heavily financed influence peddler, but most members of Congress recognize the useful byproduct—the resources lobbyists offer.

For example, imagine a North Carolina representative has a meeting with a tobacco lobbyist, who is concerned about a pending bill that further taxes and regulates the sale of cigarettes. The tobacco company sees the bill as dangerous to its bottom-line profits.

The lobbyist presents the legislator with the results of an opinion poll—an expensive endeavor—that shows 57 percent of registered voters in his district oppose the bill. The lobbyist also points out that the tax increase will increase black market sales. The lobbyist then hands the lawmaker a complete report at the end of the meeting. Could the poll or report be bogus? Probably not. Lobbyists have an agenda, but they are generally looking to foster a long-term relationship. "[T]hey know that if they lie, they lose," Congressman Barney Frank once declared. "They will never be allowed to come back to this office."

Imagine further that the following day the lawmaker meets with a representative from the American Heart Association. He provides a medical research study about cigarette prices as a deterrent to new smokers. He also provides poll results from a nationwide survey on smoking in public places.

The elected official has now spent only a couple hours to obtain valuable information with no money spent by his office. With that information, he can represent more of his constituents while considering attitudes and factors across the country. "I help my boss the most," declared one congressional staffer, "when I can play the good lobbyists off each other."

Key Targets and Strategizing No one is more effective in lobbying a legislator than another lawmaker. In the early stages of a legislative fight, influential members of Congress, especially those serving on key committees, become interest group targets. Some legislators give cues to other members, so lobbyists target them first.

To what degree do lobbyists move legislators on an issue? Do they persuade members to change their votes? Little evidence exists, Cigler and Loomis offer, to show that lobbyists actually change legislators' votes. Most findings do not prove lobbyists are successful in "bribing" legislators. Also, lobbyists tend to interact mostly with those members already in favor of the group's goals. So the money didn't bring the legislators over to the interest group; the legislator's position on the issue brought the interest group to him or her.

BY THE NUMBERS How Lobbyists Spend Their Time	
Activity	**Percent**
Client interaction: informing clients, discussing strategy	14%
Legislative activity: providing information/researching bills/ drafting bills	35%
Implementation: testifying on bills/filing amicus briefs	10%
Electoral activity: advertising, making PAC donations	11%
Other activity: meetings, business development/media commentary, etc.	31%

Source. Rogan Kersh, in Cigler and Loomis, *Interest Group Politics*, 2002

What do the numbers show? What activities dominate a congressional lobbyist's workload? What different skills must congressional lobbyists have? What percent of a lobbyist's time involves campaigns and elections?

Researcher Rogan Kersh conducted a unique two-year study of corporate lobbyists. "I'm not up here to twist arms and change somebody's vote," one lobbyist told him in a Senate anteroom crowded with lobbyists from other firms, "and neither are most of them." These lobbyists seem more concerned with waiting, gossiping, and rumor trading. A separate study conveyed that lobbyists want information or legislative intelligence as much as the lawmakers do. "If I'm out playing golf with some congressman or I buy a senator lunch, I know I'm not buying a vote," one lobbyist declared before recent reforms. The lobbyist is simply looking for the most recent views of lawmakers in order to act upon them. Kersh tabulated congressional lobbyists' legislative activities. A lobbyist attempting to alter a legislator's position occurred only about 1 percent of the time.

Research and Expertise Large interest groups have created entire research departments to study their concerns. "How many lives would be saved if government raised the drinking age from 18 to 21?" Mothers Against

Drunk Driving wanted to know. "What kind of a Supreme Court justice would nominee Clarence Thomas make?" the American Bar Association pondered. These are the kinds of questions that members of Congress also asked as they contemplate legislative proposals. During the investigatory phase of lawmaking, experts from these groups testify before congressional committees to offer their findings.

Campaigns and Electioneering

As extended congressional careers have become more common, interest groups have developed large arsenals to help or hinder a legislator's chances at election time. Once new methods—TV ads, polling, direct mail, and marketing—determined re-election success, politicians found it increasingly difficult to resist interest groups that had perfected these techniques and that offered greater resources to loyal officials.

Endorsements and Ratings A powerful interest group can influence the voting public with an endorsement. The Fraternal Order of Police can usually speak to a lawmaker's record on law enforcement legislation and financial support for police departments. The NRA endorses its loyal congressional allies on the cover of the November issue of its magazine, printed uniquely for each district. Groups also rate members of Congress based on their roll call votes, some with a letter grade (A through F), others with a percentage. Americans for Democratic Action and the American Conservative Union, two ideological organizations, rate members after each congressional term.

Political Action Committees Many interest groups create **political action committees (PACs)**. Typically defined as the political arm of a labor union, interest group, or corporation, PACs involve themselves in a wide array of election season activities, such as sending direct mail, creating advertising, staging rallies, and campaigning door-to-door. Politicians and party-driven organizations can also form what are known as **leadership PACs**. Leading up to her 2008 presidential run, Hillary Clinton created Hill-PAC, a committee to raise money that she distributed to other candidates in return for support in her presidential campaign.

Interest groups, corporations, and unions are forbidden from donating directly to candidates, but their PACs can contribute up to $5,000 per election cycle ($10,000 combined for primary and general elections). Since costly television advertising dramatically impacts elections, PAC support is a valuable asset. To get a return on their investment, PACs tend to support incumbents that side with them. The 1970s campaign finance laws caused a drastic increase in the number of PACs. In 1974, 608 committees registered with the Federal Elections Commission. Ten years later, 4,009 did so. Direct contributions rose from $23 million in 1975–76 to nearly $260 million in the 1999–2000 cycle. In 2008, contributions to House and Senate candidates reached nearly $400 million.

		BY THE NUMBERS			
		Growth in Political Action Committees, 1974–2012			
Year	Corporate	Labor	Trade/Member	Other	Total
1974	89	201	318	NA	608
1978	433	224	489	873	1,146
1982	1,469	380	649	873	3,371
1984	1,682	394	698	1,235	4,009
1988	1,816	354	786	1,312	4,268
1992	1,735	347	770	1,343	4,195
1996	1,642	332	838	1,267	4,079
2000	1,523	316	812	1,055	3,706
2004	1,555	303	877	1,305	4,040
2008	1,551	264	962	1,474	4,251
2012	1,851	300	1,033	2,319	5,503

Source: Federal Elections Commission. "Other" includes nonconnected, privately owned companies and leadership PACs.

What do the numbers show? To what extent have PACs grown since 1974? When did the total PAC count peak or level off? What types have grown at the fastest rates?

Interest groups and their PACs can also spend money to affect the election without directly writing a check to the candidate. These soft-money contributions or independent expenditures pay for fund-raisers, meet-and-greets, ads, and other campaign activities.

Grassroots Lobbying

Grassroots lobbying, generally an outsider technique, takes place when an interest group tries to inform, persuade, and mobilize large numbers of people. Originally practiced by the more modest citizens and issue advocacy groups, Washington-based interests are increasingly relying on grassroots techniques to influence officials inside the Beltway.

Insiders Mobilizing the Masses Grassroots lobbying focuses on the next election, regardless of how far away it might be. In 1982, soon after Republican Senator Bob Dole and Democratic Representative Dan Rostenkowski introduced a measure to withhold income taxes from interest earned on bank accounts and dividends, the American Banking Association went to work encouraging banks to persuade their customers against the measure. *The Washington Post* called it the "hydrogen bomb of modern day lobbying." Banks used advertisements and posters in branch offices; they also inserted flyers in monthly bank statements mailed out to every customer, telling them to contact their legislators in opposition to the proposed law. Banks generated nearly 22 million constituent communications. Weeks later the House voted 382–41, and the Senate 94–5, to oppose the previously popular bipartisan proposal.

Framing the Issue When the debate over the Clean Air Bill of 1990 began, *Newsweek* asked how automakers could squash legislation that improved fuel efficiency and reduced both air pollution and America's reliance on foreign oil. A prominent grassroots consultant reasoned that smaller cars—which would be vital if the act were to be successful—would negatively impact child safety, senior citizens' comfort, and disabled Americans' mobility. Opponents of the bill contacted and mobilized senior organizations and disability rights groups to create opposition to these higher standards. What was once viewed as an anti-environment vote soon became a vote that was pro-disabled people and pro-child.

Television and Telephones Television and telephones have encouraged grassroots lobbyists and issue advocacy groups. Depending on their tax classification, some groups cannot suggest a TV viewer vote for or against a particular congressperson. So instead they provide some detail on a proposed policy and then tell the voters to call the senator and express their feelings on the issue. Such ads have become backdoor campaigning. They all but say, "Here's the congressperson's position. You know what to do on election day."

The restaurant industry responded rapidly to a 1993 legislative idea to remove the tax deduction for business meals. Everyday professionals conducting lunchtime business in restaurants are able to write off the expense at tax time. As Congress debated changing that deduction, special interests acted. The National Restaurant Association (sometimes called "the other NRA") sponsored an ad that showed an overworked waitress-mother: "I'm a waitress and a good one….But I might not have a job much longer. President Clinton's economic plan cuts business-meal deductibility. That would throw 165,000 people out of work. I need this job." Opposition to eliminating the tax benefit no longer came from highbrow, lunchtime dealmakers but instead from those wanting to protect hardworking waitresses, cooks, and dishwashers. At the end of the ad, the waitress directed concerned viewers to call a toll-free number. Callers were put through to the corresponding lawmaker's office with the push of a button. The "other NRA" successfully stopped the bill.

Grasstops Interest groups increase their chances of success when they reach the masses, but they also target opinion leaders, those who can influence others. Lobbying firms try to connect with business owners or lesser officials in a community—the **grasstops**—to shape opinion on the local level. Some lobbyists charge $350 to $500 for getting a community leader to communicate his or her feelings to a legislator in writing or on the phone. They also set up personal meetings between high-profile constituents and members of Congress. Grasstops lobbying sometimes shifts public opinion in the desired direction; for example, it might cherry-pick selected opinions that create an artificial view, sometimes called "Astroturf."

Congressional lobbyists sometimes also use grassroots techniques in tandem with their Washington, D.C., operations. Once they determine a legislator's anticipated position, especially if it is undecided, lobbyists can pressure that congressperson by mobilizing constituents in his or her district. Interest group leaders send out letters that provide an outline or talking points so their members can easily create a factual letter to send to their representative. With email, this technique became easier, cheaper, and more commonly used than ever before. With the click of a mouse, interest group members can forward a message to a lawmaker to signal where they stand and how they will vote.

Is That Constitutional? *Citizens United v. FEC* (2010)

Does a government limitation on groups' advertising or spending constitute a denial of free speech? Yes. In part, the BCRA prevented corporations or nonprofit agencies from engaging in "electioneering communications," primarily TV campaign ads 60 days before the general election. The Court said this violated the First Amendment's free speech clause.

In 2008, the conservative group Citizens United produced *Hillary: The Movie*, which was meant to derail Clinton's chance for the presidency. The law prevented the film's airing, but the group appealed to the Supreme Court. The Court ruled in January 2010 in a 5–4 majority that corporations, labor unions, and other organizations could now use funds from their treasuries to endorse or denounce a candidate at any time provided ads are not coordinated with any candidate.

The Court, like the country, split along ideological lines. Free speech advocates, libertarians, and many Republicans view most campaign finance regulations as infringements on their freedoms. President Obama criticized the ruling at his 2010 State of the Union address as a decision that would "open the floodgates to special interests."

Connecting with the Executive

Interest groups and industry representatives also lobby the executive branch. Leaders of major organizations, from the civil rights groups of the 1960s to business leaders today, visit the White House and gain access to the president. Martin Luther King Jr., Roy Wilkins of the NAACP, and others met with Lyndon Johnson to shape civil rights legislation and enforcement. And President Obama heard from members of the Chamber of Commerce as he fashioned his health care bill. More often, liaisons from powerful interest groups connect with White House staffers to discuss policy. This practice is particularly useful in view of the fact that so much policy—legislation and enforcement—comes from the president.

Bureaucratic agencies write and enforce specific policies that regulate industries. High-level experts at television networks might connect with the Federal Communications Commission as it revises its rules. Representatives of the National Association of Manufacturers may attempt to influence the implementation of environmental legislation by meeting with officials at the Environmental Protection Agency.

In the Courts

Interest groups also shape policy in the courts. Federal judges are not elected and cannot accept donations from PACs, and lobbyists don't try to woo judges over lunch or in their closed chambers. Yet an open and honest presentation by an interest group in a trial or in an appeals court hearing is quite common. This can be done in three major ways: representing clients in court, filing an *amicus curiae* brief, and challenging executive regulatory action.

Representing Clients Established interest groups have legal departments with expert attorneys who both seek out clients to represent and accept those who request them. Compassionate groups defend those who cannot provide their own counsel or those who are wrongly accused, to assure justice. The NAACP Legal Defense Fund has represented scores of wrongly accused African-American defendants. The ACLU has defended free speech rights and regularly defends those facing the death penalty. At other times, cases are taken to establish a higher principle or to declare an unjust law unconstitutional. If an interest group wins a case in the Supreme Court, the victory can create a new national policy.

Amicus Curiae Legal departments often file an **amicus curiae**, or "friend of the court," brief in cases in which they have an interest but no client. The amicus brief argues why the court should side with one party in the case. In this instance, the interest group acts as a third party merely expressing an outside opinion. Groups include their research findings in these briefs as experts on matters that are important to them to persuade judges.

ACLU Action in Supreme Court		
Year	Case	Outcome
1961	*Engle v. Vitale*	Outlawed New York's state-sponsored school prayer
1967	*Loving v. Virginia*	Ended state laws against interracial marriage
1969	*Tinker v. Des Moines*	Overturned student suspensions for protesting Vietnam War
1971	*New York Times v. US*	Prevented government prior restraint of news publication
1997	*Reno v. ACLU*	Internet speech gained full First Amendment protection
2003	*Lawrence v. Texas*	Overturned state laws against same-sex intimacy

The ACLU has represented clients or filed *amicus* briefs in the above cases.

Challenging Regulatory Decisions Federal regulatory agencies such as the Food and Drug Administration or the Environmental Protection Agency can issue fines and other punishments to companies that violate regulations. Corporations can challenge these decisions in the U.S. Circuit Court of Appeals.

Ethics and Reform

Lobbyists work for many different interests. The Veterans of Foreign Wars seeks to assist military veterans. The Red Cross, United Way, and countless public universities across the land employ lobbyists to seek funding and support. Yet the increased number of firms that have employed high-paid consultants to influence Congress and the increased role of PAC money in election campaigns have given lobbyists and special interests a mainly negative public reputation. The salaries for successful lobbyists typically outstrip those of the public officials they seek to influence. Members of Congress and their staffs can triple their salaries if they leave Capitol Hill to become lobbyists. This situation has created an era in which careers on **K Street**—the noted Washington street that hosts a number of interest group headquarters or lobbying offices—are more attractive to many than careers in public service. Still, old and recent bribery cases, lapses of ethics, and conflicts of interest have led to strong efforts at reform.

Scandals

Bribery in Congress, of course, predates formal interest groups. In the 1860s Credit Mobilier scandal, a holding company sold nominally priced shares of railroad stock to congressmen in return for favorable votes on pro-Union Pacific Railroad legislation. A century ago, *Cosmopolitan* magazine ran a series entitled "Treason in the Senate" that exposed nine senators for bribery. In the late 1940s, the "5 percenters," federal officials who offered government favors or contracts in exchange for a 5 percent cut, went to prison. Over the years, Congress has had to pass several laws to curb influence and create greater transparency.

Congressional Acts on Lobbying
• Federal Regulation of Lobbying Act (1946)
• Lobbying Disclosure Act (1995)
• Honest Leadership and Open Government Act (2007)

The high-profile cases of congressmen Randall "Duke" Cunningham and William Jefferson and lobbyist Jack Abramoff created headlines in 2006 that exposed lawlessness taking place inside the lawmaking process. Cunningham, a San Diego Republican representative, took roughly $2.4 million in bribes to direct Pentagon military defense purchases to a particular defense contractor. A California contractor supplied Cunningham with lavish gifts and favors such as cash, a Rolls-Royce, antique furniture, and access to prostitutes. He was convicted in 2006. In Louisiana Congressman William Jefferson's case, an FBI probe uncovered $90,000 in cash hidden in his home freezer, which led to his bribery conviction.

A more publicized scandal engulfed lobbyist Jack Abramoff, whose client base included several Native American casinos. He pled guilty in January 2006 to defrauding four wealthy tribes and other clients of nearly $25 million as well as evading $1.7 million in taxes.

Recent Reform

Congress responded with the **Honest Leadership and Open Government Act** in 2007. New rules banned all gifts to members of Congress or their staff from registered lobbyists or their clients. It also banned members from flying on corporate jets in most circumstances and restricted travel paid for by outside groups. The 2007 law also outlawed lobbyists from buying meals, gifts, and most trips for congressional staffers. Lobbyists must now file reports quarterly instead of twice a year. The new law also requires members to report the details of any bundling—raising large sums from multiple donors for a candidate. Lobbyists that bundle now have to report it if the combined funds equal more than $15,000 in any six-month period. Also, for the first time ever, lobbyists that break ethics rules will face civil and criminal penalties of up to $200,000 in fines and five years in prison. The Abramoff scandal brought an end to former House and Senate members' Capitol Hill gym privileges. Many of those former members had become lobbyists, and the gym had become a place where both heavy lifting and heavy lobbying took place.

Revolving Door

Another key problem with lobbying is known as the **revolving door**. Many officials leave their jobs on Capitol Hill or in the Executive Branch to lobby the government they departed. Some members of Congress take these positions after losing an election. Others realize they can make more money by representing industry instead of citizens. While serving in the House or Senate, legislators gain hands-on understanding of the legislative process. When they leave office, they have the phone numbers of key committee chairmen already in their cell phones. Later as lobbyists, they can serve their clients with both expertise and immediate access. Congressional staffers, too, are known for seeking jobs as lobbyists—especially if they have worked on key committees. The average term for a congressional staffer is about two years. Many who work under the president also find it lucrative to leave the Pentagon to lobby for defense contractors or to leave the Department of Agriculture to lobby for large agricultural firms.

A Public Citizen study found that half the senators and 42 percent of House members who left office between 1998 and 2004 became lobbyists. Another study found that 3,600 former congressional aides had passed through the revolving door. The Center for Responsive Politics identified 310 former Bush and 283 Clinton appointees as lobbyists working in the capital. As of late 2014, 143 former members of Congress serve as registered lobbyists.

As author Robert Kaiser explains, when former Senate Majority Leader Trent Lott abruptly announced his retirement, it soon became clear why. He wanted to leave within a year of his new six-year term to avoid the impact of a 2007 law and join friend and former Louisiana senator John Breaux to start a lobbying firm. Recent reform requires outgoing senators, their senior aides, and officials in the executive branch to wait two years before becoming lobbyists. House members must wait only one year. This period is meant to at least slow down the revolving door. Lott got around the requirement by leaving office just before the new reform law took effect.

After Citizens United

Not long after, the **super PAC**, known in legal terms as an independent expenditure-only committee, became a player in national politics. Powerful PACs receive unlimited donations, and they can raise and spend as much as they want on electioneering communication provided they disclose their donors and don't coordinate with any candidate. The 501(c)(4) groups, so named for the relevant part of the tax code, need not disclose donors but cannot spend as freely. Critics refer to them as dark money groups. They accounted for more than one-fourth of outside group spending in 2012.

The spending by nonparty outside groups tripled during the period 2008–2012 and topped the historic outside group record at $1 billion. Super PACs accounted for more than $600 million of that, according to Andrew Mayersohn at OpenSecrets.org. Michael Beckel and Russ Choma of the Center for Responsive Politics report that conservative groups were responsible for 69 percent of outside spending and liberal groups for 28 percent. For American Crossroads, one of the largest and best-funded groups, only 7 percent of the money spent went to candidates who actually won.

According to Molly Ball of *The Atlantic*, during the 2012 campaign, "groups on the left were some of the most skilled exploiters of the 2010 Citizens' United decision." The AFL-CIO had actually filed an *amicus curiae* brief with the court to allow unions to campaign to the general public. This action returned labor to a powerhouse position during campaigns.

REFLECT ON THE ESSENTIAL QUESTION

Essential Question: *How do citizens, businesses, and other interests influence lawmaking and policy in this country, and how has government regulated their actions?* On a separate paper, complete a chart like the one below to gather details to answer that question.

How Groups Influence Lawmaking	Government Regulations

THINK AS A POLITICAL SCIENTIST: DETERMINE RELATIONSHIPS, PATTERNS, OR TRENDS

To contextualize historical and present-day events and ideas, researchers need to be able to determine relationships, patterns, and trends among them over time. To do so, they use both qualitative and quantitative research methods.

Qualitative research is a type of exploratory research that helps researchers understand human motivations and other underlying factors and reasons for how and why events, problems, or ideas take shape. It is subject to interpretation. Qualitative research presents a broad, mostly verbal view of a research topic. Examples of qualitative research include focus groups and one-on-one interviews. It typically uses only semistructured research techniques and small sample sizes.

Quantitative research, on the other hand, generates data that can be charted numerically to arrive at relevant statistical information. It is used to narrow a qualitative research topic. Quantitative research most often relies on surveys and polls. These can be given in person, online, or by telephone.

Practice: Choose two well-known super PACs—one liberal and one conservative—such as Americans for Prosperity (Koch brothers) or Workers' Voice (AFL-CIO). Use quantitative information from online sources and/or print media to track and compare the issues and causes these super PACs support and the levels of funding they apply to influence American politics. Illustrate your findings in a graph or chart.

KEY TERMS, NAMES, AND EVENTS

access	K Street	Seventeenth Amendment
amicus curiae	leadership PACs	single-issue group
Citizens United v. FEC (2010)	lobbying	Sixteenth Amendment
501(c)(4)	lobbyist	solidary incentives
501(c)(3)	material incentives	super PAC
direct lobbying	Nineteenth Amendment	think tanks
free rider	outsider strategy	Thirteenth Amendment
grassroots lobbying	pluralism	trade associations
grasstops	political action committees (PACs)	Twenty-sixth Amendment
Honest Leadership and Open Government Act (2007)	professional associations	*United States v. Harriss* (1954)
insider strategies	public interest group	upper-class bias
intergovernmental lobby	purposive incentives	Wagner Act (1935)
	revolving door	

MULTIPLE-CHOICE QUESTIONS

1. Which type of interest group represents the largest share of political action committees (PACs) operating in Washington?

   (A) Labor unions

   (B) Consumers unions

   (C) Corporations

   (D) Public interest groups

   (E) The gun lobby

2. Interest groups are regulated in all of the following ways EXCEPT

   (A) government officials cannot at the same time serve as lobbyists

   (B) lobbyists that lobby members of Congress must register with the House and/or Senate

   (C) corporations cannot make contributions to candidates, but their political action committees can

   (D) interest groups cannot advertise on television

   (E) PAC contributions to federal candidates cannot exceed $5,000 per election

3. Which of the following interest groups has the largest membership?

(A) American Federation of Labor-Congress of Industrial Organizations (AFL-CIO)

(B) American Association of Retired Persons (AARP)

(C) Mothers Against Drunk Driving (MADD)

(D) National Rifle Association (NRA)

(E) American Medical Association (AMA)

4. When interest groups offer new members benefits such as a monthly magazine or discounts, they are providing

(A) purposive incentives

(B) material incentives

(C) legislative incentives

(D) regulatory incentives

(E) required incentives

5. Which interest group action would most greatly influence policy in the courts?

(A) Rating senators and representatives based on roll call votes

(B) Directly lobbying House and Senate members

(C) Filing an *amicus curiae* brief in a pending case

(D) Purchasing an ad in a newspaper

(E) Writing an op-ed column for a newspaper

6. Which statement about recent trends in grassroots lobbying is true?

(A) Only citizen groups employ grassroots lobbying.

(B) Grassroots lobbying uses mail and telephone, but not television.

(C) This technique is often used to target particular congressional districts.

(D) The average citizen and the grasstops are of equal value to a lobbyist.

(E) Grassroots lobbying was pioneered by corporations.

7. All of the following are reasons for the growth of interest groups EXCEPT

(A) social movements tend to generate interest groups

(B) the consumer movement of the 1960s resulted in an organized effort to assure product safety

(C) the Constitution's separation of powers has ultimately created more groups trying to affect policy

(D) federalism has caused special interest groups to target lawmakers at both the state and federal level

(E) the government began funding all interest groups in the 1970s

8. Which advocate started a series of public interest groups to protect consumers and to guarantee fair and open government?

   (A) Hugo Black

   (B) Ralph Nader

   (C) Samuel Gompers

   (D) Trent Lott

   (E) Jack Abramoff

9. Which of the following statements about interest groups and lobbying is true?

   (A) Lobbying is protected by the Fourth Amendment.

   (B) Lobbyists spend most of their time persuading lawmakers to change their political views.

   (C) A Capitol Hill lobbyist's most precious asset is access.

   (D) Free riders rarely benefit from interest group activity.

   (E) Interest groups can influence policy in the legislative and judicial branches, but not in the executive branch.

PAC Campaign Donations (in millions)			
	2000	2004	2008
Incumbents	$195.4	$246.8	$304.7
Challengers	$27.5	$22.3	$48.8
Open Seats	$36.9	$41.3	$32.4

Source: FEC

10. Which trend does the table above support?

   (A) PAC donations tend to change legislators' votes.

   (B) PAC donations have diminished in recent years.

   (C) Republican candidates receive more donations from labor PACs than do Democrats.

   (D) Interest group PACs tend to donate to incumbents more than challengers.

   (E) Interest group PACs spend more on open seat races than to protect incumbents.

Question

1. Interest groups have grown in both overall number and in membership to have great influence in American politics.

   (a) Identify and explain two reasons why the number of interest groups has grown in the United States.

   (b) Select one of the following groups and describe this group's primary concern and one policy goal it has achieved.
   - National Rifle Association
   - American Civil Liberties Union
   - National Organization for Women
   - Common Cause

   (c) Explain one incentive for citizens to join an interest group.

Question

2. Interest groups employ several activities in an attempt to shape national policy through government institutions.

   (a) Identify a federal government institution and explain how interest groups use a particular activity to influence policy via that institution.

   (b) Identify another federal government institution and explain how interest groups use a different activity to influence policy via that institution.

   (c) Explain two factors that guide or limit the relationship of interest groups and government officials.

WRITING: ANSWER COMPLETELY

Jot down the skeleton of each question so you remember to answer it entirely. For example, as you begin to think about the answer to the first free-response question, you might jot the following on your paper:

   (a) Identify and explain

   (b) Select group and describe goal

   (c) Explain incentive

Then as you write your answer, you can check off each part of the question and double check that you are not leaving anything out.

8

The Media

"Were it left to me to decide whether we should have a government without newspapers, or newspapers without government, I should not hesitate a moment to prefer the latter."

—Thomas Jefferson, letter to a friend, 1787

Essential Question: What are the roles of the media in the political system and the impact of the media on public affairs?

Soon after Johannes Gutenberg created the printing press, reporting and commenting on government became commonplace. In late colonial America, pamphleteers and newspaper editors printed ideas that helped to bring about the American Revolution. Since that time, the media have evolved from a world of thin, hard-copy publications intended for elite audiences to one of instant reporting and citizen interaction via the Internet. Governments tend to have a love-hate relationship with the press, probably because what journalists and commentators report affects public opinion, government operation, and policy. In fact, the media wield power that rivals that of the three branches of government. The media are therefore sometimes referred to as the "Fourth Estate," meaning a force that influences society and politics but is not officially recognized as such. In this chapter, you will learn about the history of news reporting, the Federal Communications Commission, the media's role, and contemporary trends in a free press.

History of Government and the Press

In 1734, New York writer and publisher John Peter Zenger faced an American colonial court on a charge of seditious libel. Zenger had criticized the royal governor in his weekly *New York Journal*, which constituted an illegal action at the time. Zenger's attorney argued that the truth, which was not a legitimate defense under the law at the time, should be an absolute defense. The jury agreed and found Zenger not guilty. This verdict marked the beginning of an American **free press**—an uninhibited institution that places an additional check on government to maintain honesty, ethics, and transparency—later enshrined in the First Amendment.

Newspapers and the Party Press

Colonial newspapers served a major function during the Revolution and later fostered a spirit of unity for the new nation's course. Only large cities could maintain a regular newspaper, and the first daily paper did not appear until 1784. Most were four-page weeklies that reported on the ratification debate, *The Federalist* essays, and events in Europe.

Subsidizing Newspapers President Washington and Secretary of the Treasury Alexander Hamilton wanted a newspaper to convey Federalist party ideas. They hired printer John Fenno to create the *Gazette of the United States*, which became an organ of the Washington administration and the infant party. Thomas Jefferson's followers responded by securing publisher Philip Freneau to start the *National Gazette*. The warring political factions held debates and issued attacks as part of public discourse in these printed journals. During the first two decades of the 1800s, a different publication, the *National Intelligencer,* was the preferred paper among presidents. The seat of government became the center for national reporting. Government officials awarded lucrative printing jobs; as a result, a close patronage relationship grew between the parties and the newspapers.

Source: Clipart

The *National Gazette* was first published on October 31, 1791. Federalists criticized then-Secretary of State Thomas Jefferson when he hired Freneau as a translator for the state department—a public position—as a way to encourage him to move to Philadelphia and publish a newspaper that was consistently critical of the Washington administration.

An Independent Press

The partisan press dominated until newspapers began to expand their circulation. The factors that drove the expansion were the development of the inexpensive, mass-produced papers collectively known as the **penny press** and the creation of national news organizations. The 1860 opening of the **Government Printing Office**—a permanent federal agency to print government publications—broke the patronage relationship between government and publishers.

Newspapers Seek a Mass Audience In 1833, Benjamin Day launched the *New York Sun,* the first successful daily newspaper for readers with modest incomes. He charged a penny per copy and sold the paper at the outdoor city markets. The *Sun* included everything from recipes to human-interest stories, which were the kind of items average readers desired. Government activity no longer dominated the front pages, and other papers began to thrive as America's readership grew. Over the next decade, the invention of the rotary press and the development of news organizations expanded newspapers. Editors began to send their own correspondents to cover Washington.

The Telegraph Samuel Morse's telegraph altered communication even more. In 1841, Congress funded Morse's telegraph line from Washington to Baltimore—the government's first direct involvement in private-sector telecommunications.

Associated Press In 1848, New York's leading editors gathered in the *New York Sun* offices to finalize plans for a formal news organization, the **Associated Press (AP).** By pooling resources, they could gather, share, and sell the news beyond their city. With expanding telegraph lines, their reporters could send information quickly from the location of the action (whether it was Washington or elsewhere) to AP headquarters. Editors could then shape the story and send it out to client newspapers in cities across the country.

During its first year, the Associated Press covered the presidential campaign, a women's rights convention, and other national stories. It set up **bureaus**, offices beyond newspaper headquarters, in Albany and Washington to cover state and national government. Writing for a national audience and so many different client newspapers, the AP departed from partisan preferences and standardized its unbiased reporting to gain and keep customers. This **wire service** set the standard for others to follow. Today, other wire services—United Press International and Reuters—compete with the Associated Press.

Yellow Journalism

As technology allowed newspapers to thrive, a new style of reporting developed, driven by influential publishers' quests for larger profits. **Yellow journalism**—exaggerated stories filled with sensational crime and scandal—dominated the front pages.

Pulitzer and Hearst In the late 1800s, publishers William Randolph Hearst and Joseph Pulitzer competed for readers and soared to the top of the newspaper industry while cultivating an aggressive form of yellow journalism. Hearst's *New*

York Journal and Pulitzer's *World* exaggerated and sometimes fabricated news stories to grab audiences' attention. These papers printed lurid accounts of murders, railroad wrecks, fires, lynchings, political corruption, and scandals.

Spanish-American War Both Hearst and Pulitzer took their creativity too far during U.S. hostilities with Spain in 1898. Cubans sought independence from their mother country. As Spanish-American friction increased, Hearst sent his illustrator and writer to describe and depict alleged Spanish atrocities inflicted on the Cuban people. Hearst reportedly told his personnel, "You furnish the pictures and I'll furnish the war." When the *U.S.S. Maine* exploded in the Caribbean in February, Hearst laid the blame squarely on the Spanish. Pulitzer joined Hearst's crusade. By April both the *World* and the *Journal* had mobilized America against Spain and encouraged Congress to declare war.

Contemporary Sensationalism The unusual sells. The tabloid weeklies at grocery checkout counters do not have the influence Hearst and Pulitzer enjoyed a century ago, but they tend to practice the same kind of **sensationalism**. The flagship tabloid the *National Enquirer* initially shaped its publication, in the words of founder Generoso Pope Jr., to appeal to "those women in hair curlers who pass through the checkout lines." In more recent decades, tabloids broke stories about the love affairs of Bill Clinton and presidential hopeful John Edwards, among other celebrities.

Progressive Journalism

In the early twentieth century, Washington became a common **dateline**— the locale listed atop an article in a newspaper. Dispatches from the capital described such major news stories as the progress of the pure food and drug legislation, the efforts at trust busting, and the controversy over railroad rates.

Magazines of Opinion Progressive Era journalism fostered integrity in reporting and a publication's ability to create change. Magazines such as *McClure's*, *The Nation,* and *The New Republic* offered in-depth stories on national issues. They employed aggressive reporters and projected a social conscience. **Investigative reporting** became a new genre as reporters went undercover to expose corruption in government and other institutions. Ida Tarbell wrote an honest and extremely damaging **exposé** of John D. Rockefeller's Standard Oil monopoly. Lincoln Steffens wrote stories and Jacob Riis published photos that revealed the tragic street conditions in cities. These reporters changed the national mindset to bring about reforms. Breaking up monopolies became easier once the public was aware of the harsh and sometimes illegal business practices of some industries.

Teddy Roosevelt shared the progressive spirit of these investigative journalists but did not always appreciate how they threatened his image or that of the United States. He dubbed them **muckrakers**, a derogatory charge that compared them to "the man with the muck rake" in the novel *Pilgrim's Progress*. They were too busy looking down and stirring up the filth to gaze upon the stars. Lincoln Steffens proudly reflected on the label years later, "The makers of muck ... bade me to report them."

Broadcasting

As progressive journalists began to retire, radio and then television emerged as powerful new media. Stations included journalism in their programming and developed news departments to shape an industry that competed with, and later surpassed, newspapers and magazines. Print media continued to feature more in-depth articles than the rather brief radio and television news reports. As broadcast's influence rose, the federal government began regulating it.

Radio After World War I, radio stations began to appear across the nation. KDKA in Pittsburgh is generally credited with being the first of these. Few people purchased "radio sets," the large, primitive radios available at that time, so radio manufacturers began creating stations to boost sales.

A Broadcast Network The concept of a **broadcast network**—broadcasting from one central location to several stations, then on to people's living rooms—reached a new level in 1926 when the National Broadcasting Company (NBC), a subsidiary of the Radio Corporation of America, operated 24 stations, or affiliates. Its first coast-to-coast hookup came in 1927. Early newscasts had reporters from *Time* magazine read essential tidbits from the magazine's stories. News dramatizations featured narrators and radio voice-over artists playing the parts of the world leaders.

World War II transitioned radio journalism into a clear, just-the-facts style of reporting that kept the public interest in mind. Edward R. Murrow was a key pioneer of this form of journalism, and, by the war's end, he had shaped the industry and given it the most familiar voice in the business. The Columbia Broadcasting System (CBS) sent him to Europe to cover Germany's attack on England. In 1940, broadcasting from a rooftop in London, Murrow made the first of his many reports on Adolf Hitler's massive bombing effort, the Blitz. The bombing had stopped temporarily, but listeners could hear anti-aircraft guns and air raid warnings. Against this background, Murrow provided a vivid ad-lib description.

Films of the war appeared in movie theaters as well. But as Murrow biographer Bob Edwards put it, "Newsreel footage of the Blitz is in black and white; Ed's radio reports were in color." In 1937, Murrow had not even been allowed to attend the Foreign Correspondents' Association (FCA) in London because radio was not yet considered a legitimate journalism-based medium. By 1944, the FCA had made him its president.

Early Television and the Big Three In the postwar period, broadcast companies shifted many of their efforts toward television. RCA had demonstrated a TV set to President Franklin Roosevelt at the 1939 World's Fair. By 1951, 10 million American homes had television. Entertaining shows dominated the schedule.

Conventional News The networks worked to develop news departments, and they covered the 1948 Democratic and Republican conventions. Television reporters wore headsets, carried 30-pound transmitters on their backs, and roamed the convention floor to interview delegates. Presidential contenders highlighted their credentials in front of the TV cameras.

Over the next few years, the **Big Three networks** (CBS, NBC, and ABC) set the tone and developed a standard news formula that is still largely followed today. Initially, the evening news was only 15 minutes long and reporters read the news with accompanying footage. Soon, however, the networks began using film technology that could simultaneously record sound, making interviews and on-the-scene reports more immediate and compelling.

The term "anchorman" first came into use when CBS covered the 1952 political conventions. The first anchorman was Walter Cronkite, who sat in the broadcast booth and coordinated reports coming in from the convention floor and beyond the convention hall.

The networks began to create in-depth programming to look into national affairs, international relations, and the lives of celebrities. Edward R. Murrow moved to television to host *See It Now*, a forerunner to *60 Minutes*. Murrow exposed Senator Joseph McCarthy by presenting examples of the senator's abusive tactics against alleged communists. Murrow's on-air indictment helped to bring about McCarthy's downfall. Television journalism had asserted itself as a watchdog, which made it an even more influential medium.

A Television President In 1960, Senator John F. Kennedy became America's first president to use the power of television to his advantage. The televised debates between Kennedy and opponent Richard Nixon began a new era of campaigning. Interestingly, those who viewed the debates on TV felt Kennedy had won, while those who listened to the debate on the radio favored Nixon. Once elected president, Kennedy proved a master of the medium, working with reporters and holding the first live press conferences. CBS extended its 15-minute broadcast to 30 minutes in 1963 with Walter Cronkite interviewing President Kennedy. By the end of that year, Cronkite announced the president's death to the nation. Days later, millions watched as Jack Ruby stepped out of a crowd and shot suspect Lee Harvey Oswald on live television. Kennedy's assassination had become the largest television event ever, and it remains embedded in the nation's collective memory.

Changes Brought by Vietnam and Watergate

Perhaps more than any other two events in modern times, the Vietnam War and the Watergate scandal shaped the press's role and relationship to government. An **adversarial press**—a press that skeptically questions government action— became the reporters' obligation. Unlike the patriotic press corps of both world wars and the Korean War, journalists stationed in Vietnam began to question information presented by U.S. military and diplomats. Television images, of course, altered perceptions. The Watergate scandal unfolded on the small screen, especially with Senate Select Committee hearings from 1972 to 1974, which elevated the public's trust in the media well above its trust in the president.

Vietnam Roughly 10 American journalists were assigned to Vietnam in 1960. By 1968, 500 full-time correspondents representing print, TV, and radio were in the country. "Government's interpretations of events did not coincide with what we learned on our own," recalls NBC Vietnam Bureau Chief Ron Steinman.

"We listened, hoping to discover a kernel of truth in a fog of lies." But in reality, **journalistic integrity**—the obligation of a journalist to present the unbiased truth—did not always play out. Camera crews were pressured to get good footage, and some correspondents exaggerated the truth. Steinman recalls, "It took extra effort on my part to keep them from going overboard and leaping into the land of hyperbole." One of the most obvious examples of this type of reporting came in the aftermath of the January 1968 Tet Offensive, when the television media characterized what was essentially a U.S. tactical victory as a grave loss.

About one month later, after a trip to Vietnam, CBS anchor Walter Cronkite—known as the "most trusted man in America"—closed the evening news with an opinionated report that had big consequences. "We have been too often disappointed by the optimism of American leaders, both in Vietnam and Washington, to have faith any longer in the silver linings they find in the darkest clouds." President Lyndon Johnson reportedly remarked that if he had lost Cronkite, he had also lost America. Months later, Johnson refused to seek re-election.

Watergate In 1972, while covering a burglary of the Democratic National Committee office located in the Watergate Hotel, *Washington Post* reporters Bob Woodward and Carl Bernstein found out that the defendants had close ties to the White House. The duo kept tracking the break-in with investigative stories until they were able to ascertain that the burglars had broken the law in order to steal information that would help Nixon's re-election campaign. Whatever trust had existed between the Nixon White House and the Washington press corps vanished.

The Roles of Media

Journalists and the media serve three basic roles: gatekeeper, scorekeeper, and watchdog. In other words, they decide what is newsworthy when they present events or focus on certain issues. They judge, or allow the public to judge, successes and failures of government officials, businesses, and celebrities. And they expose action, or inaction, that public officials or leaders might prefer to keep hidden.

Gatekeeper

Every evening, often mere minutes before news anchors go on the air, they and their producers decide what to broadcast. Much more is happening than the 30-minute broadcast (actually about 23 minutes without commercials) will allow. In determining what is newsworthy and what will be aired, the news media act as a **gatekeeper**. Print and radio journalists fulfill the same function. They set the news agenda, which often later becomes the government's policy agenda. If an outbreak of Ebola becomes national news, for example, the government will likely be more compelled to act because the American people are aware of the problem and will demand action.

Scorekeeper

As **scorekeepers**, the media track political successes and failures. During campaign season, reporters update readers and viewers on the relative success of competing candidates. This **horse race journalism** tends to focus on the field of candidates. At a racetrack, using measurements like "a length" or "a nose," an announcer reveals how far ahead or behind each horse is as the race goes on. Similarly, reporters emphasize public opinion polls, mainly because these are the only data that tend to change from day to day. Candidates' ideas, policies, or biographies remain fairly static, so once those are reported, they are no longer considered newsworthy. The scorekeeping continues after an election as well. When President George W. Bush's poor handling of Hurricane Katrina was reported, for example, his approval rating fell precipitously.

Watchdog

Journalists' obligations to keep an eye on government or industry is part of the press's **watchdog** function. Reporters look for corruption, scandal, or inefficiency. Congress often addresses an issue after the press has highlighted it. In the age of muckrakers, *McClure's* magazine published a series entitled "Railroads on Trial," which ultimately led to the passage of the 1906 Hepburn Act to strengthen railroad regulations. *Washington Post* reporters Woodward and Bernstein served as watchdogs throughout the Watergate scandal.

When the U.S. Army discovered its soldiers were mistreating Iraqi prisoners at Abu Ghraib in 2004, reporter Seymour Hersh reported the horrific abuses in *The New Yorker* magazine. The TV show *60 Minutes* aired the story with photographic evidence. Among other things, U.S. soldiers had forced Iraqi prisoners to strip, thrown cold water on them, threatened them with military dogs, and forced them to assume humiliating poses. These abuses, which occurred halfway around the world, would never have reached the American public if not for the Fourth Estate's check on government.

Government's Relationship with the Media

The press's ability to influence public opinion has always kept government officials on their toes, and the adversarial relationship between journalists and government officials often creates a rift between the two. Though candidates and office holders cannot do without the press, a writer's words can sometimes make or break an official's reputation.

Presidents and the Press

The press delves into the president's mind, his relations with fellow policymakers, his family activity, and his interactions with other world leaders. Beyond the regular 60 or so top reporters who cover the president daily, another 2,000 have White House press credentials. Some travel on *Air Force One* or on the chartered press plane that follows it.

BY THE NUMBERS Reported Scandals, 2007–2009	
Accused of Scandal, Date	**Newshole**
Gov. Rod Blagojevich, Dec. 8–14, 2008 (accused of selling Senate seat)	28%
Gov. Eliot Spitzer, Mar. 10–16, 2008 (hired a prostitute, caught in sting)	23%
Sen. Larry Craig, Aug. 26–31, 2007 (charged with lewd conduct, MN airport)	18%
Alberto Gonzales, Mar. 18–23, 2007 (accused of political firings of U.S. Attorneys)	18%
VP Chief of Staff "Scooter" Libby, Mar. 4–9, 2007 (leaked secret CIA agent's identity)	13%
Gov. Mark Sanford, June 22–28, 2009 (affair with Argentine mistress)	11%
VP Dick Cheney, June 24–29, 2007 (overstepped executive authority)	5%

Source: Pew Center Project for Excellence in Journalism

What do the numbers show? What scandals received more or less coverage during that week? What types of officials committed what types of scandals? What percentage of the newshole (the amount of space available for news in a daily newspaper) do scandals fill when they surface? What role does the press play in delivering this news?

In the early 1900s, as national newspapers were on the rise, Theodore Roosevelt developed a unique relationship with the press. He referred to the presidency as a **bully pulpit**, a stage from which he could persuade the public who then would persuade Congress. With his colorful remarks, unique ideas, and vibrant persona, Roosevelt always provided good copy. He and his cabinet officials distributed speeches and photos to journalists to use in their stories, and he saved the richest pieces of information for his favorite newsmen.

In the 1930s, Franklin Roosevelt pioneered the radio message with his fireside chats and chummy relationships with reporters. The media allowed him to show the nation his flamboyant, energetic style rather than his disabled condition. He conducted press conferences twice weekly under an agreement that reporters would not quote his answers, but only his distributed press releases.

John F. Kennedy did the first live televised press conferences in the early 1960s. Richard Nixon's paranoia, complicated by the release of the Pentagon Papers and his Watergate scandal, had pitted him directly against the press. He had offending reporters' phones tapped, his vice president spoke publicly about "disloyal" reporters, his Department of Justice tried to subpoena reporters' notes, and a White House aide threatened antitrust lawsuits against TV networks if they did not let more conservatives on the air.

White House Press Secretaries Since President Herbert Hoover appointed the first full-time press secretary, a number of presidents' chief spokesmen have developed unique customs and have become familiar national figures. Some pundits consider the White House press secretary's position the second toughest job in Washington. Perhaps for this reason, and because of the fast-paced, intense nature of the job, modern-day presidents tend to go through multiple press secretaries over the course of their term.

The press secretary holds almost daily **press conferences** in the James Brady Press Briefing Room (named for President Reagan's press secretary, who was shot in an assassination attempt on the president in 1981). The White House controls these media events. TV networks and wire services get preferential seating, as do the other major outlets, such as the *New York Times* and the *Washington Post*. The president's communication team can alter or revoke press credentials or seating assignments to discipline hostile reporters. The more senior reporters are called on first, and the press secretary typically signals the close of the session by calling on the senior wire service reporter.

Presidents appear at a podium to field questions much less frequently than their press secretaries do, usually only a few times each year. Administrations occasionally hold more formal, planned press conferences in the larger East Room during primetime television. In addition to videotaped or televised conferences, press secretaries hold more informal sessions with small groups of reporters in their office.

Spin and Manipulation The press conference is in many ways a staged event. Press secretaries and presidents anticipate questions and rehearse in advance with planned answers. President George W. Bush's critics complained that his press relations were an affront to the media. Reporter and media expert Eric Alterman and others reported how the Bush administration was caught manipulating the news process. The president's administration distributed government-prepared "news reports" to local TV stations across the country to promote his programs, planted a fake reporter in the briefing room to throw softball questions at the president's press secretary, and paid large sums of public money to writers to promote their programs. The most notable example was the $240,000 that went to conservative columnist and radio host Armstrong Williams to promote Bush's No Child Left Behind Act.

Media and Congress

The House of Representatives voted during the first Congress to open its doors to the public and the press. In the late 1800s, many reporters preferred to cover Congress instead of the White House. In the 1950s, Americans became familiar with Congress during Senator McCarthy's House Un-American Activities Committee hearings and later during Watergate hearings and the effort to impeach Nixon.

Getting the deepest insight into a particular issue depends on the ability to formulate and refine inquiries to push your thinking—and your research—forward.

To **formulate an inquiry**, you begin by reading and recognizing where questions are possible and necessary. What is it you want to know or verify? Where do you start, and where do you go from there? A strong question will guide your research process and help you see patterns of information in what you read to identify valid and relevant inquiries.

But formulating an inquiry is just the start. With additional research, you will see new patterns and issues emerge related to your initial inquiry. Consider all the information objectively and remain alert to the specifics that will lead you to a more refined and nuanced inquiry.

In this chapter, for example, you read about the role of the press in the U.S. political system. What are some questions you might ask to create a refined inquiry question worthy of further research?

Practice: On the Internet, look up the following articles by entering the titles and publication information in a search engine: "GOP Security Aide Among Five Arrested in Bugging Affair," Bob Woodward and Carl Bernstein (*Washington Post*, June 19, 1972) and "Obama for Re-Election" (*New York Times*, October 27, 2012). Look at the headlines and dates, and consider the overall editorial slant of each of the publications. Determine the purpose of each article. Look for patterns that link and separate the two articles. Then write down a succinct theory about what they indicate about the role of the press in U.S. politics.

Congressional stories include members' roles on committees and in the legislative process—these are typically technical story lines, not easily conveyed in short headlines and TV news segments. Yet those interested in lawmaking continue to monitor the legislature closely. Two notable newspapers that cover Congress, *Roll Call* and *The Hill*, have gained national popularity with their Web sites. Large newspapers devote space to the first branch, and most TV news services have correspondents who report from the halls of Congress.

In the late 1970s, the cable industry created **C-SPAN**—the Cable Satellite Public Affairs Network—a privately funded, nonprofit public service. Cable and satellite affiliates pay fees that in turn fund the network. C-SPAN began covering the House in 1979. The Senate decided to allow cameras into its chamber in 1986, which gave rise to C-SPAN 2. Congress owns and controls the cameras in the two chambers, but C-SPAN receives the feed and can broadcast House and Senate floor debates. When Congress has no floor activity, the network covers committee hearings, seminars at university campuses and think tanks, public meetings, and political rallies.

Courts and Cameras

The press covers crime, lawsuits, courtroom activity, and appeals court decisions. The Sixth Amendment assures public trials and makes press coverage possible at these proceedings. At the national level, major newspapers and television news typically assign a legal affairs correspondent to cover the Supreme Court and high-profile trials throughout the country. Viewers often see footage of a trial from the state level, especially one involving celebrities or a horrific crime. In the federal courts, however, cameras are generally not allowed. Instead, pastel drawings depicting courtroom people and events usually appear on screen during TV news coverage.

Attempts to bring cameras into the Supreme Court for increased understanding and transparency will likely fail. For every person who sees court coverage on C-SPAN gavel-to-gavel, Justice Antonin Scalia warned in 2005, "10,000 will see 15-second takeouts on the network news, which, I guarantee you, will be uncharacteristic of what the court does." Like Scalia, most justices have reservations that cameras might undermine the institution.

Freedom of the Press

The general application of freedom of the press since the founding allows anyone to print anything, but the government can punish the publishing of "improper, mischievous, or illegal" material. This basic philosophy, combined with the reverence for the revolutionary essayists who argued for independence, has shaped a free press in America. The press, however, is not absolutely free. Governments can limit obscenity and content that promotes violence or crime. Anyone who prints false and malicious material can be sued for **libel**.

Prior Restraint

Unlike in totalitarian states where governments oversee what is printed or broadcast, the First Amendment protects against **prior restraint**—mandated government approval in advance of publication. In *Near v. Minnesota* (1931), the Supreme Court ruled out a state law that would have prevented the printing of radical propaganda.

The Pentagon Papers The issue of prior restraint came up again in 1971. Daniel Ellsberg, a high-level Pentagon analyst, became disillusioned with the war in Vietnam and released to the *New York Times* a massive report that became known as the **Pentagon Papers**. The 7,000-page classified document outlined the history of America's entry into the Vietnam conflict; it also revealed government deception. These papers put President Nixon's credibility on the line and, the president claimed, hampered his ability to manage the war.

Nixon's lawyers petitioned a U.S. district court to order the *Times* to stop the printing in the name of national security. "I think it is time," Nixon said, "to quit making national heroes out of those who steal secrets and publish them in the newspaper." The lower court obliged, and armed guards arrived at the newspaper's office to enforce the order.

New York Times v. United States The *Times* appealed, and the Supreme Court ruled in its favor. The ruling assured that the hasty cry of national security does not justify censorship in advance and that the government does not have power of prior restraint. Even Nixon's solicitor general, the man who argued his case in the Supreme Court, later said the decision came out exactly as it should. "This decision was a Declaration of Independence," claimed *Times* reporter Hedrick Smith, "and it really changed the relationship between the government and the media ever since."

The court ruled on only the newspaper's right to print these documents, not on Ellsberg's right to leak them. In fact, Ellsberg was indicted under the Espionage Act, which led to his own trial. But the *New York Times* did nothing criminal when it received the information nor when it conveyed that information to the public. After federal law enforcement mishandled the investigation and violated the law in the process, the judge threw out the charges against Ellsberg and he was cleared.

Anonymous Sources

In trying to uncover wrongdoing or find unique information, reporters cannot always find sources willing to go on record. Those with knowledge of corruption in a government agency or a large company often fear retaliation if they are discovered as the whistleblower, the source of the information on wrongdoing. Sometimes this means reporters must promise anonymity to a source to obtain the information. On the other hand, government officials sometimes leak information they want to come to light.

Journalism Terms	
On the record	Officials are willing to be quoted and named.
Off the record	The information cannot be used in any way.
On background	The information can be reported but not attributed to the source by name.
On deep background	Information can be reported, but the source demands that there be no attribution, not even a vague connection.

Unnamed sources can create a dilemma for reporters and publishers. Some of those that require anonymity may simply have an ax to grind or want to cast a negative light on some person, policy, or institution. Former President Clinton's press secretary, Mike McCurry, claims reporters are more eager to grant anonymity in pursuit of unique information than officials are to demand it. According to a 2005 Associated Press study, to avoid these problems, about 28 percent of the nation's daily newspapers refuse to use information from unnamed sources.

Branzburg v. Hayes **and Shield Laws** When anonymous sources reveal criminal activity, they hide their own identity for their safety or because of their own guilt. Police question reporters in pursuit of criminals or to find more evidence of wrongdoing. Journalists find themselves trapped between honoring a promise to keep a source anonymous and assisting police in pursuit of crime. When a reporter refuses to cooperate with police, investigators sometimes seek a court-ordered subpoena to gain access to a reporter's notes or to make him or her testify. This issue came to a head in *Branzburg v. Hayes* (1972).

The court ruled that information and knowledge a reporter collects is "everyman's evidence" and cannot legally be withheld. *New York Times* reporter Judith Miller spent 85 days in jail in July 2005 for refusing to reveal a confidential source. Journalists do not get an added privilege in the First Amendment. The court noted that legislatures could create additional protection for reporter's privilege that would apply in state law. Several states have created these **shield laws**, but so far Congress has not.

 Is That Constitutional? *New York Times v. Sullivan* (1964)

Does the First Amendment protect criticism and misstatements targeted at public officials? Yes.

In 1960, a civil rights group put an ad in the *New York Times* entitled "Heed their Rising Voices," which included some inaccuracies and false information about a Montgomery, Alabama, city commissioner, L. B. Sullivan. Sullivan sued for libel in an Alabama court and won $500,000 in damages. The *Times* appealed, arguing that the First Amendment protected against slight mistakes and these should differ from an intentional defamation. The Supreme Court sided with the newspaper. Uninhibited debate "may well include vehement, caustic, and sometimes unpleasantly sharp attacks on government and public officials," the court noted. The fear of an easy libel suit would stifle robust debate and hard reporting. Even false statements, therefore, must be protected "if the freedoms of expression are to have the proper 'breathing space' that they need to survive."

The standard to prove libel is high. The suing party must prove that they were damaged and that the offending party knowingly printed the falsehood and did so maliciously with intent to defame. Public officials are less protected and cannot recover damages for defamatory falsehoods relating to their official conduct unless they can prove actual malice, that is, reckless disregard for the truth. The court later broadened the category of "public figure" to include celebrities such as movie stars, top athletes, and business leaders.

Libel and Slander

Libel and **slander** are printed or spoken lies, respectively. It is not illegal to lie, per se, but when one lies from a strong platform, such as a newspaper or broadcast, for the express purpose of defaming another, the injured party may sue the publication or the reporter.

Regulating the Airwaves

The federal government has developed a series of regulations to assure fairness and decency on radio and TV broadcasts. Laws on print journalism are fewer because, unlike broadcasts, print media do not compete for airwaves, and print media tend to be less accessible to children. Broadcasting licenses are limited by the finite number of available radio and TV frequencies. Congress has created a system in which privately owned stations broadcast on publicly owned airwaves. Licensees accept certain obligations as trustees of the airways in exchange for the right to broadcast. These regulations began as radio became popular and continued to increase in the television era, but they have since been weakened.

Federal Communications Commission In 1934, the Communications Act created the **Federal Communications Commission (FCC),** which regulates electronic media. The original law established a commission that now has authority over radio, TV, wire, satellite, and cable broadcasts. The FCC also has jurisdiction over communications between the Internet and trains, airplanes, and ships. Since its creation, the commission has licensed stations, assured equal time to political candidates and balanced coverage of controversial issues, helped facilitate noncommercial public broadcasts, prevented rigged game shows, and assured decency on radio and television. Since radio and TV stations are generally privately owned and the First Amendment ensures free speech and press, many have argued that the airwaves should be regulated similarly to the traditional press.

Content and Monopoly Early in its existence the FCC focused on program content, network monopoly, false advertising, and profanity. In 1941, it forbade one organization from operating two networks. NBC had to sell one of its two networks, which eventually evolved into the American Broadcasting Company (ABC). The 1950s were a time of programming growth and one of the lowest points in U.S. history in terms of broadcast ethics, courage, fairness, and honesty. The blacklisting of suspected Communists and quiz show scandals left a black cloud over the industry.

FCC Today Today the FCC has five president-appointed commissioners who serve five-year terms. This commission is for the most part insulated from political pressures; however, presidents have helped to shape the FCC by naming commissioners who conform to their philosophies. Since the 1960s, its activity has fluctuated based on Kennedy's and Johnson's proconsumer attitudes to the deregulatory philosophies of Presidents Nixon, Carter, and Reagan.

Licensing and Ownership Radio and TV stations still must apply and be granted licenses to operate. Until the mid-1990s, no one could own and operate more than one station in a given media market. Radio stations must renew their licenses every seven years, and television stations must do so every five years. Applications for renewal are rarely refused.

Equal Time and Right of Reply The **equal time** rule states that any station that permits a candidate for a given office to use its broadcast facilities must provide equal opportunities for the use to all other legally qualified candidates for that same office. News and public affairs shows are exempt, an exemption that allows stations to freely cover candidates they choose without tabulating and evenly distributing coverage to all.

Equal time has evolved along with televised debates. In 1960, when Kennedy and Nixon debated, Congress modified the rule so that not all candidates, most of whom were relative unknowns, would be allowed to take the stage. Since then, organizations that are not under the authority of the FCC—for example, the League of Women Voters—host their own debates, and the stations or networks merely cover these events as news.

The **right of reply** rule guarantees a candidate a response to attacks on the air. If a radio or TV station issues a scathing criticism of a candidate, he or she is entitled to respond. The Supreme Court upheld the policy in *Red Lion Broadcasting v. FCC* (1969). The right of reply does not apply to newspaper attacks, as the court ruled in *Miami Herald v. Tornillo* (1974).

Fairness Doctrine The **Fairness Doctrine** was a policy guided by FCC rules, court decisions, congressional acts, and presidential action, which sought to ensure balance in the on-air coverage of controversial issues from 1949 through 1987.

The original 1949 FCC rule required broadcasters to devote some airtime to discussing controversial matters of public interest and to airing contrasting views. The court upheld the doctrine in the 1969 *Red Lion* decision, stating, "There is no sanctuary in the First Amendment for unlimited private censorship operating in a medium not open to all."

Yet deregulation conservatives argued the rule was the antithesis of an absolute free press. When government requires that opposing arguments be expressed, unpopular and unwarranted views clog the airwaves and disallow broadcasters their First Amendment freedoms, opponents said. Critics also argued that the Fairness Doctrine chilled debate as stations might avoid certain issues to avoid the mandates of the doctrine. In the 1970s, network television editor Peter Kohler recalls, the doctrine provided "a convenient club for politicians and interest groups itching to silence their critics."

President Reagan's deregulatory philosophies resulted in the law's removal. His FCC chairman Mark Fowler claimed, "The perception of broadcasters as community trustees should be replaced by a view of broadcasters as marketplace participants." Television is "just another appliance—it's a toaster with pictures." Realistic enforcement of the Fairness Doctrine ceased in the mid-1980s, and by 1987 the FCC had dismantled it entirely.

Should the Fairness Doctrine be reinstated? Critics on the left want the doctrine reinstated. They maintain the policy actually gave stations wide latitude. As Fairness Doctrine advocate Steve Rendall has explained, the policy did not require each program to be internally balanced, nor did it mandate equal time for opposing viewpoints. There was no 50–50 requirement. And in the entire history of the policy, the FCC only revoked one license for fairness infraction. Democratic leaders differ on it—Democratic congressional leader Nancy Pelosi said it should return, but President Barack Obama showed no signs of pushing for it.

Obscenity The Communications Act expressly prohibits censorship, yet the FCC has struggled to define indecency and obscenity without violating the law or the First Amendment. Though it was not problematic during its first decades—when married couples on TV slept in separate beds—today's free speech advocates and child advocates argue about the line of censorship.

In 1973, a New York radio station aired a 12-minute monologue from comedian George Carlin's album that included a list of the seven words one cannot say on television. The FCC soon became involved. The Carlin case, *Pacifica Foundation v. FCC*, was appealed to the Supreme Court, which narrowly sided with the FCC. It held that the radio was an intruder into the home and uniquely accessible to children, and that broadcasters must be sensitive that children might be exposed to adult material. President Jimmy Carter's FCC did not take the ruling too seriously—one commissioner sarcastically noted that each dirty word had been assigned to each of the then-seven commissioners.

Religious conservatives in the late 1980s and early 1990s, however, pushed for greater monitoring of indecency on the airwaves. More recently, "shock jock" Howard Stern came under fire and has since moved his program to a less regulated medium—satellite radio. The national debate on televised obscenity resurfaced in 2004 when CBS aired a Super Bowl halftime show that exposed too much of singer Janet Jackson's body. The alleged "wardrobe malfunction" resulted in a $550,000 fine against the network and reminded the nation that broadcasts have limits.

Corporate vs. Public Media

The concern that business interests might compromise journalistic integrity is not a new one. In 1958, Edward R. Murrow noted that network managers had been trained in advertising, sales, and show business. RJ Reynolds Tobacco Company sponsored a leading news program *Camel News Caravan* in the 1950s; it was no coincidence that cigarettes were often featured prominently in the show's filmed reports or in ashtrays on the set.

Corporation for Public Broadcasting In the late 1960s, Congress passed the Public Broadcasting Act, which created the **Corporation for Public Broadcasting (CPB)** to develop noncommercial television and radio. As he signed the bill, President Johnson declared, "It will be free, and it will be independent—and it will belong to all of our people." The CPB's goals are to reward creative risks and to bring programming to underserved audiences, especially children and minorities. The agency funds public television and radio stations directly with grants. Congress appropriates more than $400 million a year for this purpose.

Public Television and Radio The CPB subsidizes a national TV network, **Public Broadcasting Service (PBS)**, and a radio network, **National Public Radio (NPR)**. PBS has more than 350 member stations, which get most of their money from local membership drives. In addition to long-running shows like *Sesame Street*, PBS has aired public affairs programming and news including *PBS NewsHour* and *Frontline*. According to public TV pioneer Bill Moyers, "From the outset, we believed there should be one channel not only free of commercials but free from commercial values. . . . One channel—at least one—whose success is measured not by the numbers who watch but by the imprint left on those who do."

National Public Radio (NPR) opened in 1971, broadcasting from the nation's capital. Today a broad cross section of America tunes in daily. For more than four decades, NPR's flagship evening news program, *All Things Considered*, and its morning show, *Morning Edition*, have served to keep Americans informed during their commutes to and from work.

Telecommunications Act In 1996, Congress passed and President Clinton signed into law the **Telecommunications Act**, which deregulated ownership and allowed large corporations to purchase more media outlets in almost every form. This change has resulted in the consolidation of media by a handful of major corporations. AOL merged with Time Warner in 2000, and the conglomerate took over movie studios, book publishers, news magazines, and entire cable channels, including CNN. Viacom owns and directly influences CBS TV, MTV, Paramount Pictures, and some of the nation's largest book publishers. Together, the seven largest media companies control about 80 percent of America's access to information. Some people have claimed that the consolidation hamstrings honest news delivery in favor of corporate interests or news as entertainment. They argue that news journalists may now create copy for the purpose of gaining the most viewers, selling the most products, or bowing to advertisers. In short, they believe that consolidation has damaged journalistic priorities and diminished honest, critical reporting.

The Telecommunications Act exacerbated the corporate conflict of interest that PBS and NPR sought to remove. Network news programs now are expected to promote many other business endeavors. With major film producers and book publishers under their company umbrella, news broadcasts feature promotional material on upcoming movies and new books created by their sister companies. How critical can *Good Morning America* or *60 Minutes* be of the power structure that keeps it on the air? Network news outlets also spend airtime to promote their own programming. When NBC carried the Olympics, *NBC Nightly News* found the event far more newsworthy than its competitors did, giving it 69 minutes of news coverage versus 30 minutes at ABC and 10 minutes at CBS. Similarly, CBS's *Early Show* regularly covers contestants from its reality shows *Survivor* and *The Amazing Race*. According to researchers Jackson, Hart, and Coen, ABC gave the show *The Bachelor* more coverage than it gave the midterm congressional elections.

Contemporary Reporting and New Media

Changes in law, regulatory philosophy, and rapid developments in technology continue to shape the media world. The 24-hour cable news cycle brings a need for more frequently breaking news. The Internet and blogosphere have created a rapid-fire national news conversation. And print newspapers are fighting to stay alive.

Print Newspapers and Magazines

Nationally influential newspapers such as the *Washington Post*, the *New York Times*, the *Wall Street Journal*, and *USA Today* have played a strong role in the United States over the past generation. The *Post* and the *Times* in many ways set the news agenda for other media outlets that try to advance their stories. Former TV news producer Charles Lewis lamented that when he pitched edgy investigative stories, his boss typically passed, giving him the response, "I haven't read this in the *New York Times*."

Local Newspapers Many large city newspapers have a Washington bureau, or they may cover events only in their city and their state capital. These papers have a larger impact on local rather than national government. Most papers have an editorial board, a group of veteran journalists who guide the editorial philosophy of the paper. These writers compose **editorials**—the newspaper's opinion pieces with no byline. Political candidates seek the endorsement of these publications during election season, though most studies show endorsements make little difference in an election's eventual outcome.

National Magazines For decades, *Time, Newsweek,* and *U.S. News & World Report* dominated in-depth national news coverage with middle-of-the-road perspectives. These publications still operate today, though they have experienced a great decline in readership and profits. Other magazines cover national and international politics with a particular editorial slant. Some of the more liberal publications—*The New Republic, The Nation,* and *The Progressive*—have been around since the Progressive Era. Others, like *National Review* and *The Weekly Standard,* attract a conservative readership.

Leading Ideological Political Magazines	
Liberal	**Conservative**
The Nation	*National Review*
The New Republic	*Human Events*
The Progressive	*The Weekly Standard*
Mother Jones	*American Spectator*

Cable News

In 1980, Atlanta TV station owner Ted Turner created the Cable News Network (CNN), giving Americans access to national news 24 hours a day. The 1990s brought MSNBC and the Fox News Channel. These networks changed television news from a daily cycle with an evening peak to an all-day cycle with updates and analysis on the hour. Today, news producers and journalists must search for news to break 24 hours a day, every day.

This change explains why then-President Clinton's White House affair with Monica Lewinsky was so widely reported while previous presidential affairs had not been. Veteran White House reporter Helen Thomas explained how the Clinton administration found itself caught in a new paradigm that resulted in the Lewinsky scandal. "[I]t was a different era," she says of prior presidents' affairs. "Although gossip was also rampant about previous presidents, it remained just that—gossip—and reporters did not attempt to verify it."

These competing news outlets try to appeal to niche audiences in what is commonly known as **narrowcasting**. Fox News, headed by Nixon's 1968 ad man and GOP media consultant Roger Ailes, has created a lineup of conservative hosts, including Bill O'Reilly and Sean Hannity. They are friendly to Republicans and host GOP office holders. MSNBC has countered Fox from the left using hosts Chris Matthews and Lawrence O'Donnell, both of whom have past experience working for Democrats. According to the Pew Research Center, Fox has led in viewership for several years. Recall from Chapter 3 the discussion of the American division of conservative, moderate, and liberal camps. Fox is likely garnering most conservative cable viewers, while left-leaning viewers are divided among CNN, MSNBC, and others. This narrowcasting trend has also blurred the line between news and commentary. Broadcast reporters from a more objective era accuse the cable anchors of political partisanship in commentary that aims to solicit a highly profitable following. Meanwhile, many American viewers are merely confirming their already biased notions. These viewers practice **selective attention**—favoring sources of information that adhere to their beliefs, thus reinforcing those beliefs, while ignoring other important sources.

Internet

In the early days of the Internet, journalists and news-savvy citizens scoffed at news traveling across the Web. When conservative Internet reporter Matt Drudge broke the Monica Lewinsky scandal, President Clinton's spokespersons painted him as an Internet "rumor monger." Because the Internet is free and accessible, skeptics originally feared merging the news business with the new medium. But major newsmagazines, dailies, and others have had to turn to the Internet because much of their audience has done so. People under 30 have made the Web their preferred news source. Baby Boomers still form the core of newspaper readers, though many of them use the Web as well.

Newspapers are suffering from their readership's increased reliance on the Internet as a news source. This revolution is by no means a rejection of newspaper content or journalistic skill, but in many ways newspapers have become an anachronism. Traditional print media now make their Web presence central to their business models. Web sites such as the *Huffington Post* and *Politico* are setting the standards for online political reporting. These and other digital media organizations, such as Yahoo News and BuzzFeed, have spent millions to bring well-known print and TV journalists into their ranks. According to the Pew Research Center, in 2013 roughly 5,000 full-time professionals worked at about 500 digital media outlets. Internet news moved ahead of newspapers as a leading source for national and international news but remains second to television news.

Because the Internet has offered such vast alternatives, cable news experienced an overall drop in viewership of 11 percent in 2013. That same year, the Big Three TV networks experienced an increase in viewers of 2.3 percent, and local TV is still the chief source for most people when obtaining news. Remember, many viewers are more interested in local weather, crime reports, and community news than national politics.

The changes in news delivery combined with recent economic challenges have turned most cities into essentially one-newspaper towns, and printed newspapers have become an endangered species. Newspapers are now about half the size they were 20 years ago. The costs of running extra bureaus and distributing the news from printing press to doorstep are simply too high. Putting information on the Internet instead of in print speeds delivery and avoids the need for paper and gas. The budgetary challenges of printed news combined with readers' diminished desire for content has brought newsroom layoffs and closings of century-old newspapers. Full-time newsroom employment at newspapers declined another 6.4 percent in 2012. Magazine circulation is experiencing the same hard times. *Time* has cut staff as well as its overseas reporting; *U.S. News & World Report* has gone to a monthly format; and *Newsweek*, nearing bankruptcy, sold in 2010 for $1.

These organizations have turned to digital platforms to compete and remain afloat. Promoting their mobile apps, hiring full-time online editors and graphic designers, and selling digital versions of their newspapers has helped ease the transition somewhat. In 2013, newspapers actually increased their total daily circulation by 3 percent, but this increase includes digital-only paying subscribers as well. One analysis of 15 major newspapers shows that only about 55 percent of their subscribers are still receiving a paper on their doorsteps.

Instant, Ever-Changing News The shift from print to electronic journalism and the intense competition to "scoop" competitors in a fast-paced news environment have sped up publishing, shortened stories, encouraged sloppy reporting, and caused journalists to seek out anything unique on an almost hourly basis. The shift has not only encouraged sensationalism, but it also has increased the number of errors and after-story corrections.

Social Media and News In recent years, social media such as Facebook and Twitter have played a role in shaping news presentation and consumption. Roughly 64 percent of Americans use Facebook, and about 30 percent get some level of news from it. However, 78 percent of Facebook users see most news on the site for reasons other than staying informed, and only 34 percent of these news consumers "like" a news organization or a particular journalist. This trend indicates that these viewers see news coming from friends, and the most common type of news that Facebook users absorb from friends—about 73 percent—is entertainment news. About 55 percent look at Facebook for stories on national government or politics.

Ethical Lapses in Journalism

In the past decade, ethical lapses in journalism that would have infuriated Murrow and Cronkite have sullied the media's reputation. Editors and reporters at otherwise respected outlets have carelessly reported and in some instances fabricated news reports. A young *New York Times* reporter, Jayson Blair, created quotes, plagiarized, provided geographic datelines he never visited, and told outright lies that required the *Times* to issue 54 corrections. In 1998, writer Stephen Glass was found to have altered direct quotes, made up fictional characters and organizations, and plagiarized in many of the supposedly fact-based articles he had published in the *New Republic*. In September 2004, Dan Rather reported on *60 Minutes II* that President George W. Bush had never completed his National Guard duty decades earlier. Rather and his producers failed to do some basic fact checking from a partisan source and relied on forged documents. Both Rather and the story's producer soon left CBS.

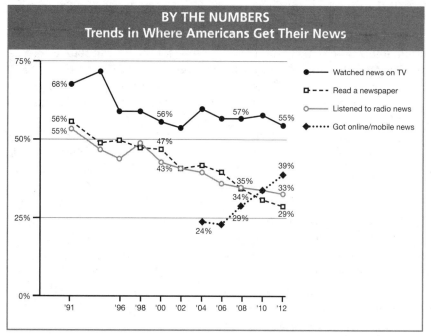

Source: Pew Center for Excellence in Journalism

What do the numbers show? From what media platform do Americans obtain news the most? What portion of citizens obtain some news via the Internet? What percentage might read a printed newspaper? What forms have become more, and less, popular in recent years?

Since 1985, the number of Americans who regard news organizations as "professional" declined from 72 to 49 percent. Those who considered their daily newspapers believable fell from 80 to 59 percent. Today, many Americans consider journalists sloppier, less professional, less caring, more biased, and generally more damaging to democracy than they were in the 1980s.

Ideological Bias

Starting in 1848, the Associated Press began efforts to make news reporting standard, accurate, and objective. The trend continued into the twentieth century with national publications and later with TV news. Today, America's perception is that of a "liberal media," especially since the early 1970s, when the press became President Nixon's whipping boy. But that is a simplistic characterization that circumvents the impossibility of defining and measuring media bias. First, as discussed in Chapter 3, the terms "conservative" and "liberal" are difficult to define, which makes any objective analysis based on such subjective characterizations very difficult. Second, with so many media platforms, it is challenging to define "the media."

A generation ago when the Big Three networks, the *Washington Post*, the *New York Times*, and the newsweeklies ruled reporting, a political scientist or a journalism professor could reasonably measure media bias. Today, with thousands of national reporters for every entity from Fox News to the *Huffington Post*, a sound method to determine the question conclusively is nearly impossible. The term **mainstream media** has become the common label for the traditional media leaders who strive to adhere to time-honored standards of objectivity.

The Press Corps One way to examine bias is to look closely at the people who report the news. Overwhelmingly, national reporters who shape political coverage vote with the Democratic Party and have done so for a generation. A 1972 poll showed that 70 percent of reporters voted for the antiwar candidate, Democrat George McGovern, while 25 percent voted for Nixon. Yet Nixon won the largest landslide ever and McGovern won only Massachusetts and the District of Columbia. In 1985, a *Los Angeles Times* survey offered a comprehensive comparison of journalists to Americans and found that 55 percent of journalists were self-described liberals, while only 23 percent of average Americans were.

Findings in the 1990s revealed a greater disparity in the political affiliations of reporters and average citizens. In a 1992 election study, 89 percent of reporters voted for Bill Clinton (who received only 43 percent of the popular vote), 7 percent voted for George H.W. Bush (37 percent in the election), and 2 percent voted for Ross Perot (who received 19 percent). In the same study, 50 percent of the media said they were Democrats and 4 percent said they were Republicans.

A 2000 *Orlando Sentinel* study looked at some 3,400 journalists and found that journalists are less likely to get married, have children, volunteer in communities, own homes, or go to church than others living within their respective communities.

More recently, David Horowitz and Joseph Light found that Democrats outnumber Republicans 15 to 1 at Columbia University's journalism school, and 10 to 0 at the University of California. A 2004 Pew study found that at national news outlets, liberals outnumbered conservatives 34 percent to 7 percent.

Additional studies have found a liberal bias in the media. David Brady and Jonathan Ma found that the *New York Times* and the *Washington Post* tend to treat liberal senators as bipartisan and malign conservative senators. The newspapers defined Senator Tom Harkin as a "kindred liberal Democrat from Iowa," and Ted Kennedy as the party's "old-school liberal" or a "liberal spokesman." Conservatives, on the other hand, *Times* reporters cast as belligerent and extreme, using phrases like "the most unyielding conservative," "arch-conservative," and "contentious conservative." The *Washington Post,* Brady and Ma say, described liberal senators as bipartisan lawmakers and iconic leaders of a noble cause, but portrayed conservatives as hostile, combative, and out of the mainstream.

Quantifying Bias In a study of 20 major print and TV news outlets, Tim Groseclose and Jeffrey Milyo of the University of Missouri found that two leaned conservative, Fox News and *The Washington Times*, but the other 18 ranged from slightly to substantially left of center. In an analysis that studied only segments classified as news, not editorials or talk shows, the finding revealed *PBS NewsHour* to be as close to the middle as any they examined.

Recent Presidential Campaigns Using a large sample of national stories from the 2008 and 2012 campaigns and a system to classify news stories as positive or negative (many had no distinction), Pew's Project for Excellence in Journalism compared the reporting on the major party candidates. In 2008, Pew found a bias in favor of Obama. They found 36 percent of Obama's coverage was positive, while only 14 percent of McCain's was. About 57 percent of McCain coverage was decidedly negative, while only 29 percent of Obama was. The variance in 2012 was not as great. About 19 percent of Obama stories were favorable and 30 percent unfavorable. For Romney, 15 percent were positive and 38 percent negative. When discounting horse race journalism, virtually no difference existed. Another interesting finding from the 2012 report shines light on narrowcasting. Only 3 percent of MSNBC stories painted Romney positively and 71 percent showed him negatively. Only 6 percent of Fox News segments presented Obama positively and 46 percent negatively.

These studies reveal members of the media as left of center. Yet some argue that since Nixon's media siege, the claim of "liberal bias" over and over has caused reporters to overcompensate toward the right. Eric Alterman, author of *What Liberal Media?* compares this constant cry of "liberal media" to the practice of "working the ref" and alleges the tactic causes members of the media to overcompsenate because they are too wary of the liberal accusation.

Talk Radio Lifting the Fairness Doctrine has contributed to the growth of political **talk radio**. Since 1987, the removal of constraints on balanced broadcasting has created an opening for conservatives. In fact, conservatives have gained a near monopoly on the AM radio channels. Rush Limbaugh has led the way. For 20 years the self-proclaimed conservative has led in ratings across the nation. Sean Hannity, Glenn Beck, Laura Ingraham, and others have syndicated their talk shows that mostly host Republican interviewees and conservative commentators. Air America, a left-leaning radio venture that tried to counterbalance this conservative domination, went bankrupt in the process. The number of talk radio stations has grown from about 500 in 1990 to about 2,500.

REFLECT ON THE ESSENTIAL QUESTION

Essential Question: *What are the roles of the media in the political system and the impact of media on public affairs?* On a separate paper, complete a chart like the one below to gather details to answer that question.

Roles of the Media	Impact of the Media

KEY TERMS, NAMES, AND EVENTS

adversarial press
Associated Press (AP)
Big Three networks
bully pulpit
bureaus
Corporation for Public Broadcasting (CPB)
C-SPAN
editorials
equal time
exposé
Fairness Doctrine
Federal Communications Commission (FCC)
free press

gatekeeper
horse race journalism
investigative reporting
journalistic integrity
libel
mainstream media
muckrakers
narrowcasting
National Public Radio (NPR)
New York Times v. United States (1971)
off the record
on the record
Pentagon Papers
press conferences

prior restraint
Public Broadcasting System (PBS)
right of reply
scorekeeper
selective attention
sensationalism
shield laws
slander
talk radio
Telecommunications Act
watchdog
wire service
yellow journalism

1. The first generation of newspapers in the United States was mostly influenced by
   (A) political parties
   (B) the Associated Press
   (C) yellow journalists
   (D) the executive branch
   (E) the clear threat of prior restraint

2. The Supreme Court's decision in *New York Times v. United States*
   (A) allowed for public protest of the war
   (B) declared for the first time that newspapers could criticize government action
   (C) prevented the government from blocking publication of leaked information
   (D) raised the threshold for government officials to sue for libel
   (E) required reporters to reveal anonymous sources to law enforcement

3. When a local TV station broadcasts a report of the mayor embezzling public money, the media has served the function of
   (A) scorekeeper
   (B) watchdog
   (C) gatekeeper
   (D) disseminator
   (E) regulator

4. Some states have passed shield laws to
   (A) limit the exposure of corrupt government
   (B) assure government officials the First Amendment as well
   (C) assure candidates the right to reply
   (D) protect a reporter's right to keep anonymous sources confidential
   (E) assure no prior restraint

5. Academics and researchers who point to a liberal media bias usually cite
   (A) the ideological views and voter registration of reporters
   (B) the corporate influence of the business community
   (C) the influence of talk radio
   (D) attitudes espoused in the *Wall Street Journal*
   (E) the reporting of Fox News

6. Which of the following media is supported with congressional funding?
   (A) *New York Times*
   (B) CBS-TV
   (C) National Public Radio
   (D) *USA Today*
   (E) AM talk radio

7. All of the following are recent concerns about the news media EXCEPT
   (A) blurring news reporting with opinion and commentary
   (B) intense, fast-paced competition that results in sloppy reporting
   (C) corporate concern for bottom line profits that hampers journalistic integrity
   (D) the removal of the Fairness Doctrine, which prevents broadcaster independence
   (E) the Internet diminishing the role and impact of print newspapers

8. The primary reason for the growth of yellow journalism in the late 1800s was
   (A) passage of the Communications Act
   (B) increased efforts by investigative reporters
   (C) sensationalism increased the profits of national newspapers
   (D) objective standards set by the Associated Press
   (E) an increase in political parties financing newspapers

Leading Newsmakers of Midterm Campaign (Jan. 1–Oct. 31, 2010)	
Name, Office or Office Sought (Party) State	**Election Stories**
Barack Obama, President (D)	343
Christine O'Donnell, Senate candidate (R) DE	160
Meg Whitman, Governor candidate (R) CA	90
Rand Paul, Senate candidate (R) KY	88
Joe Sestak, Senate candidate (D) PA	85
Sharron Angle, Senate candidate (R) NV	80

Source: Pew Center for Excellence in Journalism

9. The table above reflects which media trend?
   (A) The media covers only poll numbers and not substance.
   (B) The national media covers candidates for congressional, not state, races.
   (C) The president doesn't get involved in midterm elections.

(D) The liberal media tends to paint Democrats positively.

(E) The media covers the president disproportionately compared to other offices and races.

10. Which of the following created a high threshold of proof for those suing for libel?

(A) *United States v. Nixon*

(B) *New York Times v. United States*

(C) The Fairness Doctrine

(D) *Red Lion Broadcasting v. FCC*

(E) *New York Times v. Sullivan*

FREE-RESPONSE QUESTIONS

Question

1. The nature and role of of the media have evolved in the United States.

(a) Identify and describe one form of news media.

(b) Identify one trend and explain its impact in the development of the form of news media described in (a).

(c) Identify and explain one basic role of the press.

Question

2. The federal government has initiated several policies that impact radio and television broadcasts.

(a) Identify and describe two federal institutions that can impact broadcast regulations and describe how each can regulate broadcasts.

(b) Identify one policy created by each institution you described in (a) and describe how each policy impacts broadcast.

(c) Identify and discuss one constraint that broadcast regulations create.

WRITING: USE PROPER NAMES

Real names of individuals or organizations will give a crispness to your response, though they are not typically expected. For example, for #1 above, any of the following proper nouns from Chapter 8 would enhance your response: Associated Press, William Randolph Hearst, National Gazette, Edward R. Murrow, Fox News, or MSNBC.

UNIT 3: Conclusion

The chapters in Unit 3 have explored how political parties, interest groups, and the media are conduits to democracy. If it weren't for parties, interest groups, and the press, many American voices would never be heard, and fewer citizens would understand government. Political parties, very broad coalitions, choose candidates and try to place them into office. Countless people also have more narrowly tailored interests, and they coalesce to create interest groups. These groups represent everyone from police officers to Wall Street financiers. Many form PACs and develop relationships with lawmakers. The pluralist theory holds that many interests are better than few and that they create opposing political forces and operate like a check and balance outside the Constitution.

Because there is so much interest in who will govern and winning elections takes so much money and public effort, the government has passed laws to properly and fairly administer elections. Most notably, the Congress created the FEC to monitor campaign finance limits.

The media report on government, help set a national agenda, and often give their opinions. They have gone from party-financed printed publications to a fast-paced, interactive platform. Select language or images can heavily enhance or ruin candidates or stop a policy idea. Since the Supreme Court has ruled that government has no right to prior restraint, the freedom of the media to express a wide range of ideas is guaranteed. The Court's ruling that public figures claiming libel must prove it to a high threshold further extends the media's right to free expression.

THINK AS A POLITICAL SCIENTIST: ANALYZE, INTERPRET, AND SYNTHESIZE EACH PARTY'S PLATFORM

On their respective Web sites, www.democrats.org and www.gop.org, you will find the parties' most current platforms with carefully worded position statements on selected issues. Excerpts of these are on pages 120-121. The language explaining their positions is more nuanced than simply "pro-death penalty" or "anti-tax." You can either click through a Web version or find and download the party platform in PDF format. Using either method, select two issues and analyze and interpret how each party proposes to address these. What are the similarities in addressing the issue? How distinct are their differences? What buzz words or select language do they use? How specific are their proposals, and is it challenging for independents to disagree?

Synthesize your findings by making a simple grid or table that explains these differences. Quote relevant phrases or sentences from the platforms.

UNIT 4: Institutions of National Government

Chapter 9   Congress

Chapter 10   Presidency

Chapter 11   Bureaucracy

Chapter 12   Judiciary

The responsibilities of the three branches of government are carried out by four institutions: Congress, defined in Article I; the president and the executive branch's large bureaucracy, deriving from Article II; and the courts, more vaguely mentioned in Article III.

Congress is the most representative branch. Its 535 members, delegates, committees, staffers, and agencies determine policy in the areas of national defense, the economy, trade, and an array of government services. The House and Senate have developed unique leadership roles and legislative procedures to carry out their business.

The American Presidency is an iconic and powerful institution on a world scale that has become much more influential over time. Presidents administer the law through a large hierarchy of law enforcement, military, trade, and financial agencies. The chief executive meets with world leaders, designs a national budget, and campaigns for his party's candidates.

The Judicial Branch was created to settle federal disputes (criminal and civil), to ensure justice, and to interpret the law. A loosely defined branch at the founding, the Judiciary has become a three-level court system. The vast majority of federal cases are tried by U.S. district courts and end there. The appeals process, however, takes cases to the circuit and Supreme Courts where much U.S. law is shaped.

As you read these chapters, notice how each institution's unique customs and rules define it, and notice how the branches interact with one another.

Key Concepts

Institutions of National Government: The Congress, the Presidency, the Bureaucracy, and the Federal Courts

- The major formal and informal institutional arrangements of power
- Relationships among these four institutions and varying balances of power
- Linkages between institutions and voters, interest groups, and political parties

Source: *AP®United States Government and Politics Course and Exam Description*

9

Congress

"I served with, not under, eight presidents."

—Sam Rayburn, Speaker of the House of Representatives

Essential Question: How are American citizens represented, and how does Congress put policy ideas into effect?

The United States Congress is perhaps the world's most democratic governing body. As defined in Article I of the Constitution, Congress consists of the Senate and the House of Representatives. These governing bodies meet in Washington, D.C., to craft legislation that sets out a sound national policy for the benefit of U.S. citizens. Congress creates statutes, or laws, that become part of the United States Code. Its 535 members and roughly 30,000 support staff operate under designated rules to carry out the legislative process, to build and enhance highways and other public works, and to protect American citizens.

History of Congress

The U.S. Congress was officially established in 1789. The two houses of Congress performed their legislative business in several different places before settling in the current Capitol Building in Washington, D.C., in the 1850s. Congress struggled to keep the Union intact through a generation of compromises before the Civil War in 1861. Congress also passed laws in the late nineteenth and early twentieth centuries to regulate industry and trusts to protect Americans from unfair business practices. It also financed and helped manage two world wars.

The Framers' Plan

Inadequate representation in the government of Great Britain was a main cause of the Revolutionary War and the desire for independence. To ensure representation in the new government, the Framers carefully designed a legislature that would be responsive to the people as a whole while also responsive to the states. When delegates gathered to discuss their individual ideas about government, they ultimately agreed to make the new Congress the chief policymaking branch.

NOTE: This book refers to both male and female leaders of committees and groups as "Chairmen." Addressing females as "Madam Chairman" dates back to the mid-1970s when the powerful Leonor Sullivan of Missouri chaired the House Merchant Marine and Fishers Committee. She insisted that Chairman was a title of rank, not gender, and she demanded the same rank as her male counterparts.

Article I proves the Framers wanted the most democratic branch to dominate policymaking. More than half of the debates at the Constitutional Convention concerned the proposed Congress. The Framers gave Congress the power to check the other two branches by overriding a presidential veto, to change the jurisdiction and size of the courts, to fund (or refuse to fund) the other two branches, to impeach and remove presidents and judges, and most important, to draft, debate, and pass most laws that govern the country.

Bicameralism The **bicameral**, or two-house, legislature resulted from a dispute among small and large states, each desiring different forms of representation. The Great Compromise dictated the number of House seats would be allotted based on the number of inhabitants living within each state. Article I's provision for a census every 10 years assured states an allotment of these seats proportionately. States would send the same number of delegates, two, to the U.S. Senate.

Unique Houses The Framers also designed each house to have a different character and separate responsibilities. The House of Representatives was designed to represent the general populace, while the Senate was originally composed of men elected by state legislatures. Senators are somewhat insulated from public opinion by their longer terms, and they have more constitutional responsibilities than members of the House. In geographic terms, the smaller congressional districts allow House members to have a more intimate constituent-representative relationship, while senators must represent an entire state and therefore typically face a more diverse electorate.

Cautious Lawmaking The simple fact that Congress has two chambers that must approve legislation helps prevent the passage of rash laws. Madison pointed out "a second house of the legislature, distinct from and dividing the power with the first, must always be a beneficial check on the government. It doubles the people's security by requiring the concurrence of two distinct bodies."

The House The more representative House of Representatives is designed to reflect the will of the people and to prevent the kinds of abuses of power experienced in the colonial era. The House has the power to impeach federal officers, the priority to create revenue (tax) laws, and the privilege to select the president if no candidate wins the Electoral College. Some states sent their House members as an at-large, statewide delegation in the early years, but now they draw congressional districts, so representatives are responsible to smaller geographic areas. With their two-year terms, House members are forced to consider popular opinions lest they be replaced by an unsatisfied electorate.

The Senate The Senate's six-year terms offer a way to temper the popular ideas adopted by the House, since Senators cannot so quickly be voted out of office for opposing popular acts. The upper house has additional, elevated responsibilities. Its **advice and consent** power allows Senators to recommend or reject executive branch appointees. The Senate must ratify international treaties, and it is the ultimate judge on removing impeached officials.

Collectively, these two bodies pass legislation. Bills can originate in either chamber, except for tax laws, which must originate in the House. Bills must pass both houses by a majority vote to become law (with the president's signature). Congress has the power of the purse (spending), to declare war, and to oversee the general management of the federal government.

Constitutional qualifications differ for each house.

QUALIFICATIONS FOR HOUSE MEMBERS
Serve 2-year terms
Are elected by the people
Must be 25 years old
Must reside in the state they represent
Must be a citizen for at least 7 years
Have the sole power of impeachment
Have priority on tax law

QUALIFICATIONS FOR SENATE MEMBERS
Serve 6-year terms
Were elected by state legislatures (by the people since 1913)
Must be 30 years old
Must reside in the state they represent
Must be a citizen for at least 9 years
Have advice and consent power on presidential appointments
Judge impeachments and can remove officials

First Congress to the Civil War

The first Congress met in New York City on March 4, 1789, and was composed of 65 members. However, because of slow transportation, not enough members arrived to constitute a **quorum**—the required number in attendance to do business, which the Constitution defines as a simple majority. For this reason, the opening date for the House session was postponed until April 1 and for the Senate until April 6, when a quorum was finally present.

One of the first power plays between Congress and the president occurred when George Washington brought a proposed treaty with southeastern Indian tribes into the Senate for ratification. Vice President John Adams, serving as the president of the Senate, immediately called for a vote. But two senators claimed the Senate should take some time to discuss the treaty's complexities instead. Though it did eventually ratify the treaty, the Senate had asserted itself and maintained an independence from the executive. President Washington fumed and never again entered the Senate chamber, nor has any president since.

That first Congress went on to pass the Bill of Rights, set the president's annual salary at $25,000, define the federal judicial system, and approve the president's first Cabinet. After a year in New York, Congress moved to Philadelphia. By 1800, it had grown to 106 seats and relocated permanently to Washington, D.C.

Henry Clay During the first half of the nineteenth century, Congress became the dominant branch, mostly from the influence of Speaker of the House Henry Clay of Kentucky. When Clay arrived in the House on November 4, 1811, the nation was on the brink of another war with Great Britain. He had served a partial term in the Senate and had already earned a solid reputation as an outstanding debater.

A meeting of pro-war members gathered before Congress opened and decided Clay should lead them. Along with President Madison, Clay marshaled the country into the War of 1812. He went on to author the Missouri Compromise of 1820 that eased the debate on slavery and delayed the Civil War. On the issue of that compromise, he gave an impassioned speech that completely consumed the members of the House. His speeches often drew crowds from among Washington elites, foreign ambassadors, and even adoring senators from across the Capitol.

A Generation of Compromise Other developments strengthened the House during its first generation. **Congressional caucuses**, or informal groups of like-minded members, began nominating candidates for president. During the antebellum period, the Senate became a respected hall of great oratory and a venue for even more compromises between the North and South. Giants such as Daniel Webster, proslavery advocate John C. Calhoun, and Henry Clay dominated the upper house. Congress generally managed to maintain a balance of slave and free states as new states were admitted into the Union.

The late 1850s brought national tensions and congressional incivility to new levels. In 1856, South Carolina Representative Preston Brooks violently attacked Massachusetts Senator Charles Sumner, the most vocal abolitionist in the Senate, beating him with his cane. Brooks claimed his actions were to avenge insults Sumner had hurled at the South, and more specifically at his cousin, in a floor speech the day before. Brooks received scores of canes from proslavery admirers from across the South. Sumner left for England for medical treatment.

After the 1860 election of Abraham Lincoln, southern state legislatures recalled their senators and representatives. After an emotional speech in January 1861, Mississippi Senator Jefferson Davis led several men from the South out of Congress. Their seats remained empty throughout the Civil War and for some time after.

Reconstruction Through Progressive Era

Congress's primary objective in the post–Civil War era was to reconstruct the nation and address economic issues brought on by industrialization and interstate commerce. A handful of African Americans from the South served in Congress. But this trend abruptly ended as federal officers pulled out of the former Confederacy and as southern states began instituting legal loopholes to prevent black suffrage.

In the late 1800s, powerful leaders attained House seats to heavily influence the people's chamber. The Senate became known as the "Millionaires' Club," a body of elite, well-to-do industrialists and political bosses who sided with big business.

Speakers Thomas Reed and Joseph Cannon Two autocratic Speakers of the House defined the position at the turn of the century and ran roughshod over other members. Republican Thomas Reed, a successful Maine lawyer, served from 1889 to 1899. He was a larger-than-life presence at six feet two inches and 275 pounds, with a strong voice that could override any uproar in the chamber. One colleague said Reed had a "tongue that at one stroke sliced whiskers off his opponents' faces." Reed's mastery of the rules—he had served on the Rules Committee for years—became a key weapon in his legislative arsenal. After a decade as Speaker, "Czar Reed" stepped down in opposition to the Spanish-American War.

By 1903, Representative Joseph Cannon of Illinois had risen to the Speaker's position. Cannon ruled the House with an iron fist. With 28 years in Congress and full control of the Rules Committee, this anti-reformer prevented much legislation from ever reaching the House floor. "Foul-Mouthed Joe" was a brazen man who constantly chewed or smoked a cigar and used indecent language. One *New York Times* reporter described his delivery as "a slashing sledgehammer, full of fire and fury." Cannon maintained control by rewarding the faithful and punishing the disloyal. With authority to appoint committee members and chairmen, Cannon followed the established seniority system when it suited him and refused when it did not. When a concerned constituent asked his representative for a copy of the House rules, the member sent him a picture of Joe Cannon.

Reforming the Speaker's Role The Speaker's role was changed when a combination of Democrats and progressive Republicans proposed rules changes. Representative George Norris of Nebraska introduced a resolution he had held in his pocket for weeks. On St. Patrick's Day, while Cannon's Irish allies were absent from the House, Norris made his move. Knowing Cannon would simply refer the proposal to the committee to be disposed, Norris claimed the Constitution ultimately states the House may determine its own rules. His proposal increased the size of the Rules Committee and mandated that the entire House, not the Speaker, would select the committee's members and its chairman. After 26 hours of debate and some compromise, the resolution passed over Cannon's opposition.

The Twentieth Century

Many reforms followed, including the **Seventeenth Amendment**, which fundamentally transformed the Senate. Senators were no longer held to the whims of a hundred or so state legislators, but to the voting citizens of the states instead. Members of Congress were provided a staff that grew from one assistant to several. Through major crises—two world wars and the Great Depression—Congress ceded much of its power to popular presidents. During the mid-twentieth century, Congress was transformed from a lesser-known, clubby institution of white men to a highly publicized branch that gradually began to look more like the nation at large. Representatives and senators began serving longer tenures through re-election. And, in an era of scandal, Congress became less civil, and less appreciated, by the public.

Television In the 1950s, Congress, its outspoken leaders, and its committee function were ushered into living rooms across the country. Anti-Communist hearings led by Senator Joe McCarthy and investigations into organized crime spearheaded by Tennessee Senator Estes Kefauver became vivid dramas. Such public hearings continued into the late 1960s as popularity for the Vietnam War faded and as Congress began to rein in some of the executive's war-making authority.

The growth of the television medium coincided with the professionalization of Congress. The Framers intended for lawmakers to serve a few years, but many congressional service tenures stretched to 20 and 30 years. Individual annual salaries went from $12,500 in 1947 to $42,500 in 1970. Members in both houses began to take full advantage of the lack of **term limits**, which limit the number of terms an incumbent may serve, and began to appear on television regularly as a campaign and fund-raising tool. With increased and affordable air flights, members departed Washington more frequently.

Minority Members Though some African Americans served in Congress during Reconstruction, and the first female was elected to the House after the 1916 campaign, Congress had remained almost exclusively a collection of elite white men. The women's and civil rights movements that followed World War II changed all that. A number of female senators began their congressional service not by election but through appointments by governors to seats previously held by their deceased husbands. Margaret Chase Smith of Maine earned her way into the upper house and served as the only Senate female during the 1950s. Women continued to be elected, and when the 114th Congress opened in January 2015, 20 women were representing their states in the upper house.

As the Jim Crow era began, fewer blacks were elected to Congress. When North Carolina's George White left the House in 1901, it was nearly 30 years before another man of color was sworn in. From 1928 to 1970, 13 African Americans were elected to Congress, none from the South, and only one to the Senate. (Barack Obama was only the fifth black senator ever when elected in 2004.) In the 114th session of Congress, there were 44 African Americans in the House and two in the Senate.

When women and blacks broke barriers by winning elections in their home districts, they did not always find Congress a welcoming place. As House historian Robert Remini reports, Congresswoman Pat Schroeder recounts the experience she and Ron Dellums, an African-American member from California, had in the early 1970s as the first minorities on the Armed Services Committee. The committee chairman reportedly said that women and blacks were worth only half a typical member, so he added only one chair to the committee room table for Schroeder and Dellums to share. "Nobody else objected and nobody offered to scrounge up another chair," Schroeder recalls.

As Congress diversified, it also gained a reputation for seeking equality. A series of civil rights laws under Lyndon Johnson's administration gave the federal government oversight of state elections and school desegregation. In the 1970s, Title IX put women's college programs on the same footing as men's, and the House and Senate finally passed the Equal Rights Amendment (though the states never fully ratified it).

Scandal Despite these positive changes, the post–World War II era was tainted by a series of scandals that colored Congress as the nation's interrogator and sullied the people's impression of their national government. Twenty years after the McCarthy hearings, America watched as the House Speaker's staffers were convicted of crimes involving the stock market and other financial institutions. A long list of congressional members received outrageously large donations from influential individuals and outlandish perks from corporations. The House Ways and Means Committee chairman was discovered late at night, drunk, in a car with an exotic dancer.

The scandals and the revelations brought about some positive changes, however. Committee votes were made public, FEC laws limited campaign donations, the seniority system was weakened, and Congress reclaimed some of its war powers.

Powers of Congress

The Framers assigned a basic list of powers to Congress in the spirit of limited government. Since then, advancements in society, Supreme Court interpretations, and altered expectations of government have greatly expanded Congress's powers.

Expressed Powers

Expressed powers are congressional powers expressly stated in the Constitution. Article I, Section 8 lists the scope of the federal legislature's authority. These enumerated powers include the power to tax, regulate interstate commerce, declare war, operate the military, define the naturalization process (become a citizen), and several other powers.

The Commerce Clause Congress has the power "to regulate commerce among the states, with other nations, and with Indian tribes." Recall the 1824 dispute in *Gibbons v. Ogden,* discussed in Chapter 2, over the regulation of navigable waterways. The Court sided with the national government, which began a series of debates on the depth of Congress's power over commerce that has never ended. Congress's commerce power has been contested in the Supreme Court more than any other power. It came into contention during the New Deal and was a constitutional justification for the 1964 Civil Rights Act, as Congress required proprietors of lunch counters to accept customers of all races. In more recent years, Congress has assumed wide authority over nearly every type of both interstate and intrastate commerce.

Power of the Purse Article I provides that no money can be drawn from the Treasury, "But in consequence of appropriations made by law." Congress appropriates, or allots, how public money will be spent. The Congress works in concert with the administration in determining the budget. Both the House and Senate have committees for budgeting and appropriations. Ultimately, Congress has the "power of the purse."

Members of Congress set their own salaries. Like anyone else, congressional members love a pay raise but absolutely hate voting for it. Pay raises typically become campaign issues, as the election challenger can easily point to an incumbent member's "salary grab." The **Twenty-seventh Amendment**, passed in 1992, prevents any pay raises from taking effect until the following Congress. In 2015, members of Congress earned $174,000 per year.

Foreign Affairs and the Military Congress is a key player in U.S. foreign policy, and it oversees the military. It can raise armies and navies, legislate or enact conscription procedures, and mandate a military draft. Congress determines money spent on military bases and, through an independent commission, has authority over base closings. It sets the salary schedule for all military personnel.

Congress plays a part in foreign policy as well. Both houses have a foreign policy committee. The Senate has more foreign relations duties than the House does. The Framers gave the upper house the power to ratify or deny treaties with other countries. The Senate also approves U.S. ambassadors. In *Federalist #75*, Madison argued for the Senate, not the House, to handle treaties and foreign affairs due to its continuity. "Because of the fluctuating and . . . multitudinous composition of the House, we can't expect it to have the qualities essential to properly executing such a trust." The chairman of the Senate Foreign Relations Committee works with the president and secretary of state to forge U.S. foreign policy.

Implied Powers

The "necessary and proper" clause, or elastic clause, gives Congress the power "To make all Laws which shall be necessary and proper for carrying into Execution the foregoing Powers." Basically, Congress's **implied power** is its ability to make the laws necessary to carry out its expressed powers.

The elastic clause first came into contention in the case of *McCulloch v. Maryland* in 1819. Congress created a national bank, and the state of Maryland and strict constructionists felt it lacked the power to do so. The word *bank* cannot be found in the enumerated list of expressed powers, critics pointed out. Nationalists argued in response that a bank was essential, since Congress can borrow money, coin money, regulate commerce, and deal in other finances. On appeal, the Supreme Court found for McCulloch and the United States. This opinion also stated that the states cannot tax the national government due to the supremacy clause. Congress had won a massive victory.

The Legislative Institution

Congress has structures and procedures that define the election process, the conduct of business, distribution of House seats, rules of debates and voting, and the support systems that assist the legislative process.

Congressional Elections

"A congressman's first obligation is to get elected," said Senator Russell Long of Louisiana; "his second is to get re-elected." Running for Congress today is no easy task. In most cases, candidates need more than $1 million to survive a primary campaign and a general election. Good candidates have some type of prior elected experience, such as serving in the state legislature or in county-level positions. Some successful first-time candidates with a grasp of the issues and a pipeline to money can earn a seat in the Congress, too. In more competitive congressional races and most Senate contests, both Republican and Democratic candidates face fellow party members in primary elections. Then, in November of even-numbered years, party-nominated candidates go head-to-head in the general election. The 435 House races plus elections for one-third of the Senate seats make for many independent contests. The national political parties have little influence in how many of these campaigns operate. For the closer contests, the party assists local candidates via the party-driven Democratic and Republican campaign committees.

Congress's Image Americans generally view Congress negatively and give it low approval ratings. Yet most individual members of Congress enjoy about a 60 percent approval rating from their constituency. This dynamic causes challengers to point to the "mess in Washington," but the composition of Congress changes very little every two years. Well over 90 percent of incumbents seeking re-election in the House win their seats. The average tenure in the House for current members is 9.1 years. Senators serve an average of 10.2 years. Representative John Dingell Jr. of Michigan served the longest in the House, 58 years. Robert Byrd of West Virginia was the longest serving Senator at 51 years.

Incumbency Members of Congress have the advantage of **incumbency** over election rivals who run to replace them. Incumbents win re-election because they are familiar names and faces. Even negative press coverage reminds casual voters of their legislator. The **franking privilege**, or free use of the mail with a "frank," or signature, facilitates communication with constituents and allows members to take credit for their activity. Senators and representatives can provide **constituent services**, such as addressing a senior citizen's Medicare concern or arranging a tour of the Capitol for a visiting constituent. In many states, the majority party in the state legislature has created congressional districts that favor one party. Districts in which a party consistently tends to win by more than 55 percent of the vote are considered **safe seats**; those districts with closer elections are referred to as **marginal seats**.

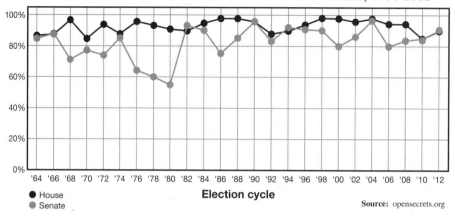

U.S. HOUSE AND SENATE RE-ELECTION RATES, 1964–2012

● House
● Senate

Election cycle

Source: opensecrets.org

To combat incumbents' advantage in retaining their seats for consecutive terms, critics have called for term limits. A movement to enact term limits gained attention in the 1990s in several states. However, in the 1995 *U.S. Term Limits, Inc. v. Thornton* case, the Supreme Court ruled that term limits for federal office require a constitutional amendment.

Membership of Congress

Today's Congress has 535 members (with nonvoting House delegates from Washington, D.C., Guam, Puerto Rico, Virgin Islands, and American Samoa). Most members are men; an overwhelming majority are college educated and from households with above-average incomes. More than half of the members of Congress have a net worth of over $1 million. The average age in the House is 57; in the Senate it is 62. The dominant professions of these members before entering Congress were prior public service, law, and business. Congress has become increasingly diverse, but it by no means mirrors the ethnic, gender, or socioeconomic divisions in America at large.

Democrat and Republican majorities have alternately dominated Congress over the years. Since World War II, the Democratic Party most often has held the majority of seats in both houses. Democrats controlled the House from 1955 to 1995 as well as the Senate for most of those years, except the early 1980s. In the 1994 elections, however, the Republicans handily won the majority in both houses and typically held control of them until the 2006 elections.

Source: Gage Skidmore / Flickr

Representative Mia Love of Utah is the first African-American Republican female elected to Congress (2014). Here she addresses the Conservative Political Action Conference.

The House

The lower house is more responsive to the people than the Senate, and it more quickly takes on the more popular agenda items. House members take great pride in their roles to represent the underrepresented.

Reapportionment Since 1913, the House has been composed of 435 members, with the temporary exception of adding two more for the annexation of Alaska and Hawaii. Each congressional district has more than 700,000 inhabitants. The Reapportionment Act of 1929 mandates the periodic **reapportionment**, or distribution, of U.S. congressional seats according to changes in the census figures. Each decade, the U.S. Census Bureau tabulates state populations and then awards the proportional number of seats to each state. Every state receives at least one seat. States gain, lose, or maintain the same number of seats.

Redistricting The state legislatures must alter congressional district maps to reflect these changes. The **redistricting** process in each state can be competitive and contentious. The party in power in the state legislature ultimately determines the new statewide map of congressional districts and does so to benefit the party in the following election. Too often, there are illogical district lines drawn to give the advantage to one party, a process called **gerrymandering**. Countless districts across the United States have been carved out to guarantee safe seats and one-party rule, which has often made the primary election the determining race for members of the House. To counter this tactic, several states have created independent commissions to remove the parties' dominance in the process.

REAPPORTIONED MAP AFTER 2010 CENSUS, FOR 2012 ELECTIONS

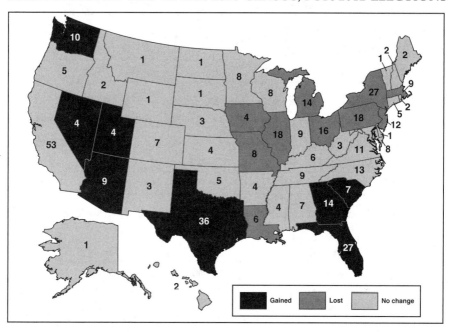

"One Man, One Vote" Rule In the 1960s, two Supreme Court cases addressed fairness in the reapportionment and redistricting process. The Tennessee General Assembly had not redrawn its legislative map since 1900, in violation of the Tennessee State Constitution that required redistricting every 10 years. The 1960 census showed drastic demographic shifts had occurred in the state. In *Baker v. Carr* **(1962)**, the Court ruled that Tennessee violated the equal protection clause of the Fourteenth Amendment because districts were not proportionately represented. In another case, out of Georgia, *Wesberry v. Sanders* **(1964)**, voters pointed to the state's malapportioned congressional districts. The Court came to basically the same conclusion. These districts had to be drawn so that roughly the same population existed in one district as in another. These two decisions collectively create the "one man, one vote" principle for representation.

Discharge Petition The creation and function of the **discharge petition** prove an expansion of democracy in the House. The discharge petition can bring a bill out of a reluctant committee. The petition's required number of signatures has altered over the years. It now stands at a simple majority to discharge a bill out of committee and onto the House floor. Thus, if 218 members sign, no chairman or reluctant committee can prevent the majority's desire to publicly discuss the bill. This measure may or may not lead to the bill's passage, but it prevents a minority from stopping a majority on advancing the bill.

Is That Constitutional? *Shaw v. Reno* (1993)

Can states draw new congressional districts with race in mind? That was the question in ***Shaw v. Reno*** (1993). After the 1990 census, North Carolina submitted its congressional district map to the U.S. Attorney General, Janet Reno, to comply with the 1965 Voting Rights Act. Reno and the Justice Department required the state to reconfigure the districts because there was only one majority black district. The state complied and redrew lines, yielding a very bizarrely shaped district. It was called the "I-85 District" because at one point it barely straddled each side of Interstate 85. North Carolina residents challenged the plan as a violation of the equal protection clause. The litigants argued that these unusually shaped districts, drawn with race in mind, violated their rights. The Court narrowly agreed with the plaintiffs. The bizarrely shaped district, which was not compact and barely contiguous, may have resulted from a noble effort but exceeded what was reasonably necessary to avoid racial imbalance.

NORTH CAROLINA'S "I-85 DISTRICT"

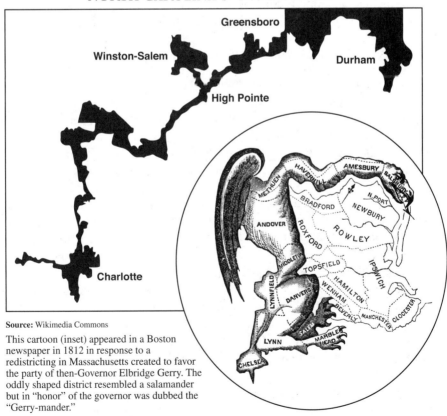

Source: Wikimedia Commons

This cartoon (inset) appeared in a Boston newspaper in 1812 in response to a redistricting in Massachusetts created to favor the party of then-Governor Elbridge Gerry. The oddly shaped district resembled a salamander but in "honor" of the governor was dubbed the "Gerry-mander."

C-SPAN The airing of C-SPAN (Cable Satellite Public Affairs Network) opened the House to a national audience in 1979. In 1986 C-SPAN-2 began covering the Senate. Congress controls and owns the cameras, while C-SPAN, an independent, nonprofit, private organization, determines all of the programming. Speaker Tip O'Neill called it "one of the best decisions I ever made," in pushing for cameras, claiming it revealed to constituents how hardworking, intelligent men and women dedicated themselves in Congress.

The Senate

The Senate has been called "the world's greatest deliberative body." George Washington explained the character of the U.S. Senate: "We pour our coffee into a saucer to cool it, we pour legislation into the senatorial saucer to cool it." The Framers wanted a cautious, experienced group to handle foreign affairs and presidential appointments. Additionally, only one-third of the Senate is up for re-election every two years, making it a **continuous body**. In *The Federalist*, Madison argued, "By leaving a lot of old ones (senators) in place, uniformity and order, as well as a constant succession of official information, will be preserved."

The Senate, with its smaller numbers, has fewer rules and few restrictions on what members can do. Debate can go much longer. The Senate uses measures that require higher thresholds for action and that slow it down. These include unanimous consent and the hold. When the Senate takes action, unanimous consent is typically requested—that is, "Does anyone object?" If anyone does, then the motion is put on hold or at least stalled for discussion. For years senators abused this privilege, as a few senators, even one, could stop popular legislation. Then and now, senators can place a hold on a motion or on a presidential appointment.

Delaying legislation in this way brought about changes in the rules. As the United States stepped closer to war in 1917, President Woodrow Wilson called for changes in Senate procedures so that a small minority of senators could not block U.S. action in arming merchant ships for defense. A **filibuster**, a lengthy speech to delay action on a bill, blocked his armed neutrality plan before America's entrance into World War I. President Wilson was enraged. The Senate, he said, "is the only legislative body in the world which cannot act when its majority is ready for action. A little group of willful men," Wilson went on, "have rendered the great government of the United States helpless."

Rule 22 Wilson called the Senate into special session and demanded the rules change. The Senate created Rule 22, or the **cloture rule,** which enabled and required a two-thirds supermajority to close up or stop debate on a bill and call for a vote. In 1975, the Senate lowered the standard to three-fifths, or 60 out of 100 senators. Once cloture is reached, each senator has the privilege of speaking for up to one hour on that bill or topic.

Advice and Consent The Senate also has the prerogative of advising and consenting with the president on appointments such as Cabinet secretaries and federal judges. The upper house, over the years, has approved most appointees quickly. Senators often recommend people for positions in the executive branch or judges to serve in their states. High-level appointments must first clear a confirmation hearing, where the appropriate committee essentially interviews the nominee. If the committee votes in favor of the nominee, then the entire Senate will take a vote. A simple majority is required.

How Congress Votes

Many legislators say one of the hardest jobs is voting. Determining exactly what most people want in their home state is nearly impossible. Legislators hold town hall meetings, examine public opinion polls, hold focus groups, and read stacks of mail and emails to get an idea of their constituents' desires. Members also consider a variety of other factors in deciding how to vote.

Representing "Very often [lawmakers] are not voting for or against an issue for the reasons that seem apparent," historian David McCullough once explained. "They're voting for some other reason. Because they have a grudge against someone . . . or because they're doing a friend a favor, or because they're willing to risk their political skin and vote their conscience." There are multiple views on what impacts members' votes. Those members trying to reflect the will of their constituency follow the **representative (or delegate) model**. At a town hall meeting in one member's district, an irritated and upset constituent shot down his representative's explanation for an unpopular vote. "We didn't send you to Washington to make intelligent decisions," the angry voter said, "we sent you to represent us."

Other members follow the general beliefs of their party. Party leaders encourage members to follow the party-line vote, especially if political favors are expected. Other members are ideologically aligned with certain groups who back them at election time. Those following the lead of their party or some other group are operating in an organizational way. Some members simply follow their conscience or the general public attitude toward the issue. This more independent approach is often called the **trustee model**. Voters have elected their representative and entrust them with the job.

Logrolling—trading votes to gain support for a bill—is another factor affecting lawmaking. By agreeing to back someone else's bill, members can secure a vote in return for a bill of their own.

Staffers and Capitol Hill

In 1907, the first House office building was completed. It had 397 offices, one for each member at that time, and 14 committee rooms. Today, each senator employs an average of 40 staffers, and each House member has about 17. Some of these assistants answer constituents' phone calls from a district office. Most swarm Capitol Hill in a complex network that supports the legislative process. Senators and representatives can assign various titles and responsibilities to their staffers. Most will have a chief of staff (the lawmaker's chief aide), one or more communications experts, and constituent liaisons. Legislative assistants familiarize their boss with details on large bills. Press secretaries connect with the media and schedule interviews. Most Washington staffers are young, single, and willing to work long hours for relatively low pay.

Capitol Hill has several structures beyond the Capitol Building, such as the Dirksen and Russell Office Buildings, that hold committee hearings and members' offices. These buildings, which are named for former notable leaders, house much of the inner workings of the institution. Besides Senate staffers, some committees also have independent staffs as well. The Capitol has an infrastructure all its own that includes everything from a police department to food services.

Organization of the Legislative Process

Congress is organized by house, party, leadership, and committee. The parties create leadership positions to coach the party members, to move legislation, and to carry out the parties' goals. Congress's formalized groups include both lawmaking committees and partisan or ideological private groups. Some of the powerful committees are institutions unto themselves, as committees are where the real work of Congress is done.

Leadership

The only official congressional leaders mentioned in the Constitution are the Speaker of the House, the President of the Senate, and the President *Pro Tempore* of the Senate. The document states that the House and Senate "shall choose their other Officers." Both have done so.

Positions and Roles The Constitution originally set early December as the opening for Congress. Since ratification of the Twentieth Amendment, however, Congress has opened on January 3 in odd-numbered years, or on a day prescribed by law (another day Congress sets). Each house's first order of business is to elect leaders. The party caucuses—that is, the entire party membership within each house—gather privately days or weeks before to determine their choices for Speaker and the other leadership positions. These party caucus meetings, in a way, parallel a primary election. In a closed-door meeting and often by secret ballot, members vote their choices of who will lead them. The actual public vote for leadership positions takes place when Congress opens and is invariably a party-line vote.

In his 2014 memoir, South Carolina Representative James Clyburn recalls campaigning for the Democratic whip position. Expecting his party to win the majority in 2006, Clyburn announced his desire for the job to the Congressional Black Caucus well before the November elections. His campaign against Rahm Emanuel and others required many phone calls, connections with the right people, and a lot of follow-up meetings and calls. The campaign became heated when Clyburn accused Emanuel or his supporters of "playing the race card, though no means openly," by planting a story that, "as a black southerner, I did not have the ability to raise money." Emanuel later stepped out of the race, and Clyburn was elected whip.

Once the leaders are elected, they oversee the organization of Congress, form committees, and proceed with the legislative agenda.

Speaker of the House The Speaker of the House has lost power since the demise of Joe Cannon, but it still is a powerful position. In January 2007,

Nancy Pelosi, a Democrat from California, became the first female Speaker of the House. After a Republican midterm victory in November 2010, John Boehner of Ohio was elected Speaker as the 112th Congress opened in January 2011. The Speaker recognizes members for speaking, organizes members for conference committees, and has great influence in most matters of lawmaking.

Floor Leaders On the next rung down in the House are the majority and minority leaders. These are the **floor leaders** that lead debate among their party and guide the discussion from their side of the aisle. They are the first recognized in debate. Party leaders have also become spokespersons for the party in press conferences and in interviews on Sunday talk shows.

Whips The deputy floor leader, also known as the **whip**, is in charge of party discipline. The whip keeps the tally of votes among his or her party members, which aids in determining the optimum time for a vote. Whips have also strong-armed party members to vote with the party. Political favors or even party support during an election can have a persuasive influence on representatives contemplating an independent vote. The whip also ensures his or her own party members' good standing in an ethical and professional capacity. When scandals or missteps occur, the whip may ask a member to step down from a chair position or to leave Congress entirely.

Senate Leaders In the Senate, a similar structure exists. The Constitution names the vice president of the United States as the nonvoting President of the Senate. In case of a tie, the vice president can vote to break it. He or she is also meant to rule on procedure and organize the Senate. For years, the vice president was more like the Speaker, organizing committees and running floor debate. However, now the vice president is rarely in the Senate chamber and usually delegates the responsibility of moderating debate to other members. The Constitution also provided for the **president** *pro tempore*, or temporary president. The "pro tem" is traditionally the most senior member in the majority party.

The Senate majority leader wields much more power in the Senate than the vice president and pro tem. He or she is, in reality, the chief legislator. As the first recognized in debate, he or she sets the legislative calendar, basically determining which bills get to the floor and which ones do not. The majority leader also guides the party caucus on issues and party proposals. Senate leaders are not sovereign coaches of a team; every member makes his or her own independent choice, and many members within the same party have different and specialized interests in framing legislation. Some former Senate leaders have expressed frustration. Bob Dole once said the letter "P" was missing from his title, "Majority Pleader."

The Senate whips serve much the same way as their House counterparts. They keep a tally of party members' voting intentions and try to maintain party discipline. Each party also has a **conference chairman**, like a party chairperson, in each house below the whip. This chairman takes care of party matters, such as heading the organization of party-centered groups in each house.

Caucuses

The formal, nongovernmental groups of like-minded people organized in Congress are called caucuses. These groups usually unite around a particular belief. As stated earlier, each party has a caucus, sometimes called the "party conference," among the entire party membership to set legislative agendas and select committee members. Many other smaller caucuses are organized around specific interests, even some that cross party lines, such as agriculture, business, or women's issues. Members can belong to multiple caucuses.

The Blue Dog Coalition is traditionally composed of fiscally conservative Democrats, many from the South, who view some concerns more conservatively than their Democratic colleagues. The Congressional Black Caucus gathers around issues of concern for African Americans, such as education, employment, and discrimination. These caucuses cannot create law, even though caucus members are also members of Congress. They can, however, work to enhance the chances of passing their desired policies.

Committees

Committees are not mentioned in the Constitution, but they have been a fixture in Congress since it first met. Smaller groups can tackle tough issues and draft more precise laws than the entire House or Senate can. Committees allow for expertise and make moving legislation manageable. Today the intricate committee system handles a vast amount of legislation. Committees dealing with finance, foreign relations, the judiciary, and other common topics have become permanent. The Democrats and Republicans can create their own private committees, much like the caucuses, to further party goals. Recall from Chapter 6 the committees designed to elect party members to each house, such as the Democratic Congressional Campaign Committee. The committees discussed below, however, are public, lawmaking groups that fall into different committee types.

Standing committees are permanent and cover a particular subject. For example, the House Energy and Commerce Committee has wide authority on utilities and gasoline, as well as almost any business matter. The Committee on Transportation and Infrastructure oversees the creation and maintenance of U.S. highways.

Standing committees are chaired by a senior experienced member in the majority party. The vice chair or "ranking member" is the senior committee member in the minority party. The majority party always holds the majority seats on each committee and therefore controls the flow of legislation. Members of Congress can specialize on a few topics and become experts in these areas. Committee members discuss and polish, or reject, a variety of bills. Before the entire House or Senate votes, a bill must first clear committee with a majority vote.

The Senate's committees often hold confirmation hearings for presidential appointments. For example, a nominated secretary of defense must appear before the Armed Services Committee to answer individual senators'

LEADERSHIP IN CONGRESS

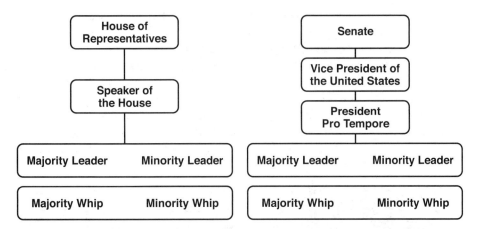

The Congressional leadership shown above results from a mix of constitutionally defined positions, congressional customs, and party decisions. The Speaker is in charge in the House, while the Majority Leader has much control and influence in the Senate.

questions. After this hearing, a majority can recommend the nominee to the full Senate for approval. The **House Judiciary Committee** drafts crime bills that define illegal behavior and outline appropriate punishments. It also handles impeachments.

In the House, the **Ways and Means Committee** and the **Rules Committee** both wield an inordinate amount of power. Ways and Means, a committee exclusive to the House, determines tax policy. When raising or lowering income taxes, the Ways and Means Committee decides the details first.

The Rules Committee has an impact on every bill because this committee assigns bills to the appropriate standing committees, determines which bills are scheduled for debate, and decides when votes take place. It can easily dispose of a bill or define the guidelines for debate. The Rules Committee generally reflects the will and sentiment of House leadership and the majority caucus. The majority party typically holds a disproportionately higher number of seats on this committee; thus the controlling party can control the flow of legislation.

The strength of the majority party—which dominates committee chairs and holds a majority of seats in committees—has made Congress a one-sided affair. "In recent years," retired Congressman Mickey Edwards said, "to be in the minority is essentially to be made a nonfactor in the legislative process."

Most standing committees are within one chamber, but a few permanent **joint committees** exist that unite members from the House and Senate, such as one to manage the Library of Congress and the Joint Committee on Taxation.

In addition to the standing committees, **select committees** are put together periodically for some particular short-lived reason. Select committees are common when investigating a scandal, such as Watergate or the Iran-Contra scandal in the 1980s. These groups also investigate issues to determine if further congressional action is necessary. Should Congress mandate seat belts in cars? Should Congress regulate/intervene in Major League Baseball to prevent steroid abuse? Recently the House created a select committee on Energy Independence and Global Warming. Select committees can be exclusive to one house, or they can combine members from both.

Conference committees are created temporarily to iron out differences on bills that passed each house but in slightly different forms. In the legislative process, provisions of bills are added and deleted. Therefore, when two similar bills pass each house, usually a compromise can be reached, and members from both houses gather for a **markup session,** a process by which the bill is amended. The final draft must pass both houses and receive the president's signature to become law.

Selected Congressional Committees, 113th Congress Chairman, Membership, and Role	
House	**Senate**
Ways & Means Dave Camp (R-MI) Rep: 23; Dem: 16 Determines tax policy	**Finance** Ron Wyden (D-OR) Dem: 13; Rep: 111 Spending and budgeting
Rules Pete Sessions (R-TX) Rep: 9; Dem: 4 Determines House proceedings	**Armed Services** Carl Levin (D-MI) Dem: 14; Rep: 12 Oversees the military
Armed Services Howard McKeon (R-CA) Rep: 34; Dem: 29 Oversees the military	**Foreign Relations** Robert Menendez (D-NJ) Dem: 10; Rep: 8 Guides U.S. foreign policy
Judiciary Robert W. Goodlatte (R-VA) Rep: 23; Dem: 18 Drafts crime bills, impeachments	**Judiciary** Patrick Leahy (D-VT) Dem: 10; Rep: 8 Approves judges, oversees courts
Energy & Commerce Fred Upton (R-MI) Rep: 31; Dem: 23 Regulates energy and business	**Agriculture, Nutrition, and Forestry** Debbie Stabenow (D-MI) Dem: 1; Rep: 10 Addresses farming, food, and nature

In the 113th Congress, there were 21 independent standing committees in the House and 16 in the Senate.

Committee Types
Standing: permanent committees that handle most of Congress's work
Joint: members of both houses that address a long-term issue or program
Select: temporary committee that handles a particular issue or investigation
Conference: House and Senate members who reconcile similar bills

The House of Representatives has the **Committee of the Whole**, of which every representative is a member. Evolved from the British House of Commons, this "committee" is more of a state of operation in which the House rules are relaxed to speed business. For example, no roll call voting took place during the Committee of the Whole until 1971. Additionally, the otherwise nonvoting delegates from U.S. territories can vote when present during the Committee of the Whole. Only 100 members must be present for the Committee of the Whole to act, but a full quorum must be present to vote on final passage of bills.

Committee Assignments Representatives and senators seek particular committee appointments because they likely arrive to Congress with an expertise in a certain field, or they are from a state or district that has a high interest in certain congressional matters. Several members have served in the Armed Forces and want to shape the military. Some arrive with high-level business experience and therefore want to employ their experience in commerce or international trade. Veterans of Congress have usually served on a variety of committees and are senior and influential members of some powerful ones.

The parties put forth certain members for committee assignments, but ultimately each full house votes to approve committee membership. The Democrats and Republicans each have a committee for the purpose of assigning members to standing committees to create favorable bills and points and to develop legislative strategy. The Democrats' **Policy and Steering Committee** and the Republicans' **Committee on Committees** both recommend committee assignments. "The campaign for committee assignments," recalls Senator Sherrod Brown, "is the most important task a new member performs between November and January."

In addition to creating bills and confirming presidential appointments, committees also oversee how the executive agencies administer the laws Congress created. Therefore, Congress, through its committees, conducts **congressional oversight** to ensure executive branch agencies, such as the FBI or the IRS, are carrying out the policy or program as Congress intended. When corruption or a less-than-adequate job is suspected, committees call agency directors to testify. Other oversight hearings may simply be fact-finding exchanges between lawmakers and cabinet secretaries or agency directors about funding, efficiency, or just general updates.

Committee Reforms   The **committee chairmen** absorbed much of the power that the Speaker lost. They became the gatekeepers of much legislation for two generations. For decades, southern conservatives in the Senate prevented civil rights proposals. The seniority rule made it difficult to unseat autocratic chairpersons who bottled up legislation they did not favor. Seniority has gradually waned in importance as majorities have watched minorities stop them.

Congress finally addressed the problem of committee rules and procedures. It required all committee roll call votes and Committee of the Whole votes to be made public. It implemented electronic voting and permitted television and radio to cover House hearings with approval of a majority of committee members.

THINK AS A POLITICAL SCIENTIST: PRESENT ACCURATE INFORMATION ABOUT CONGRESSIONAL COMMITTEE LEADERSHIP, MEMBERS, AND ACTIVITIES

Political scientists construct graphics to organize and communicate accurate information and present relationships among facts, concepts, or ideas visually. Graphic information includes graphs, diagrams, tables, maps, charts, and timelines. Often, writers will use graphic information to compare and contrast facts given in the text or to present related facts or ideas so that they can be understood quickly. A reader can quickly scan graphics to find key information instead of searching for it in a text.

For example, bar graphs are used to compare data between different groups. Line graphs can be used to show how variables change over time. A pie chart shows sections of a whole and the percentages that each section represents of the whole. Tables and graphs are used to organize information and to show patterns and relationships.

Practice: Construct a table of up-to-date congressional committee leadership, members, and activity similar to the table on page 232. Go to https://www.congress.gov/committees or to Senate and House Web pages on committees and select at least two committees from each house to examine. Who chairs the committees you chose? Examine the list of committee members. What topics, issues, or pending bills have these committees recently discussed? What occurred at the last few meetings? What's on the agenda for the next meetings?

Then create a table with the committee's name atop each column. For each committee you choose, list the chairman and his or her party. Also list the committee members, their home states, and party affiliation. Then list their recent meeting topics or actions. Consider: How do the House and Senate committees differ? Which party holds more seats on these committees? Why? Write two or three paragraphs to accompany your table that answers those questions.

Legislative Process

Only House or Senate members can introduce a bill. Today, however, the actual authors of legislation are more often staffers with expertise, lobbyists, White House liaisons, or outside professionals. When a bill's **sponsor** (the member who introduces it) presents it, the bill is officially numbered. Numbering starts at S.1 in the Senate or H.R.1 in the House at the beginning of each biennial Congress. A bill can originate in either chamber, but an identical bill must pass both houses by a majority and be signed by the president to become law. Several events take place in the process, creating several opportunities for a bill to drastically change along the way. Additional ideas and programs usually are attached.

How each house, the president, and the public view a bill will determine its fate. The rough and tumble path for legislation often leads to its death. In a typical two-year Congress over the last generations, about 10,000 bills are introduced, and about 500 new laws are passed. Over the last three terms, Congress passed on average 284 bills during each two-year period.

Assigning Bills to Committee

The Senate majority leader and the House Rules Committee assign bills to committees in their respective chambers. Sometimes multiple committees have overlapping jurisdiction. A military spending bill may be examined by both the Armed Services Committee and the Appropriations Committee. In that case, the bill may be given **multiple referral** status, allowing both committees to address it simultaneously. Or it might have **sequential referral** status, giving one committee priority over others. Frequently, subcommittees with a more narrow scope are involved.

If the committee is "ordering the bill," the bill is under consideration. Hearings, expert testimony, and thorough discussion of the bill will take place. The chairman will call for a published report, a summary, and analysis of the proposal with views of the other participants, such as the executive branch or interest groups. Once the bill passes the vote in the committee, the ratio of "yeas" to "nays" often speaks to the bill's chances on the House or Senate floor. In the House, the Rules Committee would first define the parameters of debate on the bill and set the calendar for its discussion and potential vote. Then floor debate begins and amendments are likely added. From this point, many factors can lead to passage, and many more can lead to the bill's failure.

Source: Department of Defense, Staff Sgt. Sean K. Harp

Here the president's secretary of defense and another ranking Pentagon official testify before a House Appropriations subcommittee.

Amendments

In the House, amendments to bills typically have to be approved by the committee overseeing the bill. In the Senate, an individual senator can introduce an amendment to a bill on the floor. Formal changes to a bill require a vote. Amendments of all kinds get tagged onto bills. The additional points of a law may not even relate to the original. These are called **non-germane amendments**. Congressmen add these **riders**, additional points that ride onto an often unrelated law, to benefit their own agendas or programs, or to enhance the political chances of the bill. Mo Udall, a representative from Arizona, once expressed frustration when he had to vote against his own "Udall bill," because it had evolved into legislation he eventually opposed. When a bill grows to mammoth size and takes care of several facets of law or addresses multiple programs, it is referred to as an **omnibus bill**. A long string of riders will earn the nickname "Christmas Tree bill."

HOW A BILL BECOMES A LAW

Pork and Earmarks

One product of these add-ons is **pork barrel spending**. Federal dollars are spent all across the nation to fund construction projects, highway repair, new bridges, national museums and parks, university research grants, and other programs. Members of Congress try to send federal dollars, also known as pork, back to their district—referred by some as "bringing home the bacon." The funds directed for a specific purpose, known as **earmarks,** have generated a national debate. Constituents who benefit from pork barrel spending obviously appreciate it. Yet, in recent years the competition for federal dollars has tarnished Congress's reputation. Citizens Against Government Waste reported an explosion of earmarks from 1994 to 2004. Congress passed more than five times as many projects, and spending rose from $10 billion to $22.9 billion.

Equally appalling are the hidden trips to the pork barrel. Riders are inserted onto bills sometimes literally in the dark of night by powerful leaders, sometimes within days or hours before a final vote. The most egregious example of pork barrel politics came when Alaska Senator Ted Stevens added a rider to send more than $400 million dollars to his state to build a bridge to connect the mainland to an island with 60 inhabitants. The rider's primary purpose was to fund and provide armor for U.S. troops in Iraq. Critics dubbed the construction project "The Bridge to Nowhere."

Contemporary Congress

If those men who served in the First Congress could take part in the modern legislature, "They would probably feel right at home," says historian Raymond Smock. Other observers disagree and point to burgeoning federal government responsibilities. Congress has created a Department of Education, defended marriage, and addressed various other modern issues outside the scope of Article I's enumerated powers. Other surprises might include Congress's negative image, its intense polarization, and the degree to which legislation develops outside the House and Senate.

An Unpopular Congress

The late 1960s and early 1970s proved a trying time for the nation and the legislature. People had come to distrust national politicians. Since then, conflicts of interest among congressional members have reached new levels, and an increased number of scandals has given the institution a black eye.

When people asked humorist Will Rogers where he got his jokes, he replied, "Why I just watch Congress and report the facts." Critics from Mark Twain to comedian Jon Stewart have cast Congress in a bad light. The media have also contributed to its tarnished reputation. Controversial battles in the legislature receive prime coverage, while routine compromises do not. Finally, the lawmaking process is simply slower and more complicated than what most citizens expect. All of these factors help to create an image of an uncaring, "do nothing" Congress.

Party Polarization

The legislature has descended into a partisan and sometimes uncivil institution. A variety of factors has driven a wedge between liberal and conservative members. Regular flights to home states or districts and the need to constantly campaign have resulted in a hectic workweek, which ends with a weekend exodus from D.C. The constant travel and split focus allows for few bipartisan friendships. The primary election system of nominating the more conservative, or more liberal, candidates by the more ideological and active primary voters has shrunk the number of moderates in Congress. As House historian Robert Remini explains, a generation ago, representatives and senators overlooked ideological difference in their personal encounters. "Despite our various disagreements in the House," Speaker Tip O'Neill once reflected, "we were always friends after six o'clock and on weekends."

Judicial nominations, especially when the president and the Senate majority represent opposing parties, have become contentious battles. After the Republican ascendancy with the 1994 elections (after 40 years of being in the minority in the House), the GOP took a tone of "getting even" under the leadership of the divisive Speaker Newt Gingrich. Real floor debate has been replaced by carefully orchestrated speeches, while combative media-hungry lawmakers face off in head-to-head confrontations on cable TV news shows. As historian Lewis Gould put it, "In this hectic atmosphere of perpetual campaigning, the older values of collegiality and comity, though rarer than senatorial memory had it, eroded to the point of virtual disappearance."

Congress's approval rating, as measured by Gallup, hovered in the mid-30 percent range in the early 1970s. Over the past few terms, it has generally fallen below 15 percent.

Inconsistent Leadership

In the House, competing leadership made for unharmonious transitions. Democrat Jim Wright of Texas became Speaker in 1987. Wright frayed the relationship between the parties by preventing Republican involvement in House business. Some called Wright's partisan squabbles bitter, unlike O'Neill's. House Republican leader Newt Gingrich took aim at Wright. Gingrich went on tour, calling Wright a "crook" and eventually filed ethics charges against the Speaker regarding Wright's personal finances. An inquiry ousted Wright, and he became the only sitting Speaker ever to abdicate his position. He was replaced by Tom Foley of Washington.

Clinton Impeachment In addition to polarizing the House and pushing the impeachment of President Clinton, Speaker Gingrich eventually faced his own problems. He was brought up on ethics charges for financial indiscretions with a book deal and other conflicts of interest. The House eventually fined and reprimanded him. His conflicts and power play with Clinton encouraged a New York newspaper to lampoon him as a crybaby. Gingrich eventually resigned.

An Overworked Congress

Sam Rayburn, Speaker of the House in the 1950s and 1960s, advised newcomers to keep a low profile. "Don't ever talk until you know what you are talking about. . . . If you want to get along, go along." That has changed. The modern Congress is busier than ever before, and a lawmaker's job has become more challenging and time consuming. Legislators act as independent agents more often than they once did.

More Constituents With enhanced technology, more people are watching Congress, and more constituents have access to their legislators. Congress now receives well over 50 million email messages and 200 million pieces of mail annually, whereas it received about 10 million letters in the late 1960s. Meanwhile the average population of House districts has risen 40 percent. Interest groups and PACs have brought more participants into the policymaking arena. There is simply more pressure on members. This increased interest and visibility has made the race for re-election more challenging than ever. The campaign calendar has shifted earlier and earlier.

Demands The scheduled days in Washington and number of votes on the House and Senate floors have dropped. During the 1960s and 1970s, the average Congress (two-year term) was in session 323 days. Now Congress meets about 250 days per two-year period. But this change is largely due to the other business a member of Congress must take care of and the expectation of spending time in home districts. Veteran Congressman Lee Hamilton once suggested this help-wanted ad to better define the job description: "Wanted: A person with wide-ranging knowledge of scores of complex policy issues. Must be willing to work long hours in Washington, then fly home to attend an unending string of community events. Applicant should expect that work and travel demands will strain family life, and that every facet of public and private life will be subject to intense scrutiny and criticism."

Visibility and Political Forces The Framers would be most surprised at how television, PACs, and networks of nonelected policy experts impact the legislative process. The introduction of C-SPAN and access of video clips from the House and Senate floors have had a downside. Instead of lively, impassioned discourse, House representatives and senators rarely engage in old-fashioned debate and instead rely on scripted speeches. The persuasion that took place on the floors of both chambers for two centuries has nearly disappeared. Members of Congress rarely change a single colleague's vote through oratory, and they are more likely to direct their speeches at a national television audience instead of fellow members.

Much of what goes on within the institution is affected by forces coming from outside its doors. Bills aren't written, debated, and tweaked like they used to be. Members of Congress are hardly the authors of much of the legislation that becomes law. Major bills that would require weeks of hearings and days of markups in the past are now often reviewed within days and with no visible time before a committee. Much of the drafting and altering of bills takes place behind closed doors by a small group of leaders, staffers, industry representatives, and majority party members before they are hurried through committee and on to the floor of Congress.

REFLECT ON THE ESSENTIAL QUESTION

Essential Question: *How are American citizens represented, and how does Congress put policy ideas into effect?* On separate paper, complete a chart like the one below to gather details to answer that question.

How Citizens Are Represented	How Policy Goes Into Effect

KEY TERMS, NAMES, AND EVENTS

advice and consent
Baker v. Carr (1962)
bicameral
caucuses
cloture rule
committee chairmen
Committee of the Whole
Committee on Committees (Republican)
conference chairman
conference committees
congressional oversight
constituent services
continuous body
discharge petition
earmarks
expressed powers
filibuster
floor leaders
franking privilege

gerrymandering
House Judiciary Committee
House Ways and Means Committee
implied powers
incumbency
joint committees
logrolling
marginal seats
markup session
multiple referral
non-germane amendments
omnibus bill
Policy and Steering Committee (Democratic)
pork barrel spending
president *pro tempore*
quorum
reapportionment

redistricting
representative (or delegate) model
riders
Rules Committee
safe seats
select committees
sequential referral
Seventeenth Amendment
Shaw v. Reno (1993)
sponsor
standing committees
term limits
trustee model
Twenty-seventh Amendment
Wesberry v. Sanders (1964)
whip

1. Which of the following are standing committees in Congress?
   I. Ways and Means Committee

   II. Congressional Campaign Committee

   III. Committee on Committees

   IV. House Judiciary Committee

   (A) I and II
   (B) I and III
   (C) I, II, and III
   (D) I and IV
   (E) IV only

2. Which of the following shows the Framers' commitment to bicameralism?
   (A) The presidential veto
   (B) Different rules for the House and Senate
   (C) Congressional oversight
   (D) Advice and consent power
   (E) The powers delegated to Congress

3. The current Congress differs from prior generations in that
   (A) Congress is now less white and less male than it used to be
   (B) Congress's demographic character mirrors the United States at large
   (C) today individual members have less impact on lawmaking than they used to
   (D) Congress takes on fewer issues than it did in decades past
   (E) Congressmen have fewer responsibilities than in years past

4. One reform that weakened the power of House Speaker Joe Cannon was
   (A) giving some of the Speaker's authority to the entire House of Representatives
   (B) the initial creation of the committee system
   (C) the creation of the cloture rule
   (D) ratification of the Seventeenth Amendment
   (E) the airing of C-SPAN to a national audience

5. In which case did the Supreme Court first uphold Congress's commerce power?

(A) *Marbury v. Madison*

(B) *McCulloch v. Maryland*

(C) *Gibbons v. Ogden*

(D) *Dred Scott v. Sandford*

(E) *Lochner v. New York*

6. All of the following typically enhance a congressional incumbent's chances at re-election EXCEPT

(A) the franking privilege

(B) regular press coverage

(C) providing constituent services

(D) name recognition

(E) a bad economy

7. The desire for congressional term limits has generated some controversy. Term limits do not exist now because

(A) the Constitution does not provide for term limits

(B) voters never vote an incumbent out of office

(C) like federal judges, congressmen must quit, retire, or be dismissed

(D) no state has ever wanted term limits for their members

(E) the Supreme Court has never ruled on it

8. Which of the following committees is most likely to address a bill when the House and Senate both pass different versions of the same bill?

(A) A standing committee

(B) A select committee

(C) Rules Committee

(D) Ethics Committee

(E) A conference committee

9. Which of the following is a responsibility of the party whip?

(A) Scheduling the legislative calendar

(B) Determining the rules for debate

(C) Encouraging partisan support for a bill

(D) Ruling on parliamentary procedure

(E) Selecting party chairmen

10. The modern Congress is known for all of the following EXCEPT
   (A) harmonious relationships among the parties
   (B) partisanship and polarization
   (C) isolation from each party
   (D) scandal and investigation
   (E) low approval ratings

FREE-RESPONSE QUESTIONS

1. The United States Congress is governed by Article I of the Constitution and by particular rules or customs each house has developed.

   (a) Identify and explain two provisions in Article I of the U.S. Constitution that guide the Congress.

   (b) Identify and explain two legislative rules or customs developed since the ratification of the Constitution.

   (c) Select one rule or custom from (b) and identify and explain the impact it has had on the legislative process.

2. Congressional reapportionment and redistricting are meant to foster representative democracy and are impacted by several factors.

   (a) Explain the reapportionment and redistricting process, identifying one relevant government organization and its specific roles in this process.

   (b) Select two factors below and explain what role each plays in the redistricting process.
   - gerrymandering
   - race
   - political parties
   - *Wesberry v. Sanders*

   (c) Identify and explain one solution to the recurring reapportionment and redistricting controversies.

WRITING: PLAN

Before you start writing, take a few minutes to plan your responses. The time you spend planning will pay off in careful and complete answers.

10

The Presidency

"The office of the President requires the constitution of an athlete, the patience of a mother, and the endurance of an early Christian.... The President is a superior kind of slave."

—Woodrow Wilson, President 1913–1921

Essential Question: How does the chief executive make decisions, enforce the laws, and represent the nation's citizens?

The American presidency is filled with ceremony, custom, and expectation. Presidential institutions, such as the White House, Air Force One, the First Lady, and the State of the Union address, are likely familiar to you. Signing ceremonies and photo opportunities with foreign dignitaries are common images. The Constitution lays out the president's job description, yet since the creation of the office, American citizens have come to expect more and more from the president. In this chapter, you will become more familiar with the design of the executive branch, the process the president uses to choose advisers, and the daily responsibilities of the president.

Creating and Developing the Presidency

The presidency is shaped by Article II and five amendments to the Constitution, federal law, Supreme Court decisions, customs, and precedents. The Framers designed a limited executive office meant to carry out the ideas put into law by Congress. The office, however, has become the seat for a powerful captain of the ship of state, empowered by support institutions and American expectation.

Framers' Vision

In laying out the presidential powers, the Framers debated whether or not to make the nation's executive a singular leader or a small group of leaders. The delegates in Philadelphia voted seven to three to make the office a singular executive. Fears arose because skeptics saw this office as a potential "fetus of monarchy." One delegate tried to allay such fears, explaining "[i]t will not be too strong to say that the station will probably be filled by men preeminent for their ability and virtue." The concern, however, led Framers to include specific roles and several provisions to limit the powers of the strong, singular leader.

Qualifications, Office, and Term The Constitution requires the president to be a natural-born citizen, at least 35 years old, and a U.S. resident for at least 14 years before taking office. They designated the president as the people's top military commander and empowered the president to issue pardons and reprieves and to appoint ambassadors, judges, and other public ministers. They gave the office a key role in the lawmaking process—the president can recommend legislative measures to Congress, veto or approve proposed bills, and convene or adjourn the houses of Congress. The Framers defined a four-year term with no limit for re-election. Term limits, the Federalists argued, "would be a reduction of inducements for good behavior." The Framers also created the Electoral College to elect the nation's key leader.

Presidential Powers Some presidential powers are explicit and clear, while others are fairly vague. Presidents and scholars have argued about the gray areas of a president's job description. Most presidents have claimed **inherent powers**, those that may not be explicitly listed but are essentially in the jurisdiction of the executive. This debate has taken place during nearly every administration. Presidents have fought battles for expanded powers, winning some and losing others. There are several constitutional checks on a president—the Senate has the power to provide advice and consent on appointments, for example, and the presidential salary cannot increase or decrease during the elected term.

Impeachment The Framers defined the **impeachment** process to check the chief executive. The Constitution gives the House sole power of impeachment (the accusation), which it can declare with a simple majority. The impeached official then receives a trial in front of the Senate. After sitting as the jury, the Senate votes to convict or acquit the official. A two-thirds vote is required to remove the president. Only two presidents have been impeached—Andrew Johnson for violating the Tenure of Office Act after the Civil War and Bill Clinton for perjury and obstruction of justice in 1998. Johnson escaped removal by one vote. The Senate voted to remove Clinton by votes of 55–45 and 50–50, neither vote reaching the required two thirds. The House nearly voted on an impeachment bill during Richard Nixon's presidency after the Watergate affair. The measure cleared the House Judiciary Committee, but Nixon resigned before it reached the full House. To date, no president has ever been removed.

Early Administrations

As the office was conceived, most Americans predicted General Washington would serve as the head of the newly formed Republic. This prediction eased the people's concerns, as they expected Washington to set the correct tone and standards for the office. Washington was revered at home and abroad, and thus he served as both an admirable chief of state and a strong communicator to other European nations. His role as commander in the Revolutionary War and his trusted character gave the presidency immediate credibility.

Article II: Qualifications, Duties, and Limits of the Presidency

- Must receive a majority of Electoral College votes to win the office
- Shall hold office for a four-year term
- Must be a natural-born citizen, at least 35 years old, and have lived in the United States for 14 years
- Shall be the commander in chief of the Army and Navy
- May require opinions of advisers and department heads
- Shall have the power to pardon convicted persons for federal offenses
- Shall appoint ambassadors and judges, and make treaties with Senate approval
- May recommend measures he finds necessary
- May convene or adjourn Congress

Pioneering the Office The Constitution gave Washington's new position a mere five-paragraph job description. He took on the role with modesty and accepted being addressed as "Mr. President," though some suggested more lofty titles.

Washington's key accomplishments include putting down an insurrection against a whiskey tax, working out treaties with Native American tribes and the British, and, perhaps most important, instilling public confidence in the nation's constitutional experiment. Though he surely would have won a third term, Washington chose to leave government after his second term to allow others to serve and to allay any fears of an overbearing executive.

The presidents that followed Washington had moments of questionable initiative and international confrontation. Most early presidents, however, faithfully carried out congressional acts, exercised the veto minimally, and followed Washington's precedent to serve no more than two terms. John Adams succeeded Washington and completed one term. The next three presidents—Thomas Jefferson, James Madison, and James Monroe, all Virginians—were strong leaders that served two terms each. Jefferson purchased the Louisiana Territory without congressional approval. Madison led the nation in a second war against Great Britain. And Monroe established a foreign policy with which the United States dominated the Western Hemisphere. For the most part, however, these powerful men let the Congress fill its role as the main policymaking institution while the presidents executed the laws it created.

The Imperial Presidency

Yielding to Congress, however, began to fade as stronger presidents came to office. The president's strength relative to that of Congress has grown steadily, with occasional setbacks, to create a kind of **imperial presidency**, a powerful executive position guided by a weaker Congress. *Webster's Dictionary* defines an imperial presidency as "a U.S. presidency that is characterized by greater powers than the Constitution allows." Historian Arthur Schlesinger Jr. popularized the term with his 1973 book of the same name. The book was published in the shadow of an overreaching Nixon presidency.

Reasons for Expanded Powers A century before the U.S. founding, John Locke argued that in emergencies reasonable rulers should be able to resort to exceptional power. Legislatures were too big, too unwieldy, and too slow to cope with crisis. On occasion, "a strict and rigid observation of the laws may do harm," Locke said. Every president, once in office, has agreed with this assessment. War and international conflict have necessitated the commander in chief's strong, rapid, and sometimes unilateral response to enemies and hostile

BORN TO COMMAND.

OF VETO MEMORY.

HAD I BEEN CONSULTED.

KING ANDREW THE FIRST.

Source: Library of Congress

President Andrew Jackson's critics often questioned if he had stepped outside his authority. What symbols does the cartoonist use to signal this accusation? What is at Jackson's feet? What does he hold in his hand?

nations. Economic and other domestic crises have raised popular expectations for strong leadership and new ideas. Sometimes a president's personality and popularity have also helped to expand executive powers.

Andrew Jackson A noticeable shift in presidential power took place during Andrew Jackson's presidency (1829–1837). Jackson was a forceful military general who had led the southern expedition that evacuated the Native Americans. He served in both the House and Senate but took office with greater influence from his days as a military hero and stern commander. As president, he blazed a path of executive dominance. He used the veto 12 times, more than any president ever before. Jackson's opposition to a national bank, combined with his headstrong demeanor, created a rift between the president and other branches. His popularity among farmers and workers in an age of expanded suffrage and increased political participation enhanced his power even more.

The presidents that served after Andrew Jackson and before Abraham Lincoln are often forgotten. None of the eight presidents that served between Jackson and Lincoln served more than one term, and two died in office. It was a time of relative peace, with the exception of the Mexican-American War. Franklin Pierce and James Buchanan, who preceded Lincoln, are noted for their lack of presidential leadership and for allowing the nation to drift toward Civil War. Historians rank Buchanan and Pierce at the bottom of the list of effective presidents.

Abraham Lincoln After the southern states seceded, Abraham Lincoln (1861–1865) assumed sweeping presidential powers to save the Union and to limit slavery. During the four years of the conflict, writes historian Arthur Schlesinger, "Lincoln ignored one constitutional provision after another. He assembled the militia, enlarged the Army and Navy beyond the congressional appropriation, suspended habeas corpus, arrested 'disloyal' people, asserted the right to proclaim martial law behind the lines, to arrest people without warrant, to seize property, to suppress newspapers." Lincoln is generally excused for these constitutional violations because he stretched the powers of his office in the name of saving the United States and emancipating the slaves.

Theodore Roosevelt Through Reconstruction and after, a host of Union officers, mostly Republicans, served as chief executives. In the late 1800s, the United States began to compete on an international stage with the industrial and imperial powers of Europe. President William McKinley, for example, sent 5,000 American troops to China to help put down the Boxer Rebellion.

McKinley's successor, Theodore Roosevelt (1901–1909), continued this presidential trend in the name of advancing the nation and serving the people. Roosevelt's popularity at the turn of a new age served him well. His gallant Rough Rider background from the Spanish-American War and his brash, forward manner made people respect his strong persona. His progressive actions for environmental conservation and against corporate giants contributed greatly to both his reputation and his legacy.

On international affairs, Roosevelt strengthened the Monroe Doctrine with his foreign policy motto that the United States would "speak softly and carry a big stick." During his tenure, he sent troops to Cuba and the Philippines, and he sent the U.S. Navy around the world. He acquired property from Panama to build a canal. His so-called **stewardship theory** of governance presumed that presidential powers are only strictly limited by the actual limits listed in the Constitution. Like a good steward, Roosevelt insisted, the president should exercise as much authority as possible to take care of the American people.

Woodrow Wilson Roosevelt stepped down after serving nearly two full terms, and conservative William Howard Taft succeeded him. Taft supported business and corporate interests, and he believed in limited constitutional government. After Taft's one term, Roosevelt again threw his hat in the ring for the presidency. Unable to secure the Republican nomination, he ran as a third-party candidate with the "Bull-Moose" party and thereby diluted the Republican vote, a move that allowed Democrat Woodrow Wilson to win the presidency in 1912. Wilson became a strong leader with an international voice.

A scholar, Princeton University president, and New Jersey governor, Wilson was another two-term president. His progressive policies worked to mandate the eight-hour workday and to prevent child labor abuses. When he delivered the **State of the Union** address to the Congress, the first such in-person delivery of the report since John Adams had done it, he created for himself yet another platform from which to present and gain popularity for his ideas. His involvement in international affairs became inevitable as America entered World War I. Within two years, he led a successful American mission and became a world leader. His celebrity in Paris for the Treaty of Versailles elevated his stature in the United States and around the world.

Wilson's final years as president were marred by his conflict with the Republican Party and his failed postwar plans. The Senate refused to ratify his treaty to join the new League of Nations. In the war's aftermath, Wilson became sick and reclusive. He finished his term as an invalid.

Franklin Delano Roosevelt In a discussion of presidents who expanded the reach of the office, there is perhaps no better example than Franklin Delano Roosevelt (1933–1945). He became president during the Great Depression, the most severe economic crisis in history. The large coalition that rallied behind him included people from nearly every walk of life who had been harmed by the Depression. His New Deal programs promised to bring the nation out of despair. His unprecedented third term began as the United States was getting closer to entering World War II.

FDR arrived in Washington with revolutionary ideas that fundamentally changed the role of government. He recommended and Congress passed laws that required employers to pay a minimum wage, created the Social Security system, and started a series of public works programs to stimulate the economy. In trying to prevent a conservative Supreme Court from striking down his self-described liberal legislation, he moved to increase the number of seats on the Court with plans to place judges favorable to his proposals on the bench. His plan failed, but it illustrates that Roosevelt had a few imperial tendencies as president.

The foreign policy dilemma that resulted in war with Germany and Japan only strengthened his leadership and America's reliance on him as the federal government took on a greater role. As Roosevelt mobilized the nation for an overseas war, he overpowered civil liberties in the name of national security by relocating Japanese-Americans to internment camps. At the time, FDR acted as a commander in chief, not as an administrator concerned about constitutional rights. What would have seemed autocratic in peacetime was accepted as an appropriate measure during wartime.

Americans accepted most of his measures and elected him to a fourth term, but he died just months later. Since that time, the **Twenty-second Amendment,** ratified in 1951, prevents any president from serving more than two consecutive terms or a total of 10 years.

Cold War The state of political and military tension that became known as the **Cold War** came about in the aftermath of World War II and lasted into the 1990s. The Cold War only strengthened the president's role as commander in chief. Presidents from Harry Truman through George H.W. Bush took strong measures in the name of national security or international influence that Washington, Jefferson, and Madison would surely have questioned. The creation of the peacetime Central Intelligence Agency (CIA) in 1947 gave presidents insight into other nations and potential threats long before those threats fully materialized. Presidents and their main intelligence organization infiltrated foreign governments to influence or anticipate problems. The United States has at times supported the overthrow of foreign leaders, to prop up leaders more favorable to U.S. interests.

Presidential Elections

Because of the U.S. president's global influence, the contest for the American presidency is one of the most closely watched events in the world. Long before anyone formally declares a run for this high office, media pundits and political speculators begin to discuss worthy candidates. The Great Mentioner—a mythical entity that could be any high level political player, pundit, national reporter, or the collective media and punditry—often serves to open the door for candidates by circulating rumors of their interest in running before there is any announcement.

Modern Presidential Campaigns

After declaring candidacy, a presidential hopeful begins the long road to winning the presidency, which includes raising millions of dollars, competing against fellow party members for the nomination, proposing original solutions to important national and international problems, and sustaining a campaign that runs 24 hours a day, seven days week. Practical requirements include some degree of independent wealth and an ability to raise campaign donations.

Electoral System The Electoral College system makes the campaign a state-by-state contest. The states choose **electors**, people entrusted to vote for the president of the United States, who later cast electoral votes. In modern times, these electors follow the popular vote in their states. In the winner-take-all system used by all but two states—Maine and Nebraska—the candidate that gets a plurality of the popular vote from a state wins all the state's electoral votes. The candidate that wins a majority of electoral votes (50 percent + 1, or 270 electoral votes or more) becomes president.

The **Twelfth Amendment**, passed in 1804, provided that each elector gets one vote for president and one for vice president. Candidates from opposite parties could feasibly serve together, but since these candidates now run on the same ticket, pledged, partisan electors vote accordingly. Washington, D.C., did not have electors until the 1964 election because the Framers did not want the seat of government to have undue influence. The **Twenty-third Amendment** allots electors for the District of Columbia, but never any more electors than those of the smallest state.

Running Against Washington In 1976, the presidential contest pitted a nonelected president, Gerald Ford, who had assumed office after Nixon's scandalous departure, against Georgia governor Jimmy Carter. Ford had developed a reputation as a bumbling executive, a holdover from a tainted administration. Carter, on the other hand, was in effect running against the Washington establishment. At a time when the nation had lost confidence in the presidency and the federal government in general, Carter used an outside strategy to win the Democratic nomination and then the presidency. No sitting member of Congress was elected president after John F. Kennedy in 1960 until Barack Obama in 2008. Four of the six past presidents had previously served as state governors. George H.W. Bush had been vice president, and Barack Obama had been a senator. A candidate's distance from Washington and success as a governor have been assets in electability, while experience in Congress has been a drawback.

Incumbents and Intraparty Challengers Incumbent presidents invari- ably receive their party's nomination. But those who have been challenged from within their party during primary season have maintained the nomination but lost re-election. Ronald Reagan challenged Ford for the Republican nomination in 1976. Democratic Senator Ted Kennedy challenged Jimmy Carter in 1980. Conservative Pat Buchanan challenged George H. W. Bush in 1992. None of the challengers won the party nomination, but Ford, Carter, and Bush failed to win a second term.

In 1976, President Gerald R. Ford (right) and Jimmy Carter met at the Walnut Street Theater in Philadelphia to debate domestic policy during the first of three Ford-Carter debates.

Source: Gerald R. Ford Library

	BY THE NUMBERS			
	Selected Presidential Elections			
Historic				
Year	Candidates	Popular Vote (%)	Electoral Vote	Outcome
1789	Washington & others	None	69–0	Washington becomes first president.
1800	Jefferson Burr Adams Pinckney	Unknown	73 73 65 64	House elects Jefferson.
1824	J. Q. Adams Jackson Crawford Clay	30.9 41.3 11.0 13.0	84 99 41 37	Though Jackson wins a plurality of popular and electoral votes, the House awards presidency to Adams.
1860	Lincoln Douglas Breckinridge Bell	39.9 29.5 18.1 12.6	180 12 72 39	Without a single popular vote from the South, Lincoln takes office, and the southern states secede.
Modern				
1960	Kennedy Nixon	49.7 49.5	303 219	The closest popular vote margin ever; Kennedy wins by a razor-thin margin.
1972	Nixon McGovern	60.7 37.5	520 17	George McGovern wins only one state. Nixon is later investigated for the election-season Watergate break-in.
1992	Clinton G.H.W. Bush Perot	43.0 37.4 18.9	370 168 0	Clinton defeats incumbent Bush; third-party candidate Ross Perot gets almost 19 percent of the popular vote but no electoral votes.
2000	G.W. Bush Gore	47.9 48.4	271 266	After a disputed election in Florida, George W. Bush wins the electoral vote.
2008	Obama McCain	52.9 45.7	365 173	Obama becomes first African-American president.
2012	Obama Romney	51.1 47.2	332 206	Amid debate on health care, Obama wins re-election.

What do the numbers show? When has a candidate won the Electoral College while another candidate won more popular votes? How do the variances of the electoral vote and popular vote differ? What presidents have won the presidency while winning less than 50 percent of the popular vote? What were the closest elections? When did landslides occur?

Transition, Succession, and Continuity

Modern presidents usually win an election with about 50 to 55 percent of the popular vote and a much larger portion of the electoral vote. Some minority presidents—those winning with less than half of the popular vote, such as Harry Truman or Bill Clinton—faced at least one viable third-party candidate.

One testament to the American presidency is the time-honored guarantee of certainty in leadership. The United States has never experienced major problems during a transfer of presidential power. Presidents have smoothly transitioned, whether at the dawn of the Civil War, at the end of World War II, after Nixon's resignation, and after a disputed election in 2000 deeply divided the nation. Such presidential transitions are a result of both constitutional provisions and a focus on the rule of law.

The **Twentieth Amendment** moved the presidential inauguration date from March 4 to January 20 in 1933. An outgoing president, especially an unpopular one, is sometimes referred to as a "lame duck"—that is, a duck that can't fly—because by that point in the term the president's power and ability to get things done have greatly diminished. The **lame duck period** typically begins after the nation has elected a new president and before the exit of the old one. The Twentieth Amendment shrank this period because the country no longer required as much time for presidential transition.

From Campaigning to Governing The first days of a president's term begin with the oath of office at noon on January 20. These first days are known as the **honeymoon period** because, much like a new husband and wife, the president and the people get to know one another more intimately. Typical news stories at this time include how the new president plans to fulfill campaign promises and how the first family will decorate the White House.

Presidents who win with large margins claim the electorate gave them a mandate to fulfill their campaign promises. They begin by naming their chief administration officials, such as Cabinet secretaries and agency directors. They also create an inner circle of close advisers to help them form policies and programs to achieve their goals. Much depends on how they set up their White House and administration, as well as their relationship to Congress and the public.

Succession The 1947 **Presidential Succession Act** prevents any doubt about the identity of the person who will assume the presidency in the event that the vice presidency and lower offices also become vacant. In fact, the law assigns succession to 18 positions beyond the president. The succession order goes from the vice president to congressional leaders and then to the Cabinet secretaries in the chronological order of each department's creation. The **Twenty-fifth Amendment,** passed in 1967, provides for the vice president to assume presidential duties if the president is incapacitated or disabled.

Presidential Succession
Vice President
Speaker of the House
President Pro Tempore of the Senate
Secretary of State
Secretary of the Treasury
Secretary of Defense
Attorney General
Remaining Cabinet Secretaries

Based on the Presidential Succession Act of 1947, in the event of presidential vacancy, the next office assumes the presidency. All vacancies except the presidency are filled in the normal routine of such vacancies.

Constitutional Amendments Defining the Presidency

- **Twelfth Amendment**: (1804) Electors vote for president and for vice president.
- **Twentieth Amendment**: (1933) Inauguration date moved from March 4 to January 20.
- **Twenty-second Amendment**: (1951) Limits a president's tenure to two terms or ten years.
- **Twenty-third Amendment**: (1961) Awards electors to the District of Columbia.
- **Twenty-fifth Amendment**: (1967) Addresses presidential vacancy and disability.

Presidential Roles

The president of the United States takes on many roles based on constitutional powers and the demands of the office. The president becomes an architect of new laws and programs formulated during the campaign. A president cannot introduce legislation on the House or Senate floor but in many ways still serves as the nation's chief lawmaker. As the head of state, the president becomes the nation's chief ambassador and the public face of the country. As commander in chief, the president manages the military. Running a federal bureaucracy that resembles a company with more than two million employees, the president has become chief executive and chief administrator. And finally, as the de facto head of the party, the president becomes the most identifiable Republican or Democrat.

Source: The White House photostream
President Barack Obama, Vice President Joseph Biden (L), and former Speaker of the House Nancy Pelosi

Chief Legislator

The Constitution provides that the president "may recommend [to Congress] such measures as he shall judge necessary and expedient." Presidents make such recommendations in their State of the Union address or at other events, calling on Congress to pass their proposals.

Presidents have asked Congress to pass laws to clean up air and water, amend the Constitution, create a national health care system, and declare war. A president with a strong personality can serve as the point person and carry out a vision for the country more easily than any or all of the 535 members of Congress. The media's attention on the president provides a **bully pulpit**—a brightly lit stage to pitch ideas to the American people. Article II also gives the president the option to convene or adjourn Congress at times.

The president meets with the leaders of Congress on occasion to discuss pending bills or to compromise on particular proposals. During the 1950s, President Eisenhower developed an Office of Congressional Relations. But bringing ideas in congruence with those of lawmakers on Capitol Hill can be tricky. Modern presidents realize they need a staff to research, draft, and manage legislation, and most presidents have appointed liaisons with Congress to carry out those tasks. The current White House Office of Legislative Affairs works with senators and representatives and their staffs to promote the president's legislative priorities.

Constitutional Lawmaking Authority From the beginning, presidents have to some extent been able to influence legislation. The Framers empowered the president with the final stamp of approval (or rejection) of congressional bills, known as the executive **veto**. After a bill has passed both House and Senate, the president has 10 days (not including Sundays) to sign it into law. Though the president cannot change the wording of a bill, several presidents have offered **signing statements** that explain their interpretation of a particular bill. Critics of the signing statement argue that it violates the basic lawmaking design and overly enhances a president's last-minute input on a bill.

Veto Regarding presidential veto of a bill, the Constitution states, "He shall return it, with his objections to that House in which it shall have originated." This provision is meant to create a dialogue between the two branches and encourage Congress to consider the president's critique. It requires some accountability on the part of the executive, and it also encourages consensus policies. Congressional proponents of a bill will work cooperatively to pass it, reshaping it if necessary to avoid a veto. The use of the veto has fluctuated over presidential history. When there is a divided government—one party dominating Congress and another controlling the presidency—there is typically a corresponding increase in the use of the veto. During President George W. Bush's first six years, his party also held the majority of seats in Congress. His first veto came only after the Democrats won the House and Senate in 2006.

The president can also opt to neither sign nor veto. Any bill not signed or vetoed becomes law after the 10-day approval period. However, if a president receives a bill in the final 10 days of a congressional session and does nothing, the bill dies, an outcome known as a **pocket veto**. Since much legislation arrives at the end of a session, the president can eliminate congressional plans with a pocket veto.

Line-Item Veto Many state governors have the option of a **line-item veto**. This measure empowers an executive to eliminate a line of spending from an appropriations bill, vetoing part, but not all, of the bill. Since the founding, presidents have argued for the right to a line-item veto. In 1996, Congress granted that right with the **Line-Item Veto Act**, which gave the president line-item veto authority with regard to appropriations, new direct spending, and limited tax benefits. As the chief representative of the nation, the president has no loyalties to a particular district and can thus make difficult spending cuts without fear of local political repercussions.

Under the new act, President Clinton cut proposed federal monies earmarked for New York City. The city sued, arguing that the Constitution gave Congress the power of the purse, and this new law suddenly gave away that power to the president. The Court agreed in ***Clinton v. City of New York*** (1998), and the act was struck down. Presidents and fiscal conservatives continue to call for a line-item veto to reduce spending. There is little doubt that such power would reduce at least some spending. However, it is difficult to convince lawmakers (who can currently send pork barrel funds to their own districts) to provide the president with the authority to take away that perk.

Executive Order An **executive order** empowers the president to carry out the law or to administer the government. Unlike creating a criminal law or making a monetary appropriation, which requires Congress to act, the president can issue a directive that falls within his authority as head of the executive branch. For example, the president can define how the military and other departments operate. These executive orders have been issued for about a century, and since 1946, all executive orders have been published in the *Federal Register*, a compendium of administrative law.

Executive orders address issues ranging from security clearances for government employees to smoking in the workplace. In 1942, for example, FDR issued the infamous Executive Order 9066, which empowered the FBI to intern Japanese-Americans in West Coast camps during World War II. In 1948, an executive order issued by President Truman brought racial integration to the Armed Forces. Truman realized that making such a change through legislative means would create a fiery, uncivil debate and probably would not have succeeded. More recently, onlookers wondered if President Obama might, through executive order, lift the "don't ask, don't tell" policy for gays in the military. In December 2010, Congress lifted the ban, so Obama did not have to make the choice.

Chief Diplomat

The Constitution says the president shall have the power "to make treaties," and "he shall receive **ambassadors** and other public ministers" from other countries. The Framers gave the president much foreign policy power because the philosophers that inspired the American Revolution also argued that the executive—kings at that time—should be assigned the primary role in foreign affairs. The U.S. secretary of state has become the president's main diplomat, overseeing an array of ambassadors to foreign countries.

According to author Bradley Patterson, nearing the end of his presidency, George W. Bush had more than 750 phone conversations with other chiefs or world leaders, participated in more than 675 face-to-face meetings, and conducted 15 video teleconferences. The balance of power between the president and Congress on foreign relations, however, is sometimes uncertain. For example, Congress can fund or refuse to fund a diplomatic endeavor. The Senate can reject a president's appointed ambassadors and must ratify the president's treaties.

Treaties vs. Executive Agreements Through treaties, presidents can facilitate trade, provide for mutual defense, help set international environmental standards, or prevent weapons testing. President Wilson could not get the Senate to fully ratify America's entry into the League of Nations. Franklin Roosevelt called the Senate "a bunch of incompetent obstructionists," and claimed the only way to pass anything in the American government was to bypass the Senate.

An **executive agreement** resembles a treaty yet does not require the Senate's two-thirds vote. It is a simple contract between two heads of state: the president and a prime minister, king, or president of another nation. Like any agreement, such a contract is only as binding as each side's ability and willingness to keep the promise. These compacts cannot supersede prior treaties or congressional acts.

Presidents have come to appreciate the power of the executive agreement. President Washington found it extremely cumbersome and perhaps dangerous to confer with the Senate during each step of a delicate negotiation. It compromised confidentiality and created delays. As the Senate has grown with the addition of each new state, so has its potential for inefficiency.

From 1889 to 1939, of 1,441 international compacts, 917 were executive agreements and only 524 were treaties. "The biggest matters," Teddy Roosevelt wrote as he left the White House in 1909, "I managed without consultation with anyone; for when a matter is of capital importance, it is well to have it handled by one man only."

Cuban Missile Crisis Executive agreements are a preferred diplomatic path to ensure secrecy or speed or to avoid senatorial egos. During the Cuban Missile Crisis, President Kennedy discovered the Soviet Union's plan to install nuclear missiles in Cuba. Intelligence reports estimated these would soon be operational. After days of contemplation, negotiation, and a naval standoff in the Caribbean, the United States and the USSR made a deal. The agreement stated that the Soviets would remove their offensive missiles from Cuba if the United States would remove its own missiles that had been installed in Turkey. Had Kennedy relied on the full Senate, a different outcome could very well have occurred. Many U.S. leaders wanted no deals with the enemy. Time, strong words on the Senate floor, or an ultimate refusal could have drastically reversed this historic outcome.

Commander in Chief

The Framers named the president the **commander in chief** and gave the president much control over the military. The Constitution, however, left the decision of declaring war strictly to the Congress. Congress has declared war only a few times—against Britain in 1812, against Mexico in 1846, against Spain in 1898, and against U.S. adversaries in both world wars. The question of what constitutes a war, however, is not always clear. The United States conducted military campaigns against Native Americans and against pirates on the seas without congressional declaration. The U.S. Civil War, the Union and President Lincoln insisted, was not a war with another state, but merely a southern rebellion or insurrection. Calling it a war would have legitimized the Confederacy as a sovereign state.

Senator Barry Goldwater proclaimed in the waning days of the Vietnam War, "We have only been in five declared wars out of over 150 that we have fought." His point was fair, if his estimate was high. The questions remain: Should all troop landings be considered wars that require congressional declarations? What about eavesdropping or covert military operations carried out in other countries?

There is no consensus on when military action is strictly defensive. FDR ordered U.S. troops to Greenland in 1940 after the Nazis marched into Denmark but before any U.S. declaration of war. President Kennedy conducted an invasion of the Bay of Pigs in Cuba in hopes of overthrowing dictator Fidel Castro. Harold Krent and others explain how President Clinton bombed Iraq after finding out about the failed assassination attempt on his predecessor, the elder President Bush. Some believe that actions such as these stretch the meaning of "defensive" too far and are really acts of war.

Though undeclared encounters took place before the 1940s, World War II greatly expanded the president's authority as commander in chief. Since that time, Harry Truman attacked North Korea without congressional authority, Lyndon Johnson mobilized the Army in Southeast Asia in 1964, and President

George H.W. Bush claimed he needed no congressional authorization to join the United Nations in 1991 in forcing Saddam Hussein out of Kuwait. He later got congressional approval but not a congressional declaration of war.

Vietnam The Cold War and intense fear of nuclear weapons helped to grow the president's war powers relative to Congress. In the early 1960s, one senator conceded that the president must have some war powers because "the difference between safety and cataclysm can be a matter of hours or even minutes."

The theory of defense against imminent as well as actual attack began to obliterate the distinction the Framers had set and added an increasingly elastic theory of defensive war to the president's diplomatic arsenal. As recent presidents tried to assume more power, they argued the world was figuratively much larger in 1789, meaning that travel and communication were much slower. This, some have argued, allowed the commander in chief more time to react to perceived aggressors and to consult with Congress. Today, with so many U.S. interests abroad, an attack on American interests or an ally far from U.S. shores can directly and immediately impact national security.

Empowering the President The Congress yielded some of its war-making authority with the **Tonkin Gulf Resolution** in 1964. After reports of a naval skirmish off the coast of Vietnam in the Tonkin Gulf (which were later found to be untrue), Congress quickly gave the president the green light "to take all necessary measures to repel any armed attack against the forces of the United States to prevent further aggression." Congressional leaders rushed the resolution in a stampede of misinformation and misunderstanding. This rapid reaction to aggressive Communists led to the nation's longest, most unpopular war. In 1973, Congress decided to fix this constitutional mistake and passed the **War Powers Act.** The law maintains the president's need for urgent action or to defend the United States while preserving the war-declaring authority of Congress. The president can order the military into combat 48 hours before informing Congress. In turn, Congress can vote to approve or disapprove any presidential military action at any time, with the stipulation that the vote must take place within 60 days.

Chief of Party

The president is the face of his political party. That makes him the highest-ranking member of the team that put him in office. Once in office, the president continues to advance the party's goals and the philosophies espoused in its platform. Most presidents have been strong, loyal, and influential party members.

During election season, the president hits the campaign trail, whether during midterm elections to support fellow party members or for his own re-election. The White House is drawn deeply into electoral contests across the nation because such contests can have a direct effect on the success or failure of enacting presidential policy. It is in the president's best interest to have as many like-minded partisans in Congress as possible to help implement his programs.

Public opinion polls gauge the standing of both the president and his party. Presidents tend to publicly disparage public opinion polling when it goes against their position, while emphasizing their courageous independence and assertive decision making. Yet presidents also measure public opinion and can become fixated on polls. The RNC spent more than $3 million on such polling during President George W. Bush's first two years.

Chief Magistrate

The president has some judicial powers and can shape the courts. In addition to giving the president the power to appoint federal judges and enforce the law, the Constitution gives the president the power "to grant reprieves and pardons for offenses against the United States, except in cases of impeachment." These checks on the courts make the president the last resort for those convicted of federal criminal offenses. The Department of Justice prosecutes accused defendants, and a federal court determines their guilt. Of the thousands of prosecuted federal cases, the president rarely gets directly involved with individual crimes or trials. On occasion a president will issue an act of clemency through pardon, commutation (lessening sentences), or amnesty (pardoning a large group). Notable pardons include George Washington's pardon of participants in the Whiskey Rebellion and Lincoln's pardon of some southern sympathizers. President Ford pardoned Nixon after he left office to put the Watergate scandal in the past. And President Carter issued a general amnesty for Vietnam draft dodgers.

Presidents tend to issue controversial pardons during the lame duck period to avoid political fallout. For example, Americans generally frown upon releasing convicted criminals, yet on his final day in office, Bill Clinton granted 140 pardons, including one for his brother Roger Clinton, who had been convicted of drug charges and other crimes.

Chief Administrator

The president oversees 15 departments and countless agencies to carry out the law. The executive branch, with its vast bureaucracy, builds roads, defends the nation, educates the populace, and tracks down criminals. The president is essentially the CEO of a company with more than two million employees and a massive budget. Cabinet-level executives and advisers act as upper management. Agency heads also ultimately serve this CEO. The president designs a budget to spend the nation's funds on programs from the military to education grants.

Executive Privilege Presidents have at times asserted **executive privilege,** the right to withhold information or advice they received from their subordinates. Sometimes the input is offered confidentially, which presents a problem for a president if he is asked to reveal the source. Some presidents have declined to identify a source, claiming that the information is privileged. They argue that their right to executive privilege comes from the separation of powers and point out that nothing in the Constitution requires the president to reveal any part of the decision-making process en route to an official act.

If controversial input from subordinates can simply be demanded by another branch, presidents argue further, then subordinates may refuse to give worthy advice and thereby weaken a president's ability to lead.

United States v. Nixon The power of executive privilege, however, has its limits. In 1972, as the Watergate scandal developed, investigators subpoenaed the White House tapes that contained President Nixon's confidential conversations. Nixon refused to hand over the tapes, claiming through executive privilege that his conversations were confidential. The Court disagreed. In a unanimous vote, the Court acknowledged a president's right to confidentiality in decision making, but declared that there is no absolute, unqualified presidential privilege of immunity from prosecution. This was not another branch simply looking for his conversations en route to official presidential action; instead, it was a court seeking evidence in a criminal investigation. Allowing a president to assert such a right in this instance would have thwarted law enforcement. Presidents can still withhold information, but they cannot do so in cases in which they are under criminal investigation.

Presidents' Experiences and Legacies		
President	**Prior Position**	**Legacies**
Dwight D. Eisenhower (R)	General in U.S. Army	Interstate highways, firm stance with Soviets
John F. Kennedy (D)	Senator from Massachusetts	Cuban Missile Crisis, space program, Bay of Pigs
Lyndon B. Johnson (D)	Vice President, Senate Majority Leader	Civil Rights laws, Great Society Programs, Vietnam
Richard M. Nixon (R)	Vice President, Congress	De-escalation, improved relations with China, Watergate
Gerald R. Ford (R)	House Minority Leader	Pardoning Nixon
James E. Carter (D)	Governor of Georgia	Camp David Accords, inflation, Iran Hostage Crisis
Ronald W. Reagan (R)	Governor of California	Stronger defense, relations with USSR
George H.W. Bush (R)	Vice President	Gulf War
William J. Clinton (D)	Governor of Arkansas	Prosperous economy, impeachment
George W. Bush (R)	Governor of Texas	September 11, War on Terror, Civil liberties infringements
Barack H. Obama (D)	Senator from Illinois	National health care, killing Osama bin Laden

The Vice President

To many, the vice presidency appears to be the second most powerful government position in America, but in reality the VP is an assistant to the president with little influence and a somewhat undefined job description. Different presidents have given their vice presidents differing degrees of authority and roles. Vice presidents have more often become presidents through succession than through election.

Balancing the Ticket

Presidential nominees select their running mates after the primary campaign, and the party confirms the choice at the convention. The main concern is how the vice presidential candidate can balance the ticket to increase the chance of electoral success. This balance can be geographic or ideological or it can be based on complementary experiences. John F. Kennedy chose Lyndon B. Johnson because Johnson's status as a southern Senate leader counterbalanced Kennedy's appeal to northern liberals, labor, and civil rights advocates. Johnson was a Texas Democrat who brought with him southern electoral votes. In 1980, Ronald Reagan asked George H.W. Bush to join his ticket after the two competed for the Republican presidential nomination. Reagan had served as California's governor and was committed to downsizing government. Bush was a Washington insider who had, over the years, served in the House and as CIA director, United Nations ambassador, and party chairman. In 2008, Barack Obama announced that Joe Biden, a career senator with foreign relations expertise, would run as his vice president to balance out Obama's inexperience in international affairs. Quite often, presidential hopefuls who fail to receive the nomination join the ticket. All of the vice presidents mentioned above had sought their party's nomination the same year they were asked to join the winning ticket.

The Role of Vice President

The Constitution assigns the vice president to preside over the Senate without a vote, except in cases where the Senate vote is equally divided. The vice president has historically led Senate floor debate much like the Speaker of the House and at times still does so today. Article II declares that in case of presidential removal, death, resignation, or inability, the president's duties and powers "shall devolve on the vice president."

A vice president's role and scope of practical power is generally determined by the president. Some vice presidents have been frontmen for both domestic and international causes. Some have taken more active roles or have closely advised the chief executive; others have kept their distance and had cool relations with the chief executive. The office is generally described as a "heartbeat away from the presidency" yet is actually relatively weak unless that unfortunate moment arrives. The first vice presidents, especially Adams, lamented that the office was worthless. Not until 1918 was the vice president even regularly invited to Cabinet meetings.

The Twenty-fifth Amendment states that the vice president, with the support of a majority of the Cabinet, can declare a president incapable of discharging the powers and duties of the office. After declaring this disability, a vice president can assume presidential powers. Different from an impeachment, this process is meant to guarantee that a constitutionally sanctioned leader is in charge at all times. Presidents have undergone surgery that required them to be incapacitated for several hours and have officially handed power off to their vice presidents for the duration of the medical procedure. To date, no president has been declared unable to carry out duties by the vice president and Cabinet.

A total of nine vice presidents have immediately succeeded presidents. But only three sitting vice presidents have been elected president—John Adams, Martin Van Buren, and George H.W. Bush.

The importance of the office of vice president was elevated during World War II when Harry Truman had to take over for Franklin Roosevelt and immediately became the commander in chief of the allied powers. No longer was the vice presidency irrelevant. Years later, President Eisenhower employed his vice president, Richard Nixon, to serve as an international expert and an emissary to foreign heads of state.

Recent vice presidents have taken stronger and more active roles in assisting the president. Both Dick Cheney and Joe Biden have had strong roles in policy development. Cheney was a key player in Bush's war on terror, and Biden has been an active manager in U.S.-Afghanistan policy and a congressional liaison on the issue of the federal budget.

Since 1974, vice presidents have resided at the official residence at the U.S. Naval Observatory.

Administering the Executive Branch

The hierarchy of the executive branch consists of the president at the top, the Cabinet secretaries, and then the federal agencies. In addition to these offices, the president has immediate staff and entire organizations to assist him.

Cabinet

The **Cabinet** is a defined group of presidential advisers. Most of them also run large departments that take care of a wide range of national concerns. For example, the Department of Defense oversees the military, and the Department of Transportation oversees the federal interstate highway system and air traffic control. The Framers discussed the term "cabinet" but did not include it in the Constitution. Article II mentions "the principal officers in each of the executive departments."

Today's Cabinet consists of 15 department heads and a few additional members the president may assign. President Obama added his chief of staff, the EPA director, the budget director, U.S. trade representative, the UN ambassador, and his chief economic adviser. When appointing secretaries for the Cabinet, presidents try to create some balance based on geography, gender, ethnicity, and even party membership. Recently, presidents have included

EXECUTIVE HIERARCHY
Selected Cabinet Level Departments and Agencies

Executive Office of the President	**President** **Vice President**	**White House Office**
Council on Economic Advisors Office of Management & Budget Central Intelligence Agency National Security Council Others	15 Cabinet Secretaries	White House Staff Chief of Staff Press Secretary Legal Counsel

State	**Treasury**	**Defense**	**Justice**	**Labor**	**Homeland Security**
Regional Offices, Economic & Business Affairs Ambassadors United States Agency for International Development	IRS, Comptroller of Currency, Engraving & Printing, U.S. Mint Financial Crimes Enforcement Network	Joint Chiefs of Staff Army, Navy, Air Force, Marine Corp, National Guard, Defense Intelligence Agency NSA	Solicitor General FBI, DEA, ATF, Civil Rights Division, Bureau of Prisons, U.S. Attorneys, Marshals	Bureau of Labor Statistics Mine Safety & Health Disability Employment	FEMA, TSA, Customs & Border Protection Coast Guard Secret Service USCIS

Independent Agencies and Government Corporations	**Independent Regulatory Agencies**
NASA Post Office AMTRAK Corporation for Public Broadcasting Tennessee Valley Authority Others	FCC: Federal Communications Commission FEC: Federal Elections Commission FDA: Food & Drug Administration EPA: Environmental Protection Agency SEC: Securities & Exchanges Commission

token members from the opposite party. When President Obama came to office, he kept Bush's secretary of defense, Robert Gates, and appointed two new Republicans to his Cabinet; one declined. Historically, Cabinets have taken a backseat to the president; they are rarely seen as an influential driving force of an administration unless dominated by strong personalities or long-time loyal aides.

History During George Washington's presidency, Congress set up the Department of State, the Department of the Treasury, and the Department of War. Washington also named an attorney general, though Congress did not officially create the Department of Justice until 1870. Washington appointed talented men who differed widely on the key issues of the day. In the 1860s, President Lincoln assembled a team of able rivals, including his political antagonists who had also sought the presidency, in order to create a strong team and vibrant discussion. The Cabinet typically works as an advisory panel; the president is the one that makes the top decisions. When Lincoln's Cabinet differed from him on a particular question, he proclaimed, "Seven nays and one aye—the ayes have it."

President Eisenhower expanded his Cabinet in the 1950s to more than 20 representatives from areas of government beyond the department secretaries. Eisenhower prided himself on long, deliberate meetings to fully flesh out the concerns of government. John F. Kennedy preferred more frequent meetings with fewer, more specialized members in attendance. "Cabinet meetings are simply useless," Kennedy once said in frustration. "Why should the postmaster general sit here and listen to a discussion of the problems of Laos?" Many presidents use the Cabinet as a forum for discussion or transmission of information more than as a decision-making body. Lyndon Johnson used these Cabinet meetings to create the impression of consensus within his administration.

Structure and Conflict Some observers divide the Cabinet into "inner" and "outer" circles. The more influential inner cabinet is consulted more often; it handles the more traditional issues. It includes the national security diplomatic wing, the secretaries of state and defense, and the legal and economic side dominated by the attorney general and the treasury secretary. The outer cabinet comprises those more modern departments and secretaries that oversee commerce, labor, and housing and urban development. The secretary of Homeland Security, though the newest Cabinet member, typically shares seats with the state and defense secretaries on the inner cabinet.

Agencies

Federal agencies are subcabinet entities that carry out specific government functions. The Federal Bureau of Investigation (FBI), the Coast Guard, the Food and Drug Administration (FDA), the Internal Revenue Service (IRS), the Central Intelligence Agency (CIA), and the Postal Service are prime examples. These agencies are staffed by thousands of people in Washington and across the country. They carry out laws Congress has passed with funds Congress has allotted.

White House

The president is assisted on a daily basis by the **Executive Office of the President** (EOP) and the White House Office. The EOP carries out most constitutional duties, with a large group of advisers and supporting agencies that handle the budget, the economy, and staffing. The president's immediate staff of specialists runs the White House Office. It is divided into different teams for national security, the economy, and communications. These staffers require no Senate approval and tend to come from the president's inner circle or campaign team. They generally operate out of the West Wing.

Just trying to count how many people work in or directly for the White House is difficult. Patterson in 2008 estimated that there were 74 separate policy offices. Once the Secret Service, telephone operators, and others are added, the total of White House employees reaches 6,574. Following is a look at the key assistants and their jobs:

Executive Office of the President Created in 1939 when FDR needed an expanded presidential staff, the EOP now includes the Office of Management and Budget, the Central Intelligence Agency, the Council of Economic

Advisers, and others. Over the years, the Executive Office has changed from president to president. Congress has added many offices, and presidents have added some others via executive order. The Executive Office has included more than 60 offices, boards, or councils at one time or another. The main divisions appear below.

Office of Management and Budget Originally the Bureau of the Budget, the **Office of Management and Budget** (OMB) was created in 1970 as the president's principal accounting office. The president is charged with spending and managing billions of dollars each year. The OMB has a strong relationship with sister organizations such as the Internal Revenue Service, which collects income taxes, and the Congressional Budget Office. The OMB's budget director is the president's right-hand adviser on federal spending and revenue.

National Security Council Congress created the **National Security Council** with a 1947 law to redefine how the United States defends itself. This council consists of the president's principal advisers on matters of national security, defense, intelligence, and war. Officials sitting on this council include the president (who serves as the chair), the vice president, the national security adviser, the CIA director, secretaries of state and defense, and others. The NSC is an advisory board, but the president still functions as the commander in chief. The modern National Security Council has a support staff of about 250 persons.

Council of Economic Advisers The Congress created the Council of Economic Advisers in 1946. It is a unique three-person committee, one person serving as chair and each member appointed by the president and approved by the Senate. The president names one adviser as chair of the council. The CEA is more independent than most White House offices. This council assists the president in preparing an annual economic report for Congress. It also assesses federal government spending.

Office of U.S. Trade Representative Essentially an ambassador to other nations, the trade representative negotiates treaties regarding international commerce. He or she connects with business interests and works to formulate international law.

There are additional offices in the Executive Office of the President, such as the Office of National Drug Control Policy, and presidents have continued to add and remove offices to shape the EOP based on their beliefs and management styles.

White House Office The president has a **White House staff** composed of fairly permanent advisers and staffers brought to the White House from other executive departments to make the president's inner circle. These staffers are close to the president because many are long-time friends or loyal aides. They are independent from the Congress because most do not set policy but instead work in an advisory capacity. Therefore, the Senate does not need to confirm them. Presidents sometimes come to rely on their staffs more than their

Cabinets or agency heads because staff members serve the president directly. White House staffers, unlike secretaries, do not have loyalties to departments or agencies and do not compete for funding.

Development After Congress created the protocol for the modern-day White House operation in the late 1930s, presidents continued to develop it. Unlike other leaders in the executive branch, the president can alter, shape, and assign various levels of authority to staff members. A staffer's influence is determined by his or her individual relationship and access to the president. Some leading staffers include the press secretary, the chief of staff, the chief legal counsel, congressional liaisons, and the national security adviser.

Chief of Staff In the 1950s, President Eisenhower's **chief of staff** became his gatekeeper, responsible for the smooth operation of the White House and the swift and accurate flow of business, paper, and information. Though the chief of staff has no official policymaking power, a president seeks the chief of staff's opinion on many issues, giving the position a great deal of influence.

Richard Nixon's chief of staff, H. R. Haldeman, once noted that when the president decides that other staffers or Cabinet secretaries must be let go, he dispatches the chief of staff to do the firing. The chief of staff also clears up presidential misstatements and corrects errors. Chiefs of staff tend to be tough, punctual, detail-oriented managers, and these qualities allow the president to concentrate on big-picture decisions. An exception was Bill Clinton's chief, Thomas "Mack" McLarty, who was so easygoing and amicable that he became known as "Mack the Nice."

White House Counsel The attorney general heads the Department of Justice and oversees the nation's law enforcement and federal prosecutions. Though the attorney general can and does advise the president on legal matters, the president also must have a dedicated personal lawyer that does not also have to manage a department of more than 100,000 employees.

The White House counsel provides a wide range of legal advice. He or she reviews legislation before it is sent to Congress, checks over treaties or executive agreements, reviews pardon recommendations, and may advise on bold presidential initiatives to determine constitutionality.

National Security Adviser The national security adviser oversees the National Security Council. This adviser is the president's key point person regarding the safety of the nation. He or she coordinates information coming to the president from the CIA, the military, and the State Department to assess any security threat to the United States.

Legislative Affairs As chief legislator, the president needs a team to draft bills and assist the legislative process. Many senior White House aides have friends and colleagues serving on congressional staffs. Bonds formed years before contribute to the development of policy between the two branches. Sometimes the aides employ techniques to push public opinion in a lawmaker's home district in the direction of a desired presidential policy. White House political staffers know just which groups to contact in which to generate interest in a particular program or position.

Communications Staff Beyond the press secretary, a position discussed in Chapter 8, contemporary presidents have an entire communications office that includes speechwriters and public relations experts. Since the 1930s, the White House has had a day-to-day challenge regarding the 50 or more assigned journalists clamoring for the president's view of various current issues. The expansion of the media has redefined the communications office. President Eisenhower held nearly 200 press conferences and gave speeches and remarks at some 700 occasions over his two terms. President Clinton gave about the same number of press conferences but made speeches and remarks approximately 4,500 times in his eight years in office. In the White House, speechwriters and wordsmiths are nearly always hard at work.

Appointments and Removals

The president has more than 3,000 positions to staff. For each agency director, Congress can define the term of office. Most serve at the pleasure of the president and some are kept on when a new president is elected. Other positions are protected by statute or Supreme Court decisions. Because the founders did not anticipate that Congress would convene as frequently as it does in modern times, they provided for **recess appointments**. If the Senate is not in session when a vacancy arises, the president can appoint a replacement that will serve until the Senate reconvenes and votes on that official. This recess appointment is particularly necessary if the appointee is to handle urgent or sensitive work.

The president cannot remove federal judges at all but can remove upper-level executive branch officials at will, except those that head independent regulatory agencies. (This will be discussed further in the next chapter). A president's power of removal has been the subject of debate since the founding. Founder Alexander Hamilton argued that the Senate should, under its advice and consent power, have a role in the removal of appointed officials. James Madison, however, disagreed and argued that to effectively administer the government the president must retain full control of his subordinates. The Article II phrase that grants the president the power to "take care that the laws be faithfully executed" suggests the president has a hierarchical authority over secretaries and other administrators.

This issue brought Congress and the president to a major conflict in the aftermath of the Civil War. President Andrew Johnson dismissed Secretary of War Edwin Stanton, congressional Republicans argued, in violation of the Tenure of Office Act. This act led to Johnson's impeachment. Johnson remained in office, but subsequent presidents became wary of the law and refrained from using the power of removal.

Is That Constitutional? *Humphrey's Executor v. United States* (1935)

Can the president remove his appointed officials? That depends on several factors.

The question of removal resurfaced in 1926—this time with regard to President Wilson's earlier removal of a postmaster in violation of an 1876 law. The Supreme Court answered the controversy in *Myers v. United States*. Presidential appointees serve at the pleasure of the president. The Court tightened this view a few years later when it came to regulatory agencies in the case of *Humphrey's Executor v. United States* (1935). Franklin Roosevelt removed a conservative member of the Federal Trade Commission. The member in question, William Humphrey, contested his removal in the U.S. Court of Claims but died before his case was fully adjudicated. The executor of Humphrey's will continued to appeal it to the Supreme Court. The act that created the FTC stated that presidents could only remove commissioners for causes specified in the act. Roosevelt probably had the right to release Humphrey on a cause so specified, but he stated instead that they did not "go along together . . . on administering of the FTC."

The *Humphrey's* decision dictated that if the appointee oversees an agency with a mixture of executive and legislative or judicial powers, as was the FTC's jurisdiction, then Congress could shield that officer from the president's removal. The Court's opinion was much praised for liberating commissioners and heads of regulatory agencies from the political pressures that a president might impose. Such insulation allows them to do their job more effectively.

Management Styles

With such flexibility in structuring the White House, presidents have the opportunity to create a management style that reflects their persona and their operation. A president's experience, personality, and chosen appointees help to determine White House character and management style. President Obama's, for example, is that of a reasoned manager—logical like Mr. Spock on the 1960s TV show *Star Trek*, according to analyst Jonathan Alter— who reluctantly engages Washington institutions. Most observers categorize management styles into three groups: pyramid, circular, or ad hoc.

Pyramid The **pyramid system** follows a rigid top-down approach that features the president at the top of the pyramid, with his chief of staff just below serving as gatekeeper, followed by the department heads and then the lesser offices. This system creates a clear chain of command and allows for an orderly flow of information traveling up the pyramid, as well as clarity in directives coming down from the president. The pyramid system encourages specialization at the various levels and emphasizes control and authority at the top.

President Eisenhower used a very clear pyramid structure, which paralleled the military hierarchy he had experienced throughout his career. It mirrored his belief that "a president who doesn't know how to decentralize will be weighted down with details and won't have time to deal with the big issues." Others have followed Eisenhower's example. Richard Nixon arrived at the White House in 1969 and created a similar structure. Nixon's paranoid and controlling personality was well suited to a top-down system. He was also a policy-oriented intellectual who preferred to work in private rather than in large meetings with subordinates.

Though a pyramid approach can be an effective management style, it may also serve to isolate the president or create unwanted stops in the flow of information. The chief of staff or others in the pyramid may prevent pertinent information from reaching a president, disallowing him to make effective decisions.

Circular The **circular system** of executive administration can be thought of as a large wheel with many spokes. The president is the wheel's hub while the principal officers are at the many points along the rim. Twentieth century presidents Kennedy, Johnson, and Carter used this more casual method in order to get more and stronger input from advisers. Because staffers and secretaries have greater access to the president than others, information flows along the spokes of the wheel, and the chief of staff acts as less of a gatekeeper.

President Kennedy was known for running a harmonious White House. He wanted a faster flow of information and more original voices in the decision-making process. President Johnson followed a similar method, keeping much of Kennedy's Cabinet intact and continuing some of his established customs. Johnson's folksy manner and wheeler-dealer persona probably influenced his management style as well. He particularly liked to meet with key staffers in his bedroom either first thing in the morning or late at night right before he went to bed.

This more open communication system can sometimes give officers and staffers too much access to the president. Critics argue that there is simply not enough of the president to go around. A circular arrangement can become excessively casual and cause the presidency to lose its perspective. The Constitution designates one person to ultimately make the national decisions, and a circular arrangement can result in "groupthink" that may lead the nation to bad decisions with no accountability.

Ad Hoc Some administrations are defined by rigid hierarchy and flow charts; others operate with a great deal more flexibility. Bill Clinton took a fairly casual approach to setting up his advisers. Clinton, an affable, gregarious executive, liked to talk to people. This resulted in an organizational façade during his first year in office. The new president kept assigning new people and new groups to handle an ever-widening array of specific issues. Task forces and new committees were created to deal with the pressing issues. In fact, he put his wife, who was relatively inexperienced in Washington at the time, in charge of his national health care proposal.

Such a system has its benefits—the flexibility to bring in alternatives or shift gears in handling an issue—but Clinton's operation struck many as disorganized and out of control. He eventually appointed House Representative Leon Panetta to be his chief of staff. Panetta soon improved the administration's efficiency. Clinton's staff operation reflected both the president's enormous energy and his habit of moving restlessly from problem to problem, another strong reminder that White House operation is highly reflective of the president.

THINK AS A POLITICAL SCIENTIST: EVALUATE THE PRESIDENT'S CABINET

Presidents—and all officials—face big questions every day. Before they can begin to answer such questions, they need to establish *how* to answer them. What are the possible **methods** and **techniques** for gathering information and **evidence** necessary to answer a question? Are there existing studies to research, or should a new study be undertaken? If a new study, how can it be set up to yield appropriate and accurate information? Or should expert opinion be sought? After identifying the various ways to pursue an inquiry, decision-makers must then evaluate those approaches to determine which method or combination of methods will yield the best results.

Students of political science follow the same general approach for identifying and evaluating methods, techniques, and evidence for the inquiries they pursue.

Practice: Suppose you have identified the following inquiry for research: What does the current president's Cabinet reveal about the president's administration? Before you can begin to answer that, you need to determine the best methods and techniques for finding answers to that question. Begin with some preliminary research by going to the Web page of the president's Cabinet at www.whitehouse.gov/administration/cabinet. Select two or three Cabinet secretaries and follow the links to their respective departments. Read their biographies and ask yourself some basic questions: When were they appointed? What line of work were they in before serving the president and heading a department? Did they serve in government or in the private sector? What recent actions have they taken?

Then ask yourself what else you need to know to answer your research inquiry: what do these leaders reveal about the president's administration? Identify several paths to pursue to answer that question. Evaluate them and determine the best approach for gathering the information you need. In a paragraph, summarize the research plan you believe would be most appropriate for addressing your inquiry.

Essential Question: *How does the chief executive make decisions, enforce the laws, and represent the nation's citizens?* On a separate paper, complete a chart like the one below to gather details to answer that question.

Make Decisions	Enforce Laws	Represent Citizens

KEY TERMS, NAMES, AND EVENTS

ad hoc

ambassadors

bully pulpit

Cabinet

chief of staff

circular system

Clinton v. City of New York (1998)

Cold War

commander in chief

electors

executive agreement

Executive Office of the President

executive order

executive privilege

honeymoon period

Humphrey's Executor v. United States (1935)

impeachment

imperial presidency

inherent powers

lame duck period

line-item veto

Line-Item Veto Act (1996)

Myers v. United States (1926)

National Security Council

Office of Management and Budget

pocket veto

Presidential Succession Act (1947)

pyramid system

recess appointments

signing statements

State of the Union

stewardship theory

Tonkin Gulf Resolution (1964)

Twelfth Amendment

Twentieth Amendment

Twenty-second Amendment

Twenty-third Amendment

Twenty-fifth Amendment

United States v. Nixon (1974)

veto

War Powers Act (1973)

White House staff

Source: Kevin Kallaugher, Kaltoons.com

1. With which of the following statements would the cartoonist agree?

    (A) President Carter gained popularity with the Iran Hostage Crisis.

    (B) Bill Clinton maintained integrity and honesty in the White House.

    (C) President Reagan raised federal income taxes.

    (D) George W. Bush will be remembered for a failed and burdensome Iraq policy.

    (E) Presidential actions are typically forgotten after presidents leave office.

2. The most important factor for a presidential candidate in selecting a vice presidential running mate is

    (A) the vice presidential candidate's military experience

    (B) a balanced ticket that can win the election

    (C) the vice presidential candidate's prior experience in the federal government

    (D) selecting someone of the opposite gender

    (E) concern about removing the vice president if it is deemed necessary

3. Which Supreme Court decision declared that presidential appointees serve at the president's pleasure?

(A) *Marbury v. Madison*

(B) *United States v. Nixon*

(C) *Youngstown Sheet & Tube v. Sawyer*

(D) *Myers v. United States*

(E) *New York Times v. United States*

4. Which requirement to serve as president did the Framers include in the original Constitution?

(A) New presidents must be sworn in on January 20.

(B) A president cannot serve more than two terms.

(C) Presidential candidates must have prior experience in federal or state government.

(D) All presidents must be at least 35 years old.

(E) Presidential candidates must belong to a political party.

5. Presidents have used executive orders to establish policies over the years. Which of the following changes came about due to an executive order?

(A) Establishing a national minimum wage

(B) Integrating the races in the military

(C) Guaranteeing women the right to vote

(D) Creating the Social Security system

(E) Mandating limits on campaign contributions

6. The Framers devised the Electoral College system in order to

(A) bring the nation's electors together in one place to select the president

(B) ensure that the candidate earning the most popular votes will be the nation's leader

(C) give all states the same electoral voting strength

(D) give members of Congress the power to select the president

(E) maintain the primacy of the states in electing the nation's leader

7. All of the following have contributed to the growth of the imperial presidency EXCEPT

(A) constitutional limits of four-year terms and impeachment

(B) domestic crises that require effective leadership

(C) cooperative Congresses

(D) war or national security threats

(E) the overlapping constitutional responsibilities of the president and Congress

8. Which of the following is true regarding presidents and their White House management?

(A) The pyramid structure allows for a more structured, controlled White House operation.

(B) Bill Clinton ran an orderly top-down administration during his presidency.

(C) The press secretary is usually the chief gatekeeper between the president and his appointed executives.

(D) More structured presidential administrations tend to use an ad hoc system.

(E) Presidents always maintain the same structure throughout their time in the office.

9. Which statement regarding the presidential veto is true?

(A) All presidents have made frequent use of the veto.

(B) Presidents using the veto must explain their reasoning to Congress.

(C) A president can veto part of a bill, while not vetoing the entire bill.

(D) The pocket veto can be an effective tool to stop legislation throughout the year.

(E) President George W. Bush used the veto frequently during his first term.

10. Which statement illustrates the chief difference between the president's Cabinet and the White House staff?

(A) Unlike Cabinet members, White House staff must be approved by the Senate.

(B) The Cabinet typically comes more from the president's campaign team than the staff.

(C) When seeking advice, presidents are more reliant on their staffs than their Cabinet.

(D) White House staffers are in the line of succession for a president, but Cabinet secretaries are not.

(E) One group is elected for two-year terms, the other for four-year terms.

Question

1. The Framers of the Constitution shaped the presidency with a series of qualifications, duties, and checks.

   (a) Identify one constitutional qualification for the president of the United States and explain the reason for its inclusion in the Constitution.

   (b) Identify one constitutional duty for the president of the United States and explain how the president carries out the duty.

   (c) Identify one constitutional check on the president of the United States and explain how that check limits the president.

Question

2. Some presidential historians and contemporary scholars claim that expanded presidential powers have led to an imperial presidency. Yet, Congress and the Judiciary have acted to limit presidential power.

   (a) Explain two reasons for a president's expansion of power, and provide an example for each.

   (b) Explain how two of the following limit a president's power.
   - *Clinton v. City of New York*
   - *United States v. Nixon*
   - War Powers Act
   - Twenty-second Amendment

WRITING: CONSIDER YOUR OPTIONS

Many FRQs have multiple possible responses. Take #1 above as an example. You probably didn't have a difficult time coming up with presidential duties or checks. Explaining these, however, may be another story. Before you write your response, create a short list of what you think are possible answers. Step back a moment and review and evaluate your list. Choose the answers you are most certain about and the ones you will find easiest to explain.

The Bureaucracy

*"You are laboring under the impression that I read these
memoranda of yours. I can't even lift them."*

—President Franklin Delano Roosevelt to an appointed bureaucrat

Essential Question: How does the executive branch administer the machinery
of government and provide services to American citizens?

The federal government provides many services, such as interstate highways, air traffic coordination at airports, border protection, law enforcement, and mail delivery. For each of these services, Congress has passed a law and created one or more executive branch departments or agencies to carry out the law. The federal bureaucracy is the vast, hierarchical organization of executive branch employees—more than 2.6 million people ranging from members of the president's Cabinet to accountants at the Internal Revenue Service—that takes care of the federal government's business. Sometimes referred to as the "fourth branch of government," the bureaucracy is composed of experts with specialized roles, such as soldiers, tax collectors, and letter carriers. Additional personnel support the federal system from the private sector or as employees of state and local government who are paid with federal funds and guided by federal directives.

History, Growth, and Reform

The bureaucracy has grown from a four-man council and a few hundred employees at the nation's founding to a massive administration of expansive programs. As the nation has grown, so have its responsibilities. The bureaucracy became a place to reward loyal party leaders with federal jobs, a practice known as **patronage**. Congress reformed the system several times, most recently in the 1970s. In the modern era, the anonymous bureaucrat has become the symbol of government inefficiency and impersonality.

George Washington established the first Cabinet by appointing an attorney general and secretaries of state, treasury, and war. Congress created a military, a coast guard, and a postal system, thereby creating many quality federal jobs for President Washington to fill. Washington set high ethical and competency standards for his appointees during that formative administration. He also considered his appointees' commitment to the revolution and their military experience. What's more, when others recommended candidates, Washington asked, "Is he a Federalist?"

Presidents Adams and Jefferson allowed personal prejudice and party politics to influence them even more than Washington. When Jefferson took office in 1801 atop a developing party organization, he filled every vacancy with a member of his party until achieveing a balance of Federalists and Jeffersonians.

The National Spoils System

The 1820 Tenure of Office Act legally ended a presidential appointee's term unless the incoming president allowed the incumbent officeholder to remain. The growing impact of political parties caused a "rotation system" of appointments regardless of merit or performance. The outgoing president's appointees left with him. On Jackson's Inauguration Day in 1829, job-hungry mobs pushed into the White House, snatching refreshments as aggressively as they sought patronage jobs. Congressmen began recommending fellow party members, and senators—with advice and consent power—asserted their influence on the process.

The Post Office became the main agency for the president to run party machinery. Nearly every city had a branch office, creating an established organizational hierarchy across the United States. Presidents appointed local postmasters based on their efforts to help elect the presidents and with an expectation of loyalty after the appointment. This patronage system became known as the **spoils system**. "To the victor belong the spoils," claimed President Jackson and other proponents.

The Civil War Era The Civil War and its aftermath brought an even greater need for bureaucracy, an enlarged federal staff, and, ultimately, an opportunity for corruption in government. President Abraham Lincoln, once a postmaster himself, made a clean sweep of his predecessor's appointees and filled those openings with choices from his own party. During his term, Lincoln managed to fund a war that enlisted thousands of soldiers. Droughts and other agricultural challenges led him to establish the Department of Agriculture. After the Civil War, Congress created the Pension Office to manage soldiers' payments. Reconstruction also added to the federal bureaucracy, since rebuilding and governing the former Confederate states required more money, more personnel, and new federal responsibilities.

The Heyday of the Machine As party strength and influence grew, cities and states developed their own bureaucracies to fill with patronage appointments. Political machines—organized party-based clubs—rose in importance and influence. A party boss, who may or may not have been an elected or appointed official, controlled the jobs through political influence or established party protocol. Members of government, especially in President Ulysses Grant's administration, engaged in scandal and nepotism. By the 1870s, the spoils system was thoroughly entrenched in state and federal politics.

Considering Merit

The desire for the best government rather than a government of friends became a chief concern among certain groups and associations. Moral-based movements such as emancipation, temperance, and women's suffrage also encouraged taming or dismantling the spoils system. Reformers called for candidate appointments based on merit, skill, and experience.

In 1870, leading Republican Senator Lyman Trumbull included a rider to a law that authorized the president to create rules and regulations for a civil service. The system, the law said, would "best promote the efficiency thereof, and ascertain the fitness of each candidate in respect to age, health, character, knowledge, and ability." President Grant appointed a commission of seven people to draw up these regulations.

Garfield's Assassination Reformers' efforts temporarily faded, however, until a murder of national consequence brought attention back to the issue. Soon after James Garfield was sworn in as president in 1881, an eccentric named Charles Guiteau began insisting Garfield appoint him to a political office. Garfield denied his requests. On July 2, only three months into the president's term, Guiteau shot Garfield twice as he was about to board a train. Garfield lay wounded for months before he finally died.

The Pendleton Civil Service Act

Garfield's assassination brought attention to the extreme cases of patronage and encouraged more comprehensive legislation. Congress passed the **Pendleton Civil Service Act** in 1883 to prevent the constant reward to loyal party members. The law established the principle of hiring federal employees on the basis of merit rather than political affiliation or loyalty. The government created the **merit system**, which included competitive, written exams for many job applicants. The law also created the bipartisan **Civil Service Commission** to oversee the process and prevented officers from requiring federal employees to contribute to political campaigns.

The establishment of the civil service and an attempt by the U.S. government during the Industrial Era to regulate the economy and care for the needy brought about the modern administrative state. The bureaucratic system became stocked with qualified experts dedicated to their federal jobs. These workers served across administrations to create a continuity and expertise that professionalized the institution.

The federal government began more frequently to legislate on business and corporations. With the Interstate Commerce Act of 1887, the government created its first regulatory commission, the Interstate Commerce Commission, to enforce Congress's laws regarding train travel and products traveling across state lines. Progressives, led by Republican Teddy Roosevelt, came into office. Roosevelt pushed for the establishment of the Department of Labor and Commerce. Organized labor unions had become a force in public policy, and the all-powerful corporations responded. Having these two forces represented in one department proved difficult, however, so Labor and Commerce was split into two departments. The Pure Food and Drug Act brought attention to the meatpacking industry and other industries producing consumable goods. The Sixteenth Amendment, which gave Congress the power to collect taxes on income, put more money into the Treasury's coffers, which helped the federal bureaucracy expand.

Over the next several decades, the United States survived two world wars and an economic depression that resulted in an entirely new view of government's administrative role. New Deal programs of the 1930s gave the government more responsibility and worked to strengthen the Democratic Party in ways the Pendleton Act was meant to prevent. The Pendleton Act placed only a segment of the federal civilian workforce under an examination system. Leading federal officeholders across the country were still wrapped up in politics. At the 1936 Democratic National Convention, a majority of the delegates were postmasters, U.S. marshals, revenue collectors, or close relatives. FDR won renomination and handily defeated his Republican challenger. After taking a beating in the elections and watching the residual workings of the patronage system, congressional Republicans joined reform-minded Democrats to create another regulation meant to curb the overlap of politics and profession.

The Hatch Act Congress passed statutes in 1939 and 1940 that are collectively referred to as the **Hatch Act.** Sponsored by Democratic Senator Carl Hatch of New Mexico, the law distanced federal employees, as well as state employees paid with federal funds, from politics. It prohibited federal workers from becoming directly involved in federal political campaigns. The law, however, interfered with the First Amendment rights of free speech and free association. The Hatch Act was criticized on these grounds and was eventually softened by the Federal Employees Political Activities Act of 1993. Today, federal employees cannot use their official position to influence or interfere in an election. They cannot engage in political activity while on duty, while using a government vehicle, or while in official uniform. They can, however, express opinions about candidates, contribute to a campaign fund, join political parties, and attend political functions after hours.

The 1960s and 1970s

The same movements that increased interest group growth in the 1960s also increased the size and scope of the bureaucracy. Laws that ensured the equal rights of minorities and women brought on the need for new offices to guarantee them. The Justice Department established the Office of Civil Rights and later the Equal Employment Opportunity Commission. A push for consumer rights and product safety led Congress to create the Consumer Product Safety Commission. Concerns for clean air and water brought about the establishment of the Environmental Protection Agency.

1978 Reforms President Carter ran for office promising to change Washington and to reform the bureaucracy. With experience as an engineer and as a governor, he spent much time analyzing systems. He tinkered with the structure of the federal government as much as any other president. What became the **Civil Service Reform Act** (1978) altered how a bureaucrat is dismissed, limited preferences for veterans in hopes of balancing the genders in federal employment, and put upper-level appointments back into the president's hands.

Senior Executive Service The law also created the **Senior Executive Service,** a system that placed more emphasis on a bureaucrat's skills and experiences than on the job. The administration paid the recruited and incoming senior executives a standard salary, but the president had the right to move these officials laterally or put them in a lesser job with no loss of pay. Carter's reforms increased managerial flexibility and gave political leaders the tools to carve and mold the senior civil service.

The Bureaucracy Today

Today's bureaucracy is a product of two hundred years of increased public expectation and increased federal responsibilities. It touches every issue the nation handles and provides countless services to U.S. citizens. Like all bureaucracies, the federal bureaucracy is characterized by hierarchies, a distinct division of labor or specialization, and highly tailored rules.

Departments

The president oversees the executive branch through a structured system of 15 departments. Newer departments include Energy, Veterans Affairs, and Homeland Security. Departments have been renamed and divided into multiple departments. The largest department is by far the Department of Defense.

Federal Departments	
Department	**Established**
Department of State	1789
Department of Treasury	1789
Department of Defense	1789
Department of Interior	1849
Department of Agriculture	1862
Department of Justice	1870
Department of Commerce	1903
Department of Labor	1913
Department of Health and Human Services	1952
Department of Housing and Urban Development	1965
Department of Transportation	1967
Department of Education	1979
Department of Energy	1979
Department of Veterans Affairs	1989
Department of Homeland Security	2003

Overseeing each department is a Cabinet secretary who shares the name of his or her department. At formal Cabinet meetings, the secretaries sit in seats based on the age of their department, with the oldest departments seated closest to the president. Though different secretaries handle different issues, they are all paid the same salary.

Agencies

The departments contain agencies that divide the department's goals and workload. In addition to the term *agency*, these sub-units may be referred to as divisions, bureaus, offices, services, administrations, and boards. The Department of Homeland Security oversees the Border Patrol, the Coast Guard, and the Transportation Security Administration. These agencies deal with protecting the country and its citizens. There are hundreds of agencies, many of which have headquarters in Washington, D.C., and regional offices in large U.S. cities. The president appoints the head of each agency, typically referred to as the "director."

Federal Bureau of Investigation The Federal Bureau of Investigation celebrated its 100th birthday in 2008. This Justice Department law enforcement agency first dealt with immigration violations, national banking, and antitrust violations. Then interstate crimes—transporting stolen property, bank robbery, and fraudulent schemes—became federal crimes. The FBI professionalized its forces and opened branch offices throughout the nation. Director J. Edgar Hoover, the longest serving agency director, strongly ruled the bureau from the 1920s until his death in 1972. Today, the FBI works with state and local law enforcement to find America's most wanted criminals. The bureau also has helped to track and uncover terrorist organizations that threaten the United States.

Internal Revenue Service After Congress began to tax individuals' incomes, it then established an agency to collect the taxes. Originally named the Bureau of Internal Revenue, the Internal Revenue Service is the nation's tax collector within the Treasury Department. Its mission is to help Americans understand and fulfill their tax responsibilities and to enforce the tax code fairly. With its Criminal Investigation Division, the IRS also prosecutes those who evade their taxes.

Independent Agencies and Commissions

In addition to departmental agencies, independent agencies have unique duties and an independence from others in the executive branch. For example, the National Aeronautics and Space Administration (NASA) is an independent agency that has distinct authority beyond the reaches and influence of the military.

Regulatory Authority Some independent agencies have a regulatory capacity. Congress has vested regulatory authority in agencies, commissions, and boards to oversee or regulate a particular industry or interest. They can make narrow, industry-specific rules, and they can adjudicate (process and punish) violators. In a sense, these bodies have powers normally divided among the three federal branches.

Interstate Commerce Commission Exercising its authority under the commerce clause, Congress created the Interstate Commerce Commission to oversee the expanding interstate trade and the practices that accompanied it in the 1880s. The creators of this model wanted to remove political influence, and they stipulated that the president appoint the commission, but the appointed commissioners did not have to please the president.

Commissions typically have an odd number of seats to avoid a tie vote, and their membership is meant to be balanced according to party. Their fixed terms are also staggered to create continuity in government that overlaps presidential administrations.

Federal Trade Commission The U.S. government created the Federal Trade Commission in 1914 to prevent overly powerful corporations from engaging in unfair business practices. This commission came about during the battle between the trusts and a progressive government seeking to tame big business. Since then, Congress has enhanced the FTC's authority and power. It also has under its jurisdiction consumer protection laws, and it has regulated telemarketing.

Federal Elections Commission The early 1970s election reforms brought about the Federal Elections Commission (Chapter 6). The FEC has monitored elections and campaigns ever since.

Selected Independent Regulatory Agencies and Commissions	
Organization	**Established**
Interstate Commerce Commission	1887
Federal Reserve System	1913
Federal Trade Commission	1914
Federal Communications Commission	1934
Securities and Exchange Commission	1934
Federal Aviation Administration	1948
Environmental Protection Agency	1970

Government Corporations

Government corporations are a hybrid of a government agency and a private company. These started to appear in the 1930s, and they usually come into being when the government wants to overlap with the private sector. Some examples include the Federal Deposit Insurance Corporation, Amtrak, the Tennessee Valley Authority, and the Corporation for Public Broadcasting. All of these organizations receive funding from the private sector and the government.

Commercial banks join the FDIC by paying a fee to insure their bank accounts. As train travel plummeted and the nation's rail system became unsustainable, Congress stepped in to purchase rail and operate Amtrak. This agency receives an annual appropriation from Congress, while private citizens—the passengers—purchase tickets. Congress also funds the Corporation for Public Broadcasting, which finances National Public Radio and PBS-TV. Member stations across the country raise funds and pay an annual fee to receive PBS and NPR programs.

Executive Branch Organization
• **Cabinet-Level Departments**: 15 departments, plus others the president names to the Cabinet
• **Agencies Within Departments** (selected): Coast Guard in Homeland Security; FBI in the Justice Department
• **Independent Agencies** (selected): NASA and the Postal Service
• **Independent Agencies and Regulatory Commissions** (selected): EPA, FCC, FEC
• **Government Corporations** (selected): Amtrak and FDIC

Staffing the Bureaucracy

Federal bureaucrats include anyone in the executive branch carrying out some decision or applying some law. Bureaucrats sit on the president's Cabinet, and they work in regional offices throughout the country. Some are upper-level problem solvers and administrators. Others are lawyers, doctors, and educators. Still others are plumbers, carpenters, and drivers. Many lower-level bureaucrats must follow heavily scripted routines to assure consistency in government's application of the law.

Cabinet Secretaries and Deputies The spoils system will never fully disappear. Presidents still name friends and campaign managers to upper-level White House jobs as well as to Cabinet and subcabinet positions that require Senate confirmation. Most presidents appoint more than 2,000 upper-level management positions, deputy secretaries, and bureau chiefs who are the leaders and spokespeople for the executive branch. Many of these people tend to be in the president's party and have experience in a relevant field of government or the private sector.

The Cabinet historically has been a place for political appointees. Former senators, governors, and other elected officials took Cabinet posts when they lost re-election. In more recent years, the Cabinet has become a place for academics, university presidents, and other experts. For example, President John Kennedy appointed Ford Motor Company CEO Robert McNamara as his secretary of defense.

An "old boy" network of federal officers, mostly white males, dominates these upper level posts. They tend to go in and out of government depending on which party controls the White House. The lower levels of the executive branch are composed of people from all walks of life and all ideologies. The more traditional organizations—the military and the Department of Agriculture, for instance—employ more conservatives. The more activist reforming agencies, those protecting the environment and defending laborers, tend to employ more liberal bureaucrats.

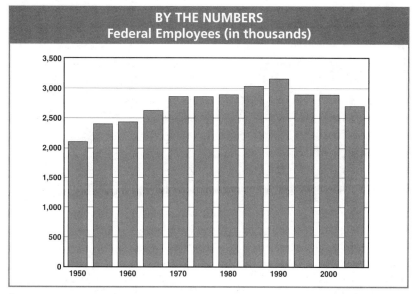

BY THE NUMBERS
Federal Employees (in thousands)

Source: Data 360 (U.S. Census Bureau)

What do the numbers show? In the last generation, how many people has the federal government employed? How has the total number of employees fluctuated? Where do you see trends of growth or decline? What brought on these increases or decreases? Do these changes correspond with presidential or congressional action?

Executives' Background President Nixon's administration had sizable numbers of African-American appointees, especially in the more liberal agencies in which Nixon allowed directors to select subcabinet appointees. However, only three percent of Nixon appointees were women. Nearly 20 years later, roughly 27 percent of the appointees of George H. W. Bush (1989–93) were women. The upper-level executives tend to come from privileged backgrounds. It is no mystery, then, that top-level appointees come from prestigious universities. Most fathers of presidential appointees had worked in managerial or professional jobs. Roughly 72 percent of appointees have some postgraduate training and advanced degrees.

Comparisons of top-appointed federal officials with those in the top ranks of the private sector reveal that officials in government earn considerably lower salaries. Private sector leaders earned 15 to 16 times as much as their government counterparts. Department and agency leaders are 50 percent more likely to have attended graduate school than top corporate executives, and they are three times as likely to have a Ph.D.

When a new position is created, bureaucrats recommend and recruit some of their own people who have experience in that area. This is called a name-request job, a job for which those doing the hiring already have someone in mind. Additionally, members of Congress will contribute to this process by recommending a colleague who can fit this position.

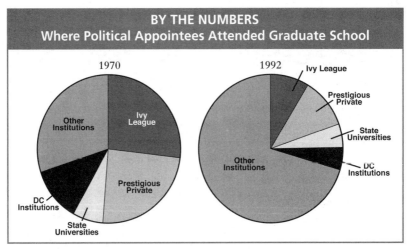

BY THE NUMBERS
Where Political Appointees Attended Graduate School

Source: Aberbach and Rockman, *In the Web of Politics*, 2000

What do the numbers show? At what kinds of institutions do top-level executives attend graduate school? About what percentage of these institutions were Ivy League schools in 1970? In 1992? What factors might explain this difference? What might have caused an expansion of the "Other Institutions" category?

Competitive Service The **competitive service** includes those jobs that require some type of exam or competitive hiring process. These are the merit-based jobs that began with the Pendleton Act. Foreign Service officers, the State Department workers who represent the United States abroad, must pass a challenging and competitive test. The **excepted service** includes all the others, providing hiring options when the competitive service is not practical. The ratio of competitive versus excepted positions in the civilian bureaucracy has fluctuated with different laws and different presidents. In recent years, the two groups have been about even.

Office of Personnel Management The Civil Service Commission established by the Pendleton Act operated until the 1978 reforms replaced it with the **Office of Personnel Management (OPM).** The OPM runs the merit system and coordinates federal application for jobs and the hiring process. The OPM's goals include promoting the ideals of public service, finding the best people for federal jobs, and preserving merit system principles. Many of the larger, more established agencies do their own hiring.

Rules

As mentioned previously, the constitutional basis for any bureaucratic department or agency stems from Congress's power to invent and empower them. Congress must create, define, guide, and fund each department and agency. The legislative branch decides on principles for law and debates the details as it develops policies.

The level of power or influence that any executive branch agency has is largely determined by its **discretionary authority**. This is the agency's ability to make decisions and to take, or not take, courses of action. Much as a beat police officer has the prerogative to issue or not issue a ticket for a moving violation, a Justice Department prosecutor—an arm of the executive branch at the county or city level—can decide to prosecute or not prosecute a suspected criminal based on the available evidence in the case.

Congress has given the executive branch significant authority in three areas: Congress creates agencies to pay subsidies to groups, such as farmers or Social Security recipients. It also creates a system to distribute federal dollars going to the states, such as the grant program discussed in Chapter 2. Finally, it gives many federal offices the ability to devise and enforce regulations for various industries or issues. This quasi-legislative power enables the Federal Communications Commission to determine what one can or cannot say on TV or the EPA to create emission standards for factories.

As laws are made in a public manner, the agency rulemaking process and schedule must also be available to the public in advance to allow relevant players to participate in the rulemaking. Companies or others can submit arguments or appear and testify before a commission, much as an expert might appear before a congressional committee.

Enforcement Commissions and boards can make rulings or enforce the laws for those who have violated them. Playing the traditional role of a court, the bureaucracy has quasi-judicial authority as well. Like a court, it can adjudicate and impose a fine or other punishment. This administrative adjudication targets industry or particular companies, not individual citizens.

Interaction

It is often difficult to determine who is responsible for a bureaucratic decision. Congress creates the big-picture laws and regulations, the president shapes the staff, and interest groups try to influence the bureaucracy. With so many players interacting with these executive branch sub-units, it is difficult to tell to whom the bureaus, administrations, and offices are beholden.

Bureaucratic agencies interact with other governmental offices and nongovernmental organizations. In trying to follow prescribed law, these executive branch bodies still face political constraints and challenges. Cabinet secretaries serve at the pleasure of the president but have to please many people. These secretaries and their subordinates report to Congress and thus must please members, especially when funding decisions arise.

Within the Executive Branch Departments and agencies have to compete with others for funding and for the president's ear. Similar departments and agencies compete to attain the same or overlapping goals. They all contend that with more money they could better complete their missions.

Sometimes the different beliefs or approaches can create friction between departments when the United States must state a position or make a decision. The Departments of State and Defense have had differences on foreign policy. The Department of State is the diplomatic wing of the government; the Department of Defense trains the military and prepares the country for armed conflict. These differing perspectives can make it challenging for the United States to develop and advance coherent goals.

Cabinet secretaries tend to be experienced high-level managers who enter government as a director of an agency. Sometimes presidents appoint them to shake up the agency or to put it on a new course. Even a talented leader will find it challenging to drastically alter an agency staffed by career bureaucrats who know and understand the politics and procedures of the agency better than their new boss.

Competition among agencies rises when they have similar goals. Law enforcement agencies sometimes cooperate to find criminals, but they are also protective of their methods and desire credit in a way that breeds dissention. The lack of information sharing among the government's many intelligence agencies before September 11 may have increased the terrorists' chances of a successful attack.

Loyalties Sometimes upper-level bureaucrats get caught between their boss and the many people who work for them. The president has certain policy goals, irrespective of some of the practical constraints of the bureaucracy. **Going native** occurs when an appointed bureaucrat sides with his or her own department or agency instead of with the president. Presidents have at times rotated appointees from agency to agency to assure loyalty to the administration.

Federal employees sometimes see corruption or inefficiency in their offices but are tempted to keep quiet. Exposing illegal or improper government activities can lead to reprisals from those in the organization or retaliation that can lead to firing. However, citizens in a democracy want transparency in government and often encourage such exposure. That is why Congress passed the **Whistleblower Protection Act** in 1989, which prohibits a federal agency from retaliating, or threatening to retaliate, against an employee or applicant for disclosing acts that he or she believes was illegal or dishonest.

Removal Going native is a risky proposition, and many who have publicly disagreed with the president have been replaced. As discussed in the previous chapter, most presidential appointees serve at the pleasure of the president, owing to the *Myers* decision (page 269). But heads of regulatory commissions are protected. Congress and the Supreme Court removed these appointees from the influence of politics to assure their adherence to their defined jobs, not the president's wishes. The president can, however, remove them "for cause," an explanation that suggests incompetence. Short of a neglect of duty, these officials have been protected since the *Humphrey's* case.

Congressional Oversight Congress has wide authority over departments and agencies. In addition to assigning their jurisdiction, Congress checks up on them occasionally, determines how much funding they receive, asks top-level bureaucrats how they can improve their goals, and sometimes tries to constrain agencies.

Most interaction with agencies is at the committee level. A list of standing House and Senate committees parallels a list of notable agencies. For example, the Senate Committee on Agriculture, Nutrition, and Forestry oversees the National Parks Service. Committees and subcommittees receive reports from directors and call them to testify.

Funding With the power of the purse, Congress can determine the financial state of an agency and its success when it allocates the money. The agency cannot spend public funds until a committee or subcommittee first passes **authorization of spending** measures. These measures state the maximum amount the agency can give on a certain program. The distribution of money defined in such an authorization may be a one-time allotment of funds, or it could be a recurring annual allotment. The agency will not receive the actual funds until each house's appropriations committee also approves the spending. These **appropriations** are typically made annually as part of the federal budget.

The Final Say Congress and agencies share a good deal of authority. This sharing has created an unclear area of jurisdiction. One procedure that has developed to sort out any overlap is **committee clearance**. Some congressional committees have secured the authority to review and approve certain agency actions in advance. Where these actions are not spelled out in law, few executive branch leaders will ignore Congress's request, knowing the same committee determines its funding.

Congress established the **legislative veto** in the 1930s to control agencies. The legislative veto is a requirement that certain agency decisions must wait for a defined period of either 30 or 90 days. During the Vietnam War, the legislative veto became extremely attractive as a tool to control executive excesses.

 Is That Constitutional? *INS v. Chadha* (1983)

Is the legislative veto a violation of the separation of powers?

Jagdish Chadha, born in Kenya of Indian descent, immigrated to the United States in the 1960s to study. When his U.S. visa expired, neither country would accept him, so he applied for permanent residency in the United States. The Immigration and Naturalization Service approved his application. Two years later, the House rejected it.

continued

Chadha sued to retain his U.S. residency. The public interest groups that had fought to create regulatory agencies in the 1960s watched agencies' lawful decisions being stopped by one house of Congress. They joined Chadha in his quest to prevent the legislative veto. Chadha's fight to remain in the United States became a power play between the president and Congress over the constitutionality of the legislative veto.

In 1983, the Supreme Court sided with Chadha and against Congress's use of this procedure. The veto was intended only for the president, not the legislative branch. The Court stated that when the House rejected Chadha's application, it exercised a judicial function by expressing its opinion on the application of a law, something reserved for the courts. The legislative veto was a violation of separation of powers.

Iron Triangles and Issue Networks Over time, congressional committees and agencies become well acquainted. Lawmakers and leaders in the executive branch may have worked together in the past. At the same time, interest groups target agencies for pressing their agendas. Industry, especially, creates political action committees to impact policy and its success. As discussed in Chapter 7, they meet with and make donations to members of Congress as elections near. They also meet with bureaucrats during the rule-making process in an ongoing effort to shape rules that affect them.

The relationship among these three entities—an agency, a congressional committee, and an interest group—is called an **iron triangle**. The three points of the triangle join forces to create policy. Iron triangles establish tight relationships that are collectively beneficial. Bureaucrats have an incentive to cooperate with congressional members who fund and direct them. Committee members have an incentive to pay attention to interest groups that reward them with PAC donations. What's more, interest groups and agencies generally are out to advance similar goals.

More recently, scholars have observed the power and influence of **issue networks**, which parallel iron triangles. Issue networks include committee staffers (often the experts and authors of legislation), academics, think tanks, advocates, and/or members of the media. These experts and stakeholders—sometimes at odds with one another—collaborate to create specific policy. The policymaking web has grown because of so many overlapping issues, the proliferation of interest groups, and the influence of industry.

Bureaucratic Culture and Contemporary Issues

The traits and operation of government bureaucracies create a unique culture. Professionally trained and educated bureaucrats occupy the higher levels of government. Each agency has developed its own persona based on influential directors and the organization's goals. Bureaucratic culture and processes define the administration and help form public impressions. The concern for efficient and limited government has brought continual efforts to reshape or reform the administration.

Cultures, Perceptions, and Political Forces

The structures, rules, and overlapping jurisdictions seem an inevitable byproduct of government. Career bureaucrats and the strong leaders who rise to the top of the executive hierarchy are instrumental in setting a tone throughout their organizations. These qualities of bureaucracy have led to some cumbersome challenges for citizens, policymakers, and bureaucrats themselves.

Duplication Congress has a tough time establishing clear laws and clear goals; as a result, it creates multiple entities to manage or oversee important activities with only marginal differences. It is a rare agency that has exclusive authority over a particular responsibility. For example, both the FBI and the Drug Enforcement Administration seek to apprehend drug dealers. Both the Army and the Navy protect America militarily. Both the CIA and the National Security Agency seek foreign intelligence. This kind of duplication creates competition among agencies and causes jurisdictional issues. This also creates redundancy that expands government cost and frustrates taxpayers because two or more agencies that overlap responsibilities might handle matters differently. The very specific rules of dealing with government can slow things down.

Red Tape The most common complaint among U.S. citizens about government is **red tape**. Red tape is the vast amount of paperwork, procedures, forms, and formal steps citizens must take to accomplish a government-mandated task. Any driver who has stood in a long line at the local state bureau of motor vehicles with proof of insurance, an emissions check, and other paperwork to receive a drivers' license can understand red tape.

Governmental restrictions on agency decisions and purchases contribute to slowing down bureaucratic decision making. In many cases, agencies must meet contingencies before they can move ahead with projects. For example, Congress mandates that government contracts must be with American firms. The federal government institutes targets and guidelines to encourage companies to work with minority-owned businesses. Agreements dictate that the federal government hire prolabor firms and pay prevailing wages. Major construction firms require impact studies to determine the project's effect on the environment and the local economy before spending public money.

Inertia Another concern for the operation of the bureaucracy is accountability. Presidents and their subordinates have ordered performance reviews and assessments for decades. Trying to enhance responsiveness and effectiveness while also seeking to boost efficiency can be counterproductive. A government of laws is one that avoids arbitrary or capricious rule, but the more an agency is held accountable, the more forms, guidelines, and systems are required. Accountability, therefore, increases red tape and decreases responsiveness.

The Paperwork Reduction Act of 1979, one of President Jimmy Carter's reforms, sounded like a good idea when it was proposed. To enforce it, Congress created the Office of Internal Regulatory Affairs, which created numerous obstacles for agencies issuing regulations. It decreased the flow of paper by increasing regulations on the federal bureaucracy itself.

FEMA and Katrina When Hurricane Katrina hit New Orleans and its surrounding area in 2005, the Federal Emergency Management Administration (FEMA) became ensnared in controversy. FEMA allocates federal aid to areas that suffer from national disasters. The hurricane devastated the Gulf shores and many areas inland. An estimated 1,800 people died. The after-effects included social chaos and public displacement. Critics quickly pointed to FEMA as a nonresponsive agency. Jurisdictional divisions complicated the situation and FEMA's director stepped down. FEMA's image and that of the federal bureaucracy reached a new low when a photograph surfaced showing some 300 FEMA trailers sitting in a muddy Arkansas lot unable to reach the victims who needed housing.

Public Impression Fierce public criticism, such as that which followed the FEMA problems, has helped to erode the positive impression of the bureaucratic system. But bashing bureaucrats has been fashionable for decades. Outspoken Alabama Governor George Wallace, for one, was known for attacking the "pointy-headed bureaucrats." Presidents Nixon, Carter, and Reagan taught the American populace to distrust them. The bureaucracy has become a favorite scapegoat of politicians promising to reform government, largely because so many people have had negative experiences with red tape. Politicians and commentators have primed citizens to focus their resentments on this amorphous, faceless entity, despite the fact that most citizens desire the government services that agencies offer and tend to speak positively about individual bureaucrats they have encountered.

Modern Reforms

Various presidents and congresses have tried to improve their administration organization and structure. Presidents have created commissions to streamline the executive branch or to reassign government priorities. Occasionally, Congress merges, splits, or dissolves agencies. Both the legislative and the executive branches focus reforms to improve representativeness and responsiveness. They have emphasized markets, efficiency, and transforming citizens into customers. Below are three such laws.

Congressional Acts and the Bureaucracy
• **Freedom of Information Act** (1966): Gives the public the right to request access to records or information
• **Sunshine Act** (1976): Requires most federal agencies to hold their meetings in publicly accessible places
• **Whistleblower Protection Act** (1989): Protects federal workers who report or disclose evidence of illegal or improper government action

Presidential Initiatives in the 1980s

The bureaucracy can be an impediment or a vehicle for presidential goals. Presidents rely on the bureaucratic system to work well for them. When bureaucracy works against or impedes the administration's ideas and goals, presidents are encouraged to shake up or restructure the system.

President Carter's landmark revisions encouraged subsequent presidents to address some of the same concerns, partly because some dated back to George Pendleton's day. Two studies in the 1980s estimated that about one-third of all Democratic delegates and 21 percent of Republican delegates to the national party conventions were full-time government employees. The continued effort to curb bureaucratic waste also continued because of the popularity of the idea.

President Ronald Reagan, who arrived in Washington in 1981, stated in his inaugural address, "Government is not the solution to our problem; government is the problem." To gain greater control over departments and agencies, he put people who agreed with the Reagan agenda into top positions. He sought officials who would show a loyalty to the White House and reduce administrative personnel.

Volcker Commission The Volcker Commission on the bureaucracy, headed by former Federal Reserve Chairman Paul Volcker in the late 1980s, reported that the bureaucracy was in a "quiet crisis." The report confirmed some suspicions about "an erosion in the quality of American public service." It was deemed not as attractive as it once was nor as effective in meeting perceived needs. The report called for more civility from critics after three straight presidents blamed bureaucracy for a variety of the nation's problems.

Clinton and Reinvention President Clinton promised early in his administration to address government inefficiency. However, he used a more careful tone than his predecessors did, conveying that problems in a large administration came not from bureaucrats but rather from the outdated systems and inefficient institutions. His vice president, Al Gore, headed the effort to investigate and revamp the administration. The Clinton-Gore team signaled that the administration was doing something to make government work better and cost less. The president ultimately promised to "reinvent" rather than dismantle the bureaucracy system.

National Performance Review In 1993, Clinton announced a six-month review of the federal government. The **National Performance Review (NPR)** became Clinton's key document in assessing the federal bureaucracy. The review was organized to identify problems and offer solutions and ideas for government savings. The group focused on diminishing the paperwork burden and placing more discretionary responsibility with the agencies. The report made almost 400 recommendations designed to cut red tape, put customers first, empower employees, and produce better and less-expensive government.

One report, "From Red Tape to Results," characterized the federal government as an industrial-era structure operating in an information age. The bureaucracy had become so inundated with rules and procedures, so constrained by red tape, that it could not perform the way Congress had intended.

The review differed from prior ones that had sought to increase efficiency, accountability, and consistency. The NPR review pushed for greater customer satisfaction and a more businesslike manner of running government. Clinton also, by way of executive order, told heads of executive agencies to expand flex options so federal workers could better balance the demands of job and family.

REFLECT ON THE ESSENTIAL QUESTION

Essential Question: *How does the executive branch administer the machinery of government and provide services to American citizens?* On separate paper, complete a chart like the one below to gather details to answer that question.

Functions of the Bureaucracy	Examples of Services

KEY TERMS, NAMES, AND EVENTS

appropriations	Federal Trade Commission	National Performance Review (NPR)
authorization of spending	Freedom of Information Act (1966)	Office of Personnel Management (OPM)
Civil Service Commission	going native	patronage
Civil Service Reform Act (1978)	government corporation	Pendleton Civil Service Act
committee clearance	Hatch Act (1939)	red tape
competitive service	*INS v. Chadha* (1983)	Senior Executive Service
discretionary authority	iron triangle	spoils system
excepted service	issue networks	Sunshine Act (1976)
Federal Bureau of Investigation	legislative veto	Whistleblower Protection Act (1989)
Federal Elections Commission	merit system	

MULTIPLE-CHOICE QUESTIONS

1. One key way Congress has influence over the bureaucracy is through
   (A) competitive service
   (B) executive order
   (C) oversight function
   (D) going native
   (E) removal power

2. Which of these departments or agencies would employ staff with a more conservative ideology?

   (A) Environmental Protection Agency

   (B) Department of Labor

   (C) Department of Housing and Urban Development

   (D) Department of Agriculture

   (E) National Labor Relations Board

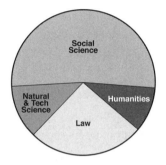

FIELDS OF STUDY FOR APPOINTED EXECUTIVES

3. Which statement supports information presented in the above graph?

   (A) Choosing engineers is more common than not in staffing the executive administration.

   (B) Most presidential appointees entered the federal workplace when college degrees were uncommon.

   (C) Business leaders make up the majority of bureaucrats.

   (D) Those with degrees in law and social science constitute a majority of bureaucrats.

   (E) A law degree is required to serve as an executive in the federal government.

4. All of the following are reasons for long-term growth of the bureaucratic system EXCEPT

   (A) an expanded United States has required more governmental services

   (B) the creation of the federal income tax has given the government more funds to spend

   (C) the American citizenry has developed increased expectations of the federal government

   (D) presidential initiatives and new programs have spawned new programs

   (E) fiscal conservatism in the federal government has created new agencies

5. President Garfield's assassination led to

   (A) the *Humphrey's* decision

   (B) the Pendleton Civil Service Act

   (C) the creation of the Internal Revenue Service

(D) the Whistleblower Protection Act

(E) the creation of the Central Intelligence Agency

6. Which of the following laws limit a bureaucrat's activity in political campaigning?

(A) The Pendleton Civil Service Act

(B) The Hatch Act

(C) *Humphrey's Executor v. United States*

(D) The War Powers Act

(E) The Presidential Succession Act

7. Independent regulatory agencies have quasi-legislative and quasi-judicial powers. This means

(A) a president has no influence on regulatory agencies

(B) agency rulings cannot be challenged in court

(C) these agencies can create policies and can issue fines or punishments

(D) Congress has no control or influence over these agencies

(E) members of Congress and active judges can also serve on regulatory agencies

8. All of the following are government corporations EXCEPT

(A) the U.S. Postal Service

(B) Amtrak

(C) the Federal Deposit Insurance Corporation

(D) the Corporation for Public Broadcasting

(E) the U.S. Army

9. Which of the following is true about the legislative veto?

(A) It allows the president to veto acts of the legislature.

(B) It was upheld in the case of *INS v. Chadha.*

(C) For some time it allowed congressional committees to veto regulatory agency decisions.

(D) It was included in the Constitution.

(E) It was used to block the Freedom of Information Act.

10. A loose collaboration of congressional staffers, researchers, academics, advocates, and/or journalists to develop public policy in a certain area is known as

(A) an iron triangle

(B) an issue network

(C) bureaucratic madness

(D) gold plating

(E) going native

FREE-RESPONSE QUESTIONS

Question

1. Bureaucratic departments and government agencies must interact with different groups to implement policy.

   (a) Define an iron triangle.

   (b) Select one agency or department listed below. Identify and describe two ways in which Congress can exercise authority over this agency.

   Department of State   Environmental Protection Agency

   Department of Defense   Federal Bureau of Investigation

   (c) Identify and explain two ways in which interest groups interact with or impact the other members of the iron triangle.

Question

2. Independent regulatory agencies and commissions differ from most federal executive branch agencies.

   (a) Identify and describe two ways regulatory agencies or commissions differ from other federal agencies.

   (b) Identify one independent regulatory agency or commission and define its basic authority.

   (c) Explain how Congress influences or interacts with this organization.

   (d) Explain how the president influences or interacts with this organization.

WRITING: MAKE CLEAR DIVISIONS

In your responses, clearly show where one idea ends and another begins. Either start a new paragraph by indenting when making a new point, or label each section of your answer (a), (b), and so on, skipping a line between each. Use transitional words or phrases (page 74) to move on to another point. For example, in #1 (c) you might write, "Another way interest groups interact . . ." or in #2 (a) you might write, "A second way regulatory agencies are unique . . . ."

The Judiciary

"It is emphatically the province and duty of the judicial department to say what the law is."

—John Marshall for the Supreme Court in *Marbury v. Madison, 1803*

Essential Question: How do the nation's courts settle legal controversies and establish public policy?

From an early age you developed some understanding of courtrooms in which accused criminals are innocent until proven guilty and one party sues another. Courtroom drama has been popular since Perry Mason—a 1950s television defense attorney who lost only one case in a nine-year run. More recently, TV has stereotyped small claims courts with the feisty, tell-it-like-it-is judge, a beefy courtroom bailiff, and litigants who yell and are rude to each other. The true picture of the judiciary shows a revered institution shaped by Article III of the Constitution, the Bill of Rights, and federal and state laws. The courts handle everything from speeding tickets to death penalty cases. State courts handle most disputes, whether criminal or civil. Federal courts handle crimes against the United States, high-dollar lawsuits involving citizens of different states, and constitutional questions.

Article III and the Federal Courts

Today's three-level federal court system is made up of the **U.S. District Courts** on the lowest tier, the **U.S. Circuit Courts of Appeals** on the middle tier, and the **Supreme Court** alone on the top. These three types of courts are known as **constitutional courts** because they are either directly or indirectly mentioned in the Constitution. All federal judges are appointed by presidents and approved by the Senate to serve life terms.

No national court system existed under the Articles of Confederation, so the Framers decided to create a national judiciary in basic terms while empowering Congress to expand and define it. Because states had existing courts, many delegates saw no reason to create an entirely new, costly judicial system to serve essentially the same purpose. Others disagreed and argued that a national judicial system with a top court for uniformity was necessary. "Thirteen independent [state] courts of final jurisdiction over the same cases, arising out of the same laws," *The Federalist* argued, "will produce nothing but contradiction and confusion."

Article III

Article III defines an independent, multilevel court system. "The judiciary," Alexander Hamilton argued in *Federalist #78*, "will always be the least dangerous to the political rights of the Constitution because it will have the least capacity to annoy and injure them." He envisioned that courts would settle disputes or hold trials only for federal offenses, not be key players in determining the law. The only court actually mentioned in the Constitution is the Supreme Court, though Article III empowered Congress to create "inferior" courts.

All federal judges "shall hold their offices during good behavior." Although this term of office is now generally called a "life term," judges can be and have been impeached and removed. The Supreme Court has **original jurisdiction**—in other words, it is the court in which the case originates—in cases affecting ambassadors and public ministers and those in which a state is a party. For the most part, however, the Supreme Court acts as an appeals court with **appellate jurisdiction**.

Treason Article III also defined *treason* as "levying war" or giving "aid or comfort" to the enemy. Treason is the only crime mentioned or defined in the Constitution. Because the accusation of treason had been used as a political tool in unfair trials to quiet dissent against the government, the founders wanted to ensure that the new government could not easily prosecute that charge just to silence alternative voices. At least two witnesses must testify in open court to the treasonous act in order to convict the accused.

Judiciary Act of 1789

The first Congress quickly defined a three tier federal court system with the Judiciary Act of 1789. The law established one district court in each of the 13 states, plus one each for the soon-to-be states of Vermont and Kentucky. The law also defined the size of the Supreme Court with six justices, or judges. President Washington then appointed judges to fill these judgeships. In addition to the district court, the Congress created three regional circuit courts designated to take cases on appeal from the district courts. Two Supreme Court justices were assigned to each of the "circuits" and were required to hold circuit court twice per year in every state. The presiding district judge joined them to make a three-judge intermediate panel. In a given period, the Supreme Court justices would hold one court after another in a circular path, an act that became known as "riding circuit."

Source: Library of Congress

The Supreme Court is the only federal court named in Article III of the Constitution, yet it did not operate in its own building—shown here in a drawing before it was built—until 1935.

Federal Court System

U.S. Supreme Court

- Created by Article III of Constitution
- Nine justices
- Hears 80–100 cases from October through June
- Has original jurisdiction in unique cases
- Takes appeals from circuits and top state courts

U.S. Circuit Courts

- Created by Congress
- 11 regional courts
- 2 courts in Washington (D.C. and Federal)
- Nearly 200 total justices
- Take appeals from district courts
- Justices sit in panels of three

U.S. District Courts

- Trial courts created by Congress
- 94 districts
- Nearly 700 total justices
- Hear federal criminal and civil matters

U.S. District Courts

There are 94 district courts in the United States—at least one in each state, and for many western states, the geographic district is the whole state. Each district court may have several federal courthouses and several federal district judges. There are nearly 700 district judges nationwide who preside over trials concerning federal crimes, lawsuits, and disputes over constitutional issues. In 2013, the district courts received more than 375,000 case filings nationwide, most of a civil nature.

A Trial Court U.S. district courts are trial courts with original jurisdiction over federal cases. The litigants in a trial court are the **plaintiff**—the party initiating the action—and the **defendant**, the party answering the action. Others who may be part of a trial court are witnesses, jury members, and a presiding judge. Trial courts are finders of fact; that is, these courts determine if an accused defendant did in fact commit a crime, or if a civil defendant is indeed responsible for some mistake or wrongdoing.

Federal Crimes The U.S. district courts try federal crimes, such as counterfeiting, mail fraud, or evading federal income taxes—crimes that fall under the enumerated powers in Article I, Section 8 of the Constitution. Most violent crimes, and indeed most crimes overall, are tried at the state level. Congress has declared illegal some violent crime and interstate actions, such as drug trafficking, bank robbery, terrorism, and acts of violence on federal property. For example, in the *United States v. Timothy McVeigh*, the government argued that McVeigh exploded an Oklahoma City federal building and killed 168 victims. The court found him guilty and sentenced him to death.

The defendant has a constitutional right to a jury and defense lawyer and several other due process rights included in the Bill of Rights. The judge or jury must find the defendant guilty "beyond a reasonable doubt" in order to convict and issue a sentence. Many cases are disposed of when a defendant pleads guilty before the trial. This process is known as a **plea bargain,** whereby the government and the defendant bargain for a lesser sentence in exchange for a guilty plea. A plea bargain saves courts time and taxpayers money, and it guarantees a conviction. For example, FBI agent Robert Hanson was discovered to have sold government secrets to the Russians for years. He was charged with espionage crimes and pleaded guilty in order to avoid the death penalty.

U.S. Attorneys Each of the 94 districts has a U.S. attorney, appointed by the president and approved by the Senate, who represents the federal government in federal courts. These attorneys work in the Department of Justice under the **attorney general.** They serve as federal prosecutors, and with assistance from the FBI and other federal law enforcement agencies they prosecute federal crimes committed within their districts. Nationally, they try close to 80,000 federal crimes per year. Of those, immigration crimes and drug offenses take up much of the courts' criminal docket. Fraud is third.

Civil Cases Citizens can also bring civil disputes to court to settle a business or personal conflict. Some plaintiffs sue over **torts**, civil wrongs that have damaged them. In a lawsuit, the plaintiff files a complaint (a brief that explains the damages and argues why the defendant should be held responsible). The party bringing suit must prove the defendant's liability or negligence with a "preponderance of evidence" for the court to award damages. Most civil disputes, even million-dollar lawsuits, are handled in state courts. The U.S. district courts have jurisdiction over disputes involving more than $75,000 with **diversity citizenship**—cases in which the two parties reside in different states.

Disputes involving constitutional questions also land in this court. In these cases, a federal judge, not a jury, determines the outcome because these cases involve a deeper interpretation of the law than more general cases do. Sometimes a large group of plaintiffs claim common damage by one party and will file a **class action suit**. After a decision, courts may issue an **injunction**, or court order, to the losing party in a civil suit, making them act or refrain from acting to redress a wrong.

Suing the Government Sometimes a citizen or group sues the government. Technically, the United States operates under the doctrine of **sovereign immunity**—the government is protected from suit unless it permits such a claim. Over the years, Congress has made so many exceptions that it even established the U.S. Court of Claims to allow citizens to bring complaints against the United States. Citizens and groups also regularly bring constitutional arguments before the courts. One can sue government officials acting in a personal capacity. For example, the secretary of transportation could be sued for causing a traffic accident that resulted in thousands of dollars in damage. But the secretary of defense or Congress cannot be sued for the loss of a loved one in a government-sanctioned military battle.

Special Legislative Courts In addition to the constitutional courts, the federal judiciary has some additional obscure courts. Congress has created a handful of special courts to hear matters of expert concern. These are known as the **special legislative courts** because they are created by the legislature as opposed to the Constitution. The judges are appointed by the president and approved by the Senate, typically for a 15-year fixed term. These courts deal with specific issues, and therefore an experienced judge in that area of law is desired. Since the body of law around taxation or intelligence gathering changes with the times, these judges aren't given indefinite terms.

U.S. Circuit Court of Appeals

Directly above the district court is the U.S. Circuit Courts of Appeals. The circuit courts have appellate jurisdiction, taking cases on appeal. In 1891, Congress made the circuit court of appeals a permanent body. By this time, the country had expanded to the Pacific Coast and Supreme Court justices still had to travel across the now distant and expansive circuits. The increasing caseload, too, made this task unmanageable for justices based in Washington.

Appellate Courts Appeals courts are especially influential because they don't determine facts; instead, they shape the law. The losing party in a trial can appeal based on the concept of *certiorari,* Latin for "to make more certain." Thousands more cases are appealed than accepted by higher courts. The appellant must offer some violation of established law or procedure that led to the incorrect verdict in the prior court. Appeals courts look different and operate differently from trial courts. Appeals courts have a panel of judges sitting at the bench. There is no witness stand or jury box since the court does not entertain new facts but decides instead on some narrow question or point of law.

The **petitioner** appeals the case, and the **respondent** responds, claiming why and how the lower court ruled correctly. The hearing lasts about an hour as each side makes oral arguments before the judges. Appeals courts don't declare guilt or innocence when dealing with criminal matters, but they may order new trials for defendants. After years of deciding legal principles, appeals courts have shaped the body of U.S. law.

The U.S. Courts of Appeals consist of 11 geographic circuits, each with one court in cities such as Atlanta, New Orleans, and Chicago. Nationwide, there are nearly 200 circuit court justices who sit in panels of three to hear both criminal and civil appeals. On important matters, an entire court will sit *en banc;* that is, every judge on the court will hear and decide a case. Appeals courts' rulings stand within their geographic circuits.

FEDERAL CIRCUITS AND DISTRICTS

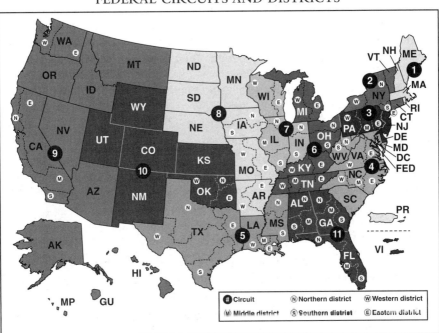

In addition to the 11 circuits, two other appeals courts are worthy of note. The Circuit Court for the Federal Circuit hears appeals dealing with patents, contracts, and financial claims against the United States. The Circuit Court of Appeals for the District of Columbia handles appeals from those fined or punished by executive branch regulatory agencies. The D.C. Circuit is considered the second most important court in the nation and has become a feeder for Supreme Court justices.

The United States Supreme Court

Atop this hierarchy is the U.S. Supreme Court, with the chief justice and eight associate justices. The Supreme Court hears mostly cases on appeal from the circuit courts and also decisions appealed from the state supreme courts. The nine members determine which appeals to accept, they sit *en banc* for attorneys' oral arguments, and they vote to decide whether or not to overturn the lower court's ruling. The Court overturns about 70 percent of the cases it takes. Once the Supreme Court makes a ruling, it establishes a legal precedent.

Common Law and Precedence

Courts follow a judicial tradition begun centuries ago in England. The **common law** refers to the body of court decisions that make up part of the law. Court rulings often establish a **precedent**—a ruling that firmly establishes some legal principle. These precedents are generally followed later as other courts consider the same legal logic in similar cases. The concept of *stare decisis*, or "let the decision stand," governs common law.

Lower courts must follow higher courts' rulings. Following precedence establishes continuity and consistency in law. Therefore, when a U.S. district court receives a case that parallels an already decided case from the circuit level, the district court is obliged to rule in the same way due to **binding precedent**. Even an independent-minded judge who disagrees with the higher court's precedent is guided by the fact that an appeal of his or her unique decision will likely be overruled by the court above. That's why all courts in the land are bound by U.S. Supreme Court decisions. Judges also rely on **persuasive precedent**. That is, they can consider past decisions made in other districts or rulings in other circuits as a guiding basis for their decision. Precedents can of course be overturned. No two cases are absolutely identical, and for this reason differing considerations come into play. Attitudes and interpretations differ and evolve over time in different courts.

History of the Supreme Court

The Supreme Court's authority of binding precedent combined with its power of **judicial review**—the ability to declare a legislative act or an executive branch action void—makes it a powerful institution and often the final arbiter of national law. With these two powers, the Court has had an amazing history of establishing national policy. Early on, it addressed national supremacy and states' rights. Later, it defined the relationship between government and industry. Most recently, the Court has extended and protected individual rights and liberties.

Defining Federalism

The Supreme Court in its early years was a nondescript, fledgling institution that saw little action and was held in low esteem. President Washington appointed Federalist John Jay as the first chief justice. For its first year the Court was given a second-floor room in a New York building and convened for only a two-hour session. Several early justices didn't stay on the Court long. Jay resigned in 1795 to serve as governor of New York. The Court's reputation and role would soon change.

John Marshall Once President John Adams appointed Federalist **John Marshall** as chief justice, the Court began to assert itself under a strong, influential leader. Marshall remained on the Court from 1801 until his death in 1835, establishing customs and norms and strengthening national powers. Marshall was a Virginian who acquired a strong sense of nationalism and respect for authority and discipline during his service in the Revolutionary

War. After independence, he became an ardent Federalist and attended the Virginia ratifying convention to vote in favor of ratification.

The Marshall Court John Marshall might as well be considered the father of the Supreme Court as he established its customs and solidified a strong nation under the Framers' plan. Throughout his 34 years as chief justice, he and his colleagues lived in a convivial atmosphere at a boarding house in Washington. Most who knew Marshall liked him. The Supreme Court, seven members at the time, simply shared a small room in the Capitol with Congress. It held hearings in a designated committee room on

Source: Library of Congress
Chief Justice John Marshall

the first floor for seven years until it was given more spacious quarters. It did not have its own building until the 1930s.

Marshall created a united court that spoke with one voice. When he arrived, he found the Supreme Court functioning like an English court, where multiple judges issued separate opinions when deciding a case. Marshall insisted that this brotherhood of justices agree and unite in their rulings to shape national law. The Court delivered mostly unanimous opinions written by one judge. In virtually every important case during his time, that one judge was Marshall. "He left the Court," Chief Justice William Rehnquist wrote years later, "a genuinely coequal branch of a tripartite national government . . . the final arbiter of the meaning of the United States Constitution." He fortified the Union and the powers of the federal government with rulings that strengthened national supremacy and the Congress's commerce power.

Judicial Review One of the Court's first landmark cases was *Marbury v. Madison* (1803), a case involving the eleventh-hour appointments by outgoing President John Adams, who appointed several fellow Federalists in addition to Marshall to fill judicial vacancies. In deciding the case, the Court struck down part of the Judiciary Act and exercised judicial review.

The concept of judicial review existed before *Marbury*. Though the term or concept was not included in the U.S. Constitution, the idea was circulating among those creating it. In *Federalist #78*, Publius argued, "The Courts will have the right to pronounce legislative acts void because they are contrary to the Constitution." And during a debate at the Virginia ratifying convention,

John Marshall himself warned, "If Congress were to make a law not warranted by any of the powers enumerated, it would be considered by the judges as an infringement of the Constitution which they are to guard . . . they would declare it void."

Shaping a Strong Nation Marshall developed a legacy of siding with the national legislature when controversies regarding federalism arose, strengthening the national government and opening Congress's powers more than Jeffersonian Republicans wanted. The *McCulloch v. Maryland* (page 33) and *Gibbons v. Ogden* (page 34) cases empowered Congress to create a bank and to regulate interstate commerce.

The Taney Court and Slavery Chief Justice Roger Taney replaced John Marshall. The Court's operation altered somewhat with new leadership and new members. In 1837, Congress increased its membership to nine justices to ease the workload and created new circuits. It also took up questions regarding slavery during the antebellum period. Taney and his fellow justices were determined to protect slavery and to suppress any threats to the institution's expansion. In *Prigg v. Pennsylvania*, the Court upheld a congressional fugitive slave act and refuted any state's attempt to alter such law.

In 1857, as the North and the South grew further apart, the Court decided the Dred Scott case. The slave Dred Scott had traveled with his master into free territory and claimed, with the help of abolitionist lawyers, that having lived in free northern territory, he should have his freedom. Taney and the Courts majority shocked abolitionists with their decision and left one of the Court's worst legacies. The ***Dred Scott v. Stanford*** ruling held that Scott wasn't even a citizen and thus had no standing, or right, to be a party in federal court, much less the country's top tribunal. The Court went further, stating that a slave owner's constitutional right to due process and property prevented depriving him of that property, regardless of where he traveled. It would take a civil war and constitutional amendments to overturn this ruling and free the slaves.

Congress increased the size of the Supreme Court to ten members in 1863 and then in 1867 decreased it back to nine, where it has been ever since.

Corporations and the State

In the late 1800s, the Court found itself occupied with concerns over business, trade, and workplace regulations. The nation had expanded its commercial power, and with it came more factories, railroads, and production of goods and services. Workers were subjected to long hours in unsafe conditions for modest pay. Congress tried to address these issues under its power to regulate interstate commerce. State legislations also devised laws creating safety bureaus, barring payment in company scrip, setting maximum daily working hours, and preventing women and children from working in certain industries.

While lawmakers tried to satisfy workers' groups such as the Grangers or labor unions, their counterparts—typically strong businesses dominant in the northeastern United States—argued that minimal government interference and a *laissez-faire* approach to governance was the constitutionally correct path.

When pressed by corporations to toss out such laws, the Court had to decide two principles: what the Constitution permitted government to do, and which government—state or federal—could do it.

Liberty of Contract The Court began to overturn various state health, safety, and civil rights laws in 1877. It threw out a congressional act that addressed monopolies. It also ruled Congress's income tax statute null and void. By the turn of the century, the Court had developed a conservative reputation as it questioned business regulation and progressive ideas. In *Lochner v. New York* (1905), the Court overturned a New York state law that prevented bakers from working more than 10 hours per day. The law was meant to counter the pressures from the boss that mandated long hours in an era before overtime pay. In *Lochner,* the Court ruled that liberty of contract—a worker's right to freely enter into an agreement—superseded the state's police powers over safety and health. By 1908, however, the Court considered research and sociological data submitted by noted attorney Louis Brandeis, who later became a justice on the Court. The Brandeis brief persuaded the Court to uphold a maximum-hours law for women working in laundries.

During the Progressive Era, the Court made additional exceptions but quickly returned to a conservative, **strict constructionist** view of business regulation. A strict constructionist interprets the Constitution based on a literal or narrow definition of the language of the Constitution without taking into account changes and social conditions since ratification. The Court held that neither the state nor federal commerce power could be used to suppress child labor. The Court's conservative viewpoint turned further to the right when former president William Howard Taft was appointed chief justice. In *Adkins v. Children's Hospital*, it said that minimum wage law for women also violated liberty of contract.

The New Deal and Roosevelt's Court Packing Plan During the Depression, the Court transformed. Charles Evans Hughes replaced Taft as chief justice in 1929. Hughes managed a mixed group with a strong conservative four, nicknamed the "Four Horsemen," which overturned several New Deal programs. The Court struck down business regulations, invalidated the National Recovery Act, ruled out New York's minimum wage law, and restricted the president's powers to remove commissioners on regulatory boards.

The Court's status was raised with a new building that represented its authority, ceremony, and independence. In 1935, the justices moved into their current building with its majestic façade and familiar red-curtained courtroom. The Court also went through another transformation as it changed ideologically to solidify New Deal laws for the next generation.

After his 1936 landslide re-election, Roosevelt responded by devising a plan to "pack the Court." He proposed legislation to add one justice for every justice currently over the age of 70, which would have allowed him to appoint up to six new members. FDR claimed this would relieve the Court's overloaded docket, but in reality he wanted to dilute the power of the "nine old men" who had been unreceptive to his New Deal proposals. The sitting Court denied any need for more justices. Conservatives and liberals alike felt such a plan amounted to an attack on the Court's independence.

The Court changed ideologically, however, when one of the conservatives took an about-face in *West Coast Hotel v. Parrish*, which sustained a Washington state minimum wage law. Justice Owen Roberts became "the switch in time that saved nine." After the *West Coast Hotel* decision, the Court upheld every New Deal measure that came before it. Roosevelt pressed ahead with more legislation, including a national minimum wage that has withstood constitutional scrutiny ever since. Winning four elections, he was able to appoint nine new justices to the Court friendly to his policies before his death in 1944.

A Court Dedicated to Individual Liberties

During the 1940s and in the post-World War II years, the Court protected and extended individual liberties. It delivered mixed messages on civil liberties up to this point—holding states to First Amendment protections while allowing government infringements in times of national security threats. It upheld executive action that placed Japanese Americans in internment camps after Pearl Harbor. The Court, however, began a fairly consistent effort to protect individuals' liberties when the rights of minorities and accused criminals came before it. This pattern started after a Jehovah's Witness student refused to salute the American flag in violation of a West Virginia law. It crested in 1973 when the Court upheld a woman's right to an abortion.

The Warren Court The Court extended many liberties under Chief Justice **Earl Warren** after President Dwight Eisenhower appointed him in 1953. As an FBI official during the war, Warren oversaw the internment of Japanese Americans, and in 1948 he was the Republican's vice presidential nominee. But any expectations that Warren would act as a conservative judge were lost soon after he took the bench.

Civil Rights and Civil Liberties Warren's first major case was *Brown v. Board of Education* in 1954. When the National Association for the Advancement of Colored People argued that the "separate but equal" standard set by the Court in the 1896 *Plessy v. Ferguson* decision was outdated and in violation of the Constitution's equal protection clause, Warren rallied his fellow justices to a unanimous opinion. As the particulars of the integration process were worked out in the courts, the High Court issued several subsequent unanimous pro-integration rulings over the next decade.

Warren was flanked by civil libertarians Hugo Black, William O. Douglas, and Felix Frankfurter. With them, the Court set several precedents to guarantee rights to accused defendants that ultimately created a national criminal justice system. They declared courts could throw out evidence obtained unlawfully by the police. States had to now provide defense attorneys for indigent (poor) defendants at state expense. And arrested suspects had to be formally informed of their rights with the so-called *Miranda* ruling.

The Supreme Court also placed a high priority on the First Amendment's protection against a government-established religion and protection for citizens' free speech. It outlawed school-sponsored prayer and upheld students' rights to protest the Vietnam War in schools. The Court upheld the press's protection against charges of libel. The Warren Court legacy is that of an activist, liberal court that upheld individual rights of minorities and the accused.

Warren's legacy did not please traditionalists because his Court overturned state policies created by democratically elected legislatures. Several Warren Court decisions seemed to insult states' cultures and threaten to drain state treasuries. Some argued that Earl Warren should be impeached. Meanwhile, the counterculture of the 1960s outraged conservative America. President Nixon won the 1968 election, in part by painting Warren's Court as an affront to law enforcement and local control. After winning, Nixon tilted the Court to the right.

The Burger Court Nixon's first appointment replaced Warren with U.S. appeals court justice Warren Burger. But Burger by no means satisfied Nixon's quest to instill a conservative philosophy, and he largely failed in judicial leadership. While serving as a lackluster manager of the Court, Burger continued American law on the same path Warren had begun.

Burger had a difficult time leading discussions "in conference"—the Court's closed chambers discussions. Some suspected that Burger at times switched his opinion toward the end of the process in order to gain control and to draft or assign the writing of the opinion. The chief often couldn't round up enough agreement to get a five-justice majority. Thus cases went undecided while the Court took on additional ones. The justices became overworked and took as many as 150 appeals in a year.

In *Roe v. Wade*, Burger joined six others on the Court to outlaw states' anti-abortion laws as a violation of due process. With this ruling, a woman could now obtain an abortion, unconditionally, through the first trimester of a pregnancy. He also penned a unanimous opinion to uphold school busing for racial enrollment balance.

Supreme Court historian and former clerk Edward Lazarus refers to Burger as "an intellectual lightweight" who had "alienated his colleagues and even his natural allies." By 1986, Burger had proven pretentious and chafing to his colleagues, and he had simply become tired. At the press conference where he announced his retirement, a reporter asked him what he would miss most on the Court. Burger stalled, sighed, and said, "Nothing."

The Rehnquist Court At the same press conference, President Reagan elevated Associate Justice **William Rehnquist** to the chief's position. Rehnquist had attended Stanford Law School and clerked for Supreme Court Justice Robert Jackson in the 1950s. In considering him as a nominee in 1972, President Nixon was taken aback by Rehnquist's awkward appearance. The president's counsel John Dean recalls the encounter and aftermath. He was wearing a pink shirt and a psychedelic tie. "That's a hell of a costume he's wearing," Nixon said after he left a meeting in the Oval Office, "just like a clown." Nixon looked to Rehnquist's strict constructionist view instead of his style and nominated him anyway. The Senate did not confirm him easily and accused him of racism, as he had recommended upholding the "separate but equal" doctrine when clerking for a justice in the early 1950s en route to the *Brown* ruling. This same controversy arose in 1986 as he accepted the chief's position.

Initially, Rehnquist found himself in dissent and all alone on several cases, earning him the nickname "the Lone Ranger." When Rehnquist took over for Burger, however, additional strict constructionists soon joined him. He improved the conference procedures and decreased the Court's caseload. All the justices, liberals and conservatives alike, welcomed the changes. In the 1990s, Rehnquist's Court upheld states' rights to place limitations on access to abortions and limited Congress's commerce clause authority.

The Modern Supreme Court

The Supreme Court is known more for continuity than for change. Membership is small and justices serve long tenures. The Court's customs are established through consensus and remain over generations. The contemporary group operates in many ways as the Marshall, Warren, and Rehnquist courts did. When Justice Sandra Day O'Connor announced her retirement in 2005, the Court had not received any new members since 1994. President George W. Bush named John Roberts as her replacement. Before Roberts was confirmed, Chief Justice Rehnquist died. President Bush quickly altered his nomination to name Roberts as chief, and named his White House counsel, Harriet Miers, as the associate justice to replace O'Connor. Roberts was confirmed, but Miers withdrew her nomination after pressure from Bush's conservative base. He awaited Roberts's confirmation and then appointed Samuel Alito to the Court. President Barack Obama appointed two new justices within his first year in office, circuit judge Sonia Sotomayor and U.S. Solicitor General Elena Kagan. The Court that had not changed in 12 years now had four new members appointed by presidents from both parties.

A Diverse, Experienced Court

Originally, the Court was a white Protestant man's institution. Some diversity came when presidents appointed Catholics and Jews. Justice Taney (1835) was the first Catholic member. Justice Louis Brandeis (1916) was the first Jewish member. President Lyndon Johnson appointed the first African American, Thurgood Marshall, in 1967. Ronald Reagan appointed the first woman, Justice O'Connor, in 1981.

The current Court is as diverse and as experienced as it has ever been. One African American, Clarence Thomas, and three females serve on the Court. There are six Catholics, three Jews, and no Protestants. Historically, many Supreme Court justices had never served as judges before their nomination. Presidents from FDR through Nixon tended to nominate highly experienced political figures and presidential allies. Since 1969, however, that trend has changed to naming lesser-known jurists who have served on other federal courts.

Ideology The latter-day Rehnquist Court and the current Roberts Court have been difficult to predict. The conservative and liberal wings have been balanced by the swing votes of O'Connor and now Justice Anthony Kennedy. For the past decade or so, most experts have been quick to characterize the Court as leaning conservative. However, the Court has limited states' use of the death penalty and has upheld government's eminent domain authority for economic development in the *Kelo v. New London* ruling.

Chief Justice John Roberts Chief Justice **John Roberts** has guided the Court with judicial minimalism. "Judges and justices are servants of the law, not the other way around. Judges are like umpires," he said during his confirmation hearing. "Umpires don't make rules; they apply them . . . nobody ever went to a ball game to see the umpire." The conversations and conferences go longer. He has achieved more unanimity in decisions and has written more narrow opinions to address the questions before the Court.

Current and Recent Supreme Court Justices				
Current Justices	**President**	**Senate vote**	**Prior Job**	**Law school**
John Roberts, Chief	G.W. Bush	78—22	DC Circuit	Harvard
Antonin Scalia	Reagan	98—0	DC Circuit	Harvard
Anthony Kennedy	Reagan	97—0	Ninth Circuit	Harvard
Clarence Thomas	G.H.W. Bush	52—48	DC Circuit	Yale
Ruth Bader Ginsburg	Clinton	96—3	DC Circuit	Harvard
Stephen Breyer	Clinton	87—9	First Circuit	Harvard
Samuel Alito	G.W. Bush	58—42	Third Circuit	Yale
Sonia Sotomayor	Obama	68—31	Second Circuit	Yale
Elena Kagan	Obama	63—37	Solicitor General	Harvard
Recent Justices				
William Rehnquist	Nixon	68—26	Justice Dept.	Stanford
John Paul Stevens	Ford	98—0	Seventh Circuit	Northwestern
David Souter	G.H.W. Bush	90—9	First Circuit	Harvard
Byron White	Kennedy	Voice vote	Justice Dept.	Yale
Sandra Day O'Connor	Reagan	99—0	Arizona Court of Appeals	Stanford
Harry Blackmun	Nixon	94—0	Eighth Circuit	Harvard
Lewis Powell	Nixon	89—1	ABA President	Harvard
Warren Burger	Nixon	74—3	DC Circuit	St. Paul
Thurgood Marshall	Johnson	69—11	Solicitor General	Howard

Operation

The Supreme Court is guided by Article III, congressional acts, and its own rules. Congress is the authority on the court's size and funding. The Court began creating rules in 1790 and now has 48 formal rules. These guide the submission of briefs, the Court's calendar, deadlines, fees, paperwork requirements, jurisdiction, and the handling of different types of cases. Less formal customs and traditions it has developed also guide the Court's operation.

Jurisdiction The Court has both original and appellate jurisdiction. It serves as a trial court in rare cases, typically when one state sues another over a border dispute or to settle some type of interstate compact. When such cases are filed, the Court appoints a "special master," typically a former judge, to determine the facts and to recommend an outcome. Both states still appear before the Court for a hearing. It also accepts a plethora of *in forma pauperis* briefs, filings by prisoners (in the form of a pauper) seeking a new trial.

New Jersey v. New York. One of the rare original jurisdiction cases came in 1998 when New Jersey sued New York for rights to Ellis Island. The island sits in the harbor between the two states, and it served as the main port of entry for a generation of European immigrants. New Jersey was interested in revenues, about $500,000 in annual taxes and fees. More importantly, the state wanted bragging rights to the island that defines America as a nation of immigrants. The Court heard the case in May 1998 and ruled for New Jersey.

Appeals Process As the nation's highest appeals court, the Court takes cases from the 13 circuits and the 50 states. Two-thirds or more of appeals come through the federal system. The Supreme Court has a more direct jurisdiction over cases starting in U.S. district courts.

Like the circuit courts, the Supreme Court accepts appeals each year from among thousands filed. The petitioner files a **petition for certiorari**, a brief arguing why the lower court erred. The Supreme Court reviews these to determine if the claim is worthy and if it should grant the appeal. To be more efficient, the justices share their clerks, who review the petitions for certiorari and determine which are worthy. This cert pool becomes a gatekeeper at the Supreme Court. If a certiorari is deemed worthy, the justices add the claim to the **discuss list**. From time to time, all nine justices gather in conference to discuss these claims. They consider past precedents and the real impact on the petitioner and respondent. The Supreme Court does not consider hypothetical or theoretical damages; the claimant must show actual damage. Finally, the justices consider the wider national and societal impact if they take and rule on the case. Once four of the nine justices agree to accept the case, the appeal is granted. This **rule of four**, a standard less than a majority, reflects courts' commitments to minorities.

The Court then issues a **writ of certiorari** to the lower court, informing it of the Court's decision and to request the full trial transcript. The justices spend much time reading the case record. Then a date is set for oral arguments. When the Court opens on the first Monday in October, the nine justices enter to hear the petitioner and respondent make their cases, each having 30 minutes for argument. A Supreme Court hearing is not a trial but a chance for each side to persuade justices on one or more narrow points of law. Justices will ask questions, pose hypothetical scenarios, and at times boldly signal their viewpoints. Sometime after the hearing the justices will reconvene in conference to discuss the arguments and make a decision. A simple majority rules.

Opinions

Chief Justice John Marshall's legacy of unanimity has vanished. The Court comes to a unanimous decision only about 30 to 40 percent of the time. Therefore, it issues varying opinions on the law. Once the Court comes to a majority, the chief justice, or the senior-most justice in the majority, either writes the Court's opinion or assigns it to another justice in the majority. In making that decision, the assigning justice considers who has expertise on the topic, who is passionate about the issue, and what the nature of the discussions were that took place in conference. The **majority opinion** is the Court's

Source: Wikimedia Commons / Collection of the Supreme Court of the United States

John Roberts (seated center) became Chief Justice of the Supreme Court in 2005. Associate Justice Anthony Kennedy (seated beside him on the right) has become an often-deciding swing vote on the Court.

opinion. It is the judicial branch's law much as a statute is Congress's law or an executive order is law created by a president. The majority opinion sums up the case, the Court's decision, and its rationale. These opinions often include colorful legal language.

Justices who find themselves differing from the majority can draft and issue differing opinions. Some may agree with the majority and join that vote but have reservations about the majority's legal reasoning. They might write a **concurring opinion**. Those who vote against the majority often write a **dissenting opinion**. The dissenting opinion has no force of law but allows a justice to explain his disagreements with his colleagues. While these have no immediate legal bearing, dissenting opinions send a message to the legal community or to America at large and are often referenced in later cases when the Court might revisit the issue or reverse the precedent. On occasion, the Court will issue a decision without the full explanation. This is known as a *per curium* **opinion**.

BY THE NUMBERS Supreme Court's Recent Caseload									
Term	2004	2005	2006	2007	2008	2009	2010	2011	2012
Cases Filed	7,496	8,521	8,857	8,241	7,738	8,159	7,857	7,713	7,509
Cases Argued	87	87	78	75	87	82	86	79	77

Source: http://www.supremecourt.gov/

What do the numbers show? Roughly how many cases are appealed to the Supreme Court each year? How many cases does the Court generally accept? What fraction or percent of cases appealed does the Court take? Recall the reasons the Supreme Court will or will not accept an appeal.

Clerks' Role Each justice typically employs four law clerks to assist them with handling briefs and analyzing important cases. These bright young attorneys typically graduate high in their classes at Ivy League law schools and have a prosperous legal career ahead of them. In fact, several Supreme Court Justices of the modern era served as clerks in their earlier days. They preview cases for the justices and assist them with writing the opinions.

Judicial Activism vs. Judicial Restraint

After the Supreme Court established judicial review in *Marbury*, it only checked the legislature once more in the government's first full century, in the Dred Scott case. Other courts have since reserved the right to rule on government action in violation of constitutional principles, whether by the legislature or the executive. Judicial review has since become a vehicle that has strengthened all courts. It has placed the Supreme Court, in some ways, above the other branches, making it the final arbiter on controversies of federalism that typically have made the federal government supreme while defining what states, the Congress, and the president can or cannot do.

When judges strike down laws or reverse public policy, they are said to be exercising **judicial activism**. To remember this concept, think *judges acting* to create the law. Activism can be liberal or conservative, depending on the nature of the law that is struck down. When the Court threw out the New York maximum-hours law in 1905 in *Lochner*, it acted conservatively because it rejected an established liberal statute. In *Roe v. Wade*, the Court acted liberally to remove a conservative anti-abortion policy in Texas. Courts at all levels have struck down state and federal statutes.

The Court's power to strike down parts of or entire laws has encouraged litigation and changes in policy. Gun owners and the NRA supported an effort to overturn a ban on handguns in Washington, D.C., and got a victory in the *Heller* decision. Several state attorneys general who opposed the Affordable Care Act sued to overturn it. In a 5–4 decision, in *National Federation of Independent Business v. Sebelius*, the Court upheld the key element of the Affordable Care Act, the individual mandate. That mandate is the federal requirement that all citizens must purchase health insurance or pay a penalty.

Critics of judicial activism tend to point out that, in a democracy, policy should be created by the elected representative legislatures. These critics advocate for **judicial self-restraint**. Chief Justice Harlan Fiske Stone first used the term in his 1936 dissent when the majority outlawed a New Deal program. The Court should not, say these critics, decide a dispute unless there is a concrete injury to be relieved by the decision. The current Court's outspoken conservative strict constructionist Antonin Scalia once claimed, "A 'living' Constitution judge [is] a happy fellow who comes home at night to his wife and says, 'The Constitution means exactly what I think it ought to mean!'" Justices should not declare a law unconstitutional, strict constructionists say, when it merely violates their own idea of what the Constitution means, but only when the law clearly and directly contradicts the document.

Not Ideologically Exclusive The idea that judicial activists are liberal and that self-described conservatives are strict constructionists is an outdated overgeneralization. As historian David Garrow has observed, "Both highly conservative and relatively liberal justices have repeatedly embraced judicial activism." Conservatives and strict constructionists tend to criticize judges who make liberal activist decisions with "legislating from the bench." In several cases, however, the Court has exercised a conservative brand of judicial activism. In striking down limits on when a corporation can advertise during a campaign season, it struck down parts of Congress's campaign reform act in *Citizens United v. FEC*.

Ideology aside, still other critics argue judicial policymaking is ineffective as well as undemocratic. Wise judges have a firm understanding of the Constitution and citizens' rights, but they don't always study issues over time. Most judges don't have special expertise on matters of environmental protection, operating schools, or other administrative matters. They don't have the support systems of lawmakers, such as committee staffers and researchers, to fully engage an issue to find a solution. So when courts rule, the outcome is not always practical or manageable for those meant to implement it. Additionally, many such court rulings are just unpopular.

The Courts and the Other Branches of Government

Congress and the president interact with the judiciary in many ways. From the creation of various courts to the appointment of judges to implementation of a judicial decision, the judiciary often crosses paths with the other two branches.

Appointing the Judiciary

With hundreds of judgeships in the lower courts, presidents will have a chance to appoint several judges to the federal bench over their four or eight years in office. When a vacancy occurs, or when Congress creates a new seat on an overloaded court, the president carefully selects a qualified judge because that person can shape law and will likely do so until late in his or her life. Since John Adams's appointment of the Federalist "midnight judges" in 1801, presidents have tried to shape the judiciary with jurists who reflect their political and judicial philosophy.

District and circuit appointments receive less news coverage and have less impact than Supreme Court nominees but are important nonetheless. In appointing them, presidents tend to consider candidates from the same or nearby geographic areas. Law school deans, high-level state judges, and successful lawyers in private practice make excellent candidates. The president's White House legal team and the Department of Justice in conjunction with the Senate seek out good candidates to find experienced, favorable nominees.

Senate's Advice and Consent The Senate Judiciary Committee looks over all the president's judicial appointments. Sometimes the nominee appears before the committee to answer senators' questions about their experience or their views on the law. Less controversial district judges are confirmed without notice based largely on the home state senators' recommendations. The more controversial, polarizing Supreme Court nominees will receive greater attention during contentious and dramatic hearings. The quick determination of an appointee's political philosophy has become known as a **litmus test**. Much like testing a solution for its pH in chemistry class, presidents, senators, or pundits may ask pointed questions on controversial issues to determine a candidate's ideology on the political spectrum.

Senatorial Courtesy The Senate firmly reserves its right of advice and consent. "In practical terms," said George W. Bush administration attorney Rachel Brand, "the home state senators are almost as important as—and sometimes more important than—the president in determining who will be nominated to a particular lower-court judgeship." This practice of **senatorial courtesy** is especially routine with district judge appointments, as districts are entirely within a given state. When vacancies occur, senators typically recommend judges to the White House.

Blue Slip Senate procedure and tradition basically give individual senators veto power over nominees located in their respective states. For U.S. district court nominations, each of the two senators receives a blue slip—a blue piece of paper they return to the Judiciary Committee to allow the process to move forward. To derail the process, a senator can return the slip with a negative indication or never return it at all. The committee chairman will usually not hold a hearing on the nominee's confirmation until both senators have consented. This custom has encouraged presidents to consult with the home state senators early in the process. President George W. Bush asked senators to offer three recommendations when vacancies occurred.

All senators embrace this influence. They are meant to be guardians and representatives for their states. The other 98 senators tend to follow the home state senators' lead, especially if they are in the same party, and vote for or against the nominated judge based on the senators' views. This custom is somewhat followed with appeals court judges as well. Both George W. Bush and President Obama have considered the views of senators representing states within judicial circuits. Appeals courts never encompass only one state, so the privilege of senatorial courtesy is less likely.

Confirmation When a Supreme Court vacancy occurs, a president has a unique opportunity to shape American jurisprudence. Of the 159 nominations to the Supreme Court over U.S. history, 35 were not confirmed. Eleven were rejected by a vote of the full Senate, 23 were postponed or never acted on by the Judiciary Committee, and a few withdrew on their own or by request of the president. Few confirmations brought rancor or public spectacle until the Senate rejected President Nixon's first two nominees. Since then, the Court's influence on controversial topics, intense partisanship, the public nature of the confirmation process, and contentious hearings have made confirmation a partisan event.

Interest Groups The Senate's role and the increasingly publicized confirmation process has also involved interest groups. Confirmation hearings were never public until 1929. In recent years, they have become a spectacle and may include a long list of witnesses testifying about the nominee's qualifications. The most active and reputable interest group to testify about judicial nominees is the American Bar Association. This powerful group represents the national interest of attorneys and the legal profession. Since the 1950s, the ABA has been involved in the process. They rate nominees as "highly qualified," "qualified," and "not qualified." More recently, additional groups weigh in on the process, especially when they see their interests threatened or enhanced. Interest groups also target a senator's home state when they feel strongly about a nominee, urging voters to contact their senators in support or in opposition to the nominee. Indeed, interest groups sometimes suggest or even draft questions for senators and assist them at the confirmation hearings.

Getting "Borked" The confirmation process became more ideological during the Reagan and first Bush administrations and has continued since. The process took a turn when Reagan chose U.S. Appeals Court Justice **Robert Bork** in 1987. Bork was the conservative's leading intellectual in the legal community. At 60 years old, he had been a professor at Yale Law School, U.S. solicitor general, and a successful corporate lawyer. He was an advocate of original intent, seeking to uphold the Constitution as intended by the Framers. He made clear how he despised the rulings of the activist Warren Court. He spoke against decisions that mandated legislative reapportionment, upheld affirmative action, and placed citizen privacy over state authority.

When asked about his nomination, then-Senator Joe Biden, chair of the Senate Judiciary Committee, warned the White House that choosing Bork would likely result in a confirmation fight. Within hours of Reagan's nomination, Senator Edward Kennedy drew a line in the sand at a Senate press conference.

"Robert Bork's America," Kennedy said, "is a land in which women would be forced into back alley abortions, blacks would sit at segregated lunch counters, rogue police could break down citizen's doors in midnight raids, and school children could not be taught evolution."

Kennedy's warning brought attention to Judge Bork's extreme views that threatened to turn back a generation of civil rights and civil liberties decisions. What followed was a raucous, lengthy confirmation hearing. Bork himself jousted with Senator Biden for hours. This contest drew attention as it was a pivotal moment for the Court when every liberal and conservative onlooker in the country had chosen sides. After a go with the committee, the full Senate, which had unanimously confirmed Bork as an appeals court judge in 1981, rejected him by a vote of 58 to 42. The term "to bork" entered the American political lexicon, defined more recently by the *New York Times*: "to destroy a judicial nominee through a concerted attack on his character, background, and philosophy."

Clarence Thomas In 1991, Justice Thurgood Marshall, the first African American on the Court, resigned. President George H.W. Bush and his advisors opposed affirmative action but simply could not let the Court return to a completely white institution. After some consideration, Bush introduced Marshall's replacement, conservative African-American judge Clarence Thomas. What followed was Clarence Thomas's controversial confirmation process that centered on ideology, experience, and sexual harassment.

By naming Thomas, Bush satisfied the left's penchant for diversity, while also satisfying his conservative base with a strict constructionist. As Jeffrey Toobin, author of *The Nine*, says, "The list of plausible candidates that fit both qualifications pretty much began and ended with Clarence Thomas." After onlookers expressed concern for Thomas's ideology, they then pointed at his lack of experience. He had never argued a single case in any federal appeals court, much less the Supreme Court. He had never written a book, an article, or legal brief of any consequence. He had served as an appeals judge on the D.C. Circuit for about one year. The ABA gave him only a "qualified" rating, a rarity among nominees to the High Court.

Then Anita Hill came forward. Hill had some years earlier worked on Thomas's staff in the administration and accused him of an array of sexually suggestive office behavior. The Judiciary Committee then invited her to testify. In a highly televised carnival atmosphere, Hill testified for seven hours on the harassing comments Thomas had dealt her and the pornographic films he discussed. Thomas denied many of the allegations and called the hearing a "high-tech lynching." After a tie vote in committee, the full Senate barely confirmed him.

"The Nuclear Option" During George W. Bush's first term, Democrats did not allow a vote on 10 of the 52 appeals court nominees that had cleared committee. Conservative nominees were delayed by Senate procedure. The Democrats, in the minority at the time, invoked the right to filibuster judges. One Bush nominee waited four years. Bush declared in his State of the Union message, "Every judicial nominee deserves an up or down vote." Senate Republicans threatened to change the rules, which could be done with a simple majority. The threat to the filibuster became known as a drastic "nuclear option." A bipartisan group of senators dubbed the "Gang of 14" joined forces to create a compromise that kept the Senate rules the same while confirming most appointees. President Obama had a lower confirmation rate than Bush. Late in his first term, about 76 percent of Obama's nominees had been confirmed, while nearly 87 percent of Bush's nominees were confirmed. Bush nominees waited, on average 46 days to be confirmed; Obama's waited 115 days.

President	Supreme Court	Appeals Courts	District Courts	Total
BY THE NUMBERS Recent Presidents' Judicial Appointments				
Nixon	4	45	182	231
Ford	1	12	52	65
Carter	0	56	206	262
Reagan	3	78	292	373
G.W.H.Bush	2	37	149	188
Clinton	2	62	306	370
G.W. Bush	2	61	261	324

Source: U.S. Courts. Excludes Court of International Trade

What do the numbers show? What presidents appointed more judges than others? On average, how many Supreme Court judges does a president appoint? How many lower court judges? Which president of recent years appointed the most? How do a president's judicial appointees impact law and government in the United States?

Reforming Judicial Confirmation With all the interested parties focused on the potential impact of a new Supreme Court justice, confirmation has become a public and hotly debated event for an otherwise private, venerable institution. Joyce Baugh of Central Michigan University offers a solution to tame the confirmation process: Limit the number of participants at the hearings, prevent nominees from testifying, prevent senators from offering specific hypotheticals to conduct a litmus test, and base confirmation solely on nominees' written records and testimony from legal experts. Chief John Roberts spoke to the persistent problem of filling judicial vacancies in an age of partisanship. In his annual report on the judiciary, he declared, "Each party has found it easy to turn on a dime from decrying to defending the blocking of judicial nominations, depending on their changing political fortunes."

Surprising Their Appointers Not all appointees prove to be as controversial in practice as suspected during the power play. And not all confirmed judges follow the philosophy the appointing president expected. Once confirmed, judges are independent from the executive. Several have disappointed the presidents who appointed them. Eisenhower did not bring

Earl Warren to the Supreme Court to make liberal, activist decisions. Warren Burger disappointed Nixon when he voted to legalize abortion and to promote school busing for racial balance. Justice David Souter, appointed by Republican George H.W. Bush in 1990, proved to be a reliably liberal vote until he resigned in 2009.

Congress and the Courts

Impeachment The same process for accusing and removing a president also exists for federal judges who have acted improperly. The first judicial impeachment came in 1804 against John Pickering, an abusive, partisan drunkard on his way to insanity. Pickering refused to yield the bench, so Congress ousted him. Almost immediately, Thomas Jefferson's party moved to impeach Supreme Court Justice Samuel Chase. In an age of partisan attacks, Jefferson's party wanted to weaken the remaining presence of Federalists on the federal bench. Chase had vigorously supported convictions under the Sedition Acts. Wanting to avoid making the impeachment process a political tool to rid the third branch of opponents, Jefferson withdrew his support for the endeavor and Chase survived the Senate vote. Impeachment has served as Congress's check on the so-called life terms. Since these early cases a total of 15 federal judges have been impeached. The most recent was District Judge Thomas Porteous, whom the Senate later found guilty of corruption and perjury and voted to remove.

Congressional Oversight and Influence Beyond the Senate's advice and consent and removal powers, Congress can influence the judiciary in other ways. It sets and pays judges' salaries. Congress budgets for the construction and maintenance of federal courthouses. It has passed an entire body of law that helps govern the judiciary. This includes regulations about courtroom procedures to judicial recusal—judges withdrawing from a case if they have a conflict of interest. Occasionally Congress creates new seats in the 94 district courts and on the 13 appeals courts. Congress has more than doubled the number of circuit and district judges over the last 50 years.

Selected U.S. Courts of Special Jurisdiction
• U.S. Court of Appeals for the Armed Services
• U.S. Court of Federal Claims
• U.S. Court of International Trade
• U.S. Tax Court
• U.S. Court of Appeals for Veterans Claims

Department of Justice

In addition to appointing the judiciary, the executive branch enters the federal courts to enforce criminal law and to weigh in on legal questions. The president's **Department of Justice**, headed by the attorney general, investigates federal crimes with the FBI or DEA, and U.S. attorneys prosecute the accused criminals. These attorneys are also the legal authority for federal civil law on a more local basis. When a party sues the federal government, it is the U.S. attorneys who defend the United States. In appealed criminal cases, these attorneys present the oral arguments in the circuit courts.

Another high-ranking figure in the Department of Justice is the **solicitor general** who works in the Washington office. Appointed by the president and approved by the Senate, the solicitor general determines which cases to appeal to the U.S. Supreme Court and represents the United States in the Supreme Court room. When you see a Supreme Court case entitled the *United States v. John Doe*, it means the United States lost in one of the circuit courts and the solicitor general sought an appeal. At times, this official will submit an *amicus curiae* **brief** (friend of the court brief) to the Supreme Court in cases where the United States is not a party. As discussed in Chapter 7, an amicus brief argues for a particular ruling in the case. Several solicitors general have later been appointed to the High Court, notably Stanley Reed, Thurgood Marshall, and the newest member Elena Kagan.

Judicial Implementation

When a court orders, decrees, or enjoins a party, it can do so only from the courtroom. Putting a decision into effect, however, is another matter. Judges alone cannot implement the verdicts and opinions made in their courts. Nine robed justices in Washington simply cannot put their own decisions into effect. They require at least one of several other potential governing authorities—police, regulatory agencies, or other government agencies—to carry out their decisions. Legislatures may have to rewrite or pass new laws.

The implementing population, those charged with putting a court's decision into effect, doesn't always cooperate with or follow courts' orders. When the Supreme Court makes decisions it surely assesses potential enforcement and cooperation. When John Marshall's court deemed that Georgia could not regulate Cherokee Indian lands in its state because such regulation was exclusive to the federal government, President Andrew Jackson strongly disagreed and allegedly said, "John Marshall has made his decision, now let him enforce it." In the late 1950s, after the Court ruled that a Little Rock high school had to integrate, the executive branch sent federal troops to escort the claimants into the formerly all-white school.

REFLECT ON THE ESSENTIAL QUESTION

Essential Question: *How do the nation's courts settle legal controversies and establish public policy?* On separate paper, complete a chart like the one below to gather details to answer that question.

System for Settling Legal Controversies	How Courts Establish Public Policy

KEY TERMS, NAMES, AND EVENTS

amicus curiae brief	injunction	Roberts, John
appellate jurisdiction	judicial activism	rule of four
attorney general	judicial review	senatorial courtesy
binding precedent	judicial self-restraint	solicitor general
Bork, Robert	litmus test	sovereign immunity
certiorari	majority opinion	special legislative courts
class action suit	Marshall, John	*stare decisis*
common law	original jurisdiction	strict constructionist
concurring opinion	*per curium* opinion	Supreme Court
constitutional courts	persuasive precedent	torts
Department of Justice	petition for certiorari	U.S. Circuit Court of Appeals
discuss list	petitioner	U.S. District Courts
dissenting opinion	plaintiff	Warren, Earl
diversity citizenship	plea bargain	writ of certiorari
defendant	precedent	
Dred Scott v. Stanford	respondent	
in forma pauperis	Rehnquist, William	

MULTIPLE-CHOICE QUESTIONS

1. Which of the following statements concerning the Supreme Court's acceptance of an appeal is true?
   - (A) The chief justice's vote to accept an appeal is stronger than that of the other justices.
   - (B) A majority is necessary to grant the appeal.
   - (C) Four justices must agree to accept the appeal.
   - (D) A majority of the Court and the solicitor general must accept the appeal.
   - (E) Most appealed cases are accepted by the Supreme Court.

2. Special legislative courts differ from constitutional courts in that
   - (A) judges on special courts have fixed terms, while constitutional court judges serve during good behavior
   - (B) legislative courts try federal crime, and constitutional courts determine only constitutional questions
   - (C) special courts are state courts but constitutional courts are federal
   - (D) special courts try defendants for breaking federal law, and constitutional courts hear only cases on appeal
   - (E) constitutional court judges are appointed by the president, but special court judges are elected by the people

3. The Senate blocked which of President Reagan's Supreme Court nominees after a rather partisan confirmation battle?
   - (A) John Roberts
   - (B) William Rehnquist
   - (C) Antonin Scalia
   - (D) Robert Bork
   - (E) Sandra Day O'Connor

4. The quote below from the *Federalist Papers* refers to what trait of the national judiciary?
   "Nothing contributes so much to its firmness and independence as permanency in office."–*Federalist #78*
   - (A) Senatorial courtesy
   - (B) Judges' terms
   - (C) Judicial implementation
   - (D) Precedence
   - (E) Certiorari

5. Which of the following cases is NOT likely to land in U.S. District Court?
   - (A) A suspended student challenges a school's ruling on free speech grounds
   - (B) A criminal counterfeiting case
   - (C) A high-dollar lawsuit involving parties that live in different states
   - (D) A violent crime such as murder or rape
   - (E) A crime arising on the seas just off the U.S. coast

6. All of the following about the United States solicitor general are true EXCEPT
   - (A) the solicitor general is appointed by the president and approved by the Senate
   - (B) the solicitor general argues cases and represents the United States when the U.S. is a party to a hearing in the Supreme Court

(C) some solicitors general have later served on the Supreme Court

(D) the solicitor general can file an *amicus curiae* brief as a third party in Supreme Court

(E) the solicitor general works in the judicial branch

7. Which statement is a valid criticism of judicial activism?

   (A) With judicial activism, appointed officials override a democratically established policy.

   (B) The practice of judicial activism results in exclusively liberal policies imposed on Americans.

   (C) The overwhelming amount of public policy is created through judicial activism.

   (D) The practice was common in the Supreme Court's early years but not since.

   (E) Judicial activism is only possible at the Supreme Court level.

8. Which statement accurately reflects the Supreme Court under Chief Justice Earl Warren (1953–1969)?

   (A) Judicial restraint was the order of the day.

   (B) Warren's long career as a judge gave him the experience to later succeed as chief justice.

   (C) Rulings during Warren's era reflect a commitment to civil rights and civil liberties.

   (D) States generally gained relative power during the Warren Court era.

   (E) Warren was typically a dissenting justice in the minority.

9. Which of the following determines the size of the Supreme Court?

   (A) The Constitution

   (B) Congress

   (C) President

   (D) Chief Justice of the United States

   (E) Senate Judiciary Committee

10. All of the following regarding the judicial branch are true EXCEPT

   (A) most criminal cases are heard in state courts

   (B) many states elect judges, while federal judges are appointed

   (C) the only court mentioned by name in the Constitution is the Supreme Court

   (D) there are no juries in federal criminal trials

   (E) the Supreme Court takes more cases from the circuit courts than from the state court systems

Question

1. The United States Supreme Court operates according to provisions in the Constitution and the Court's customs and rules.

    (a) Identify two provisions regarding the Supreme Court in the Constitution and explain how these provisions guide the Court.

    (b) Identify two customs or rules the Supreme Court has adopted since ratification of the Constitution and explain how these guide the Supreme Court.

Question

2. The United States Judiciary is a three-tier court system that follows certain concepts and procedures in its operation.

    (a) Identify one type of a case that goes to U.S. District Court, and explain why the district court has jurisdiction over that type of case.

    (b) Describe one characteristic or responsibility of the U.S. Circuit Courts.

    (c) Describe two of the following and explain how these two affect the appeals process in the federal judiciary.
    - *stare decisis*
    - *certiorari*
    - solicitor general

WRITING: USE CONCISE LANGUAGE

You've already read about the impact of the active voice on strong and clear writing (page 50). Other ways to improve the clarity of your writing include eliminating wordy phrases and avoiding inflated language.

For example, instead of the wordy phrases "due to the fact that" and "in light of the fact that," use the simpler, clear word "because." And instead of such inflated language as "is cognizant of" and "is desirous of" use the simpler and clearer "knows" and "wants."

UNIT 4: Review

Our national institutions govern the United States through constitutional designs, historic customs, and practical relationships. Congress's bicameral set-up provides an additional check within the legislature to assure the legitimacy and popularity of most legislation. The many committees in the House and Senate determine particulars of our national laws and handle the day-to-day business on Capitol Hill. Congress has become less a white man's institution and more a democratic and inclusive body with the Seventeenth Amendment, the one-man, one-vote rule, and legislative measures such as the discharge petition and the decreased threshold to break a filibuster.

The Executive Branch carries out Congress's laws. Presidents have become stronger with increased media attention, international face-offs, and their handling of domestic crises. The president is the chief executive of government and the chief of military and foreign policy as well as a manager of the nation's funds. Able and experienced advisors help the president develop policies and manage large departments and agencies. These sub-units range from the mammoth Department of Defense to the Federal Communications Commission.

The Judiciary adjudicates federal crimes and high-dollar civil disputes between citizens of different states. The Circuit Courts hear appeals and interpret law in their respective circuits. Special legislative courts hear unique cases dealing with specialized areas of law. The less visible, nine-judge Supreme Court hears about 80 cases a year to rule on constitutionality and national policy.

Together these institutions govern the United States.

THINK AS A POLITICAL SCIENTIST: ANALYZE AND INTERPRET A PRESIDENT'S INAUGURAL ADDRESS

Presidential inaugural speeches are part of the public record and available in books and on the Internet. A convenient place to find them is at The American Presidency Project at the University of California-Santa Barbara at http://www.presidency.ucsb.edu/inaugurals.php. This Web site has a wealth of data, records, and primary documents. From the complete catalog of presidential inaugural addresses, pick one speech to analyze and interpret. Consider such elements as the ideology and promises espoused in the speech, its historical context, foreign policy points addressed, programs introduced, and memorable words and phrases.

Using additional sources on this site or elsewhere, look into this same president's administration and legacy. Did he accomplish goals set forth in the inaugural address? What kind of legacy does he have?

UNIT 5: Civil Rights and Civil Liberties

Chapter 13 *Civil Rights*

Chapter 14 *Civil Liberties*

In a diverse America, minority groups have used the institutions of government to seek equality and individual liberties. African Americans overcame the notorious legacy of slavery and persevered through a century of discrimination before experiencing equality and fair representation in the halls of government. Other minority groups and brave individuals have turned to Congress and, more often, to the courts to ensure that government follows the Constitution.

The National Association for the Advancement of Colored People has led the charge for racial equality, due process for black defendants, school desegregation, and voting rights for over 100 years. By lobbying Congress, organizing public protests and voter registration drives, and pressing their cases in the courts, the NAACP and other civil rights groups dismantled Jim Crow. Today, President Barack Obama serving in the White House and the number of African Americans serving in Congress are a testament to the accomplishments of this long quest. Women, Asian Americans, Latinos, gays and lesbians, people with disabilities, and other minorities have also taken a path from harsh discrimination toward equality via congressional laws, presidential directives, and court decisions.

Government often infringes on citizen liberty. But the Bill of Rights guarantees fundamental freedoms and prevents government from denying citizens free speech, free religion, privacy, a fair trial, and other essential liberties. The American Civil Liberties Union and other rights groups have fought to prevent government from squelching free expression, banning the teaching of evolution, punishing war protesters, and executing prisoners. For both equal treatment and due process, advocates have emphasized the Fourteenth Amendment and turned to the courts as the most useful institution to secure these rights. The Supreme Court has ordered that states, too, must refrain from infringing on most of the same rights.

Key Concepts

Civil Rights and Civil Liberties

- The development of civil liberties and civil rights by judicial interpretation
- Knowledge of substantive rights and liberties
- The impact of the Fourteenth Amendment on the constitutional development of rights and liberties

Source: *AP®United States Government and Politics Course and Exam Description*

Civil Rights

"Our Constitution is colorblind, and neither knows nor tolerates classes among citizens. In respect of civil rights, all citizens are equal before the law."
—Supreme Court Justice John Marshall Harlan's dissent in *Plessy v. Ferguson, 1896*

Essential Question: How have minorities and women sought equality and fair treatment from our government institutions?

United States political culture places a high priority on freedom and equality. These principles are evident in the Declaration of Independence, the Constitution, the Bill of Rights, and later amendments. Civil rights organizations representing African Americans and women have pushed for governments to deliver on the promises these documents laid out. In more recent years, additional groups—Latinos, people with disabilities, gays and lesbians—have petitioned the government for fundamental fairness and equality. All three branches have responded in varying degrees to address civil rights issues. Even so, racism, sexism, and other forms of bigotry have not disappeared. Today, a complex body of law brought on by Supreme Court decisions, federal statutes, and executive directives defines civil rights in America.

Civil Rights for African Americans

In the United States, federal and state governments generally ignored civil rights policy before the Civil War. The Framers of the Constitution left the legal question of slavery up to the states, allowing the South to strengthen its plantation system and relegate slaves and free blacks to subservience. The North had a sparse black population and little regard for fairness to African Americans. Abolitionists, religious leaders, and progressives sought to outlaw slavery and advocated for African Americans in the mid-1800s.

A major setback for the antislavery movement came with the Supreme Court's Dred Scott decision, also known as *Dred Scott v. Sandford*. Dred Scott, a skilled slave who assisted Army surgeon John Emerson, his master, had lived in free territory and saw an opportunity for freedom when Dr. Emerson died. With the assistance of abolitionists, Scott sued for his freedom in the courts, but Emerson's brother-in-law, John Sandford, claimed to inherit the slave. The Supreme Court heard the case in 1857 and quickly denied Scott his quest for freedom. This blow strengthened support for abolition on a national level and helped to bring about the Civil War. After the North defeated the Confederacy, Congress passed a host of federal measures during the Reconstruction Era to make gains for former slaves.

Reconstruction

The Republican Party was created in part to abolish slavery or slow its spread. During the war, a Republican-dominated Congress outlawed slavery in the capital city, and President Lincoln issued the Emancipation Proclamation. After the Confederacy surrendered, Radical Republicans took the lead. The House and Senate passed legislation to reconstruct the Union and to protect the freed slaves, including three constitutional amendments.

The **Thirteenth Amendment** outlawed slavery across the United States, trumping the Tenth Amendment's reserved power that before had enabled states to have slavery. The **Fourteenth Amendment** had a host of provisions to protect the newly-freed slave. It promised U.S. citizenship to anyone born or naturalized in the United States. It required states to guarantee privileges and immunities to its own citizens as well as those from other states. The due process clause (which will be discussed further in Chapter 14) ensured all citizens would be afforded due process in court as criminal defendants or in other areas of law. The amendment's **equal protection clause** guaranteed that government—state and federal—would treat all citizens the same.

Later sections of this long amendment prevented those members of the U.S. government who fled to serve the Confederacy from serving easily again in the federal government. It also prohibited payments to war contractors who aided the Confederacy, and it prevented southern slave owners from making claims against the United States.

As with the other Reconstruction amendments, the Fourteenth was obviously directed at protecting the newly freed slaves, making them citizens and ensuring equal treatment from the states. But since neither slaves nor African Americans are specifically mentioned in the amendment, several others—women, other ethnic minorities, gays—have benefitted from it in their search for equality. Criminal defendants have made claims against states to establish new legal standards. Immigrants, documented or undocumented, who bear children in the United States will see their offspring become U.S. citizens.

The **Fifteenth Amendment** prohibited states from denying the vote to anyone "on account of race, color, or previous condition of servitude." It was meant to give the vote to black men.

Reconstruction Amendments
• The **Thirteenth Amendment** (1865) abolished slavery.
• The **Fourteenth Amendment** (1868) guaranteed citizenship, privileges and immunities, due process, and equal protection.
• The **Fifteenth Amendment** (1870) prevented state denial of suffrage on account of race.

In addition to these constitutional protections, Congress also created the Freedmen's Bureau and led Reconstruction programs to rebuild the southern states. The federal government dispatched Union soldiers to monitor elections and to prevent lawlessness toward freed slaves. Confederate leaders—those who had sworn to uphold the U.S. Constitution and then joined the Confederacy—were temporarily removed from the political process. These two factors allowed African Americans to vote and to serve in elected positions. Another expansion of civil rights looked imminent after the **Civil Rights Act of 1875** made it illegal for privately-owned places of public accommodation—trains, hotels, and taverns—to make distinctions between black and white patrons. The law also outlawed discrimination in jury selection, public schools, churches, cemeteries, and transportation.

Civil Rights Fade

These measures created a relative equality for the emancipated slave. The franchise (the right to vote) greatly expanded the black man's rights. African Americans sent men from their own ranks to state capitals and to Washington. Virginia had at least some black representation in the state assembly every year from 1869 to 1891. Between 1876 and 1894, North Carolina elected 52 black representatives to its state legislature. Ten black men were sent to Congress during Reconstruction; ten others were elected afterward.

The black presence in elected bodies and federal protections, however, soon disappeared after federal troops departed from the South and after a conservative Supreme Court took away Congress's authority over civil rights. An electoral commission awarded the 1876 contested presidential election to Rutherford B. Hayes, and the new president agreed to withdraw federal troops from the South, essentially ending the federal occupation. When Union troops departed, so did the freed slaves' protection. Additionally, the Supreme Court reviewed the civil rights law. In a series of decisions collectively dubbed the *Civil Rights Cases* (1883), the Court struck down the 1875 statute. It declared the Fourteenth Amendment did not confer new powers—such as that of preventing discrimination by private businesses—on Congress and ruled that the equal protection clause was meant to protect the African Americans against unfair state action, not to guide a shopkeeper's service policy.

Disenfranchisement, economic reprisals, and discrimination against blacks followed. States created a body of law that segregated the races in the public sphere. These **Jim Crow laws** separated blacks and whites on trains, in theaters, in public restrooms, and in public schools.

Circumventing the Fifteenth Amendment As former Confederates returned to power, the southern states circumvented the Fifteenth Amendment. Disenfranchising African Americans, southern whites believed, would return them to second-class status. The South began requiring property or literacy qualifications to vote. Several other states elevated the **literacy test** into their state constitutions. The **poll taxes**—a simple fee required of voters—became one of the most effective ways to discourage the potential black voter. And the **grandfather clause**, which allowed states to recognize a registering voter as it would have recognized his grandfather, prevented thousands of blacks from voting while it allowed illiterate and poor whites to be exempt from the literacy test and poll tax. The **white primary**, too, became a popular method for states to keep African Americans out of the political process. Though primary elections empowered greater numbers of rank-and-file voters, primaries in the South became another method used to **disenfranchise** blacks early in the electoral process.

These state-level loopholes did not violate the absolute letter of the Constitution because they never prevented blacks from voting "on account of race, color, or previous condition of servitude," as the Fifteenth Amendment prohibits.

"Separate But Equal"

Policymakers continued to draw lines between the races. They separated white and black citizens on public carriers, in public restrooms, in theaters, and in public schools. This institutionalized separation was tested in *Plessy v. Ferguson* **(1896)**. Challenging Louisiana's separate coach law, Homer Adolph Plessy, a man with one-eighth African blood and thus subject to the statute, sat in the white section of a train. He was arrested and convicted and then appealed his conviction to the Supreme Court. His lawyers argued that separation of the races violated the Fourteenth Amendment's equal protection clause. The Supreme Court saw it differently, however, and sided with the state's right to segregate the races in public places. The Court claimed that **"separate but equal"** facilities satisfied the amendment. One lone dissenter, Justice John Marshall Harlan, decried the decision (as he did in the *Civil Rights Cases*) as a basic violation to the freed African Americans. Unfortunately, Harlan's dissent was only a minority opinion. Segregation and Jim Crow continued for two more generations.

The NAACP Seeks Justice and Equality

State-sponsored discrimination and a violent race riot in Springfield, Illinois, led civil rights leaders to create the **National Association for the Advancement of Colored People (NAACP)** in 1909. On Abraham Lincoln's birthday, a handful of academics, philanthropists, and journalists sent out a call for a national conference. Harvard graduate and Atlanta University professor Dr. W. E. B. DuBois was among those elected as the association's first leaders.

Taking Action

The NAACP soon opened its national headquarters in New York and brought Dr. DuBois on as its full-time director of research and publications. He began publishing the association's magazine, *The Crisis*. DuBois declared in the first issue that the publication "will stand for the rights of men, irrespective of color or race, for the highest ideals of American Democracy." The publication revealed racial injustices, printed academic findings on race, and editorialized on civil rights issues. By 1912, the organization printed 16,000 copies of *The Crisis* that were sent to subscribers and members in nearly every state.

Before World War I, the group pressed President Woodrow Wilson to overturn segregation in federal agencies and departments. The NAACP had also hired two men as full-time lobbyists in Washington, one for the House and one for the Senate. The association joined in filing the case of *Guinn v. United States* (1915) to challenge the grandfather clause. The Supreme Court ruled the practice a violation of the Fifteenth Amendment. Two years later, the Court again sided with the NAACP in *Buchanan v. Warley* (1917), which ruled government-imposed residential segregation a constitutional violation.

The Campaign Against Lynching After these two successes, the NAACP sought legal prevention of the horrific act of lynching. Lynch law—mobs of vengeful whites hanging African Americans who were often wrongly accused of crimes—became common in the South and around northern cities. Lynch mobs grabbed alleged offenders from their homes in the middle of the night or from jail cells as they awaited trial and hanged them, often leaving the corpses for public display. The sight of a lynched victim served as a constant warning to aspiring blacks not to step outside their boundaries. Lynching had waned somewhat since 1900, but as of 1920, an average of about 60 known lynchings took place each year. The NAACP began hanging a large flag out of its New York office window to inform passersby "A Man was Lynched Today." The association also researched and documented lynching cases to expose the problem and to push for federal legislation to stop the heinous practice.

In the early 1920s, the NAACP and Representative L. C. Dyer of St. Louis backed a bill to make lynching a federal crime. Of course, assault and murder were already criminal offenses under state statutes, but state or local police rarely enforced those laws in cases of lynchings. At times, the local sheriff or constable was in attendance at a lynching or conspicuously unavailable. The bill passed the House on a partisan basis; most Republicans voted for it and most Democrats voted against. The bill faced greater opposition in the Senate, where southern men dominated committee chairmanships. The chairman of the Senate Judiciary Committee, James Eastland of Mississippi, delayed the bill in committee. This delay as well as filibusters on the Senate floor prevented a 20-year attempt to make lynching illegal at the federal level.

Legal Defense Fund The NAACP regularly argued cases in the Supreme Court. It added a legal team led by Charles Hamilton Houston, a Howard University law professor, and his worthy assistant, Baltimore native Thurgood Marshall. The association's Legal Defense Fund employed capable lawyers. They argued for the Scottsboro Nine—nine black youths falsely accused of rape—to have the right to counsel in a death penalty case. They defended helpless and mostly innocent black defendants across the South in front of racist judges and juries. Finally, they successfully convinced the Supreme Court to outlaw the white primary.

The great-grandson of a slave, Thurgood Marshall was a leader in shaping civil rights law well before he became the first African-American justice on the Supreme Court in 1967.

Desegregating Schools

The NAACP next developed a legal strategy to chip away at state school segregation. The federal judiciary was the ideal place to start since federal judges served life terms and could issue an unpopular decision in the South without fear of losing their positions. Thurgood Marshall and other attorneys would prove that states and local school boards did not follow the Fourteenth Amendment's equal protection clause while creating segregated schools. Marshall argued that the *Plessy v. Ferguson* principle of "separate but equal" simply did not result in equal education.

Higher Education The NAACP filed suits to integrate college and graduate schools first and then K-12 schools. Early success came with the case of *Missouri ex. Rel. Gaines v. Canada* (1938), with which the NAACP won Lloyd Gaines's entrance into the University of Missouri's Law School. The state had offered to pay his out-of-state tuition at a neighboring law school, but the Fourteenth Amendment specifically requires states to treat the races equally, and failing to provide the "separate but equal" law school, the Court claimed, violated the Constitution. The state created an all-black law school within the University of Missouri campus.

In 1950, the NAACP won decisions in the companion cases of *McLaurin v. Oklahoma* and *Sweatt v. Painter*. The Court found inequalities between the white and black graduate and law schools of Oklahoma and Texas. Beyond the obvious differences in the facilities and tangible materials, the Court recognized stark differences in discourse and the professional connections essential to success in the field after graduation. The Supreme Court ruled that separate schools were not equal and that states had to admit blacks seeking advanced degrees.

Overturning *Plessy* As the Supreme Court delivered the *Sweatt* and *McLaurin* decisions, the NAACP had already filed several suits in U.S. district courts to overturn K-12 segregation. With assistance from sociologists Kenneth and Mamie Clark, two academics from New York universities, the NAACP improved its strategy. In addition to arguing that segregation was morally wrong, they argued separate schools were psychologically damaging to black children. In experiments, when black children were shown two dolls identical except for their skin color and asked to choose the "nice doll," they chose the white doll. When asked to choose the doll that "looks bad," they chose the dark-skinned doll. With these results, the Clarks proved how the segregation system caused feelings of inferiority in the black child. Attorneys sought strong, reliable plaintiffs who could withstand the racist intimidation and reprisals that followed the filing of a lawsuit.

Brown v. Board of Education Among the damaged plaintiffs was Linda Brown of Topeka, Kansas, who had received an inferior education far from her home and with outdated textbooks. The segregation left her with a general feeling of inferiority. On May 17, 1954, the Supreme Court issued its opinion on five cases, including hers. The cases were from Delaware, South Carolina, Virginia, the District of Columbia, and her own Kansas, collectively referred to as ***Brown v. Board of Education of Topeka, Kansas***. Newly appointed Chief Justice Earl Warren had a significant role in this decision and rallied the Court to a unanimous vote. In the opinion, Warren wrote, "We conclude, in the field of public education, the doctrine of 'separate but equal' has no place." The Court overturned *Plessy* and declared the southern segregation laws void. The Court also agreed with the assertion that separating students "solely because of their race generates a feeling of inferiority … unlikely ever to be undone."

Brown II The Court knew its decision would bring complicated adjustments for the southern community. Integrating the southern schools would be complex and dangerous. The Supreme Court invited both the NAACP and the southern states to return to argue for the proper implementation timetable. In *Brown II* (1955) the Court declared that states should work "with all deliberate speed" to integrate black and white students. Realizing not all schools could integrate immediately, the *Brown II* order empowered U.S. district court judges to determine compliance locally on a case-by-case basis.

The southern response to the decision ranged from civil dissent to violent massive resistance. Southerners began a campaign to impeach members of the Supreme Court and quickly promised to defy the order. In all, 101 southern members of Congress signed the Southern Manifesto, a document denouncing the ruling and promising to use all legal means to maintain "separate but equal" as the status quo. Racist organizations such as the Ku Klux Klan revived, and the White Citizens Council—sometimes referred to as "the white-collar Klan"— was born. Most school administrators across the segregated South stalled while a few brave African Americans enrolled in token compliant school districts. Another decade passed before congressional legislation brought meaningful integration and full compliance with the *Brown* order.

Civil Rights in Congress

Over the next decade, Congress struggled but succeeded in passing legislation to fulfill the promise of the Fifteenth Amendment, to prevent discrimination in employment, and to enforce the school integration order. The NAACP had more than 300,000 members in the late 1950s, and other grassroots movements were visibly pushing for equality. The Urban League, the Congress on Racial Equality (CORE), and the Southern Christian Leadership Conference (SCLC) headed by Martin Luther King Jr. also petitioned Congress to enact laws to bring equality to African Americans. In the spring of 1956, more than 2,000 delegates from various civil rights organizations traveled to Washington for a national convention on civil rights.

President Eisenhower had a less than aggressive record on civil rights, and the NAACP did not see him as an ally. Though many may recall Eisenhower's order to send the 101st Airborne into Little Rock to enforce a desegregation order, he is also remembered for criticizing Chief Justice Earl Warren's *Brown* ruling. In his January 1957 State of the Union address, he failed to note that four Montgomery, Alabama, churches had been bombed the night before.

In his second term, however, the president advocated for a civil rights bill. The proposal would create a civil rights commission to investigate voter discrimination, establish a civil rights division within the U.S. Justice Department, empower the attorney general to sue noncompliant school districts refusing to desegregate, and protect African Americans' right to vote in federal elections. After some debate (and by a vote of 286–126), the House passed a modified version that accomplished three of Eisenhower's four goals; not until passage of a later, more comprehensive law would the attorney general be able to sue noncompliant school districts.

Source: A. Y. Owen / Getty Images

Soldiers from the 101st Airborne division were sent to protect students during a desegregation order in Little Rock, Arkansas.

Passing the bill in the Senate was a much more difficult task. Recall the Senate's filibuster of anti-lynching bills. Now, with Mississippi's James Eastland chairing the Senate Judiciary Committee, the bill had little chance making it out of committee. However, a handful of southern senators—Lyndon Johnson among them—maneuvered the bill to passage. On August 29, the **1957 Civil Rights Act** passed the Senate following the longest filibuster in history.

The passage of this act proved northern Democrats and Republicans could work together to overcome southern obstructionism. Over the next few years, a series of organized protests, the rise and fall of a presidential ally, and national media attention to white-on-black violence in the South brought the most sweeping civil rights package in American legislative history.

Outlawing Discrimination

The civil rights movement had a pivotal year in 1963, with both glorious and horrific consequences. On the one hand, James Meredith, a 29-year-old black man, enrolled in the University of Mississippi, Martin Luther King assisted the grassroots protests in Birmingham, and more than 200,000 people gathered in the nation's capital for the March on Washington. On the other hand, Mississippi NAACP leader Medgar Evers was shot and killed, Meredith's entrance into Ole Miss was only possible with the help of a federal escort, and in Birmingham, brutal police chief Bull Connor turned fire hoses and police dogs on peaceful African-American protesters.

President Kennedy As these events unfolded, President John F. Kennedy had a change of heart that made him a strong ally for civil rights leaders. He had avoided the topic in the 1960 campaign and let Cold War concerns push civil rights to the bottom of his agenda. However, the president's brother, Robert Kennedy, the nation's attorney general, witnessed violent, ugly confrontations between southern civil rights leaders and brutal state authorities. It was Robert who persuaded President Kennedy to alter his views. JFK began hosting black leaders at the White House and embraced victims of the violence. By mid-1963, Kennedy buckled down to battle for a comprehensive civil rights bill. Kennedy's empathy for the plight of blacks, later followed by President Johnson's commitment to the civil rights cause, proved crucial to the enforcement of ideas written into the Reconstruction amendments a century earlier.

The White House Bill Kennedy addressed Congress on June 11, 1963, informing the nation of the legal remedies of his proposal. "They involve," Kennedy stated, "every American's right to vote, to go to school, to get a job, and to be served in a public place without arbitrary discrimination." Kennedy's bill became the center of controversy over the next year and became the most sweeping piece of civil rights legislation to date. The proposal barred unequal voter registration requirements and prevented discrimination in public accommodations. It empowered the attorney general to file suits against discriminating institutions, such as schools, and to withhold federal funds from noncompliant programs. Finally, it outlawed discriminatory hiring practices.

As Kennedy began to push for this omnibus bill, he faced several dilemmas. How strong should it be? The president had served in both the House and the Senate and knew the difficult path for such a controversial bill becoming a law. Should he put forth a fairly moderate bill that had better chances of passage, or should he push forward with a stronger civil rights proposal that the NAACP, Urban League, and SCLC desired? Should the process begin in the House or the Senate? And where exactly was the nation on civil rights?

Civil Rights Act of 1964 By this point, nationwide popular opinion favored action for civil rights. In one poll, 72 percent of the nation believed in residential integration, and a full 75 percent believed in school integration. Kennedy's popularity, however, was dropping; his 66 percent approval rating had sunk below 50 percent. The main controversy in his plan was the bill's public accommodations provision. Many Americans— even those opposed to segregation in the public sphere—still believed in a white shop owner's legal right to refuse service to a black patron. But Kennedy held fast to what became known as Title II of the law and sent the bill to Capitol Hill on June 19, 1963.

Days later, Attorney General Robert Kennedy arrived to the House Judiciary Committee's hearing. The House was the preferred starting ground for this controversial measure, largely because the Senate Judiciary Committee was known as the "graveyard for civil rights proposals."

Public Opinion By mid-1963, the national media had vividly presented the civil rights struggle to otherwise unaffected people. Shocking images of racial violence published in the *New York Times* and national newsweeklies such as *Time* and *Life* were eye-opening. Television news broadcasts that showed violence at Little Rock, standoffs at southern colleges, slain civil rights workers, and Bull Connor's aggressive Birmingham police persuaded northerners to care more about the movement. Suddenly the harsh, unfair conditions of the South were very real to the nation. In a White House meeting with black labor leader A. Phillip Randolph and Martin Luther King, John Kennedy reportedly joked when someone criticized Connor, "I don't think you should be totally harsh on Bull Connor. After all, Bull Connor has done more for civil rights than anyone in this room."

Johnson Takes Over Soon after Kennedy had championed the cause of civil rights, he was slain by a gunman in Dallas on November 22, 1963. Within an hour, Lyndon Johnson was sworn in as the thirty-sixth president. Onlookers and black leaders wondered how the presidential agenda might change. Johnson had supported the 1957 Civil Rights Act, but only after he moderated it. Civil rights leaders hadn't forgotten Johnson's southern roots nor the fact that he and Kennedy had not seen eye to eye.

Fortunately, President Johnson took the helm and privately told two of his top aides that the first priority would be passage of Kennedy's bill. As Johnson and other Democratic leaders drafted his speech for his first televised presidential address, they paid tribute to Kennedy by supporting his civil rights package. "No memorial oration or eulogy could more eloquently honor President Kennedy's memory," Johnson stated to the nation, "than the earliest passage of the civil rights bill for which he fought so long." Days later, on Thanksgiving, Johnson promoted the bill again: "For God made all of us, not some of us, in His image. All of us, not just some of us, are His children."

Johnson was very likely a much better shepherd for this bill than Kennedy would have been. Johnson, having been a leader in the Congress, was skilled at both negotiation and compromise. He had a better chance as the folksy, towering Texan than Kennedy would have had as the elite, overly polished, and often arrogant patriarch. Johnson was notorious for "the treatment," an up-close-and-personal technique of muscling lawmakers into seeing things his way. Johnson beckoned congressmen to the White House for close face-to-face persuasion that some termed "nostril examinations."

With LBJ's support, the bill had a favorable outlook in the House; it was more representative of popular opinion and more dominated by northerners. On February 10, after the House had debated for less than two weeks and with a handful of amendments, the House passed the bill 290 to 130.

The fight in the Senate was much more difficult. A total of 42 senators added their names as sponsors of the bill. Northern Democrats, Republicans, and the Senate leadership formed a coalition behind the bill which made passage of this law possible. After a 14-hour filibuster by West Virginia's Robert C. Byrd, a cloture vote (page 226) was finally taken. The final vote came on June 19 when the bill passed by 73 to 27, with 21 Democrats and six Republicans in dissent.

Civil Rights Act of 1964
• Banned discrimination in public accommodations
• Outlawed discrimination in hiring based on race, color, religion, sex, or national origin
• Cut off federal funding for discriminating organizations, including schools
• Empowered the U.S. Department of Justice to initiate suits against noncompliant programs

Is That Constitutional? *Heart of Atlanta Motel v. United States* (1964)

Does the commerce clause give Congress the authority to require a proprietor to accept all patrons?

That was the question in *Heart of Atlanta Motel v. United States* (**1964**). Congress had just passed the Civil Rights Act when a Georgia motel owner refused service to African Americans and challenged the law. He claimed that the new law exceeded Congress's authority and violated his constitutional right to operate his private property as he saw fit. In debating the bill, Congress asserted that its power over interstate commerce granted it the right to legislate in this area. Most of this motel's customers had come across state lines. By a vote of 9–0, the Court agreed with Congress. In the companion case of *Katzenbach v. McLung*, the Court also decided that a small, essentially intrastate restaurant was still subject to the law because many of the restaurant's supplies came from out of state.

Focus on the Franchise

The 1964 Civil Rights Act addressed discrimination in voting registration but lacked the necessary provisions to fully guarantee African Americans the vote. Before World War II, about 150,000 black voters were registered throughout the South, about 3 percent of the region's black voting-age population. In 1964, African-American registration in the southern states varied from 6 to 66 percent but averaged 36 percent.

Twenty-fourth Amendment In 1962, Congress passed the **Twenty-fourth Amendment**, which outlaws the poll tax in any federal, primary, or general election. At the time, only four states still charged such a tax. By January of 1964, the required number of states had ratified it. The amendment did not address any taxes for voting at the state or local levels, but the Supreme Court ruled those unconstitutional in 1966.

Selma Many loopholes to the Fifteenth Amendment had been dismantled, yet intimidation and literacy tests still limited the number of registered African-American voters. Martin Luther King Jr. had focused attention on Selma, Alabama, a town where blacks made up about 50 percent of the population but only 1 percent of registered voters. Roughly 9,700 whites voted in the town compared to only 325 blacks. To protest this inequity, King organized a march from Selma to Alabama's capital, Montgomery. Alabama state troopers violently blocked the mostly black marchers at the Edmund Pettus Bridge as they tried to cross the Alabama River. Mounted police beat these activists and fired tear gas into the crowd. Two northerners died in the incident.

Again the media offered vivid images that brought great attention to the issue of civil rights. President Johnson had handily won the election, and the Democratic Party again dominated Congress. In a televised speech before Congress, Johnson introduced his voting rights bill, ending with a line that defined the movement: "We shall overcome."

Voting Rights Act of 1965 The **Voting Rights Act** was signed into law on August 6, 1965, one hundred years after the Civil War. It passed with greater ease than the 1964 Civil Rights Act. The law empowered Congress and the federal government to oversee state elections in southern states. It addressed or "covered" states that used a "test or device" to determine voter qualifications or any with less than 50 percent of its voting-age population actually registered to vote. The policy effectively ended the literacy test.

BY THE NUMBERS Registered African-American Voters Before and After the 1965 Voting Rights Act		
	1964	**1971**
Alabama	18%	54%
Arkansas	42%	81%
Florida	51%	54%
Georgia	28%	64%
Louisiana	32%	56%
Mississippi	6%	60%
North Carolina	44%	43%
South Carolina	33%	45%
Tennessee	66%	65%
Virginia	38%	52%

What do the numbers show? What impact did the 1965 Voting Rights Act have on black voter registration? Which states had the lowest voter registration before the law? Which states experienced major increases in registration? Is there a regional trend regarding registration among these southern states?

The law also required these states to ask for **preclearance** before they could require any new voter qualifications. The controversial preclearance provision empowered the U.S. Justice Department to be a watchdog for the Fifteenth Amendment. If southern states attempted to invent new, creative loopholes to diminish black suffrage, the federal government could stop them.

Impact The Voting Rights Act was the single greatest improvement for African Americans in terms of access to the ballot box. The law shifted the registration burden from the victims to the perpetrators. Under the 1957 Civil Rights Act, the victim had to prove the discrimination and could only do so in relation to federal elections. By 1967, black voter registration in six southern states increased from about 30 to more than 50 percent. African Americans soon held office in greater numbers. Within five years of the law's passage, several states saw marked increases in their numbers of registered voters. In fact, in 1971, the same southern states averaged over 50 percent for registered black voters. The original law expired in 1971, but Congress has renewed the Voting Rights Act several times, most recently in 2006.

More recent, racially charged voting rights controversies have arisen around a Supreme Court decision on part of the Voting Rights Act and the fairness of voter identification laws. Remember, the preclearance provision of the Voting Rights Act states that any voting district that had a voting test in place and less than 50 percent turnout in 1964 cannot change voting laws—which is usually a state power—without the approval of the Justice Department. Seeking to reclaim local control, Shelby County, Alabama, sued. In a 5–4 ruling in *Shelby County v. Holder*, the Court struck down the formula that determines which districts are covered, stating that it imposes burdens that "must be justified by current needs."

State laws requiring voters to present identification at the voting booth have also brought criticism and constitutional challenges. Since 2011, 13 mostly Republican-dominated states have introduced voting ID laws. Conservative supporters of voter ID laws cite occasional instances of voter fraud and the goal of restoring integrity in election. Liberal opponents say these laws simply create another voting impediment and unfairly disenfranchise the lower socioeconomic groups—minorities, workers, the poor, immigrants—who also typically vote for Democrats. They point out that very little coordinated voter fraud actually goes on in the United States. A 2007 Justice Department study found virtually no proof of organized skewing of elections. A 2014 Loyola Law School study of elections since 2000 found just 31 examples of voter impersonation.

Are these voter ID requirements suppressing the vote? The Brennan Center for Justice says about 25 percent of eligible black voters and 16 percent of Hispanics do not have IDs compared to 9 percent of whites. It's likely that at least some of the 33 to 35 percent of eligible African-American voters who did not participate before the voter ID requirements are among those without IDs. Participation among these groups has generally grown over the period, and voter ID laws could interfere with that growth. At the same time, voting ID laws seemed to serve as a rallying cry against voter suppression and actually help increase turnout. Congressional Quarterly reports that 35 states have some variation of a voter ID law on the books, though some are pending, and more are suspended while in court proceedings.

Fulfilling the Spirit of *Brown*

After gaining civil rights protections and increasing black voting via Congress, interest groups and civil rights activists questioned the effectiveness of the *Brown* decision on schools across the nation. The ruling met with varying degrees of compliance from state to state and from school district to school district. North and South, a great degree of segregation still existed. **De jure segregation** (segregation by law) had been struck down, but **de facto segregation** (segregation by fact) remained.

The *Brown* ruling and the *Brown II* clarification spelled out the Court's interpretation of practical integration, but a variety of reactions followed. To avoid the Court's ruling, school officials created measures such as the **freedom-of-choice plans** that placed the transfer burden on the black student seeking an accepting, modern white school, a rare place indeed. Intimidation, too, prevented the otherwise willing student to ask for a transfer.

In short, "all deliberate speed" had resulted in a deliberate delay. In 1964, only about one-fifth of the school districts in the previously segregated southern states taught whites and blacks in the same buildings. In the Deep South, only 2 percent of the black student population had entered white schools. And in many of those instances, there was but one or two token black students willing to stand up to an unwelcoming school board and face intimidation from bigoted whites. Rarely did a white student request a transfer to a historically black school. Clearly, the intention of the *Brown* ruling had been thwarted.

Bearing the Burden of Brown

Activists and civil rights lawyers took additional cases to the Supreme Court to ensure both the letter and the spirit of the *Brown* ruling. From 1958 until the mid-1970s, a series of lawsuits—most filed by the NAACP and most resulting in unanimous prointegration decisions—brought greater levels of integration in the South and North.

The Little Rock Nine faced violent confrontations as they entered school on their first day at Central High School in 1957. School officials and the state government asked for a delay until tempers could settle and until a safer atmosphere would allow for smoother integration. The NAACP countered in court and appealed this case to the high bench. In *Cooper v. Aaron*, the Court ruled potential violence was not a legal justification to delay compliance with *Brown*.

By the late 1960s, the transfer option had yielded few integration results. In a case out of a New Kent, Virginia, school district, the Court found the transfer option had brought only 15 percent of the black student population to white schools and not one white student requested a transfer to the black schools. In *Green v. County School Board New of Kent County*, the Court ruled the freedom-of-choice plans, by themselves, were not a satisfactory remedy for integration.

BY THE NUMBERS Desegregated Districts 1964		
Percent of African Americans Attending School with Whites		
South	Alabama	0.03
	Arkansas	0.81
	Florida	2.65
	Georgia	0.37
	Louisiana	1.12
	Mississippi	0.02
	North Carolina	1.41
	South Carolina	0.10
	Tennessee	5.33
	Texas	7.26
	Virginia	5.07
Border	Delaware	57.8
	DC	86.0
	Kentucky	62.5
	Maryland	51.7
	Missouri	44.1
	Oklahoma	31.7
	West Virginia	88.1

What do the numbers show? What percentage of African-American students attended with whites? How effective was the *Brown v. Board* ruling in integrating previously segregated schools? What states reached higher integration levels? What kept the percentage of African Americans in traditionally white schools low?

Balancing Enrollments Three years later, in ***Swann v. Charlotte-Mecklenburg* (1971)**, the Supreme Court addressed a federal district judge's solution to integrate this North Carolina school district. The judge had set a mathematical ratio as a goal to achieve higher levels of integration. The district's overall white-to-black population was roughly 71 to 29 percent. So the district judge ordered the school district to assign students to school buildings across town to reflect roughly the same proportion of black to white students in each building. The Supreme Court sanctioned mathematical ratios to achieve school integration in yet another unanimous decision.

Busing The *Swann* opinion ended a generation of litigation necessary to achieve integration, but it did not end the controversy. A popular movement against busing for racial balance sprang up as protesters questioned the placement of students at distant schools based on race. Ironically, though the constitutionality of busing grew out of a southern case, cases from Indianapolis, Dayton, Buffalo, Detroit, and Denver brought much protest, sabotaged buses, and legal means to stop this ruling. President Nixon denounced the ruling. The antibusing movement grew strong enough to encourage the U.S. House of Representatives to pass a constitutional amendment to outlaw busing for racial balance, though the Senate never passed it. White parents in scores of cities transferred their children from public schools subject to similar rulings or relocated their families to adjacent, suburban districts to avoid rulings. This situation, known as **white flight,** became commonplace as inner cities became blacker and the surrounding suburbs became whiter.

Women's Rights

Women's quest for equal rights began formally at the Seneca Falls Convention in 1848, was enhanced with a suffrage amendment, and reached new levels when Congress passed legislation that mandated equal pay, fairness in property and family law, and a more even playing field in education.

The western states, beginning with Wyoming, allowed women to vote in some or all elections. In the late 1800s, women entered the workplace, and they became a valued part of the workforce during World War I. After the war's end, women secured the right to vote. It wasn't until the 1950s and 1960s, however, that women organized to gain full independence, equal protection, and civil liberties.

Seeking Women's Suffrage

Obtaining the franchise was key to altering public policy toward women, and Susan B. Anthony led the way. In 1872, in direct violation of New York law, she walked into a polling place and cast a vote. An all-male jury later convicted her. She authored the passage that would eventually make it into the Constitution decades later as the Nineteenth Amendment.

Women and Industry At the end of the 1800s, industrialization brought large numbers of women into the workplace. They took jobs in urban factories for considerably lower pay than men. Oregon passed a law that set a maximum number of work hours for women, but not for men. The law was largely to prevent harsh supervisors from overworking female employees. In *Muller v. Oregon* (1908), attorney Louis Brandeis, representing Oregon's right to create such a law, presented social science findings that proved a woman's physical makeup made her less suited to work lengthy days in rough conditions. The Court decided the state had a right to create such a law that allowed it to treat women differently from men. This was a bittersweet victory for women. On the one hand, progressives sought to protect the health and safety of women; on the other, this double standard gave lawmakers ammunition to hold back women's advancement and suffrage.

Nineteenth Amendment Suffragists still pressed on. By 1914, 11 states allowed women to vote. In the 1916 election, both major political parties endorsed the concept of women's suffrage in their platforms, and Jeanette Rankin of Montana became the first woman elected to Congress. The following year, however, World War I completely consumed Congress and the nation, and the issue of women's suffrage drifted into the background.

Organized groups pressured President Woodrow Wilson. Suffrage leader Alice Paul had organized public picket lines in the nation's capital. Women were arrested and jailed—usually for minor charges such as disturbing the peace—in the name of seeking a stronger political voice. The perpetual picket lasted for more than a year until President Wilson, after pardoning the arrested suffragists, supported the amendment. The measure passed both houses in 1919 and was ratified as the **Nineteenth Amendment** in 1920.

From Suffrage to Action

What impact did the amendment have on voter turnout for women, how did it impact elections after 1920, and what did it do for the overall quest for women's rights? An in-depth study of a Chicago election from the early 1920s found that 65 percent of potential women voters stayed home, many responding that it wasn't a woman's place to engage in politics or that the act would offend their husbands. Men outvoted women by roughly 30 percent.

Voting laws were not states' only unfair practice. The Supreme Court had ruled that states could prevent women from tending bar, and states were allowed to have all-male juries. The 1960s, however, witnessed advancements for women in the workplace. In 1963, Congress passed the **Equal Pay Act** that required employers to pay men and women the same wage for the same job. The 1964 Civil Rights Act protected women from discrimination in hiring.

In addition, Betty Friedan, the author of *The Feminine Mystique*, encouraged women to speak their minds, to apply for male-dominated jobs, and to organize for equality in the public sphere. Friedan went on to create the **National Organization for Women (NOW)** in 1966.

Women and Equality

In the 1970s, Congress passed legislation to give equal opportunities to women in schools and on college campuses. Pro-equality groups pressed the Court to apply strict scrutiny standards to policies that treated the genders differently. In addition, after *Roe v. Wade* (1973), states could no longer have an outright ban on abortion.

The women's movement, however, fell short of a couple of its goals. The Court never declared that legal gender classification deserves the same level of scrutiny as policies that differentiated classes based on race or national origin. Additionally, women were unable to amend the Constitution to declare absolute equality of the sexes. All in all, though, the 1970s was a successful decade for women gaining legal rights and elevating their status in society.

Title IX Most people agreed that young women should have the same educational opportunities as men. This concept became law with **Title IX** of the Education Amendments of 1972, which amended the 1964 Civil Rights Act. Two congresswomen, Patsy Mink (Democrat, Hawaii) and Edith Green (Democrat, Oregon), introduced the bill, which passed with relative ease. The law states, "No person in the United States shall, on the basis of sex, be excluded from participation in, be denied the benefits of, or be subjected to discrimination under any education program or activity receiving federal financial assistance." This means colleges must offer comparable opportunities to women. Schools don't have to allow females to join football and wrestling teams—though some have—nor do schools have to have precisely the same number of student athletes from each gender. However, any school receiving federal dollars must be cognizant of the pursuits of women in the classroom and on the field and maintain gender equity.

To be compliant with Title IX, colleges must make opportunities available for male and female college students in substantially proportionate numbers based on their respective full-time undergraduate enrollment. Additionally, schools must try to expand opportunities and accommodate the interests of the underrepresented sex.

The controversy over gender equality, especially in college sports, has created a conundrum for many that work in the field of athletics. Fair budgeting and maintaining programs for men and women that satisfy the law has at times been difficult. Some critics of Title IX claim female interest in sports simply does not equal that of young men, and therefore a school should not be required to create a balance. In 2005, the Office of Civil Rights began allowing colleges to conduct surveys to assess student interest among the sexes. Title IX advocates, however, compare procedures like these to the burden of the freedom-of-choice option in the early days of racial integration. Federal lawsuits have resulted in courts forcing Louisiana State University to create women's soccer and softball teams and requiring Brown University to maintain school-funded varsity programs for girls.

In 1972, about 30,000 women competed in college varsity-level athletics. Today, more than five times that many do. When the USA women's soccer team won the World Cup championship in 1999, President Clinton referred to them as the "Daughters of Title IX."

The Right to Choose The year after Title IX passed, the Supreme Court made its landmark *Roe v. Wade* (1973) decision. Many women's groups and the ACLU felt state restrictions on abortion denied a pregnant woman and her doctor the right to make a highly personal and private medical choice. In Texas, where abortion was a crime, prochoice attorneys provided assistance to a pregnant young woman, given the alias of Jane Roe, who sought an abortion.

The Court in *Roe v. Wade* decided that a state cannot deny a pregnant woman the right to an abortion during the first trimester of the pregnancy. In a 7–2 decision, the *Roe* opinion erased or modified statutes in most states, effectively legalizing abortion. Since then, however, the battle over abortion has continued. States can still regulate abortion by requiring brief waiting periods and other restrictions that will be explained in Chapter 14.

Strict Scrutiny Also during the 1970s, women pressed the Supreme Court to give gender-based laws the same level of scrutiny it required of laws that distinguish classes of citizens based on race or national origin. Authorities may find there is a compelling state interest in distinguishing classes of race, but any such law deserves **strict scrutiny**. In 1971, activists looked on as the Supreme Court heard the case of *Reed v. Reed* (1971). In an Idaho case, both the mother and the father of their deceased child wanted to administer the child's will. Idaho law gave preference to the father when both parents made equal claims. Then-ACLU attorney Ruth Bader Ginsburg argued that the law arbitrarily favored men over women and thus created a legal inequity. The Court agreed. The law was struck down because it "establishes a classification subject to scrutiny under the equal protection clause." For the first time, the Court concluded sex-based differences of policy were entitled to some degree of scrutiny. Feminists won this case but felt somewhat of a loss in that the Court did not conclude that gender classifications deserved "strict scrutiny." Ginsburg's brief devoted 46 pages to applying the strict scrutiny standard. Only four of the eight in the majority wanted to make gender a suspect classification.

Five years later, an Oklahoma law was at issue in *Craig v. Boren* (1976). The statute prevented the sale of beer to men under 20 and women under 18. In other words, young women could purchase beer two years before young men could. The Court ruled that this violated the equal protection of the law and that the state would have to set the same drinking age for both men and women. But more importantly, the Court established what has become known as the intermediate or **heightened scrutiny test**.

To this day, the Court has not given the same kind of deference to laws that create classes of gender as it has to those that distinguish people of different races and has instead offered a **reasonableness standard** for treating the sexes differently. For example, it is deemed reasonable for the federal government to require men, but not women, to register for the military draft and to assign men, but not women, to combat roles in the armed services.

Equal Rights Amendment Feminists and their supporters also fell short of adding the **Equal Rights Amendment** to the Constitution. Alice Paul, suffragist and founder of the National Woman's Party, actually managed to get the Equal Rights Amendment introduced into Congress in 1923. The proposed amendment stated, "Equality of rights under the law shall not be denied on account of sex," and gave Congress power to enforce this. The amendment was introduced in every session of Congress with various degrees of support until 1972, when it passed both the House and the Senate. Both major parties supported the amendment. Thirty of the 38 states necessary to ratify the amendment approved the ERA within one year. At its peak, 35 states had ratified the proposal, but when the chance for full ratification expired in 1982, the ERA failed.

Why would anyone vote against the idea of equality of the sexes? Several reasons will explain what seems to be an unfair position. Though it was easy for Congress to reach the two-thirds requirement, it was hard to overcome the concerns of traditionalists and conservatives on treating women equally. Policymakers concerned about the military feared that an absolute equality in military affairs, such as the draft, coed bunking of men with women, and other potentially delicate matters made the ERA an unfavorable scenario. The *Roe v. Wade* decision, though seen as a victory among feminists, was not approved by masses of people in the 1970s. The *Roe* decision likely harmed the credibility of the ERA's allies, such as NOW and the ACLU. Finally, the proposition of absolute equality caused opponents to argue the amendment might hurt women, especially in cases involving assault, alimony, and child custody. Though women had gained equality on so many policy fronts, the Equal Rights Amendment was unable to pass.

Women have continually become more involved in the political process. Since 1980, women have outvoted men by small margins in national turnouts. In the 2012 election, women outvoted men by 6 points. About 55 percent of women voted Democrat, and 52 percent of men voted Republican.

Gay Rights and Equality

Like African Americans and women, gays and lesbians have been discriminated against and have therefore sought legal enforcement of equality. The state and federal governments had long set policies that limited the freedoms and liberties of gays. In the 1950s, some state and local authorities closed gay bars and prevented liquor sales to gays. Meanwhile, the military intensified its exclusion of homosexuals. It wasn't until 1973 that psychiatrists removed homosexuality as a mental disorder from their chief diagnostic manual.

Throughout the 1970s and 1980s, to seek legal protections and gain a political voice, homosexuals began publicly proclaiming their sexual identity. Governments make a host of legal decisions regarding sexual behaviors, relationships, and family law. When states must define and regulate marriage, morality, public health, adoption, and wills, controversy is likely to follow. State and federal legal definitions also may determine the way gay couples are allowed to file their taxes.

Debates regarding these issues are extremely complex, with a wide array of overlapping constitutional principles. The states' police powers and the individual's right to self-expression, privacy, and equal protection under the law are all at stake. Federalism and geographic mobility intensify the issue. To what degree should the federal government intervene in governing marriage, which is a reserved power of the states? After all, when affected people move from one state to another, differing state laws concerning marriage, adoption, and inheritance can bring legal standoffs when the Constitution's full-faith-and-credit clause and the states' reserved powers principle are at odds.

The LGBT (lesbian, gay, bisexual, and transgender) community has fought for and earned the legal rights to intimacy and military service. Some states and localities have passed antidiscrimination laws that prevent employers from discriminating against gays. Many states have legalized some form of same-sex marriage. The initial states that legalized gay marriage did so after court orders. More recently, state legislatures and statewide ballot initiatives have done so. In many localities, a confusing legal situation still exists in terms of when gays can adopt a child, enter into matrimony, and serve in the Armed Forces. Courts and legislatures have partially aided gays in their quest for equal protection, but recent polling data and statewide elections show that America has not yet reached consensus on this issue.

Seeking Legal Intimacy

Traditionalists responded to the growing visibility of gays by passing laws that criminalized homosexual behavior. Though so-called antisodomy laws had been around for more than a century, it was not until the 1970s when state laws were passed that specifically criminalized same-sex relations and behaviors and subjected them to prosecution. Georgia's law, which outlawed sodomy for both gays and heterosexuals, was tested in the U.S. Supreme Court in the case of *Bowers v. Hardwick* (1986). The fact that the law applied to anyone committing the act made it difficult to prove an equal protection violation, so Michael Hardwick's attorney emphasized his client's right to privacy. The Court was divided. Can a state regulate such behavior as part of its police powers? Or is this kind of activity instead protected by the same privacy principles emphasized in other opinions?

The Court ruled in a 5–4 decision that a state's authority over sexual behavior superseded any claims to privacy in this instance. Justice Harry Blackmun, who authored the *Roe* opinion, wrote a vigorous dissent in which he declared that preventing the most private forms of sexual intimacy was beyond government's legal reach.

Lawrence v. Texas The Court heard the issue again and reversed itself in the case of ***Lawrence v. Texas*** (2003). Law enforcement officers had entered John Lawrence's home based on a reported weapons disturbance only to discover homosexual activity. The Texas law declared, "a person commits an offense if he engages in deviate sexual intercourse with another individual of the same sex." Lawrence's attorneys argued that the equal protection clause voided this law because the statute specifically singled out gays and lesbians. The Court agreed. It had changed its makeup since 1986, adding a few judges who were more open to the idea of gay equality. Writing for the majority, Justice Anthony Kennedy stated, "*Bowers* was not correct when it was decided, and it is not correct today." This decision further opened the door for gay rights activists to seek legal same-sex marriage in the courts.

Culture Wars of the 1990s

The battle between the religious right—those social conservatives who coalesced in the early 1980s around an anti-*Roe*, pro-family values platform—and the social liberals of the Democratic party created major friction between gays and traditionalists. These competing interests continue to battle over who should serve in the military and in what capacity, to what degree gays and lesbians should be protected, and which organizations can lawfully exclude gays.

Gays in the Military The U.S. Armed Forces has addressed the issue of gays within its ranks since the creation of the United States. In 1917, the War Department made sodomy illegal. In 1949, the military banned any "homosexual personnel" and began discharging known homosexuals from service. Over recent years, high-ranking officers and the civilian personnel in the Pentagon have spoken on the impact—real or perceived—that homosexuals would have on the military's morale, unit cohesion, discipline, and combat readiness.

The issue became heated once again during the 1992 presidential election when Democratic candidate Bill Clinton promised to end the ban on gays in the military. Clinton won the election, but as president, he soon discovered that neither commanders nor the rank and file welcomed the idea of reversing the ban. In a controversy that mired the first few months of his presidency, President Clinton compromised as the Congress passed the **"don't ask, don't tell"** policy. This rule mandated that the military be kept in the dark about the private lifestyles of its personnel. It prevented the military from asking new recruits about their sexual orientation and put a stop to unworthy investigations. In short, "don't ask, don't tell" was meant to cause both sides to ignore the issue and focus on defending the country. The debate continued for 17 years. More recent surveys conducted among military personnel and leadership have shown a more favorable response to the idea of allowing gays to serve openly. During the lame duck Congress of December 2010, and with President Obama's support, the House and Senate voted to remove the "don't ask, don't tell" policy so members of the LGBT community can openly serve their country.

Discrimination Gays have faced discrimination in the workforce and in the private sector as well. During the 1960s Civil Rights Movement, the federal government had a hard time outlawing discrimination from the private sector because the Fourteenth Amendment's equal protection clause does not prohibit nongovernmental discrimination. In the 1970s and 1980s, states and cities began passing laws to prevent discrimination against homosexuals. These policies surfaced in urban areas and in states with higher numbers of gay residents. Conservatives argued that these policies created a special class for the gay community and were thus unequal and unconstitutional.

In 1992, Colorado passed a state constitutional amendment that disallowed the state or any of its political bodies to enact a policy that defined homosexuals with minority status in order to claim discrimination. This amendment prevented cities from protecting gays. The amendment was challenged in the Supreme

Court in *Romer v. Evans* (1996). The Court ruled that the new policy ran afoul of the U.S. Constitution because it singled out homosexuals for unequal treatment.

The Court, however, did not stop private organizations from discriminating against gays. When scoutmaster James Dale was discovered to be homosexual, the Boy Scouts of America quickly invoked its policy and dismissed Dale. He sued, arguing the Boy Scouts, though nongovernmental, amounted to a public accommodation under the state's civil rights acts. Dale won at the state level, but after the Boy Scouts appealed, the U.S. Supreme Court disagreed. It upheld the Boy Scouts' right to create and enforce its own policies with regard to membership under free speech and free association ideals.

Same-Sex Marriage

While Dale failed to secure equal treatment from the Boy Scouts, other activists pursued gaining the right to marry. Even before the *Lawrence* decision, few states enforced their sodomy statutes. Thus, gay partners lived with one another yet lacked formal legal recognition and the legal benefits that come with a state-sanctioned marriage. Gays and lesbians believe they deserve the same recognition of marriage as do straight men and women. Since the founding, states have defined and regulated marriage. The states set age limits, marriage license requirements, divorce law, and other policies. If members of the LGBT community could legally marry, they could begin to enjoy the benefits granted to those in heterosexual marriages: purchasing a home together, accessing the same inheritance law, and securing spousal employee benefits. In order for this to happen, states would have to change their marriage statutes. Advocates of traditional marriage supported the 1996 congressional **Defense of Marriage Act (DOMA)**, which keeps the power to define marriage at the state level and declares states need not recognize same-sex unions from other states. The law also barred federal recognition of same-sex marriage for purposes of social security, federal income tax filings, and other points of law.

The first notable litigation occurred in 1971 when Minnesota's highest court heard a challenge to the state's refusal to issue a marriage license. The state court dismissed the plaintiff's argument that preventing gays from marrying paralleled state laws preventing interracial marriage, which the Supreme Court's struck down. "In common sense and constitutional sense," the state court said, "there is a clear distinction between a marital restriction based merely on race and one based upon the fundamental difference in sex." This opinion also relied on the simple definitions from *Webster's Dictionary* and *Black's Law Dictionary* to uphold the legislature's definition.

These may seem like simple sources for courts to consult, but this issue is very basic: should the state legally recognize same-sex partnerships, and if so, should the state refer to it as "marriage"? Most contend that gay couples deserve equal access and should not be discriminated against in the workplace. However, most also see marriage as a union of one man and one woman. Thus, in general, many are ready to afford equal protection of the law to gay couples, but many more refrain from placing the label of "marriage" on the relationship.

Vermont was the first state to legally recognize same-sex relationships. The process there started in the state court system and reached a pinnacle when the Vermont Supreme Court ruled the traditional marriage statute violated the state's constitution. The legislature then passed Vermont's "civil unions" law, which declared that gay couples have "all the same benefits, protections and responsibilities under law ... as are granted to spouses in a civil marriage."

The 2004 Ballot Initiatives This law, and a national push for same-sex marriage, encouraged conservatives in 11 states to counter with ballot measures in November of 2004. Most of these statewide initiatives added to their respective state constitutions a distinct definition of traditional marriage to prevent state courts from overturning general marriage statutes. President George W. Bush supported the movement and, in his pursuit of a second term, called for a national constitutional amendment to do the same. Conservatives turned out on election day to pass these various ballot issues and to re-elect Bush.

Since the 2004 elections, however, more states have legalized same-sex marriage than have ruled it out, and public opinion has become increasingly accepting of it. Several court decisions in state and federal courts have struck down state statutes outlawing same-sex marriage. Citizens responded with statewide initiatives to reinstate traditional marriage only and campaigned to oust state judges who ruled in favor of gay marriage. Activists on both sides of this issue continue to challenge laws in federal courts based on the equal protection, full-faith-and-credit, and reserved powers clauses. A handful of legislatures have voted to legalize gay marriage as have some statewide initiatives. In 2012, the Supreme Court ruled the federal Defense of Marriage Act unconstitutional and thus made federal employees eligible for marriage benefits in states where same-sex marriage is legal. During this time, public opinion "has solidified," according to Gallup, just above 50 percent in favor of legalizing same-sex marriage. Until the Supreme Court makes a nationwide ruling, however, the states and various courts will develop and define this policy.

Affirmative Action

Affirmative action is the label placed on institutional efforts to diversify by race or gender. Presidents Kennedy and Johnson helped define the term as they developed policy in the hope of creating an equal environment for the races. Both men knew that merely overturning "separate but equal" would not bring true equality. Kennedy issued an executive order to create the Committee on Equal Employment Opportunity and mandated that federal projects "take affirmative action" to ensure hiring free of racial bias. Johnson took it a step further in his own executive order requiring federal contractors to "take affirmative action" in hiring prospective minority contractors and employees. President Johnson also said in a speech at Howard University, "You do not take a man who for years has been hobbled by chains, liberate him, bring him to the starting line of a race, saying, 'you are free to compete with all the others,' and still justly believe you have been completely fair."

Seeking Diversity

Civil rights organizations, progressives, and various institutions agree with Kennedy's ideas and Johnson's noble statements. The federal government, states, colleges, and private companies have echoed these sentiments in their hiring and admissions practices. Yet, affirmative action has been mired in controversy since the term was coined.

Two current schools of thought generally follow a pro- and anti-affirmative action line, though neither willingly accepts those labels. One is that our government institutions and society should follow the *Brown* and *Reed* decisions and be blind to issues of race and gender. Another group, influenced by feminists and civil rights organizations, asks government and the private sector to create policies that will create parity by elevating those who have been discriminated against in the past.

These two groups have divergent views on college admissions and hiring practices. Colleges and companies have set aside spots for applicants with efforts to accept or hire roughly the same percent of minorities that exist in a locality or in the nation. Institutions that use such numeric standards refer to these as targets, while those opposed call them **quotas**.

Supreme Court and Affirmative Action The issue of affirmative action came to a head in the decision in ***Regents of the University of California v. Bakke*** (1978). This case addressed the UC-Davis medical school and its admission policy. The school took in 100 applicants annually and had reserved 16 spots for minorities and women. Alan Bakke, a white applicant, was denied admission and sued to contest the policy. He and his lawyers discovered that his test scores and application in general were better than some of the minorities and women who were admitted ahead of him. He

Source: Mike Keefe, InToon.com

Affirmative action policies have created tricky problems of constitutional interpretation. What point does the cartoonist make about these problems?

argued that the university violated the equal protection clause and denied his admission because of his race.

A Gray Area of Law In this reverse-discrimination case, the Court sided with Bakke in a narrow 5–4 ruling, leaving the public and policymakers wondering what was constitutional and what was not. As far as mandatory quotas are concerned, this case made them unconstitutional. Yet the Court, through its nine different opinions (all justices gave an interpretation), made it clear that the concept of affirmative action was permitted, provided the assisted group had suffered past discrimination and the state has a compelling governmental interest in assisting this group. Clearly, recruitment of particular groups could continue, but government institution could not be bound by hard and fast numeric quotas.

The ruling was a victory for those who believed in equality of opportunity, but it by no means ended the debate. Since *Bakke*, the Court has upheld a law that set aside 10 percent of federal construction contracts for minority-owned firms. It overturned a similar locally sponsored set-aside policy. Then it upheld a federal policy that guaranteed a preference to minorities applying for broadcast licenses.

Legal scholars and government students alike are confused by this body of law. Quotas have a hard time passing the strict scrutiny test that is applied to them. To give preference, a pattern of discriminatory practices must be proven. And federal affirmative action programs usually withstand greater scrutiny because of particulars in the Fourteenth Amendment.

The Court heard two more cases regarding admissions policies from the University of Michigan. The Michigan application process worked on a complex numeric point system that instantly awarded 20 extra points for ethnic minorities including African Americans, Hispanics, and Native Americans. By contrast, an excellent essay was awarded only one point. Though the school did not use a quota system per se, the point breakdown resembled something rather close to what *Bakke* banned. The Court reaffirmed its 1978 stance and made it plain by rejecting the University of Michigan's use of fixed quotas for individual applicants. In 2012, the Court ruled against race-based admissions at the University of Texas, arguing that they did not pass strict judicial scrutiny.

REFLECT ON THE ESSENTIAL QUESTION

Essential Question: *How have minorities and women sought equality and fair treatment from our government institutions?* On separate paper, complete a chart like the one below to gather details to answer that question.

Groups Seeking Equality	Methods Used and Legal Milestones

THINK AS A POLITICAL SCIENTIST: ANALYZE, INTERPRET, AND SYNTHESIZE INFORMATION ON AFRICAN-AMERICAN SUFFRAGE

When you **analyze** a source, you closely examine the components that make it up. For example, think about how Chapter 13 is constructed. To analyze the larger subject of the chapter topic "Civil Rights," the chapter presents four main subtopics: African-American rights, women's rights, gay rights, and affirmative action. Each is presented in the context of past history, evolving legislation, and the present day.

When you **interpret** a source, you employ critical thinking skills to better understand its meaning. When using historical sources, you might be tempted to believe most of what an author says as undisputed fact. But some sources may be simplistic, invalid, or biased, whether consciously or unconsciously. When interpreting historical material, ask the following questions: (1) Is the source reliable and credible? (2) Are there obvious biases in the source? (3) What *facts* can you take from the source? (4) In what historical context was the source created?

When you **synthesize** information, you gather together relevant facts, ideas, and perspectives you have gleaned from various sources and combine that information with any prior knowledge you may have had in order to form a new, deeper understanding.

Practice: Analyze, interpret, and synthesize information from the Fifteenth Amendment (page 329), the 1965 Voting Rights Act at at www.ourdocuments.gov, and the table below. Then, referring to information from these sources, write an explanation of the change in southern African-American voter registration during the period shown in the table.

African-American Voter Registration in Southern States			
State	**1960**	**1964**	**1968**
Alabama	14%	23%	57%
Arkansas	38%	54%	68%
Florida	39%	64%	62%
Georgia	n/a	39%	56%
Louisiana	40%	32%	59%
Mississippi	6%	7%	59%
North Carolina	38%	47%	55%
South Carolina	n/a	39%	51%
Tennessee	64%	69%	73%
Texas	34%	58%	83%
Virginia	23%	46%	58%

From Piven, et al. *Keeping Down the Black Vote,* 2009

KEY TERMS, NAMES, AND EVENTS

affirmative action

Brown v. Board of Education of Topeka, Kansas (1954)

Civil Rights Act (1875)

Civil Rights Act (1957)

Civil Rights Act (1964)

Civil Rights Cases (1883)

de facto segregation

Defense of Marriage Act (DOMA)

de jure segregation

disenfranchise

"don't ask, don't tell"

Equal Pay Act (1963)

equal protection clause

Equal Rights Amendment

Fifteenth Amendment

Fourteenth Amendment

freedom-of-choice plans

grandfather clause

Heart of Atlanta Motel v. United States (1964)

heightened scrutiny test

Jim Crow laws

Lawrence v. Texas (2003)

literacy test

National Association for the Advancement of Colored People (NAACP)

National Organization for Women (NOW)

Nineteenth Amendment

Plessy v. Ferguson (1896)

poll taxes

preclearance

quotas

reasonableness standard

Regents of the University of California v. Bakke (1978)

"separate but equal"

strict scrutiny

Swann v. Charlotte-Mecklenburg (1971)

Thirteenth Amendment

Title IX

Twenty-fourth Amendment

Voting Rights Act (1965)

white flight

white primary

MULTIPLE-CHOICE QUESTIONS

1. All of the following contributed to the success of the civil rights movement EXCEPT
   (A) Earl Warren's role as Chief Justice
   (B) the efforts of the NAACP
   (C) the chairman of the Senate Judiciary Committee
   (D) national media coverage
   (E) President Lyndon Johnson supporting the Voting Rights Act

2. The Supreme Court ruled in *Heart of Atlanta Motel, Inc. v. United States* that Congress can outlaw discrimination in public accommodations based on the Constitution's
   (A) equal protection clause
   (B) supremacy clause
   (C) commerce clause

(D) full-faith-and-credit clause

(E) establishment clause

3. The primary effect of the Supreme Court's decision in *Regents of the University of California v. Bakke* was that

   (A) schools and colleges remained separate but equal

   (B) universities could no longer consider race as a factor in college admissions

   (C) southern schools integrated for the first time

   (D) colleges could no longer use quotas in admissions

   (E) it drastically decreased the number of women and minorities attending college

4. A key difference between the Civil Rights Acts of 1957 and the Civil Rights Act of 1964 is

   (A) one passed into law unanimously, but the other barely passed at all

   (B) in 1957 the president supported the bill, but in 1964 the president vetoed the bill

   (C) the 1957 law empowered the federal government to intervene in federal elections, and the 1964 law created comprehensive antidiscrimination legislation

   (D) most southern congressmen supported the 1957 proposal, while they denounced the 1964 law

   (E) the 1957 law addressed business practices, and the 1964 act addressed fair housing

5. Which of the following Supreme Court decisions gained legal rights for gays and lesbians?

   (A) *Bowers v. Hardwick*

   (B) *Regents of the University of California v. Bakke*

   (C) *Craig v. Boren*

   (D) *Lawrence v. Texas*

   (E) *Boy Scouts of America v. Dale*

6. Which of the following statements is true?

   (A) Race cannot be a factor in determining college admissions.

   (B) All laws must address men and women in the same exact manner.

   (C) No women in the United States could vote before ratification of the Nineteenth Amendment.

   (D) Public accommodations, such as restaurants and hotels, cannot discriminate on the basis of race or gender.

   (E) Private clubs cannot discriminate on the basis of race or gender.

7. The decision in *Swann v. Charlotte-Mecklenburg*
   (A) prevented affirmative action
   (B) integrated schools at the college level
   (C) approved court-ordered racial enrollment ratios which led to busing
   (D) admitted gays into the military
   (E) found the Civil Rights Act of 1957 unconstitutional

8. Which of the following policies extended rights to women in the 1970s?
   I. Equal Rights Amendment
   II. The "strict scrutiny" standard
   III. The *Roe v. Wade* decision
   IV. Title IX
   (A) I
   (B) I and II
   (C) I, II, and III
   (D) I, II, III, and IV
   (E) III and IV

9. Which group is most responsible for integrating the nation's public schools?
   (A) Congress on Racial Equality
   (B) NAACP
   (C) Urban League
   (D) Southern Christian Leadership Council
   (E) White Citizens Council

10. During President Clinton's administration, the Congress established which policy for gays in the military?
    (A) "Don't ask, don't tell"
    (B) Separate but equal
    (C) A ban on homosexuals in the military
    (D) Gay couples in the military can get married
    (E) Gays can join the armed services but are barred from combat

Question

1. Before 1954, several states segregated their citizens according to race. Activists fought a long battle to desegregate schools in the United States before and after the *Brown v. Board of Education* ruling.

   (a) Identify the constitutional provision that allowed states to segregate their citizens.

   (b) Identify the constitutional provision that allowed civil rights activists to overturn racial segregation in the courts.

   (c) Identify two factors that delayed the full implementation of the Supreme Court's *Brown v. Board of Education* school desegregation ruling.

   (d) Explain two factors that have assisted the desegregation process since the *Brown* ruling.

Question

2. Women's rights advocates have sought equality through Congress and through the Supreme Court with varying degrees of success.

   (a) Define the Nineteenth Amendment to the Constitution and explain how the amendment altered the struggle for women's rights.

   (b) Identify and explain one act of Congress that enhanced equality for women and discuss the effect of that act.

   (c) Identify and explain two relevant Supreme Court decisions and discuss how the Court's decisions affected women's quest for equality.

WRITING: AVOID FIRST PERSON

In your responses to questions, establish and maintain a formal style. Avoid using the first-person pronoun "I," which is commonly associated with informal, personal writing. Formal writing also tends to have longer sentences, more academic vocabulary, and a more serious tone than informal writing.

14

Civil Liberties

"Ways someday may be developed by which the government … will be enabled to expose to a jury the most intimate occurrences in the home."
—Justice Louis Brandeis's dissent in *Olmstead v. United States*, 1928

Essential Question: How has the government defined freedoms and protected civil liberties?

Americans have held liberty in high regard since lost liberties spurred the break from Great Britain. The original Constitution includes a few basic protections against government—Congress could pass no bill of attainder and no ex post facto law, and *habeas corpus* could not be suspended in peacetime. Article III guarantees a defendant the right to trial by jury. However, the original Constitution lacked many fundamental protections, so critics and Anti-Federalists pushed for the Bill of Rights to protect civil liberties—those civic rights protected from arbitrary governmental interference or deprivations. The United States has struggled to fully interpret and define phrases such as "free speech," "unreasonable searches," and "cruel and unusual punishments." Citizens, leaders, and courts have interpreted these ideas differently over time. Justice Brandeis's quote above—from his dissent in *Olmstead v. United States*, an early FBI wiretapping case—speaks to his concern for citizens' rights to privacy and protection from government intrusion into the home. This chapter explores that and other civil liberties and how our courts have interpreted them.

A Culture of Civil Liberties

The freedoms Americans enjoy are about as comprehensive as those in any Western democracy. As long as it doesn't violate existing laws, anyone can practice or create nearly any kind of religion. Expressing opinions in public forums or in print is nearly always protected. Just outside the Capitol building, the White House, and Supreme Court, ever-present protestors criticize law, presidential action, and alleged miscarriages of justice without fear of punishment or retribution. Nearly all Americans enjoy a great degree of privacy in their homes, and, unless suspected of some crime, can generally trust that governments will not enter unannounced. When civil liberties violations have occurred, individuals and groups such as the American Civil Liberties Union (ACLU) have challenged them in court. Both liberals and conservatives hold civil liberties dear, although they view them somewhat differently.

Selective Incorporation

All levels of government adhere to most elements of the Bill of Rights, but that wasn't always the case. The Congress passed the Bill of Rights to protect the people from the *federal* government. The First Amendment begins, "Congress shall make no law…" that violates freedoms of religion, speech, press, and assembly. The document then goes on to address additional liberties the Congress cannot take away. Most states had already developed bills of rights with similar provisions, but states did not originally have to follow the national Bill of Rights. Through a process known as **selective incorporation**, the Supreme Court has insisted states must also follow several Bill of Rights provisions through the Fourteenth Amendment's due process clause.

Due Process The right to **due process** dates back to England's Magna Carta (1215), when nobles limited the king's ability to ignore their liberties. Due process ensures fair procedures when the government burdens or deprives an individual. It prevents arbitrary government decisions to avoid mistaken or abusive taking of taxes, fees, land, or freedom from individuals and to ensure that accused persons are given a fair trial. Due process is a fundamental fairness concept that ensures a legitimate government in a democracy. The **Fifth Amendment** declares, among other points, that no person shall be "deprived of life, liberty, or property without due process of law; nor shall private property be taken for public use, without just compensation."

Barron v. Baltimore When wharf owner John Barron arrived in the Supreme Court in 1833, he anticipated relief. The city of Baltimore had diverted a series of streams that lowered water levels in the harbor and damaged Barron's property and much of his business. Barron argued that the Fifth Amendment's "takings clause" entitled him to "just compensation" for his dock, which Baltimore had rendered useless. Barron had lost in the lower courts because Maryland's state constitution had no takings provision. Most would agree that Baltimore caused Barron's financial woes. Chief Justice John Marshall, on the other hand, declared the Bill of Rights restrained the federal, not the state, government, and Barron lost. This precedent made clear that the Bill of Rights, at least for a while, did not restrain state action.

Fourteenth Amendment The ratification of the **Fourteenth Amendment** (1868) in the aftermath of the Civil War changed this precedent. Before the war, southern states had made it a crime to speak out against slavery or to publish antislavery materials. Union leaders questioned the legality of these statutes. During Reconstruction, Union leaders complained that southerners denied African Americans, Unionists, and Republicans basic liberties of free speech, criminal procedure rights, and the right to bear arms. They questioned whether the losing rebel state governments would willingly follow the widely understood principles of due process, especially with regard to freed slaves. Would an accused black man receive a fair and impartial jury at his trial? Could an African-American defendant refuse to testify in court? Could the southern states inflict the same cruel and unusual punishments on freed men

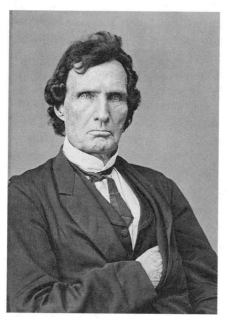

Speaker of the House Thaddeus Stevens (left) and Massachusetts Senator Charles Sumner crafted and led passage of the Fourteenth Amendment to, in part, ensure newly freed African Americans due process of law.

that they had inflicted on slaves? To ensure the states followed these commonly accepted principles in the federal Bill of Rights and in most state constitutions, the House Republicans drafted the most important and far-reaching of the Reconstruction Amendments, the Fourteenth, which declares that "all persons born or naturalized in the United States … are citizens" and that no state can "deprive any person of life, liberty, or property, without due process of law."

Early Incorporation In an 1897 decision, a Chicago rail line sued the city, which had constructed a street across its tracks. The Court held that the newer due process clause compelled Chicago to award just compensation when taking private property for public use.

Later, the Supreme Court declared that the First Amendment prevents states from infringing on free thought and free expression. In a series of cases that addressed state laws designed to crush radical ideas and yellow journalism, the Court began to hold states to First Amendment standards. Benjamin Gitlow, a New York Socialist, was arrested and prosecuted for violating the state's criminal anarchy law. The law prevented advocating a violent overthrow of the government. Gitlow was arrested for writing, publishing, and distributing thousands of copies of pamphlets called the *Left-wing Manifesto* that called for strikes and "class action … in any form."

In one of its first cases, the ACLU appealed Gitlow's case and argued that the due process clause of the Fourteenth Amendment compelled states to follow free speech and free press ideas in the First Amendment. In *Gitlow v. New York*

(1925), the Court actually upheld the law and Gitlow's conviction, but it did address the question of whether or not the Bill of Rights did or could apply to the states. In the majority opinion, the Court said, "for present purposes, we may and do assume that freedom of speech and of the press...are among the fundamental personal rights and liberties protected by the due process clause of the Fourteenth Amendment from impairment by the states." Gitlow went to jail, but the Court put the states on notice.

In 1931 the Court applied its earlier warning. Minnesota had attempted to bring outrageous newspapers under control with a public nuisance law, informally dubbed the Minnesota Gag Law. This statute permitted a judge to stop obscene, malicious, scandalous, and defamatory material. A hard-hitting paper published by the unsavory J. M. Near printed anti-Catholic, anti-Semitic, antiblack, and antilabor stories. Both the ACLU and Chicago newspaper mogul Robert McCormick came to Near's aid on anticensorship principles. The Court did too. In *Near v. Minnesota* it declared that the Minnesota statute "raises questions of grave importance.... It is no longer open to doubt that the liberty of the press ... is within the liberty safeguarded by the due process clause of the Fourteenth Amendment."

It is appropriate that the Court emphasized the First Amendment freedoms early on in the incorporation process. The basic American idea that free religion, speech, and press should be protected from all governments dates back to the founding. In creating the Bill of Rights in 1789, James Madison and others had strongly supported an early draft that stated, "No state shall infringe on the equal rights of conscious, nor the freedom of speech, or of the press." It was the only proposed amendment directly limiting states' authority. As biographer Richard Labunski reveals, Madison called it the most valuable amendment on the list as it was "equally necessary that [these rights] should be secured against the state governments."

In case after case, the Court has required states to guarantee fair and impartial juries, warnings against self-incrimination, free speech, and freedom of religion and to prevent the death penalty under certain circumstances. Though states have incorporated nearly all rights in the document, a few remain exclusively to the federal government.

Rights Not Yet Incorporated
• Third Amendment protections against quartering troops in homes
• Fifth Amendment right to a grand jury indictment in misdemeanor cases
• Seventh Amendment right to jury trials in civil cases
• Eighth Amendment protection against excessive bail

Free Speech and Free Press

Once the Court, through the incorporation doctrine, had required states and localities to follow the First Amendment, it took two generations of cases to define "free speech" and "free press." When does one person's right to free expression violate others' right to peace, safety, or decency? Most precedents and interpretations regarding the media came in the 1960s when the Court addressed libel, the press's access to trials, and federal broadcast regulations. Free speech is not absolute, but both federal and state governments have to show substantial or compelling governmental interest to curb it.

The creators of the First Amendment meant to prevent government censorship. Many revolutionary leaders came to despise the accusation of seditious libel—a charge that resulted in fines and/or jail time for anyone who criticized public officials or government policies. Because expressing dissent in assemblies and in print during the colonial era led to independence and increased freedoms, the members of the first Congress preserved this right as the very first of the amendments.

The Court has not made much distinction between "speech" and "press" and ordinarily provides the same protective standards for both rights. "Speech" includes an array of expressions—actual words, the lack of words, pictures, and actions. An average citizen has as much right to free press as does a professional journalist. The First Amendment does not protect all speech, especially speech that invites danger, that is obscene, or that violates an existing law.

The government has no prerogative of **prior restraint**—the government's right to stop publication in advance—first declared in *Near* and later reaffirmed in *New York Times v. United States* (page 195). Governments cannot suppress a thought from entering the marketplace of ideas just because most people see the idea as repugnant or offensive. A government that can squelch ideas is one that violates the very essence of a free democracy. The Court, however, has never suggested that its reverence for free expression means that all expression should be tolerated at all times under all conditions. In addition to what the federal government prevents on the airwaves, which is discussed in Chapter 8, there are exceptions that allow state and federal governments to limit or punish additional forms of speech.

National Security and Public Danger

One exception is that government can limit speech more in wartime or when national security is threatened. As first explained by Justice Oliver Wendell Holmes in 1919, when speech poses a threat to society, weakens the nation's ability to defend itself, or threatens the safety of citizens, government can step in to curb it.

Clear and Present Danger The first time the Court examined a federal conviction on a free speech claim was in *Schenck v. United States* (1919). As the United States entered World War I, the 1917 Sedition and Espionage Acts prevented publications that criticized the government, advocated treason or insurrection, or brought disloyal behavior in the military. A U.S. district court tried and convicted Charles Schenck, the secretary of the Socialist Party, when he printed 15,000 antidraft leaflets for Philadelphia-area draftees. The government was deeply concerned about the Socialist Party, German Americans, and anyone who questioned America's military draft and war effort.

Schenck appealed the verdict. The Court drew a distinct difference between speech that communicated honest opinion and speech that incited unlawful action. In a unanimous opinion delivered after the war's end, the Court upheld the government's right to define prohibited speech and convict citizens for using it. The question in every case, Justice Holmes wrote, "is whether words ... are of such a nature as to create a clear and present danger that they will bring about the substantive evils that Congress has the right to prevent." Schenck went to prison, as did defendants in five similar cases. The **clear and present danger test** became the balancing act between competing demands of free expression and a government's need to protect a free society.

Free Speech and the Cold War Congress's attempts to suppress speech temporarily subsided but rose again during Cold War threats. In 1949, President Truman's justice department convicted 11 Communist Party leaders under the Smith Act—a law that made advocating the overthrow of any government in the United States a criminal act. After a nine-month trial, the jury convicted the Communists. On appeal, the Supreme Court upheld the conviction in *Dennis v. United States* (1951). Similar trials for Communist leaders a few years later brought the Smith Act back to the Supreme Court. In *Yates v. United States* (1957), it considered two major points. The act made it illegal to organize for the purposes of overthrowing the government. The Court drew a line between advocating a government change in the abstract versus calling for actual illegal action to cause an overthrow. The Court did not toss out the Smith Act, but it overturned these convictions and weakened the Justice Department's efforts to prosecute Communists for expressing unpopular ideas.

Vietnam War Era As the Court softened its restrictions on free speech, Americans became more willing to protest. The 1960s witnessed a revolution in free expression. As support for the Vietnam War waned, young men burned their draft cards to protest the military draft. Congress quickly passed a law to prevent the destruction of these government-issued documents.

David O'Brien burned his Selective Service registration card in front of a Boston courthouse. After his conviction, he appealed to the Supreme Court, arguing that his protest was a symbolic act of speech that government could not infringe. The Court, however, upheld his conviction and sided with the government's right to prevent this behavior in order to protect Congress's authority to raise and support an army. O'Brien was disrupting the draft effort and publicly encouraging others to do the same. Others continued to burn draft cards, but after *United States v. O'Brien* (1968), this symbolic act was not protected.

The clear and present danger standard, however, did not prevent all forms of speech, nor was the claim always a justification for criminal charges. In the late

1960s, the Court refined the standard and held the First Amendment in higher regard. When a Ku Klux Klan member used harsh language at a televised rally in 1969, he was arrested and convicted. On appeal in *Brandenburg v. Ohio* (1969), the Court ruled that the government may not punish a speaker unless it can prove the speech was directed at inciting or producing imminent lawless acts.

Obscenity

Some language and images are so offensive to the average citizen that governments have banned them. Though obscenity is difficult to define, two trends prevail regarding **obscene speech**: the First Amendment does not protect it, and no national standard defines what it is.

In the nineteenth century, some states and later the national government outlawed obscenity. Reacting to published birth control literature, postal inspector and moral crusader Anthony Comstock pushed for the first national antiobscenity law in 1873, which banned the circulation and importation of obscene materials through the U.S. mail. Yet the legal debate since has generally been over state and local ordinances brought before the Supreme Court on a case-by-case basis. The Court has tried to square an individual's right to free speech or press and a community's right to ban filthy and offensive material.

A Transformational Time From the late 1950s until the early 1970s, the Supreme Court heard several appeals by those convicted for obscenity. In *Roth v. United States* (1957), Samuel Roth, a long-time publisher of questionable books, was prosecuted under the Comstock Act. He published and sent through the mail his *Good Times* magazine, which contained partially airbrushed nude photographs. On the same day, the Court heard a case examining a California obscenity law. The Court upheld the long-standing view that both state and federal obscenity laws were constitutionally permissible, because obscenity is "utterly without redeeming social importance." In *Roth*, the Court defined speech as obscene and unprotected when "the average person, applying contemporary community standards," finds that it "appeals to the prurient interest" (having lustful or lewd thoughts or wishes).

The new rule created a swamp of ambiguity that the Court tried to clear up over the following 15 years. Before Roth finished his prison term, the law was on his side. The pornography industry grew apace during the sexual revolution of the 1960s and 1970s. States reacted, creating a battle between those declaring a constitutional right to create or consume risqué materials and local governments seeking to ban smut. The Court struggled to determine this balance. In his frequently quoted phrase from a 1964 case regarding how to distinguish acceptable versus unacceptable pornographic expression, Justice Potter Stewart said, "I know it when I see it." Although the Court could not reach a solid consensus on obscenity, from 1967 to 1971 it overturned 31 obscenity convictions.

In April 1968, Paul Robert Cohen wore a jacket bearing the words, "F — the Draft" while walking into a Los Angles courthouse. Local authorities arrested and convicted him for "disturbing the peace ... by offensive conduct." The Supreme

Court overturned the conviction in *Cohen v. California* (1971). As opposed to its stance on the act of burning a draft card, the Court declared the state could not prosecute Cohen for this particular speech. The phrase on the jacket in no way incited an illegal action. "One man's vulgarity is another's lyric," the majority opinion stated.

Defining Obscenity The conflict continued in ***Miller v. California*** (1973). After a mass mailing promoting adult materials, a number of recipients complained to the police. California authorities prosecuted Marvin Miller under the state's obscenity laws. On appeal, the justices reaffirmed that obscene material was not constitutionally protected, but they modified the *Roth* decision saying in effect that a local judge or jury should define obscenity by applying local community standards. Obscenity is not necessarily the same as pornography, and pornography may or may not be obscene. The following year, the Court overturned Georgia's conviction of a theater owner for showing the film *Carnal Knowledge*. The Court has heard subsequent cases dealing with obscene speech, but the *Miller* test has served as the standard in obscenity cases.

The *Miller* Test
Speech or expression may be obscene if
• the average person applying contemporary community standards finds it appeals to the prurient interest
• it depicts or describes in a patently offensive way sexual conduct specifically defined by state law
• it lacks serious literary, artistic, political, or scientific value

Symbolic Speech

People cannot invoke **symbolic speech** to defend an act that might otherwise be illegal. For example, a nude citizen cannot walk through the town square and claim a right to symbolically protesting textile sweatshops after his arrest for indecent exposure. Symbolic speech *per se* is not an absolute defense in a free speech conflict. That said, the Court has protected a number of symbolic acts or expressions.

In evaluating regulations of symbolic expression, the Court looks primarily at whether the regulation suppresses the content of the message or simply regulates the accompanying conduct. Is the government ultimately suppressing what was being said, or the manner, time, or place in which it was expressed? Compare the *Cohen* and *O'Brien* rulings. In both cases, someone spoke against the Vietnam-era draft. O'Brien burned a government-issued draft card. The Court didn't protect the defendant's speech but rather upheld a law to assist Congress in its conscription powers. Cohen publicly expressed his dislike for the draft with an ugly phrase printed on his jacket, but he did nothing to incite public protest and did not himself refuse to enlist when drafted.

Flag Burning The Court struck down both state and federal statutes meant to prevent desecrating or burning the U.S. flag in *Texas v. Johnson* (1989) and *United States v. Eichman* (1990), respectively. The Court found that these laws serve no purpose other than ensuring a government-imposed political idea—reverence for the flag. (See Chapter 1 for more on these cases.)

Free Speech in Schools Do students have a right to free speech in schools? What if this expression is symbolic? Two important cases help illustrate where students' rights to free expression begin and end. In 1965, Mary Beth Tinker, her brother, and others wore black armbands to their Des Moines, Iowa, school to protest America's war in Vietnam. The school saw this protest as a distraction and a potential problem. The principal instructed the students to remove the armbands. The students, with support from their parents, refused. The school then suspended them.

The Tinkers sued in U.S. district court on free speech grounds and eventually appealed to the Supreme Court. The High Court sided with the Tinkers in 1969, declaring that "students' constitutional rights do not stop at the schoolhouse gate." The decision in ***Tinker v. Des Moines Independent Schools*** upheld this speech because the suspension was intended to quiet their antiwar message.

Source: Granger, NYC

Writing the majority opinion in the Tinker case, Justice Abe Fortas stated that schools could forbid conduct that would "materially and substantially interfere with the requirements of appropriate discipline" but not activities that merely create "the discomfort and unpleasantness that always accompany an unpopular viewpoint."

The Tinkers' protest of a war was a brand of political speech. A different brand of speech was at the center of another case involving a school suspension, **Bethel Schools v. Fraser**, settled in 1986. High school student Matt Fraser gave a speech to a student assembly at his Bethel, Washington, school that showcased student government candidates. In introducing his friend, Fraser delivered a speech riddled with sexual innuendo that caused a roaring reaction and led the school to suspend him.

Fraser challenged his suspension. The Court, after fully analyzing Fraser's sexually suggestive language, upheld the school's punishment. The Court considered the *Tinker* precedent, but unlike the speech in *Tinker*, the speech in this case had no real political value and was designed to entertain an audience of high school students. Students still do not shed their rights at the schoolhouse gates, but neither are they entitled to lewd or offensive speech. A similar case reached the Court in 2007. In Alaska, a student body gathered outside a school to witness and cheer on the Olympic torch as runners carried it by. In a quest for attention, one student flashed a homemade sign that read "BONG HITS 4 JESUS" as the torch passed the school. The student was suspended, and he lost his appeal challenging the suspension. The Court ruled that the school was reasonable to see his sign as promoting illegal drug use.

Fighting Words Can government prevent words that might cause a fight or a breach of the peace? That question was settled in a 1942 case entitled *Chaplinsky v. New Hampshire*. A Jehovah's Witness was distributing religious literature when a crowd formed around him. When police arrived, Chaplinsky called a cop a "damned racketeer" and a "damned fascist." He was then arrested and convicted on a state law against offensive speech or name calling in public. The Court unanimously upheld his conviction and the state's right to prevent such provocative speech.

Commercial Speech Commercial speech receives a lesser degree of protection than noncommercial speech. In the mid-1970s, the Court outlawed a Virginia statute that prevented the public advertising of prescription drug prices. It declared that in a capitalistic free market, there should be a free flow of ideas and information as expressed in the list of drug prices. It also has said that deceptive and misleading advertising, even if not directly false, does not serve any social interest and is therefore not protected. When the Court has upheld commercial speech, it has been in the interest of the audience or consumer, not the advertiser or merchant.

Libel A charge of **libel** refers to false statements that defame someone in print. Much negativity can be printed about someone of a critical, opinionated, or even speculative nature before it qualifies as libel. American courts have typically allowed for a rather high standard of defamation before rewarding a suing party. The main decision that defined the First Amendment's protection of printed speech against the charge of libel was *New York Times v. Sullivan* (1964), discussed fully in Chapter 8. This and subsequent decisions have generally ruled that to win a libel suit in a civil court, the suing party must prove actual damages, that the offending writer either knowingly lied or presented information with a reckless disregard for the truth, and that the writer did so with malicious intent to defame.

Church and State

The First Amendment also guarantees freedom of religion. The Founders wanted to stamp out religious intolerance and to outlaw a nationally sanctioned religion. The Supreme Court did not address congressional action on religion for most of its first century, and it did not examine state policies that affected religion for another generation after that. As the nation became more diverse and more secular over the years, the Supreme Court constructed what Thomas Jefferson called a **"wall of separation"** between church and state. In this nation of varied religions and countless government institutions, however, it is easy for church and state to encroach on each other. Like other interpretations of civil liberties, those addressing free religion are nuanced and sometimes confusing. In more recent days, the Court has addressed laws that regulate the teaching of evolution, the use of school vouchers, and the public display of religious symbols.

Freedom of Religion

Both James Madison and Thomas Jefferson led a fight to oppose a Virginia tax to fund an established state church in 1785. Madison argued that no law should support any true religion nor should any government tax anyone, believer or nonbeliever, to fund a church. During the ratification battle in 1787, Jefferson wrote Madison from Paris and expressed regret that the proposed Constitution lacked a Bill of Rights, especially an expressed freedom of religion. The First Amendment allayed these concerns because it reads in part, "Congress shall make no law respecting an *establishment* of religion, or prohibiting the *free exercise* thereof." In 1802, President Jefferson popularized the phrase "separation of church and state" after assuring Danbury, Connecticut, Baptists that the First Amendment builds a "wall of separation between church and state." Today some citizens want a stronger separation; others want none.

Members of the First Congress included the **establishment clause** to prevent the federal government from establishing a national religion. More recently, the clause has come to mean that governing institutions—federal, state, and local—cannot sanction, recognize, favor, or disregard any religion. The **free exercise clause** prevents governments from stopping religious practices. This clause is generally upheld, unless an unusual religious act is illegal or deeply opposes the interests of the community. Today, these two clauses collectively mean people can practice any religion they want, provided it doesn't violate established law or harm others, and the state cannot endorse or advance one religion over another.

Mormons brought the first freedom of religion issue to the Supreme Court in the case of *Reynolds v. United States* (1879). Under President

Ulysses S. Grant, the federal government pushed to end Mormon polygamy common in the Utah Territory. U.S. marshals rounded up hundreds of Mormons who had violated a congressional antipolygamy law. George Reynolds, secretary to Mormon leader Brigham Young, brought a test case that argued the free exercise clause prevented such law. The Mormons lost, and the Court said the federal government could limit religious practices that impaired the public interest.

The Court Erects a Wall In the 1940s, New Jersey allowed public school boards to reimburse parents for transporting their children to school, even if the children attended parochial schools—those maintained by a church or religious organization. Some argued this constituted an establishment, but in *Everson v. Board of Education* (1947), the Court upheld the law. State law is not meant to favor or handicap any religion. This law gave no money to parochial schools but instead provided funds evenly to parents who transported their children to the state's accredited schools. Preventing payments to parochial students' parents would handicap them. Much like fire stations, police, and utilities, school transportation is a nonreligious service available to all taxpayers.

Though nothing changed with *Everson*, the Court did signal that the religion clauses of the First Amendment applied to the states via the Fourteenth Amendment in the incorporation process. The Court also used Jefferson's phrase in its opinion and began erecting the wall of separation.

Prayer in Public Schools In their early development, public schools were largely Protestant institutions; as such, many began their day with a prayer. But the Court outlawed the practice in the early 1960s. The ACLU argued that a 22-word, nondenominational New York state–sanctioned prayer was unconstitutional. The Court agreed in *Engle v. Vitale* (1962). A year later it outlawed a daily Bible reading in the Abington schools in Pennsylvania and thus in all public schools. In both cases, the school projected or promoted religion, which constituted an establishment.

The Court later ruled that a Wisconsin mandatory high school law violated Amish parents' right to teach their own children under the free exercise clause. The Court found that the Amish's alternative mode of informal vocational training paralleled the state's objectives. Forcing these children to attend high school violated the basic tenets of the Amish faith because it forced their children into unwanted environments.

Lemon v. Kurtzman In 1971, the Court created a measure of whether or not the state violated the establishment clause. Both Rhode Island and Pennsylvania passed laws to pay teachers of secular subjects in religious schools with state funds. The state mandated such subjects as English and math and reasoned that it should assist the parochial schools in carrying out a state requirement. In trying to determine the constitutionality of this statute, the Court decided these laws created an "excessive entanglement" between state and the church. The Court said that teachers in these parochial schools may improperly involve faith in their teaching. Even if the state monitored them, such a relationship would cause an entanglement. In the unanimous opinion,

Chief Justice Warren Burger further articulated Jefferson's "wall of separation" concept, and "far from being a wall," the policy made a "blurred, indistinct, and variable barrier." To guide lower court decisions and future controversies that might reach the High Court, the justices developed the *Lemon* test to determine excessive entanglement.

The *Lemon* Test
To avoid an excessive entanglement, a policy must
• have a secular purpose that neither endorses nor disapproves of religion
• have an effect that neither advances nor prohibits religion
• avoid creating a relationship between religion and government that entangles either in the internal affairs of the other

Contemporary Issues

Excessive entanglements, real and perceived, have continued. Can government funding go to private schools or universities at all? Does a display of religious symbols on public grounds constitute an establishment of religion? As with so many cases, it depends.

Funding Many establishment cases address whether or not state governments can contribute funds to religious institutions, especially Roman Catholic schools. Virtually every one has been struck down, except those secular endeavors that aid higher education in religious colleges, perhaps because state laws do not require education beyond the twelfth grade and older students are not as impressionable.

Vouchers Supporters of private parochial schools and parents who pay tuition argue that the government should issue vouchers to ease their costs. Parents of parochial students pay the same taxes as public school parents while they also ease the expenses at public schools. A Cleveland, Ohio, program offered as much as $2,250 in tuition reimbursements for low-income families and $1,875 for any families sending their children to private schools. The Court upheld the program largely because the policy did not make a distinction between religious or nonreligious private schools, even though 96 percent of private school students attended a religious-based school. This money did not go directly to the religious schools but rather to the parents for educating their children.

Moment of Silence Since the *Engle* and *Abington* decisions, any formal prayer in public schools is a violation of the establishment clause. The Court has even ruled against student-led prayer at official public school events. However, popular opinion has never endorsed these stances. Gallup consistently found that strong majorities of American citizens still approved of a daily form of prayer in public schools. In the 1980s, Alabama created a policy to satisfy community wishes without violating the 1960s precedents. The state provided that schools give a moment of silence at the beginning of the school day to facilitate prayer or meditation. In a 1985 ruling, however, the Court said this constituted an establishment of religion. Though the law offered a degree of choice and flexibility, using the *Lemon* test, the Court found no secular purpose in the law. The Court left open the possibility that an undefined, occasional moment of silence might pass constitutional muster. In 2014, Gallup found that 61 percent of Americans supported allowing daily prayer, down from 70 percent in 1999.

Students can still operate extracurricular activities of a religious nature provided these take place outside the school day and without tax dollars. The free exercise clause guarantees students' rights to say private prayers, wear religious T-shirts, and discuss religion. Public teachers' actions are more restricted because they are employed by the state.

Religious Symbols in the Public Square Freedom of religion cases often deal with government coercion instead of endorsement. Coercion results in a deprivation of physical liberty, such as laws that take away a merchant's right to conduct business on Sunday or to secure a liquor license near a church. When religious activity, such as a school prayer or a religious ceremony, has been declared optional, too often the nonbeliever must decide between participation and ridicule—an unfair expectation for a child. The Court is reluctant to permit governing bodies to simply offer an opt-out system to avoid an establishment clause violation. Religious symbols are considered in the same vein but have been defined differently in different circumstances.

Christmas A Rhode Island town annually adorned its shopping district with Christmas decor, including a Christmas tree, a Santa's house, and a nativity scene. Plaintiffs sued, arguing that the nativity scene created government establishment of Christianity. The Court upheld the city's right to include this emblem because it served a legitimate secular purpose of depicting the historical origins of the Christmas holiday. A few years later in another case, the Court found the display of a crèche (manger scene), when standing alone without other Christmas decor, a violation because it was seen as a Christian-centered display. "Endorsement sends a message to nonadherents that they are outsiders, not full members of the political community," the Court wrote, while it signals that adherents are favored insiders.

Ten Commandments In 2005, the Court ruled two different ways on the issue of displaying the Ten Commandments on government property. One case involved a large outdoor display at the Texas state capitol. Among 17 other monuments sat a 6-foot tall rendering of the Ten Commandments. The other case involved the Ten Commandments hanging in two Kentucky courthouses, accompanied by several historical American documents. The Court said the Texas display was acceptable because of the monument's religious and historical function. It was not in a location that anyone would be compelled to be in, such as a school or a courtroom. And it was a passive use of the religious text in that only occasional passersby would see it. The Kentucky courtroom case brought the opposite conclusion because an objective observer would perceive the displays as having a predominantly religious purpose in state courtrooms—places where some citizens must attend and places meant to be free from any prejudice.

Supreme Court's First Amendment Rulings and Standards	
Case	Ruling
Reynolds v. United States (1879)	Government can limit religious practices that impair the public interest.
Schenck v. United States (1919)	Government can limit speech that causes a clear and present danger.
New York Times v. Sullivan (1964)	To prove libel, the suing party must prove falsehoods, a malicious intent, and actual damage.
Tinker v. Des Moines (1969)	Students' right to free speech does not stop at the schoolhouse gate.
Lemon v. Kurtzman (1971)	States cannot have an excessive entanglement of church and state.
Miller v. California (1973)	States can prohibit obscene speech that lacks literary, artistic, political, or scientific value.
Bethel v. Fraser (1986)	Schools can punish speech that administrators find lewd or offensive.

Due Process

There are two types of due process, procedural and substantive. Both apply to the federal and state governments through the Fifth and Fourteenth Amendments. These measures prevent government from unfairly depriving citizens of "life, liberty, or property without due process of law." The concept ensures that government does not act arbitrarily on unstable whims and is consistently fair. The government *can* take away life, liberty, and property, but only in a highly specific, prescribed manner. Democratically elected legislatures must define criminal offenses before they are committed, and the government must follow prescribed procedures to ensure defendants' rights en route to prosecution. As one Supreme Court justice wrote in an early decision, "The fundamental requisite of due process of law is the opportunity to be heard." As the Court interpreted and defined due process in various cases, it also selectively required states to follow additional rights from the Bill of Rights, thus expanding the incorporation doctrine discussed earlier in this chapter.

Procedural Due Process

Procedural due process addresses the manner in which the law is carried out. For example, did the local court give the defendant a fair trial? Did the zoning board accurately appraise the citizen's house before seizing it under eminent domain powers? Were the suspended students given a chance to explain their side of the story? Such questions arise in cases that have defined the concept nationally. Under the leadership of Chief Justice Earl Warren (1953–1969), the Court extended liberties and limited states' authority in areas of **search and seizure**, the right to counsel, and the right against self-incrimination during police interrogations.

Fourth Amendment The Fourth Amendment prevents law enforcement from conducting unreasonable searches and seizures. Before American independence, the mother country cracked down on smugglers who tried to avoid taxes. To do so, Britain used writs of assistance—blanket search warrants—that empowered British soldiers to search any warehouse, vessel, or home at any time. This practice violated any sense of privacy or respect to personal property. The Fourth Amendment seeks to prevent the emergence of such an overpowering police state and requires courts to issue search warrants and arrest warrants only "upon probable cause" supported by a witness on record and under oath. The warrant, if issued, must list the place(s) to be searched and the persons or items to be seized. There are exceptions to the warrant requirement, especially when police see or quickly respond to crimes.

Exclusionary Rule In 1914, in *Weeks v. United States*, the Court established the **exclusionary rule**, which states that evidence the government finds or takes in violation of the Fourth Amendment can be excluded from trial. This decision protected the citizenry from aggressive federal police by reducing the chances of conviction. The justice system rejects evidence that resembles the "fruit from the poisonous tree."

In 1961, the Court applied the exclusionary rule to state law enforcement. Seven police officers broke into Dollree Mapp's Cleveland house in search of a fugitive suspect and gambling paraphernalia. The police found no person or evidence related to either suspect or paraphernalia, but they did find some obscene books and pictures. Mapp was convicted on obscenity charges and sent to prison. When her case arrived in the Supreme Court, the justices ruled the police had violated her rights and should never have discovered the illegal contraband. Since *Mapp v. Ohio* (1961), states must follow the Fourth Amendment.

Exceptions Law enforcement can still conduct searches without warrants, but they need to establish probable cause. Other exceptions to the warrant requirement include the consent of the person being searched and searches in airports and at U.S. borders.

Chief Justice Burger's Court refined the exclusionary rule to include the "inevitable discovery" and "good faith" exceptions. The inevitable discovery exception is when police find evidence in an unlawful search but would have eventually made the same discovery in a later, lawful search. The good faith exception addresses police searches under a court-issued warrant that is proven unconstitutional or erroneous later. In such instances, the police conducted the search under the good faith that they were following the law and thus have not abused or violated the Fourth Amendment. Evidence discovered under these exceptions will likely be admitted at trial.

Searches in Schools As the *Tinker* decision upheld, students' constitutional rights do not stop at the schoolhouse gate. Students' rights against unreasonable searches, however, are more limited in school than average citizens' rights against unreasonable searches in public or in their home.

This issue was decided in *New Jersey v. TLO* (1985). After a student informed a school administrator that another student, TLO (the Court used only initials to protect this minor's identity), had been smoking in the restroom, an assistant principal searched TLO's purse. He found cigarettes, as well as marijuana, rolling papers, plastic bags, a list of students who owed her money, and a large amount of cash. The administrator turned this evidence over to the police, who prosecuted the student. She appealed her conviction on exclusionary rule grounds. The Court ruled that although the Fourth Amendment does protect students from school officials, in this case the search was reasonable. School officials are not required to have the same level of probable cause as police. Students are entitled to a "legitimate expectation of privacy," the Court said, but this must be weighed against the interests of teachers, administrators, and the school's responsibility and mission. The *New Jersey v. TLO* ruling gave administrators a greater degree of leeway than police in conducting searches, requiring that they have reasonable cause or suspicion.

Right to Counsel In 1963, with *Gideon v. Wainright*, the Court addressed the legal meaning of the Sixth Amendment's right to an attorney in state prosecutions. Clarence Earl Gideon, a drifter who had served jail time in four previous instances, was arrested for breaking and entering a Florida pool hall. He came to his trial expecting the local court to appoint him a lawyer because he simply could not afford one. The Supreme Court had already ruled that states must provide counsel in the case of an indigent defendant facing the death penalty, or in a case where the defendant has special circumstances, such as illiteracy, or psychological incapacity. At the time of Gideon's trial, 45 states appointed attorneys to all indigent defendants. Florida, however, did not.

Gideon was quickly convicted. In prison, he studied the law and applied to the Supreme Court *in forma pauperis* ("in the form of a poor man"), drafting his handwritten appeal in pencil. The Court took his case and declared that a defendant cannot receive a fair trial without an attorney. Since this decision in *Gideon v. Wainwright*, all states must pay for public defenders in cases where defendants cannot afford one.

Self-Incrimination "You have the right to remain silent…" goes the famed Miranda warning. This statement also reminds arrested suspects that "anything you say can and will be used against you." Since 1966, this statement has become familiar, mostly through TV crime dramas. The warning resulted from an overturned conviction of a rapist who confessed to his crime in *Miranda v. Arizona*.

For years, the Court handled a heavy appellate caseload addressing the problem of police-coerced confessions. Many losing defendants claimed during appeal that they had confessed only under duress, while police typically insisted the confessions were voluntary. The Fifth Amendment states, "nor shall [anyone] be compelled in any criminal case to be a witness against himself." With so many different law enforcement units across the country employing tactics that landed them in the Supreme Court, the justices took Miranda's case and created a new standard.

Ernesto Miranda, an indigent man who never completed the ninth grade, was arrested for the kidnapping and rape of a girl in Arizona. The police questioned Miranda for two hours until they finally emerged from the interrogation room with a signed confession. The confession was a crucial piece of evidence at Miranda's trial.

There had been some question as to when the Fifth Amendment right against self-incrimination begins. It clearly meant no defendant was compelled to take the witness stand at trial. In *Miranda*, the Court declared the right applies once a suspect is in custody. It declared that custodial interrogation carries with it a badge of intimidation. If such pressures from the state are going to occur, the police must inform the suspect of his or her rights.

Source: © Bettman/CORBIS

The Warren Court, shown here in 1953, extended individual liberties and limited states' authority in the areas of search and seizure, the right to counsel, and self-incrimination.

Civil libertarians hailed the *Miranda* ruling, while conservatives and law enforcement saw it as tying the hands of the police. Miranda received a new trial that did not use his confession. Additional proof, it turned out, was enough to convict this rapist. He went to prison while changing national due process law.

Death Penalty The Eighth Amendment prevents cruel and unusual punishments and excessive bail. Capital punishment, or the death penalty, has been in use for most of U.S. history. A handful of states, as well as most western and developed countries, have banned the practice. States can use a variety of methods of execution; lethal injection is the most common. From 1930 through the 1960s, 87 percent of death penalty sentences were for murder, and 12 percent were for rape. The remaining 1 percent included treasonous charges and other offenses. In the United States, strong majorities have long favored the death penalty for premeditated murders.

The Court put the death penalty on hold nationally with the decision in *Furman v. Georgia* in 1972. In a complex 5–4 decision, only two justices called the death penalty itself a violation of the Constitution. The Court was mostly addressing the randomness of the death penalty. Some justices pointed out the disproportionate application of the death penalty to the socially disadvantaged, the poor, and racial minorities.

With the decision of *Gregg v. Georgia* in 1976, the Court began reinstatement of the death penalty as states restructured their sentencing guidelines. No state can make the death penalty mandatory by law. Rather, aggravating and mitigating circumstances must be taken into account in the penalty phase, a second phase of trial following a guilty verdict. Character witnesses may testify in the defendant's favor to affect the issuance of the death penalty. In recent years, in cases of murder, the Court has outlawed the death penalty for mentally handicapped defendants and those defendants who were under 18 years of age at the time of the murder.

Substantive Due Process

The idea of **substantive due process** dates back to the English constitution. In the 1873 *Slaughterhouse Cases*, the majority opinion pointed to rights not directly stated in the Bill of Rights, such as the right to pursue lawful employment and other lawful pursuits of life. During the Court's second historical phase, when it addressed business regulation in the industrial period, it developed the substantive due process doctrine in relation to state and federal regulations in the workplace. Substantive due process places substantive limits on what laws can actually be created. If the substance of the law—the very point of the law—violates some basic right, even one not listed in the Constitution, then a court can declare it unconstitutional. State policies that might violate substantive due process rights must meet some valid interest to promote the police powers of regulating health, welfare, or morals. The right to substantive due process protects people from policies for which no legitimate interest exists. These policies became a thorny issue as labor unions and corporations debated the Constitution and while legislatures tried to promote the health and safety of citizens.

Right to Privacy In the 1960s a new class of substantive due process suits came to the Court. These suits sought to protect the individual's rights, especially in terms of privacy and lifestyle. In *Griswold v. Connecticut* (1965), the Court ruled an old anti–birth control state statute in violation of the Constitution. The law even barred married couples from receiving birth control literature. The Court for the first time emphasized an inherent **right to privacy** that, though not expressly mentioned in the Bill of Rights, could be found in the penumbras (shadows) of several amendments.

The Court further bolstered the right to privacy in the ***Roe v. Wade*** (1973) decision. Primarily a question of whether Texas or other states could prevent a woman from aborting her unborn fetus, the decision rested on a substantive due process right against such a law. Whether a pregnant woman was to have or abort her baby was a private decision between her and her doctor and outside the reach of the government. These two cases together revived the substantive due process doctrine first laid down a century earlier.

***Roe* and Later Abortion Rulings** Before 1973, abortion on demand was legal in only four states. The *Roe* decision made it unconstitutional for a state to ban abortion for a woman during the first trimester, the first three months of her pregnancy. An array of other state regulations developed in response. States passed statutes to prevent abortion at state-funded hospitals and clinics. They adjusted their laws to prevent late-term abortions. In 1976, Congress passed the Hyde Amendment (named for Illinois Congressman Henry Hyde) to prevent federal funding that might contribute to an abortion.

The Court has addressed a series of cases on abortion since *Roe,* and the abortion issue inevitably comes up at election time and during Supreme Court nominees' confirmation hearings. The Court outlawed a Pennsylvania law designed to discourage women from getting abortions that could expose patients via public records. In *Planned Parenthood v. Casey*, the national pro-choice organization fought to overturn Pennsylvania Governor Bob Casey's enforcement of state abortion restrictions. The *Casey* decision upheld state requirements, such as a mandatory waiting period, parental (or judge's) consent for pregnant teens, and the provision of information on abortion alternatives at clinics. But it did not uphold the "informed consent" portion of the law that required the aborting woman (mother), married or unmarried, to inform and secure consent from the father.

Civil Liberties and National Security

The Court has typically sided with governmental restrictions on liberties that protect national security during times of war or international threat. Two months after the Japanese bombed Pearl Harbor, the federal government created internment camps to relocate Japanese immigrants and Japanese Americans for the remainder of the war. When internee Fred Korematsu challenged this in the Supreme Court, he lost. The Congress curtailed First Amendment liberties during the Cold War and during the Vietnam War. Since the September 11th attacks in 2001, the United States has wrestled with the issue of protecting the nation from terrorism while also maintaining constitutional rights.

September 11

Not long after al Qaeda terrorists hijacked four U.S. commercial aircraft to fly them into selected targets in New York and Washington, President George W. Bush addressed a joint session of Congress, stating, "Whether we bring our enemies to justice, or we bring justice to our enemies, justice will be done." Faced with an adversary that generally operated underground and not under the flag of any sovereign nation, the United States modified its laws and defense operations to create a series of federal policies to eradicate threats, which fueled an ongoing debate about proper recognition of the Bill of Rights.

USA PATRIOT Act Administration officials began to deliberate about how the United States might locate the perpetrators of the September 11th attacks and, further, how to prevent future attacks. By late October 2001, the Congress passed the USA PATRIOT Act (Uniting and Strengthening America by Providing Appropriate Tools Required to Intercept and Obstruct Terrorism). The law covered intelligence gathering and sharing by executive branch agencies, points of criminal procedure, and border protection. It allowed government agencies to share information about significant suspects, and it widened authority on tapping suspects' phones. Government can now share grand jury testimony and proceedings, detain illegal immigrants for longer periods, and monitor email communications. The new bipartisan law passed with strong majorities in both houses. Soon after its passage, however, people began to question the law's constitutionality and its threat to civil liberties.

Executive Branch Initiatives U.S. armed forces quickly invaded Afghanistan, where al Qaeda operated under the ruling Taliban regime. The terrorist network, however, also operated in cells throughout the Middle East and beyond. Some members were in the United States. President Bush issued an executive order authorizing trials of captured terrorists to take place via military tribunals rather than civilian courts.

A debate about handling terrorists created controversy. Should the United States seek out these terrorists as criminals who violated federal law under the established criminal justice system, or should the federal government treat this as a war against an outside adversary? In both cases, the government must follow established laws. If done through law enforcement, the government arrests terrorists and tries them in U.S. district courts to put them away in prison if convicted. This approach requires the government to follow standard criminal justice due process rights. If done as part of a war effort, the federal government has fewer restrictions but still must recognize U.S. law and international treaties. Depending on the circumstance, the government currently acts in both ways and employs tactics that critics declare violate the Constitution and international law.

When President Bush declared a "war on terror," questions arose. For example, does the 1949 Geneva Convention, the international treaty that governs the basic rules of war, apply? Al Qaeda is not a nation-state and is not a signatory (signer) of the Geneva Convention or any international treaty. In that case, does the United States have to honor Geneva provisions when acting against al Qaeda? And does the Constitution apply to U.S. action beyond U.S. soil (especially when acting against enemies)? The Bush administration categorized those captured on the terror battlefield—meaning basically anywhere—as "enemy combatants" and treated their legal condition differently than either an arrested criminal or a conventional prisoner of war.

Guantanamo Bay and Interrogations The U.S. military set up a detention camp at its naval base in Guantanamo Bay, Cuba, to hold terror suspects. Placing the camp at this base provided stronger security, minimal press contact, and less prisoner access to legal aid than if it had been within U.S. borders. Administration officials believed that the location of the camp and interrogations outside the United States allowed a loosening of constitutional restrictions.

Soon after 9/11, administration officials signaled that unconventional tactics would be necessary to prevent another devastating attack. In trying to determine the legal limits of an intense interrogation, President Bush's lawyers issued the now infamous "torture memo." In August of 2002, President George W. Bush's Office of Legal Counsel offered the legal definition of torture, calling it "severe physical pain or suffering." The memo claimed such pain "must be equivalent in intensity to the pain accompanying serious physical injury, such as organ failure, impairment of bodily function, or even death." One of the notorious techniques employed to gather information from reluctant detainees is waterboarding—an ancient method that simulates drowning.

As these policies developed and became public, some people became outraged. Civil libertarians in the United States questioned the disregard for both *habeas corpus* rights and the Eighth Amendment's prohibition of cruel and unusual punishment. The international community, too, was aghast.

In the Courts

These legal complications and competing views on how to apply international law and the Bill of Rights in a war against an enemy with no flag have caused detainees and their advocates to challenge the government in court. A lower court has declared part of the PATRIOT Act unconstitutional. The Supreme Court has addressed *habeas corpus* rights.

The right of *habeas corpus* guarantees that the government cannot arbitrarily imprison or detain someone without formal charges. Could detainees at Guantanamo Bay question their detention? The president said no, but the Court said yes. *Rasul v. Bush* (2004) stated that because the United States exercises complete authority over the base in Cuba, it must follow the Constitution. Fred Korematsu, who lost his own *habeas corpus* claim in 1944, submitted an *amicus curiae* brief in support of Rasul. "It is during our most challenging and uncertain moments that our nation's commitment to due process is most severely tested," Justice Sandra Day O'Connor wrote, "and it is in those times that we must preserve our commitment at home to the principles for which we fight abroad."

In *Hamdi v. Rumsfeld* (2004), the Court overruled the executive branch's unchecked discretion in determining the status of detainees. After this, the

United States could not detain a U.S. citizen without a minimal hearing to determine the suspect's charge. In a separate case, *Hamdan v. Rumsfeld*, the Court found that Bush's declaration that these detainees should be tried in military tribunals violated the United States Code of Military Justice. The commissions themselves, wrote Justice John Paul Stevens, violated part of the Geneva Convention that governed noninternational armed conflicts before a "regularly constituted court ... affording judicial guarantees ... by civilized peoples." As summed up in *Hamdi*, "We have long since made clear that a state of war is not a blank check for the president when it comes to the rights of the nation's citizens."

Source: Rena Schild / Shutterstock

Citizens rally to protest mass surveillance policies.

BY THE NUMBERS Supreme Court Votes in Due Process Decisions		
Case	**Decision**	**Vote**
Mapp v. Ohio (1961)	States must follow the exclusionary rule.	6 to 3
Gideon v. Wainwright (1963)	States must supply defense attorneys to indigent defendants.	9 to 0
Miranda v. Arizona (1966)	States must inform the accused of their rights.	5 to 4
Griswold v. Connecticut (1965)	Privacy rights prevent state anti–birth control law.	7 to 2
Roe v. Wade (1973)	States cannot outlaw abortion in first trimester.	7 to 2
Hamdi v. Rumsfeld (2004)	The U.S. cannot hold terror suspects without following *habeas corpus* rights.	6 to 3
Hamdan v. Rumsfeld (2006)	The U.S. must follow Geneva Convention and cannot rely strictly on military commissions in prosecuting terror suspects.	5 to 3

What do the numbers show? In which decisions did the Court have stronger majorities or unanimous opinions? Which cases brought narrow decisions? What do the narrow decisions say about the view of civil liberties? Which cases altered or shaped law enforcement? Which ones dealt with privacy? Which amendments were at issue in each case?

REFLECT ON THE ESSENTIAL QUESTION

Essential Question: *How has the government defined freedoms and protected civil liberties?* On separate paper, complete a chart like the one below to gather details to answer that question.

Fundamental Liberties	Court Cases

THINK AS A POLITICAL SCIENTIST: INTERPRET *SNYDER V. PHELPS*

Almost no idea has meaning in isolation; it is instead subject to interpretation. When you **interpret** information, you attempt to understand and explain the meaning of an idea or event in context. You consider the time period in which the author created the work and the place where it was created. You use critical thinking skills and prior information to help you interpret and understand the overall meaning of the work. Similarly, to understand an event, you analyze the facts as you understand them and interpret them according to such factors as the politics and social trends of the day, as well as other related events that may have happened around the same time or that may have engendered or resulted from the event you are studying.

In legal proceedings, courts analyze events and claims to interpret the law. Supreme Court justices must be able to examine the facts of each case—time, place, and extenuating circumstances—and interpret them in context of existing law to reach complex decisions on how a given law is or should be carried out.

Practice: In 2006, a young U.S. Marine named Matthew Snyder was killed in a noncombat-related accident in Iraq. Later, Westboro Baptist Church of Topeka, Kansas, picketed Snyder's funeral as part of the church's ongoing protest of the U.S. military's increasing tolerance of homosexuality among its personnel. Matthew Snyder's father, Albert Snyder, sued the church, its pastor Fred Phelps, and two members of Phelps's family for, among other things, defamation and intentional infliction of emotional distress. Use the Internet to research the events and decisions involved in this case since it first went to trial in 2007. Then write an interpretation of the Supreme Court's ruling.

KEY TERMS, NAMES, AND EVENTS

Barron v. Baltimore (1833)	*Gideon v. Wainwright* (1963)	prior restraint
Bethel Schools v. Fraser (1986)	*Griswold v. Connecticut* (1965)	procedural due process
clear and present danger test	*Lemon v. Kurtzman* (1971)	right to privacy
due process	libel	*Roe v. Wade* (1973)
Engle v. Vitale (1962)	*Mapp v. Ohio* (1961)	search and seizure
establishment clause	*Miller v. California* (1973)	*Schenck v. United States* (1919)
exclusionary rule	*Miranda v. Arizona* (1966)	selective incorporation
Fifth Amendment	*New Jersey v. TLO* (1985)	substantive due process
Fourteenth Amendment	obscene speech	symbolic speech
free exercise clause		*Tinker v. Des Moines Independent Schools* (1969)
		wall of separation

MULTIPLE-CHOICE QUESTIONS

Source: Clay Bennett, Cartoonist Group

1. With which of the following statements would the creator of the cartoon above be most likely to agree?

   (A) The government should be able to impose religion on its citizens.

   (B) Members of government cannot be religious.

(C) There is a constant struggle to define the separation of church and state.

(D) The government should provide more help to churches.

(E) The government is too rigid in its effort to separate church and state.

2. The decision in *Texas v. Johnson* prevented governments from banning flag burning because such a law violates

(A) property rights

(B) free speech rights

(C) free religion rights

(D) procedural due process rights

(E) public opinion polls

3. Which statement about the Supreme Court under Chief Justice Earl Warren and procedural due process rights is true?

(A) A "police-state" grew out of the Supreme Court's interpretations.

(B) Warren's Court elevated several rights of the accused.

(C) The Court claimed the state violated the defendants' procedural due process rights in *Roe v. Wade*.

(D) State-sponsored school prayer was upheld under the free exercise clause.

(E) The Court declared indigent defendants are not entitled to an attorney.

4. Which constitutional right is NOT specifically listed in the First Amendment?

(A) Freedom of religion

(B) Freedom of the press

(C) The right to privacy

(D) The right to assemble

(E) Freedom of speech

5. Which type of speech has the Supreme Court most consistently protected?

(A) Commercial

(B) Obscene

(C) Political

(D) Fighting words

(E) Students' speech in schools

6. The Supreme Court held that arrested criminal suspects should be informed of their rights in
   (A) *Gideon v. Wainwright*
   (B) *Miranda v. Arizona*
   (C) *Mapp v. Ohio*
   (D) *Roe v. Wade*
   (E) *Gitlow v. New York*

7. To win a libel lawsuit, the suing party must prove
   (A) another person insulted them
   (B) a factual mistake was made in reporting
   (C) the libeling party acted maliciously
   (D) an unfair criticism of public officials
   (E) only that his or her reputation was tarnished

8. The Supreme Court's contemporary interpretation of the death penalty
   (A) prevents states from using the death penalty
   (B) disregards international trends about executions
   (C) focuses on the method of execution
   (D) prevents the practice because it is cruel and unusual
   (E) prevents state execution of minors and the mentally handicapped

9. In the decision in *Barron v. Baltimore* (1833), Chief Justice John Marshall
   (A) declared that Baltimore had to reimburse Barron under the Fifth Amendment
   (B) began the incorporation doctrine
   (C) upheld the Fourteenth Amendment
   (D) ruled the Bill of Rights did not apply to the states
   (E) made free speech an absolute right

10. Today, police can conduct searches
    (A) only if a court issues a warrant
    (B) if they have slight suspicion of wrongdoing
    (C) as long as they have probable cause of criminal activity
    (D) in public schools at any time, for any reason
    (E) if they follow provisions in the Second Amendment

Question

1. The incorporation doctrine limits state action and enhances civil liberties.

    (a) Explain the Supreme Court's incorporation doctrine, addressing the relevance of the Fourteenth Amendment and judicial precedence.

    (b) Select two constitutional rights below and for each identify and explain one Supreme Court decision that required states to uphold these liberties.
    - Right to counsel
    - Right against self-incrimination
    - Freedom of the press

Question

2. The First Amendment guarantees freedom of religion in the United States.

    (a) Identify and describe the two clauses in the First Amendment that make religious freedom or separation of church and state a challenging standard.

    (b) Describe two standards the Supreme Court has made regarding the interaction of government and religion.

    (c) Identify one controversial public policy issue that divides citizens on freedom of religion, and explain why the issue is divisive.

WRITING: USE DISCIPLINARY CONVENTIONS

Use the style conventions of political science when answering your questions. For example, Supreme Court cases are italicized when they appear in print. If you are writing by hand, underline them. Use a small v. with a period for "versus." When citing a constitutional provision, name the parts in order (Article I, Section 8, for example) or describe it in enough detail so it will be easily understood (the Fourteenth Amendment's equal protection clause, for example, or the Fourteenth Amendment's due process clause).

UNIT 5: Review

Women, African Americans, and other ethnic and political minorities have pushed for fairness and equality because they were overlooked at the U.S. founding and by state and federal governments during the decades that followed. The Bill of Rights, later amendments, and subsequent laws were meant to afford these groups and individuals real justice and freedoms. Brave, principled leaders and organized groups had to press the government to fully deliver these.

The Supreme Court's evolving interpretation of the Fourteenth Amendment's equal protection clause eventually required states to treat citizens equally. From *Brown v. Board of Education* to the current debate about affirmative action, civil rights have been on the front burner of public policy. Women's rights came partially with the ratification of the Nineteenth Amendment in 1920 but more fully after Congress mandated equal pay and a fair footing in college. Gays have successfully sought to serve openly in the military and have won the right to marry in many courts.

In addition to rights, noted groups and individuals have pushed for the civil liberties promised in the Bill of Rights. Though at times states have infringed on free speech, free religion, and rights of the accused, the Supreme Court has generally restored these liberties. This process has occurred on a case-by-case basis via the selective incorporation doctrine. The Court has prevented government censorship, protected people from aggressive police and overzealous school administrators, set standards to allow localities to define public obscenity, and prevented excessive entanglements of church and state.

THINK AS A POLITICAL SCIENTIST: APPLY DISCIPLINARY THEORIES AND CONCEPTS IN RESEARCHING A CIVIL RIGHTS ORGANIZATION

Select a notable civil rights or civil liberties organization.

- Find the organization's official Web site. Read the "About" and/ or "History" pages for an overview of the organization. What issues or controversies are front-and-center on its agenda today?

- Find historic or recent primary sources about your organization. Use digital databases and national online newspapers.

- Consider your sources and analyze the evidence. How does the organization gather and mobilize members? How does the organization interact with Congress, state legislatures, and other elected officials? What court cases, if any, did you learn about?

- Present your findings in a short paper that explains the group's activity, assesses its effectiveness, and shows your understanding of government and politics.

UNIT 6: Public Policy

Chapter 15 *Domestic Policy*

Chapter 16 *Foreign and Military Policy*

Our institutions of national government interact with the citizenry, organized interests, financial institutions, and other nations to craft domestic and international policy. Different types of policies are forged through different political processes. Earlier chapters explored how interest groups, think tanks, industry leaders, and the general populace interact with Congress, the executive branch, and the courts to enact and shape policy. The institutional framework of the U.S. government has allowed for the implementation of social welfare policy to protect citizens in need and an environmental policy to protect the earth and regulate polluting industries.

The national government carries out economic policy as well as it determines how much to tax its citizens, its corporations, and products shipped into the United States. It also determines how to spend tax revenues, how much currency to put into circulation, what nations to trade with, and what rules businesses must follow. Chapter 15 explains social welfare policy, environmental policy, labor policy, taxes, and the budget-making process.

Article I of the Constitution empowers Congress to raise and maintain a military, and Article II names the president as commander in chief. This shared responsibility for military matters has caused a constant, if intended, struggle between the executive and legislative branches even as the United States has gained much influence in world affairs. Chapter 16 explores foreign and military policy, addressing the defense budget, U.S. relations with other countries, civil liberties in wartime, and the national security apparatus.

Key Concepts

Public Policy

- Policymaking in a federal system
- The formation of policy agendas
- The role of institutions in the enactment of policy
- The role of the bureaucracy and the courts in policy implementation and interpretation
- Linkages between policy processes and 1) political institutions and federalism, 2) political parties, 3) interest groups, 4) public opinion, 5) elections, and 6) policy networks

Source: *AP®United States Government and Politics Course and Exam Description*

Domestic Policy

"Balancing the budget is like going to heaven. Everybody wants to do it, but nobody wants to do what you have to do to get there."

—Senator Phil Gramm in televised interview, 1990

Essential Question: How does the federal government set and carry out domestic policy?

You have been reading about public policy and the policymaking process throughout this book. The linkage institutions discussed in Unit 3 show how the public selects its leaders and communicates its desires. Political parties and interest groups act within their legal and practical means to push for their desired policies. Our national institutions of government enact policies when Congress passes a new law, when the president issues an executive order, or when the Supreme Court determines a new legal standard. Remember, public policy is simply the laws of the land and the manner in which government does business. America's domestic policy includes everything the government takes care of within U.S. borders. The United States has developed policy to take care of its people, especially the less fortunate, to protect the environment, to finance government, and to enhance the state of the economy.

Policymaking

Policy is created and shaped every day in the federal government, even in small ways: when a congresswoman inserts language into a bill, when the president discusses relations with another head of state, when the Postal Service changes its delivery schedule, or when a court sets a precedent, for just a few examples.

Theories of Public Policy

Public policy arises in a variety of ways depending on the political situation at the time. Following are some of the key theories or pathways to policy.

Majoritarian Politics   Majoritarian politics come from the interaction of people with government in order to put into place and carry out the will of the majority. Democratic government, a foundational principle in America, is meant to represent the people's views through elected representatives. Popular ideas will work their way into the body politic via our state and national legislatures. A president seeking a second term will go with public opinion when there is an outcry for a new law or a different way of enforcing an existing law. State referenda and initiatives, too, are a common way for large grassroots efforts to alter current policy when state assemblies refuse to make the public will the public law.

This democratic system sounds fair and patriotic. But the Framers also put into place a republic of states and a system to ensure that the tyranny of the majority did not run roughshod over the rights of the minority. Additionally, the Framers warned, factions—often minority interests—will press government to address their needs, and at times government will comply.

Elite Theory The elite theory of politics asserts that there is an inequity in the spread of power among the populace, and that the elites—people with resources and influence—dominate. Dominating influence by the elites, a trait of the new nation, weakened somewhat in the Progressive Era, when the masses became more involved in politics. Yet in many ways, elite-dominated politics prevail today. Individuals with the most time, education, money, and access to government will take more action than the less privileged, and, because of their resources, they will be heard. People who serve in the leadership of a political party, whether on the local or national level, are usually of a higher socioeconomic level, well-known, and well educated.

Interest Group Politics Interest groups have an undue influence and interact with all three branches while government officials search for consensus among competing interests. Interest groups, such as organized labor PACs or the gun lobby, raise and spend money in elections to ensure that people friendly to their ideas are elected. These groups send professional researchers and experts to testify at congressional committee hearings in hopes of shaping or stopping a bill. They monitor the government as it enforces existing law. Interest groups—from AARP to Public Citizen—push for specific areas of policy to satisfy their members and their philosophy.

Pluralist Theory Pluralist theorists believe that the ideas and viewpoints in the United States are so scattered and so varied that no single view can control the shaping and administration of policy. We live in a world of so many policymakers putting into effect so many rules and procedures at the local, state, and federal levels that no single input shapes our body of law. We are a nation of immigrants, both ethnically and ideologically diverse, and the large variety of viewpoints results in public policy that is usually established by a consensus.

Decision Making Model/Process

In creating policy, public officials follow a general routine. Legislators and bureaucrats constantly develop and reshape an **agenda**—a list of potential policy ideas, bills, or plans to improve society. These could be new methods of law enforcement, alterations of the tax system, or a long-term plan to improve relations with a foreign nation. With each new policy idea comes a cost-benefits analysis, a full look into the strains and efforts that come with a new policy compared to the benefits the new policy would bring. Of course building an overhead skywalk at every intersection would reduce pedestrian injuries and deaths, but the costs—the actual price, the disruption caused by their construction, the unsightliness, and pedestrian confusion from such a network of skywalks—simply outweigh the benefits.

Sequence Governments at all levels recognize an issue, study it, and try to solve it. First an issue gets attention because there is enough concern about it or enough support for a policy change. It may come from a widespread citizen push to ban smoking in public places, for example, or it may come from a defense contractor's proposed design for new fighter jets. Once the issue is made public, the government investigates it. Congress will exercise its investigatory power to better understand the issue. The relevant committee(s) will hear experts testify. Ideally all sides of the issue and particular concerns about solving the problem will be heard.

Then, government formulates the policy on paper, whether it is a comprehensive proposed new bill or just a new way for police to enforce existing law. As the topic is discussed in theory and the language of a bill or an executive directive is developed and refined, the government will work toward adopting the policy. Sweeping changes in law usually come incrementally, with the most obvious, passable ideas coming before any major overhauls.

The government must also figure out a way to finance the enforcement of new laws. Each new policy requires the executive branch to enforce it, which means either creating an additional agency to oversee the law or putting more responsibilities on an existing one. Finally, the government will evaluate the new policy sometime after its implementation. This evaluation could be done through required agency reports or with congressional oversight (pages 233 and 289).

Challenges to new policies quickly come from those who oppose the law. Opponents often file suit to overturn the law in the courts. Many times a state legislature will pass a controversial bill with a marginal vote only to see the citizenry rise up and repeal it through a referendum. In Ohio, for example, the state legislature had passed a bill (Senate Bill 5) limiting collective bargaining for 400,000 public workers employed by the state, preventing them from striking and limiting their ability to do collective bargaining for better pay and benefits. The bill was signed into law on March 31, 2011. Opponents of the law, however, collected more than one million signatures to put the law on the ballot as a referendum. The voters repealed the law in November 2011.

Social Welfare Policy

The Preamble to the Constitution declares that the government will "promote the general welfare" of its citizens. The nation's social welfare policy has enacted that goal, especially the New Deal programs of the 1930s and the Great Society programs of the 1960s. More recently, Congress passed and President Obama signed into law a national health care law.

A Social Safety Net

Other Western nations provide more social welfare services to their needy citizens than does the United States and began providing them much earlier. Factors such as federalism and differing views on responsibility have slowed the United States in this regard. Nonetheless, American society, to some degree, has always taken care of its elderly and its poor. Philanthropists and most states had some type of programs to support widows, orphans, and the less fortunate.

Social Security Amid the Great Depression, Franklin Roosevelt and his team of advisors created a federal safety net for the elderly and supported those who were put out of work. The economic disaster bankrupted local charities and state treasuries, forcing the national government to act. **The Social Security Act of 1935** created an insurance program that required the employed to pay a small contribution via a payroll tax into an insurance fund designed to assist the unemployed and to help financially strapped retirees. An additional assistance program helps blind, elderly, and less fortunate people. The act guaranteed that all who paid into the system would collect retirement benefits via Social Security checks at age 65. But for the less fortunate under 65, only those who did not have the means to survive would be provided benefits. The government developed a **means test** to determine which citizens qualify for this aid.

Officially called Old Age, Survivors, and Disability Insurance (OASDI), Social Security requires most employed citizens to pay 12.4 percent (the employer pays 6.2 percent and the employee pays 6.2 percent) into a trust fund that is separate from the general treasury to protect it. The Social Security Administration is an independent agency that handles the fund and distributes the checks. It is a large agency composed of almost 60,000 employees and more than 1,400 offices nationwide.

Medicare and Medicaid FDR's plan to pay for the elderly's medical care was tabled until Congress passed the **Medicare** law in 1965. It helps ease the medical costs of disabled seniors over the age of 65. It is administered by an agency in the Department of Health and Human Services and is funded by a payroll tax of 1.45 percent paid by both employer and employee. For those earning more than $200,000 per year, the rate has recently increased to 3.8 percent. The law, which has since been amended, is broken into four parts that cover hospitalization, physicians' services, a public-private partnership known as Medicare Advantage that allows companies to provide Medicare benefits, and a prescription drug benefit. For those over age 65 who qualify, Medicare can cover up to 80 percent of their health care costs. **Medicaid** provides health insurance coverage for the poorest Americans. To be eligible for Medicaid services, the applying citizen must meet minimum-income thresholds or be disabled or pregnant.

Health Care American citizens purchase health care insurance coverage either through their employer or on their own. Health insurance eases the cost of doctor's visits, prescription medicines, operations, and other medical costs. Many politicians and several presidents have favored the idea of a government-based health care system for decades. Some health insurance regulations have existed for years, sometimes differing from state to state. Recently, with the continual increases in insurance prices and the diminishing level of coverage, more Americans have bought into the idea of expanding government regulation of health insurance and making the service more affordable to average Americans.

This idea finally became law with the passage of the **Patient Protection and Affordable Care Act** in 2010. Sometimes referred to as "Obamacare" because of President Obama's support for the law, the Affordable Care Act is comprehensive and often confusing. It became a divisive issue in party politics, with opponents concerned about the overreach of government.

The Patient Protection and Affordable Care Act
• Prevents health insurance companies from denying coverage for pre-existing conditions to those under the age of 19
• Allows young adults to remain on their parents' insurance plan until they are 26 years old
• Prevents insurers from canceling coverage arbitrarily
• Prevents insurers from setting a lifetime limit on coverage
• Requires all Americans above a basic income level to buy insurance or pay a penalty

Environmental Policy

A conservation movement developed at the end of the nineteenth century, as John Muir, Teddy Roosevelt, the Sierra Club, and others pointed to the need to protect our environment. National parks and forest preserves became mainstays on our American landscape. But it was not until the 1960s and 1970s that the environmental movement took off and Congress began to strongly regulate industry to assist this effort. As Congress imposed environmental standards, the business community opposed regulations. Over the ensuing decades, environmental policy in the United States became a competition between environmental activists and conservative free-market thinkers. Today, millions of members of the Sierra Club, the National Wildlife Federation, Greenpeace, and the World Wildlife Fund push for greater regulations, while the manufacturing and construction sectors fight regulations that slow job development.

Environmental Legislation

The National Environmental Policy Act requires any government agency, state or federal, to file an environmental impact statement with the federal government every time the agency plans a policy that might harm the environment, dams, roads, or existing construction. The 1970 amendments to the Air Pollution Control Act, commonly known as the **Clean Air Act**, call for improved air quality and decreased contaminants. The act ultimately requires the Department of Transportation to reduce automobile emissions. The **Clean Water Act** of 1972 regulates the discharges of pollutants into the waters of the United States and monitors quality standards for surface waters. The Endangered Species Act established a program that empowers the National Fish and Wildlife Service to protect endangered species.

After the catastrophic Love Canal toxic waste disaster in western New York in the mid-1970s, the federal government forced industry to pay for the insurance necessary to manage their dangerous by-products. In that disaster, a company had dumped toxic chemicals in the area that later became a residential development. Heavy rains washed some of the chemicals out of the ground. Adults and children developed serious liver, kidney, and other health problems. The company responsible for this had already gone out of business. In response, Congress created the **Superfund**. Essentially, industry pays into the fund set aside for waste cleanup. Under the law, the guilty polluter pays for the cleanup, but when the guilty party is unknown or bankrupt, the collective fund will cover these costs, not the taxpayer.

Environmental Protection Agency Over the years since the 1970 creation of the Environmental Protection Agency, it and the federal government in general have required states to set air quality standards, to reduce the damage done by automobiles, to measure city smog, and to set environmental guidelines. The EPA oversees the Superfund and toxic waste cleanup.

A more recent environmental concern centers on greenhouse gases which result from the burning of fossil fuels. This concern has heightened attention to global warming, an increase in average global temperatures. Melting polar ice caps, unusual flooding in certain areas, animal habitat destruction, and a damaged ozone layer have caused the scientific community, including the Intergovernmental Panel on Climate Change, to conclude that the use of these damaging fuels should be limited and regulated. One international attempt to combat this problem came with the 1997 Kyoto Protocol, a multi-country agreement that committed the signing nations to reduced greenhouse gas emissions. Most industrialized nations joined the treaty and President Bill Clinton agreed to it. But the conservative-leaning U.S. Senate at the time did not achieve the two-thirds support necessary for ratification.

Labor Policy

As you read in Chapter 7, corporations and workers struggled as the labor union movement developed from the late 1800s into the Great Depression. Congress passed various laws that prevented collusion by corporations, price fixing, trusts, and yellow dog contracts (forcing newly hired employees into a promise not to join a labor union). Different presidents implemented these laws with varying degrees of enforcement. As part of the New Deal program, Congress passed the **Wagner Act** (also known as the National Labor Relations Act) in 1935 and the **Fair Labor Standards Act** in 1938. The Wagner Act

THINK AS A POLITICAL SCIENTIST: ANALYZE AND INTERPRET A POLITICAL CARTOON ON ENVIRONMENTAL POLICY

Political cartoons are one way people express their views. Funny or somber, they shed light on political events, issues or people, and reflect the cartoonist's viewpoint. The artist decides how much of the message is carried by the text and how much by the image.

To **analyze** a political cartoon, study its elements: Who are the people in the cartoon and how are they portrayed? Take note of the cartoon's symbols and labels. How would you describe the artist's style? What is the mood or tone of the cartoon?

To **interpret** a political cartoon, draw inferences: make an educated guess based on the evidence presented and your own knowledge. What meaning can you draw from the cartoon that is not explicitly stated? How is this information presented textually and visually?

Finally, when you **synthesize** information, you pull together the information in a unified and coherent understanding. What is the author's point of view on the topic based on your analysis and the evidence?

Practice: Analyze, interpret, and synthesize the cartoon below to fully understand its text and visual information. Then use an online resource to find two more cartoons on the same subject. Compare and contrast how the artists address the issue of environmental policy. In what ways are the cartoons similar and different? Sum up your analysis, interpretation, and comparison in a brief essay.

"IF ONLY WE COULD HARVEST THE WIND COMING OUT OF THERE."

Source: Cartoonstock

created the **National Labor Relations Board**, a federal executive branch commission that regulates labor organization and hears complaints of unfair labor practices. It also ensured workers' rights to collectively bargain with management. The second law established minimum wage, defined the 40-hour work week, and required companies to pay employees overtime pay.

After World War II, the **Taft-Hartley Act** (1947), generally favored by business, partly counteracted the labor movement. It enabled states to outlaw the closed shop—a company policy or labor contract that requires all employees to join the local union. States could now pass "right to work" laws. Taft-Hartley also allowed the federal government to block any labor strike in an industry that might put into jeopardy the "national health or safety." In 1970, Congress created the **Occupational Safety and Health Act**, which established the Occupational and Safety and Health Administration, or OSHA. OSHA inspects factories and other workplaces for occupational hazards. Like other regulatory agencies, OSHA can fine a company or can close it down until problems are fixed.

Source: Getty Images

President Ronald Reagan (C), with his Transportation Secretary Andrew L. Lewis (R) and Attorney General William French Smith, spoke out against the August 1981 strike by air traffic controllers. He declared it illegal because they were public employees and fired them. Their union was later decertified. Reagan was in general a supporter of workers' rights to collective bargaining but his firm stand against the air traffic controllers, according to labor expert Joseph A. McCartin, "shaped the world of the modern workplace," which has seen dramatically fewer participants in labor walkouts.

Economic Policy

The philosophy of the president and the collective attitude of Congress can drastically impact the value of the dollar, trade relationships with foreign nations, taxes paid into the federal purse, and the federal budget. Nonetheless, the president and Congress can impact the economy only so much. Countless other market forces are at work every day. But one thing is for sure: whether or not the federal government is fully responsible for a good or bad economy, voters will hold incumbents accountable at election time.

The president is praised or blamed for a good or bad economy more so than Congress. Presidents mostly rely on three advisors who assist in making financial decisions, such as taxing and spending. They include the chairman of the **Council of Economic Advisors** (a three-person panel in the White House Executive Office), the director of the **Office of Management and Budget (OMB),** and the Secretary of the Treasury. All three serve at the president's pleasure. The Secretary of the Treasury has constitutional authority as the head of an entire department. The Council of Economic Advisors forecasts economic trends and makes predications on the economy. The budget director of the OMB serves as the president's chief accountant charged with determining how much the federal government should spend year to year.

Pocketbook Issues and Elections

Except for partisan identification, there are no greater determiners on election day than a voter's view of the economy and the economic scorecard for politicians in power. Incumbent presidents who sought re-election during a bad economy have invariably lost their chances for a second term. The classic example is Herbert Hoover, who in 1932 sought re-election during the worst economy in history and suffered a landslide loss to Franklin Roosevelt. Presidents Ford in 1976, Carter in 1980, and Bush Sr. in 1992 all lost their quests for a second term during poor economic times. In 1992, with the Cold War over and the economy in bad shape, Bill Clinton's campaign manager, James Carville, reminded his candidate, "It's the economy, stupid." People who are adversely affected by the economy will vote against the incumbent party.

Governing economic and budgeting issues is challenging, especially considering the general desires of the citizenry. Most people have three desires for government finances: lower taxes, no national debt, and enhanced government services. Having all three is impossible, as Senator Graham's quote at the opening of this chapter reveals. So how do politicians satisfy these wants? "Don't tax me, don't tax thee, tax that fellow behind the tree," Senator Russell Long of Louisiana allegedly used to say. Long came from a family of adept Louisiana politicians that knew the answer was to raise taxes on "other people." For example, governments create excise taxes on particular products or services, such as cigarettes or gambling (often called "sin taxes"), hitting only a few people, many of whom won't cease making such purchases even when taxes lead to higher prices.

Economic Ideology

The manner in which the government can approach the economy spans a wide range of ideologies. Many divide the political approach to governing the economy along a continuum of more or less government interference.

Keynesian Economics English economist John Maynard Keynes (1883–1946) offered a theory regarding the aggregate demand (the grand total spent) in an economy. Keynes theorized that if left to its own devices, the market will not necessarily operate at full capacity. Not all persons will be employed and the value of the dollar may drop. Much depends on how much people spend or save. Saving is wise for individuals, but when too many people save too much, companies will manufacture fewer products and unemployment will rise. When people spend too much, conversely, their spending will cause a sustained increase in prices and shortages of goods. Keynes believed that the government should create the right level of demand. When demand is too low, the government should put more money into the economy by reducing taxes and/or increasing government spending, even if doing so requires borrowing money. If demand is too high, the government should take money out of the economy by taxing more (taking wealth out of citizens' pockets) and/or spending less.

Franklin Roosevelt based his New Deal concept largely on the Keynesian model. The federal government built an array of public works during the era. Agencies such as the Works Progress Administration, the Public Works Administration, and the Civilian Conservation Corp built new schools, dams, roads, libraries, and other capital investments. The government had to borrow money while it pumped money into the economy and provided jobs.

Multiplier Effect Keynesian economics also recognizes a multiplier effect. Output increases by a multiple of the original change in spending that caused it. For example, a $10 billion increase in government spending could cause the total output to rise by $15 billion (if a multiplier of 1.5 is possible). When the government begins construction projects, for example, not only are unemployed builders potentially put to work, but bricklayers, electricians, and plumbers are too.

Supply-Side Theory On the opposite end of the economic ideological spectrum are the supply-side theorists, or supply-siders. Harvard economist Arthur Laffer, a key advisor to President Ronald Reagan, came to define **supply-side economics**. Supply-siders—fiscal conservatives—believe that the government should leave as much of the money supply as possible with the people. This approach means taxing less and leaving that money in the citizens' pockets. Such a stance serves two purposes: 1) people will have more money to spend and will spend it, and 2) this spending will increase purchasing, jobs, and manufacturing. Under this concept, the government will still earn large revenues via the taxes collected from this spending. The more people spend, the more the state collects in sales taxes from store cash registers. The federal government will take in greater amounts of income tax because more people will be employed to earn higher salaries. Government will also take in greater revenues in corporate taxes from companies' profits. Supply-siders try to determine the right level of tax to strengthen firms and increase overall governmental revenues.

Keeping taxes low also provides incentives for people to work more and earn more, knowing they will keep larger amounts of money. They will also invest more in other ways. If they are not spending money at the store, they are putting more money into the economy with larger investments, such as purchasing stocks or bonds, activities that boost the economy and show consumer confidence.

Monetary Policy

The basic forces of supply and demand that determine prices on every product or service from lemonade to cars also determine the actual value of the U.S. dollar. Of course, a dollar is worth 100 cents, but what will it buy? Diamonds and gold are worth a lot because they are in short supply. Paper clips are cheap for the opposite reason. These same principles affect the value of money. **Monetary policy** is how the government manages the supply and demand of its currency and thus the value of the dollar. How much a dollar is worth depends on how many printed dollars are available and how much people (both Americans and those around the world) want them.

Inflation (rising prices and devaluation of the dollar) occurs, monetarists will tell you, when there are too many dollars in circulation. If a government prints few dollars or closely monitors how much currency makes its way into circulation, the value of a dollar will remain relatively high.

The Federal Reserve System

Congress created the Federal Reserve System in 1913. It has a unique structural design. It consists of the **Federal Reserve Board**, its most powerful component, the Federal Open Market Committee, and 12 regional Federal Reserve Banks. The Treasury Department is in charge of collecting taxes and printing U.S. currency, but the Federal Reserve Board sets U.S. monetary policy.

The Federal Reserve Board is a board of seven "governors" appointed by the president and approved by the Senate for 14-year staggered terms. One governor serves as the chairman for a four-year term. Typically referred to as "The Fed," this agency sets monetary policy by buying and selling securities, regulating money reserves required at commercial banks, and setting interest rates.

The 12 Federal Reserve Banks serve as the intermediaries for money traveling from the government printing press to the commercial banks in your hometown. The letter code in the Federal Reserve seal on the face of a dollar bill represents one of these 12 banks. The U.S. government loans these printed dollars to the commercial banks.

Bond Rates The Fed also determines the rates for government **bonds,** or securities (government IOUs), and when to sell or purchase these. In addition to taxes, our federal government takes in revenue when individual Americans or even foreign governments purchase U.S. bonds or other Treasury notes on a promise that the United States will pay them back later with interest. The Fed both sells these to and purchases these from commercial banks. When it buys them back with interest, it is giving the banks more money with which to operate and to loan out to customers.

Discount Rate The Fed also sets the **discount rate**, the interest rate at which the government loans actual dollars to commercial banks. Since 1990, this rate has fluctuated from 4 to 6 percent; more recently it has dropped below 1 percent. Raising or lowering the discount rate has a direct impact on commercial banking activity and the economy in general. Commercial banks will borrow larger sums when the rate is lower and drop their interest rates accordingly. When banks can offer lower interest rates to consumers, people purchase more cars and houses. When more homes or cars are purchased, employment rises as more car sales associates, realtors, and housing contractors are needed, and demand is generated for lumber, bricks, rubber, and gasoline.

Reserve Requirements The Fed also regulates how much cash commercial banks must keep in their vaults. While these banks give you an incentive to keep your money with them by offering small interest rates on savings or checking accounts, they charge higher rates to those borrowing from them. The Fed sets reserve requirements, the amount of money that the bank must keep on hand as a proportion of how much money the bank rightfully possesses (though much of it is loaned out to borrowers). These reserves and this requirement have a direct effect on how much the bank can loan out. If the reserve requirement goes from 16 dollars on hand for every 100 it loans out to 12 on hand, the bank will be encouraged to loan out more. If the reserve requirement rises, the interest rates will also rise.

The Federal Reserve and the Economy
• The Fed sets the terms for U.S. bonds and Treasury bills.
• The Fed can raise or lower the discount rate.
• The Fed can alter banks' reserve requirement.

Independence and Stability As you can see, decisions at the Fed can have monumental impact on the value of the dollar and the state of the economy. That is why the Federal Reserve Board is an independent agency in the executive branch with a unique structural design. Presidents can shape the Fed with appointments, but once confirmed, these governors and the chairman act in the best interest of the nation, not at the whims of the president or of a political party. Their lengthy, 14-year terms allow for continuity. The chairman's term is a four-year period that staggers the president's term to prevent making the appointment an election issue. The president can remove these governors for stated causes if they are proven to act in poor interest of the nation. No president, however, has ever done so.

Fiscal Policy

The manner in which the government taxes and spends is what defines its fiscal policy. Each year the federal government creates an annual budget just as many families create household budgets. A family must estimate how much money it will earn in a year, mostly through salary or wages, and then consider what to purchase. Individuals or families must first allot for the most essential expenditures—house payments or rent, food, clothing, car payments, household repairs, and utilities. Only then can they decide where to spend leftover, disposable income—by going out to dinner, for example, or taking a vacation, or investing for the future. Husbands and wives, parents and children, differ on what expenses are most important. Unforeseen costs can arise, prices can go up, and sometimes people don't earn what they expected.

Some of these same complications cloud the federal budgeting process, as do differing economic theories, differing priorities, powerful interest groups, and political considerations. The government brings in revenue, largely through taxes, and spends on services—interstate highways, national parks, military defense, law enforcement, the arts and sciences, and others. Congress and the president determine the amounts of these expenditures, or outlays, with nearly every relevant entity weighing in.

Competing political parties and hundreds of interest groups have different views on how much citizens should pay in to this system and where this money should be spent. Several governmental actors in the executive and legislative branches help determine fiscal policy. Unforeseen disruptions, such as war or natural disasters, can drastically affect spending from the government treasury.

Revenue

Article I of the Constitution gives Congress the power to lay and collect taxes and to borrow money. It is through this power that the United States taxes, charges fees, and borrows money to collect revenue. Most government receipts today come from the national income tax. In addition to taxing, the United States is good at borrowing. In fact, the United States has been out of debt only once in its entire history. It sells bonds and securities, or government IOUs, to individual investors. Grandparents purchase U.S. savings bonds for their grandchildren. Large investment firms and foreign nations make large-scale investments by buying large bonds, confident that the federal government will pay it off with interest. The United States has always managed to do so. U.S. bonds are some of the safest and most sound investments in the world.

Tax Policy When the Framers empowered Congress to lay and collect taxes, they only vaguely defined how Congress would assess and collect those taxes. For the first several decades, customs duties on imports supplied most of the government revenues. During this time, however, the federal government provided many fewer services than it does in modern times.

One of the few exclusive powers the House of Representatives has over the Senate is its priority on tax bills. The **House Ways and Means Committee** is where tax policy begins. Such bills must also pass the Senate and be signed by the president to become law.

 Is That Constitutional? *Pollock v. Farmers' Loan and Trust Co.* (1892)

Does Article I, Section 8, empower Congress to lay and collect a tax on individual incomes?

No. That's what the Court said in *Pollock v. Farmers' Loan and Trust* in 1892. Congress passed the first income tax to support the Union cause during the Civil War without much citizen opposition because the tax was only temporary. In the later 1800s, Congress instituted the first-ever peacetime income tax to support the growing federal government. The Supreme Court ruled it unconstitutional because Article I did not specifically grant Congress the power to directly tax individuals. This was a classic case that exemplified the Court's late-1800s adherence to *laissez-faire* thought. This decision would soon be overriden by a constitutional amendment.

Federal Income Tax To trump the decision in *Pollock*, Congress passed and the states ratified the **Sixteenth Amendment** (1913), which allows Congress to tax people's incomes "from whatever source derived." Soon after, Congress began defining the income tax system and later created the **Internal Revenue Service (IRS)** to oversee the collection process. Today, the largest share of federal revenue comes from these income taxes on individual citizens.

Most people generally think of an income tax as an "earnings tax," a tax on wages or salaries. The amendment's wording, however, also allows the federal government to tax incomes from successful investments, gambling winnings, earned interest, and stock dividends. Even when people receive an inheritance, Congress can tax this income. This is known as an **estate tax** and is sometimes referred to as a "death tax" by its critics. In 2015, the federal estate tax applied only to inheritances over $5.4 million.

Over the last century, Congress has regularly altered the tax code for a variety of reasons. Our national income tax is a **progressive tax**, meaning one's tax rate increases, or progresses, as one's income increases. During World War II, the highest tax bracket required the richest Americans to pay 94 percent of their income in tax. Since President Kennedy encouraged a major drop in the tax rate in 1962, the top tax bracket has gradually diminished. In the 1970s, it hovered around 70 percent. While Ronald Reagan was in office in the 1980s, it fell to below 30 percent, and in the most recent decades, it has hovered between 35 and 40 percent.

Individual Federal Income Tax Rates, 2010		
Taxable Income	Federal Income Tax	Percent
25,000	3,331	13
50,000	8,681	17
100,000	21,709	28
500,000	152,644	31
1,000,000	327,644	33

Source: Senate Committee on Finance, JCX-51-10, 2010

Paying nearly 40 percent of what one earns to the national government seems high, but only the richest Americans do so. Today, only people earning hundreds of thousands of dollars per year are paying at this high rate. In fact, more than 18 million people in the United States need not even file a tax return, and well over 30 million others still end up paying no federal income tax at all. Middle-class Americans pay roughly between five and 15 percent of their incomes to the federal government. Public opinion supports a mildly progressive tax code, and that has been the standard since the Progressive Era. Some conservatives on the far right, however, argue for a **flat tax**, one that taxes citizens at the same rate.

Complicated Tax Code Congress has used its taxing power to create incentives and punishments. Special interest groups have pushed for loopholes in the tax code to favor certain people. Congress has used taxing power not only as a revenue source but also as a way to draft social policy, by encouraging certain behaviors and discouraging others.

For example, homebuilders' associations have successfully pushed for tax breaks for people taking out a mortgage on a new house. Laws that encourage home ownership also encourage stability in society. Most agree that attending college is a good thing and that the government should help ease that cost. Congress has arranged for students taking financial aid to receive government-sponsored, interest-deferred loans. Congress has created incentives to encourage people to purchase energy-efficient cars, appliances, solar panels, doors, and windows for their homes in order to protect the environment.

In 1995, the federal tax rules and regulations covered 40,500 pages. In 2006, it had reached more than 66,000 pages. In trying to determine one's annual federal income taxes, most taxpayers go through more than 70 lines on the 1040 tax form before they know their actual tax liability.

Other Taxes Corporations and small businesses also have incomes and are taxed on these. When McDonalds or Wal-Mart makes a profit, these firms earn money that is taxed, just as the local mom-and-pop shops are in your hometown. The corporate tax rate in the United States has varied between 15 and 35 percent. About 10 percent of overall federal revenue comes from corporate taxes. The United States also creates **excise taxes** on particular products or services. About three percent of the national budget comes from excise taxes imposed on such items as alcohol, tobacco, airline travel, and gasoline, all of which require certain government attention. Most states also have their own income taxes as well as sales taxes, additional taxes on hotels, and other luxury items such as cars and boats.

FEDERAL RECEIPTS BY SOURCE

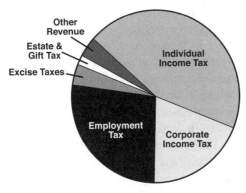

Source: OMB Historical tables, FY 2011

Most U.S. citizens realize that taxes are necessary but typically want lower ones. What about the tax rates in other countries? Most industrialized nations have a tax burdens well above that of the United States. In one survey of the overall tax burden by the Organization for Economic Cooperation and Development, the United States ranked 15th among selected countries as a percent of income, with U.S. citizens paying 25.4 percent of their incomes to a combination of income, sales, and other taxes.

The Federal Budget

The Constitution states "no money shall be drawn from the Treasury but in consequences of appropriations made by law." This provision creates a constitutional constraint on fiscal policy by giving Congress the "power of the purse." It simply means federal dollars cannot be spent unless Congress says so. The Framers wanted the most democratic branch to have authority over spending. Congress has guided spending over the years. The executive branch, however, may have a better idea of what expenditures are necessary in carrying out the nation's business.

The federal government grew large enough to warrant an agency just for planning and keeping track of spending. In 1921, Congress created the Bureau of the Budget. This executive branch agency gave the president authority to prepare an annual budget to submit to Congress for approval. A more complicated, multistep process exists today that includes both houses of Congress, a handful of agencies, and considerations that make annual budgeting a year-long process.

The Budget Process By the early 1970s, Congress had created the Office of Management and Budget (OMB) and modified the process with the **Congressional Budget and Impoundment Control Act (1974)**. The OMB is the president's budgeting arm. Headed by a director who is essentially the president's accountant, the OMB considers the needs and wants of all the federal departments and agencies, the fiscal and economic philosophy of the president, federal revenues, and other factors to arrange the annual budget.

Preparing a spending plan for an entire department or just one federal agency is a complex process in itself. The FBI, the Navy, and all other agencies create annual operating budgets to cover federal employees' salaries, equipment, services, and many more expenses. As a yardstick, these agencies consider their spending in the prior year. If their goals are similar, and inflation has not taken off, they will require about the same amount. They submit their spending requests up to their department secretaries. The 15 departments consider these requests, perhaps tweak them, and then send these up to the president's OMB. The budget director, in consultation with the president, his Council of Economic Advisors, and the Treasury Secretary, draft what becomes the president's budget proposal to Congress.

Budgeting Guidelines This spending plan is for the **fiscal year**, the time frame from October 1 through September 30. For example, FY 2013 ended on September 30, 2013. The president typically makes his budget plan public and sends it to Congress in early February so it can be finalized by the time the fiscal year begins on October 1.

This process continues under the 1974 law, which returned more control to Congress. Presidents had impounded funds, refusing to spend monies Congress had appropriated. President Nixon, particularly, impounded funds in an attempt to curb spending. Yet, saving federal dollars by refusing to spend what Congress deemed necessary was seen as undemocratic and a violation of separation of powers. The Congressional Budget and Impoundment Control Act outlawed such **impoundments**.

In Congress The law also defines the stages in reconciling the budget. It calls for Congress to set overall levels of revenues and expenditures, the size of the budget surplus or deficit, and spending priorities. Each chamber also has an appropriations committee that allots the money to federal projects. The Senate Finance Committee is a particularly strong entity in federal spending. Congress also created a congressional agency made of nonpartisan accountants called the **Congressional Budget Office (CBO)**. This professional staff of experts examines and analyzes the budget proposal and serves as a check on the president's OMB.

Another relevant player in the budgeting process is the **Government Accountability Office (GAO)**, an independent, nonpartisan arm of Congress. The GAO serves as a watchdog of congressional funds and keeps track of where and how money is spent. Sometimes viewed as Congress's accounting firm, it is headed by the U.S. Comptroller General. The comptroller is a presidential appointee chosen from a slate of nominees recommended by Congress. The

GAO's work is based on requests from committees and committee chairmen. The agency audits federal spending, examines efficiency, and in many ways acts as policy developer in the spending process.

The congressional committees examine the president's budget, and by May they usually adopt resolutions that define a budget ceiling. After this point, the various legislative committees (those with jurisdiction over particular areas, such as education, transportation, or the military) take up appropriations bills for the coming fiscal year, ideally staying within the guidelines set by the budget resolution. After each of these committees considers and passes these appropriations bills, and after Congress passes the overall budget bill, it then goes back to the president for his signature.

Federal Organizations with Budgetary Influence
• Office of Management and Budget
• Congressional Budget Office
• House and Senate Budget Committees
• House and Senate Appropriations Committees
• Senate Finance Committee
• Department of the Treasury
• Council of Economic Advisors

Partisanship and Political Philosophy The budget process has become more partisan as Republicans and Democrats differ on spending priorities. Those in the GOP tend toward fiscal conservatism; Democrats tend to spend federal dollars more liberally on social programs to help the disadvantaged or to support the arts.

Members of Congress from the party opposite the president commonly claim the president's budget plan is "dead on arrival." The reality is that typically both parties vote to spend more than the federal government takes in, while they bicker about philosophical differences on parts of the budget that make up a fraction of the total. For example, some argue that the NASA program and other scientific endeavors aren't worthy. For the 2006 budget, all funds going to science, space exploration, and technology totaled 23.6 billion, a huge sum, but less than 1 percent of the overall budget. The National Endowment for the Arts, a favorite whipping boy for fiscal conservatives, received $124 million and the National Endowment for the Humanities got $141 million, together a mere 0.009 percent of the budget. Welfare programs, an easy slice of the federal pie to rile taxpayers, typically amounts to between one and two percent.

Debt and Deficits

The national debt is what the United States owes to those who have loaned it money. Several factors in our political system and in this budgeting process have driven the nation further into debt. The government's needs and wants are much bigger than the government's means (revenue), individual members of government seek to appease certain constituents, and Congress must pay entitlements. These are just some of the practical constraints that make the budgeting process challenging.

The **debt** is the grand total the United States owes at any one time, more than $18 trillion in 2015. The **deficit** is the year-to-year difference between what the government takes in versus what it spends. Occasionally, the United States runs a **surplus**, taking in more in taxes than it must spend. The last budget surpluses existed under President Bill Clinton and lasted into the first years of President George W. Bush's term. During this time, the United States still owed a debt, but it was taking in more than it was spending annually. The government has not been without some level of debt since 1836.

In 2006, the annual interest on the debt exceeded $226 billion and was the third largest area of federal spending. Congress must make the interest payments to have any credibility in order to borrow more in the future, just as an individual citizen must make at least a minimum monthly payment on a large credit card bill.

Entitlements One major contributor to both annual deficits and the overall debt is **entitlements**—government services Congress has promised by law to citizens. Congress frequently defines criteria that will award cash to individuals, groups, and state or local governments. Congress must cover this **mandatory spending**, paying those who are legally "entitled" to these funds. Entitlements include Social Security, Medicare, Medicaid, block grants, financial aid, food stamps, money owed on bonds, and other contractual obligations.

The largest entitlement program is Social Security. This mandatory government-run retirement plan constitutes more than 20 percent of the budget. Compared to the 1930s, Americans are living much longer. When the Baby Boom generation fully retires, there will be more people in retirement than working to support them. Some predict the Social Security trust fund—an account set aside and protected to help maintain the system—will become exhausted in 2042. At that time, the annual tax income for the program is projected to drop by 25 percent.

Politicians began realizing the potential hazards with this program years ago. Political daredevils have discussed privatizing the program or raising the retirement age. However, people who have paid into the system for most of their lives become upset when they hear politicians planning to tamper with Social Security or to change the rules. As discussed in earlier chapters, older citizens vote reliably, and AARP is the largest and one of the most influential interest group in the nation. These factors have made Social Security the "third rail" of politics: nobody wants to touch the third rail of a train track because it carries the electrical charge, and no politician wants to touch Social Security because of the shockwave in constituent disapproval.

Combined, Medicare and Medicaid make up nearly 20 percent of the federal budget. Once a patient is 65 years old, the government pays for most doctor visits, hospitalization, and prescription drugs. Medicare is largely administered by the states while the federal government pays the bill.

Congress must pay entitlements, but these could be altered. The rules and criteria around them can change to trim the payments to those entitled. And, for the future, some could surely be scrapped. The problem is that most entitlements are on autopilot, and the government need not review them annually. And, like the third rail of Social Security, politicians have little nerve to take away money from those to whom they have given for so long.

Discretionary Spending All told, entitlements make up about two-thirds of the federal budget. That leaves the remaining one-third that can be altered, cut, or increased. This **discretionary spending** parallels the optional spending in the household budget. The vast majority of this wedge of the pie is spent on national defense. With well over one million full-time employees in the Defense Department and countless contractors, the defense budget makes up about one-fifth of the total pie.

Wasteful spending is always a concern. In their book *Where Does the Money Go?* authors Scott Bittle and Jean Johnson offer the top three reasons why money gets thrown away—fraud and abuse, waste, and pork. A recent sampling includes nearly $2 billion in wasted funds allocated for victims of Hurricane Katrina; $100 billion in unused refundable airline tickets for which the Pentagon never sought refunds; Department of Agriculture credit cards used to purchase concert tickets, tattoos, and lingerie; and nearly 1,000 pork barrel projects that cost $29 billion.

HOW FEDERAL REVENUE IS SPENT, 2001–2010

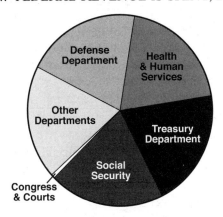

Facing the Debt The national debt grew to new proportions in the 1980s. Before that, the government ran budget deficits typically under $60 billion annually. In the 1980s, these deficits averaged $150 billion. Not only had these increased, but they quickly expanded the national debt. The overall national debt stood at $909 billion in 1980 and skyrocketed beyond $2.87 trillion in 1989. This increase occurred for a variety of reasons. One key reason was the dramatic inflation in the 1970s—one of the greatest in U.S. history—that made government purchases more costly.

Reaganomics In 1980, Ronald Reagan campaigned for the presidency, arguing against government interference and high taxes. Once he took office, he developed an economic program that became known as **Reaganomics.** The program was a combination of widespread tax cuts, deregulation, supply-side economics, decreased social spending, and increased defense spending. During Reagan's first term, Congress dropped the highest income tax rate from 70 to 50 percent and later to below 30 percent. His administration cut several domestic programs that assisted the poor, while it ramped up defense spending as a signal of strength intended for the Soviet Union.

During Reagan's second term, Congress began to address the rising debt and passed legislation to reduce deficit spending. The first was the **Gramm-Rudman-Hollings Act** in 1985. Sponsored by fiscally conservative senators and also known as the 1985 Balanced Budget Act, the law required annual overall budget cuts until the deficit disappeared. It mandated a **sequester**, or automatic across-the-board cuts in all programs except entitlements. The plan, however, failed.

In a second attempt, Congress raised income taxes and passed the 1990 Budget Enforcement Act. This law set limits on discretionary spending. It required that for any increases in spending in one category there had to be a decrease in another to limit the overall budget. This "pay as you go" procedure was meant to limit the deficit.

Other events addressed the growing debt. After the Soviet Union collapsed in 1991, military spending was cut. With Republican victories in the House and Senate after 1994, fiscal cuts and reform of social welfare programs enabled President Clinton in his final years in office to create the first modern balanced budget. In more recent years, the deficit and overall debt have skyrocketed again. The September 11, 2001, tragedy forced the federal government to rethink and increase its spending to protect its citizens and its shores. The Iraq and Afghan wars, too, have been extremely costly.

Amending the Process Two recent proposals to contain the national debt involve amending the Constitution to add a **balanced budget amendment** and **line-item veto.** The United States has no legal or constitutional obligation to spend less than it takes in, and it has rarely done so. Most people believe the nation should have to balance its budget, but to ensure this practice, a constitutional amendment would be necessary.

The line-item veto would empower the president to strike through Congress's excessive pork barrel spending. For example, individual representatives and senators seek to direct federal funds to their home districts and states, but with this power, the president could simply say no to what he deems unnecessary or excessive. The president has no particular geographic constituency and therefore would not have the same political concerns of upsetting small portions of the country by denying it funds. Americans have debated the line-item veto since the early years of the Republic. Congress gave this power to the president in the late 1990s, only to watch the Supreme Court declare it unconstitutional. At this point only a constitutional amendment could give the president this power.

Globalization

Globalization is the process of an ever-expanding and increasingly interactive world economy. Nations have increased their trading over the past two generations. Today, most products you find in your local department store were produced overseas. The U.S. government, mostly through Congress, can decide to increase or decrease this trade. A government wants to encourage its firms to export to larger, world markets so that wealth from other nations enters the U.S. economy. A nation that exports more than it imports has a favorable **trade balance**. One that purchases more goods from other nations than it sends out has a trade deficit. The size of this surplus or deficit is but one measure of U.S. economic success. On the other hand, Congress imposes import duties on products coming into the country to protect U.S. manufacturers.

According to Article I, Section 9, to encourage American production, Congress cannot tax exports. The Framers did, however, expect Congress to tax imported goods, charging fees to foreign manufacturers in order to give American manufacturing an advantage. Import taxes require foreign firms to raise prices on the goods once they arrive in the United States. The idea was to create a favorable trade balance, hoping Americans would produce and export more than they imported.

NAFTA The **North American Free Trade Agreement** lifted trade barriers among the three largest North American countries: the United States, Canada, and Mexico. This agreement effectively removed import taxes among these powers. The debate about this agreement created a battle between corporations and labor unions. The business community, manufacturing firms, and economic conservatives generally favor free trade. To *laissez-faire* economists, lifting barriers and government interference will create a free flow of goods and services on a global scale. These same proponents of globalization argue that the process has decreased poverty and enhanced the general quality of life in foreign nations. Many laborers, however, feared that American firms would outsource their labor requirements, which they have done. The auto industry suffered a major blow over the past decade and the automakers in Detroit closed plants and laid off workers. The free traders responded that the Mexican economy has grown and Mexico has bought more goods and services from the United States.

REFLECT ON THE ESSENTIAL QUESTION

Essential Question: *How does the federal government set and carry out domestic policy?* On separate paper, complete a chart like the one below to gather details to answer that question.

Types of Policy	How Each Is Set, with Examples

KEY TERMS, NAMES, AND EVENTS

Affordable Care Act

agenda

balanced budget amendment

bonds

Clean Air Act

Clean Water Act

Congressional Budget and Impoundment Control Act (1974)

Congressional Budget Office (CBO)

Council of Economic Advisors

debt

deficit

discount rate

discretionary spending

Elite Theory

entitlements

Environmental Protection Agency (EPA)

estate tax

excise taxes

Fair Labor Standards Act (1938)

Federal Reserve Board

fiscal year

flat tax

Government Accountability Office (GAO)

Gramm-Rudman-Hollings Act (1985)

House Ways and Means Committee

impoundments

Inflation

interest group politics

Internal Revenue Service (IRS)

mandatory spending

majoritarian politics

Medicaid

Medicare

Monetary policy

National Labor Relations Board

North American Free Trade Agreement (NAFTA)

Occupational Safety and Health Act (1970)

Office of Management and Budget (OMB)

pluralist theory

progressive tax

Reaganomics

sequester

Sixteenth Amendment

Social Security Act (1935)

Superfund

supply-side economics

surplus

Taft-Hartley Act (1947)

trade balance

Wagner Act (1935)

1. Which federal institution is most directly in charge of arranging the president's budget proposal each year?
   (A) House Ways and Means Committee
   (B) Senate Budget Committee
   (C) House Appropriations Committee
   (D) Office of Management and Budget
   (E) Congressional Budget Office

2. The single largest source of revenue for the United States comes from
   (A) custom duties
   (B) individuals' income taxes
   (C) corporate income taxes
   (D) national sales tax
   (E) estate taxes

3. About two-thirds of the federal budget consists of
   (A) entitlements
   (B) discretionary spending
   (C) military spending
   (D) salaries for members of Congress
   (E) education

4. Franklin Roosevelt followed the ideas of which economist in planning for the New Deal?
   (A) Arthur Laffer
   (B) Milton Friedman
   (C) John Maynard Keynes
   (D) Allen Greenspan
   (E) John Kenneth Galbraith

5. Congress responded to the Love Canal disaster by
   (A) creating the Environmental Protection Agency
   (B) placing an embargo on goods and services to Canada
   (C) creating the Superfund
   (D) passing the North American Free Trade Agreement
   (E) deregulating industry

6. Supporters of supply-side economics argue that
   (A) the more revenue the government takes in and spends the better off the economy will be
   (B) leaving more money in the citizens' pockets will stimulate the economy and generate government revenues via other taxes
   (C) the federal government should follow the ideas of John Maynard Keynes
   (D) the government should increase the supply of currency into circulation to bring down inflation
   (E) the demand for U.S. dollars will go up if the supply of those dollars is increased

7. Presidential impoundments of congressional appropriations have been viewed unconstitutional because
   (A) the president is not part of the budget process
   (B) a national debt makes a healthy impact on the economy
   (C) tax-and-spend policies create inflation
   (D) they tend to drive up the deficit
   (E) they violate the separation of powers

8. In an attempt to bring down the national debt, which congressional law sought to make across-the-board cuts via sequesters?
   (A) Gramm-Rudman-Hollings Act
   (B) Congressional Budget Act
   (C) Fair Labor Standards Act
   (D) Social Security Act
   (E) Recovery Act

9. Which federal labor policy act was LEAST favored by labor unions?
   (A) Wagner Act
   (B) Fair Labor Standards Act
   (C) Taft-Hartley Act
   (D) Occupational Safety and Health Act
   (E) Social Security Act

Source: Mike Keefe, InToon.com
Social Security Cartoon

10. Which of the following statements about the above cartoon is true?
   (A) Both of these leaders are very happy with the Social Security program.
   (B) The cartoonist believes there is no political danger to altering Social Security.
   (C) One president is trying to undo another president's policies.
   (D) A president is sending the nation into greater debt.
   (E) President Roosevelt is removing a federal program.

FREE-RESPONSE QUESTIONS

Question

1. The two dominant political parties in the United States differ in their approach to economic and budgetary goals.

   (a) Identify one difference in how the major parties approach tax policy.

   (b) Identify one difference in how the major parties approach budgeting.

   (c) Beyond differing partisan philosophy, identify and explain one constitutional constraint in setting fiscal policy that makes this process challenging.

   (d) Beyond differing partisan philosophy, identify and explain one pratical constraint in setting fiscal policy that makes this process challenging.

Question

2. The Federal Reserve Board largely determines monetary policy, while the legislature and the president share the responsibility of establishing fiscal policy.

   (a) Identify two ways in which the Federal Reserve Board determines monetary policy.

   (b) Identify one structural design that makes the Federal Reserve Board independent and stable, and explain why this agency is designed to be independent and stable.

   (c) Identify one government actor within the legislative or executive branch who helps determine fiscal policy, and explain how that actor determines fiscal policy.

WRITING: USE STRONG AND VARIED EXAMPLES

When you find yourself wanting to offer repetitive examples, or those that are precisely opposite each other for two separate points, think twice. For example, in Question 1 (a), you wouldn't want to simply say, "Republicans want lower taxes while the Democrats want higher taxes." This may even be true, but you'd want to offer greater differences in distinguishing the varied party philosophies on taxation and strong examples showing that variety.

In question 2 (a), you wouldn't want to simply offer, "One way the Fed determines monetary policy is by taking money out of circulation to raise the value of the dollar. Another way it alters the value of the dollar is to put more dollars into circulation to lower the value of the dollar." If you find an answer for two examples being this close together, you want to search for a more varied response and some strong examples to provide specificity.

Foreign and Military Policy

*"We must guard against the acquisition of unwarranted influence,
whether sought or unsought, by the military-industrial complex."*

—Dwight Eisenhower in his farewell address, 1961

Essential Question: How does the United States interact with other nations
and ensure national security?

America's foreign and military policy is defined by how the United States interacts with other nations and how it manages its defenses. International relationships develop from the views nations have of one another, their trade customs, and the interaction of their leaders. Countries engage in every level of diplomacy, from open-door policies to war. U.S. foreign and military policy is developed largely by the president, Congress, many executive branch agencies, and other governmental entities. This chapter explores the roles and relative power of the first two branches, their sub-units, the defense budget, historic conflicts, and the influence of nongovernment actors in creating foreign and defense policy.

Creating Foreign and Military Policy

The formulation of foreign policy is an ongoing process that reflects the current needs and interests of the country. It dictates how the United States deals with actors outside our national borders. It determines where our troops or sailors are located and which weapons Congress will purchase.

U.S. military policy is determined by how the federal government defends the country and how it uses the armed forces to influence international relations. In addition to the president and Congress, several key players impact foreign and military policy. The Department of Defense (originally the Department of War) has more than one million uniformed personnel in the Army, Navy, Air Force, and Marines. It is by far the largest department in the executive branch. The United States has military installations and bases placed in strategic locations in the United States and throughout the world. About one-fifth of the U.S. annual budget is devoted to defense.

The United States recognizes nearly every other country in the world. This recognition means our government will talk with, trade with, and acknowledge these other governments. Occasionally, nations refuse to recognize one another in any friendly manner, and some do not acknowledge others at all. For every nation that we recognize, the president names an ambassador to that nation. This diplomat operates a foreign office in an embassy in that nation's capital. Currently, the United States does not have an embassy in Iran or North Korea.

No matter how carefully assessed, not all foreign policy decisions will result in the desired consequences. Decisions are made from information that may or may not be accurate. For example, communiqués or cables from a foreign nation trying to strike a deal with the United States will have at the very least a bias and at times may even be fabricated. Intelligence reports are based on a spying game that involves questionable characters and endless intrigue.

The Constitutional Framework

Foreign and military policy is determined jointly by Congress and the president. The Constitution grants Congress the ultimate authority to "declare war." The Framers wanted a system that would send the United States to war only when deemed necessary by the most democratic branch, rather than allowing a potentially tyrannical or power-hungry executive to make a solo decision to invade another country. Yet the Framers also wanted a strong military leader who was responsible to the people, so they named the president the "commander in chief" of the armed forces. Presidents have assumed much authority over the military, perhaps more than was originally intended.

Foreign and Military Powers
Congress
• Congress has the power to declare war.
• Congress funds the military, foreign endeavors, and foreign aid.
• The Senate must approve appointed ambassadors and high-ranking military personnel.
• The Senate must ratify treaties with other nations by a two-thirds vote.
• Congress has oversight of the State and Defense Departments and relevant agencies.
• Congress can institute a mandatory military draft to staff the Armed Forces.
The President
• The president is commander in chief of the Armed Forces.
• The president appoints ambassadors and receives foreign ministers.
• The president negotiates treaties with other nations.
• The president issues executive orders that can impact foreign policy.
• The president makes executive agreements with other heads of state.
• The president commissions the military officers of the United States.

The War Powers Act of 1973 The president and Congress have not always agreed on the balance of their powers. The Vietnam experience provides a clear example of their disagreements. As tensions rose between the United States and North Vietnam in 1964, the United States found itself nearly embroiled in war. After what was perceived to be an attack on a U.S. ship in the Tonkin Gulf off the coast of Vietnam, Congress quickly passed the **Gulf of Tonkin Resolutions**, which empowered the president to use "all necessary measures" to prevent further aggression in Southeast Asia. With this broadly worded resolution, Congress gave the president wide latitude to conduct a war, because in the nuclear age, the delay required for lengthy congressional debate about "declaring war" could drastically endanger the United States. Within months, President Lyndon Johnson had fully engaged the North Vietnamese Communists to prevent the takeover of democratic South Vietnam. What resulted was America's longest war up to that point.

As the Vietnam War dragged on and public support for it dropped, Congress repealed this resolution and then passed the **War Powers Act** in 1973. This law tries to reign in the power the president gained in 1964 while still understanding the need for sudden, perhaps secret military action in the name of protecting the United States. The act gives the president 48 hours in which to engage in urgent combat without informing Congress. Congress, which had too quickly ceded its war authority to the president in 1964, had also abdicated the responsibility of checking the president. To correct this problem, the law mandates that after 60 days from the start of combat, Congress must vote to either approve or stop the engagement. This requirement forces Congress to act and guarantees the American people representation in approving or disapproving the action.

The law strikes a balance between the Framers' intended checks and balances and the need for quick action in the days of modern warfare. However, this relationship has been anything but clear since the law's passage. President Nixon vetoed the bill, only to be overridden. And no president has acknowledged the law's validity. In fact, most presidents have viewed it as an unconstitutional law that takes away powers the Constitution granted to them.

The Practical Framework

To achieve a coherent foreign policy, our national leaders must shape ideas and initiatives and then navigate them through the framework outlined above. In addition to the established constitutional authorities, several other governing bodies, committees, and advisory groups examine foreign policy questions and develop strong opinions on how to resolve them. These governmental sub-units are influential in the process.

The president has become the dominant player in foreign policy. President Truman's Secretary of State Dean Acheson stated in his memoir, "The Constitution makes the president the piano player of foreign policy." The president's role as a facilitator of foreign policy comes from the developing nature of warfare and diplomacy, the strong personalities of those holding the office, and the president's ability to be a much more effective communicator with the American people than a faceless Congress.

Strong public support for any foreign policy or warlike measure is unlikely until the president has brought attention and interest to it by publicly promoting or redefining U.S. national interests. When there is a real or even perceived threat to the United States, it is not difficult to rally support or to quickly retaliate and engage the new enemy. Most Americans will oppose a U.S. intervention in a foreign country until it starts; then they tend to favor presidential action. Gaining solid support for U.S. assistance to foreign nations or involvement in distant armed conflicts when there is no obvious threat to the United States is far more difficult. The president must persuade the American people that such an action is in the nation's best interest.

BY THE NUMBERS Declarations of War		
Year	Action	Vote
1812	War of 1812	House: 79-49; Senate: 19-13
1846	Mexican-American War	House: 174-14; Senate: 40-2
1898	Spanish-American War	House: voice; Senate: voice
1917	WW I Against Germany	House: 373-50; Senate: 82-6
1941	WW II Against Japan	House: 388-1; Senate: 82-0

Source: Congressional Research Service

What do the numbers show? Which historical foreign conflicts brought Congress to declare war? By what margins did the House and Senate vote for these actions? Which declarations had the strongest support? Which declared wars had noticeable opposition?

State Department Besides the president, the most important diplomat is the Secretary of State, who administers the State Department. Secretaries of state sometimes meet with foreign ministers from other nations. The State Department has thousands of employees working in Washington and abroad in U.S. embassies.

Several assistant and deputy secretaries of state have broad authority over a region or over a topic of concern. For example, the U.S. ambassador to the United Nations is generally seen as the nation's third most important diplomat. There are also deputy secretaries that oversee U.S. affairs with an entire region or continent, such as the assistant secretary for African affairs. The U.S. Agency for International Development (USAID), a State Department agency, helps determine how to allocate U.S. resources to aid foreign nations. These resources often come in the form of economic aid, food, medical supplies, or engineering know-how to enhance other countries' otherwise underdeveloped infrastructures.

Defense Department The Defense Department is headquartered at the Pentagon, just outside Washington, D.C., and contains four divisions—Army, Navy, Air Force, and Marines—with well over one million uniformed military personnel stationed around the United States and overseas. Congress issued a mandatory military draft with the Selective Service Act in 1917, and it maintained a draft from WWII through the Vietnam War. Since 1973, however, the military has become an all-volunteer force. The Secretary of Defense is the top civilian officer in the military below the president. The president typically names an able leader who is not a career military officer. The Secretary of Defense oversees the Secretary of the Army and the secretaries for the other divisions as well, who are also civilian officers.

Source: Mariordo Camila Ferreira & Mario Duran, Wikimedia Commons

Construction on the Pentagon began on September 11, 1941. Sixty years later, to the day, terrorists flew a commercial airliner into the Pentagon.

Department of Homeland Security In the aftermath of the attacks on September 11, 2001, Congress, the president's administration, and an array of experts created the Department of Homeland Security. Many believe that the United States might have been able to prevent the horrific terrorist attack had the various agencies charged with protecting America operated within one department and shared information better. So Congress created the government's 15th department, an umbrella department that oversees the Border Patrol, the Coast Guard, and immigration services. The department protects U.S. borders, monitors activity in airports and on planes, and assesses terror threats.

Joint Chiefs of Staff (JCS) Each military division has a chief of staff, a career general or admiral. These uniformed officers are involved in planning and policy for their respective divisions, and they work collectively to develop military policy. The **Chairman of the Joint Chiefs** is the top uniformed official in the United States and, along with a vice chairman, oversees the other chiefs of staff. Each division chief is primarily responsible for ensuring the readiness of his or her division and participating in an advisory panel for the president.

National Security Council Amid the beginnings of the Cold War, the **National Security Act of 1947** restructured the administration and shaped foreign and military policy. This law merged the Departments of War and Navy into the Department of Defense and created the **National Security Council (NSC).** The law states that "the function of the council shall be to advise the president with respect to the integration of domestic, foreign, and military policies relating to the national security." The NSC is an advisory board composed of top civilian and military personnel dedicated to ensuring the president considers a variety of viewpoints before making crucial national security decisions. Today, the council includes the president, the vice president, the director of national intelligence, the Chairman of the Joint Chiefs of Staff, Secretaries of State and Defense, and others. Presidents can choose to include additional members on the council, such as the attorney general or the FBI director. Also, a large NSC staff assesses national security worldwide and creates reports for council members and the president.

Foreign Relations Committees Both the House and the Senate have committees dedicated to the nation's relationships with other countries: the **House Committee on Foreign Affairs** and the **Senate Committee on Foreign Relations.** These standing committees discuss U.S. relations with other nations, consider how much foreign aid to provide countries in need, and hear testimony from ambassadors and cabinet secretaries. The Senate's committee is the more powerful and influential as it confirms presidential appointees and considers treaties before they go to the full Senate. The Chairman of the Senate Foreign Relations Committee is the most powerful legislator in the area of foreign policy. Historically, some of these chairmen have later served as Secretary of State.

Armed Services Committees The House and Senate Armed Services Committees are key architects of defense policy. They examine and consider a variety of issues, such as the development of weapons systems, military research, openings and closings of military bases, salaries of military personnel, and defense contracts. Senators and representatives serving on these committees have a special interest in U.S. defense, and several served in the military before running for Congress.

Intelligence In determining foreign or military policy, presidents rely on intelligence gathered from foreign nations and sometimes from within the United States. Gathering intelligence on both enemies and friends is essential in determining how to engage, attack, or ignore them. The president's chief intelligence agency has been the **Central Intelligence Agency (CIA)** since its creation in 1947. The CIA collects information from officials and agents spying abroad in the field. The CIA Director sits on the National Security Council. After September 11, 2001, Congress restructured the intelligence community—the many U.S. intelligence agencies including the CIA—to encourage a greater level of information sharing. The Director of National Intelligence oversees the intelligence community and serves the president directly, providing accurate assessments and fostering a good relationship among these otherwise competitive agencies.

Principals of Foreign and Military Policy	
Authority/Entity	**Role/Function**
President of the United States	Chief diplomat, commander in chief of armed forces
Senate Foreign Relations Committee	Handles treaties; confirms presidential appointees (Secretary of State, ambassadors)
House Foreign Relations Committee	Oversees the State Department; makes some foreign policy decisions
Senate Armed Services Committee	Oversees the military; confirms presidential appointees (Secretary of Defense, top military commanders)
House Armed Services Committee	Oversees military, bases, funding
Department of State	Coordinates the daily business of U.S. foreign policy; runs embassies abroad
Department of Defense	Manages the divisions of the military; creates military policy
National Security Council	Advises the President on national security and international affairs
Joint Chiefs of Staff	Uniformed head of each branch of the military; advises the president
U.S. Agency for International Development	Assists underdeveloped countries with foreign aid
Central Intelligence Agency	Gathers intelligence on other nations; advises president

Non-Government Organizations and Think Tanks

Across the globe, numerous organizations are concerned with foreign policy. A recent count shows nearly 2,000 U.S. think tanks, about 400 in Washington, that deal with foreign policy.

Perhaps the most influential is the **Council on Foreign Relations.** Headquartered in New York, the Council is a nonpartisan think tank that studies international issues of trade, security, and relationships. Leading members include current and past members of Congress, the State Department, journalists, and scholars on international affairs. The Council on Foreign Relations was created from a less formal band of academics and researchers who gathered information about the world to advise President Woodrow Wilson after World War I. Wilson, an academic, historian, and past president of Princeton University, relied on deep inquiry in making foreign policy decisions. The council was formally chartered in 1921 and has since served as a valuable resource in the policymaking process. It publishes the leading journal on the topic, *Foreign Affairs.* Its current board of directors includes two past Secretaries of State, other past Cabinet members, leading military generals, and well-known international journalists.

Another leading think tank in foreign policy and defense is the RAND Corporation. An abbreviation for "research and development," RAND was started after World War II by the Douglas Aircraft manufacturer in Santa Monica, California, and has since become a nonprofit, independent organization.

Foreign Policy Think Tanks
• Council on Foreign Relations
• Brookings Institution
• Carnegie Endowment for International Peace
• Center for Strategic and International Studies
• The RAND Corporation
• Woodrow Wilson International Center for Scholars

International Organizations

World organizations are chief in formulating and shaping international relations. By far the largest and most influential is the **United Nations.** Created after World War II and headquartered in New York City, the UN has 193 member nations and is involved with peacekeeping, humanitarian assistance, and working toward human rights. The UN consists of the General Assembly, which is the entire membership with broad authority over general issues and programs, and the Security Council, which is composed of 15 nations. The United States, the United Kingdom, China, Russia, and France are permanent members of the Security Council with the power to veto any Security Council resolutions. The other 10 seats rotate among other nations of the world.

The **North Atlantic Treaty Organization,** or NATO, is a smaller organization dominated by western European countries, the United States, and Canada. NATO also engages in foreign policy programs, peacekeeping missions, and humanitarian endeavors. NATO led the mission to remove from power the ruthless dictator Slobodon Milosovic in Serbia. More recently, NATO led an endeavor to assist revolutionaries in Libya in overthrowing dictator Muammar Gaddafi.

The Defense Budget

Historically, America's defense budget rose in times of war and largely disappeared in peacetime. Military drafts were instituted only when war was imminent or underway. That all changed with World War II and the global politics that followed. The weapons and the stakes became more consequential, and the United States wanted to remain ready for, if not ahead of, any potential enemies. The nation's main adversary, the USSR, thought the same way. This mutual stance resulted in an intense arms race and a costly military buildup.

During the 1960s, the defense budget comprised more than 40 percent of the overall federal budget. After the Vietnam War and into the 1980s, the defense portion constituted about 25 percent of federal expenses. During these times, most citizens supported a strong military and national defense as an essential role of government. Both Democrats and Republicans were on board with supporting and funding the military as their highest priority. But the demise of the Soviet Union in 1989 changed attitudes, and a new foreign policy dynamic emerged. Overall defense spending dropped to below 20 percent, where it has remained since. The spending includes personnel (the most expensive part of the military budget), machinery, and a host of other costs.

Military-Industrial Complex President Eisenhower's quote at the beginning of the chapter warns of the **military-industrial complex**, that network of large defense manufacturers and government defense leaders who purchase and use the best possible war materiel, always trying to stay on top of technological changes. Defense contractors have a stake in exaggerating the threat of war or the need for advanced weapons. Many private-sector defense industry leaders once served in the Pentagon or as weapons experts in the military. Corporations hire these former officers for their expertise and connections to clients. For example, Defense Secretary Dick Cheney left government to work for the defense contractor Halliburton and then later returned as the U.S. vice president. This revolving door (page 176) creates a conflict of interest.

Another factor that increases the defense budget is cost overruns. From the time the military plans, designs, and then finally completes a new ship or tank, the actual costs almost always surpass the estimated costs. Unrealistically low estimates and competition among designers and builders are two reasons why costs tend to inflate. Another important factor is **gold plating**—Pentagon officials pressuring Congress for premium war machines.

Military bases—where they are located and how well they are funded—cause controversy in Congress. Military bases bring jobs and boost a local economy. Members of Congress, even those who believe in cutting defense, will fight to bring a base to their district or to keep on old base open and operating at capacity. Congress has ultimate authority over these bases, but the politics of base openings and closings has caused Congress to put these decisions in the hands of an independent commission.

Both Democrats and Republicans want to protect America and support the troops. There essentially was no partisan divide on military policy during World War II and well into the 1980s. But since the diminished threat from the Soviet Union, the two parties have deviated on defense spending. Differing approaches to the War on Terror and the invasion of Iraq have caused a split in defense support. Overall, the Republicans are usually more willing to spend on defense than are lawmakers in the Democratic Party.

A Brief History of War and Diplomacy

The American founders not only planned for a robust foreign and military policy but also believed in minimal engagement with other nations, except in a commercial sense. They desired the economic advantages that come with trade but not the political and military alliances that could drive America into unwanted war. President Washington and Secretary of State Thomas Jefferson advocated what scholars have called a "policy of aloofness," or a detachment. Washington warned in his farewell address that the United States should "steer clear of permanent alliances with any portion of the foreign world." He asked why we should "entangle our peace and prosperity in the toils of European ambition, rivalship, interest, humor, or caprice." The United States was ready to advance domestically and to thrive in international trade, but it also wanted to avoid obligations and international friction. As you read the following brief history of U.S. diplomacy, notice the different foreign policy tactics, techniques, and approaches the nation has used over the years.

Expansion

The expansion of the United States from 13 coastal colonies to 50 states was the result of diplomatic land purchases and violent conflict. After the 1803 Louisiana Purchase, the idea of **Manifest Destiny** took hold—an incontestable belief in the destiny of the United States to spread across the continent. The belief held that Americans had a higher purpose—a charge to protect liberty and promote freedom. This destiny manifested itself through negotiations, wars, and purchases with other nations that ultimately led to the territorial holdings that are today the United States.

Beyond Louisiana Territory The Republic of Texas had earned its independence from the Mexican government and governed itself as an independent state. President John Tyler pushed to add Texas as a state, but the Senate refused to ratify the treaty. James Polk campaigned for office on a platform of expansion as attitudes in Congress shifted toward annexation. A month before Polk's inauguration in 1845, Congress fully annexed Texas, making it the twenty-eighth state in the Union.

The United States and Mexico subsequently squabbled over the location of the country's western border. In an effort to settle this dispute and to acquire more Mexican lands, President Polk sent Ambassador John Slidell to Mexico City with an offer of $30 million to purchase New Mexico and California. The Mexican government refused to receive Slidell. In response, Polk sent American troops into the disputed area. A skirmish between U.S. and Mexican forces gave Polk the card he needed to play to obtain a declaration of war. By war's end, the United States had acquired not only the disputed territory but also most of the land stretching from Texas to California.

The United States acquired a substantial amount of land through peaceful negotiations with Spain (Florida, 1819) and Great Britain (Oregon, 1846)— and the Gadsden Purchase (southern New Mexico and Arizona, 1858). The territory of the lower 48 states had been entirely acquired within 75 years of U.S. independence.

United States on a World Stage

Contrary to President Washington's wishes, the United States eventually became a world power aligned with other Western powers. The process was gradual and involved three wars that took place mostly beyond U.S. borders. By the end of this process, the United States had become not only a major world power but also the leader of the free world.

Monroe Doctrine President James Monroe delivered an address to Congress in 1823 that established a U.S. posture against European colonialism in the Americas. His speech came in response to a British proposal to align against Spain and France. The **Monroe Doctrine** defined the U.S. position: The United States would continue to stay out of European affairs, but Europe should also avoid further colonization of lands in the Western Hemisphere. "It is impossible that the allied powers should extend their political system to any portion of either continent without endangering our peace and happiness," said Monroe. Relying on some of the fundamental ideas carried out in the American Revolution, the United States had declared its sphere of influence.

Imperial America Within the following decades, the United States had acquired more land, sent Commodore Matthew Perry to open trade relations with Japan, and purchased Alaska from Russia. By the end of the nineteenth century, the United States had mounted the stage with the European powers. An age of **imperialism** prevailed in the Western Hemisphere and indeed throughout the world. The United States had interests beyond the mainland. After the brief Spanish-American War of 1898, the United States took on a more aggressive foreign policy and an expanded view of U.S. territory.

Spanish-American War With Spanish influence in the Americas waning, the United States recognized newly independent Latin American governments. U.S. involvement in Cuban affairs had partly evolved from a humanitarian effort—an estimated 200,000 Cubans had died of starvation or disease while trying to free themselves from Spanish rule. The United States sent the *USS Maine* to show a presence near Havana to protect Americans on the island. After American business interests and President McKinley supported freeing the Cuban peoples from Spain, the perfect opportunity presented itself for the United States to show its power and gain more territory.

That opportunity was an explosion that sank the *Maine.* Though the cause of the explosion was unknown, the national press pushed for war. In April of 1898, McKinley asked Congress for action against Spain. The war lasted only a short time and ended with American territorial gains. Spain gave Cuba its independence and ceded Puerto Rico and Guam to the United States. The United States then purchased the Philippines for $20 million. After going to war on a perceived attack in the Caribbean, the United States ran the last European power out of the hemisphere and grabbed valuable strategic territories in the Pacific.

Theodore Roosevelt The rapid, decisive end to the Spanish-American War caused world powers to view the United States in a new light. Congress soon annexed Hawaii and Samoa. The United States asserted that it, too, was a power player in the global system. After President McKinley's assassination, Teddy Roosevelt arrived at the White House and moved expansion and international influence atop his agenda.

After some European pressures on Venezuela, Roosevelt declared the United States would interfere only when the United States had been violated and only as a last resort. Citing the Monroe Doctrine, he said, "We have acted in our own interest as well as in the interest of humanity at large." In what became known as the **Roosevelt Corollary** to the doctrine, he summed up his policy with an old African proverb, "Speak softly and carry a big stick." The president played peacemaker at the end of a conflict between Russia and Japan, earning a Nobel Peace Prize while also tempering Japan's strength. He acquired the Isthmus of Panama to create a canal to connect the Pacific and the Atlantic Oceans. Roosevelt's successors continued the nation's growth to dominance in the Western Hemisphere.

World Wars and Isolation

The battles of World War I began in August of 1914. President Woodrow Wilson proclaimed U.S. neutrality to remain out of the war. German submarines fought with Great Britain and on more than one occasion sank British ships carrying American passengers.

Wilson had called for an end to these hostilities in his State of the Union address. He wanted to "create a peace that is worth guaranteeing and preserving," in the interest of all humanity, not just in the interest of those countries involved. Although the United States had declared neutrality, it still somewhat assisted Great Britain's war effort. In February of 1917, the attack on a U.S. merchant ship by German U-boats encouraged Wilson to ask Congress for a declaration of war against Germany. Wilson put the move toward war in idealistic and moral terms, stating, "The world must be made safe for democracy." Congress declared war against Germany, it enacted a mandatory draft with the Selective Service Act, and it prosecuted radical denunciations of the draft and the war effort.

League of Nations With the end of the war in sight, Wilson offered his **Fourteen Points**, a plan designed to prevent future conflict. His blueprint for an association of nations dedicated to "political independence and territorial integrity" would allow large and small states to protect one another from imperialists or expansionist invaders. This concept of **collective security**—the power of a united group to stand down an aggressor—was the basis for his plan. While at Versailles, France, to negotiate the treaty to end World War I, Wilson pushed to create the **League of Nations,** a postwar peace organization designed to provide a forum for resolving international disputes. Article 10 of the treaty stated that an attack on any member of the league was to be regarded as an attack on all members of the league, and therefore all should be prepared to go to war in response. The U.S. Senate, however, refused to ratify the Treaty of Versailles or to fully agree with its membership terms. This was one of the rare occasions when a foreign policy decision promoted by a popular president was checked by Congress.

Isolationism The United States had further asserted itself on the world stage, but the Senate's reluctance to enter the League of Nations parallels the American attitude that prevailed after the war. World War I was the most widespread, destructive encounter among nations up to that point. Americans supported the endeavor, but soon shied away from involvement in overseas conflicts. This attitude led to a movement for **isolationism**. For some people, the large number of refugees and immigrants who had been arriving in the United States for more than a generation raised concerns about national safety. The first Red Scare made the mainstream very wary of leftists, communists, socialists, and other intellectual radicals.

Congress passed a series of immigration laws that severely limited the number of people allowed to enter the United States from countries in eastern and southeastern Europe, especially Russia, Poland, and Italy. A 1924 law placed additional restrictions on immigrants, favoring those from northern and western European countries while barring those from China, Japan, and other Asian countries.

In the 1920s and 1930s, the United States sought arms limitations agreements. The chances for war, many believed, decrease when nations possess fewer weapons. But such agreements were difficult to enforce. In 1928, the **Kellogg-Briand Pact,** signed by 65 countries, tried to outlaw war, stating that settlements to international disputes should never be sought except by peaceful means. In an effort to avert another world war, Congress also passed a series of laws that prohibited the United States from providing arms or money to belligerents engaged in war or from sending ships into harm's way. The Great Depression had shifted America's concern from controlling lands and resources abroad to assisting the poor and the jobless at home. In this time of peace, however, other dangerous military and imperial giants began to rise.

World War II Adolf Hitler's Nazi Party had expanded in Germany, and Hitler was elected chancellor in 1933. Hitler's Germany had encroached upon neighboring countries in an effort to reclaim much of what Germany felt it lost after the armistice ending World War I. Hitler marched on and annexed part of Czechoslovakia. At the **Munich Conference,** Britain and France met with Hitler and agreed on a policy of **appeasement**, granting concessions in the hope Hitler would stop the aggression. He didn't. In 1939, the Nazis marched on Poland and soon began the Blitz—the air campaign against Great Britain.

Meanwhile, Japan had risen as the chief aggressor in Asia. It attacked China twice in the 1930s. Some gruesome attacks were unprovoked, designed to bring the Chinese citizenry to its knees. In trying to expand its imperial holdings, Japan started to colonize more and more nations in Asia. Serious tensions grew between the United States and Japan over aggression in the Pacific.

Taking Sides The developing world conflict caused President Franklin Roosevelt to say the United States would "extend to the opponents of force the material resources of this nation." After winning an unprecedented third term, FDR gave his message to protect the "Four Freedoms"—freedom of speech or expression, freedom of worship, freedom from want, and freedom from fear. He reminded Americans why the United States went to war in the past: for the maintenance of American rights and for the principles of peaceful commerce. "As long as the aggressor nations maintain the offensive, they—not we—will choose the time and the place and the method of their attack." He called on U.S. citizens to sacrifice to protect their four essential freedoms. Two months later, Congress passed the Lend-Lease Act to enable the United States to assist countries whose defense was seen as vital to U.S. interests. In August, British Prime Minister Winston Churchill and FDR met in Newfoundland, Canada, to confirm common principles in what became known as the **Atlantic Charter**.

Declaring War On December 7, 1941, Japan attacked the U.S. naval base at Pearl Harbor, Hawaii. The next day, FDR called on Congress to declare war against Japan, which it did with only one "no" vote. The conflict continued and expanded across the globe. Millions died as the war was fought on multiple continents. The Allies, led by the United States, the Soviet Union, the United Kingdom, France, and China, began to see turning points in 1944. By May of 1945, Germany surrendered. Over the next few months, the United States successfully tested the new atomic bomb. FDR's successor, President Harry Truman, ordered the bombs dropped on the Japanese cities of Hiroshima and Nagasaki, and these bombings brought Japan's unconditional surrender. The world's worst conflict was over. The United States prevailed as the preeminent world power by leading in the defeat of what were considered aggressive, evil enemies. A new world order had developed, with the United States displaying a weapon that it exclusively possessed, at least for the moment.

The United Nations Some of Woodrow Wilson's World War I collective security proposals and the ideas in the Atlantic Charter became a reality with the creation of the United Nations. Once committed to stopping the Nazi menace and the violent Japanese attacks on innocent Pacific nations, the leading allies began discussing a postwar concept for the United Nations. First conceived at a Washington, D.C., conference in 1944, the United Nations was officially created in San Francisco in April 1945. Delegates from 46 nations gathered to shape the UN charter. President Truman submitted it to the Senate, which ratified it in July 1945. This new organization was charged with maintaining peace and fostering cooperation among nations but committed to using force if necessary to stop aggressor nations.

The Cold War

The United States, with its superb military and exclusive possession of nuclear weapons, was well suited to lead a new world order. It was not physically and economically devastated like the other leading countries. Additionally, the United States had taken a moral high ground in defeating a Nazi empire in Europe and ruthless Japanese aggression in the Pacific. Committed to defend and befriend, the United States began to aid the smaller war-torn nations with economic aid. Meanwhile, the Soviet Union sought to influence and control neighboring nations to bring them under Communist influence. These cross purposes marked the beginning of the Cold War between the two superpowers. A global competition between democratic free-market capitalism and Communist totalitarianism put the United States and the USSR at odds. This competition created a bipolar world in which the two powers competed in an arms race, a space race, and a race for world allies.

Containment The United States became concerned about the Soviet Union's aggressive march into eastern European countries. This concern led to the U.S. policy of **containment**—limiting Soviet influence. *Containment* was a term first coined in a 1946 communiqué from American diplomat George F. Kennan stationed in Moscow. Containment guided U.S. foreign policy over the next 40 years. Kennan's "Long Telegram" explained Russian tactics and predicted how America must deal with them. The telegram became a blueprint for both the State and Defense departments in trying to understand Communist Russia. "I wrote this long telegram, which for some reason struck this very, very responsive bell back in Washington," Kennan reflected in a 2004 interview with *Foreign Service Journal*, "and it was circulated all around . . . for officers of the armed services in the Pentagon." Kennan transformed the telegram into an influential article in 1947 in *Foreign Affairs* under the pseudonym Mr. X. He warned of a long struggle with the Soviets, noting that "the main element of any United States policy toward the Soviet Union must be that of long-term, patient but firm and vigilant containment of Russian expansive tendencies."

Truman Doctrine Kennan's concern for containment helped shape President Harry Truman's approach to U.S. policy. The president had already claimed in a postwar speech that all citizens should be able to choose their own form of government. He later compared nations becoming Communist to falling dominoes, and he insisted the United States needed to stop this trend. The **Truman Doctrine,** a policy meant to halt Soviet expansion by providing aid to all democratic nations threatened by communism, arose from an address to Congress in 1947. Truman identified Greece and Turkey as two major areas of concern because Communist forces were trying to overthrow them. "I believe it must be the policy of the United States to support free peoples who are resisting attempted subjugation by armed minorities or by outside pressures," the president declared. He then asked Congress for $400 million for this effort based on the **Domino Theory**—the idea that if the United States allowed another country to fall to communism, additional, adjacent countries would follow.

Marshall Plan and Economic Aid Secretary of State George Marshall, in a commencement speech at Harvard University, outlined basic principles for a postwar Europe. Only an economically stable Europe could resist and withstand any attempt at Communist insurgency. Britain, France, and other European nations proposed a plan for recovery to present to the United States. The Soviet Union and its allies refused to participate. In April of 1948, Truman signed the European Recovery Act, more commonly known as the **Marshall Plan**. Over the next two years, the United States provided $12 billion in economic aid to Europe, more than half of which went to Britain, France, and Germany. Economic aid has since become a cornerstone of American foreign policy.

The Soviet Union conducted its first successful detonation of a nuclear bomb in 1949. Over the following years, the United States and the USSR began an arms race and created ways to launch missiles at great distances. While the Soviet acquisition of nuclear weapons increased tensions between the two superpowers, it also created somewhat of a stalemate. Having seen the destruction at Hiroshima and Nagasaki in 1945, neither nation wanted such a catastrophe. One of the guiding principles throughout the era was **mutually assured destruction**, or **MAD**. Both sides realized the devastation nuclear war would cause and thus refrained from using such weapons.

 ## Is That Constitutional? *Youngstown Sheet & Tube v. Sawyer* (1952)

Can the president take over an industry in the name of wartime national security?

The answer is no. On the heels of a national steel strike while the United States fought against North Korea in the early 1950s, President Harry Truman issued an executive order to nationalize the steel industry. Steel plants had been contracted to produce war materiel. A labor strike, Truman argued, would put America's national security in jeopardy. "We are in one of the greatest emergencies the country has ever been in," Truman declared. "I feel sure that the Constitution does not require me to endanger our national safety by letting all the steel mills shut down." He ordered the Secretary of Commerce to seize and operate most steel plants under his authority to "take care that the laws be faithfully executed" and to act as commander in chief. Steel companies immediately sought to reverse this in court.

continued

The Supreme Court struck down the president's executive order and rebuffed Truman's exercise of nonstatutory power in the Korean War. Justice Hugo Black stated, "Our Constitution . . . refutes the idea that he is to be lawmaker. The Constitution limits his functions in the lawmaking process to the recommending of laws that he thinks wise and the vetoing of laws he thinks bad." The president was neither empowered by the Constitution nor from an act of Congress to seize property or to nationalize an industry in the name of national security.

Vietnam and Disengagement

During the 1950s and early 1960s, a series of events intensified the Cold War. Under the authority of the United Nations, the United States joined South Korea in defending itself at the thirty-eighth parallel against the encroaching North Korean Communists. China had recently fallen to a Communist takeover, and the USSR had influenced North Korea since the end of World War II. This undeclared war ended in an armistice between the two sides. Today, roughly 25,000 U.S. troops assist South Korea in patrolling the southern side of the DMZ, or demilitarized zone, which straddles the armistice line.

The USSR launched the first satellite in 1957 and the first man into space in 1961. More dominoes fell. Communist regimes were established in Europe and in the Western Hemisphere. Most concerning was Cuba. After a Communist takeover in Cuba led by Fidel Castro, the United States felt threatened by adversaries within miles of Florida and by Cuba's disregard of warnings and the ideals in the Monroe Doctrine. The most suspenseful moments came during the 1962 **Cuban Missile Crisis.** After the United States confirmed that the Soviet Union had installed missiles in Cuba, just 90 miles from the United States, it formed a blockade to prevent further missile shipments. The tense standoff between the United States and the USSR resulted in an executive agreement and eventual treaties on disarmament.

Soon Vietnam became central to American concerns. North Vietnamese Communists had successfully defeated their nation's colonial parent, France, in 1954 and began entering the Democratic Republic of South Vietnam. From 1964 until 1973, the United States became embroiled in a long defensive war, characterized in part by televised reports of deaths in the field and public dissent back home. Congress continued the mandatory military draft and altered it with a lottery to make it fair and equal to all eligible men. Eventually, Congress began to question U.S. involvement in Vietnam and debated what became understood as unnecessary funding. The United States eventually pulled out and lost Vietnam to Communism. Since then, the public has tended to view foreign policy through the Vietnam prism. Over the following years, a policy of **disengagement** largely prevailed as the United States became more careful about how and when it engaged adversaries.

Détente and Arms Limits The draining experiences in Korea and Vietnam and the looming fear of nuclear annihilation led the United States and the USSR to begin a process of **détente**—a softening of tensions, a willingness to begin a better dialogue between the United States and its communist adversaries. The arms control process began in the 1960s as both sides looked to cooperation instead of competition. The process was helped by the United States playing the two leading communist nations—the USSR and China—against each other.

President Kennedy had called the Soviets "not to an arms race, but to a peace race." The Cuban Missile Crisis caused leaders on both sides to realize how close they were to global destruction. The United States agreed to the **Limited Nuclear Test Ban Treaty** in 1963. This treaty prohibited nuclear weapons tests under water, in the atmosphere, or in outer space. It also included a pledge by the signatories to work toward complete disarmament.

SALT This new attitude and the fear of mutually assured destruction led to the **Strategic Arms Limitations Talks (SALT).** The brinkmanship of the Cuban Missile Crisis and the high cost of the arms race made nations willing to talk. The Soviet Union, the United States, and Great Britain signed the first **Nuclear Non-Proliferation Treaty,** which prevented the transfer of nuclear technology from one country to another. Soon after, the United States and the USSR announced that an arms limitation, including a reduction in both offensive and defensive systems, would follow.

At a 1972 summit in Moscow, President Nixon and the new Soviet Premier Leonid Brezhnev signed the **Anti-Ballistic Missile (ABM) Treaty**, which barred the United States and the USSR from deploying nationwide defenses against strategic ballistic missiles. Such a move, the treaty's preamble explains, prevents either side from gaining an incentive to build arms. **SALT I** ushered in a new era of détente between the Soviet Union and the United States and essentially froze the military balance between the two nations.

In the late 1970s, President Jimmy Carter engaged Brezhnev in hopes of both nations agreeing to ban the manufacture of new weapons systems and encourage more weapons reduction. The first and only meeting between Carter and Brezhnev took place at a Vienna summit in 1979 and ended with the signing of the treaty **SALT II.** When Carter returned to the United States, those on the conservative right felt he had acted as an appeaser. The Senate Armed Services Committee recommended against the treaty, and the Senate failed to ratify SALT II.

Nixon and China Much of this idealist approach of cooperation is credited to Nixon's chief foreign policy advisor, Henry Kissinger, who in many ways was the ultimate realist. The United States refused to recognize "Red China," or mainland China, after the 1949 Communist revolution. Instead, it recognized Nationalist Chiang Kai-shek's government in exile in Taiwan as the legitimate Chinese government. By 1971, the United States began to rethink its position. Nixon sent Henry Kissinger to China to begin **normalization** with its adversary. Though some criticized the process, Nixon felt an improved U.S.-China relationship would allow him to play a card against the USSR and to weaken Soviet-China connections.

The following year, Nixon traveled to China for a two-week tour, the first American president to do so. After the visit, Nixon issued what became known as the Shanghai Communiqué. This communiqué tries to strike a balance between keeping the same close bond with the Republic of China (Taiwan) while also cooperating with mainland China, creating a "One China" policy that remains in place today. President Carter (1977–1981) followed up and established full diplomatic relations with China.

Carter and Reagan

Jimmy Carter's one-term presidency is remembered for two major foreign policy events—one a high point and one a very low point. The high point was an agreement between the leaders of Egypt and Israel. The Middle East had proven to be the next powder keg waiting to explode during the Cold War. The United States had a difficult time in the post-World War II years in both helping to create the Jewish state of Israel while also befriending Arab nations that held so much of the world's oil. Territorial and ideological disputes between these powers had raged for decades, resulting in frequently redrawn maps.

Camp David Accords In 1979, Carter finally brought Egyptian President Anwar al-Sadat and Israeli Prime Minister Menachem Begin together at Camp David, the presidential retreat in Maryland. Both sides had been at odds for more than a decade over control of the strategic Sinai Peninsula between the Mediterranean and Red Seas. Carter spent 12 days of negotiations trying to bring the two leaders together. Finally, the three signed the **Camp David Accords** in a ceremony back at the White House. Israel agreed to withdraw from the Sinai Peninsula. Carter won the Nobel Peace Prize for his work in this grand accomplishment.

Iran Hostage Crisis A horrific disaster for the Carter administration followed. The United States had sided with the shah of Iran, a dictator in power since the 1950s. When radical revolutionaries managed to overthrow the shah's regime in 1979, they also took the U.S. embassy and held U.S. State Department workers hostage. The hostage situation dragged on and on while Carter began to lose the confidence of the American people. Network news coverage began nightly announcing how many days these Americans had been imprisoned. A covert military attempt to retrieve them failed, with American forces dying in the process. This conflict contributed to Carter's loss to Ronald Reagan in the 1980 election. The Iranians returned all the hostages after 444 days, on the day that Carter left office and Reagan was sworn in.

Reagan President Ronald Reagan campaigned on promises of a harder line on the Soviet Union and other communists and extremists abroad. He soon pushed for increased defense spending. Meanwhile, Reagan's speeches included statements that characterized the Soviet Union as "an evil empire," ramping up Cold War tensions. Reagan's increasingly hostile rhetoric and an arms buildup returned the United States to a pre-détente, pre-arms-control policy.

Star Wars Star Wars was the common term for Reagan's **Strategic Defense Initiative (SDI)**. This multibillion-dollar plan meant to create a system to intercept Soviet missiles headed for U.S. targets. The program, though heavily researched and advocated by his administration, never came to fruition because of its high cost, diplomatic impact, and unproven influence on mutual deterrence.

Iran-Contra Scandal The most embarrassing Reagan policy culminated in the **Iran-Contra scandal**. A 1980 revolution in Nicaragua brought a Marxist regime, the Sandanista government, to power. Another domino had fallen and threatened U.S. interests in Latin America. Reagan's administration soon embarked on assisting Nicaraguan rebels, the Contras, with overthrowing the new Marxist government. Wanting to avert another Vietnam, the American public opposed any military involvement. In fact, Congress expressly stated so in the Boland Amendments, congressional acts that forbade such activity. Ignoring these laws, Reagan's National Security Council staff began devising undercover plans to assist the Contras anyway.

In 1986, stories of the United States selling arms to the Iranian government and of a CIA plane shot down in Nicaragua raised serious questions for the president. A plan had been hatched to sell arms to Iran in return for the release of American hostages held in Lebanon. It also involved funneling the money secretly to the Nicaraguan Contras. When asked about this illegal plan, Reagan denied any knowledge and created a commission to investigate. Most of the blame fell on Reagan's National Security Adviser Robert McFarlane and staffer Lt. Col. Oliver North. Apparently, the scheme was arranged to keep the knowledge from the president, or so it appeared. The nation became divided over the Iran-Contra affair, largely along partisan lines: conservatives embraced the ultimate objective of saving Americans and defeating Communists while Democrats saw an abuse of presidential power over Congress's foreign policy prerogative. In the end, the Tower Commission Report declared that the ultimate responsibility of such international paramilitary action rests with the president, even if the plan came to be without his knowledge.

Human Rights and Strategic Interest

After the Cold War, a series of events in the 1980s led to the demise of the Soviet Union and the end of the era. Reagan and USSR Premiere Mikhail Gorbachev began constructive exchanges. The Soviet economy was faltering. Gorbachev's policies of *perestroika* (economic reconstruction) and *glasnost* (understanding, or openness) greatly contributed to the improved relations and the eventual fall of the USSR. The Berlin Wall was taken down and reunited a Germany that had been divided on east-west ideas for a generation. When the Soviet Union broke up, the United States drastically altered its views on foreign and military policy.

The long effort to outpace the Soviet Union on arms while making alliances throughout the world paid off. The United States now had a **peace dividend**, the payoff of peace after so much investment to win the ideological and political struggle. With this victory, the United States turned more of its focus to humanitarian efforts far beyond U.S. borders.

Gulf War

The United States became more interested in tyrannical dictators who posed threats to U.S. interests. In 1990, President George H.W. Bush led an effort to oust Iraqi dictator Saddam Hussein from the small, neighboring, oil-rich country of Kuwait he had recently invaded. The international community agreed that Hussein's invasion of his much smaller neighbor was a violation worth addressing. The United Nations Security Council passed a resolution that authorized member nations to "use all necessary means to uphold and implement and to restore international peace and security in the area." It set a six-week deadline for Iraq to withdraw from Kuwait. In an effort to avert war, U.S. Secretary of State James Baker met with Iraqi Deputy Prime Minister Tariq Aziz in Geneva, warning him that the only way to prevent an armed conflict was to completely withdraw. Hussein refused the warning.

Bush sought approval from Congress to assist with the UN resolution, which passed the House and Senate on January 12, 1991, by votes of 250 to 183 and 52 to 47. When the deadline arrived, the United States began an attack on Iraqi forces in Kuwait. After only 43 days, Iraq withdrew and **Operation Desert Storm** had succeeded. Military historian Fred Kagan says, "Desert Storm became the exemplar of the 'come-as-you-are' war, the war that breaks out with little notice, lasts a short time, and ends with a decisive United States triumph." Joint Chiefs of Staff Chairman Colin Powell was determined never to allow U.S. troops to get into a Vietnam quagmire. The **Powell Doctrine** offered the model for a successful military campaign: have a clear objective, use overwhelming force, and get out quickly.

WORLD MAP OF TROOP LEVELS

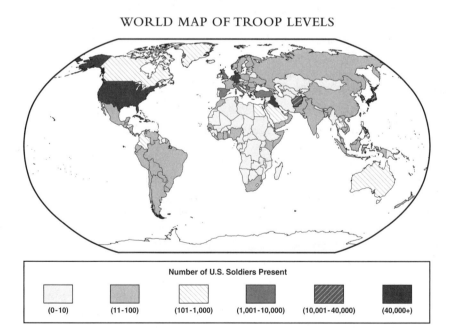

Clinton and Enlargement

After Bill Clinton won the 1992 presidential election, his national security advisor took a prominent role in articulating the administration's philosophy, which he called a strategy of engagement, providing diplomatic and humanitarian engagement in the world, and **enlargement**, increasing the zone of democracy. In 1995, U.S. aircraft bombed Bosnia-Herzegovina to allow U.S. peacekeepers to enter. The Air Force and Navy conducted a massive bombing campaign against Serbia, followed by a large-scale deployment of U.S. peacekeeping forces to enforce the peace in Kosovo.

Another influential member of the Clinton national security and diplomatic team was Secretary of State Madeleine Albright. Biographer Michael Dobbs explains that Secretary Albright came from a family who had fled Hitler and developed a worldview colored more by the Munich experience than by Vietnam. She became an advocate for more forceful intervention to balance the president's administration populated by a number of more cautious officials. In a speech before her appointment as the first female Secretary of State, she said, "Broad-based coalitions, multinational sanctions, internationally approved use of force will prove to be key tools for dealing with those who threaten their neighbors with weapons of mass destruction." A believer in the tools of the Cold War, she said, "Containment has succeeded—integration is next."

One high point of the Clinton foreign policy came with the **Dayton Accords,** a peace treaty between the presidents of Bosnia, Croatia, and Serbia to end the conflict in the Balkans. The negotiations took place at Wright-Patterson Air Force base outside Dayton, Ohio.

September 11 and After

The terrorist attacks of September 11, 2001, reshaped the way the United States creates and implements policy. Osama bin Laden, the leader of al Qaeda and the sponsor of these attacks, sought revenge on the United States for its presence in the Middle East and its involvement in the Muslim world. Operating from a safe haven in Afghanistan, bin Laden and his al Qaeda network conducted a series of attacks against the United States in the late 1990s. These included a massive bombing of U.S. Air Force dormitories in Saudi Arabia, simultaneous bombings of U.S. embassies in Kenya and Tanzania, and the attack on the *USS Cole* off the coast of Yemen.

On the morning of September 11, al Qaeda terrorists hijacked four commercial airliners departing Boston and New York in order to fly these into selected targets. Two planes hit the World Trade Center towers in New York City, another hit the Pentagon in Washington, and the fourth crashed in a field near Shanksville, Pennsylvania, after passengers stormed the cockpit. Nearly 3,000 people were killed in these attacks.

Declaring Enemies Within weeks, the United States determined this al Qaeda plot was designed and launched from Afghanistan. The ruling Taliban party had allowed al Qaeda to operate there. President George W. Bush and Congress laid plans to invade Afghanistan with strong public support. The president had declared an unofficial "War on Terror." The U.S. military quickly ousted the Taliban regime with Operation Enduring Freedom, at least for the time being.

Bush soon expressed great concern about U.S. adversaries—Iraq, Iran, and North Korea specifically—in a noted State of the Union address. These three nations formed an "axis of evil," Bush said, and the United States would need to monitor them. The president and his administration officials ramped up support for an invasion of Iraq.

Operation Iraqi Freedom Meanwhile, Saddam Hussein continuously refused to allow—or only allowed conditionally—UN weapons inspectors. Iraq was bound by international treaties not to possess weapons of mass destruction (WMD). Hussein had carried on a weapons program and killed thousands of his own people, but he had discontinued it in the late 1990s. To keep his neighbors guessing and to assert Iraqi sovereignty, he refused inspections, while in reality he had abandoned the weapons program and actually had nothing to hide. This refusal and faulty intelligence by Iraqi dissidents and power seekers led the intelligence community to suspect that Hussein harbored WMD.

President Bush sought a resolution to use force from the House and Senate and got it in October 2002. In the spring of 2003, the United States invaded Iraq and scattered the Iraqi regime. U.S. Marines took Baghdad within months of the invasion. As Bush declared major combat operations over, a nightmare began. Hussein's soldiers had shed their uniforms but had gone underground as civilians. Over the following months and years, the battle continued as the U.S. forces had difficulty knowing who was for ousting Saddam and who was simply eager for the United States to leave. Saddam was eventually captured, and a new Iraqi government convicted and executed him.

The above series of events influenced the development of the **Bush Doctrine,** which centered largely on preemption, nation building, and humanitarian endeavors. The Bush Doctrine was a product of terrorists and state-sponsored terrorism. In many ways it defends the United States and U.S. interests at home and abroad by identifying and destroying the threat before it reaches U.S. borders.

President Obama Barack Obama was a chief critic of the U.S. war in Iraq and against the Bush administration's approach to the War on Terror. As president, he has shifted U.S. efforts and withdrawn troops from Iraq to refocus on Afghanistan. He placed killing or capturing Osama bin Laden atop the agenda for the war on terror. In a covert operation designed partly by the CIA and carried out by Navy Seals, the United States killed Osama bin Laden in a compound in nearby Pakistan on May 2, 2011. Obama has been emptying the Guantanamo Bay terrorist detention center in the hope it will be closed, but he has followed some of the Bush Doctrine. He was instrumental in supporting the overthrow of Egyptian president Hosni Mubarak and actively supported the NATO assault on Libyan dictator Muammar Gaddafi. Obama uses the phrase "War on Terror." His drone and his National Security Agency spying programs have called into question his commitment to civil liberties.

REFLECT ON THE ESSENTIAL QUESTION

Essential Question: *How does the United States interact with other nations and ensure national security?* On separate paper, make a chart like the one below to gather details to answer that question.

Role of Congress	Role of President	Role of Judiciary

THINK AS A POLITICAL SCIENTIST: ANALYZE AND INTERPRET WORLD MAPS OF U.S. FOREIGN POLICY

Maps show where places are in relation to one another and provide information about an area of land, water, or space. Many maps show land features, including rivers and mountains. Political maps show the boundaries of countries. Specialized maps illustrate information about a specific characteristic, such as climate, land use, population density, or migration. Symbols on maps represent key information about the map. A legend or map key helps readers understand the meaning of the symbols shown on the map.

By now you probably have good skills in interpreting a map. Develop them further by comparing maps to draw inferences.

Practice: The United States develops foreign policy with a variety of tools, including troops and military bases abroad and aid to foreign countries. Examine the maps below and on the next page and answer the questions that follow.

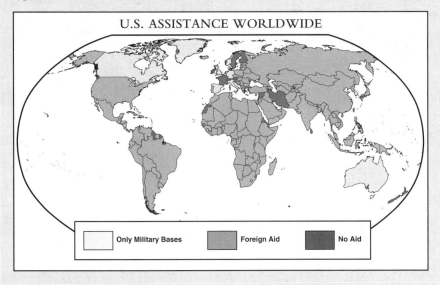

U.S. ASSISTANCE WORLDWIDE

Only Military Bases   Foreign Aid   No Aid

U.S. MILITARY TROOPS AND BASES AROUND THE WORLD

46 countries with no U.S. military presence

156 countries with U.S. troops

63 countries with U.S. military bases

7 countries host a new U.S. military base since 9/11

- What countries host U.S. military bases?
- What countries receive U.S. foreign aid?
- What areas have the strongest U.S. military presence?
- What countries or areas tend to receive the most aid? Why?

Compare the maps and write a short paragraph about the information provided. How do the two maps relate to each other? What conclusion can you draw about U.S. foreign policy by comparing the two maps? Provide evidence from the maps that supports your claim.

KEY TERMS, NAMES, AND EVENTS

Anti-Ballistic Missile (ABM) Treaty (1972)

appeasement

Atlantic Charter

Bush Doctrine

Camp David Accords (1979)

Central Intelligence Agency (CIA)

Chairman of the Joint Chiefs

collective security

containment

Council on Foreign Relations

Cuban Missile Crisis

Dayton Accords

détente

disengagement

Domino Theory

enlargement

Fourteen Points

gold plating

Gulf of Tonkin Resolutions (1964)

House Committee on Foreign Affairs

Iran-Contra scandal

isolationism

Kellogg-Briand Pact (1928)

League of Nations

Limited Nuclear Test Ban Treaty (1963)

military-industrial complex

Monroe Doctrine

Munich Conference

mutually assured destruction (MAD)

National Security Act (1947)

National Security Council (NSC)

normalization

North Atlantic Treaty Organization

Nuclear Non-Proliferation Treaty

Operation Desert Storm

peace dividend

Roosevelt Corollary

Senate Committee on Foreign Relations

Strategic Arms Limitations Talks (SALT)

Strategic Defense Initiative (SDI)

Truman Doctrine

United Nations

War Powers Act (1973)

Youngstown Sheet & Tube v. Sawyer (1951)

MULTIPLE-CHOICE QUESTIONS

1. The military's insistence on top grade war machines or defense equipment is referred to as

   (A) logrolling

   (B) pork barrel spending

   (C) military industrial complex

   (D) gold plating

   (E) overestimating

2. Of the following, which person has the LEAST power in determining U.S. foreign policy?

   (A) Secretary of State

   (B) President

   (C) Chairman of the Senate Foreign Relations Committee

   (D) House Minority Whip

   (E) Secretary of Defense

3. Some commonly referred to President Reagan's Strategic Defense Initiative as

   (A) Gold Plating the Heavens

   (B) Star Wars

   (C) The Final Frontier

   (D) Lost in Space

   (E) The Great Society

4. The military-industrial complex has been criticized

   (A) for its role during President Washington's day

   (B) for the revolving door from the Pentagon to defense contractors

   (C) because Eisenhower advocated for a strong one

   (D) for not being active in government contracts

   (E) for not creating enough weapons to defend America

5. Which of the following foreign policy principles or approaches seemed most effective in preventing deployment of nuclear weapons during the Cold War?

   (A) Collective security

   (B) Economic aid

   (C) Mutually assured destruction

   (D) Isolationism

   (E) Containment

6. Which of the following is NOT a congressional power over military authority?

   (A) Congress can declare war.

   (B) Congress appoints the top military generals.

   (C) Congress can stop military action by refusing to fund it.

   (D) The Senate has advise and consent authority over the presidents' appointed officers.

   (E) Congressional committees have oversight of military bases.

7. All of the following statements about the U.S. role during the Cold War are true EXCEPT

   (A) America attained its goals in the Vietnam War

   (B) a bipolar world emerged, with several nations aligning with the United States or the Soviet Union

   (C) the strategy of mutually assured destruction prevented actual war between the two leading nations

   (D) Congress conducted a military draft to maintain combat readiness during the post-World War II years

   (E) in spite of tensions between the United States and Communist countries, normalized relations and treaties assured some level of peace and cooperation

8. Which statement regarding foreign policy and public opinion is true?

   (A) Most Americans believe in a mandatory peacetime military draft.

   (B) Americans are generally more concerned with U.S. foreign policy than the state of the U.S. economy.

   (C) Most Americans oppose U.S. involvement in overseas conflicts until the United States actually enters such conflicts.

   (D) Most Americans opposed World War II after the Pearl Harbor attacks.

   (E) In the late 1930s, American citizens strongly favored entering the war against Germany and Japan.

9. Of the following U.S. policies, which involved the greatest open cooperation between the United States and the USSR?

   (A) SALT

   (B) Monroe Doctrine

   (C) Strategic Defense Initiative

   (D) Kellogg-Briand Pact

   (E) The arms race

10. America's intervention in Kosovo and Iraq in 1991 are based largely on which foreign policy view?

   (A) Isolationism

   (B) Containment of communism

   (C) Disengagement

   (D) Human rights

   (E) Détente

Question

1. Non-governmental linkage institutions influence the foreign policy that government institutions carry out.

    (a) Identify two non-governmental institutions that can influence foreign policy.

    (b) Identify and explain one drawback to such institutions' involvement in foreign policy.

    (c) Identify and explain one benefit to such institutions' involvement in foreign policy.

    (d) Identify and describe one foreign policy approach and how a non-governmental organization has influenced the approach.

Question

2. United States foreign policy is developed through a complex process that involves two branches of government as well as constitutional and political concerns in a democratic society.

    (a) Name and describe one constitutional and one political consideration presidents must take into account in making foreign policy decisions.

    (b) Name and describe one constitutional and one political consideration members of Congress must take into account in making foreign policy decisions.

    (c) Select two from below and explain the impact each has on the foreign policymaking process.

    - *Youngstown Sheet & Tube v. Sawyer*
    - War Powers Act
    - Senate Foreign Affairs Committee

WRITING: USE STYLE CONVENTIONS

When answering a free-response question, establish and maintain a formal style and follow style conventions. Capitalize names of congressional acts, court cases, and governing bodies. Use punctuation correctly. Try to leave enough time to proofread for correct grammar, spelling, and mechanics.

UNIT 6: Review

The federal government has instituted policies of all kinds since its beginning in 1789. Most Americans agree that the government should provide a safety net for citizens with unemployment insurance, the Social Security system, Medicaid, Medicare, food stamps, and other supportive services. Also, a heightened concern for a clean and sustainable environment in the 1960s and 1970s led Congress to set emission standards on industry, protect natural resources, and create a regulatory agency to enforce environmental standards.

The economic health of the United States is determined by a variety of factors, many of which the government can powerfully influence. Congress determines tax rates, business regulations, and government spending. The president, through his actions and words, can impact international trade and the stock market. The independent Federal Reserve Board alters interest rates, bank activity, and the value of the dollar to boost or stabilize the economy.

The United States also sets policies while looking beyond its borders. Countries interact via commerce, immigration, political agreements and struggles, and other common interests. The president and Congress cooperate and check each other in order to assure citizens' views are represented in matters of national security and interests abroad. Congress can institute a military draft and declare war, and the Senate can recommend, approve, or reject diplomats and generals. The president receives foreign ambassadors, serves as the commander in chief, and overseas the Pentagon and State Department. Through linkage institutions and with a vast variety of approaches, Americans influence government institutions to make the public's will the national policy.

THINK AS A POLITICAL SCIENTIST: FORMULATE AND REFINE RELEVANT INQUIRIES ON PRESIDENTIAL BUDGETS

Consider what you've learned about the Democrat and Republican parties' views on government taxation and spending. If you wanted to gain an in-depth understanding of how the parties tax and spend differently, what specifically would you research, and how would you carry out that research? Some of these questions may give you ideas.

- What are the large categories of federal budgets?
- What percent of the budget goes to entitlements? To defense?
- What departments, agencies, intiatives, or programs get more or fewer dollars?

Write up a specific and refined plan for researching the differences in spending between Democrats and Republicans based on recent presidents. Explain where you will find the information you need.

United States Government and Politics
Practice Examination

Section I

1. Which constitutional amendment guaranteed women the right to vote?
   (A) Fifteenth Amendment
   (B) Nineteenth Amendment
   (C) Twentieth Amendment
   (D) Twenty-sixth Amendment
   (E) State governments, alone, determine if women can vote.

2. The *Washington Post's* reporting on the Watergate scandal is an example of the media functioning in what role?
   (A) Scorekeeper
   (B) Watchdog
   (C) Overseer
   (D) Scheduler
   (E) Entertainer

3. In which case did the Supreme Court first exercise judicial review?
   (A) *Fletcher v. Peck*
   (B) *Marbury v. Madison*
   (C) *Dred Scott v. Sandford*
   (D) *Gideon v. Wainwright*
   (E) *Roe v. Wade*

4. The Great Compromise at the Constitutional Convention resulted in
   (A) a bicameral legislature that represents both the states and the people
   (B) the Virginia Plan becoming the format for government as introduced
   (C) a system for counting slaves in the census
   (D) the creation of the Bill of Rights
   (E) the system to elect the American president

5. Which of the following about the "Solid South" is true?

(A) It was a Republican stronghold from the end of the Civil War to the 1960s.

(B) It was the political power base for abolitionists.

(C) Since the Civil Rights Movement, the Solid South for Democrats no longer exists.

(D) It helped elect Abraham Lincoln.

(E) It opposed New Deal legislation.

6. The variety of American viewpoints that determines U.S. policy is known as

(A) republicanism

(B) pluralism

(C) nepotism

(D) gerrymandering

(E) coattailing

7. Which of the following U.S. offices are directly elected by the populace?

   I. House of Representatives

  II. Senate

 III. President

 IV. Supreme Court Justices

(A) I only

(B) I and II

(C) I, II, and III

(D) I and III

(E) IV only

8. Which is an accurate statement about judicial activism or restraint?

(A) The Supreme Court was an activist court during the first 50 years of its history.

(B) Judicial activism is carried out by liberals, not conservatives.

(C) The Warren Court (1953-69) is known for practicing judicial restraint.

(D) Critics of judicial activism point to judges' lack of expertise on policymaking matters.

(E) In the *Roe v. Wade* decision, the High Court exercised judicial restraint.

9. Which of the following about campaign finance is true?

(A) Free speech prevents any congressional limit on campaign donations.

(B) The Court has ruled that Congress can limit a citizen's donation to a campaign but cannot limit a candidate's own contribution to his or her campaign.

(C) The *Citizens United* ruling made donating to political campaigns an illegal act.

(D) Candidates can pay for TV ads, but others cannot.

(E) Congress addressed campaign spending mostly in the 1920s.

10. Read the following statement.

"[T]he judiciary, from the nature of its functions, will always be the least dangerous to the political rights of the Constitution because it will have the least capacity to annoy and injure them." — *Federalist #78*

In this statement, the Federalists meant

(A) judges will be independent because of their life terms

(B) the courts cannot do harm because courts don't have to accept appeals

(C) courts will have little influence in determining policy because courts cannot easily initiate policy

(D) the fact that the president appoints judges will keep courts accountable

(E) judges and courts will act responsibly or face defeat at election time

11. Which of the following is true regarding a free press in the United States?

(A) The government can prevent publication of leaked government information.

(B) Public officials are protected from public criticism.

(C) Federal law does not protect reporters from having to reveal anonymous sources to federal investigators.

(D) The FCC cannot limit what is broadcast on radio or television.

(E) Congress and the FCC currently require radio and TV networks to provide balance in their broadcasts.

12. Those who assert Thomas Jefferson's "wall of separation" idea

   (A) want absolute free speech in public

   (B) want the establishment clause strictly upheld

   (C) believe the police cannot enter a home without a warrant

   (D) want to bar obscene materials from public view

   (E) believe defendants must be protected from intense interrogations

13. Political participation in the United States

   (A) is lower than in any other industrialized nation

   (B) is higher than it has ever been, considering the relative voting-eligible population

   (C) is required by American law

   (D) takes other forms besides voting

   (E) increased dramatically after the Motor Voter law was passed

14. The Federal Reserve Board impacts the economy by

   (A) raising or lowering taxes

   (B) limiting the number of imports or exports

   (C) raising or lowering the discount rate on commercial banks

   (D) establishing the annual national budget

   (E) appointing the Secretary of the Treasury

15. A Cabinet secretary siding with his or her own department instead of the president on an issue is called

   (A) going native

   (B) gerrymandering

   (C) legislative overdrive

   (D) franking

   (E) logrolling

16. All of the following are members of the president's White House Staff EXCEPT

   (A) Press Secretary

   (B) Chief of Staff

   (C) Secretary of Defense

   (D) Senior Advisor

   (E) Office of Legal Counsel

17. Which of the following is true of the federal grants-in-aid programs?
    (A) The federal government did not award any grants until the 1960s.
    (B) Grants in aid are usually spent on the military and foreign affairs.
    (C) Categorical grants lack accountability to Congress.
    (D) Federal grants allow Congress to use federal dollars to address national concerns on matters traditionally addressed by the states.
    (E) States must participate in all federal grant programs.

18. Which of the following statements is supported by data in the table below?

United States Receipts, Outlays, and Surpluses or Deficits (in millions of dollars)			
Year	Receipts	Outlays	Surplus/Deficit
1980	517,112	590,941	-73,830
1990	1,031,958	1,252,994	-221,036
2000	2,025,191	1,788,950	+236,241
2010	2,162,724	3,456,213	-1,293,489

Source: OMB Historical Tables

    (A) The United States government has never been without a debt.
    (B) The United States tends to take in more revenue than it pays out in expenses.
    (C) The United States owes more money to Asian governments than any other creditor.
    (D) In 2000, the United States received more revenue than it had expenses.
    (E) Deficit spending was less in 2010 than in the other years presented in the table.

19. All of the following congressional committee system reforms have been instituted EXCEPT
    (A) limiting chairmen to only one two-year term
    (B) increasing frequency and influence of sub-committees
    (C) requiring publicly held committee meetings
    (D) altering committee staff size
    (E) preventing chairmen from pigeonholing popular bills

20. Which of the following is a sign that party loyalty has decreased during the last generation?

(A) Republican dominance in Congress and the presidency over the past generation

(B) Democratic dominance in the Congress and the presidency over the past generation

(C) Split-ticket voting that results in divided government

(D) An increase in voter turnout in primary elections

(E) Minor party candidates winning the Electoral College in recent years

21. Upon ratification of the original Constitution in 1788, which of the following happened?

(A) The Bill of Rights went into effect.

(B) The states gave up a degree of power to the United States.

(C) States regained powers from the national government.

(D) The American colonists were able to win the Revolutionary War and independence.

(E) States declared a level of sovereignty greater than they had before.

22. Which of the following concepts do courts follow when adhering to precedent?

(A) *Certiorari*

(B) *Stare decisis*

(C) Senatorial courtesy

(D) Recusal

(E) *Amicus curiae*

23. Which of the following is necessary for a presidential candidate to win the party nomination?

(A) The candidate must win the Iowa caucuses.

(B) The candidate must win the New Hampshire Primary.

(C) The candidate must win a majority of electoral votes.

(D) The candidate must win the necessary delegates at the party convention.

(E) The candidate must win the endorsement of party leaders.

24. In the reapportionment process, which government entity is responsible for drawing new congressional district lines?

(A) The U.S. Census Bureau

(B) The U.S. Congress

(C) The U.S. House of Representatives

(D) State legislatures

(E) State governors

25. In which case did the U.S. Supreme Court uphold the "necessary and proper" clause?

(A) *Marbury v. Madison*

(B) *McCulloch v. Maryland*

(C) *Gibbons v. Ogden*

(D) *United States v. Lopez*

(E) *Dred Scott v. Sandford*

26. A voter's beliefs tend to be most influenced by his or her

(A) views on the environment

(B) income

(C) experience with the justice system

(D) schooling

(E) parents/family

27. According to the 1947 Presidential Succession Act, in the event that the presidency and vice presidency become vacant, which federal officer becomes president?

(A) Secretary of State

(B) Secretary of Defense

(C) President *Pro Tempore* of the Senate

(D) Secretary of Treasury

(E) Speaker of the House

28. To effectively desegregate public schools in the South, the federal government had to do all of the following EXCEPT

(A) the Supreme Court had to overturn prior precedents

(B) Congress had to withhold federal money until southern schools proved meaningful integration

(C) the executive branch had to enforce court orders

(D) courts had to issue or approve plans that created more balanced racial enrollments

(E) the federal government had to take over full school administration

29. Which congressional power has been the most contested over the years?

(A) Declaring war

(B) Printing money

(C) Regulating commerce

(D) Defining immigration

(E) Setting weights and measures

30. Today, which voting bloc has the highest percentage of people who identify with the Democratic party?

(A) African Americans

(B) Evangelicals

(C) Southerners

(D) 18–24 year olds

(E) Catholics

31. Which government organization is the most instrumental in altering U.S. tax policy?

(A) Federal Reserve Board

(B) Internal Revenue Service

(C) Office of Management and Budget

(D) Congressional Budget Office

(E) House Ways and Means Committee

32. The president can impact the judiciary in all of the following ways EXCEPT

(A) nominating judges who agree with the president's ideology

(B) persuading senators to confirm nominated judges

(C) having executive branch lawyers file *amicus curiae* briefs for parties in Supreme Court cases

(D) encouraging the solicitor general to appeal cases to the Supreme Court when the United States has lost in the circuit courts

(E) threatening to relieve sitting federal judges with whom the president disagrees

33. Which of the flowing statements can be determined by the graph below?

GEORGE W. BUSH APPROVAL RATING

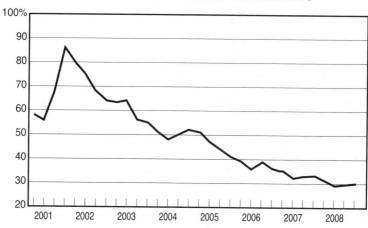

Source: The American Presidency Project

(A) President Bush left office with more political support than when he entered office.

(B) President Bush's popularity spiked after the United States was attacked but declined thereafter.

(C) President Bush left office with the lowest approval rating of any president.

(D) President Bush's approval average was higher in his second term than in his first term.

(E) As with most presidents, President Bush's approval rating hovered just above 50 percent.

34. All of the following are features of the Australian ballot EXCEPT

(A) it is of uniform size and shape

(B) all candidates are listed

(C) it is printed at government expense

(D) the parties distribute this official ballot in advance of the elections

(E) voting is done in secret

35. Which of the interest groups below tend(s) to represent and favor corporations?

    I. AFL-CIO
    II. U.S. Chamber of Commerce
    III. Public Citizen
    IV. Sierra Club

(A) I only

(B) I and II

(C) I, II, and III

(D) II only

(E) III and IV

36. All of these are blocks to the advancement of minor parties in the United States EXCEPT

(A) a lack of an established network of supporters and members

(B) the prevalence of single-member districts

(C) the Constitution bans minor parties from national elections

(D) the Electoral College discourages minor party candidates

(E) established major party committees finance and support major party candidates

37. Which of the following responsibilities is held primarily by the Senate majority leader?

(A) Appointing committee members

(B) Appointing committee chairmen

(C) Ensuring party discipline

(D) Naming the Speaker of the House

(E) Scheduling the legislative agenda

38. Voter turnout in the United States during presidential elections

(A) is at the lowest point it has ever been

(B) has hovered between 50 and 60 percent for the last several decades

(C) is higher than in most Western countries

(D) is close to 80 percent of the voting age population

(E) is generally lower than other U.S. electoral contests

39. A Supreme Court justice who disagrees with the Court's decision may write and issue a

(A) majority opinion

(B) concurring opinion

(C) *per curium* opinion

(D) plurality opinion

(E) dissenting opinion

40. Interest groups take on all of the following activities to influence policy EXCEPT

(A) direct lobbying of legislators

(B) filing lawsuits in courts to remove or shape policy

(C) rallying their members to influence lawmakers

(D) contributing donations to federal judges for re-election

(E) recruiting former members of government to represent their interest

41. Which of the following statements about the Senate and foreign policy is true?

(A) The Senate has ratified every treaty that U.S. presidents have supported.

(B) Treaty ratification in the Senate requires a simple majority vote.

(C) Presidents tend to have greater influence in the foreign policy process than individual senators.

(D) Treaties deal only with peace and war.

(E) The United States entered the League of Nations in 1919 after the Senate ratified the treaty.

42. Which voter trait is most predictive of voter behavior?

(A) Religion

(B) Gender

(C) Income level

(D) Party identification

(E) Ethnicity or race

43. The creator of the cartoon below most likely agrees with which statement?

(A) Terrorists use a variety of tactics to attack Americans.

(B) Too many Americans are more concerned about gay marriage than they are about terrorism.

(C) Different cultures practice different customs.

(D) Strategy is key during a war.

(E) Some terrorist leaders have heavy influence on their followers.

44. The name for the type of primary election that allows voters to split their tickets is

(A) blanket

(B) open

(C) closed

(D) run-off

(E) invisible

45. The War Powers Act of 1973

(A) made the secretary of state the commander in chief

(B) gave the president more latitude with the military

(C) prevents the president from using the military in any way without congressional approval

(D) allows the president to mobilize U.S. troops into combat temporarily without congressional approval

(E) has been declared unconstitutional by the Supreme Court

46. Which statement is supported by the data in the table below?

PAC Contributions to House and Senate Candidates, 1998-2008 (in millions)						
	1998	2000	2002	2004	2006	2008
Senate	$48.1	$51.9	$59.2	$63.7	$68.8	$79.9
House	$158.7	$193.4	$206.9	$225.4	$279.2	$301.6

Source: Federal Elections Commission

(A) There are usually more overall contributions to Senate candidates than House candidates.

(B) Campaign limits have kept overall donations to political campaigns at a minimum.

(C) Total PAC donations to senators have increased more than total PAC contributions to House candidates.

(D) Total PAC donations to House candidates have nearly doubled over the ten-year period shown.

(E) Federal matching campaign money has encouraged PAC contributions.

47. The U.S. Supreme Court declared in *Schenck v. United States* that government can curb speech that

(A) is lewd and offensive

(B) is expressed in public schools

(C) is religious in nature

(D) causes a clear and present danger

(E) misleads consumers

48. Which statement about interest groups is true?

(A) Interest group members tend to come from all socioeconomic levels.

(B) Interest groups are not seen in a favorable light by many.

(C) All interest groups ultimately exist to earn a profit.

(D) Interest groups can only influence policy through the legislative branch.

(E) Members of government want no relationship with interest groups.

49. Which of the following is an enumerated power of Congress?

(A) Appointing ambassadors

(B) Declaring war

(C) Acting as commander in chief

(D) Determining constitutionality of laws

(E) Regulating health, safety, and morals

50. The policy that resulted in the greatest expansion of voter registration for African Americans was the

(A) Fourteenth Amendment

(B) white primary

(C) *Brown v. Board of Education* decision

(D) Civil Rights Act of 1957

(E) Voting Rights Act of 1965

51. Which federal agency currently oversees the hiring of bureaucratic employees?

(A) Office of Management and Budget

(B) Office of Personnel Management

(C) Bureau of the Budget

(D) Civil Service Commission

(E) Department of the Interior

52. The United States began a policy of "containment" to

(A) decrease military spending and to prevent cost overruns

(B) prevent another terrorist act against the United States

(C) avoid entering World War II before the Pearl Harbor bombing

(D) prevent the spread of communism led by the Soviet Union

(E) make combat safe for women in the military

53. Which Supreme Court decision established the "one man, one vote" rule?

(A) Term Limits, Inc. v. Thornton

(B) Wesberry v. Sanders

(C) Reno v. Shaw

(D) McCulloch v. Maryland

(E) Gibbons v. Ogden

54. Which of the following statements about congressional committees is true?

   (A) The two major parties share committee seats equally.

   (B) Chairmen are often newly elected members of Congress.

   (C) Most bills begin in a conference committee.

   (D) Committees carry out Congress's oversight function.

   (E) The speaker of the house assigns all House committee members.

55. As a general rule, executive branch appointees serve at the president's pleasure and can be removed without cause EXCEPT

   (A) directors of law enforcement agencies

   (B) Cabinet secretaries

   (C) the postmaster general

   (D) members of the White House Staff

   (E) directors of regulatory agencies and commissions

56. The due process clause in the Fourteenth Amendment

   (A) prevents the United States government from taking property under eminent domain

   (B) is the final right listed in the Bill of Rights

   (C) guarantees all citizens the pursuit of happiness

   (D) requires states to follow additional rights listed in the Bill of Rights

   (E) was declared unconstitutional by the Supreme Court

57. A fair criticism of the custom of senatorial courtesy is that

   (A) senators don't always make good judges

   (B) district judges do not require Senate confirmation

   (C) it gives senators too much power in nominating district judges

   (D) the Senate should not have advice and consent power over presidential appointments

   (E) judges are term-limited, and therefore senators should not have a vote

58. Which law addressed the conflict of interest among bureaucrats campaigning for their political bosses and limited their political activity?

   (A) Tenure of Office Act

   (B) Pendleton Civil Service Act

   (C) Clayton Anti-Trust Act

   (D) The Hatch Act

   (E) The Whistleblower Protection Act

59. A state asserting its right to refuse to recognize a same-sex marriage license from another state would cite the Constitution's

    (A) full faith and credit clause

    (B) protection against unreasonable search and seizure

    (C) necessary and proper clause

    (D) protection of free speech

    (E) reserved powers

60. Which of the following is a trait of independent regulatory commissions?

    (A) Regulatory commissions are usually dominated by one party.

    (B) Commission directors or chairmen serve at the pleasure of the president.

    (C) Regulatory commissioners are given Cabinet rank.

    (D) Regulatory commissions can create some policies and can issue punishments.

    (E) Commission members also serve on congressional committees.

Section II: Free-Response Questions

1. The United States has an independent news media, yet government has created policies that guide or limit the media.
   (a) Identify and explain the constitutional principle that allows the media to remain independent.
   (b) Identify the federal agency that regulates broadcast media and explain one guideline or policy the agency has issued.
   (c) Select two from below and explain how each shapes an independent media in America.
      - *New York Times v. Sullivan*
      - *New York Times v. the United States*
      - Shield laws

2. Each year, the federal government engages in a process to balance an annual budget.
   (a) Identify two key government actors in the federal budgeting process and describe the role of each.
   (b) Identify two challenges in the federal budgeting process and describe how these challenges complicate the budgeting process.
   (c) Identify and describe one solution that could assist the federal government in balancing the budget.

3. A presidential candidate must compete in many contests and must employ various strategies to win the party nomination and the general election.

Select two from below.

- Iowa caucuses
- Super Tuesday
- Party convention

(a) Explain each contest you selected and describe how each impacts the nomination process.

Select two from below.

- Televised debates
- Advertising
- Electoral College system
- Matching money

(b) Explain how each shapes a candidate's strategy in the general election campaign.

4. The legislative and executive branches share powers in creating foreign and military policy, and each branch is supported by governmental sub-units.

(a) Identify one sub-unit in the legislative branch and explain how this sub-unit impacts foreign or military policy.

(b) Identify one sub-unit in the executive branch and explain how this sub-unit impacts foreign or military policy.

(c) Explain how this division of power has affected the United States' handling of foreign or military policy in one of the areas below.

- Declaring war
- Funding
- Representative government

The Constitution of the United States of America

Note: The passages that have been amended or superseded appear in italics.

Preamble

We the people of the United States, in order to form a more perfect Union, establish justice, insure domestic tranquility, provide for the common defense, promote the general welfare, and secure the blessings of liberty to ourselves and our posterity [descendants], do ordain [issue] and establish this Constitution for the United States of America.

ARTICLE I. CONGRESS

Section 1. Legislative Power All legislative powers herein granted shall be vested in a Congress of the United States, which shall consist of a Senate and House of Representatives.

Section 2. House of Representatives

[1] The House of Representatives shall be composed of members chosen every second year by the people of the several states, and the electors [voters] in each state shall have the qualifications requisite [required] for electors of the most numerous branch of the state legislature.

[2] No person shall be a representative who shall not have attained to the age of twenty-five years, and been seven years a citizen of the United States, and who shall not, when elected, be an inhabitant of that state in which he shall be chosen.

[3] *Representatives and direct taxes shall be apportioned among the several states which may be included within this Union according to their respective numbers* [population], *which shall be determined by adding to the whole number of free persons, including those bound to service for a term of years* [indentured servants], *and excluding Indians not taxed, three-fifths of all other persons.* The actual enumeration [census] shall be made within three years after the first meeting of the Congress of the United States, and within every subsequent term of ten years, in such manner as they shall by law direct. The number of representatives shall not exceed one for every thirty thousand, but each state shall have at least one representative; *and until such enumeration shall be made, the State of New Hampshire shall be entitled to choose three, Massachusetts eight, Rhode Island and Providence Plantations one, Connecticut five, New York six, New Jersey four, Pennsylvania eight, Delaware one, Maryland six, Virginia ten, North Carolina five, South Carolina five, and Georgia three.*

[4] When vacancies happen in the representation from any state, the executive authority [governor] thereof shall issue writs of election to fill such vacancies.

[5] The House of Representatives shall choose their Speaker and other officers; and shall have the sole power of impeachment.

Section 3. Senate

[1] The Senate of the United States shall be composed of two senators from each state, *chosen by the legislature* thereof, for six years; and each senator shall have one vote.

[2] Immediately after they shall be assembled in consequence of the first election, they shall be divided as equally as may be into three classes. The seats of the senators of the first class shall be vacated at the expiration of the second year, of the second class at the expiration of the fourth year, and of the third class at the expiration of the sixth year, so that one-third may be chosen every second year; *and if vacancies happen by resignation, or otherwise, during the recess of the legislature of any state, the executive* [governor] *thereof may make temporary appointments until the next meeting of the legislature, which shall then fill such vacancies.*

[3] No person shall be a senator who shall not have attained to the age of thirty years and been nine years a citizen of the United States, and who shall not, when elected, be an inhabitant of that state for which he shall be chosen.

[4] The vice president of the United States shall be president of the Senate, but shall have no vote, unless they be equally divided [tied].

[5] The Senate shall choose their other officers, and also a president pro tempore [temporary presiding officer], in the absence of the vice president, or when he shall exercise the office of president of the United States.

[6] The Senate shall have sole power to try all impeachments. When sitting for that purpose, they shall be on oath or affirmation. When the president of the United States is tried, the chief justice [of the United States] shall preside; and no person shall be convicted without the concurrence of two-thirds of the members present.

[7] Judgment in cases of impeachment shall not extend further than to removal from office, and disqualification to hold and enjoy any office of honor, trust, or profit under the United States; but the party convicted shall nevertheless be liable and subject to indictment, trial, judgment, and punishment, according to law.

Section 4. Elections and Meetings of Congress

[1] The times, places, and manner of holding elections for senators and representatives shall be prescribed [designated] in each state by the legislature thereof; but the Congress may at any time by law make or alter such regulations, except as to the places of choosing senators.

[2] The Congress shall assemble at least once in every year, *and such meeting shall be on the first Monday in December,* unless they shall by law appoint a different day.

Section 5. Rules and Procedures of the Two Houses

[1] Each house shall be the judge of the elections, returns, and qualifications of its own members, and a majority of each shall constitute a quorum to do business; but a smaller number may adjourn from day to day, and may be authorized to compel the attendance of absent members, in such manner, and under such penalties, as each house may provide.

[2] Each house may determine the rules of its proceedings, punish its members for disorderly behavior, and with the concurrence of two-thirds, expel a member.

[3] Each house shall keep a journal of its proceedings, and from time to time publish the same, excepting such parts as may in their judgment require secrecy; and the yeas [affirmative votes] and nays [negative votes] of the members of either house on any question shall, at the desire of one-fifth of those present, be entered on the journal.

[4] Neither house, during the session of Congress, shall, without the consent of the other, adjourn for more than three days, nor to any other place than that in which the two houses shall be sitting.

Section 6. Members' Privileges and Restrictions

[1] The senators and representatives shall receive a compensation for their services, to be ascertained [fixed] by law and paid out of the treasury of the United States. They shall in all cases except treason, felony [serious crime], and breach of the peace [disorderly conduct], be privileged [immune] from arrest during their attendance at the session of their respective houses, and in going to and returning from the same; and for any speech or debate in either house, they shall not be questioned in any other place.

[2] No senator or representative shall, during the time for which he was elected, be appointed to any civil office under the authority of the United States, which shall have been created, or the emoluments [salary] whereof shall have been increased, during such time; and no person holding any office under the United States shall be a member of either house during his continuance in office.

Section 7. Lawmaking Procedures

[1] All bills for raising revenue shall originate in the House of Representatives; but the Senate may propose or concur with amendments as on other bills.

[2] Every bill which shall have passed the House of Representatives and the Senate shall, before it becomes a law, be presented to the president of the United States; if he approve, he shall sign it, but if not, he shall return it, with his objections, to that house in which it shall have originated, who shall enter the objections at large on their journal, and proceed to reconsider it. If after such reconsideration two-thirds of that house shall agree to pass the bill, it shall be sent, together with the objections, to the other house, by which it shall likewise be reconsidered, and, if approved by two-thirds of that house, it shall become a law. But in all such cases the votes of both houses shall be determined by yeas and nays, and the names of the persons voting for and against the bill shall be entered on the journal of each house respectively. If any bill shall not be returned by the president within ten days (Sundays excepted) after it shall

have been presented to him, the same shall be a law, in like manner as if he had signed it, unless the Congress by their adjournment prevent its return, in which case it shall not be a law.

[3] Every order, resolution, or vote to which the concurrence of the Senate and House of Representatives may be necessary (except on a question of adjournment) shall be presented to the president of the United States; and before the same shall take effect, shall be approved by him, or, being disapproved by him, shall be repassed by two-thirds of the Senate and House of Representatives, according to the rules and limitations prescribed in the case of a bill.

Section 8. Powers of Congress   The Congress shall have power:

[1] To lay and collect taxes, duties, imposts, and excises, to pay the debts and provide for the common defense and general welfare of the United States; but all duties, imposts, and excises shall be uniform [the same] throughout the United States;

[2] To borrow money on the credit of the United States;

[3] To regulate commerce with foreign nations, and among the several states, and with the Indian tribes;

[4] To establish a uniform rule of naturalization [admitting to citizenship], and uniform laws on the subject of bankruptcies throughout the United States;

[5] To coin money, regulate the value thereof, and of foreign coin, and fix [set] the standard of weights and measures;

[6] To provide for the punishment of counterfeiting the securities and current coin of the United States;

[7] To establish post offices and post roads;

[8] To promote the progress of science and useful arts by securing for limited times to authors and inventors the exclusive right to their respective writings and discoveries;

[9] To constitute tribunals [establish courts] inferior to [lower than] the Supreme Court;

[10] To define and punish piracies and felonies committed on the high seas and offenses against the law of nations [international law];

[11] To declare war, grant letters of marque and reprisal, and make rules concerning captures on land and water;

[12] To raise and support armies, but no appropriation of money to that use shall be for a longer term than two years;

[13] To provide and maintain a navy;

[14] To make rules for the government and regulation of the land and naval forces;

[15] To provide for calling forth the militia to execute [carry out] the laws of the Union, suppress insurrections [rebellions], and repel invasions;

[16] To provide for organizing, arming, and disciplining [training] the militia, and for governing such part of them as may be employed in the service of the United States, reserving to the states respectively

the appointment of the officers, and the authority of training the militia according to the discipline [regulations] prescribed by Congress;

[17] To exercise exclusive legislation in all cases whatsoever, over such district (not exceeding ten miles square) as may, by cession of particular states, and the acceptance of Congress, become the seat of government of the United States, and to exercise like authority over all places purchased by the consent of the legislature of the state in which the same shall be, for the erection of forts, magazines [warehouses for explosives], arsenals, dockyards, and other needful buildings; and

[18] To make all laws which shall be necessary and proper for carrying into execution the foregoing powers, and all other powers vested by this Constitution in the government of the United States, or in any department or officer thereof.

Section 9. Powers Denied to the Federal Government

[1] *The migration or importation of such persons as any of the states now existing shall think proper to admit shall not be prohibited by the Congress prior to the year 1808; but a tax or duty may be imposed on such importation, not exceeding ten dollars for each person.*

[2] The privilege of the writ of habeas corpus shall not be suspended, unless when in cases of rebellion or invasion the public safety may require it.

[3] No bill of attainder or ex post facto law shall be passed.

[4] No capitation [head] or other direct tax shall be laid, *unless in proportion to the census or enumeration herein before directed to be taken.*

[5] No tax or duty shall be laid on articles exported from any state.

[6] No preference shall be given by any regulation of commerce or revenue to the ports of one state over those of another; nor shall vessels bound to, or from, one state be obliged to enter, clear, or pay duties in another.

[7] No money shall be drawn from the treasury, but in consequence of appropriations made by law; and a regular statement and account of the receipts and expenditures of all public money shall be published from time to time.

[8] No title of nobility shall be granted by the United States; and no person holding any office of profit or trust under them shall, without the consent of the Congress, accept of any present, emolument, office, or title, of any kind whatever, from any king, prince, or foreign state.

Section 10. Powers Denied to the States

[1] No state shall enter into any treaty, alliance, or confederation; grant letters of marque and reprisal; coin money; emit bills of credit; make anything but gold and silver coin a tender [legal money] in payment of debts; pass any bill of attainder, ex post facto law, or law impairing the obligation of contracts, or grant any title of nobility.

[2] No state shall, without the consent of the Congress, lay any imposts or duties on imports or exports, except what may be absolutely necessary for executing its inspection laws; and the net produce [income] of all duties and imposts, laid by any state on imports or exports, shall be for the use of the treasury of the United States; and all such laws shall be subject to the revision and control of the Congress.

[3] No state shall, without the consent of Congress, lay any duty of tonnage, keep troops or ships of war in time of peace, enter into any agreement or compact with another state or with a foreign power, or engage in war unless actually invaded or in such imminent [threatening] danger as will not admit of delay.

ARTICLE II. THE PRESIDENCY

Section 1. Executive Power

[1] The executive power shall be vested in a president of the United States of America. He shall hold his office during the term of four years, and, together with the vice president, chosen for the same term, be elected as follows:

[2] Each state shall appoint, in such manner as the legislature thereof may direct, a number of electors, equal to the whole number of senators and representatives to which the state may be entitled in the Congress; but no senator or representative, or person holding an office of trust or profit under the United States, shall be appointed an elector.

[3] *The electors shall meet in their respective states, and vote by ballot for two persons, of whom one at least shall not be an inhabitant of the same state with themselves. And they shall make a list of all the persons voted for, and of the number of votes for each; which list they shall sign and certify, and transmit sealed to the seat of the government of the United States, directed to the president of the Senate. The president of the Senate shall, in the presence of the Senate and House of Representatives, open all the certificates, and the votes shall then be counted. The person having the greatest number of votes shall be the president, if such number be a majority of the whole number of electors appointed; and if there be more than one who have such majority, and have an equal number of votes, then the House of Representatives shall immediately choose by ballot one of them for president; and if no person have a majority, then from the five highest on the list the said House shall in like manner choose the president. But in choosing the president, the votes shall be taken by states, the representation from each state having one vote; a quorum for this purpose shall consist of a member or members from two-thirds of the states, and a majority of all the states shall be necessary to a choice. In every case, after the choice of the president, the person having the greatest number of votes of the electors shall be the vice president. But if there should remain two or more who have equal votes, the Senate shall choose from them by ballot the vice president.*

[4] The Congress may determine the time of choosing the electors, and the day on which they shall give their votes; which day shall be the same throughout the United States.

[5] No person except a natural-born citizen, *or a citizen of the United States at the time of the adoption of this Constitution*, shall be eligible to the office of the president; neither shall any person be eligible to that office who shall not have attained to the age of thirty-five years and been fourteen years a resident within the United States.

[6] *In case of the removal of the president from office, or of his death, resignation, or inability to discharge the powers and duties of the said office, the same shall devolve on the vice president, and the Congress may by law provide for the case of removal, death, resignation, or inability, both of the president and vice president, declaring what officer shall then act as president, and such officer shall act accordingly, until the disability be removed, or a president shall be elected.*

[7] The president shall, at stated times, receive for his services, a compensation, which shall neither be increased nor diminished during the period for which he shall have been elected, and he shall not receive within that period any other emolument from the United States, or any of them.

[8] Before he enter on the execution of his office, he shall take the following oath or affirmation:

"I do solemnly swear (or affirm) that I will faithfully execute the office of President of the United States, and will, to the best of my ability, preserve, protect, and defend the Constitution of the United States."

Section 2. Powers of the President

[1] The president shall be commander in chief of the army and navy [all the armed forces] of the United States, and of the militia of the several states, when called into the actual service of the United States; he may require the opinion in writing of the principal officer in each of the executive departments upon any subject relating to the duties of their respective offices; and he shall have power to grant reprieves and pardons for offenses against the United States except in cases of impeachment.

[2] He shall have power, by and with the advice and consent of the Senate, to make treaties, provided two-thirds of the senators present concur; and he shall nominate, and, by and with the advice and consent of the Senate, shall appoint ambassadors, other public ministers and consuls, judges of the Supreme Court, and all other officers of the United States whose appointments are not herein otherwise provided for and which shall be established by law; but the Congress may by law vest the appointment of such inferior officers as they think proper in the president alone, in the courts of law, or in the heads of departments.

[3] The president shall have power to fill up all vacancies that may happen during the recess of the Senate, by granting commissions which shall expire at the end of their next session.

Section 3. Duties and Responsibilities of the President
He shall, from time to time, give to the Congress information of the state of the Union, and recommend to their consideration such measures as he shall judge necessary and expedient [advisable]; he may, on extraordinary [special] occasions, convene both houses, or either of them, and in case of disagreement between them with respect to the time of adjournment, he may adjourn them to such time as he shall think proper; he shall receive ambassadors and other public ministers; he shall take care that the laws be faithfully executed, and shall commission [appoint] all the officers of the United States.

Section 4. Impeachment
The president, vice president, and all civil officers of the United States, shall be removed from office on impeachment for, and conviction of, treason, bribery, or other high crimes and misdemeanors [offenses].

ARTICLE III. THE SUPREME COURT AND OTHER COURTS

Section 1. Federal Courts
The judicial power of the United States shall be vested in one Supreme Court, and in such inferior [lower] courts as the Congress may from time to time ordain and establish. The judges, both of the Supreme and inferior courts, shall hold their offices during good behavior, and shall, at stated times, receive for their services a compensation, which shall not be diminished during their continuance in office.

Section 2. Jurisdiction of Federal Court

[1] The judicial power shall extend to all cases in law and equity arising under this Constitution, the laws of the United States, and treaties made, or which shall be made, under their authority; to all cases affecting ambassadors, other public ministers, and consuls; to all cases of admiralty and maritime jurisdiction; to controversies to which the United States shall be a party; to controversies between two or more states, *between a state and citizens of another state,* between citizens of different states, between citizens of the same state claiming lands under grants of different states, and between a state, or the citizens thereof, and foreign states, citizens, or subjects.

[2] In all cases affecting ambassadors, other public ministers, and consuls, and those in which a state shall be a party, the Supreme Court shall have original jurisdiction. In all the other cases before mentioned, the Supreme Court shall have appellate jurisdiction, both as to law and fact, with such exceptions and under such regulations as the Congress shall make.

[3] The trial of all crimes, except in cases of impeachment, shall be by jury; and such trial shall be held in the state where the said crimes shall have been committed; but when not committed within any state, the trial shall be at such place or places as the Congress may by law have directed.

Section 3. Treason

[1] Treason against the United States shall consist only in levying [carrying on] war against them, or in adhering to [assisting] their enemies, giving them aid and comfort. No person shall be convicted of treason unless on the testimony of two witnesses to the same overt [open; public] act, or on confession in open court.

[2] The Congress shall have power to declare the punishment of treason, but no attainder of treason shall work corruption of blood or forfeiture except during the life of the person attainted.

ARTICLE IV. INTERSTATE RELATIONS

Section 1. Official Acts and Records

Full faith and credit shall be given in each state to the public acts, records, and judicial proceedings of every other state. And the Congress may, by general laws, prescribe the manner in which such acts, records, and proceedings shall be proved, and the effect thereof.

Section 2. Mutual Obligations of States

[1] The citizens of each state shall be entitled to all privileges and immunities of citizens in the several states.

[2] A person charged in any state with treason, felony, or other crime, who shall flee from justice and be found in another state, shall, on demand of the executive authority of the state from which he fled, be delivered up, to be removed to the state having jurisdiction of the crime.

[3] *No person held to service or labor in one state, under the laws thereof, escaping into another, shall, in consequence of any law or regulation therein, be discharged from such service or labor, but shall be delivered up on claim of the party to whom such service or labor may be due.*

Section 3. New States and Territories

[1] New states may be admitted by the Congress into this Union; but no new state shall be formed or erected within the jurisdiction of any other state; nor any state be formed by the junction [joining] of two or more states, or parts of states, without the consent of the legislatures of the states concerned as well as of Congress.

[2] The Congress shall have power to dispose of and make all needful rules and regulations respecting the territory or other property belonging to the United States; and nothing in this Constitution shall be so construed [interpreted] as to prejudice [damage] any claims of the United States, or of any particular state.

Section 4. Federal Guarantees to the States

The United States shall guarantee to every state in this Union a republican form of government, and shall protect each of them against invasion; and on application of the legislature, or of the executive (when the legislature cannot be convened), against domestic violence [riots].

ARTICLE V. AMENDING THE CONSTITUTION

The Congress, whenever two-thirds of both houses shall deem [think] it necessary, shall propose amendments to this Constitution, or, on the application of the legislatures of two-thirds of the several states, shall call a convention for proposing amendments, which, in either case, shall be valid, to all intents and purposes, as part of this Constitution when ratified by the legislatures of three-fourths of the several states, or by conventions in three-fourths thereof, as the one or the other mode [method] of ratification may be proposed by the Congress; provided *that no amendment which may be made prior to the year 1808 shall in any manner affect the first and fourth clauses in the ninth section of the first article; and* that no state, without its consent, shall be deprived of its equal suffrage in the Senate.

ARTICLE VI. MISCELLANEOUS PROVISIONS

Section 1. Public Debts   All debts contracted and engagements [agreements] entered into before the adoption of this Constitution shall be as valid [binding] against the United States under this Constitution as under the Confederation.

Section 2. Federal Supremacy   This Constitution, and the laws of the United States which shall be made in pursuance thereof, and all treaties made, or which shall be made, under the authority of the United States, shall be the supreme law of the land; and the judges in every state shall be bound thereby, anything in the Constitution or laws of any state to the contrary notwithstanding.

Section 3. Oaths of Office   The senators and representatives before mentioned, and the members of the several state legislatures, and all executive and judicial officers, both of the United States and of the several states, shall be bound by oath or affirmation to support this Constitution; but no religious test shall ever be required as a qualification to any office or public trust under the United States.

ARTICLE VII. RATIFICATION

The ratification of the conventions of nine states shall be sufficient for the establishment of this Constitution between the states so ratifying the same.

Done in convention, by the unanimous consent of the states present, the 17th day of September, in the year of our Lord 1787, and of the independence of the United States of America the twelfth. In witness whereof we have hereunto subscribed our names.

Signed by
George Washington
[President and Deputy from Virginia]
and 38 other delegates

Amendments to the Constitution

Note: The first ten amendments to the Constitution, adopted in 1791, make up the Bill of Rights. The year of adoption of later amendments (11 to 27) is given in parentheses.

AMENDMENT I. FREEDOM OF RELIGION, SPEECH, PRESS, ASSEMBLY, AND PETITION

Congress shall make no law respecting an establishment of religion, or prohibiting the free exercise thereof; or abridging [reducing] the freedom of speech or of the press; or the right of the people peaceably to assemble, and to petition the government for a redress [correction] of grievances.

AMENDMENT II. RIGHT TO BEAR ARMS

A well-regulated militia being necessary to the security of a free state, the right of the people to keep and bear arms shall not be infringed [weakened].

AMENDMENT III. QUARTERING OF TROOPS

No soldier shall, in time of peace, be quartered [assigned to live] in any house without the consent of the owner, nor in time of war, but in a manner to be prescribed by law.

AMENDMENT IV. SEARCHES AND SEIZURES

The right of the people to be secure [safe] in their persons, houses, papers, and effects [belongings] against unreasonable searches and seizures shall not be violated; and no [search] warrants shall issue but upon probable cause, supported by oath or affirmation, and particularly describing the place to be searched, and the persons or things to be seized.

AMENDMENT V. RIGHTS OF THE ACCUSED; PROPERTY RIGHTS

No person shall be held to answer for a capital or otherwise infamous crime unless on a presentment or indictment of a grand jury, except in cases arising in the land or naval forces, or in the militia, when in actual service in time of war or public danger; nor shall any person be subject for the same offense to be twice put in jeopardy of life or limb; nor shall be compelled in any criminal case to be a witness against himself; nor be deprived of life, liberty, or property without due process of law; nor shall private property be taken for public use without just compensation.

AMENDMENT VI. ADDITIONAL RIGHTS OF THE ACCUSED

In all criminal prosecutions [trials], the accused shall enjoy the right to a speedy and public trial by an impartial [fair] jury of the state and district wherein the crime shall have been committed, which district shall have been previously ascertained by law; and to be informed of the nature and cause of the accusation; to be confronted with the witnesses against him; to have compulsory process for obtaining witnesses in his favor; and to have the assistance of counsel for his defense.

AMENDMENT VII. CIVIL SUITS

In suits at common law where the value in controversy shall exceed twenty dollars, the right of trial by jury shall be preserved, and no fact tried by a jury shall be otherwise reexamined in any court of the United States, than according to the rules of the common law.

AMENDMENT VIII. BAILS, FINES, AND PUNISHMENTS

Excessive bail shall not be required, nor excessive fines imposed, nor cruel and unusual punishments inflicted.

AMENDMENT IX. RIGHTS NOT LISTED

The enumeration [listing] in the Constitution of certain rights shall not be construed to deny or disparage [weaken] others retained by the people.

AMENDMENT X. POWERS RESERVED TO THE STATES AND PEOPLE

The powers not delegated to the United States by the Constitution, nor prohibited by it to the states, are reserved to the states respectively, or to the people.

AMENDMENT XI. SUITS AGAINST STATES (1798)

The judicial power of the United States shall not be construed to extend to any suit in law or equity, commenced or prosecuted against one of the United States by citizens of another state, or by citizens or subjects of any foreign state.

AMENDMENT XII. ELECTION OF PRESIDENT AND VICE PRESIDENT (1804)

[1] The electors shall meet in their respective states, and vote by ballot for president and vice president, one of whom at least shall not be an inhabitant of the same state with themselves; they shall name in their ballots the person voted for as president, and in distinct [separate] ballots the person voted for as vice president; and they shall make distinct lists of all persons voted for as president, and of all persons voted for as vice president, and of the number of votes for each, which lists they shall sign and certify, and transmit sealed to the seat of the government of the United States, directed to the president of the Senate.

[2] The president of the Senate shall, in the presence of the Senate and House of Representatives, open all the certificates, and the votes shall then be counted; the person having the greatest number of votes for president shall be the president, if such number be a majority of the whole number of electors appointed; and if no person have such majority, then from the persons having the highest numbers not exceeding three on the list of those voted for as president, the House of Representatives shall choose immediately, by ballot, the president. But in choosing the president, the votes shall be taken by states, the representation from each state having one vote; a quorum for this purpose shall consist of a member or members from two-thirds of the states, and a majority of all the states shall be necessary to a choice.

And if the House of Representatives shall not choose a president whenever the right of choice shall devolve upon them, *before the fourth day of March next following,* then the vice president shall act as president, as in the case of the death or other constitutional disability of the president.

[3] The person having the greatest number of votes as vice president shall be the vice president, if such number be a majority of the whole number of electors appointed; and if no person have a majority, then from the two highest numbers on the list, the Senate shall choose the vice president; a quorum for the purpose shall consist of two-thirds of the whole number of senators, and a majority of the whole number shall be necessary to a choice. But no person constitutionally ineligible to the office of president shall be eligible to that of vice president of the United States.

AMENDMENT XIII. ABOLITION OF SLAVERY (1865)

Section 1. Slavery Forbidden Neither slavery nor involuntary servitude [compulsory service], except as a punishment for crime whereof the party shall have been duly convicted, shall exist within the United States, or any place subject to their jurisdiction.

Section 2. Enforcement Power Congress shall have power to enforce this article [amendment] by appropriate [suitable] legislation.

AMENDMENT XIV. CITIZENSHIP AND CIVIL RIGHTS (1868)

Section 1. Rights of Citizens All persons born or naturalized in the United States, and subject to the jurisdiction thereof, are citizens of the United States and of the state wherein they reside. No state shall make or enforce any law which shall abridge the privileges or immunities of citizens of the United States; nor shall any state deprive any person of life, liberty, or property, without due process of law; nor deny to any person within its jurisdiction the equal protection of the laws.

Section 2. Apportionment of Representatives in Congress Representatives shall be apportioned among the several states according to their respective numbers, counting the whole number of persons in each state, excluding Indians not taxed. But when the right to vote at any election for the choice of electors for president and vice president of the United States, representatives in Congress, the executive and judicial officers of a state, or the members of the legislature thereof, is denied to any of the *male* inhabitants of such state, being *twenty-one* years of age and citizens of the United States, or in any way abridged, except for participation in rebellion or other crime, the basis of representation therein shall be reduced in the proportion which the number of such *male* citizens shall bear to the whole number of *male* citizens *twenty-one* years of age in such state.

Section 3. Persons Disqualified from Public Office No person shall be a senator or representative in Congress, or elector of president and vice president, or hold any office, civil or military, under the United States, or under any state, who, having previously taken an oath, as a member of Congress, or as an officer of the United States, or as a member of any state legislature, or as an executive or judicial officer of any state, to support the Constitution of the United States, shall have engaged in insurrection or rebellion against the same, or given aid or comfort to the enemies thereof. But Congress may, by a vote of two-thirds of each house, remove such disability.

Section 4. Valid Public Debt Defined The validity [legality] of the public debt of the United States, authorized by law, including debts incurred for payment of pensions and bounties [extra allowances] for services in suppressing insurrection or rebellion, shall not be questioned. But neither the United States nor any state shall assume or pay any debt or obligation incurred in aid of insurrection or rebellion against the United States, or any claim for the loss or emancipation [liberation] of any slave; but all such debts, obligations, and claims shall be held illegal and void.

Section 5. Enforcement Power The Congress shall have power to enforce, by appropriate legislation, the provisions of this article.

AMENDMENT XV. RIGHT OF SUFFRAGE (1870)

Section 1. African Americans Guaranteed the Vote The right of citizens of the United States to vote shall not be denied or abridged by the United States or by any state on account of race, color, or previous condition of servitude [slavery].

Section 2. Enforcement Power The Congress shall have power to enforce this article by appropriate legislation.

AMENDMENT XVI. INCOME TAXES (1913)

The Congress shall have power to lay and collect taxes on incomes, from whatever source derived, without apportionment among the several states, and without regard to any census or enumeration.

AMENDMENT XVII. POPULAR ELECTION OF SENATORS (1913)

[1] The Senate of the United States shall be composed of two senators from each state, elected by the people thereof, for six years; and each senator shall have one vote. The electors [voters] in each state shall have the qualifications requisite for electors of the most numerous branch of the state legislatures.

[2] When vacancies happen in the representation of any state in the Senate, the executive authority of such state shall issue writs of election to fill such vacancies: Provided, that the legislature of any state may empower [authorize] the executive thereof to make temporary appointments until the people fill the vacancies by election as the legislature may direct.

[3] *This amendment shall not be so construed as to affect the election or term of any senator chosen before it becomes valid as part of the Constitution.*

AMENDMENT XVIII. PROHIBITION (1919)

Section 1. Intoxicating Liquors Prohibited After one year from the ratification of this article, the manufacture, sale, or transportation of intoxicating liquors within, the importation thereof into, or the exportation thereof from the United States and all territory subject to the jurisdiction thereof, for beverage purposes is hereby prohibited.

Section 2. Enforcement Power The Congress and the several states shall have concurrent power to enforce this article by appropriate legislation.

Section 3. Conditions of Ratification This article shall be inoperative unless it shall have been ratified as an amendment to the Constitution by the legislatures of the several states, as provided in the Constitution, within seven years from the date of the submission hereof to the states by the Congress.

AMENDMENT XIX. WOMEN'S SUFFRAGE (1920)

[1] The right of citizens of the United States to vote shall not be denied or abridged by the United States or by any state on account of sex.

[2] Congress shall have power to enforce this article by appropriate legislation.

AMENDMENT XX. PRESIDENTIAL AND CONGRESSIONAL TERMS (1933)

Section 1. Terms of Office The terms of the president and vice president shall end at noon on the 20th day of January, and the terms of senators and representatives at noon on the 3d day of January, of the years in which such terms would have ended if this article had not been ratified; and the terms of their successors shall then begin.

Section 2. Convening Congress The Congress shall assemble at least once in every year, and such meeting shall begin at noon on the 3rd day of January, unless they shall by law appoint a different day.

Section 3. Presidential Succession If, at the time fixed for the beginning of the term of the president, the president-elect shall have died, the vice president-elect shall become president. If a president shall not have been chosen before the time fixed for the beginning of his term, or if the president-elect shall have failed to qualify, then the vice president-elect shall act as president until a president shall have qualified; and the Congresss may by law provide for the case wherein neither a president-elect nor a vice president-elect shall have qualified, declaring who shall then act as president, or the manner in which one who is to act shall be selected, and such person shall act accordingly until a president or vice president shall have qualified.

Section 4. Selection of President and Vice President The Congress may by law provide for the case of the death of any of the persons from whom the House of Representatives may choose a president whenever the right of choice shall have devolved upon them, and for the case of the death of any of the persons from whom the Senate may choose a vice president whenever the right of choice shall have devolved upon them.

Section 5. Effective Date *Sections 1 and 2 shall take effect on the 15th day of October following the ratification of this article.*

Section 6. Conditions of Ratification *This article shall be inoperative unless it shall have been ratified as an amendment to the Constitution by the legislatures of three-fourths of the several states within seven years from the date of its submission.*

AMENDMENT XXI. REPEAL OF PROHIBITION (1933)

Section 1. Amendment XVIII Repealed The eighteenth article of amendment to the Constitution of the United States is hereby repealed.

Section 2. Shipment of Liquor into "Dry" Areas The transportation or importation into any state, territory, or possession of the United States for delivery or use therein of intoxicating liquors in violation of the laws thereof is hereby prohibited.

Section 3. Conditions of Ratification *This article shall be inoperative unless it shall have been ratified as an amendment to the Constitution by conventions in the several states, as provided in the Constitution, within seven years from the date of the submission hereof to the states by the Congress.*

AMENDMENT XXII. LIMITING PRESIDENTIAL TERMS (1951)

Section 1. Limit Placed on Tenure No person shall be elected to the office of the president more than twice, and no person who has held the office of president, or acted as president, for more than two years of a term to which some other person was elected president shall be elected to the office of the president more than once. *But this article shall not apply to any person holding the office of president when this article was proposed by the Congress, and shall not prevent any person who may be holding the office of president, or acting as president, during the term within which this article becomes operative from holding the office of president or acting as president during the remainder of such term.*

Section 2. Conditions of Ratification *This article shall be inoperative unless it shall have been ratified as an amendment to the Constitution by the legislatures of three-fourths of the several states within seven years from the date of its submission to the states by the Congress.*

AMENDMENT XXIII. SUFFRAGE FOR WASHINGTON, D.C. (1961)

Section 1. D.C. Presidential Electors The district constituting [making up] the seat of government of the United States shall appoint in such manner as the Congress may direct:

A number of electors of president and vice president equal to the whole number of senators and representatives in Congress to which the district would be entitled if it were a state, but in no event more than the least populous state; they shall be in addition to those appointed by the states, but they shall be considered, for the purposes of the election of president and vice president, to be electors appointed by a state; and they shall meet in the district and perform such duties as provided by the Twelfth Article of amendment.

Section 2. Enforcement Power The Congress shall have power to enforce this article by appropriate legislation.

AMENDMENT XXIV. POLL TAXES (1964)

Section 1. Poll Tax Barred The right of citizens of the United States to vote in any primary or other election for president or vice president, for electors for president or vice president, or for senator or representative in Congress, shall not be denied or abridged by the United States or any state by reason of failure to pay any poll tax or other tax.

Section 2. Enforcement Power The Congress shall have the power to enforce this article by appropriate legislation.

AMENDMENT XXV. PRESIDENTIAL SUCCESSION AND DISABILITY (1967)

Section 1. Elevation of Vice President
In case of the removal of the president from office or his death or resignation, the vice president shall become president.

Section 2. Vice Presidential Vacancy
Whenever there is a vacancy in the office of the vice president, the president shall nominate a vice president who shall take the office upon confirmation by a majority vote of both houses of Congress.

Section 3. Temporary Disability Whenever the president transmits to the president pro tempore of the Senate and the Speaker of the House of Representatives his written declaration that he is unable to discharge the powers and duties of his office, and until he transmits to them a written declaration to the contrary, such powers and duties shall be discharged by the vice president as acting president.

Section 4. Other Provisions for Presidential Disability
[1] Whenever the vice president and a majority of either the principal officers of the executive departments or of such other body as Congress may by law provide, transmit to the president pro tempore of the Senate and the Speaker of the House of Representatives their written declaration that the president is unable to discharge the powers and duties of his office, the vice president shall immediately assume the powers and duties of the office as acting president.

[2] Thereafter, when the president transmits to the president pro tempore of the Senate and the Speaker of the House of Representatives his written declaration that no inability exists, he shall resume the powers and duties of his office unless the vice president and a majority of either the principal officers of the executive department or of such other body as Congress may by law provide, transmit within four days to the president pro tempore

of the Senate and the Speaker of the House of Representatives their written declaration that the president is unable to discharge the powers and duties of his office. Thereupon Congress shall decide the issue, assembling within 48 hours for that purpose if not in session. If the Congress, within 21 days after receipt of the latter written declaration, or, if Congress is not in session, within 21 days after Congress is required to assemble, determines by two-thirds vote of both houses that the president is unable to discharge the powers and duties of his office, the vice president shall continue to discharge the same as acting president; otherwise, the president shall resume the powers and duties of his office.

AMENDMENT XXVI. VOTE FOR 18-YEAR-OLDS (1971)

Section 1. Lowering the Voting Age   The right of citizens of the United States, who are 18 years of age or older, to vote shall not be denied or abridged by the United States or by any state on account of age.

Section 2. Enforcement Power   The Congress shall have power to enforce this article by appropriate legislation.

AMENDMENT XXVII. CONGRESSIONAL PAY (1992)

No law, varying the compensation for the services of the Senators and Representatives, shall take effect, until an election of Representatives shall have intervened.

Bibliography

Books

Aberback, Joel D. and Bert A. Rockman. *In the Web of Politics: Three Decades of the U.S. Federal Executive*. Washington: Brookings Institution Press, 2000.

Acheson, Dean. *Present at the Creation: My Years in the State Department*. New York: Norton, 1969.

Alter, Jonathan. *The Promise: President Obama, Year One*. New York: Simon and Schuster, 2010.

Alterman, Eric. *What Liberal Media? The Truth About Bias in the News*. New York: Basic Books, 2003.

Alvarez, R. Michael and John Brehm. *Hard Choices, Easy Answers*. Princeton: Princeton University Press, 2002.

Asher, Herbert. *Polling and the Public: What Every Citizen Should Know*. Washington: Congressional Quarterly Press, 2004.

Balz, Dan. *Collision 2012: Obama vs. Romney and the Future of Elections in America*. New York: Viking, 2013.

Balz, Dan and Haynes Johnson. *The Battle for America 2008: The Story of an Extraordinary Election*. New York: Viking, 2009.

Becker, Carl L. *The Declaration of Independence: A Study in the History of Political Ideas*. New York: Vintage Books, 1970.

Bittle, Scott and Jean Johnson. *Where Does the Money Go? Your Guided Tour to the Federal Budget Crisis*. New York: Collins, 2008.

Bowen, Catherine Drinker. *Miracle at Philadelphia*. Boston: Little, Brown and Co., 1966.

Brown, Sherrod. *Congress from the Inside*. Kent, Ohio: Kent State University Press, 2004.

Cigler, Allan J. and Burdettt A. Loomis eds. *Interest Group Politics*. Washington: CQ Press, 2002

Clyburn, James E. *Blessed Experiences: Genuinely Southern Proudly Black*. Columbia: University of South Carolina Press, 2014.

Conlan, Timothy. *From New Federalism to Devolution: Twenty-Five Years of Intergovernmental Reform*. Washington: Brookings, 1998.

Crawford. Kenneth G. *The Pressure Boys: The Inside Story of Lobbying in America*. New York: J. Messner, 1939.

David, Paul T., Ralph Goldman, and Richard Bain. *The Politics of National Party Conventions*. New York: Vintage Books (Brookings Institute), 1964.

Edwards, Bob. *Edward R. Murrow and the Birth of Broadcast Journalism*. Hoboken, NJ: John Wiley and Sons, 2004.

Elkins, Stanley and Eric McKitrick. *The Age of Federalism: The Early American Republic, 1788 to 1800*. New York: Oxford University Press, 1995.

Farazmand, Ali. *Modern Systems of Government: Exploring the Role of Bureaucrats and Politicians*. Thousand Oaks, CA: Sage Publications, 1997.

Fauntroy, Michael K. *Republicans and the Black Vote*. Boulder: Lynne Rienner Publishers, 2007.

Gillespie, Nick and Matt Welch. *The Declaration of Independents: How Libertarian Politics Can Fix What's Wrong with America*. New York: Public Affairs, 2011.

Goldberg, Bernard. *Bias: A CBS Insider Exposes How the Media Distort the News.* Washington: Regnery Publishing, 2002.

Goldman, Ralph M. *The Democratic Party in American Politics.* New York: Macmillan Company, 1966.

Goldstein, Kenneth M. *Interest Group Lobbying, and Participation in America.* Cambridge, UK: Cambridge University Press, 1999.

Gould, Lewis. *The Most Exclusive Club: A History of the Modern United States Senate.* New York: Basic Books, 2005.

Fleischer, Ari. *Taking Heat: The President, the Press, and My Years in the White House.* New York: William Morrow, 2005.

Hall, Kermit L. ed. *The Oxford Companion to the Supreme Court of the United States.* New York: Oxford, 1992.

Halperin, Mark and John Heilemann. *Double Down: Game Change 2012.* New York: Penguin Press, 2013.

___. *Game Change: Obama and the Clintons, McCain and Palin, and the Race of a Lifetime.* New York: Harper, 2010.

Hamilton, Lee. *How Congress Works and Why You Should Care.* Bloomington: Indiana University Press, 2004.

Herrnson, Paul S. *Congressional Elections: Campaigning at Home and in Washington.* Washington: CQ Press, 2000.

Hilliard, Robert L. *The Federal Communications Commission.* Boston: Emerson College, 1991.

Jensen, Merrill. *The Articles of Confederation: An Interpretation of the Social-Constitutional History of the American Revolution, 1774-1781.* Madison: University of Wisconsin Press, 1959.

Judis, John B. *The Paradox of Democracy: Elites, Special Interests and the Betrayal of Public Trust.* New York: Pantheon, 2000.

Kaiser, Robert G. *So Damn Much Money: The Triumph of Lobbying and the Corrosion of Government.* New York: Knopf, 2009.

Kallen, Stuart A. ed. *Media Bias.* San Diego: Thomson-Gale, 2004.

Kaufman, Joyce. *A Concise History of U.S. Foreign Policy.* New York: Rowan and Littlefield, 2006.

Kelly, Kate. *Election Day: An American Holiday, An American History.* New York: Facts on File, 1991.

Krent, Harold J. *Presidential Powers.* New York: New York University Press, 2005.

Labunski, Richard E. *James Madison and the Struggle for the Bill of Rights.* Oxford: Oxford University Press, 2006.

Lazarus, Edward. *Closed Chambers: The Rise, Fall, and Future of the Modern Supreme Court.* New York: Penguin Books, 1998.

Mann, Thomas and Norman Ornstein. *The Broken Branch: How Congress Is Failing America and How to Get It Back on Track.* New York: Oxford, 2006.

Marlin, George J. *The American Catholic Voter: 200 Years of Political Impact.* South Bend, IN: St. Augustine Press, 2004.

McCullough, David. *Truman.* New York, Simon and Schuster, 1992.

Medoff, Rafael. *Jewish Americans and Political Participation.* Santa Barbara, CA: ABC-CLIO, 2002.

Newport, Frank. *Polling Matters: Why Leaders Must Listen to the Wisdom of the People*. New York: Warner Books, 2004.

Nichols, David. *A Matter of Justice: Eisenhower and the Beginning of the Civil Rights Revolution*. New York: Simon and Schuster, 2007.

Nixon, Richard. *The Memoirs of Richard Nixon*. New York: Grosset and Dunlap, 1978.

Patterson, Bradley H. *The White House Staff: Inside the West Wing and Beyond*. Washington: Brookings Institution Press, 2000.

Piven, Frances Fox, Lorraine C. Minnite, and Margaret Groarke. *Keeping Down the Black Vote: Race and the Demobilization of American Voters*. New York: The New Press, 2009.

Rehnquist, William. *The Supreme Court*. New York: Vintage Books, 2001.

Remeni, Robert V. *The House*. New York: Harper Collins, 2007.

Rodman, Peter W. *Presidential Command: Power, Leadership, and the Making of Foreign Policy from Richard Nixon to George W. Bush*. New York: Alfred A. Knopf, 2009.

Safire, William. *Safire's New Political Dictionary*. New York: Random House, 1993.

Schlesinger, Arthur M., Jr. *The Imperial Presidency*. Boston: Houghton Mifflin, 1989.

Shrum, Robert. *No Excuses: Confessions of a Serial Campaigner*. New York: Simon and Schuster, 2007.

Sloan, W. David and Lisa Mullikin Parcell eds. *American Journalism: History, Principles, Practices*. Jefferson, NC: McFarland and Company, 2002.

Sorenson, Theodore C. *Kennedy*. Old Saybrook, CT: Konecky & Konecky, 1965.

Steinman, Ron. *Inside Television's First War: A Saigon Journal*. Columbia: University of Missouri Press, 2002.

Thomas, Helen. *Watchdogs of Democracy? The Waning Washington Press Corps and How It Has Failed the Public*. New York: Scribner, 2006.

Tocqueville, Alexis de. *Democracy In America*. Chicago: University of Chicago Press, 2002.

Toobin, Jeffrey. *The Nine: Inside the Secret World of the Supreme Court*. New York: Anchor, 2008.

Tribe, Laurence and Joshua Matz. *Uncertain Justice: The Roberts Court and the Constitution*. New York: Henry Holt, 2014.

Webster, Mary ed. *The Federalist Papers in Modern Language Indexed for Today's Political Issues*. Bellevue, WA: Merril Press, 1999.

Whitcover, Jules. *Party of the People: A History of the Democrats*. New York: Random House, 2003.

White, Theodore. *The Making of a President 1960*. New York: Atheneum, 1961.

Wood, Gordon S. *The Creation of the American Republic, 1776-1787*. Chapel Hill: UNC Press, 1998.

Woodward, C. Vann. *The Strange Career of Jim Crow*. New York: Oxford University Press, 2002.

Articles

Abello, Cristina. "Changes in Store at the FCC." *The News Media and the Law*. Winter 2009.

Alterman, Eric. "Bush's War on the Press." *The Nation*. May 9, 2005.

Baker, Peter. "The Education of a President." *New York Times*. October 12, 2010.

Basinger, Scott, and Maxwell Mak. "The Changing Politics of Federal Judicial Nominations." *Congress and the President*, vol. 37. 2010.

Beckel, Michael and Russ Choma. "Decision Helped Romney Neutralize Obama's Fundraising Advantage." Open Secrets <www.opensecrets.org>. October 30, 2012.

Biskupic, Joan. "Ellis Island: This Land is Whose Land?" *Washington Post*. January 11, 1998, and May 27, 1998.

Bottum, Joseph. "There is No Catholic Vote." *The Weekly Standard*. November 1, 2010.

Brand, Rachel. "Judicial Appointments: Checks and Balances in Practice." *Harvard Journal of Law and Public Policy*. Volume 33, Number 1.

Brill, Steven. "On Sale: Your Government." *Time*. July 12, 2010.

Carney, Eliza Newlin. "K Street's Sea Change." *National Journal*. September 22, 2007.

Casey, Winter. "Why They Lobby." *National Journal*. May 31, 2008.

___. "Everything You Need to Know about the Voter ID Controversy." *The Week*. October 25, 2014.

Garrow, David. "The Once and Future Supreme Court." *American History*. February 2005.

Goldmacher, Shane. "Four Years Later." *National Journal*. June 8, 2014.

Groseclose, Tim and Jeffery Milyo. "A Measure of Media Bias." Stuart Kallen ed., *Media Bias*. San Diego: Greenhaven Press, 2004.

Guldon, Bob. "Mr. X Speaks: An Interview with George Kennan." *Foreign Service Journal*. February 2004.

Jackson, Jannie, Peter Hart and Rachel Coen. "The Media are Biased Against Conservative Economic Policies." Stuart Kallen ed., *Media Bias*. San Diego: Greenhaven Press, 2004.

Johnson, Fawn. "The End of No Child Left Behind." *National Journal*. October 29, 2011.

Jost, Kenneth. "Revising No Child Left Behind." *CQ Researcher*. April 16, 2010.

___. "Voting Controversies: Are U.S. Elections Being Conducted Fairly?" *Congressional Quarterly Researcher*. February 21, 2014.

Klein, Daniel B. and Charlotta Stern. "By the Numbers: The Ideological Profile of Professors." *The Politically Correct University*. Washington: AEI Press, 2009.

Kohler, Peter. "The Unfairness of the 'Fairness Doctrine.'" *The Masthead*. Spring 2009.

Lewis, Charles. "Why I Left *60 Minutes*." *Politico Magazine*. June 29, 2014.

Mayersohn, Andrew. "Four Years After Citizens United: The Fallout." Open Secrets <www.opensecrets.org>. January 21, 2014.

Meyerson, Harold. "California's Jungle Primary: Tried it. Dump it." *Los Angeles Times*. June 21, 2014.

"New American Center," *Esquire*. November 2013.

Rendell, Steve. "The Fairness Doctrine: How We Lost It, and Why We Need it Back." *Extra!* January/February 2005.

Smock, Raymond W. "The Institutional Development of the House of Representatives, 1789–1801." Kenneth R. Bowling and Donald R. Kennon eds. *The House and Senate in the 1790s: Petitioning, Lobbying, and Institutional Development*. Athens: Ohio University Press, 2002.

Unger, Ross. "Boss Rove." *Vanity Fair*. September 2012.

Walker, Jesse. "Beyond the Fairness Doctrine." *Reason*. November 2008.

Wolfensberger, Donald R. "The Return of the Imperial Presidency?" *The Wilson Quarterly*. Spring 2002.

Reports

American National Election Study (ANES). Stanford University, University of Michigan, and the National Science Foundation, 2014.

Congressional Research Service. *Declarations of War and Authorizations for the Use of Military Force: Historical Background and Legal Implications.* March 17, 2011.

___. *Lobbying Reform, Background and Legislative Proposals*, 109th Congress. March 23, 2006.

___. *Membership of the 113th Congress: A Profile.* March 14, 2014.

Democratic National Committee. *Moving America Forward: Democratic National Platform.* 2012.

Gans, Curtis. *African-Americans, Anger, Fear and Youth Propel Turnout to Highest Level Since 1960.* American University. December 17, 2008.

___. *Testimony Before Senate Rules Committee.* March 11, 2009.

Klein, Daniel B. *By the Numbers: The Ideological Profile of Professors.* American Enterprise Institute Conference. November 14, 2007.

Lopez, Mark Hugo and Paul Taylor. *Dissecting the 2008 Electorate.* Pew Research Center. April 30, 2009.

Manning, Jennifer E. *Membership of the 113th Congress: A Profile.* March 14, 2014.

McGann, James. *The Go-To Global Think Tanks.* University of Pennsylvania. January 25, 2011.

Pew Research Center. *Dissecting the 2008 Electorate: Most Diverse in U.S. History.* April 30, 2009.

___. *Eight Takeaways About Social Media and News.* March 26, 2014.

___. *Fiscal Facts: Fiscal Year 2012 Budget of the United States Government.* March 11, 2011.

___. *Growth in Digital Reporting: What It Means for Journalism and News Consumers.* March 26, 2014.

___. *Key Indicators in Media and News.* March 26, 2014.

___. *State of the News Media*, Overview. March 26, 2014.

___. *Winning the Media Campaign 2012.* November 2, 2012.

Republican National Committee. *Republican Platform.* 2012.

U.S. Census Bureau. *Voting and Registration in the Election of November 2008.* May 2010.

U.S. Election Assistance Commission. *The Impact of the National Voter Registration Act.* June 30, 2009.

U.S. Office of Management and Budget. *The Budget for Fiscal Year 2012.*

___. Historical Tables, 2014.

U.S. Office of Personnel Management. *Biography of an Ideal: A History of the Federal Civil Service.* 2003.

___. *A New Day for the Civil Service.* Fiscal Year 2010 Annual Performance Report. 2011.

Films

Casino Jack and the United States of Money. Magnolia Home Entertainment, 2010.

The Most Dangerous Man in America: Daniel Ellsberg and the Pentagon Papers. First Run Features, 2009.

The War Room. Criterion Collection, 1994.

Index

A

AARP, 167, 391, 408
ABC (American Broadcasting Company), 188, 197
Abington School District v. *Schempp,* 371
abortion
    Planned Parenthood v. *Casey,* 379
    poll on, 63
    Roe v. Wade, 113, 120, 161, 309, 314, 345,
    346, 347, 348, 379
Abramoff, Jack, 175–176
absentee ballots, 94
Abu Ghraib, 190
access, 162, 167, 168, 173
Acheson, Dean, 420
Adams, John, 249, 263
    administration of, 32, 246
    as colonial leader, 6, 9
    court appointments of, 304–305, 316
    in election of 1800, 133, 252
    as Federalist, 106
    as Vice President, 33, 215
Adams, John Quincy, in election of 1824, 107, 252
Adams, Samuel, as Son of Liberty, 4
ad hoc administrative system, 269
Adkins v. Children's Hospital, 307
adversarial press, 188
advice and consent, 20, 214, 226, 316
affirmative action, 352–354
Affordable Care Act (2010), 164, 394
Afghanistan War, 380, 439–440
African Americans
    in bureaucracy, 230
    civil rights and, 161, 328–355
    in Congress, 217–218, 230
    as critical of political and criminal justice
    system, 65
    lynching and, 332
    suffrage for, 79–80, 111, 340
agencies, 282
    independent, 282–283
Agency for International Development, 421
agenda, 391–392
Agriculture, U.S. Department of, 278, 281, 285, 409
Ailes, Roger, 202
Air America, 207
Air Pollution Control Act (1970), 395
Alaska, blanket primaries in, 135
Albright, Madeleine, 439
Alien and Sedition Acts, 32–33
Alito, Samuel, 310
All Things Considered, 200

Allwright, S. S., 111
al Qaeda, 380, 439
Alterman, Eric, 192, 206
The Amazing Race, 200
ambassadors, 257
American Banking Association, 171
American Bar Association (ABA), 164, 170, 317, 318
American Civil Liberties Union (ACLU), 148, 159,
    167, 327, 346, 360, 362, 363, 371
American colonies
    declaration of independence by, 6–7
    original 13, 6
    ratification of Constitution, 15
American Conservative Union, 148, 170
American Crossroads, 177
American Enterprise Institute, 165
American Farm Bureau, 159
American Federation of Labor, 91, 158
    merger with Congress of Industrial
    Organizations, 160
Americans for Prosperity, 178
American Heart Association, 168
American Independent party, 124
American Legion, 159
American Medical Association, 164
American Party, 90, 122
American Railway Union, 158
American Revolution, 3, 4, 5, 6, 7, 10, 37, 183,
American Rifleman, 166
Americans for Democratic Action, 170
Americans with Disabilities Act (1990), 42
amicus curiae brief, 174, 321, 381
Amtrak, 284
anchorman, 188
Anderson, John, 124
animal rights movement, 163–164
Annapolis, Maryland, meeting in, 9
anonymous sources, 195–196
Anthony, Susan B., 80, 344
Anti-Ballistic Missile Treaty, 435
Anti-Defamation League, 159
Anti-Federalists, 16–17, 30, 32, 105, 113, 360
Anti-Masonic party, 118, 122
Anti-slavery movement, 329
antisodomy laws, 349
AOL, 200
appeasement, 431
appellate courts, 302
appellate jurisdiction, 299, 302
approval ratings, 68
arguments, formulating, 97

Articles of Confederation, 1, 4, 7–9, 29
    problems with, 8, 13, 298–299
    ratification of, 3
Asher, Herbert, 63, 65
Asian Americans, voting by, 89
Associated Press (AP), 185, 205
Astroturf, 172
The Atlantic, 177
Atlantic Charter, 431
attorney general, 301
Audubon Society, 161
Australian ballots, 84
authorization of spending, 289
automobiles, consumer movement and, 162
Automobile Theft Act (1915), 35
Aziz, Tariq, 438

B

The Bachelor, 201
backroom deals, 133
Baker, James, 438
Baker v. Carr, 224
Bakke, Alan, 353
Balanced Budget Act (1985), 410
balanced budget amendment, 410
Ball, Molly, 177
ballots
    absentee, 84, 95
    access of independents to, 126
    Australian, 84
Balz, Dan, 87
Bank of the United States, 32
Barr, Bob, 56
Barron, John, 361
Baugh, Joyce, 319
Bay of Pigs invasion, 258
Beck, Glenn, 207
Becker, Carl, 5
Begin, Menachem, 436
Bell, John, in election of 1860, 252
Berlin Wall, fall of, 437
Bernstein, Carl, 189, 190, 193
Bethel Schools v. Fraser, 369
bias
    ideological, 205–207
    quantifying, 206
    upper class, 165
bicameralism, 16, 214
Biden, Joe, 262, 263, 317
Big Three networks, 188, 205, 203
Bill of Rights, 1, 2, 3, 17–18, 22, 29, 55, 216, 298,
    301, 327, 360–361, 363. *See also specific*
    ratification of, 3
bills, 19
    assigning to committee, 235
    becoming law, 236

drafting and altering of, 239–240
    numbering of, 235
    origination of, 215
    riders for, 236
    sponsors of, 235
binding precedents, 304
bin Laden, Osama, 439–440
Bipartisan Campaign Reform Act (2002), 149–150,
    166
Bittle, Scott, 409
Black, Hugo, 159–160, 308, 434
Blackmun, Harry, 311, 349
Blagojevich, Rod, 191
Blair, Jayson, 204
blanket primaries, 135
block grants, 38–39
Bloomberg, Michael, 124, 125
Blue Dog Coalition, 230
blue slip, 316
Board of Elections, 136
Boehner, John, 229
Boland Amendments, 437
bolter parties, 122
bond rates, 400–401
bonds, 400
Border Patrol, 282, 422
Bork, Robert, 317
Bosnia-Herzegovina, 439
Boston Massacre, 3
Boston Tea Party, 3
Bowers v. Hardwick, 349
Boxer Rebellion, 248
Boy Scouts of America, 351
Brady Bill, 167
Brady, David, 206
Brady, James, Press Briefing Room, 192
Brand, Rachel, 316
Brandeis, Louis, 307, 310, 344
Brandenburg v. Ohio, 366
Branzburg v. Hayes, 196
Breckenridge, John C., in election of 1860, 252
Brennan, William, 21
Breyer, Stephen, 311
Brezhnev, Leonid, 435
broadcasting, 187–188
broadcasting licenses, 197
broadcast networks, 187
Brown, Linda, 334
Brown, Sherrod, 136, 233
Brown II, 334, 342
Brown v. Board of Education, 308, 309, 334, 343
Bryan, William Jennings, 56, 109
Buchanan, James, 108
    administration of, 248
Buchanan, Pat, 125, 251
Buchanan v. Warley, 332
Buckley, James, 148

Buckley v. Valeo, 148
budget, defense, 426
budget committees, 407, 412
Budget Enforcement Act (1990), 410
budgeting guidelines, 406
budget process, 406
Bull Moose party, 123
bully pulpit, 191, 255
bureaucracy, 277–294
    agencies in, 282–283
    commissions in, 283
    culture in, 290–294
    departments in, 281–282
    government corporations in, 284
    history, growth, and reform of, 277–281
    interaction in, 287–290
    rules for, 287
    staffing of, 284–287
    today, 281–290
Bureau of the Budget, 266, 405
bureaus, 185
Burger, Warren, 309, 320
    as Chief Justice of Supreme Court, 372
Burns, James McGregor, 114
Burr, Aaron, 133
    in election of 1800, 252
Bush, George H. W., 115, 259, 263
    administration of, 68, 92, 114, 250, 285
    court appointments of, 311, 318, 319–320
    in election of 1980, 141
    in election of 1992, 251, 252, 398
    foreign policy of, 258, 437
    lobbying and, 177
    media support for, 205
    as Republican party chairperson, 116
    as vice president, 262
Bush, George W., 115, 261
    administration of, 19, 63, 69, 114, 256, 408
    court appointments of, 310–311, 316, 317
    diplomacy and, 257
    election of, 93
    in election of 2000, 126, 143, 149
    media coverage of, 190, 204
    press relations and, 192
    same-sex marriage and, 352
    September 11 and, 380–381
    War on Terror and, 439–440
Bush Doctrine, 440
business community, voting participation and, 91
Business Roundtable, 165
BuzzFeed, 203
Byrd, Robert C., 221, 338

C

Cabinet, 263–265
    of Adams, John, 278
    of Eisenhower, Dwight D., 264

    evaluating, 271
    of Jackson, Andrew, 278
    of Jefferson, Thomas, 278
    of Johnson, Lyndon, 265
    of Kennedy, John F., 265, 285
    of Lincoln, Abraham, 264
    of Obama, Barack, 263
    secretaries and deputies of, 282–284
    of Washington, George, 106, 264, 277
Cable news, 201
Cable News Network (CNN), 200
Calhoun, John, 33, 216
California
    blanket primaries in, 135
    nonpartisan primaries in, 135
Camp, Dave, 232
Camp David Accords, 436
candidates, showcasing of, 137–138
Cannon, Joseph (Joe), 217, 228
capitalism, 112
    laissez faire, 306, 403, 411
Capitol Building, 213, 228
Capitol Hill, 227–228
Carlin, George, 199
Carnal Knowledge (film), 367
Carnegie Steel, 158
Carson, Rachel, 161
Carter, Jimmy, 115, 260
    administration of, 270, 435–436
    civil service reforms of, 280
    court appointments of, 319
    in election of 1976, 251
    in election of 1980, 251, 398
    press relations and, 197
Carville, James, 398
Casey, Bob, 379
Castro, Fidel, 434
categorical grants, 38
Catholics, 59
    political parties and, 110
    voting participation and, 90
caucuses, 106, 117–118, 228
    congressional, 133
    Iowa, 141
Caveat emptor, 162
CBS (Columbia Broadcasting System), 187, 188, 199
CBS Paramount TV, 200
census, 214
Center for Responsive Law, 166
Central Intelligence Agency (CIA), 250, 265, 291, 424
certiorari, 302
Chadha, Jagdish, 289–290
Chairman of the Joint Chiefs, 423
Chaplinsky v. New Hampshire, 369
Chase, Samuel, 319–320

checks and balances, 12, 19
Cheney, Dick, 191, 263, 426
Chiang Kai-shek, 435
Chicago, 1968 Democratic Convention in, 118–119
chief of staff, 267
child labor, 36, 157–158
China, Nixon and, 435
Chisholm, Shirley, 132
Christian Coalition, 112
Christian fundamentalists, 109
Christmas displays, 373
Christmas tree bill, 236
Churchill, Winston, 431
circuit courts of appeals, 298
circular system, 270
citizens, expectations and involvement of, 162
Citizens Against Government Waste, 237
Citizens United, 173
Citizens United v. FEC, 150, 173, 315
civil cases, 301
Civilian Conservation Corps, 399
civil liberties, 360–383
    church and state in, 370–374
    civil rights and, 306–307
    due process in, 374–379
    free speech and free press in, 364–370
    national security and, 379–383
    selective incorporation in, 361–363
civil rights
    affirmative action and, 352–355
    for African Americans, 327–330
    civil liberties and, 308–309
    in the Congress, U.S., 334–343
    gay rights and, 348–352
    interest groups and, 159
    political party realignment and, 113
    women's rights and, 344–348
Civil Rights Act (1875), 330
Civil Rights Act (1957), 80, 336, 337
Civil Rights Act (1964), 80, 112, 161, 220, 337
Civil Rights Cases (1883), 330, 331
Civil Rights Movement, 59
Civil Service Commission, 279, 286
Civil Service Reform Act (1978), 280
civil unions, 352
Civil War, 59, 328–329
    need for bureaucracy, 278
Clark, Kenneth, 333
Clark, Mamie, 333
class action suits, 301
Clay, Henry, 107, 118, 216
    in election of 1824, 107–108, 252
Clean Air Act (1964), 161
Clean Air Act (1970), 46, 395
Clean Air Act (1990), 172
Clean Water Act (1963), 161
Clean Water Act (1972), 395

clear and present danger test, 364–365
Cleveland, Grover, 108
Cleveland, Ohio, Hanna, Mark, in, 134
Clinton, Hillary
    creation of Hill-PAC, 170
    fund-raising and, 137
Clinton, Roger, 260
Clinton, William (Bill), 115, 252, 260, 398
    administration of, 43, 55, 114, 172, 267–268,
        293–294, 408, 410, 438
    court appointments of, 311, 317
    in election of 1992, 141–142, 252
    foreign policy of, 258
    gay rights and, 350
    impeachment charges against, 20, 238, 245
    legislation signed by, 200
    lobbying and, 177
    love affairs of, 186, 202
    pardons issued by, 260
    press relations and, 195, 205, 268
    women's rights and, 346
Clinton v. City of New York, 256
closed primaries, 135
cloture, 226–227
Clyburn, James, 228
coalitions, 107
    Christian, 112
    New Deal, 110, 111
Coast Guard, 265, 282, 422
coattail effect, 140
Cohen, Paul Robert, 366–367
Cohen v. California, 367
Cold War, 44, 250, 259, 365, 423, 432–434
collective security, 430
colleges, 337, 346
commander in chief, 246–247
Commerce, U.S. Department of, 279, 281
Commerce Clause, 13, 217–218
    Supreme Court on, 36, 219–220
commercial speech, 369
commissions, 282
committee chairmen, 234
committee clearance, 289
Committee of the Whole, 233
Committee on Committees (Republican), 233
Committee on Equal Employment Opportunity,
    352
committees
    budget, 407
    conference, 232
    Hill, 116
    joint, 231
    select, 230–231, 232
    standing, 229–230, 231
Common Cause, 166
common law, 304
Communications Act, 197

Community Development Block Grants, 39
compact theory, 33
competitive service, 286
Comprehensive Employment and Training Act
  (1973), 39
Comstock, Anthony, 366
Concord, battle of, 3, 6
concurrent powers, 30
concurring opinion, 313
conditions of aid, 39
Confederation Congress, 15
conference chairman, 229
conference committees, 229, 232
Congress, U.S., 211–238. *See also* House of
  Representatives, U.S.; Senate, U.S.
  African Americans in, 217–218, 230
  assigning bills to committee in, 235
  civil rights in, 334–343
  committees in, 228–235
  contemporary, 237–240
  demographics of 113th, 223
  elections for, 219–221
  first, 215
  in foreign and military policy, 418
  Framers' plan for, 213–215
  history of, 213–219
  image of, 221
  incumbency and, 221–222
  leadership of, 228–230, 238
  legislative process in, 235–237
  media and, 191–192
  membership of, 222–227
  national voting regulations and, 92–93
  oversight and influence on Supreme Court,
    320
  as overworked, 239–240
  party polarization and, 237
  powers of, 219–221
  staff for, 227–228
  television coverage of, 218
  voting in, 227
  women in, 218
Congressional Black Caucus, 228, 230
Congressional Budget Office (CBO), 266, 406
congressional campaigns, 136
  connecting with the public in, 137–138
  fund-raising for, 136–137
congressional caucuses, 133, 216
congressional oversight, 233–234, 289
Congress of Industrial Organizations, merger with
  American Federation of Labor, 160
Congress on Racial Equality (CORE), 161, 335
Congress Watch, 166
Connally, John, in election of 1980, 149
Connecticut, ratification of Constitution, 16
Connecticut Compromise, 11
Connor, Bull, 336

The Conscience of a Conservative
  (Goldwater), 55
Conservatism, 54, 112–113
conservatives, 206
constituent services, 221
Constitution, U.S., 1
  Article I, 12–13, 20, 22, 29, 30, 34, 212, 219,
    301
  Article II, 13, 30, 144, 244, 255, 262
  Article III, 13, 20, 30, 298, 298, 311, 360
  Article IV, 13, 29
  Article V, 14
  Article VI, 14, 21, 29, 30
  Article VII, 14–15
  Bill of Rights to, 17–18
  commerce clause in, 13, 36, 219–220
  elastic clause in, 13, 220–221
  enumerated powers in, 12
  flexibility of, 18, 22
  full faith and credit clause, 13, 29
  necessary and proper clause in, 13, 22,
    220–221
  opposition to, 16–17
  in practice, 18–22
  Preamble to, 12, 18, 392
  privileges and immunity clause in, 29–30
  ratification of, 2, 15–17
  support for, 15–16
constitutional amendments, 14, 22. *See also* Bill of
  Rights; *specific by number*
  suffrage and, 78–83
Constitutional Convention (1787), 3, 9–12
  creation of political parties in, 105–106
constitutional courts, 298
Consumer Federation of America, 162
consumer movement, interest groups and, 162
Consumer Product Safety Commission, 280
Consumers' Bill of Rights, 162
Consumer's Union, 162
containment, 432, 439
Continental army, 9
Continental Congress, 3, 6, 7–8
continuous body, 226
convenience voting, 95
conventional news, 187–188
Coolidge, Calvin, as conservative, 123
cooperative federalism, 36
Cooper v. Aaron, 342
Corporation for Public Broadcasting (CPM),
  199–200, 284
corporations
  lobbyists and, 163
  state and, 304–306
cost-benefits analysis, 391–392
Council of Economic Advisers, 266, 397, 406
Council on Foreign Relations, 425
counter-mobilization, 163–164

courts. *See also* judiciary
    lobbying and, 174
    media coverage of, 194
Craig, Larry, 191
Craig v. Boren, 347
Crawford, Kenneth, 159–160
Crawford, William H., in election of 1824, 252
Credit Mobilier scandal, 175
The Crisis, 331
critical elections, 108
Cronkite, Walter, 188, 189, 204
cross-mobilization, 163–164
"Cross of Gold" speech, 56
C-SPAN (Cable Satellite Public Affairs Network), 193–194, 226, 239
C-SPAN 2, 194, 226
Cuba
    Bay of Pigs invasion of, 258
    Communist takeover of, 434
    independence of, 429
Cuban Missile Crisis (1962), 258, 434
culture wars of the 1990s, 350–351
Cunningham, Randall "Duke," 175
Cuyahoga River, 162
Czechoslovakia, 431

D

Dale, James, 351
dateline, 186
Davis, Jefferson, 216
Davis, John W., 118
Day, Benjamin, 185
Dayton Accords, 439
DC Circuit, 303
DEA, 321
dealignment, 114
Dean, Howard, 116
Dean, John, 309
death penalty, 377–378
debates, political, 138
    Kennedy-Nixon, 146, 188, 198
Debs, Eugene, 158
debt, 408
    facing the, 410
decision making model/process, 391–392
Declaration of Independence, 1, 3, 6–7, 10
Declaration of Independents (Gillespie and Welch), 56
de facto segregation, 342
defendants, 300
Defense, U.S. Department of, 263, 281, 288, 326, 418, 423
defense budget, 426
Defense of Marriage Act (DOMA) (1996), 350–351
deficit, 408
de jure segregation, 340

Delaware, ratification of Constitution, 16
delegated powers, 30
delegate model, 227
Dellums, Ron, 219
democracy, 19, 35
    Jacksonian, 106–107
Democracy in America (Tocqueville), 75
Democratic Congressional Campaign Committee (DCCC), 117, 230
Democratic National Committee (DNC), 116, 126
Democratic National Convention, of 1936, 280
Democratic Party, 54–57, 107
    African American support for, 88
    budget process and, 406
    civilian workforce and, 280
    in Congress, 222
    domination of southern politics following Civil War, 330
    foreign and military policy and, 424–425
    geographic location and, 60, 61
    Great Depression and, 110, 146
    ideology and platform of, 120–121, 126
    under Jackson, Andrew, 106–107
    McGovern-Fraser Commission and, 119
    minor parties and, 125
    national conventions of, 107, 117–119
    national party structure of, 116
    Policy and Steering Committee of, 233
    realignment and, 113
    state and local, 117
Democratic Senatorial Campaign Committee (DSCC), 117
Democrats-Republicans, 32, 106
Dennis v. United States, 365
desegregation of schools, 38, 333–334
détente, 434–435
devolution, 42–43
Dewey, Thomas, 124
Dingell, John, Jr., 221
direct lobbying, 167
direct primary, 134
Dirksen Office Building, 228
discharge petition, 224–225
discount rate, 401
discretionary authority, 287
discretionary spending, 409
discrimination
    against gays, 349–350
    reverse, 352–353
    in voter registration, 339–340
discuss list, 312
disenfranchisement,330
disengagement, 434–436
dissenting opinion, 313
district courts, 298
District of Columbia, suffrage in, 81–82
diversity citizenship, 301
divided government, 114–115

Dixiecrats, 112, 124
Dobbs, Michael, 439
Dole, Bob, 116, 171, 229
    as Republican Party chairperson, 116
domestic policy, 390–397
Domino Theory, 433
don't ask, don't tell policy, 257, 350
Douglas, William, 308
    in election of 1860, 252
draft cards, burning of, 365
Dred Scott v. Sandford, 306, 314, 328
Drug Enforcement Administration, 291
dual federalism, 34
DuBois, W. E. B., 331
due process, 361, 374–377
    procedural, 375–377
    substantive, 378–379
due process clause of fourteenth Amendment,
    362–363
Dukakis, Michael, 68, 88, 115
Dunn v. Blumstein, 83–84
Dyer, L. C., 332

E

Early Show, 220
earmarks, 237
Eastland, James, 332, 336
economic ideology, 398–399
economic policy, 397–400
economic protest parties, 122, 123
economy, role of, in elections, 140
editorials, 201
education. *See also* schools
    desegregation of, 77
    enrollment ratios in, 43
    federalism and, 44–45
    growth of colleges, 37
    No Child Left Behind Act and, 44, 192
    in political socialization, 58–59
    Race to the Top initiative, 45
    Title IX and, 161, 219, 346
Education, U.S. Department of, 281
    creation of, 44
Edwards, Bob, 187
Edwards, John, 186
Edwards, Mickey, 231
eighteen-year-olds, suffrage for, 78, 87
Eighth Amendment, 18, 363, 377–378
Eisenhower, Dwight, 261, 263
    administration of, 114, 255
    cabinet of, 264–265
    chief of staff of, 267
    civil rights under, 335–336
    court appointments of, 308, 319
    Farewell Address of, 418
    press conferences of, 268
    pyramid structure used by, 270

elastic clause, 13, 220–221
electioneering, 170–171
elections, 132–151
    congressional, 136–140, 221–222
    contemporary, 135–136
    critical, 106
    financing, 145–150
    general, 134, 143–145
    history of, 132–136
    interest groups and, 170–171
    midterm, 136
    presidential (*See* presidential elections)
    primary, 134–136
    runoff, 135, 140
Electoral College, 12, 19, 53, 60, 144, 214, 245,
    251
    alterations to, 144
    benefits of, 145
    drawbacks of, 145
electorate, 76
    expanding, 77–78
electors, 144, 251
Elementary and Secondary Education Act (1965),
    44
elites, 118, 119
elite theory of politics, 391
Elkins, Stanley, 32
Ellsberg, Daniel, 194, 195
Emancipation Proclamation, 329
Emanuel, Rahm, 228
Emerson, John, 328
employment of women, 343–344
en banc, 303
Endangered Species Act, 395
endorsements, 170
Energy, U.S. Department of, 281
Engle v. Vitale, 174, 371
enlargement, 439
enlightenment, 2
    influence of, 5–6, 7
entitlements, 408
enumerated powers, 12–13
environmental movement, interest groups and,
    161–162
environmental policy, 394–395
Environmental Protection Agency (EPA), 162, 173,
    280, 395
Equal Employment Opportunity Commission, 280
Equal Pay Act (1963), 161, 345
Equal protection clause of Fourteenth Amendment,
    7, 80, 224, 329, 331, 333, 350
Equal Rights Amendment, 161, 219, 347–348
equal time rule, 198
Espionage Act, 195, 364–365
establishment clause, 370
estate taxes, 403
ethics, lobbying and, 175–177

ethnicity. *See also specific*
    in political socialization, 59
European Recovery Act (1948), 433
Evangelical Christians, 59, 89
    voting participation of, 89
Evers, Medgar, 336
Everson v. Board of Education, 371
evidence, appropriate, 97
e-voting, 94
excepted service, 286
excise taxes, 404
exclusionary rule, 375
executive agreements, 257–258
executive branch. *See also* presidency
    lobbying of, 172
Executive Office of the President (EOP),
    265–266
Executive Order 9066, 257
executive orders, 256–257
executive privilege, 260–261
exit polls, 67, 68, 88, 91
exposé, 186
ex post facto laws, 13
expressed powers, 219–221
extradition, 8, 14, 30

F

Facebook, 203–204
factional parties, 122
Fair Labor Standards Act (1938), 36, 395
Fairness Doctrine, 198–199, 206
Falwell, Jerry, 113
Family and Medical Leave Act, 42
family in political socialization, 58
federal, 12
federal budget, 405–408
Federal Bureau of Investigation (FBI), 35, 265,
    282, 291, 321
Federal Communications Commission (FCC), 173,
    197–199, 287
    equal time rule, 198
    Fairness Doctrine, 198–199, 206
    licensing and ownership and, 198
    monopoly and, 197
    obscenity and, 199
    right of reply rule, 198
federal crimes, 301
Federal Deposit Insurance Corporation, 284
Federal Elections Campaign Act (FECA) (1971),
    147
Federal Elections Commission, 91, 136, 147–149,
    170, 283
Federal Emergency Management Administration
    (FEMA), 292
Federal Employees Political Activities Act (1993),
    280
federal government, powers delegated to the, 31

federal grant program, 36–38, 164
federal income taxes, 403–404
federalism, 28–45, 162–164, 304, 348
    contemporary, 38–41
    cooperative, 36, 38
    defined, 28–31, 304–306
    dual, 34, 38
    education and, 44–45
    fiscal, 36, 38
    marble cake, 39, 164
    new, 38, 42
    provisions defining, 29
    Supreme Court in shaping, 33–35
The Federalist Papers, 15–18, 17, 18, 32, 33, 106,
    162, 184, 226, 245, 298, 316
Federalist #10, 15, 23, 157, 160
Federalist #51, 15–16, 23
Federalist #75, 220
Federalist #78, 299, 305
Federalists, 1, 15, 20–21, 105–106, 113
    newspapers and, 184
Federal Open Market Committee, 400
Federal Regulation of Lobbying Act (1946), 176
Federal Reserve Banks, 400
Federal Reserve Board, 400, 401
Federal Reserve System, 400–402
Federal Trade Commission, 283
Feingold, Russ, 149
The Feminine Mystique (Friedan), 161, 345
Fenno, John, 184
Fifteenth Amendment, 78, 79–80, 111, 329, 330,
    331, 340
Fifth Amendment, 18, 361, 363, 377
filibusters, 226, 318
fireside chats, 191
First Amendment, 18, 21, 33, 148, 157, 163, 167,
    173, 183, 194, 196–199, 280, 308, 361,
    362–364, 366, 370–371, 374
fiscal federalism, 36
fiscal policy, 402–412
fiscal year, 406
501(c)(3) organizations, 164
501(c)(4) organizations, 164, 173
flag burning, 368
Flag Protection Act, 21
flat taxes, 404
floor leaders, 229
focus groups, 68, 137, 177–178, 227
Foley, Tom, 238
Food and Drug Administration (FDA), 264–265
Ford, Gerald, 115, 143, 261
    assumption of office, 251
    court appointments of, 311, 319
    in election of 1976, 251, 398
    pardoning of Nixon by, 260–261
Foreign Affairs, 425, 432
foreign and military policy, 418–440
    Congress, U.S., and, 220

Constitutional framework for, 418–427
defense budget in, 426–427
history of war and diplomacy in, 425–435
human rights and strategic interest in, 435–438
international organizations in, 423
non-government organizations and think tanks in, 422–423
practical framework for, 418–422
Foreign Correspondents Association (FCA), 187
Foundation for Animal Health, 164
Four Horsemen, 307
Fourteen Points, 430
Fourteenth Amendment, 329, 333, 361–363
citizenship clause in, 81
due process clause of, 362–363
equal protection clause of, 7, 80, 224, 329, 331, 333, 350
Fourth Amendment, 18, 375–376
Fourth Estate, media as the, 183, 190
Fowler, Mark, 198
Fox News Chanel, 202, 205–206
franchise, 77, 330, 339, 344
Frank, Barney, 168
Frankfurter, Felix, 308
franking privilege, 221
Franklin, Benjamin
as colonial leader, 2, 4, 6, 9
Fraser, Matt, 369
Fraternal Order of Police (FOP), 162–164, 170
Freedmen's Bureau, 330
freedom-of-choice plans, 346
Freedom of Information Act (1966), 292
freedom of the press, 194–201
Freedom Rides, 161
Free exercise clause, 370–371
free press, 183
free response questions, xxiv, 27, 50, 73,101, 130, 173, 155, 182, 210, 243, 276, 297, 325, 359, 387, 416, 446, 464
free rider problem, 165
Free Soil party, 108, 122, 123
free speech, 148, 364–370
in schools, 368–369
Fremont, John C., as Free Soiler, 108
Freneau, Philip, 184
Friedan, Betty, 161, 345
Friends of the NRA, 166–167
Frontline, 200
frontloading, 142
full faith and credit clause, 8, 13, 29, 31, 51, 352
Fulton, Robert, 34
fundamental Christians, 121
fundamentalists, 59, 89
fund-raising, for congressional campaigns, 136–137
Furman v. Georgia, 378

G

Gaddafi, Muammar, 426, 440
Gadsden Purchase, 428
Gaines, Lloyd, 333
Gallup, George, 53, 62
Gallup Poll, 62, 67, 74, 88, 145, 238, 352, 372
Gang of 14, 318
Gans, Curtis, 95
Gardner, John, 166
Garfield, James, assassination of, 279
Garrow, David, 315
gatekeeper, media's role as a, 189
Gates, Robert, 264
gay rights and equality, 348–352
Gazette of the United States, 184
gender gap, 87
general elections, 134, 136, 143–145, 170, 339
General Motors, 162, 166
Geneva Convention (1949), 380, 381–382
George III, King of England, 2, 4
Georgia, ratification of Constitution, 16
Gerry, Elbridge, 14, 225
gerrymandering, 223, 225
Gibbons v. Ogden, 34–35, 219–220, 306
Gideon, Clarence Earl, 376
Gideon v. Wainright, 376, 382
Gillespie, Nick, 56
Gingrich, Newt, 43, 238
Ginsburg, Ruth Bader, 311, 347
Gitlow, Benjamin, 362–363
Gitlow v. New York, 362–363
GITMO, 381
glasnost, 435
Glass, Stephen, 204
globalization, 411–412
going native, 288
gold plating, 426
Goldwater, Barry, 55, 112, 147, 258
Gompers, Samuel, 158
Gonzalez, Alberto, 191
good faith exception, 375–376
Goodlatte, Robert W., 232
Good Morning America, 200
Good Times magazine, 366
Gorbachev, Mikhail, 437
Gore, Al, 93, 115, 126, 154
in election of 1992, 252
in election of 2000, 145
as vice president, 293
Gould, Lewis, 238
government, relationship with the media, 190–194
Government Accountability Office (GAO), 406–407
government corporations, 284
Government Printing Office, 185
Graham, Phil, 390, 398
Gramm-Rudman-Hollings Act (1985), 410

grandfather clause, 79, 80, 331
Grand Old Party (GOP), 108
Grant, Ulysses S.
    administration of, 278, 279, 371
    in election of 1872, 122
grants, federal, 36–38, 164
grants-in-aid programs, 36–37
grassroots lobbying, 171–172
grasstops, 172–173
Great Britain
    acquisition of Oregon and, 428
    American colonies of, 2–4
    American declaration of independence from,
        6–7
    American Revolution and, 4–5, 7
    Parliament in, 3, 4, 5, 7
    search and seizures and, 375
    World War I and, 429
    World War II and, 431–432
Great Compromise, 11, 214
Great Depression, 38, 159, 393, 428
    Democratic Party and, 110–113, 146, 159
Great Mentioner, 250
Great Society, 36, 114, 163, 261, 392
Greece, Truman Doctrine and, 432–433
Green, Edith, 346
Greenback Party, 109, 118, 122, 123
Green Party, 125, 127, 128
Greenpeace, 394
Green v. County School Board Kent County, 342
Gregg v. Georgia, 378–379
Griswold v. Connecticut, 378, 382
Groseclose, Tim, 206
Guam, Spanish American War and, 421, 428–429
Guinn v. United States, 80, 332
Guiteau, Charles, 279
Gulf of Tonkin Resolution, 259, 420
Gulf War, 438
gun control issue, 55, 121, 125, 166
Gun-Free School Zones Act (1990), 43, 50
Gutenberg, Johannes, 183

H

habeas corpus, 13, 17, 248 360, 381–382
Haldeman, H. R., 267
Halliburton, 426
Hamdi v. Rumsfeld, 381, 382
Hamilton, Alexander, 268, 299
    as delegate to Constitutional Convention,
        9, 15
    as Federalist, 15, 31
    newspapers and, 184
    as Secretary of the Treasury, 32, 106
Hamilton, Lee, 239
Hammer v. Daggenhart, 36, 37
Hanna, Mark, 134, 145
Hannity, Sean, 202, 207

hard money, 149
Hardwick, Michael, 349
Harkin, Tom, 206
Harlan, John Marshall, 328, 331
Harris, Lou, 62
Harris Interactive, 62
Harrison, William Henry, 107
    in election of 1840, 133
Hatch, Carl, 280
Hatch Act (1939, 1940), 280
Hayes, Rutherford B.
    administration of, 79
    in election of 1876, 330
Health and Human Services, U.S. Department of,
    281, 393
health care, 393–394
Hearst, William Randolph, 185–186
Heart of Atlanta Motel, Inc. v. United States, 339
heightened scrutiny test, 347
Help America Vote Act (2002), 91, 93–95
Henry, Patrick, 4, 16
Heritage Foundation, 165
Herrnson, Paul, 54, 139
Hill, Anita, 318
The Hill, 193
Hillary: the Movie, 173
Hill Committees, 116–117, 140
Hill-PAC, 170
Hiroshima, 431, 433
Hispanics, voting participation and, 59, 88–89
Hitler, Adolf, 91, 187, 431, 439
Holmes, Oliver Wendell, 36, 364
Homeland Security, U.S. Department of, 281, 282,
    284, 422
Homestead, strike at, 158
Honest Leadership and Open Government Act
    (2007), 175, 176
honeymoon period, 253
Hoover, Herbert
    in election of 1928, 109
    in election of 1932, 398
    press and, 192
Hoover, J. Edgar, 282
Horowitz, David, 206
horse race journalism, 190, 206
House of Representatives, U.S., 11, 12, 213, 214
    See also Congress, U.S.; Senate, U.S.
    amendments to bills in, 236
    Armed Services Committee, 230–231,
        423–424, 435
    C-SPAN coverage of, 193, 226
    discharge petition and, 224, 226
    election of 1800 and, 133
    election of 1824 and, 107
    Energy and Commerce Committee, 230
    Foreign Relations Committee, 423
    impeachment and, 245

Judiciary Committee of, 231, 245
Madison as member of, 77
"one man, one vote" rule and, 224
qualifications for members of, 215
reapportionment and, 223
redistricting and, 223–224
Rules Committee of, 217, 231, 235
speakers of, 217, 229
Un-American Activities Committee hearings
of, 192
Ways and Means Committee, 219, 231, 403
whips in, 229
Housing and Urban Development, U.S.
Department of, 49, 281
Houston, Charles Hamilton, 332
Huffington Post, 203, 205
Hughes, Charles Evans, as Chief Justice of
Supreme Court, 307
human rights, 437–440
Humphrey, Hubert, 115, 143, 147
civil rights and, 124
in election of 1968, 118
Humphrey's Executor v. United States, 269, 289
Hussein, Saddam, 259, 438, 440
Hyde Amendment, 379
Hyde, Henry, 379

I

I-85 district, 225
ideological bias, 205–207
ideological interest groups, 166–167
ideological parties, 122, 123
ideology, 53–57
Democratic, 120
Republican, 121
immigrants, machine politics and, 134
Immigration and Naturalization Service, 289
impeachment, 20, 245, 320
of Chase, Samuel, 320
of Clinton, Bill, 20, 238, 245
of Johnson, Andrew, 20, 245
of Nixon, Richard, 20, 192, 245
Supreme Court and, 320
imperialism, 428
imperial presidency, 246–250
implicit powers, 13
implied powers, 34, 220–221
import taxes, 411
impoundments, 406
incentives
material, 165
purposive, 165
solidary, 165
income taxes, 38, 231, 266
federal, 403–404
incumbency, 221–222
incumbents, 69, 139–140, 251
Incurably Ill For Animal Research, 163–164

Independence Hall, 9
independent agencies, 264, 282–283
independent press, 185–186
independents, ballot access and, 126
Industrial Revolution, 35, 146, 158
inertia, 291–292
inevitable discovery exception, 375
inflation, 400
in forma pauperis, 312
information
applying, 41
synthesizing, 23, 211, 355
Ingram, Laura, 207
inherent powers, 245
initiatives, 76
injunctions, 301
inquiries, formulating, 193, 447
insider strategies, 167
institutional blocks, 125–126
institutional interest groups, 164–165
INS v. Chadha, 289–290
intelligence, 424
interest groups, 157–177, 239
confirmation of judges and, 317
early, 157–160
ethics and reform and, 175–177
ideological and single-issue, 166–167
influence on policy, 167–175
institutional, 164–165
member, 165
politics and, 391
proliferation of, 160–164
intergovernmental groups, 164
intergovernmental lobby, 164
Interior, U.S. Department of, 281
Internal Revenue Service (IRS), 265, 266, 277,
282, 403
Internet, 174, 183, 202–204
in campaign finance, 137
polling and, 66
voting and, 94
interpretation, 360, 364, 370, 374, 383
Interstate Commerce Act (1887), 279
Interstate Commerce Commission, 279, 283
intra-party challengers, 251
investigative reporting, 186
investigatory power, 392
invisible primary, 140–141
Iowa, caucuses in, 141
Iran, 417
Iran-Contra affair, 436–437
congressional investigation of, 231
Iraq War, 410, 427, 440
invasion of Kuwait, 438
iron triangles, 290
isolationism, 430
Israel, Camp David Accords and, 436
issue networks, 290

J

Jackson, Andrew, 247–248
  administration of, 77–78, 133, 248
  cabinet of, 278
  Democratic party endorsement of, 118
  in election of 1824, 106–107, 252
  spoils system and, 278
  Supreme Court and, 321
Jackson, Janet, 199
Jacksonian democracy, 106–107
Japan, World War II and, 379, 421, 431
Japanese-American internment, 250, 257, 379
Jay, John
  as Chief Justice of Supreme Court, 304
  as Federalist, 15
Jefferson, Thomas
  administration of, 246, 427
  as author of Declaration of Independence,
    6–7
  beliefs of, 54, 370
  cabinet of, 278
  as colonial leader, 4–5
  as Democrat-Republican, 32
  election of, 252
  in election of 1800, 133
  freedom of religion and, 370, 371
  on media, 183
  newspapers and, 184
  as Secretary of State, 106
  Supreme Court and, 320
  as U.S. ambassador to France, 9
  wall of separation and, 370–371
Jefferson, William, 175–176
Jeffords, Jim, 124, 125
Jews, voting participation and, 90–91
Jim Crow, 79, 218, 327, 330–331
Johnson, Andrew
  dismissal of Stanton, Edwin, by, 268
  impeachment charges against, 20, 245
Johnson, Gregory Lee, 21
Johnson, Haynes, 87
Johnson, Jean, 409
Johnson, Lyndon, 261
  administration of, 44, 88, 146, 199, 219, 270
  affirmative action and, 352–354
  cabinet of, 44, 265
  civil rights legislation and, 112, 336–338
  court appointments of, 310, 311
  in election of 1960, 135, 143
  in election of 1964, 82, 340
  Great Society of, 36, 114
  media and, 189
  press relations and, 197
  as vice president, 262
  Vietnam War and, 258, 418
Joint Chiefs of Staff, 423
joint committees, 231, 233

journalism. *See also* media; press
  horse race, 190, 206
  integrity in, 189
  progressive, 186
  radio, 187
  television, 187–188
  yellow, 185–186
judicial activism, 314–315
judicial implementation, 321
judicial restraint, 314–315
judicial review, 20, 304, 305–306
judicial self-restraint, 314–315
judiciary, 13, 298–321. *See also* Supreme Court,
    U.S.; Supreme Court, U.S., cases; *specific
    courts*
  appointing the, 316–320
  Department of Justice and, 321
  federal courts in, 298–304
  impeachment and, 320
  judicial implementation and, 321
Judiciary Act (1789), 299
Judis, John, 165
jungle primaries, 135
jurisdiction
  appellate, 299, 302
  original, 299
Justice, U.S. Department of, 260, 281, 301, 316,
    338

K

Kagan, Elena, 310, 311, 321
Kagan, Fred, 438
Kaiser, Robert, 163, 177
Kansas-Nebraska Act, 108
Katzenbach v. McLung, 339
KDKA, 187
Kefauver, Estes, 218
Kellogg-Briand Pact, 430
Kelly, Kate, 134
Kelo v. New London, 311
Kennan, George F., 432
Kennedy, Anthony, 311, 313, 349
Kennedy, Edward, 317
Kennedy, John F., 261
  administration of, 88, 162, 403, 432
  affirmative action and, 351
  assassination of, 188, 337
  cabinet of, 265, 285
  Catholic support for, 90
  choice of Johnson, Lyndon B., for vice
    president, 262
  circular structure used by, 270
  civil rights under, 336–337
  court appointments of, 311
  Cuban Missile Crisis and, 258
  debate with Nixon, Richard, 146, 188, 198
  in election of 1960, 62, 135, 146, 251, 252

invasion of Bay of Pigs, 258
press relations and, 197
televised press conferences of, 188
Kennedy, Robert, as attorney general, 336, 337
Kennedy, Ted, 206
Kentucky Resolution, 33
Kerry, John, 67, 115
African-American support for, 88
Catholic support for, 90
Kersh, Rogan, 169
Keynes, John Maynard, 399
Keynesian economics, 399
kickbacks, 134
King, Martin Luther, Jr., 161, 335, 336, 339–340
King Caucus, 117
Kissinger, Henry, 435
Know Nothing party, 90, 118, 122, 123
Koch brothers, 178
Kohler, Peter, 198
Korean Conflict, 69, 188, 433–434
Korematsu, Fred, 379, 381
Krent, Harold, 258
Ku Klux Klan, 79, 334, 366
Kuwait, Iraq invasion of, 438

L

labor. *See also* unions
child, 36, 91, 123, 157
organization of, 158, 160–161
voting participation and, 91
women's, 345–346
Labor, U.S. Department of, 279, 281
Labunski, Richard, 77, 363
Laffer, Arthur, 399
La Follette, Robert, 123, 134
laissez faire market capitalism, 306, 403, 411
lame duck period, 253
Landon, Alfred, 61–62
Lawrence, John, 349
Lawrence v. Texas, 174, 349
lawyers, right to counsel and, 376
leadership PACs, 170
League of Nations, 249, 257, 430
League of Women Voters, 159, 198
Leahy, Patrick, 232
Left-wing Manifesto, 362
legislating from the bench, 315
legislative veto, 289
legislators, lobbying of, 168–170
Lemon test, 372
Lemon v. Kurtzman, 371–372, 374
Lend-Lease Act, 431
Levin, Carl, 232
Lewinsky, Monica, 202
Lewis, Charles, 201
Lexington, battle of, 3, 6
Libby, Scooter, 191

libel, 194, 196, 197, 308–309, 369–370
seditious, 183
Liberal-Conservative Spectrum, 54–55
Liberal Republicans, 118, 122
liberals, 56, 205
Libertarian party, 55–56, 123, 126
liberty of contract, 307
Library of Congress, 231
Lieberman, Joe, 124, 125
Light, Joseph, 206
Limbaugh, Rush, 206
limited government, 22
Limited Nuclear Test Ban Treaty (1963), 435
Lincoln, Abraham, 331
administration of, 248, 258, 260
cabinet of, 264
election of in 1860, 108, 122, 216, 252
issuance of Emancipation Proclamation, 329
need for bureaucracy, 278
line-item veto, 256, 410
Line-Item Veto Act (1996), 256
literacy test, 79, 330, 339
Literary Digest's 1936 poll, 61–62, 64, 103
litigants, 300
litmus test, 316, 319
Little Rock Nine, 342
Livingston, Robert, 6
lobbying
direct, 167
exposing, 159–160
grassroots, 171–172
of legislators, 168–170
revolving door and, 176 177
Lobbying Disclosure Act (1955), 175
location in political socialization, 57–61
Lochner v. New York, 307, 314
Locke, John, 5, 6, 247
Log Cabin Campaign, 133
Log Cabin newspapers, 133
Long, Russell, 221, 398
Lopez, Alfonzo, 43
Lott, Trent, 177
Louisiana Purchase, 427
Louisiana Territory, 246, 427–428
Love Canal, 395
Loving v. Virginia, 174
Lynching, campaign against, 332

M

Ma, Jonathan, 206
MacArthur, Douglas, 69
machine politics, 134
Madison, James
administration of, 77, 106, 216, 246, 250
on appointments and removals, 268
as author of *Federalist Papers,* 220, 226
creation of Bill of Rights and, 17–18, 363

as delegate to Constitutional Convention, 9–10
as Democrat-Republican, 32
election to Virginia Legislature and, 145–146
as Federalist, 15–16, 31, 157, 160, 162
freedom of religion and, 370–371
on legislature, 214
as member of House of Representatives, 77
ratification of Constitution and, 15–16
as Secretary of State, 20
states' rights and, 106
magazines
ideological/political, 201
national, 201
of opinion, 186
Maine, split of electoral votes in, 144
mainstream media, 205
majoritarian policies, 390–391
majority opinion, 313
mandates, 42, 145
mandatory spending, 408
Manifest Destiny, 427
Mann Act (1910), 35
Mapp, Dollree, 375
Mapp v. Ohio, 375, 382
marble cake federalism, 39, 164
Marbury, William, 20
Marbury v. Madison, 20, 298, 305
March on Washington, 336
marginal seats, 221
margin of error, 64–65
markup session, 232
Marlin, George, 90
marriage, 55
same-sex, 31, 120–121, 167, 349, 351–352
Marshall, George, 433
Marshall, John, as Chief Justice of Supreme Court, 20, 28, 33–35, 298, 304–306, 313, 321, 361
Marshall, Thurgood
as attorney, 111, 332–333
as Supreme Court justice, 310, 311, 318, 321
Marshall Plan, 433
Maryland, ratification of Constitution, 16
Mason, George, 14, 16, 17
Massachusetts, ratification of Constitution, 16
matching money, 148–149
material incentives, 165
Matthews, Chris, 202
Mayersohn, Andrew, 177
McCain, John, 74, 90, 115
campaign reform and, 149–150
in election of 2008, 206, 252
presidential campaign of, 206
McCain-Feingold Act, 149, 166
McCarthy, Eugene, 118, 143, 148
McCarthy, Joseph (Joe), 188, 218
House Un-American Activities Committee hearings of, 192–194, 218

McClure's, 186, 190
McConnell v. FEC, 150
McCulloch, James, 33–34
McCulloch v. Maryland, 33–34, 51, 220–221, 306
McCullough, David, 227
McCurry, Mike, 195
McFarlane, Robert, 437
McGovern, George, 83, 115, 119
in election of 1972, 147, 252
media support for, 205
McGovern-Fraser Commission, 119
McKeon, Howard, 232
McKinley, William, 109
administration of, 248, 429
McKitrick, Eric, 32
McLarty, Thomas "Mack," 267
McLaurin v. Oklahoma, 333
McNamara, Robert, 285
McVeigh, Timothy, 301
means test, 393
media, 183–207. *See also* journalism; press
Congress and, 192–194
corporate versus public, 199–201
coverage of courts, 194
coverage of scandals by, 191
ethics and, 204–207
as the Fourth Estate, 183, 190
freedom of the press and, 194–201
government's relationship with the, 190–194
history of government and the press, 183–189
mainstream, 205
new, 201–204
polling and, 67–68
print, 185
roles of the, 189–190
social, 203–204
Medicaid, 393, 408–409
Medicare, 221, 393, 408–409
Medicare Advantage, 393
member groups, 165
Memendez, Robert, 232
men, voting participation and, 86–87
Meredith, James, 336
merit system, 279
Mexican-American War, 248
declaration of, 421
Meyerson, Harold, 135
Miami Herald v. Tornillo, 198
midterm elections, 136
Miers, Harriet, 310
military
Congress, U.S., and, 220
gays in, 350
integration of, 112, 124, 257
Military and Overseas Voter Empowerment Act, 94
military bases, 424, 427, 441
military industrial complex, 426–427
military policy. *See* foreign and military policy

Miller, Judith, 196
Miller v. California, 367, 374
Milosovic, Slobodon, 426
Milyo, Jeffrey, 206
Mink, Patsy, 346
Minnesota Gag Law, 363
minor parties, 105, 122–126
    matching money and, 148–149
Minor v. Happerset, 81
Miranda v. Arizona, 308, 376–377
Missouri Compromise (1820), 108, 216
Missouri ex. Rel. Gaines v. Canada, 333
mobilization, 163–164
moderates, 54
moment of silence, 372–373
Mondale, Walter, 115
monetary policy, 400–401
money
    hard, 149
    soft, 149, 171
Monroe, James, administration of, 77, 106, 246, 428
Monroe Doctrine, 248–249, 428–429, 434
Montesquieu, 5
Mormons, freedom of religion and, 370–371
Morning Edition, 200
Morrill Land Grant Act (1862), 37
Morris, Gouverneur, 12
Morse, Samuel, 185
Mothers Against Drunk Driving (MADD), 169–170
Motor Voter Law, 42, 91
Moyers, Bill, 200
MSNBC, 202
MTV, 200
Mubarak, Hosni, 440
muckrakers, 186, 190
Muir, John, 394
Muller v. Oregon, 344
multiple referral, 235
multiplier effect, 399
Munich Conference, 431
Murrow, Edward R., 187, 188, 199, 204
mutually assured destruction (MAD), 433
Myers v. United States, 269, 288

N

Nader, Ralph, 125, 126, 162, 166
NAFTA (North American Free Trade Agreement), 411
Nagasaki, 431, 433
narrowcasting, 202
The Nation, 162, 186, 201
National Aeronautics and Space Administration (NASA), 282
National Association for the Advancement of Colored People (NAACP), 75, 111, 161, 165, 173, 331–337, 342
    campaign against lynching, 332
    creation of, 331
    Legal Defense Fund, 174, 332
    school desegregation and, 332–334, 341–343
National Association for the Repeal of Abortion Laws (NARAL), 161
National Association of Manufacturers (NAM), 158, 165, 173
National Education Association, 164–165
National Endowment for the Arts, 407
National Endowment for the Humanities, 407
National Enquirer, 186
National Environmental Policy Act, 394–395
National Fish and Wildlife Service, 395
National Gazette, 184
National Governors Association, 164
National Intelligencer, 184
National League of Cities, 164
national magazines, 201
National Minimum Drinking Age Act (1984), 41–42
National Organization for Women (NOW), 75, 161, 345
National Performance Review (NPR), 293–294
National Public Radio (NPR), 200, 284
National Recovery Act, 307
National Republican Congressional Committee (NRCC), 117
National Republican Senatorial Committee (NSRC), 117
National Restaurant Association, 172
National Review, 201
National Rifle Association (NRA), 165, 166–167, 170
national security, civil liberties and, 379–383
National Security Act (1947), 423
national security adviser, 267
National Security Agency, 291
national security and public danger test, 364–366
National Security Council, 266, 267, 423–424, 437
national spoils system, 278
national supremacy, 14, 21
National Traffic and Motor Vehicle Safety Act, 162
National Voter Registration Act (1993), 42, 92–93
National Wildlife Federation, 394
National Woman's Party, 347
National Women's Political Caucus, 161
National Women's Suffrage Association, 81
NATO (North Atlantic Treaty Organization), 426
natural law, 5
Nazi Germany, 91
NBC (National Broadcasting Company), 187, 188, 200
NBC Nightly News, 200
Near, J. M., 363
Near v. Minnesota, 194, 363
Nebraska, split of electoral votes in, 144
necessary and proper clause, 13, 22, 220–221

New Deal, 31, 36, 55, 110, 114, 159, 163, 220, 249, 280, 307–308, 315, 392, 395, 399
New Deal coalition, 110, 111, 113
New Federalism, 41, 45
New Hampshire
    primary in, 141
    ratification of Constitution, 16
New Jersey, ratification of Constitution, 16
New Jersey Plan, 11
New Jersey v. New York, 312
New Jersey v. TLO, 376
Newport, Frank, 67
The New Republic, 186, 201, 204
news, conventional, 187–188
newspapers. *See also specific by name*
    colonial, 184
    ethics and, 204–207
    local, 201
    Log Cabin, 133
    need for mass audience, 185
    party press and, 184
    print, 201
    subsidizing, 184
    yellow journalism and, 185–186
Newsweek, 172, 201, 203
Newton, Isaac, 163
New York, ratification of Constitution, 16
New York City
    as first capital, 82
    Tweed, William Marcy in, 134
The New Yorker magazine, 190
New York Journal, 183, 185–186
New York Sun, 185
New York Times, 192, 194–195, 196, 201, 205, 206
New York Times v. Sullivan, 369–370, 374
New York Times v. United States, 174, 195, 196, 364, 369
Nicaragua, 1980 revolution in, 437
The Nine (Toobin), 318
Nineteenth Amendment, 78, 80–81, 82, 159, 343, 345–346
Ninth Amendment, 18, 29
Nixon, Richard, 112, 261, 263
    administration of, 38–40, 112, 267, 285, 344, 406, 420
    China and, 433
    civil rights and, 343
    court appointments of, 309–311, 317, 319
    credibility of, 194–195
    debate with Kennedy, John F., 146, 188, 198
    in election of 1960, 146
    in election of 1968, 119, 124
    in election of 1970, 83
    in election of 1972, 147, 252
    impeachment charges against, 20, 192, 245
    pardon for, 260
    press relations and, 188, 195, 205
        pyramid structure used by, 270
        as senator, 112
        Watergate scandal under, 114, 115, 119, 147, 189, 245
No Child Left Behind Act, 44, 192
non-germane amendments, 236
normalization, 435
Norris, George, 217
North, Oliver, 437
North Carolina
    black representation in, 330
    ratification of Constitution, 16, 17
North Korea, 419, 440
Nuclear Non-Proliferation Treaty, 435
nuclear option, 318–319
nullification, 33

O

Obama, Barack, 115, 218, 261
    administration of, 45, 88, 349, 394, 438
    cabinet of, 263–264
    Catholic support for, 90
    choice of Joe Biden as vice president, 262
    court appointments of, 310, 311
    elections of, 121, 206, 251, 252
    ethnic support for, 88, 89
    Fairness Doctrine and, 199
    Jewish support for, 91
O'Brien, David, 365
obscenity, 194, 199, 366–367
O'Connor, Sandra Day, 310, 311, 381
O'Donnell, Lawrence, 202
Office of Civil Rights, 280
Office of Congressional Relations, 255
Office of Internal Regulatory Affairs, 291–292
Office of Management and Budget (OMB), 266, 398
Office of National Drug Control Policy, 266
Office of Personnel Management (OPM), 286–287
Office of the U.S. Trade Representative, 266
off the record, 195
Old Age, Survivors and Disability Insurance (OASDI), 393
Olive Branch Petition, 4
Olmstead v. United States, 360
omnibus bill, 236
on background, 195
on deep background, 195
O'Neill, Thomas "Tip," 226, 238
"one man, one vote" rule, 224
one-on-one interviews, 178
on the record, 195
open primaries, 135
OpenSecrets.org, 177
Operation Desert Storm, 438
Operation Enduring Freedom, 440
Operation Iraqi Freedom, 440

O'Reilly, Bill, 202
Organization for Economic Cooperation and
   Development, 405
original jurisdiction, 299
Oswald, Lee Harvey, 188
outsider strategies, 167

P

Pacifica Foundation v. FCC, 199
PACs (political action committees), 104, 140,
   170–171, 211, 239, 290, 391
Paine, Thomas, 4
Panetta, Leon, 271
Paperwork Reduction Act (1979), 291
Paramount Pictures, 200
Paris, Treaty of (1783), 3, 7, 9
Parliament, 3, 4, 6, 7
Partnership for Health program, 38
party bosses, 134, 278
party chairperson, 116
party conventions, 117–118, 142–143
party identification, 58, 86
party polarization, 237
party press, newspapers and, 184
party realignment. *See* realignments
patronage, 277, 278
Patterson, Bradley, 257, 265
Patterson, William, 11
Paul, Alice, 345, 347
PBS NewsHour, 200, 206
PBS-TV, 284
peace dividend, 437
Pelosi, Nancy, 199, 229
Pendleton Civil Service Act (1883), 279–280, 286
Pendleton, George, 293
Pennsylvania, ratification of Constitution, 16
penny press, 185
Pension Office, 278
Pentagon, 422, 426
Pentagon Papers, 194–195
People for the Ethical Treatment of Animals
   (PETA), 163–164
per curium opinion, 314
perestroika, 437
Perot, H. Ross, 125, 127
   in election of 1992, 252
   media support for, 205
Perry, Matthew, 428
Personal Responsibility and Work Opportunity
   Reconciliation Act, 43
persuasive precedents, 304
petitioners, 302
petition for certiorari, 312
Pew Research Center, Project for Excellence in
   Journalism, 206
Phelps, Fred, 383

Philadelphia
   Constitutional Convention in, 2, 9–12
   as early capital, 82
Philippines, Spanish American War and, 429
Pickering, John, 320
Pierce, Franklin, administration of, 248
Pilgrim's Progress, 186
Pinckney, Charles, in election of 1800, 252
plaintiffs, 301
Planned Parenthood v. Casey, 379
platforms, 120–121
plea bargain, 301
Plessy, Homer Adolph, 331
Plessy v. Ferguson, 328, 331, 333
pluralism, 160, 179
plurality, 144
pocket veto, 19, 256
police powers, 30, 35
policy, influence of interest groups on, 167–175
Policy and Steering Committee (Democratic), 233
policymaking, 390–392
political campaigns, 132–150
   congressional, 136–140
   financing, 145–150
   history of, 132–136
   interest groups and, 171–173
   presidential, 140–145
   rise of, 133–134
political cartoons, interpreting, 109, 396
political efficacy, 84–85
political machines, 134, 278
political participation, 75–96
   voting and, 75–86
   voting blocs and behaviors and, 86–91
   voting reform and current trends, 91–96
political parties, 105–127. *See also specific*
   contemporary, 116–121
   defined, 105
   history of, as two-party system, 105–115
   minor, 122–126
   patterns in, 126–127
   realignments in, 106, 107, 108, 109, 111–113
political socialization, 57–61
Politico, 203
politics, machine, 134
Polk, James, administration of, 427–428
polling, 56–57, 61, 67–69, 137
   exit, 67, 68, 87, 89
   history of, 61–62
   media and, 67–68
   methodology in, 62–66
   tracking, 68
polling place, 76
poll taxes, 77, 78, 80, 330
poll workers, 135
Pope, Generoso, Jr., 186
popular sovereignty, 18, 19, 108

Populist Party, 55–56, 109, 122, 123
pork barrel spending, 237
Porteous, Thomas, 320
Post Office, 265, 278
Powell, Colin, 438
Powell Doctrine, 438
Powell, Lewis, 311
power of the purse, 215, 220
powers
    concurrent, 30
    delegated, 30
    enumerated, 12–13
    expressed, 219–220
    implicit, 13
    implied, 34, 220–221
    inherent, 245
    police, 30, 35
    reserved, 21
    separation of, 10, 19
prayer in public schools, 371, 372–373
Preamble, 12, 18
precedents, 304
    binding, 304
    persuasive, 304
precincts, 76
preclearance, 80, 340
preponderance of evidence, 301
presidency, 244–271
    administration of executive branch by, 263–271
    appointments and removals and, 268–269
    creating and developing, 244–254
    duties and limits of, 246
    Framers' vision of, 244
    imperial, 246–250
    management styles in, 269–271
    powers of, 245
    qualifications, office, and term, 245
    roles of, 254–261
president(s). See also specific by name
    in foreign and military policy, 418–419
    press and, 190–191
    running for, 140–141
presidential elections, 140–145, 250–254
    of 1789, 252
    of 1800, 106, 133, 252
    of 1824, 106–107, 252
    of 1828, 107
    of 1832, 118
    of 1840, 133
    of 1860, 108, 122, 216, 252
    of 1872, 122
    of 1876, 330
    of 1896, 109
    of 1912, 108, 125
    of 1916, 134
    of 1928, 109
    of 1932, 110, 111, 398
    of 1952, 147
    of 1956, 147
    of 1960, 135, 146, 147, 252
    of 1964, 112, 147, 341
    of 1968, 118–119, 125, 143, 147
    of 1972, 147, 252
    of 1976, 141, 252, 398
    of 1980, 141, 252, 398, 436
    of 1992, 141, 252, 252
    of 1996, 252, 398
    of 2000, 126, 252
    of 2004, 126, 138
    of 2008, 121, 206, 252
    of 2010, 115
    of 2012, 121, 142, 206, 252
Presidential Succession Act (1947), 253–254
president pro tempore, 228, 229, 231, 254
press. See also journalism; media
    adversarial, 188
    free, 183
    freedom of the, 194–201
    independent, 185–186
    penny, 185
    presidents and, 190–191
    rotary, 185
press conferences, 268
    televised, 191
Press Corps, 205–206
The Pressure Boys (Black and Crawford), 159–160
Priebus, Reince, 116
Prigg v. Pennsylvania, 306
primaries, 134–135
    blanket, 135
    closed, 135
    invisible, 140–141
    jungle, 135
    New Hampshire, 141
    open, 135
    white, 111, 333
printing press, invention of, 183
print media, 187
prior restraint, 194–195, 364
privacy, right to, 378–379
privileges and immunity clause, 29–30
procedural due process, 375–378
professional associations, 164
The Progressive, 201
Progressive Era, 36, 54, 84, 157–160, 186
progressive journalism, 186
Progressive Movement, 35, 56–57
Progressives, 56, 123
    organizing, 158–159
progressive taxes, 403
Prohibitionists, 118
Prohibition party, 123
Public Affairs Act, 65

Public Broadcasting Act, 199–201
Public Broadcasting Service (PBS), 200
Public Citizen, 166, 176–177, 391
public interest groups, 166
public opinion, 52, 53–69
    measuring, 61–69
    methodology and, 62–66
    roots of, 53–57
public policy, 389
    theories of, 390–392
public television and radio, 200
Public Works Administration, 399
Publius, 15
Puerto Rico, Spanish American War and, 429
Pulitzer, Joseph, 185–186
The Pulse of America (Gallup), 62
Pure Food and Drug Act, 279
purposive incentives, 165
push polling, 65
Putting People First, 164
pyramid system, 269–270

Q

qualitative research, 178
quantitative research, 178
Quinnipiac University, 62
quorum, 10, 215

R

race. See also specific
    in political socialization, 58
Race to the Top initiative, 45
racism, 328
Radical Republicans, 108, 122, 329
radio, 187
    fireside chats on, 191
    public, 200
Radio Corporation of America, 187
radio journalism, 187
radio sets, 187
Ramsey, David, 4
RAND Corporation, 425
Randolph, A. Phillip, 337
Randolph, Edmund, 10, 11, 14
random-digit dialing, 64
random sample, 64
rank and file, 110, 118, 133
Rankin, Jeanette, 81, 345
Rasmussen Reports, 62
Rasul v. Bush, 381
Rather, Dan, 204
rationalism, 5
Rayburn, Sam, 213, 239
Reagan, Ronald, 115, 261
    administration of, 21, 41, 112, 113, 114, 293,
        403, 410, 436–437

choice of Bush, George H.W., as vice
    president, 262
court appointments of, 310, 311, 319
deregulatory philosophy of, 198
in election of 1976, 251
in election of 1980, 141
press relations and, 192
supply-side theory and, 399
Reaganomics, 410
realignments, 107, 108, 111–115
    of 1896, 109
    defined, 106
    partial, along issues and region, 111–113
    types of, 106
reapportionment, 223
Reapportionment Act (1929), 223
reasonableness standard, 347
recall, 76
Reconstruction, 108, 217, 278, 329
Reconstruction Amendments, 79, 362
Red Cross, 175
redistricting process, 223–224
Red Lion Broadcasting v. FCC, 198
Red Scare, 91, 430
red tape, 291
Reed, Stanley, 321
Reed, Thomas, 217
Reed v. Reed, 347
referendum, 76
Reform Party (United We Stand America), 124
Regents of the University of California v. Bakke,
    353–354
Rehnquist, William, as Chief Justice of Supreme
    Court, 43, 305, 309, 310
    as clerk, 314
religion
    freedom of, 370–372
    in political socialization, 58
    voting alignment and, 114
    voting participation and, 89
religious right, 89, 113, 126, 350
religious symbols, public display of, 373
Remeni, Robert, 219, 238
Rendell, Ed, 116
Rendell, Steve, 199
Reno, Janet, 225
Reno v. ACLU, 174
representative model, 227
representative republic, 19
Republican National Committee (RNC), 116
    fund raising and, 126
Republican Party, 54–57, 105
    ascendency of, in 1850s, 108
    budget process and, 407
    call for devolution, 43
    Committee on Committees, 233
    in Congress, 222

conservatism and, 112
creation of, 329
foreign and military policy and, 424–425
geographic location and, 60–61
ideology and platform of, 120–121, 126
Liberal faction of, 122
minor parties and, 122, 125
national conventions of, 117–118
national party structure of, 116–117
radical, 108, 329
Radical faction of, 122
realignment and, 113
split into north-south factions, 108
state and local, 117
Wall Street and, 114
reserved powers, 21, 30, 41
reserve requirements, 401
respondents, 302
Reuters, 185
revenue, 402–405
revenue sharing, 36, 38, 45
reverse discrimination, 354
revolving door, 176
Reynolds, George, 371
Reynolds v. United States, 370–371, 374
Rhode Island, ratification of Constitution, 3, 16
riders, 236, 237
riding circuit, 299
right of reply rules, 198
right to privacy, 378–379
Riis, Jacob, 186
Roaring Twenties, 159
robber barons, 145
Roberts, John, as Chief Justice of Supreme Court, 310–311
Roberts, Owen, 308
Robertson, Pat, 113
Rockefeller, John D., 186
Roe v. Wade, 113, 161, 309, 314, 345, 346, 347, 348, 358, 379, 382, 384
Rogers, Will, 237
Roll Call, 193
Romer v. Evans, 351
Romney, Mitt, 68, 91, 115
in election of 2012, 252
Roosevelt, Franklin D., 38, 187, 263
administration of, 257
African American support for, 88
bureaucracy and, 277
court packing plan of, 307–308
election of, 110
in election of 1932, 398
in election of 1936, 61–62
fireside chats of, 191
labor unions and, 91
New Deal of, 31, 36, 55, 110, 114, 159, 249–250, 399

on the Senate, 257
Social Security and, 393
Supreme Court and, 269
World War II and, 258, 429–430
Roosevelt, Theodore
administration of, 123, 146, 248–249, 257–258, 279, 429
in election of 1912, 125
environmental policy and, 394
muckrakers and, 186
press and, 191
Progressives and, 123
Roosevelt Corollary, 429
Roper, Elmo, 62
Rostenkowski, Dan, 171
rotary press, 185
rotation system of appointments, 278
Roth, Samuel, 366
Rousseau, Jean-Jacques, 5
Rubio, Marco, 119
Ruby, Jack, 188
Rule 22, 226
rule of four, 312
Rules Committee, 217, 231, 235
runoff elections, 135, 140
Russell Office Building, 228

S

Sadat, Anwar al-, 436
safe seats, 221
Safe Streets program, 38
saliency, 54
SALT I, 435
SALT II, 435
same-sex marriage, 31, 349, 351–352
sample, 63
random, 64
sampling error, 64–65
Sandford, John, 328
Sanford, Mark, 191
Scalia, Antonin, 194, 311, 315
scandals
Abramoff, 176
Clinton-Lewinsky, 202
Credit Mobilier, 175
lobbying and, 175–176
machine politics and, 134
McCarthy hearings and, 219
media coverage of, 191
Schenck, Charles, 365
Schenck v. United States, 364–365, 374
Schlesinger, Arthur, Jr., 247, 248
school busing, 42, 309, 320, 344
schools. *See also* education
desegregation of, 333–336, 343
establishment clause, 371–372
free speech in, 368–369

funding of, 372
political socialization and, 58
prayer in public, 308–309, 371, 372–373
searches in, 376
vouchers for, 372
Schroeder, Pat, 219
Schultz, Debbie Wasserman, 116
Scientific Revolution, 5
Scopes, John, 167
Scopes Trial (1925), 56
scorekeeper, media's role as a, 190
Scott, Dred, 306, 328
Scottsboro Nine, 332
search and seizure, 375
secession, 33
Second Amendment, 18
Secret Service, 265
Sedition Acts, 320, 364–365
seditious libel, 183
See It Now, 188
segregation. *See also* desegregation of schools
de facto, 342
de jure, 342
select committees, 231–232, 233
selective attention, 202
selective exclusiveness, 35
selective incorporation, 361–363
Selective Services Act (1917), 422, 430
self-incrimination, 376–377
Selma march, 339
Senate, U.S., 11, 12, 213, 214–215. *See also*
Congress, U.S.; House of Representatives,
U.S.
advice and consent and, 20, 214–215,
226–227, 316
Armed Service Committee, 423, 424
cloture in, 226
Committee on Foreign Relations, 423
C-SPAN coverage of, 193–194
filibusters in, 226
Foreign Relations Committee, 220, 423
impeachment and, 245
Judiciary Committee, 316, 317, 318, 336, 337
leaders in, 229–230
as Millionaire's Club, 217
qualifications for members of, 215
Select Committee hearings, 188
Seventeenth Amendment and, 218
whips in, 229
senatorial courtesy, 316
Seneca Falls Convention, 344
Senior Executive Service, 281
seniors, voting participation and, 88
sensationalism, 186
"separate but equal" facilities, 309–310, 331, 333
separation of powers, 10, 19

September 11, 2001, terrorist attacks, 379, 380–382,
410, 439–440
sequential referral, 235
sequester, 410
Serbia, bombing of, 439
Sesame Street, 200
Sessions, Pete, 232
Seventeenth Amendment, 35, 158, 218, 363
Seventh Amendment, 18
sexism, 328
Shanghai Communiqué, 435–436
Shaw v. Reno, 225
Shays, Daniel, 9
Shays Rebellion, 3, 9
Sherman, Roger, 6, 11
shield laws, 196
Shrum, Bob, 138
Sierra Club, 161, 394
signing statements, 255–256
Silent Spring (Carson), 161
single-issue interest groups, 166–167
single-issue parties, 123
single-member districts, 125–126
60 Minutes, 188, 190, 200
60 Minutes II, 204
Sixteenth Amendment, 35, 158, 279, 403
Sixth Amendment, 18, 194
slander, 197
Slaughterhouse Cases, 378
slavery
Taney court and, 306, 310
three-fifths compromise and, 11
Slidell, John, 428
Smith Act (1940), 365
Smith, Al
Catholic support for, 90
in election of 1928, 109
Smith, Hendrick, 195
Smith, Lonnie, 111
Smith, Margaret Chase, 218
Smith v. Allwright, 80, 111
Snyder, Albert, 383
Snyder, Matthew, 383
social contract, 2–3
The Social Contract (Locke), 5
Socialist Party, 122–123
socialists, 91, 123
social media, 203–204
social movements, 160–162
Social Security, 393, 408–409
Social Security Act (1935), 393
social welfare policy, 393–394
soft money, 149, 171
solicitor generals, 321
solidary incentives, 165
Solid South, 108, 111, 114

Sons of Liberty, 4, 5
Sotomayor, Sonia, 310–311
sound bites, 132
source
    analyzing, 23
    interpreting, 23
Souter, David, 311, 320
South Carolina
    primary elections in, 142
    ratification of Constitution, 16
South Dakota v. Dole, 42
Southern Christian Leadership Conference
    (SCLC), 161, 335, 337
Southern Manifesto, 334
sovereign immunity, 302
Soviet Union
    Cold War and, 432–433
    Cuban and, 434
    SALT and, 435
    Vietnam War and, 434–436
Spain, acquisition of Florida and, 428
Spanish-American War, 248, 428–429
    declaration of, 421
    yellow journalism and, 186
special interest groups, 39, 75
special legislative courts, 302, 320, 326
special revenue sharing, 39
speech. *See also* First Amendment
    commercial, 369
    free, 148, 364–370
    obscene, 366
    symbolic, 367–368
spending
    discretionary, 409
    mandatory, 408
spin, 192
Spitzer, Eliot, 191
splinter parties, 122, 123
split tickets, 135
spoilers, 125
spoils system, 278, 284–285
sponsor, 235
spots, 138
Stabenow, Debbie, 232
Stamp Act (1765), 3, 4
Standard Oil monopoly, 186
standing committees, 230–231, 233
Stanton, Edwin, 268
stare decisis, 304
Star Wars, 436–437
State, U.S. Department of, 281, 288, 419, 421
state delegates, 142
State of the Union address, 244, 249, 255
states
    corporations and the, 306–308
    powers reserved to the, 18, 31
    returning authority to the, 41–45
    in U.S. Constitution, 31

States' Rights Party, 112, 124
Steffens, Lincoln, 186
Steinman, Ron, 188, 189
Stern, Howard, 199
Stevens, John Paul, 311, 382
Stevens, Ted, 237
stewardship theory, 249
Stewart, Jon, 237
Stewart, Potter, 366
Stone, Harlan Fiske, 315
The Strange Career of Jim Crow (Woodward), 486
Strategic Arms Limitations Talks (SALT), 435
Strategic Defense Initiative, 436–437
stratification, 64
straw polls, 61
strict constructionist view, 32, 307
strict scrutiny, 345, 347, 354
strings, 38
Student Non-Violent Coordinating Committee
    (SNCC), 161
substantive due process, 378–379
succession, 253–254
suffrage, 75
    for 18-year-olds, 78, 83, 166
    for African Americans, 79–80, 88, 111,
        339–341, 354–355
    Constitutional amendments and, 78–83
    in District of Columbia, 81–82
    expansion of, by 1828, 107
    for women, 80–82, 158, 278–279
Sugar Act (1764), 3, 4
Sullivan, L. B., 196
Sullivan, Leonor, 213 (note)
Sumner, Charles, 216
Sunshine Act (1976), 292
superdelegates, 119, 142
Superfund, 395
super PACs, 177, 179
Super Tuesday, 142
supply-side theory, 399–400
supremacy clause, 14, 30
Supreme Court, U.S., 13, 298, 300, 303
    affirmative action and, 352–354
    appeals process in, 312–313
    under Burger, Warren, 375–376
    caseload of, 314
    cases
        Abington School District v. Schempp, 372
        Adkins v. Children's Hospital, 307
        Baker v. Carr, 224
        Bethel Schools v. Fraser, 369, 374
        Bowers v. Hardwick, 349
        Brandenburg v. Ohio, 366
        Branzburg v. Hayes, 196
        Brown II, 334, 342
        Brown v. Board of Education, 308, 310,
            334, 335, 342
        Buchanan v. Warley, 332

Buckley v. Valeo, 148
Chaplinsky v. New Hampshire, 369
Citizens United v. FEC, 150, 173, 315
Civil Rights Cases (1883), 330, 331
Clinton v. City of New York, 256
Cohen v. California, 367
Cooper v. Aaron, 342
Craig v. Boren, 347
Dennis v. United States, 365
Dred Scott v. Sandford, 306, 328
Dunn v. Blumstein, 83–84
Engle v. Vitale, 174, 371, 372
Everson v. Board of Education, 371
Furman v. Georgia, 378
Gibbons v. Ogden, 34–35, 219–220, 306
Gideon v. Wainright, 376, 382
Gitlow v. New York, 362–363
*Green v. County School Board Kent
    County,* 342
Gregg v. Georgia, 378
Griswold v. Connecticut, 348, 378–379,
    382, 384
Guinn v. United States, 80, 332
Hamdan v. Rumsfeld, 382
Hamdi v. Rumsfeld, 381–382
Hammer v. Daggenhart, 36, 37
*Heart of Atlanta Motel, Inc. v. United
    States,* 339
Humphrey's Executor v. United States,
    269, 289
INS v. Chadha, 289–290
Katzenbach v. McLung, 339
Kelo v. New London, 311
Lawrence v. Texas, 174, 349, 351
Lemon v. Kurtzman, 371–372, 373, 374
Lochner v. New York, 307, 314
Loving v. Virginia, 174
Mapp v. Ohio, 375, 382
Marbury v. Madison, 20, 305
McConnell v. FEC, 150
McCulloch v. Maryland, 28, 33–34,
    220–221, 306
McCutcheon v. FEC, 150
McLaurin v. Oklahoma, 333
Miami Herald v. Tornillo, 198
Miller v. California, 367, 374
Minor v. Happerset, 81
Miranda v. Arizona, 376–377, 382
Missouri ex. Rel. Gaines v. Canada, 333
Muller v. Oregon, 344–345
Myers v. United States, 269
Near v. Minnesota, 194, 363
New Jersey v. New York, 312
New Jersey v. TLO, 376
New York Times v. Sullivan, 369–370, 374
New York Times v. United States, 174,
    195, 196, 364

Olmstead v. United States, 360
Pacifica Foundation v. FCC, 199
Planned Parenthood v. Casey, 379
Plessy v. Ferguson, 328, 331, 333
Prigg v. Pennsylvania, 306
Rasul v. Bush, 381
Red Lion Broadcasting v. FCC, 198
Reed v. Reed, 347
*Regents of the University of California v.
    Bakke,* 353, 356
Reno v. ACLU, 174
Reynolds v. United States, 370–371, 374
Roe v. Wade, 113, 161, 309, 314,
    345, 346–347, 348, 379, 382
Romer v. Evans, 350
Schenck v. United States, 364–365, 374
Shaw v. Reno, 225
Slaughterhouse Cases, 378
Smith v. Allwright, 80, 111
South Dakota v. Dole, 42
Swann v. Charlotte-Mecklenburg,
    343–344
Sweatt v. Painter, 333
Texas v. Johnson, 21, 368
*Tinker v. Des Moines Independent
    Schools,* 174, 368, 374
United States v. Eichman, 368
United States v. Harriss, 163
United States v. John Doe, 321
United States v. Lopez, 36, 43
United States v. Nixon, 261
United States v. O'Brien, 365, 367
United States v. Timothy McVeigh, 301
United States v. Eichman, 21
U.S. Term Limits, Inc. v. Thornton, 222
Weeks v. United States, 375
Wesberry v. Sanders, 224
West Coast Hotel v. Parrish, 308
Yates v. United States, 365
clerks' role in, 314
commerce clause and, 36
history of, 304–310
under Hughes, Charles Evans, 307
under Jay, John, 304
judicial activism versus judicial restraint in,
    314–315
jurisdiction of, 299, 312
under Marshall, John, 20, 28, 33–35, 298,
    304–306, 310, 313, 321
modern, 310–315
operation of, 312–314
opinions of, 313–314
original jurisdiction of, 299
under Rehnquist, William, 43, 305, 309–310
under Roberts, John, 310, 311
Roosevelt, Franklin D., and, 249
in shaping federalism, 33–35

under Taft, William Howard, 307
under Taney, Roger, 306, 310
under Warren, Earl, 308–310
surplus, 408
Survivor, 200–201
Swann v. Charlotte-Mecklenburg, 343
Sweatt v. Painter, 333
symbolic speech, 367–368

T

Taft, Robert, 112
Taft, William Howard
administration of, 123, 249
as Chief Justice of Supreme Court, 307
in election of 1912, 158
Taft-Hartley Act (1947), 146, 397
takings clause in the Fifth Amendment, 361
talk radio, 206–207
Taney, Roger, as Chief Justice of Supreme Court, 306, 310
tarmac primary, 142
taxes
estate, 403
excise, 405
flat, 404
import, 411
income, 38, 403–404
poll, 77, 78, 330
progressive, 403
tax policy, 402–403
Taylor, Zachary, 107
Tea Act, 4
Teamsters, 160
Telecommunications Act (1996), 200
telegraph, 185
telephones
grassroots lobbying and, 171
lobbying and, 172
television
coverage of Congress, 218
early, 187–188
grassroots lobbying and, 171
lobbying and, 172
political appearances on, 138
public, 200
television journalism, 188
temperance movement, 158
Ten Commandments, 373–374
Tennessee Valley Authority, 264, 284
Tenth Amendment, 18, 20, 22, 29, 30, 31, 38
Tenure of Office Act, 245, 268, 278
term limits, 218, 222
Tet Offensive, 189
Texas v. Johnson, 21, 368
think tanks, 165, 425
Third Amendment, 18, 363
"Third House," 158

Third parties, 109, 122
Thirteenth Amendment, 329
Thomas, Clarence, 310, 311, 318
Thomas, Helen, 202
three-fifths compromise, slavery and, 11–12
Thurmond, Strom, 112, 124
Ticket splitting, 114
Time, 187, 201, 203
Time Warner, 200
Tinker, Mary Beth, 368
Tinker v. Des Moines Independent Schools, 174, 368, 369, 374
Tippecanoe, Battle of, 133
Title IX, 161, 219, 346
Toobin, Jeffrey, 318
Tocqueville, Alexis de, 75, 133
torts, 301
torture memo, 381
Tower Commission Report, 437
tracking polls, 68
trade associations, 158
trade balance, 411
trade deficit, 411
Transportation, U.S. Department of, 281
Transportation Security Administration, 282
treason, 299
Treasury, U.S. Department of, 281
treaties, 257
trial courts, 300
Truman Doctrine, 432–433
Truman, Harry, 253
administration of, 91, 112, 250, 420, 431
attack on North Korea, 258–259
decision to drop atomic bombs, 68–69
integration of military by, 112, 124, 259
Jewish support for, 91
justice department of, 365
succession to presidency, 263
World War II and, 431
Trumbull, Lyman, 279
trustee model, 227
Turner, Ted, 202
Twain, Mark, 237
Tweed, William Marcy, 134
Twelfth Amendment, 144, 251, 254
Twentieth Amendment, 228, 253, 254
Twenty-fifth Amendment, 254, 263
Twenty-first Amendment, 14
Twenty-fourth Amendment, 78, 80, 339
Twenty-second Amendment, 250, 254
Twenty-seventh Amendment, 220
Twenty-sixth amendment, 78, 83, 166
Twenty-third Amendment, 78, 82, 144, 251, 254
Twitter, 203–204
two-party system, 105–115, 125, 126
two-thirds override, 19
Tyler, John, 133
administration of, 427

U

Udall, Mo, 236
Unfunded Mandates Reform Act, 43
Urban League, 159, 161, 335
Union Pacific Railroad, 175
unions
    AFL-CIO and, 160–161, 177
    strikes and, 158
    voting participation and, 91
unitary governments, 28
United Mine Workers, 161
United Nations, 421, 425, 431–432
    General Assembly, 425
    Security Council, 425, 432, 437
United Press International, 185
United States, politics and political parties in, 107
U.S. attorneys, 301
U.S. Census Bureau, 75, 85, 223
U.S. Chamber of Commerce, 158, 159, 165
U.S. Circuit Court of Appeals, 302–303
U.S. Circuit Courts, 300
U.S. Conference of Mayors, 164
U.S. Court of Claims, 302
U.S. District Courts, 298–302
U.S. News & World Report, 201, 203
U.S. Office of Civil Rights, 80
U.S. Term Limits, Inc. v. Thornton, 222
U.S Agency for International Development, 421
United States v. Eichman, 368
United States v. Harriss, 163
United States v. John Doe, 321
United States v. Lopez, 36, 43
United States v. Nixon, 261
United States v. O'Brien, 365, 367
United States v. Timothy McVeigh, 301
United States v. Eichman, 21
United Way, 175
United We Stand America, 124
universe, 63
Unsafe at Any Speed (Nader), 162
upper class bias, 165
Upton, Fred, 232
Urban League, 159, 335, 337
USA PATRIOT Act, 380, 381
USA Today, 201
USS Cole, attack on, 439
USS Maine, 186, 429

V

valence issues, 54
Valeo, Francis, 148
Van Buren, Martin, 263
    in election of 1840, 133
Ventura, Jesse "The Body," 124
Versailles, Treaty of, 249
Veterans Affairs, U.S. Department of, 281

Veterans of Foreign Wars, 159, 175
veto, 16, 19, 255, 256
    legislative, 289
    line-item, 256, 411
    overriding, 19
    pocket, 19, 256
Viacom, 200
vice president, 262–263
    balancing of ticket and, 262
    role of, 262–263
Vietnam War, 114, 258, 420, 426
    free speech and, 365–366
    Gulf of Tonkin Resolution and, 259, 420
    legislative veto during, 289
    media coverage of, 188–189
Virginia
    black representation in, 330
    ratification of Constitution, 16
Virginia Plan, 10, 11, 14–15
Virginia Resolution, 33
Virginia's Declaration of Rights, 14
visuals, 138
Volcker Commission, 293
Volcker, Paul, 293
voter apathy, 84–85, 95–96
voter disillusionment, 127
voter registration, 76
    discrimination in, 336–337, 341
voter turnout, 75
    measuring, 84–86
voting, 76
    convenience, 95
    political participation and, 75–83
voting-age population, 75
voting blocs, 86
voting rights. *See* suffrage
Voting Rights Act (1965), 80, 83, 225, 340–341

W

Wagner Act (1935), 159
Wallace, George, 124, 125, 292
wall of separation, 370, 371, 372
Wall Street Journal, 201
Wall Street Republicans, 114
war chest, 136–137
wards, 76
War of 1812, 216
    declaration of, 421
War on Terror, 380–381, 427, 440
War Powers Act (1973), 259, 420
Warren, Earl, as Chief Justice of Supreme Court,
    143, 308–310, 320, 334, 335, 372, 375
Washington, D.C.
    corporate offices in, 165
    King's March on, 336

Washington, George
    administration of, 31–32, 77, 215–216, 245,
        246, 250, 260, 427, 428
    cabinet of, 106, 216, 264, 277
    election of, 3, 132–133, 252
    farewell address of, 105
    as Federalist, 106–107
    judge appointments by, 299
    newspapers and, 184
    as president of Constitutional Convention,
        9–10
    on Senate, 226
Washington (state), blanket primaries, 135
Washington Post, 190, 192, 201, 205, 206
watchdog, media's role as a, 190
Watergate scandal, 114, 119, 147, 245, 260
    congressional investigation of, 233
    hearings on, 192
    media coverage of, 189
weapons of mass destruction (WMD), 440
Weaver, James, 122
Webster, Daniel, 107, 216
wedge issues, 54
The Weekly Standard, 201
Weeks v. United States, 375
Welch, Matt, 56
Wendell, Oliver, 364
Wesberry v. Sanders, 224
Westboro Baptist Church (Westminster, Maryland),
        383
West Coast Hotel v. Parrish, 308
Where Does the Money Go? (Bittle and Johnson),
        409
Whigs, 107, 113, 118
whips, 229
whiskey rebellion, 32
Whiskey Rebellion, 260
Whistleblower Protection Act (1989), 288, 292
White, Bryon, 311
White, George, 218
White Citizens Council, 334
white flight, 344
White House, 265–268
    press secretaries of, 192
White House counsel, 267
White House Office of Legislative Affairs, 255,
        267–268
white primary, 79–80, 111, 331
Wilderness Society, 161
Williams, Armstrong, 192
Wilson, James, 11
Wilson, Woodrow, 108, 244
    administration of, 81, 226, 249, 269, 425, 429
    civil rights and, 331
    election of, 123
    Jewish support for, 91
    League of Nations and, 257

on lobbyists, 159
    women's rights and, 344–348
winner-take-all system, 144
wire service, 185
women
    in bureaucracy, 285
    in Congress, 218
    employment of, 345
    equality and, 345–348
    interest groups and, 162
    rights of, 344–348
    Seneca Falls Convention of, 344
    suffrage for, 80–81, 158, 344–345
    Title IX and, 219, 345–346
    voting participation and, 86–87
Women's Christian Temperance Union, 158
Woodward, Bob, 189, 190, 193
Woodward, C. Vann, 79
Workers' Voice, 178
Works Progress Administration, 399
World, 186
World War I
    declaration of, 429–430
    entrance into, 364
World War II, 431–432
    broadcasting and, 187
    declaration of, 421
World Wildlife Fund, 394
Wright, Jim, 238
writ of certiorari, 312–313
Wyden, Ron, 232

Y

Yahoo News, 203
Yates v. United States, 365
yellow journalism, 185–186
Yorktown, Virginia, defeat of British at, 7
Young, Brigham, 371
young adults
    suffrage for, 82–83
    voting participation and, 82

Z

Zenger, John Peter, 183
Zogby International, 62